INTERNATIONAL
ENCYCLOPEDIA

of WOMEN
and SPORTS

INTERNATIONAL
ENCYCLOPEDIA

of

WOMEN
and SPORTS

VOLUME 2

Edited by

KAREN CHRISTENSEN
ALLEN GUTTMANN
GERTRUD PFISTER

Macmillan Reference USA
an imprint of the Gale Group
New York • Detroit • San Francisco • London • Boston • Woodbridge, CT

Macmillan Reference USA
1633 Broadway
New York, NY 10019

The Gale Group
27500 Drake Rd.
Farmington Hills, MI 48331

ISBN 0-02-864954-0 (set)
ISBN 0-02-864951-6 (vol. 1)
ISBN 0-02-864952-4 (vol. 2)
ISBN 0-02-864953-2 (vol. 3)

Printed in the United States of America

1   2   3   4   5   6   7   8   9   10

Library of Congress Cataloging-in-Publication Data

International encyclopedia of women and sports / edited by Karen Christensen,
    Allen Guttman, Gertrud Pfister.
        p.   cm.
    Includes bibliographical references and index.
    1. Sports for women—Encyclopedias.   2. Women athletes—Encyclopedias.
  I. Christensen, Karen, 1957–   II. Guttmann, Allen.   III. Pfister, Gertrud, 1945–

GV709.I58 2000
796'.082—dc21   00-062518

H

HACKY SACK *see* **Footbag**

HAEGGMAN, PIRJO

(1951–)

FINNISH TRACK ATHLETE AND SPORTS ADMINISTRATOR

In 1981, Pirjo Haeggman of Finland had the distinction of being one of two women (Flor Isava Fonseca of Venezuela was the other) admitted to the previously all-male ranks of the International Olympic Committee (IOC). Her appointment followed a distinguished athletic career in track and field, in Finland and internationally. Specializing in sprint events, Haeggman was a twelve-time Finnish champion in the 100- and 400-meter events. Internationally, she competed at the European Championships in Athens (1969), Rome (1974), and Prague (1978). Haeggman also represented her country at the Olympics in Munich (1972); Montreal (1976), where she finished fourth in the 400-meter; and Moscow (1980).

Haeggman became involved in the administration of her sport when in 1975, at the age of twenty-four, she became a member of the federal council of the Finnish Amateur Athletics Association. She held this position until 1980. Subsequently, she became chairperson of the association's Women's Committee (1982–1988) and later became its vice president (1984–1988). Haeggman was a member of the Finnish National Olympic Committee, and also a member of its Athletes Commission. Her administrative leadership in Finnish sport occurred at a time when few women occupied those types of positions in any sport organizations.

Pirjo Haeggman at a news conference concerning the IOC bribery scandal in January, 1999. (AP Photos)

By becoming a member of the IOC, Haeggman was a pioneer for women by breaking into what remains the extraordinarily male-dominated world of sport administration at the international level. During her tenure she was an active member, serving on numerous IOC commissions, including the Commission for the Olympic Program (winter 1982–1983), and as vice chairperson of the Athletes' Commission (1983–1984). From 1994 to 1999 she was involved with the Pierre de Coubertin Commission, which is devoted to promoting the study of the ideas and writings of the founder of the modern Olympic Games. In January 1999, Haeggman resigned as part of the scandal involving payments to IOC members by representatives of cities seeking to host the Olympic Games. News reports suggested that Haeggman's (now) ex-husband had received jobs and consulting fees from officials in Quebec and Salt Lake City and that Haeggman herself may have received rent-free accommodations. Haeggman is married and has two sons. She holds a master of sports science degree from the University of Helsinki. Outside of the athletic world, she has worked in business and as a physical education teacher.

Gordon MacDonald

Bibliography

International Olympic Committee. (1995) *Olympic Biographies 1995*. Lausanne, Switzerland: International Olympic Committee.

———. (1996) *The International Olympic Committee—One Hundred Years: The Idea—The Presidents—The Achievements*. Volume 3. Lausanne, Switzerland: International Olympic Committee.

Dorothy Hamill executes a spin on her way to a gold medal at the Winter Olympics in 1976. (Bettman/Corbis)

HAMILL, DOROTHY

(1956–)

U.S. FIGURE SKATER

Following Dorothy Hamill's gold medal at the Innsbruck Olympics in 1976, thousands of young girls copied her famous wedge haircut and headed to the skating rinks and Hamill herself ended her distinguished amateur career to become a professional skater. Known to millions of Americans through television commercials and the Ice Capades, she is a member of the U.S. Figure Skating Hall of Fame and the U.S. Olympic Hall of Fame.

Hamill was born in Riverside, Connecticut, on 26 July 1956, to Chalmers and Carol Hamill. Following the purchase of her first skates, when she was eight years old, Hamill taught herself to skate. Frustrated by her inability to learn to skate backward, she asked her parents if she could take skating lessons. Six years later, at age fourteen, she left school to pursue skating full time. (She earned her high school diploma through private tutoring.) In her first year of full-time skating, she developed her famous "Hamill Camel" movement.

As an amateur, she was the 1969 U.S. Novice Champion, runner-up for the 1970 U.S. Junior Championship, fifth in the 1971 U.S. Championship, fourth in 1972, and second in 1973. In addition, in 1973, she placed fourth in the World Championships. Her performances improved in 1974, when she won the U.S. National Championship and placed second in the World Championships, an achievement she repeated in 1975. Then, in 1976, Hamill proved herself a proficient, powerful, and graceful competitor when she won the Olympic gold medal at Innsbruck and the World Championships.

After these triumphs, Hamill retired from amateur competition and went on to win the World Professional Championships from 1983 through 1987. She also signed contracts to endorse and advertise various products and toured with the Ice Capades. In March 1993, she and her second husband, Kenneth Forsythe, bought the Ice Capades. Hamill became its artistic director and star performer. In 1995, after countless television and touring shows, Hamill retired from touring and sold the Ice Capades. Shortly after that, she filed for a divorce and then for bankruptcy.

In March 1996, she returned to professional skating and was the Legends champion in 1997. She has served on the advisory board for the Women's Sports Foundation. She continued to compete professionally and to do skating exhibitions, Hamill has one daughter, Alexandra.

Janet Luehring-Lindquist

Mia Hamm, star soccer player for the United States national team. (AP Photos)

Bibliography

Burchard, Sue H. (1978) *Sport Star, Dorothy Hamill.* New York: Harcourt Brace Jovanovich.

Dolan, Edward, F., Jr., and Richard B. Lyttle. (1979) *Dorothy Hamill, Olympic Skating Champion.* Garden City, NY: Doubleday.

Hamill, Dorothy, and Elva Clairmont. (1983) *Dorothy Hamill, On and Off the Ice.* New York: Alfred A. Knopf.

Sandford, William R., and Carl R. Green. (1993) *Dorothy Hamill.* New York: Crestwood House.

HAMM, MIA

(1972–)

U.S. SOCCER PLAYER

Mia Hamm is considered by many to have been the dominant female soccer (association football) player of the 1990s. Hamm had become the highest scorer in international soccer history (men's and women's), with a total of 109 career goals, by the summer of 1999. Her popularity on and off the field increased public interest in women's soccer and influenced attitudes toward women's sports in general.

Mariel Margaret Hamm, known as Mia, was born in Selma, Alabama, on 17 March 1972 to William and Stephanie Hamm. William, an Air Force major, was transferred to Italy when Mia was about three years old; here he shared his interest in soccer with his six children. Despite her mother's attempts to have Mia follow in her footsteps as a ballerina, Mia's passion was soccer.

Soccer enabled her, and her older brother Garrett, to make new friends every time they moved to a new town: Mia joined a peewee soccer team as a child, and over the next ten years she often found herself the only girl on the team. Her determination was rewarded when she became the youngest member of the U.S. women's team at fifteen years of age. She was a high school all-American and went on to play for the Tar Heels at the University of North Carolina at Chapel Hill (UNC).

At UNC, she led her team to four national championships and was the all-time leading scorer with 103 goals and 72 assists in 92 college games. Her college performance earned her the Hermann Award as the best female college soccer player in both 1992 and 1993. She graduated in 1994 with a political science degree.

In December 1994 Hamm married Christian Corey, a college classmate and Marine Corps second lieutenant. She played on the U.S. women's team in 1995 and 1996 and was named U.S. soccer's Female Athlete of the Year in 1995. She led the women's team in goals and assists and helped them win a bronze medal at the women's World Soccer Championship.

After soccer became an Olympic sport in 1996, Hamm led her team to a 2–1 victory over China for the gold medal. Hamm saw the victory over China as a victory for all women. Hamm's successes have been many, but she considers her efforts to support the Marrow Foundation and the Special Olympics as some of her most satisfying moments off the playing field. Hamm's brother Garrett died in April 1997 at the age of twenty-eight from a blood disease. In memory of her brother, Hamm organized the Garrett Game in 1998, an all-star exhibition game that raised more than $150,000. Her product endorsement deals have far surpassed those of most other female athletes. Major corporations in sport advertising such as Nike, Gatorade, and Power Bar have signed her on for endorsements. In a television ad campaign, she even went head-to-head with sport icon Michael Jordan in a commercial based on the song "Anything You Can Do, I Can Do Better." In 1999 Nike named the largest building on its corporate campus after her. Hamm was also hired as the official spokesperson for the soccer Barbie doll in 1999. Her book *Go for the Goal* was published in the same year.

Hamm is well known and admired for her teamwork and commitment to putting the team first at all times. Her modesty exemplifies sportsmanship so much that the U.S. Women's National Team has a saying—"There is no 'me' in Mia." Despite her individual successes, Hamm's goal has always been victory for the team. This attitude helped lead the U.S. women's team to the Women's World Cup championship in 1999. Later in the year she joined her teammates in refusing to play for the national team until a dispute over player's pay was resolved. The dispute was re-solved with increased pay for the players and more opportunity for them to make money outside the formal association structure.

Shana Stalker

Bibliography

"Get into: Soccer." (1995) *Sports Illustrated for Kids* (March): 7: 56–59.

Karlen, Neal, and Sally Jenkins. (1999) "The Champions." *Women's Sport and Fitness* (March/April): 2: 89.

Killion, Ann. (1997) "Mia Hamm Is Providing a Connection." *San Jose Mercury News* (8 May).

"Mia Hamm: Gold Medal, Soccer." (1996) *People* (19 August): 46: 44.

Starr, Mark (1999) "Keeping Her Own Score." *Newsweek* (21 June).

Wahl, Grant. (1999) "Scorecard." *Sports Illustrated* (31 May): 90: 23.

HANDBALL, TEAM

Team handball is a game played between two teams of seven or eleven players who try to throw or hit a ball into a goal at either end of a rectangular court while preventing the opposing team from doing so. In 1996 there were women's handball teams in 134 countries from 142 national federations in all parts of the world. It became an Olympic sport for women in 1976 (for men in 1972). Team handball has enjoyed the greatest popularity in Europe, but interest for the sport is growing in Asia, Africa, and South America.

HISTORY

The Czechoslovakian game hazena (from the Czech word, *haziti*, which means "to throw a ball") may be one of the precursors of team handball. The inventor of this game was supposedly Anton Kristof, a Czechoslovakian physical education teacher. The rules were published in the newspaper *Vyclova telesna* in 1905. In the beginning, the teams had seven players each, and they played on courts that measured 48 by 32 meters (52 by 35 yards). The game was mostly played by women, although men also played. The ball was thrown with one hand to the other players. Penalty throws were taken 6 meters (6.5 yards) outside the goal, and playing time was 25 minutes, which is similar to today's rules. The playing field was, however, divided into three parts with two defense areas and one central area, unlike today's handball court. The two backs and the goalie were not allowed to leave the defense area. The goalie could use arms, fists, and legs inside the penalty area. The game was considered suitable for women because it was not a contact sport. Players had to be more than 2 meters (2.2 yards) away from one another if they were going to pass the ball, and grabbing the ball running into, or jumping on an opponent were forbidden.

Kristof formed the Federal Commission of Hazena Teams in Prague in 1909. The first hazena association, the Czechoslovakian Association of Hazena and Women's Sports, was established in 1920. The International Federation of Women's Sports of 1921 included hazena in the women's sports program for the Summer Olympics in Paris. In 1923 the first international meets between Czechoslovakia, France, Yugoslavia, and Poland took place. Seven years later the first world championship in hazena took place with three national teams. The International Federation of Women's Sports was dissolved in 1927, before women's participation in the track and field events at the Olympic Games in 1928. This seemed to mark the end of hazena's growth. The last hazena match is believed to have taken place in Czechoslovakia in 1927. It is reasonable to suppose, however, that the rules and spirit of the game have influenced the development of seven-member team handball.

The first written rules for a game similar to today's handball were compiled in 1906 in Denmark by another schoolteacher, Holger Nielsen. According to Danish sources, the game was invented by his male pupils as an alternative to soccer (association football), which was forbidden because of the damage it caused to windows. The game was played by two teams comprised of eleven or sixteen players on a field that was 45 by 30 meters (49 by 33 yards). There were five or seven offense players; three or five halfbacks, or helpers, behind them; and two or three backs in front of the goal. The game was played in two halves of 25 minutes each. In contrast to today's

rules, a player was allowed to run into the goal with the ball. The goal circle was 6 meters (6.5 yards) from the goal. Boys were allowed to steal the ball out of their opponents hands, but girls were not. The first handball competitions are supposed to have taken place in 1903 for schoolboys and in 1906 for schoolgirls. Fifteen women played handball as an outdoor sport in Copenhagen at the Women's Sportsclub (Kvindelig Idraetsforening) in 1912. According to the rules of 1923, a seven-member team was suitable for women. "Handball," these rules noted, "seems to be a typical women's game. In the future the game may become one of the most important women's sports of which there are but few" (Nielsen 1923, 39).

Sports in the military contributed to the development of team handball as a sport in Denmark and Germany. The first handball tournament seems to have been a military tournament arranged for soldiers during World War I by Nielsen in 1916. In 1926 women joined these competitions, which were by then a civilian event. These competitions mark the beginning of handball as an organized sport in Denmark.

Germany's involvement in the development of the organized sport of handball contributed heavily to control of the sport by men, although at first German handball seemed to be a women's sport. Max Heiser created a handball game for women while he was coaching *Turnen*, the German version of gymnastics at that time, in Berlin. The game was played on an indoor court that measured 50 by 20 meters (55 by 22 yards). Each team had eleven players, and the game lasted for two halves of 20 minutes each. The distance from the goal circle to the goal was 6 meters (6.5 yards). Players could not hold the ball longer than 3 seconds. Hitting or striking the ball out of an opponent's hands was forbidden. Penalty throws were awarded to the opposing team each time the other team fouled. Opponents had to keep a distance of 4 meters (4.4 yards) during a penalty shot. This game was considered a typical women's sport because of the speed of the ball, the short distance between goals, and the rules against body contact. The fact that written rules for competition were compiled for women only seems extraordinary if we consider that German women did not obtain formal status as club members until 1919.

Denmark plays Japan in the 1996 Olympic team handball competition. Denmark won the gold, South Korea the silver, and Hungary the bronze. (TempSport)

Carl Schlenz, a teacher at Die Deutsche Hochskule für Leibesübungen (the German College of Physical Education), succeeded in compiling handball rules for men in the Brandenburg track and field clubs in 1920. The rules seem to have been influenced by the military. Handball was encouraged in the military because skills from the handball court could also be applied to targeting and throwing grenades. Carl Schlenz was responsible for a version of handball that resembled soccer: each team had eleven players, and they played on a field that was 90–100 meters (98–109 yards) long and 60–65 meters (66–71 yards) wide. Men stood 11 meters (12 yards) from the goal line and women, 8 meters (8.7 yards). In the beginning the game was played with a soccer ball. Players were allowed to hold the ball for 3 seconds or to run three steps with it. Men, in contrast to women, were allowed to strike the ball out of an opponent's hands, (*stossen*), whereas neither sex was allowed to hit it (*reisen*).

In its current form, the players can carry the ball for no more than three steps or hold the ball for no more than 3 seconds. The court is 32–41 meters (35–45 yards) long and 16–20 meters (18–22 yards) wide, the goal circle is 6 meters (6.5 yards) from the goal, except for penalty throws when the distance is increased to 7 meters (7.6 yards). Playing time for both sexes over eighteen years of age is two 30-minute halves.

The first German championship for men was in 1922. A championship for women was held the following year. According to German sources, this was supposed to be a game for team competition (*Kampfspiel*). Germans seemed to feel the need for team games of German, rather than English origin.

It is difficult to analyze how team handball spread among Czechoslovakia, Denmark, and Germany. One possibility is that Czech and Danish versions spread to Germany. Their versions dominated Europe until the 1960s. If this is so, the Czech version, which was originally organized for women, may have merged into the seven-member team game, which was backed by Swedish leaders in international handball before World War II and which has been governed by men ever since.

THE INTERNATIONALIZATION OF HANDBALL

The International Federation of Amateur Handball was formed in Germany in 1928, in connection with the Olympic Games in Amsterdam. Two years earlier, the Germans had managed to form a handball federation within the International Track and Field Federation. The German rules for the outdoor eleven-player team became the dominant version. The seven-player team version became an indoor game. The men's version with the eleven-member team was played as an exhibition sport in the Olympic Games in Berlin in 1936, where the German team won. Handball was also played in the Spartakiad (held at international meetings of the Red Sport International [RSI] beginning in 1921 and also international competitions within the RSI) in Antwerp in 1937. The RSI was a workers' association that sponsored international competitions. Thus, we can also see that sporting associations connected to the international workers' movement contributed to the development of international handball.

Women's handball had been played as a school sport in several countries before World War II, but wider participation in international competitions did not occur until after 1945. Its development as a competitive sport moved forward parallel to handball's becoming an indoor, seven-member team sport. The number of goals scored increased, as well as the speed and skill of the players. By the end of the 1940s the average score between two international teams was 4–2, whereas scores in the 1960s were on average 10–5; by the 1970s, 18–16; by the 1980s, 20–15; and up to 30–25 in the 1990s.

Hungary won the world championship for women in field handball (eleven-member teams) in 1949 and Romania in 1956 and in 1960. Since 1960, all handball championships have been played on indoor courts. Teams of particular note from the end of the 1950s to the end of the 1980s were those of Czechoslovakia, Romania, Hungary, the German Democratic Republic, Yugoslavia, Austria, and the Soviet Union. Korea fielded a strong team in the 1990s.

Teams from Asia, Africa, North and South America, and Europe participated in the world championships in Germany in 1997. Denmark won the championship; Norway received the silver medal and Germany the bronze. Denmark beat Norway 33–20. Not even Norway's chauvinistic sports journalists in *Dagbladet* could deny that Denmark had heavily beaten Norway. "Virtuoso victory," one declared, "Denmark's virtuoso performance in the championship finals against Norway left the spectators breathless. Even while witnessing Norway's resounding defeat, this journalist had to bow to Danish superiority on the court" (15 December 1997).

Anja Andersen, one of the best handball players in the world, was the most important player on the Danish team. After one match in which she scored 16 goals, many from seemingly impossible angles, an article in the Norwegian newspaper *VG* reported that "Anja Andersen is not only the best female handball player in the world, according to her coach . . . [but] no man on earth can score better than she does" (13 October 1997).

FEMALE AND MALE PERSPECTIVES

For the most part, men have been and still are the leaders, administrators, and important coaches in women's handball. Even though hazena in Czechoslovakia was administered and led by women, no female leaders of this seven-member team sport were elected to the board of the international body of the 1926 eleven-member team German version. For one thing, the rules of hazena are different from the more widespread version, and for another, the Czech hazena organization was not part of the national track and field federation. The influence of military logic in shaping the national competitions in Denmark and Germany also contributed to the "logic" of excluding women from its administration and organization. Most importantly, perhaps, was that in the 1920s and 1930s men and women did not cooperate in promoting women's sports. Most European countries experienced a period of segregation of the sexes during this time.

In the 1990s international handball was centered in Switzerland. Men dominated as leaders, even though they did not comprise a majority of the players. About half of the members in Denmark were women, in Norway 66 percent were women, and in Germany about 35 percent were women. Yet males were in the majority as leaders in all three countries.

If in 1923 handball was "a typically female sport," in the 1990s this statement remained true but with a different implication. The best female handball players of the 1990s were serious athletes, on professional and amateur levels. They were able to lift more weight, sustain tougher body contact, and score more points than most of the male handball players in the world. Although they did not compete with men, they were often compared to them by sport journalists. In this context, it is interesting to refer back to the quote from Anja Andersen's coach, who stated that Andersen was the best handball player in the world. His point was not that she scored more than most men, but that her playing was superior on a technical and creative level.

Gerd von der Lippe

Bibliography

Bon, Marta. (1997) "Historical Development of 'Hazena', a Typical Women's Game in Slovenia." In *La Comune Eredita dello Sport in Europa*, edited by Arnd Krüger and Angela Teja. Rome: Scuola dello Sport-CONI, 187–192.

Nielsen, Holger. (1923) *Haandbold* [*Handball*]. Copenhagen: Cityforlaget.

von der Lippe, Gerd. (1997) *Endring og motstand mot endring av feminiteter og maskuliniteter i idrett og kroppskultur i Norge: 1890–1950 med et sideblikk på Tyskland, Sverige og Danmark* [*Changing Femininities and Masculinities in Sport and Body Culture in Norway: 1890–1950—with a Side Glance to Germany, Sweden and Denmark*]. Oslo: Norges Idrettshøgskole, Institutt for samfunnsvitenskapelige fag.

HANG GLIDING

A hang glider is an unpowered flying wing made of an aluminum or carbon fiber frame and Dacron® Sail. A triangular-shaped structure below the wing allows the pilot to carry and handle the glider. The pilot wears a harness that is hooked into the glider and takes off on foot from a slope or behind a tow vehicle on flatlands.

Like sailplanes and birds, hang gliders can soar. The pilots find rising air currents and use them to climb, stay up, and fly over the landscape. With the right weather pattern, hang gliders can travel long distances—the world distance record is 488 kilometers (303 miles) flown by Larry Tudor in the western United States in 1990—and altitudes of well over 6,000 meters (20,000 feet) can be reached (individual countries set their own legal altitude limits).

HISTORY

Hang gliding is a relatively new sport. In its recent form, it started in the early 1970s, but its development is the result of a long evolution. Legends, including that of Icarus, show that mankind dreamed to fly in ancient times. The Renaissance artist and inventor Leonardo da Vinci studied flight, as did many inventors in the nineteenth century: Sir George Cayley of England, John Montgomery of California, and Otto Lilien-

A female hang glider pushes off a cliff. (Picture Network International, Ltd.)

THE WORLD HANG GLIDING SERIES

The newest form of hang gliding competition is an international series of competitions where the competitors go head-to-head in the air. First they race around a steeplechase course. Then they careen down a slope through a pylon course, sometimes only a few feet off the ground. Finally, they perform an aerial ballet that includes loops, wingovers, and spins. This challenging flying, the World Hang Gliding Series (WHGS), takes place without an engine at some of the most scenic sites around the world. The WHGS was established in 1995 by Murray Rose of England and Dennis Pagen of the United States. The WHGS is sanctioned by the International Federation of Aeronautics and includes meets in Europe, Asia, Australia, and the Americas.

There are three forms of competition in the series. First, a steeplechase requires pilots to gain altitude and race through a circuit to a goal. The next task is the freestyle in which pilots perform an aerial ballet that is judged on the basis of grace, originality, and degree of difficulty. Freestyle competition might be visualized as gymnastics in the air. Finally, speed gliding requires pilots to race through a course much like a ski slalom course.

Speed gliding is an exciting and new event. In a typical round the crowd hushes as a pilot lifts her glider and calms her nerves. Then with a short sprint, she is airborne and diving for the start gate. Her time is being clocked to the hundredth of a second so she pulls in her elbows and tucks in her chin to slip through the air. Soon she is in the pylon course and making aggressive steep-banked turns left and right while choosing the best line, though occasionally she must cut through an altitude control gate. The gates are six meters (6.56 yards) high and require a pilot to pass between them below their tops. Because of course layout, many times pilots are turning through these gates with their wingtips barely a foot off the ground. The control gates are the most spectacular vantage points for spectators. More pylons are usually in store for the racing pilot until a final glide to the finish gate which demands crossing below six meters. The best pilots cross at top speed barely a foot off the ground. Sometimes the drama is heightened as a pilot barely squeaks across the line or lands agonizingly short.

The objective of WHGS is to provide a challenge to the competitors while presenting a very visual, thrilling, and easy-to-follow event for spectators. The series format allows fans to follow their favorite competitors and monitor their progress through the season. A competitor can specialize in one of the WHGS formats or try for the combined title.

thal of Germany built successful motorless flying machines. The development of powered flight by the Wright brothers in the early 1900s started with nonpowered soaring flights from the dunes of North Carolina in the United States. But the fever for powered craft put soaring on the sidelines, and the idea only resurfaced in Germany after World War I. In the United States in the 1940s, NASA engineer Francis Rogallo and his wife, Gertrude, developed a triangular wing designed as a reentry device for spacecraft. In the 1960s, a group of Australian water skiers used the idea for flat kites towed behind boats. By the early 1970s, this design was adapted to foot launching and spread throughout the United States and Europe to give birth to the sport of hang gliding.

WOMEN IN HANG GLIDING

Women have been a minority in hang gliding (an estimated 5 percent to 10 percent of the general hang gliding population). However, the development of lighter and smaller gliders, as well as the evolution of teaching techniques have promoted the participation of women in the sport. With new materials and technology, the equipment is more adapted to lighter-weight pilots.

There are two main instruction methods used in hang gliding: training hill sessions and tandem flying. Most schools use a combination of both.

The development of safe towing practices (behind a winch or a powered ultralight) has promoted the tandem practice, which is less physically demanding and is more attractive to women. A tandem flight takes place on a larger glider specially designed for two people, a pilot (or instructor) and a passenger (or student). This allows a future pilot to learn techniques and skills with hands-on experience under the supervision of an instructor.

Some participants claim that hang gliding appeals to women because it is esthetically appealing and requires finesse in control. The glider is controlled by weight shift, which requires upper body motions but does not involve excessive strength. This sport allows the pilot to admire fantastic views in the company of soaring birds with only the rush of the wind to break the silence.

As of 1999, the world distance record for women was held by Kari Castle of the United States, who flew 338 kilometers (210 miles) from the Sierra Nevada in California in 1991. Judy Leden of England held the Guinness altitude record (men and women combined)—on 25 October 1994, she took off at 11,856 meters (38,897 feet) from a balloon in Wadi Rum, Jordan, and flew back to earth.

COMPETITION

In hang gliding competitions, men and women compete together with the exception of the Women's World Meet, held every other year. As of 1999, Judy Leden was the only woman to be gold medalist twice in her flying career (in 1987 and 1989).

There are three types of events in hang gliding competition: aerobatics, speed gliding, and cross-country. Aerobatics (or freestyle) is a routine of esthetically pleasing maneuvers judged on criteria of technique, precision, and elegance. Speed gliding, the newest form of competition, is a short race close to the ground between pylons.

The most prevalent format of competition is cross-country, which involves a long race along a course that is determined by turnpoints and a goal. Typically, competitions last one to two weeks, with a different task set every day. Each task may be on a course from 80 to 240 kilometers (50 to 150 miles) and last 2 to 6 hours. The course may be a straight line to a goal, a series of doglegs, an out and return, or a triangle. Competitors prove they have flown the task along the daily course by taking aerial photographs of the designated turnpoints or by recording their flight path with a GPS Global Positioning System. To complete the course, pilots must find rising currents on their way and strategically plan their flight so that they achieve the fastest time. This requires a thorough knowledge of large- and small-scale weather conditions and consummate soaring skills.

There are two main types of soaring: ridge soaring and thermal soaring. Ridge soaring takes place when wind strikes a slope and is deflected upward. The glider can then ride this upward component of the wind and stay up above the ridge. Thermal soaring uses rising columns of warm air, known as "thermals." They develop over dry, darker, or rocky areas of the terrain that absorb and then radiate heat from the sun. The pilot uses a thermal by circling and climbing in the column of rising air. Instruments are often used to aid efficiency in soaring. Altimeters (to measure altitude) and variometers (to measure the rate of climb or descent) are most widely used.

THE FUTURE

Like any type of aviation, hang gliding is in constant evolution. New materials and technologies cause the gliders to change form. Over the years, they have become safer and more efficient. Their rates of descent are getting slower and their speeds, greater. This increases the performance for soaring and traveling distances.

Claire Pagen

Bibliography

Cheney, Peter. (1997) *Hang Gliding for Beginner Pilots.* Colorado Springs, CO: United States Hang Gliding Association.

Hang Gliding Magazine. Colorado Springs, CO: United States Hang Gliding Association.

Leden, Judy. (1996) *Flying with Condors.* Spring Mills, PA: Sport Aviation Publications.

Pagen, Dennis. (1995) *Hang Gliding Training Manual.* Spring Mills, PA: Sport Aviation Publications.

———. (1993) *Performance Flying.* Spring Mills, PA: Sport Aviation Publications.

———. (1991) *Understanding the Sky.* Spring Mills, PA: Sport Aviation Publications.

Sky Adventures, Fantasies of Free Flight: True Stories by Pilots. (1997) Roanoke, VA: Sky Dog Publications.

Sky Adventures, Stories of our Heritage. (1998) Roanoke, VA: Sky Dog Publications.

HENIE, SONJA

(1912–1969)
NORWEGIAN FIGURE SKATER

The Norwegian figure skater Sonja Henie was one of the greatest female figure skaters of the twentieth century. She was also the woman most responsible for transforming Olympic figure skating from a technical sport into an international entertainment event and the most popular viewer sport in the Winter Olympics. In the process, she also transformed the public perception of female figure skaters—and to some extent male skaters—from that of athletes to that of entertainers whose success as athletes could be used to launch lucrative careers as celebrities.

Sonja Henie was born on 8 April 1912 into an upper-middle-class family in Oslo, Norway. Her father, Wilhelm Henie, was a successful businessman who as a young man had won the world bicycling championship for Denmark in 1894. He did not compete in the Olympic Games, however, because he was declared a professional. By the age of eight, Henie was training for more than 2 hours a day, and she soon left school to focus on her developing career. She seemed to be a natural athlete, and her father did everything he could to help her fulfill her potential. In addition to figure skating, a major sport in Norway, she showed promise as a tennis player and occasionally participated in track and field meets, soccer matches, and automobile races. She won her first Norwegian skating championship at age nine, competed in the Olympics at age eleven in 1924, finishing eighth; and finished second in the world championships in 1926.

Henie's breakthrough came in 1927 when the Oslo Skating Club hosted the world championships. A year earlier, she had finished second to the Austrian Herma Plank-Jaroz, and they were again the main contenders in 1927. In a close contest, Henie won with 369.7 points to Plank-Jaroz's 365. Her victory was not without controversy. There were rumors and even published newspaper articles suggesting that the panel of five judges, three of whom were Norwegian, had favored

Sonja Henie, skating in a pink costume, showing her talent for combining athleticism and glamour. (Bettmann/Corbis)

Henie. There was not yet any international standard for selecting judges in skating competitions, and it was accepted that the best skaters often had their own judges on the panels during competitions. Henie would probably have not won in 1927 had there been Austrian judges on the jury instead of three Norwegians. Nonetheless, her ability as a skater was not questioned, and she won by the rules of the day. Her international reputation was established by the victory.

Her next important victory came at the Olympic Games in St. Moritz, Switzerland in 1928. She won her first Olympic gold, with six of the seven judges awarding her first place. She went on to win the Olympics again in 1932 and 1936 and won ten world championships from 1928 to 1937. Neither achievement has been matched by any other female or male figure skater.

Her style, which captivated audiences as well as the judges, was described by the Norwegian sports magazine *SportsManden (23)* in 1928: "Tension filled the air. Sonja entered the ice at such an accelerating speed she took our breath away. Her elegant opening, with short, quick steps . . . and daring leaps, seemingly unperturbed by applause, proving a technically fantastic performance . . . as beautiful as the most delicate ballet . . . in perfect harmony." Before Henie, ice skating had been a competition that stressed the scrolling of figures on the ice and controlled movements by competitors wearing long skirts and black boots. Henie's seemingly endless triumphs, her athletic but flowing style, her showmanship and glamorous outfits, and her blond good looks transformed the sport to one based on style and glamour as well as athleticism.

After her 1936 Olympic victory, Henie launched her career as an entertainer in Hollywood. By this time she was an international celebrity known by various nicknames—including "Daddy's Little Girl", "The Pavlova of the Ice", and "Dear Miss Sonja"—and had made numerous command performances, including skating for the royal family of England. Her Hollywood career was a success: she starred in ten films produced by Twentieth Century Fox, among them *Thin Ice* in 1937, and also starred in her own show, the *Hollywood Ice Revue.*The show was a precursor of the modern touring ice shows that attract many of the top female and male skaters after their Olympic careers are over.

Henie's personal life was not as smooth as her professional one. She was married three times—to American financier Dan Topping from1939 to 1946, to airline executive Winthrop Gardiner from 1949 to 1956, and to art collector Niels Onstad from 1956 until her death in 1969. Henie did not have children and was sometimes criticized as being less than feminine for putting her career before her personal life. She became ill with leukemia in the 1960s and died at the age of fifty-six in 1969, while on a flight from Switzerland to Oslo in search of an effective treatment. A monument dedicated to her was unveiled in 1992, on the eightieth anniversary of her birth. It is located outside Frogner Stadium in Oslo, where her career began.

Henie's approach to skating transformed the sport. She was a fast and spectacular skater, determined and daring enough to take risks and press her own limits, and demonstrating the ability to control her nerves at decisive moments.

Henie's success changed what it meant to be a female figure skater. She showed that a female athlete could become an international celebrity, even though that celebrity required glamour and physical beauty in addition to athletic achievement. Thus, figure skating became a premier female sport, and many girls and their parents saw skating as a road to wealth and fame that could not be achieved by women in most other sports.

Gerd von der Lippe

Bibliography

Guttmann, Allen. (1996) *The Erotic in Sports*. New York: Columbia University Press.

Strait, Raymond. (1990) *Queen of Ice, Queen of Shadows: The Unsuspected Life of Sonja Henie*. Chelsea, MI: Scarborough House.

HENOCH, LILLI

(1899–?)

GERMAN TRACK AND FIELD ATHLETE

Lilli Henoch was a German track and field athlete whose successful athletic career and life were cut short by the Nazis because she was Jewish. She was born in 1899 in Königsberg (later Kaliningrad) to upper-middle-class Jewish parents; her family moved to Berlin in 1912. As a child Henoch developed a passion for athletics and team sports. After World War I she joined the Berlin Sports Club, which opened a women's section in 1919. Members participated in track and field and also played team handball. Henoch soon became the best athlete in her club, noted for her performance and her versatility. She was the captain of the handball team and a member of the field hockey team, which won the first Berlin hockey championships.

In the 1920s Henoch was among the world's best female track and field athletes. In 1924 she won the German long jump championship and was on the 4 × 100-meter relay team that set a world record in 1926. She was also a leading shot-putter and discus thrower, setting a world record in the shot put in 1925. In addition to athletic achievements, she was a full participant in club activities and held several leadership positions. She was a well-known and popular figure throughout Germany at a time when female athletes were frequently criticized for being "unfeminine."

Her promising career came to an end in 1933. Like all Jewish athletes, in accordance with National Socialist ideology Henoch was no longer allowed to be a member of a German sport club. As she thought of herself as German first and Jewish second, she was reluctant to join a club associated with the Zionist Maccabee movement. To continue her training, she became a member of the Jewish Gymnastics and Sport Club, which saw its home as being in Germany rather than in Israel. From then on Henoch competed in Jewish competitions only. To support herself, she taught physical education at a Jewish elementary school, but after the death of her stepfather she lived with her mother in poverty.

On 5 September 1942, she and her mother were deported to the East, and she presumably died in a concentration camp before 1945. Once a well-known name in German sports, Lilli Henoch is now listed only in a book of remembrance for victims of the Nazis: Missing in Riga.

Gertrud Pfister

Bibliography

Ehlert, Martin-Heinz. (1989) "Lilli Henoch." *Sozial- und Zeitgeschichte des Sports* 3, 2: 34–49.

HEPTATHLON

The heptathlon is the women's counterpart to the men's decathlon. It consists of seven events held over two days. It was introduced in 1981 to replace the pentathlon, which until then had been the major multiple-event competition for women. On the first day athletes compete in 100-meter hurdles, high jump, shot put, and 200-meter race.

On the second day the competitions are held in long jump, javelin, and 800-meter race. The men's decathlon is a ten-event contest. That the women's event increased from five to seven events is an acknowledgment of women's athletic ability and improving performances. That the women's competition is not yet ten events points out the continuing belief that women are not physically capable of meeting the demands of a ten-event competition.

HISTORY

Before the early twentieth century, women either did not participate in multiple-event competitions or their competition went completely unrecorded. Tracing the development of the heptathlon, then, becomes a matter of looking at the growth of multiple-event competitions more generally. That history has involved continuous revision of the number and type of events involved as well as the scoring systems used to compare athletes' performances.

Early multiple-event competitions were for men only and seem to have been inextricably linked with ideals of masculinity. In 708 BCE the Greeks introduced a pentathlon into their Olympic program that incorporated running, long jump, discus, javelin, and wrestling. This fast became the central event of the Games because the Greeks held versatility in high esteem. (The reverse has become true in modern times, with versatility and flexibility viewed more as feminine and specialization more as masculine. The symbolism of the event, as it relates to gender, is complex. In the nineteenth century, all-around competitions were held for men in Ireland, but it was the Americans who introduced them to formal athletics programs. The Amateur Athletics Union (AAU) championships in 1884 had a ten-event competition that incorporated a 100-yard race, shot put, high jump, 880-yard walk, hammer throw, pole vault, 120-yard hurdles, 56-pound weight lift, long jump, and one-mile run. This was all to be completed in one day.

Since that early event, several versions of multiple-event competitions have been held around the world. Some countries hold a one-hour decathlon. However, the best known are the decathlon, a track and field event for men; the modern pentathlon, which involves riding, fencing, shooting, swimming, and cross-country running; the triathlon, consisting of cycling, running, and swimming; and the women's heptathlon (and previously pentathlon).

DEVELOPMENT OF WOMEN'S MULTIPLE-EVENT COMPETITIONS

The women's pentathlon is the earliest known female multiple-event contest. National and international competitions began early in the twentieth century and consisted of the shot put, long jump, 100-meter race, high jump, and javelin; they were held over two days. The introduction of the pentathlon may be viewed as marking the beginning of an increasing tendency to accept athletic competition as a valid part of femininity. The fact that it did not form part of the Olympic program until 1964 indicates the limitations of this acceptance. After World War II the pentathlon schedule changed, with the shot put, high jump, and 200-meter race taking place on the first day and 80-meter hurdles and long jump on the second day. In 1961 the program was altered again, with the 80-meter hurdles moved to the first day and the 200-meter race to the second. In 1969 the distance for hurdles was changed to 100 meters. Beginning in 1977, all events took place on one day, the sequence being 100-meter hurdles, shot put, high jump, long jump, and 800-meter race. In 1981 the seven-event heptathlon was introduced.

Women's pentathlon events took place at the amateur level in the early twentieth century, long before their introduction to the Olympic Games. Since 1981, an increasing number of heptathlon competitions have been held at elite and nonelite levels in America, Europe, Africa, and Asia, many of them publicized on the Internet. In America college-level competitions are held. However, heptathlon is still a minority sport for women, as reflected in the lack of literature on the topic.

ELITE COMPETITION

Although they retain minority status, the pentathlon and the heptathlon have had several notable and powerful women competitors. Several notorious and closely fought contests also mark the history of the competitions. The comparison of women's performance across time is difficult because of the changing nature of the event and the different scoring systems. In 1938 the record for the pentathlon was held by Gisela Mauermayer, who scored 418 points (German table). The performance, which took place in Stuttgart, Germany, involved a 13.07-meter (43-foot) shot put, a 5.62-meter (18.5-foot) long jump, a time of 12.4 seconds in the 100-meter event, a 1.56-meter (5.1-foot) high jump, and a 36.90 meter (121.7-foot) javelin throw. Mauermayer was the top woman athlete of the prewar period. She also held world records in the shot put (Warsaw, 1934) and the discus (Berlin, 1936) and was on the relay team that broke the record at the 4 × 100-meter relay in the Berlin Olympics in 1936. Indeed, top heptathletes have often held records in other individual events.

The first record holder in the postwar version of the pentathlon was Fanny Blankers-Koen of the Netherlands. Blankers-Koen scored a total of 4,692 points from the following performance: A shot put of 11.50 meters (37.9 feet), a 1.60-meter (5.28-foot) high jump, a 200-meter run in 24.4 seconds, an 80-meter hurdle race run in 11.4 seconds, and a 5.88-meter (19.4-foot) long jump. Irena Press was a notable performer of the post-1961 formu-

HIGH SCORE SO SOON OBSOLETE

The 7,291 points scored by Jackie Joyner-Kersee of the United States at the Seoul Olympics on 23–24 September 1988 stand at the end of 1999 as the World, Olympic, and American record. The next five highest point totals were also recorded by Joyner-Kersee during her career. In 2000 her records will be replaced because the design and weight of the women's javelin, one of the heptathlon events, have been changed, rendering all existing records obsolete.

lation of the pentathlon; she ran the 80-meter hurdles in 10.7 seconds; made 17.16 meters (56.6 feet) in the shot put, 1.63 meters (5.3 feet) in the high jump, and 6.24 meters (20.5 feet) in the long jump; and ran 200 meters in 24.7 seconds. After the hurdle distance was changed to 100 meters in 1969, Burglinde Pollak of East Germany put in an outstanding performance at Erfurt in 1970. She ran the 100-meter hurdles in 13.3 seconds; made 15.57 meters (51.3 feet) in the shot put, 1.75 meters (5.7 feet) in the high jump, and 6.20 meters (20.4 feet) in the long jump; and ran 200 meters in 23.8 seconds.

The 1972 Olympics saw fierce competition between Mary Peters of Great Britain (1939–) and Heide Rosendahl of West Germany (1947–). On this occasion both athletes broke the world record, with Peters winning only marginally by 10 points in the last event, which was a 200-meter race in which Rosendahl actually finished ahead of Peters. An even closer contest took place at the Montreal Olympics in 1976, with Siegrun Siegl and Christine Laser of East Germany finishing with the same score. The decision was made on the basis of which athlete had performed better than the other in the most events, giving the victory to Siegl, who had outperformed Laser in three out of five events.

The last record in the pentathlon was held by Nadyezhda Tkachenko (1948–) for her performance in the 1980 Moscow Olympics. Her scores show the progress women had made in multiple-event competitions during the pentathlon years. She ran the 100-meter hurdles in 13.29 seconds; made 16.84 meters (55.5 feet) in the shot put, 1.84 meters (6 feet) in the high jump, and 6.73 meters (22.2 feet) in the long jump; and ran 800 meters in 2:05.2 seconds.

HEPTATHLON CHAMPIONS

Ramona Neubert of East Germany was the first world record holder in the heptathlon, but Jackie Joyner-Kersee (1962–) has been the most well-known and successful heptathlete. At the 1980 Goodwill Games in Moscow she became the first to score over 7,000 points (7,184 points). The marks she achieved in the event are indicative of women's growing achievement in the heptathlon: she ran the 100-meter hurdles in 12.85 seconds; made 1.88 meters (6.2 feet) in the high jump and

Jackie Joyner-Kersee competing in the long jump during the heptathlon World Championships in 1997. (TempSport)

14.76 meters (48.7 feet) in the shot put; ran 200 meters in 23.00 seconds; made 7.01 meters (23.1 feet) in the long jump and 49.86 meters (164.5 feet) in the javelin throw; and ran 800 meters in 2.10.02 seconds. Joyner-Kersee achieved a magnificent score in the 1988 Olympics in Seoul, where she scored 7,291 points and was 394 points ahead of her nearest rival. In her career Joyner-Kersee won three gold medals in the heptathlon. She was forced to drop out of the Atlanta Olympics due to injury and announced her retirement in 1998. The gold medal winner at Atlanta was Ghada Shouaa, who became the first Syrian gold medal winner. She also won the gold medal at the 1995 world championships.

RULES AND PLAY

The heptathlon scoring system incorporates the idea that different skills can be measured and weighted in such a way that comparison among athletes is possible. Although the heptathlon is based on the idea that participants display their all-round athleticism, it is often excellence at one or two events that may be decide the victor. The events are each assigned scores whose primary purpose is to rank competitors, not to weigh the absolute and relative value of performances in all events of track and field. Nevertheless, much controversy has surrounded the adequacy of different scoring systems, and as a consequence they have changed over time. For example, new tables were introduced for the pentathlon in 1954 and 1971. The earliest table was known as the German table.

Andrea Abbas

Bibliography

Payne, Howard, and Rosemary Payne. (1981) *The Science of Track and Field Athletics*. London: Pelham Books.

Quercetani, Robert L. (1990) *Athletics: A History of Modern Track and Field Athletics (1860–1990)*. Milan: Vallardi & Associati.

HIGHLAND GAMES

The Highland Games originated among Celtic ancestors of the Scottish people, and survived the centuries to become a customary part of Scottish life and a significant aspect of Scot culture. Their main events have always involved tests of strength among men—tossing the caber, throwing the hammer, and others—with women as spectators. Gradually, women have become key participants in other aspects of the Games, chiefly music and dance.

The games were formally recognized as a national festival in the early-nineteenth century. Scottish emigration was responsible for their dispersal beyond the land of their birth and for their subsequent popularity in many countries. They remain an international sporting festival that is still enthusiastically celebrated today. The Games thrived particularly in former colonies of the old British Empire and in the English-speaking New World of the nineteenth century. They were known as "Caledonian Games," attracting crowds of 20,000 people or more at major American and Canadian cities.

HISTORY

Legend has it that the Games' beginnings involved tests of strength between clansmen loyal to various chieftains, leading to recognized events such as putting the stone, throwing the hammer, and tossing the caber (a large wooden log). These heavy events have since formed the core of a Highland Games meeting and are featured as major attractions. High and long jumps also became part of the competitions, as did foot races over various distances, ranging from short sprints to longer races, even to the summits of nearby hills and back. Traditionally, these athletic contests were for male participants and women attended only as spectators. The most famous female spectator was Queen Victoria, whose regular enjoyment of the Braemar Highland Gathering is credited with increasing the prestige of Highland Games. Her patronage continued by subsequent generations of the British Royal Family. The attendance of other political dignitaries and celebrities elsewhere underlined the increasing seriousness of the Games, which offered valuable material and money prizes for the winners (thus earning them the modern label of "professionals"). Indeed, since the second half of the nineteenth century, famous athletes have traveled around a recognized circuit of Highland Games meetings, earning considerable sums for their efforts.

NOVELTY EVENTS AND MUSIC

There also emerged, albeit in a more slow and minor fashion, another permanent side to the Games, a practice of including less serious events for the spectators' amusement, an element of fun to balance the more serious contests. An impressively diverse and ever-changing number of novelty events have been included in Games programs over the years and have become very popular. Such events as sack races, three-legged races, wheelbarrow races, "best-dressed Highlander" competitions, greased pig races, among many others, appeared alongside the more familiar contests. These light events became as traditional as the revered heavy events. Another es-

---

HIGHLAND DRESS FOR LADIES (1931)

As far back as we can trace the records of our past, Scottish women—Highland and Lowland—gave much attention to their garments. In the higher walks of Clan life the ladies were noted for the style and elegance of their wearing apparel. The tartan skirt, sometimes flounced; the well-fitted bodice or firmly flanged middy, the colours of which varied from the crotul-brown to the deep-hued saffron; the pliant cuaran; the tilted cap and feather, make up an attire beautiful and becoming. The ladies of the Clan were the peers of their sisters in France in the matter of dress design, and were but slightly affected by foreign modes. As a rule they had an instinctive feeling for the fitness of things. A native garb was to them a garb which adapted itself to native conditions, such as climate, and the seasonal changes consequent on different avocations, pastimes, social functions or domestic usages. Queen Victoria, to whom Highland customs owe much, delighted to speak and write about the costumes of the Highland women, and did much to encourage the wearing of the distinctive Highland Dress by them on suitable occasions. Her own daughters and granddaughters, too, with her warm approval, set a fine example.

A Highland Gathering is not a vaudeville show, and responsible committees are moving for a gradual return to correct girls' dresses at their annual competitions. Already such outstanding places as Balmoral and Braemar have ruled out the incorrect dress altogether; Cowal is more or less in line; so are Toronto and other centres of Caledonian Games.

COL. JAMES ALEXANDER FRASER, LL.D.
(1931). Booklet from the Banff Highland Gathering and Scottish Music Festival.

---

sential element was also always present, the highland dancing and playing of the bagpipes that accompanied the athletic endeavors. Initially, most such musical activity was confined to the pageantry of parades and closing ceremonies; but before long dancing and piping competitions were being featured in Highland Games' programs.

WOMEN'S PARTICIPATION

In these novelty events, and in the ubiquitous Scottish music and dance, are rooted the beginnings of female participation in Highland Games. Alongside numerous accounts of large numbers of the women being present in the crowd, one or two items began to appear that signaled their actual participation in the arena. To the "Boys' Race" on the program was added a "Girls' Race." One of the earliest examples was "a running race for girls" that was featured at the New York Caledonian Club's Games of 1867, and later illustrated in *Harper's Weekly* (2 November 1867). And soon beside various races for men appeared races for "Ladies," "Married Ladies," and "Spinsters." In 1886, the *New York Times* (6 July 1886) reported that a ladies' race of 220 yards "excited immense enthusiasm and the ropes were broken down in several places by the eagerness of the crowd to get a good view." Although such races, and others, became commonplace over the years, women's athletic participation in the Highland Games has not increased dramatically, not to the significant extent, for instance, that it has in the related track and field events of the Olympic Games and other multisport festivals, over the same period. To this day, the serious athletic events of the Highland Games calendar remain a male preserve.

The same cannot be said, however, in the areas of Scottish dancing and piping at the Games. While these, too, were began as and were traditionally a male prerogative, women have made great progress since being gradually admitted, often reluctantly, into the several different categories of dance and musical competitions. The Highland Fling is probably the best known

Contest winners at the Cowal Highland Games, 1997. (Peter Turnley/Corbis)

dance among many others at Highland Games; while bagpipe-playing is more familiar than the drumming competitions or playing the harp. Emily Ann Donaldson has discussed the rise of Scottish dancing, showing that by the end of the nineteenth-century: "Females were getting onto the dancing stages at the Games, liking it, doing well, and staying there." So much so, in fact, that today male dancers are now in the minority at most Highland Games. Donaldson also mentions the successes of some female dancers; and David Webster includes individual photographs of several women champion dancers holding their respective trophies.

Any long-lasting sporting institution, particularly an international one, must adapt to survive. In so doing, inevitably it will attract some criticism and offend some traditionalists; and contemporary Highland Games may indeed exhibit the clear-cut facets of "advertising, sponsorship and the expansion of a comprehensive consumer culture which exploits many of the kitsch symbols of cultural identify." Still they endure, and continue to give pleasure to participants and spectators alike around the world, one of its best-loved festivals. Any explanation of the durability and popularity of Highland Games must include the successful participation of women as one significant factor.

Gerald Redmond

Bibliography

Colquhoun, Iain, and Hugh Machell. (1927) *Highland Gatherings*. London: Heath Cranton.

Donaldson, Emily Ann. (1986) *The Scottish Highland Games in America*. Gretna, LA: Pelican Publishing.

Jarvie, Grant. (1991) *Highland Games: The Making of the M*. Edinburgh, Scotland: Edinburgh University Press.

Logan, Jamee. (1851) *The Scotish [sic] Gael*. Hartford, CT: S. Andrews and Son.

Redmond, Gerald. (1971) *The Caledonian Games in Nineteenth-Century America*. Rutherford, NJ: Fairleigh Dickinson University Press.

———. (1982) *The Sporting Scots of Nineteenth-Century Canada*. Toronto: Associated University Press.

Webster, David. (1973) *Scottish Highland Games*. Edinburgh, Scotland: Reprographia.

HINGIS, MARTINA

(1980–)

SWISS TENNIS PLAYER

Martina Hingis seems to have dominated women's tennis since the first day she set foot on the court. As a seventeen-year-old, she was named Associated Press Female Athlete of the Year for 1997. During that year Hingis compiled a 79–6 overall record and captured three of the Grand Slam titles, winning the Australian Open, Wimbledon, and the United States Open. She was also named Women's Tennis Association Player of the Year. At age nineteen, she was already considered by many to be one of the greatest women's tennis players of all time.

Martina Hingis was born on 30 September 1980 in Kosice, Czechoslovakia. Her parents divorced when she was four years old, and she moved to Switzerland soon afterward with her mother, Melanie Molitor. Molitor, Hingis's coach and a former professional tennis player herself, named her daughter after Martina Navratilova, the great Czech and later American tennis player.

Since turning professional on 14 October 1994, Hingis dominated women's tennis throughout the rest of the decade. Through October 1998, she had already amassed eighteen career singles titles and twenty career doubles titles. In 1996, she became the youngest woman ever to win Wimbledon, teaming with Helena Sukova to win the doubles competition. In 1998 Hingis completed a doubles Grand Slam, winning all four major doubles titles in the same year. At sixteen years and six months, she became the youngest woman to hold the number-one ranking, maintaining that status for eighty weeks. Although she lost the ranking briefly in late 1998 to Lindsay Davenport of the United States, she regained it in early 1999.

Martina Hingis celebrates setting up a match point against Amelie Mauresmo of France in the women's final at the Australian Open in Melbourne in January 1999. Hingis defeated Mauresmo 6-2, 6-3 to win the Australian for the third consecutive time. (Torsten Blackwood/Corbis)

When she lost the first-place ranking, some experts predicted the end of her dominance because they believed that her game, based on precision shot-making and control of the court, was no match for the game of such power players as Davenport and Venus Williams. Although she won the Australian Open and regained the number-one ranking in early 1999, the first half of the year was a difficult time. She was criticized by other players for calling an opponent who is a lesbian "half a man" and also for saying that her former doubles partner, Jana Novotna, was too old. At the French Open she was loudly booed for her temper tantrums and complaints as she lost the final to Steffi Graf, and she was eliminated in the first round of Wimbledon. After the loss, she indicated that some time off from the game might be the cure for her problems. When Hingis returned to competition, she faced intense competition from the three leading American players—Lindsay Davenport and Venus and Serena Williams, but as of August, 2000 she remained the number one-ranked women's player.

When not traveling on the professional tour, Hingis resides with her mother in Trubbach, a Swiss village of 5,000 people. Her interests include horseback riding, skiing, and in-line skating. She is fluent in Czech, English, and German.

Mark Wood

Bibliography

Teitelbaum, Michael. (1998) *Grand Slam Stars: Martina Hingis and Venus Williams*. New York: HarperCollins.

HITOMI KINUE

(1907–1931)

JAPANESE TRACK AND FIELD ATHLETE

Hitomi Kinue, the first Japanese woman to win fame as an elite athlete, was born in a village in Okayama Prefecture on 1 January 1907. Although her first school sport was tennis, her ability as a track and field athlete was recognized by her high school principal, who persuaded her father to send her away to college. After graduation from what became Tokyo Women's College of Physical Education, she taught briefly and was then, in April 1926, hired as a journalist by Osaka's *Mainichi Shinbun*. The newspaper, one of Japan's most important, was recognized for its sponsorship of sports events.

A month later, at the national track and field championships, Hitomi competed so impressively in the 100-meter dash, the long jump, the shot put, and the baseball throw that she was chosen as Japan's only representative at the Fédération Sportive Féminine Internationale's second quadrennial International Women's Games scheduled for that August. Riding the Trans-Siberian Railroad, the teenager journeyed alone to Moscow and was then escorted to Göteburg, Sweden, by a Moscow-based *Mainichi* reporter. Competing in six events, she won the standing and the running long jump, was second in the discus, and third in the 100-yard dash. Her 5.5 meters (18.04 feet) in the running jump set a world's record. She was officially honored as the outstanding athlete of the games.

In the spring and fall of 1927, she competed in Japan and began training for the 1928 Olympic Games, which took place in Amsterdam. By June 1928, she was in peak form, setting world records in the 100-meter (12.2 seconds) and 400-meter (59.0 seconds) events. She was one of four women on the forty-one-member Japanese team. Just before the Olympics, at a meet in Osaka, she broke the world's record for the long jump with a leap of 5.58 meters (18.31 feet). This record stood for eleven years.

The competition in Amsterdam was stiffer. After finishing a disappointing fourth in the 100-meter race, Hitomi spent a sleepless night and then decided on the spur of the moment to enter the 800-meter race, which was not one of her specialties and an event usually thought too long for 100- and 200-meter sprinters. Finishing second, behind Germany's Lina Radke, she became the first Japanese woman to win an Olympic medal.

Two years later, Hitomi returned to Europe for the International Women's Games in Czechoslovakia. After the strenuous trans-Siberian journey, she arrived in Prague with a sore throat and a fever. Despite the rain, which was almost continuous, she competed in a number of events and won the long jump with a jump of 5.9 meters (19.36 feet). After the meet, the Japanese team went on to dual meets against the respective national teams in Warsaw, Berlin, Paris, and Brussels. Although she was exhausted and required almost daily medical treatment, she competed in the first three cities before deciding that she was too weak too continue. Then, to prevent her teammates from losing a meet to the Belgians, she ran still another 800-meter race. She was second, a teammate was fourth, and Japan won the meet.

Returning by ship from Marseilles to Kobe, she arrived in such wretched health that her horrified father tried to persuade her to rest. She was determined, however, to fulfill all her obligations to her employer and to the national sports federation that had sponsored her career. She drove herself to the limit, lecturing on her experiences and advising coaches on the latest European techniques in track and field. By the spring of 1931, she had begun to cough blood. Hospitalization came too late. She died of respiratory failure on the third anniversary of her Olympic medal on 2 August 1931.

Allen Guttmann

Bibliography

Ohara Toshiko. (1990) *Hitomi Kinue Monogatari [The story of Hitomi Kinue]*. Tokyo: Asahi Shinbunsha.

HOCKEY, FIELD

The modern history of field hockey began in England, where the game was introduced to the elite colleges and public schools, equivalent to America's Ivy League and private schools. The sport was quickly embraced and spread to other countries. In Europe, Asia, and other locations there is support for male and female programs. In many countries the men have very high visibility; however, this is not the case in North America. Although men do play field hockey in North America, it is mostly a women's sport. There are few opportunities for men to participate in field hockey in North America compared to the options available to women.

The growth and development of field hockey roughly paralleled changes in women's lives in the sport world. In some countries, it became socially permissible for women to play because their programs did not compete with men's programs. In other countries, women might play, but their programs did not receive the same amount of investment and support that were provided to the men's programs. The changes in the 1960s and 1970s introduced a movement toward serious competition for women, culminating in the first women's World Cup in 1975. Money and the changes in national governing bodies, inter-national federations, and the Olympics would permanently catapult field hockey into the fast-paced game it is today.

REGULATIONS AND GOVERNING BODIES

In 1894 during a playing visit to Ireland, a group of Englishwomen discovered the Irish Ladies Hockey Association. Returning to England, these women decided that it would be a good idea to form an association for England. In 1896 the Ladies Hockey Association was established. By adopting the same rules as the men's hockey association, with the addition of no hatpins allowed, the women hoped that their petition for recognition by the men would be successful. When the proposal was rejected, the women vowed not to let any men into the organization and, in 1897, changed their name to the All England Women's Hockey Association (AEWHA). They began designing their own rules and expectations for women players. For all practical purposes, women would guide the development of the sport for the next fifty years. The AEWHA was the primary organization that pushed and promoted women's field hockey for the next several decades. Because of their influence, as other countries began to play hockey, the rules established by the AEWHA were adopted, but with individual variations. Soon many of these counties inaugurated their own associations.

Decorum was imperative, and rude behavior such as abusing umpires or deliberately shooting at opponents was not tolerated. Players who exhibited these behaviors would receive reprimands and even be suspended from the club. When women began to play in public, the AEWHA declared that the public should not pay to watch games as it would taint the game and the women who played it.

The proper costume was an integral part of the women's game: skirt length, types of shoes, not using the skirt to stop the ball, and so forth were all regulated. As time passed, the costume changed to make it easier for a player to move around the field.

The Fédération Internationale de Hockey sur Gazon (FIH) was founded in 1924 as the world governing body for the sport. It represented both men and women in hockey to the Olympics, where men's field hockey has been played continuously since 1928. At the same time, plans were conceived for an international governing body for women, and in 1927 the International Federation of Women's Hockey Association (IFWHA) was formed. The major objectives of the IFWHA were to "standardize and popularize the game of field hockey among women of all nations." The founding members of the IFWHA were Australia, Denmark, England, Ireland, Scotland, South Africa, the United States, and Wales.

The IFWHA decided to have triennial conferences in different locations starting in 1930. These conferences would include meetings, workshops, and a tournament to showcase and exchange participation experiences. The focus of these events was on the essential qualities of sportsmanship, friendship, and goodwill. Under these circumstances, there were no rankings, no titles, nor an overall winner at these games. Each country's association had regional sections that would be further subdivided into local clubs. For the international conference tournaments, the various regions could field teams comprised of their best players from all the individual clubs, (as well as national representation). From 1939 to 1946, the IFWHA canceled all international activities because of the war, but field hockey continued to played in most nations.

With the establishment of the IFWHA, there were now two hockey federations, one that focused on women and one that included both genders. A love–hate relationship between the two federations arose and persisted for close to half a century. The major conflicts between the FIH and the IFWHA revolved around membership in regard to participation in the matches and the rules. As IFWHA membership expanded, the issue of how to handle the teams that were associated with the FIH arose. Since 1933 some FIH teams had been invited to join as special guests or affiliates, (but neither organization wanted to give up these other teams). Both federations would swing back and forth on which teams could play and retain membership and so on. In 1948 the FIH relented and permitted its members to join the IFWHA without having to resign from the FIH.

Besides competition for member teams, the FIH and IFWHA were divided by significant variations in the rules, offication, and regulation. Most of the national associations had established

rule and umpiring committees early on in their formation. By 1947 Ireland, England, Scotland, and Wales had joined together to form a Hockey Board that was empowered to make and confirm rules of the game for all four countries and to make international agreements. This marked the beginning of interest in having the IFWHA take a more active part in enforcing and establishing the rules of the game. Even though no action was taken, it was clear to many that uniformity by consent was critical, and on 29 September 1953 the IFWHA rules and umpiring subcommittee was formed. Also in 1953, a joint consultative committee between IFWHA and FIH was formed to promote exchanges of information, friendship, and closer cooperation between both federations. An ultimate goal was to secure as far as possible uniformity of rules and regulations and to deal with questions arising from international matches. The last issue was a sensitive one.

Besides its own set of rules, the IFWHA required that its games be governed by women officials. FIH matches, on the other hand, permitted male officials. The FIH also required that any rules of play had to be established by an independent rules-making body just like the International Hockey Rules Board (IHRB)—in other words, a comparable rules-making process, committee membership, and actual rules of play. Talks stalled because the FIH would not agree to recognize any decisions made by the IFWHA rules and umpiring subcommittee until an independent rules-making body was established. In September 1966, a constitution for the proposed independent rules-making body was accepted; in January 1967, the Women's International Hockey Rules Board was established by unanimous vote and would work in close cooperation with the IHRB. With a rules and a joint subcommittee established, on 17 October 1969 a draft document, Rules Common to the Men's and Women's Game, was issued by the FIH.

The ongoing conflict between the FIH and IFWHA was one reason that field hockey for women was not included in the Olympics until 1980. Unable to mediate between the two, the International Olympic Committee (IOC) had continuously recognized the FIH as the official organization for men's and women's field hockey. In 1979, the officers of the IFWHA began negotia-

The Dartmouth College women's field hockey team plays a game against the University of Massachusetts in Amherst in 1995. Despite the popularity of other field sports such as soccer and softball, field hockey remains a popular intercollegiate sport. (Phil Schermeister/Corbis)

tions with the FIH. As the positioning and posturing continued, it seemed that the FIH was maintaining control of power and not attempting to provide an equitable transition for the IFWHA. Finally in 1981, the IFWHA was absorbed into the FIH, and a year later 103 national associations were affiliated with the FIH. The last official competitions sponsored by the IFWHA were the Women's World Cup and the Inter-Continental Cup, in April 1983.

EARLY HISTORY AND DEVELOPMENT

The early history of field hockey for women is fragmentary. The Molesey Ladies Hockey Club is credited with adapting hockey for the enjoyment of women in 1887. At Lady Margaret Hall, one of the women's colleges of Oxford University, hockey was presumably played in the early 1880s because in 1885 the institution's administration placed a ban on hockey that remained in force until 1893. Sommerville, another women's college at Oxford, had introduced field hockey in 1885, but two years later Sommerville also banned

hockey—again, until 1893. Several public schools in Scotland and England and other clubs, both collegiate and recreational, were also formed in the late 1880s.

In 1894, the women of Newnham College of Cambridge were invited to play during Christmas vacation in Dublin, where they not only found the Irish women to be skilled in their play, but also that they had established the first women's hockey association, the Irish Ladies Hockey Association. Upon return, the Englishwomen discussed starting their own association and appealed for recognition to the men's association. Because recognition was refused, when the Ladies Hockey Association was formed on 23 November 1896, a stipulation that men would not be permitted to hold office was included. A year later, the association was renamed the All England Women's Hockey Association (AEWHA). From 1889 onward, associations in England, Wales, and Scotland were established. These associations, along with several colleges, become charter members of the AEWHA. Competitions among the member teams thrived. The first women's hockey publication, *The Hockey Field*, was started in England by Edith Thompson in 1901.

In the meantime, men's field hockey had spread to the United States, Canada, Australia, New Zealand, and several other countries by the turn of the century. Field hockey was introduced in New Zealand in 1890. Six years later, a club for women was started in Christchurch by a group of local women. Field hockey also thrived in Canadian provinces that had more influence from Great Britain. In 1896 the Vancouver (British Columbia) Ladies Hockey Club was formed. Hockey was also played in Nova Scotia and Newfoundland. In 1900 field hockey was introduced in private girls' schools in Australia.

Although sources credit hockey as being played at Goucher College as early as 1897, the establishment of women's field hockey in the United States has been primarily associated with Constance M. K. Applebee (1873–1981), who introduced the sport in 1901. At a Harvard Summer School of Physical Education, Applebee demonstrated the sport with a mix of sporting equipment. That fall, Miss Applebee was invited by Vassar's Harriet Ballantine to teach the game to students and teachers at Vassar. This led to clinics that were held at Wellesley, Mt. Holyoke, Smith, Radcliffe, and Bryn Mawr. At the end of this tour, Bryn Mawr hired "the Apple" as a physical educator of outdoor sports. By 1904, with her guidance, four local club teams in the Philadelphia area formed the Philadelphia Field Hockey Association. Philadelphia became a hotbed of hockey, and the sport was firmly established in the elite women's colleges in the East. A regional association was also formed in Boston. Applebee coached at Bryn Mawr until 1928, though she remained associated with it for her entire life. From 1923 to 1969, she ran her own field hockey camp for girls and young women in the Pocono Mountains

The sport had expanded into the Southern Hemisphere by 1903; games were played in the Australian provinces of New South Wales, South Australia, and Tasmania. Later that year, the Australian Women's Hockey Club was established in Sydney. In 1908 the New Zealand Women's Hockey Association was established, and later that year an interprovincial women's hockey tournament was played. Competitions briefly faded during World War I. In 1910 the All-Australian Women's Hockey Association was established, and they held their first interstate tournament. When the AEWHA embarked on its first long-distance tour in 1914, they traveled to Australia and New Zealand. In 1925 a demonstration game took place in Tokyo, and in 1931 Japan held its first national championship.

In 1920 a visiting team from the United States traveled to England. The American women improved their game dramatically while on tour. The following year arrangements were made for a team from England to tour and teach in the United States, including visits to Chicago and Wisconsin. In January 1922, just two months after the English tour in the United States, the United States Field Hockey Association (USFHA) was created.

Hilda Light (1889–1969) was a key player and organizer during field hockey's developmental years. A star in the All England Women's Hockey Association, Light also served as president of the AEWHA from 1931 to 1945. During her pres-

PRIMARILY A WOMAN'S SPORT

Although played by men and women in Europe and Asia, North American field hockey is primarily a woman's sport. It came to the United States around the turn of the twentieth century and became popular at elite women's colleges in the east. Eventually, it became a major sport for high school and college women, despite competition from basketball, volleyball, and soccer.

idency Light made many innovative decisions, including making and using hockey films and increasing the number of hockey publications. These efforts increased the number of spectators for women's field hockey. She also served as president of the IFWHA from 1950 to 1953.

POSTWAR HISTORY AND THE DEVELOPMENT OF OLYMPIC COMPETITION

Worldwide expansion notwithstanding, European teams have always had an advantage in opportunities for competition over other teams in other parts of the world, since Europe had the greatest concentration of women players in the smallest geographic area. In 1946 the first postwar request for women's field hockey to be added to the Olympic program was made. IOC rejection prompted the FIH to propose a World Festival of Women's Hockey. The festival, held in May 1948 in Amsterdam, was the biggest tournament held to that date with the most comprehensive representation of FIH- and IFWHA-affiliated national associations. Afterwards, the IFWHA continued to host its conference/tournament format until the 1970s.

Hockey gained popularity and expanded in Canada during the 1950s. Toronto started two women's clubs in 1955, hosted Ontario's first field hockey tournament in 1958, and saw the creation of the Ontario Women's Field Hockey Association in 1960. Alberta had women's field hockey clubs in Edmonton and Calgary firmly established by 1962. That same year, the Maritimes Women's Field Hockey Association was formed to represent New Brunswick, Nova Scotia, and Prince Edward Island. With increasing numbers, Canadian women were able to increase their participation in competitions on the international level. One of the unique developments in Canada's history was that the Greater Vancouver Women's Grass Hockey Association, founded in late 1928, for many years represented Canada to the IFWHA. In order to include other clubs and associations participating on the international scene without representation to IFWHA, on 24 September 1962 the Canadian Women's field hockey association was born and began a push for national unification.

The 1960s saw changes in attitudes that began to infiltrate the associations as politics began to influence the development of the sport. The IFWHA was faced with a decision on whether or not to hold the 1971 tournament in South Africa. Acutely aware of apartheid, the IFWHA imposed an unprecedented boycott and moved the host location. At the same time, the organization was experiencing financial pressures. In order to obtain government funding of national hockey teams, it decided to drop its noncompetitive policy and rank its member teams. So at the 1971 tournament, which was held in New Zealand, unofficial rankings as well as a winner were announced. In 1975 the tournament in Edinburgh, Scotland, was officially announced as the first World Championship for Women.

For its part, every two years since 1970 the FIH had been holding a sponsored competition, known after 1974 as the FIH Women's World Cup. Individual countries began to establish their teams' training and competition schedules around these international events. As increasing commitments of time and energy were required of players, countries were forced to think of new ways to sustain and compensate them. In particular, many persons focused on the inclusion of women's field hockey as an Olympic sport as a means to stabilize its finances and increase its exposure, as well as to give both women's field hockey and the women athletes their due regard.

The inclusion of women's field hockey in the Olympics received serious consideration by the International Olympic Committee in the 1970s. Many members of the IFWHA, however, had serious reservations due, no doubt, to its continuing noncompetitive orientation. A 1974 membership poll of thirty-four member associations revealed seventeen in favor, six opposed, and two undecided. Even within the group that supported consideration, there was concern that the high ideals of the IFWHA might be compromised by inclusion in the Olympics. While the debate on inclusion in the Olympics continued at the February 1975 meeting, the IFWHA received a letter from the FIH that the IOC had notified the FIH that the women's event had been approved. In 1976, the IOC announced that women's field hockey would be included in the 1980 Olympics.

When a sport becomes part of Olympic competition, serious investments of money and time follow. One result was the appearance of other federations, most notably the Continental European Hockey Federation. A further commitment to player development was made in 1977 when the first FIH Junior Cup for girls was held. With the Olympics on the horizon, women's hockey appeared in the Soviet Union in 1977, with teams formed in the southern Ukraine and Uzbekistan. Women were also integrated into the Soviet field hockey association. In 1978 field hockey made an appearance at the National Sports Festival in the United States. Additional monies were given to many teams when field hockey was approved to become an Olympic sport, and this also intensified many programs.

Beth Anders (1951–) is just one of many fine U.S. women players who emerged as the competitive game was blossoming in the 1980s. A 1973 graduate of Ursinus College, she was regarded as one of the premier penalty corner scorers in the world during her playing years. Anders was the team high scorer for the United States from 1969 to 1984 and a member of the World Cup team from 1971 to 1984. She was 1980 and 1981 Sportswoman of the Year for the United States Olympic Committee for field hockey and 1984 Amateur Olympic Athlete of the Year; she was named to the Ursinus College Hall of Fame in 1988 and to the United States Field Hockey Association Hall of Fame in 1989. Coaching at Old Dominion University in the 1990s, Anders amassed more than 300 victories, becoming the first Division I coach to earn this distinction.

As the caliber of play increased, new emphasis was placed on maintaining and developing the caliber of officiating. National governing bodies have officiating programs that structure specific criteria and move umpires from the apprentice or novice level to the national and international levels. Rising to the level of international umpire takes a combination of national experience and international exposure. Conferences for women umpires were offered in the 1980s.

The Soviet Union's national women's teams began to compete in 1979. Unfortunately, the Russian boycott of the 1980 Olympic Games severely disappointed many who were not allowed to participate in this event. Six teams did compete, and Zimbabwe took the gold. A year later, the first Asian cup was held. Women's field hockey improved steadily in the 1990s. By 1998 the IOC had announced that ten teams would compete in Sydney in the year 2000 and that twelve teams were expected at the 2004 Olympic Games in Athens. The IOC also made grants to assist countries that showed the potential to build solid women's field hockey programs.

Mila C. Su

Bibliography

Anders, Beth (head field hockey coach). (1998) Web site: <http://www.odusports.com>.

Applebee, Constance M. K. (1901) *Field Hockey for Men and Women.* New York: American Sports Publishing Co.

Broom, Eric F. (1980) "Innovations in International Sport: A Comparative Analysis of Women's World Championship in Field Hockey Teams." In *International Seminar on Comparative Physical Education and Sport,* 2d ed. Halifax, Nova Scotia, 345–360.

Dutch Field Hockey. (1998) Web site: <http://hockey.enschede.com/uk>.

Fédération Internationale de Hockey. (1998) Web site: <http://www.fihockey.org>.

Gerber, Ellen, ed. (1963) *American Women in Sport.* Reading, MA: Addison Wesley.

Grant, Christine H. B. (1984) "Gender Gap in Sport: From Olympic to Intercollegiate Level." *Arena Review* 8, 2: 31–47.

Home of Hockey, The. (1998) Web site: <http://www.fieldhockey.com>.

Lees, Josephine T., and Betty Shellenberger. (1969) *Field Hockey,* 2d ed. New York: Ronald Press.

Leikin, A. (1981). "USSR Hockey Association." *World Hockey* (May): 41–42.

Lodge, Peggy. (1995) "Women's Hockey." In *Hockey for Men and Women,* edited by Norman Borrett. London: Seely, Serne, & Co., 32–56.

Mackay, Helen T. (1963) *Field Hockey: An International Team Sport.* Englewood Cliffs, NJ: Prentice Hall.

McBryde, John. (1986) "The Bipartite Development of Hockey: The Bipartite Development of Men's and Women's Field Hockey in Canada in the Context of Separate International Hockey Federations." Unpublished master's thesis, University of British Columbia, Vancouver.

McCrone, Katherine E. (1986) "The 'Lady Blue' Sport at the Oxbridge Women's College from their Foundations to 1914." *British Journal of Sports History* 3, 2: 191–215.

———. (1988) *Playing the Game: Sport and the Physical Emancipation of English Women, 1870–1914.* Lexington: University Press of Kentucky.

McLauchlan, Gordon. (1989) *Illustrated Encyclopedia of New Zealand.* Auckland: David Bateman.

Park, Roberta J. (1985) "Sport, Gender and Society in a Transatlantic Victorian Perspective." *British Journal of Sports History*, 2, 1: 5–28.

———. (1983) "Symbol, Celebration and the Reduction of Conflict: Women's Field Hockey, a Game in Transition." In *Many Faces of Play*, edited by Kendall Blanchard et al. Urbana, IL: Human Kinetics, 232–246.

Pollard, Marjorie. (1985–1986) "50 Years of Women's Hockey: The Story of the Foundation and Development of the All England Women's Hockey Association 1895–1945." *Hockey Field* 73, 1 (Part 1: September 1985): 10–12; 73, 2 (Part 2: October 1985): 36–39; 73, 3 (Part 3: November 1985): 62–63; 73, 4 (Part 4: December 1985): 90–92; 73, 6 (Part 5: February 1986): 145–147; 73, 8 (Part 6: April 1986): 204–206.

Shaner, Janet P. (1975). "The History and Development of the International Federation of Women's Hockey Association." Unpublished master's thesis, Smith College, Northhampton, MA. "Significant Dates in the First 50 years of AEWHA History." (1995) *Hockey Digest* 22, 4: 33.

Talbott, Beverly. (1983) "Field Hockey." *women's SPORTS*, 39–48.

Vamplew, Wrey, et al, eds. (1994) *Oxford Companion to Australian Sport*, 2d ed. Melbourne: Oxford.

HOCKEY, FLOOR

Floor hockey is a popular recreational game played mainly in North America. Its development and popularity grew in the 1960s when many schools started using the game as an off-season training activity for ice hockey. The history of floor hockey can likely be traced back to the game of bandy, a stick-ball game played on frozen lakes and rivers in Scandinavia and elsewhere in Europe. Bandy is now one of the more popular winter games in Scandinavia and is played in a regulation arena similar those used for ice hockey in North America. Other historical roots include links to *hocquet* in France, the Scottish game *shinty*, and references as early as the 1500s in Galway to a similar game known as *hockie*. All these games are considered to belong to a family of stick-ball games. The differences center on the use of a puck or a ball and whether the game is played on ice, on a field, or in a gymnasium.

Floor hockey is played in a gymnasium with a puck, usually on a basketball court, but any indoor area with a centerline can be used. A team has six players: a goalie, a center, two forwards, and two guards. A regulation game has three 8-minute periods with a 5-minute rest between each period. Floor hockey is popular as a recreational activity, particularly in the Midwest and on the East Coast of the United States, but has never moved to a highly competitive level. Coed participation is common when the game is played in physical education classes, but interscholastic and intramural games are usually segregated by gender.

Whereas floor hockey is popular in the Midwest, street hockey or roller hockey is more popular in warmer climates. With the development of in-line skates, floor hockey was adapted to outside play, with participants wearing in-line skates and using floor hockey sticks and a ball rather than a puck. This version of the game is also primarily a recreational pursuit rather than an organized competitive sport. This is in direct contrast to the development of another adaptation to floor hockey called floorball. Floorball (or *innebandy*, as it is referred to in Sweden, where it is most popular) started as a recreational activity taught in physical education classes in elementary and secondary schools, but it soon developed into a highly competitive sport with international competitions for both women and men. It does not seem likely that floor hockey will develop to this level.

Linda S. Stanley

See also Innebandy

Bibliography

Zakrajsek, Dorothy B., Lois A. Carnes, and Frank E. Pethgrew, Jr. (1994) *Quality Lesson Plans for Secondary Physical Education.* Champaign, IL: Human Kinetics.

HOCKEY, ICE

Ice hockey is a variation of the traditional ball-and-stick games of shinny, hurley, or bandy. In all four games, players use sticks to hit a movable object, but the other three are played on grass, not ice. Players of field and ice hockey refer to their sports as hockey. Canada is the first country where women participated in ice hockey.

Ice hockey is played at many levels: international, professional, semiprofessional, senior, amateur, college, college club, intramural, recreational, academic (varsity and club), league club, travel teams, and in-house leagues. The world championships and Olympics, which are considered amateur competitions, are the highest international level at which females can compete, while men have amateur and professional opportunities. Participation in the sport is increasing at all levels. Hockey has become popular worldwide, expanding beyond North America to many other countries. Judging from the statistics available, national governing bodies in North America, such as USA Hockey, did not consistently count female registration separately until the late 1980s. The statistics that do identify females generally start with 1990 and indicate rapid growth of women's participation, with numbers in Canada and the United States quadrupling within four years. A form of ice hockey for people with disabilities, called sledge hockey, is played at the Paralympics by players of both sexes.

HISTORY

Several European countries claim to be ice hockey's place of origin, but Canada is the first nation where the sport was firmly established. The first photograph of a woman playing hockey dates from 1889. The subject is Isobel Stanley, daughter of Lord Stanley (the benefactor of the National Hockey League's award, the Stanley Cup), playing hockey outside of Ottawa's Government House. In 1891 the first account of a woman's match appeared in the *Ottawa Citizen*. Within the next five years, women's teams continued to form throughout Canada on the club, recreational, and university levels, creating their own space on the ice to play. There were several instances when men were not allowed to watch the women play. The first women's college team started at Queen's University in 1894, followed by a team at McGill two years later. In 1896, in the first intercollegiate match, the Morning Glories of Queens challenged the Blacks and Blues of the women's college in Kingston, Ontario. Before the turn of the century, teams were formed in the provinces of Alberta and Saskatchewan. In 1899 the *Ottawa Citizen* mentions an American match that took place at the Ice Palace in Philadelphia. By 1900 the province of Quebec had established the first all-women's league. Teams practiced and played games outdoors and indoors. For some teams, the modesty of the times prevailed, and they practiced and played out of men's sight. The long wool skirts that were worn provided a certain amount of protection and warmth, but women began to shorten them by a few inches to gain better mobility. Women were playing in American colleges in the early part of the 1900s, mostly on the East Coast, on a recreational basis. In the Midwest, at the University of Minnesota, women's teams existed from 1916 until the 1930s. Other teams in Minnesota thrived during the 1920s and early 1930s. The Ladies Hockey League, formed in Calgary, Canada, in 1908, showcased their talent at the Banff winter carnival for the next ten years. The University of Saskatchewan started a team in 1913, closely followed by the University of Manitoba as hockey became more popular in the West. In 1916 a Canadian team faced off against a team from the United States in Cleveland, Ohio. By the 1920s there was a move for the women players to wear hockey pants rather than wool skirts. Women's hockey associations were formed in the early 1920s in Quebec and Ontario. The first use of a goalie mask by a man or woman is attributed to Elizabeth Graham at Queens University, who in 1927 slipped on a wire fencing mask during a game. The first Dominion championship was held in 1933, when the Preston Rivulettes met the Edmonton Rustlers, resulting in Preston's first loss in three seasons. Preston's dynasty, which lasted through the 1930s, ended with a 348–2–1 record that included six Dominion titles and ten provincial and eastern titles.

The Depression and World War II greatly reduced the opportunities for women to participate in any sport in the United States and Canada, resulting in the immediate decrease in recreational and club teams outside the universities. But in the 1960s, women began to resume competition. In the United States in 1964, Brown University made history by establishing the first collegiate women's hockey team, which was awarded varsity status in 1975. The team was the precursor to the stronghold of eastern women's collegiate hockey and the eventual Ivy League championships that started in 1976. In Canada, the Dominion Tournament, also known as the Brampton Tournament, sponsored by the Brampton Canadettes Girls Hockey Association, was first held in 1967 for teams in Ontario. This tournament would eventually increase the number of divisions and teams and expand to include teams from other provinces and even teams from the United States.

The United States began to participate seriously in international competition in 1985. Soon after the 1972 passage of Title IX, which mandated equal funding for women's programs at institutions that received federal money, women's ice hockey teams began to emerge on the varsity and club level in prep schools and colleges. Community teams also began to form in the 1970s; one of the best known was the Massport (Massachusetts Port Authority) Jets, which formed two traveling teams in 1970. Two years later the Jets were traveling as far as Canada to play collegiate teams and by 1975 had amassed a record of 128–6. The program was created by Tony Marmo, who has been credited with the 1974 petitioning of the American Hockey Association of the United States (AHAUS) for Olympic consideration). Although the team had folded by the early 1980s, many other teams came into existence. Another noteworthy program, also started in the 1970s, was in the Assabet Valley in Massachusetts. Some players and coaches who participated in this program, such as Kelly Dyer and Julie Sasner, have risen to the national level and the program was still going strong at the turn of the century.

The 1980s were an exciting decade of change and opportunity in Canada and the United States. The Canadian Amateur Hockey Association (CAHA), as well as provincial courts and the Supreme Court, handed down landmark judicial decisions in Canada on participation issues. In 1955 eight-year-old Abby Hoffman had played for a year on a boy's team in the Toronto Hockey League under the name "Ab." She had fought for the right to play hockey, but pressure and other opportunities had turned her away from the sport. Gail Cummings, however, sought the right to play under the Ontario Human Rights act in 1977. The case dragged on for two years to the favor of the Ontario Minor Hockey League, and

she was not allowed to play. In 1981 the Canadian National Senior Championship was established, "senior" at that time meaning players from age fourteen to forty-five, with the first-place team being awarded the Abby Hoffman trophy, second place, the McTeer trophy, and third place, the Fran Rider Cup. In the United States, the Eastern College Athletic Conference (ECAC) hosted postseason play in 1983. In 1984 CAHA established a policy that permitted girls to play on boys' teams if there were no girls' teams available, a policy that conflicted with those of many local hockey leagues. In 1986 Justine Blainey asked to be allowed to play on a boys' team under the Human Rights Act, because she felt that playing on a boys' teams provided a better learning experience for her. The case eventually made its way to the Supreme Court of Canada, which ruled in 1987 that girls who qualified could play on the most skilled boys' teams in older age groups. In Canada the collegiate championship in 1971 transferred fifty years of sponsorship from the Women's Intercollegiate Athletic Union (WIAU) to the Ontario Women's Interuniversity Athletic Association (OWIAA).

Female memberships in hockey organizations in Canada and the United States increased rapidly in the 1990s. Title IX continued to be used to fight for the incorporation of the sport. In 1990 women on the Colgate University ice hockey team sued for varsity status and equitable financial support. A lengthy judicial process did not end until 1997, when the courts made a final ruling: the women gained varsity status and the requested financing. Women joined the professional leagues when Manon Rhéaume, a goalie playing for Trois-Rivières in the Quebec major junior league, made her debut on 23 September 1992 in an exhibition game for the Thunder Bay Lightning. Three months later she became the first woman to play in a regular season game in the East Coast Hockey League. Two other women, Kelly Dyer and Erin Whitten, also goalies, made it in the pro circuit. Whitten became the first woman with a win on 30 October 1993 while playing for the Toledo Storm. Dyer played in the Sunshine League in Florida in 1994, where the Louisville Hockey Equipment Company of Kentucky sponsored her. Another landmark occurred in 1994, when Minnesota became the first state to sanction girls' high school ice hockey as a varsity sport, and twenty-four teams participated in the inaugural year. Two years later, in an unprecedented legislative act, the state legislature passed a bill requiring that 15 percent of all ice time, in private and public rinks, be reserved for females. This increment would increase to 50 percent in 1997. The legislature also funded the Minnesota Amateur Sports Commission to build rinks and improve older ice facilities to support this action. The ECAC underwent a revision in 1995 and began to represent Division I teams, while the newly formed ECAC Alliance would represent a mix of varsity and club-level teams on the Division III level. The following year, two new associations, the Midwestern Collegiate Women's Hockey Alliance (MCWHA) and the Central Collegiate Women's Hockey Association (CCWHA), were formed. In order for the National Collegiate Athletic Association (NCAA) to sponsor a championship, there must be a minimum of forty teams at varsity level. With collegiate national championships in Canada and the United States, and more teams gaining varsity status, the college scene has a very promising future. Through perseverance and dedication to the sport, women's hockey is in North America to stay.

RULES AND PLAY

Two teams face off against one another, with players in six positions: goalie, two defense players, and three forwards called left wing, right wing, and center. How these players move or set up plays will vary by level of play and the team's preferred strategy. Games are played in three periods and the length of time for each period can range from 10 to 20 minutes, with or without the clock stopped at each whistle, depending on ice-time availability and level of play. Ice hockey is a fast-paced game of quick stops and starts and occasional end-to-end action. Shifts, the time a player spends on the ice, are kept short to allow players to recover from the action. Goals can be scored "even strength," when each team has the same number of players on the ice; "short handed," when the team that scores is missing at least one player because of an infraction, or "penalty"; or on the "power play," when that team has more players than the opposite team. Referees and linesmen enforce the rules.

The major difference between the men's game and the women's game is that women's hockey does not allow body checking. That does not mean, however, that body contact is not allowed. It is difficult not to have body contact; especially if two or more players are going for the puck, some bumping will occur. In fact, the range of contact that is allowed will vary by the interpretation of the official.

Body checking has its share of controversy. A rulebook published in the United States in 1917 notes that women who played ice hockey were allowed to body check. However, by the 1980s several changes had occurred. AHAUS, now called USA Hockey, banned females from checking in the United States except for those who played on boys' teams. In Canada, except for the national team, hockey rules and policies are decided at the community and provincial levels, and provinces decided to either discontinue or continue the support of body checking. When the first Canadian

PROFESSIONAL WOMEN'S HOCKEY

The National Women's Hockey League (NWHL) began play in Canada in the fall of 1999 with nine teams: Bampton Thunder, Beatrice Aeros (Toronto), Clearnet Lightning (Ajax), Scarborough Sting, Mississauga Chiefs, Ottawa Raiders, Montreal Wingstar, Laval Le Mistral (Montreal), Sainte-Julie Panthers (Quebec). Plans for 2000–2001 are to add a team in Vancouver and possibly also teams in Edmonton, Calgary, and the United States (Detroit, San Francisco, Los Angles, Boston). The United States is seen as a prime market because American women college hockey players have few opportunities to continue playing after graduation.

women's senior national championship was held in 1982, teams that did not body check played against teams that would body check. Great frustration and much fervor were generated by the inequity. This conflict would not be resolved until 1989, when body checking was eliminated from the women's championship. For the most part, players and others involved with the game do not agree on whether or not body checking should be permitted. On the international level, body checking is also a controversial topic. Several countries, including China and Germany, do allow body checking on the national level while other countries allow only body contact. The major issues at this level relate to the mixed levels of play each country brings to the competition and the rules they use, as well as the question of differentiating between body checking and body contact. The definition of body checking includes the interpretation of the hit to be "intentional and overt."

Women officials on the international level have been cultivated by the IIHF for women's international competition since 1995, when the first officials' seminar was held for twenty-one women officials in Andorra. Canada and the United States have more female referees compared to other countries because both have strong officiating programs. Other countries with women officials include Germany, Finland, Switzerland, Russia, Norway, Hungary, Slovakia, and New Zealand. Canada and the United States have made commitments to support and encourage women to be successful officials through ranked programs.

In Canada, much of the organizational structure occurs at the provincial level, one of the strongest programs and advocates being the Ontario Women's Hockey Association (OWHA). In the United States, the districts and regions are the primary structures. Canada established a Female Council in their hockey association in 1982. The program did not have a permanent manager until 1990. AHAUS established a girls' division in 1984 that included two senior categories and by 1989 raised the division to section status. This move has increased visibility and provides a stronger position for advocacy. As for national teams, which did not exist until 1990, Canada committed to supporting its national team a few years before the United States made its commitment in 1995. Support included financial commitment to the

women on the team, consistency of personal, improved communication, and increasing hockey development at all levels.

INTERNATIONAL COMPETITION

Teams from North America have traveled to Europe since the mid-1980s to help raise support of and interest in the sport. Various competitions had been held in Canada and the United States with visiting teams from Japan, Germany, and Finland during this time. In 1985, the Brampton Canadettes hosted an international tournament including a team from Germany and one from the Netherlands. The following year, the OWHA hosted the first (unofficial) world invitational tournament to promote interest and bring teams together for competition and to plan a strategy to lobby the IIHF for a world championship. Since that time four world championships have been held. Canada has won four gold medals; the United States, four silver; and Finland, four bronze. In 1992 the International Olympic Committee (IOC) announced that women's ice hockey would be a gold medal sport in the 1998 Olympics. On 17 February 1998 at the Winter Olympics in Nagano, Japan, the United States won the gold medal; Canada, the silver; and Finland, the bronze. The other teams that participated in this inaugural event were those of China, Sweden, and Japan.

Women from European and Asian countries face the same obstacles as women in North America concerning perceptions and attitudes. The difference is that Asian and European countries rely primarily on community, local government, or private support. Many females participate in rink bandy "field hockey on ice," a socially acceptable sport. Women who play hockey face resistance to their participation and often have trouble getting ice time, which contributes to their lack of success and makes it harder to maintain interest. Without a serious commitment from the national governing bodies and internal structures to ensure success, these countries will continue to lag behind North America in competitive ability. The following are abbreviated histories of some of the countries where women play ice hockey.

ASIAN NATIONS

The Asian championships started in 1992 and have been held every two years since. In 1995 the

Ice hockey was contested by women for the first time in the 1998 Olympics in Nagano, Japan. The dramatic 3-1 victory by the U.S. team over Canada brought much attention to the sport. (Wally Mc-Namee)

Pacific Rim Tournament, an IIHF-sanctioned event, was held, with North American and Asian countries represented. Teams in Japan and China were formed in the 1970s. By 1978 Japan had enough teams to play for championships, and in 1981 the Japanese Ice Hockey Federation (JIHF) recognized women players with the first federation-supported national tournament a year later. In 1985 the Japanese national team traveled to Canada to play teams in British Columbia and Alberta. In 1987 the first all-star team was formed. That same year the first national championships were held in China. In 1991 the Chinese national team was established, and it won the Asian championship in 1992, 1994, and 1996. In Hong Kong, women's ice hockey started in 1995 under the same auspices as men's and separated a year later to form a women's league. Ice hockey is not played in the universities and there are no national or regional competitions due to the small number of players. Other countries with teams include Korea and Kazakhstan.

EUROPEAN NATIONS

European teams have held tournaments and other competitions with one another since the 1970s. Official international competition began with the European championship in 1989, held in Germany with eight teams. Since then the championships have been held approximately every two years. The European B division was formed in 1991 to accommodate the growing number of teams. In 1998 the IIHF decided to replace the European B championship with a Pool B in the world championship. The first Swedish hockey team was formed in 1969. Body checking is not allowed, but body contact is permitted. There are three women's leagues in Sweden, and hockey is supported through private clubs. Teams were formed in Switzerland in the 1970s. The league structure of the Swiss teams expanded from two divisions in 1981 to three divisions in 1994. Women began playing hockey in Finland in the early 1970s; and by 1995, 1,500 Finnish women were playing on thirty-five teams within private clubs. With four gold medals in European championships, four world championship bronzes, and one bronze Olympic medal, the Finnish team has consistently rivaled the teams from Canada and the United States. German teams began play in 1974. By 1982 Gunther Sabezki and Wolfgang Sorge established the first official women's hockey league. These two men were also instrumental in persuading the IIHF to endorse women's ice hockey at the international level. The national team was formed in 1988–1989, and the team won the bronze at the first European championships.

The countries that came on the scene in the 1980s include Norway, the Netherlands, Denmark, France, and England. Norway participated in the European championships in 1989, finishing fourth after losing in penalty shots against Germany. They earned their first bronze in 1993, which was the same year the national team—sponsored through private clubs—was formed. The first national women's team for the Netherlands was formed in 1988. In 1994–1995, four female senior teams competed for a national championship. Starting in the 1995–1996 season, the Dutch and Belgian teams joined to play in one league. All teams in Denmark—where there are no age-determined teams—come from private clubs. There are two women's hockey divisions; at the end of each season, the top three teams from each league compete in the national championship. Hockey in France has had a sporadic history, with teams in 1917, the 1930s, and then in the 1980s. Relative newcomers include Scotland, Ireland, and Wales with at least one team each. England has the highest number of teams and the most support for their programs and has competed in the European championships.

In Russia women played rink bandy but were not encouraged to play ice hockey. As competition developed on the international level, a decision was made to support Russian women's hockey, and by 1993 a women's ice hockey association had been created. In 1995 the team won the gold in the European B championship, which then allowed them to move up to play in European A, where they won the silver medal in 1997. Other countries that have women's teams are Austria, Slovakia, Latvia, and Czech Republic.

SOUTHERN HEMISPHERE NATIONS

In the Southern Hemisphere, hockey is played in South Africa, Australia, and New Zealand. Hockey was introduced in the 1990s in South Africa. Johannesburg has a league with five women's teams. Cape Town has a team for players under twenty years old, but many of these women also play on the three senior teams. By 1993 Australia had begun forming teams. A girls' development league started in 1994 for groups under fourteen, sixteen, eighteen, and twenty-one. A year later, the first national championship, called the Joan McKowen Memorial Cup, was held. In 1999 all five states and the territory of Tasmania had teams. At the same time, women's ice hockey in New Zealand was at the formative stage, with most playing at the beginner level, ages six or seven. The New Zealand Hockey Association was working with the regional associations to start all-women hockey teams. Approximately fifty females were registered players.

CONCLUSION

Ice hockey is another sport that women can add to their sport legacy. For a number of reasons—including ignorance, lack of interest, and discrimination—it was only in the 1980s and 1990s that the media began to focus a little more attention on it, books about it were published, and major competitions on the national and international scale proclaimed that female hockey players were on the scene to make their mark. There have been

some remarkable stories of success, challenges, and many rugged moments, and through it all women found a way to continue playing. Almost a century after they began, women are still enjoying ice hockey. As hockey continues to grow and gain interest and support, more females will have chances to play and participate in this very exciting sport, at levels that range from recreational coed to elite national teams.

Women still have to contend with poor treatment and discrimination at all levels as resistance to them still exists. In spite increasing numbers and general acceptance, women still have to fight to play and fight for better funding. With increased attention, Olympic status, and the possibility of professional teams in the future, more countries may expand their support and developmental activities for women. This will result in expansion of tournaments on the international, national, and regional levels. An NCAA championship for American collegiate players seems inevitable. In this rapidly changing environment, more girls now have a chance to have hockey instruction from the time they are young, including opportunities to attend all-girl camps. Worldwide, the much-improved status of women hockey players indicates that the movement is continuing in a positive direction.

Mila C. Su

Bibliography

Avery, Joanna, and Julie Stevens. (1997) *Too Many Men on the Ice: Women's Hockey in North America.* Vancouver: Polestar.

Brooks, Janet. (1990) "Powerful in Pink." *Champion* 14, 1: 44–48.

Cohen, Andrew. (1993) "Icewomen Cometh: Minnesota Schools Move Toward Gender Equity by Adding Girls' Ice Hockey." *Athletic Business* 17, 1: 16, 18.

———. (1995) "Power Plays: The Girls' Ice Hockey Juggernaut Continues Its Romp across Minnesota." *Athletic Business* 19, 9: 16.

Cohen, Harvey T. (1994) "The 'Other' Hockey Ref Among Us." *Stripes* (Spring): 13–14.

Etue, Elizabeth, and Megan Williams. (1996) *On the Edge: Women Making Hockey History.* Toronto: Second Story Press.

Foster, Mary. (1967) "Ice Hockey Rules and Coaching Manual for Women." Unpublished master's thesis, Iowa City: University of Iowa.

Hunsaker, Lee. (1985) "A Break with Tradition?" *American Hockey Magazine* 6, 7: 26–29.

———. (1985) "They've Come a Long Way, Baby." *American Hockey Magazine* 6, 7: 21–25.

Jokinen, Jouko. (1993) "Women Take Up the Challenge." *Motion* 1: 24–25.

Kronholz, June. (1985) "Where Ice Hockey Is Popular, Women Take a Shot at It, Too—They Do a Lot of Bumping, Though Checking Is Out; After the Game, Corsages." *Wall Street Journal* (8 March): 1, 16.

Malkovich, Renee G., and Michael P. Savage. (1987) "Begging No More: A New Era in U.S. Women's Hockey." *GOAL* 14 (April): 57–59.

McFarlane, Brian. (1994) *Proud Past, Bright Future: One Hundred Years of Canadian Women's Hockey.* Toronto: Stoddart.

Morgan, Mary C., ed. (c. 1917) Girls and Athletics, Giving a Brief Summary of the Activity, Rules and Method of Administration of the Following Games in Girls' Schools and Colleges, Women's Clubs, etc.: Archery, Basket Ball, Cricket, Fencing, Field Day, Field Hockey, Gymnastics, Golf, Hand Ball, Ice Hockey, Indoor Base Ball, Rowing, Soccer, Skating, Swimming, Tennis, Track Athletics, Volley Ball, Walking, Water Polo, Water Basket Ball. New York: American Sports Publishing Company, 82–84.

"Officiating Program Feature: Learn More About USA Hockey's Olympic Officials." (1998) *Stripes* (Spring): 10–11.

Raboin, Sharon. (1998) "Games Revive Big Debate: Should Women Check?" *USA Today* (15 January): 7E.

Smith, Gwen. (1997) "The Home Team," *Macleans* (7 April): 68–69.

Teir, B. (1995) "Women's Ice Hockey: Tackling the Traditions" *Motion: Sport in Finland* 1: 11–13.

Vella, Susan. (1990) "RE: Blainey and Ontario Hockey Association: Removal of 'No Female Athletes Allowed' Signs in Ontario." *Canadian Journal of Women and the Law* 3: 634–643.

Williams, Megan. (1995) "Women's Hockey Heating up the Equity Debate." *Canadian Woman Studies* 15, 4: 78–82.

Women's Hockey Web. (1999) <http://www.whockey.com>.

HOCKEY, IN-LINE

In-line hockey is one of two types of hockey on wheels. Roller hockey is the second. Both games are played on a dry, flat surface made of concrete, hardwood, or asphalt. Women play the two sports, although men are more numerous in both. In-line hockey, the more recent variant, is closer to ice hockey, and the rise of women's ice hockey has crossed over to in-line hockey.

HISTORY

The sport of in-line hockey has a relatively brief history. The date of the first actual game is difficult to determine. Many believe the sport to be a progression of the common street hockey that is a neighborhood game. Nonprofessional in-line hockey has very strong grassroots organizations and leagues. In countries such as the United States, Canada, Argentina, Britain, and Finland, there are national organizing bodies who are working to promote the sport and create grassroots opportunities for children and adults to try. In the United States, there is a college league that has held national championships since 1995. In Canada, many universities and colleges offer in-line hockey as an intramural league for students.

Professionally, in-line hockey has been a feasible step for elite female ice hockey players. Several high-profile female players have been a part of the North American in-line hockey league, Roller Hockey International (RHI), founded in 1994. The most successful has been the Canadian goalie Manon Rhéaume, who has played in the RHI since its inception. Other players, such as Cammi Granato, the captain of the U.S. national ice hockey team who was drafted by the Chicago Cheetahs as their first pick in the RHI draft in 1995, have been involved but have not played in regular season games.

With the inclusion of women's ice hockey at the 1998 Winter Olympics, elite female in-line hockey is gaining momentum, and there are plans to hold high-profile women's in-line hockey events. The International Ice Hockey Federation (IIHF) included a women's in-line hockey exhibition challenge between Canada and the United States at the 1998 IIHF In-Line Hockey World Championship Tournament (senior men's). The 1999 in-line world championship included a full women's division.

RULES AND PLAY

In-line hockey is played on in-line skates (three, four, or five wheels aligned lengthwise). Players use wooden or aluminum hockey sticks to control a ball or an in-line hockey puck. The numerous types of in-line hockey pucks all have nubs or rollers that allow the puck to slide on the dry floor.

Most organized in-line hockey is played in ice arenas—without the ice—around the world, and therefore the dimensions are exactly the same as ice hockey rinks. Using ice arenas leaves teams with dimensions anywhere from 65 to 100 feet (19.8 to 30.5 meters) wide and 145 to 200 feet (44.2 to 61.0 meters) long. Tournament and sanctioned championship games are held on at least 80 by 180 feet (24.4 to 54.9 meters), if not the international ice hockey size of 100 by 200 feet (30.5 by 61.0 meters).

The court is called a rink. There are a number of companies who make in-line hockey flooring; typically it is a plastic ventilated interlocking square tile flooring. Although the game can be played on asphalt, concrete, ice arena floors, and so forth, the best surface to play on is the interlocking tile.

The game is played by teams of four, plus goalies. It is a wide-open game of speed and agility. Scores typically are high because of the emphasis on offense. In-line hockey is very much a scorer's dream game. With the decreased use of lines, the play is quicker to move up the surface, and with the four on four, there is more space for talented puck carriers to skate. The puck is lighter, the shots are quicker, and goalies see more shots. The two ways of playing in-line hockey are with a modified off-side and with no off-side. "No off-side" means the players and puck can move around the floor with absolutely no restriction. Rink-long passes can be made from one goal area to the other without penalty. This allows teams to break out of their zone and ultimately be in a position to score with one pass. When playing "modified off-side," again players may skate freely around the playing surface without restriction. However, they may not pass the puck across the center line; they must skate it across.

ROLLER HOCKEY

Roller hockey, or ball-and-cane hockey, is typically played with quad or roller skates (wheels sit two by two, front and back). The stick is a field hockey curved stick, and the ball is small and very hard. Ball-and-cane hockey (male teams) was played as a demonstration sport at the 1992 Summer Olympics in Barcelona.

Internationally, the sport of roller hockey is under the direction of the Fédération Internationale de Roller Skating (FIRS). The federation was founded in 1924 and sanctions international competitions. Roller hockey has a relatively long history, with records that date back to 1930 when women were playing in Kansas City, Missouri, although men had been playing since the first professional roller hockey championship in England in 1906. Women have a strong history internationally in this cousin of field hockey, lacrosse, and ice hockey. There have been Women's World Roller Hockey Championships (WWRHC) every other year since 1992. The FIRS sanctions these events, at which national teams play for the international title. In 1992 the first world championships were held in Germany and brought together ten countries. Canada won the inaugural event, with Italy finishing second. The 1994 world championship was held in Portugal and drew nineteen countries as competitors. Brazil hosted the 1996 WWRHC, with eleven competing countries.

In addition to the world championships there is the European Roller Hockey Championships, which are held during odd-numbered years. This event began in 1991 in Switzerland, where Italy won, with the Netherlands in second place followed by Spain. Italy won again when they hosted the event in 1993, with Spain coming in second and the Netherlands, third. In 1995 Spain held the event and won, with Italy finishing in second place and Switzerland in third place. Portugal held the event in 1997, where again the hosts won, Italy came second, and Spain finished third.

CONCLUSION

While roller hockey is a well-established sport, the sport of in-line hockey is in its infancy. Female ice hockey players are discovering that it is the best off-season training method. Women who do not otherwise play hockey are attracted to the sport because it is familiar and involves a social aspect. It is a sport in which women may easily participate and does not rely on facilities, structure, or organization. In-line hockey can be played at the beach, in a parking lot, or on dry floor in an arena.

Women's in-line hockey is strong in the United States, Brazil, the United Kingdom, Australia, and Canada. Many believe it will become the international hockey of the future for men and women, but with more focus on women because of more opportunities and faster growth in the structure of in-line hockey for women.

Tamara McKernan

Bibliography

Joyner, Steve. (1995) *In-Line Roller Hockey: The Official Guide and Reference Book.* Chicago: Contemporary Books.

NIHA Hockey Talk: The Official Publication of the National In-Line Hockey Association. (April 1995–December 1996) Murrietta, CA: Sportstalk Publication.

NIHA Newsletter. (November 1994–February 1995) Toronto: National In-Line Hockey Association, Canada Division.

HOLM, ELEANOR

(1913–)

U.S. SWIMMER

Eleanor Holm was a teenage swimming star in the 1920s who not only competed internationally but also challenged ideas of how female athletes should look and behave. Holm undertook several careers during her lifetime, including Olympic competitor, nightclub singer, synchronized swimmer, movie actress, and interior decorator. She was known as physically attractive, feisty, independent, and outspoken. These qualities, in addition to her athletic achievements, gained her a great deal of media attention throughout her career.

Holm was born on 6 December 1913 in Brooklyn, New York. In 1927, she garnered nine gold medals at the United States National Championships. A year later, she competed in the 1928 Olympics in Amsterdam, finishing fifth in the 100-meter backstroke. From 1928 through 1936, she continued to win races, acquiring numerous U.S. swimming titles. At the 1932 Olympics in Los

Eleanor Holm, the brash, popular swimming star and entertainer of the 1930s. (Bettmann/Corbis)

Angeles, Holm reached the peak of her athletic fame. She took the gold medal in the 100-meter backstroke, finishing nearly 2 full seconds ahead of her nearest competitor. She was considered a "sure thing" for a medal in the 1936 Olympics in Berlin.

In 1933, she married entertainer Art Jarratt, and she spent the next several years singing with his nightclub band. In a rather audacious statement for the era, Holm told *Time* magazine in 1936 that she never made any secret of the fact that she enjoyed a good time and that she was particularly fond of champagne. Just before the 1936 Olympic games, she told reporters asking about her training regimen that it consisted of "champagne and cigarettes." It was this bold, unabashed attitude that put Holm in the headlines in 1936, not her swimming performance at the games.

En route to those games on the *S. S. Manhattan,* Holm did not behave as the chaperones from the United States Olympic Committee (USOC) expected. She danced at all-night parties in the first-class section of the ship, drank champagne, and gambled with reporters. When one of the chaperones told her at 9 PM that it was time to go to bed, Holm replied that she was no stranger to parties, gambling, or drinking and as an adult member of an Olympic team, she was able to decide her own bedtime. This did not sit well with the USOC. By the time the boat arrived in Bremerhaven, Holm had been removed from the team. She was temporarily heartbroken by the decision, but she recovered her spirits and undertook to report on the games as a correspondent for the Hearst International News Service.

Because of the scandal, Holm returned from the 1936 Olympics with a heightened celebrity status that bolstered her career as an entertainer. She was featured in the 1938 Hollywood film *Tarzan's Revenge*. In 1938 she divorced Art Jarratt and a year later married Billy Rose, appearing in his *Aquacade* with Johnny Weismuller at the 1939 World's Fair in New York. Holm's appearance in this traveling "water ballet" is noted as a milestone in the introduction of synchronized swimming to the United States, paving the way for its future popularity. The media had been mesmerized by the Holm–Rose marriage, and photographs of the couple appeared in magazines and newspapers for many years. The pair divorced in 1952 in a messy, much-publicized legal battle. In the early 1960s, Holm moved to Miami Beach and became an interior decorator, still enjoying social life as she always had.

During her swimming career, Holm won twenty-nine national championships and nine national individual medley gold medals, and she set six world backstroke records. Her Olympic gold medal was for the 100-meter backstroke. Her induction into the International Swimming Hall of Fame in 1966 certified her as an athletic legend, but she is likely to be remembered for her independence, tenacity, and boldness, characteristics that helped break the restrictive stereotype of women as dependent and submissive.

Wendy Painter

Bibliography

Guttmann, Allen. (1991) *Women's Sports*. New York: Columbia University Press.

"I Like Champagne." (1936) *Time*, 28 (3 August): 21.

Newsweek. (1952) 40 (22 September): 36–37.

Newsweek. (1936) 18 (1 August): 20–21.

Pieroth, Doris Hinson. (1996) *Their Day in the Sun*. Seattle: University of Washington Press.

Sports Illustrated. (1972) 37 (17 July): 30–31.

USA Swimming. (1998) "USA Swimming Official Website–Superstars in American Swimming." <http://www.usswim.org>.

The Washington Post. (1998) "U.S. Synchronized Swimming History." <http://www.washingtonpost.com>.

HOMOPHOBIA

Homophobia is the irrational fear and hatred of lesbian, gay, and bisexual people, as manifested in prejudice, discrimination, harassment, and, in some cases, actual violence. Homophobia usually refers to the bigoted or harassing interpersonal behavior of individuals or groups of people, rather than to systemwide policies or programs that have a discriminatory effect.

Some lesbians prefer to use the gender-specific term "lesbophobia" to draw attention to the combined effects of sexism and homophobia. An example of the dual homophobia/sexism problem was provided by CBS golf commentator Ben Wright in 1995. As quoted in news sources, he suggested that: "Lesbians in the sport hurt women's golf. It's paraded. There's a defiance in them in the last decade. [Women golfers] are handicapped by having boobs. It's not easy for them to keep their left arms straight, and that's one of the tenets of the game." Additionally, it is important to recognize the ways in which other systems of oppression based on race/ethnicity, social class, and dis/ability interact with sexism and homophobia in the lives of many lesbians in sport, as in the wider society.

Examples of homophobic discrimination and harassment in women's sport include: (1) lesbian identity used as overt or covert grounds for employment practices (hiring/firing), team selection, and sponsorships; (2) name-calling, slurs, offensive jokes, stereotyping, or sexual advances; (3) physical or verbal threats, intimidation (e.g., graffiti, anonymous phone calls), touching, physical or sexual assault (rape); and (4) threats to disclose a woman's lesbian identity without her permission.

As in nonsport contexts, adolescents and young women are particularly vulnerable to sexual coercion (e.g., date/acquaintance rape), and their attackers may threaten to spread homophobic rumors if the woman resists. In the generally conservative climate of sport, young women's participation in team or other nontraditional sports often marks them as socially and sexually "nonconforming." As a result, many feel the need to establish their heterosexual credentials to counter male peers' suspicions that they are lesbian. This homophobic climate is especially damaging for the young athletes who are in fact lesbian.

While some institutional harassment policies specifically identify and prohibit homophobic harassment, many fail to provide any protection or remedies for lesbians. Sport organizations have generally lagged behind other sectors of society in developing harassment-prevention policies and procedures of any kind and have been particularly slow to engage in open discussions of homophobia. Where institutional codes of behavior do operate—in schools and universities, for example—extracurricular activities such as men's football are often erroneously seen as outside the domain of such policies.

In any discussion of homophobia in women's sport, it is important to consider the related problem of heterosexism. This term refers to the widespread assumption that heterosexuality is the only normal and natural expression of sexuality. Most social institutions and workplaces, including schools, universities, and sports organizations, operate on heterosexist assumptions about individuals and families, for example, by excluding same-sex partners and families from health insurance and pension plans.

A common manifestation of heterosexism in women's sport is the mandatory dress code. The covert (or sometimes stated) rationale for such codes is to emphasize players' heterosexual credentials and appeal, thereby raising the profile of women's sport in the male-dominated marketplace. For example, the form-fitting elasticized bodysuit now required in many Australian women's team sports has been justified on the grounds that "sex sells sport." In other words, regardless of their preferred styles of self-presentation or sexual expression, all sportswomen are expected to conform to a heterosexist image. It is assumed that (male) spectators and sponsors see female athletes first and foremost as (hetero)sexual objects—hence, the demand for heterosexual appeal.

Since the early days of women's involvement in organized sport in the Western world, homophobia and heterosexism have worked together to produce a "chilly climate" for lesbian athletes and a climate of compulsory heterosexuality for women of all sexual orientations. This climate is marked by constant overt and covert messages to sportswomen to present a heterosexually attractive image to the public and to suppress all evidence that there are any lesbians in sport.

In a 1995 example in Australian women's cricket, players' and administrators' attempts to refute rumors of a lesbian majority were characterized by disgust and outrage at the notion that

HOMOPHOBIA IN ATHLETICS

In her 1998 book, *Strong Women: Deep Closets*, sports sociologist and activist Patricia Griffin argues that opponents of women's full participation in sports have developed the homophobic image of the "lesbian bogeyman." As a stereotype, the lesbian bogeyman is a lesbian athlete who preys sexually on other women, is unidentifiable, and is disruptive to the normal functioning of society. Griffin argues that this false image of lesbians and women athletes is used to define women's sports participation as abnormal, to limit participation of women in sports, to place women in subordinate positions, and to divide women so that they cannot act as a unified force to fight for women's rights in sports.

lesbians played cricket at all. This defense—a common one in women's sport—is not only strategically unsound (because it allows the critics to "divide and rule") but also very damaging to the morale of lesbian players because it renders their presence and contribution invisible.

Homophobia has long served to divide heterosexual and lesbian women in sport, and these divisions have been largely responsible for sportswomen's general reluctance to join in feminist political struggles around sport or other women's issues in the past three decades. The feminist = lesbian equation has been especially pervasive in sport circles, and many observers would argue that sport is the past bastion of sexism and homophobia.

Sexual orientation constitutes prohibited grounds for discrimination in some jurisdictions in Canada, the United States, Australia, and the United Kingdom, but protection is by no means universal. It is to be hoped that legal battles such as the 1997 American case of a lesbian field hockey coach who was fired from her university position will help to pave the way for more widespread antidiscrimination legislation. However, the financial and emotional toll on those involved in high-profile test cases deters many lesbians from revealing the true extent of homophobic harassment and discriminatory employment practices that they experience in sport contexts. Therefore, rather than relying on social change through the legal precedent route, it is important for all progressive people in sport to challenge homophobia as it is manifested in everyday sporting practices, through educational and awareness-raising initiatives, codes of behavior, and harassment-prevention policies and procedures.

Helen Jefferson Lenskyj

See also Gay Games; Lesbianism

Bibliography

Burroughs, Angela, Liz Ashburn, and Leonie Seebohm. (1995) " 'Add Sex and Stir': Homophobic Coverage of Women's Cricket in Australia." *Journal of Sport and Social Issues* 19, 3: 266–284.

Griffin, Pat. (1989) "Homophobia in Physical Education." *CAHPER Journal* 55, 2: 27–31.

———. (1992) "Changing the Game: Homophobia, Sexism and Lesbians in Sport." *Quest* 44: 251–265.

———. (1994) "Homophobia in Sport: Addressing the Needs of Lesbian and Gay High School Athletes." In *The Gay Teen,* edited by Gerald Unks. New York: Routledge.

———. (1998) *Strong Women, Deep Closets.* Champaign, IL: Human Kinetics.

Kane, Mary Jo, and Helen Lenskyj. (1998) "Media Treatment of Female Athletes: Issues of Gender and Sexualities." In *MediaSport: Cultural Sensibilities and Sport in the Media Age,* edited by Laurence Wenner. New York: Routledge.

Lenskyj, Helen. (1986) *Out of Bounds: Women, Sport and Sexuality.* Toronto: Women's Press.

———. (1991) "Combating Homophobia in Sport and Physical Education: Academic and Professional Responsibilities." *Sociology of Sport Journal* 8, 1: 61–69.

———. (1995) "Sport and the Threat to Gender Boundaries." *Sporting Traditions* 12, 1: 47–60.

HONDURAS

Honduras is a small country in the Central American isthmus with a population of 5.6 million. The majority of Hondurans live in rural areas where there is little formal support for organized sport. Organized sport is concentrated in the main cities, Tegucigalpa and San Pedro Sula. Sport initially developed in Honduras through the influence of American and European employees of the banana companies (long the mainstay of the Honduran economy), immigrants from Europe and other Latin American nations, and students who returned home after studying at foreign universities.

Women's sports developed slowly. Until the 1950s, when some girls and young women began to play basketball, sport was a male activity, one that was not compatible with the prevailing image of women and their role in Honduran society. Women were expected to be subservient to men—at least in public—and to work mainly in or near the home. These restrictions on women began to give way in the 1970s due to the effort of feminist organizations that advocated for a greater role for women in Honduran society. In 1974 the first school of physical education was founded at the Pedagogical University to train physical education teachers. By 1988 the Independent National University offered an extended curriculum, aimed at educating professors, recreation directors, and trainers. By the end of the 1990s a third of the students were women.

PROGRESS IN SPORTS

The first sport practiced by women in Honduras was basketball, which was introduced in the 1920s by Sister Agustina Rosi, an Italian nun who taught at the Institute of Maria the Helper in Tegucigalpa. The game then spread to other schools for young women in several cities. A league was organized by the schools, and friendly games and exhibitions became the primary sport event for young women around the nation. In 1950 the Honduran women's team won the first Central American championship in basketball, going through the tournament undefeated.

Swimming and volleyball were organized in the 1970s, thus considerably increasing the participation of women in sport. But the major event that led to the development of women's sport did not occur until the late 1980s when it was announced that the 1990 Central American Sport Games would be in Tegucigalpa. Eager to have its athletes perform as well as possible in the games as a means of enhancing Honduras' regional reputation, the Honduran authorities encouraged and supported the development of women's sports and women athletes. As a result, women become visibly active in several new sports, including sprinting, weight throwing, judo, karate, artistic gymnastics, tennis, table tennis, racquetball, and fencing.

This effort to promote sports for women had the lasting effect of producing more interest in sports by women and more women participants. Basketball, swimming, and volleyball, followed by the martial arts, gymnastics, and handball, remain the most popular sports. The most successful athletes are the sisters Ana and Claudia Bunker (swimming), the sisters Izzwa and Jhalim Medina (table tennis), Dora Maldonado (judo), and Chávez Shepherd and Gina Coit (track and field). Honduras sent a total of ten women to the four Olympics in 1984, 1988, 1992, and 1996, including Ana Bunker (Seoul, 1988), Claudia Bunker (Barcelona, 1992), and Chávez Shepherd (Atlanta, 1996).

The advances in women's sport since the 1970s have been considerable. In 1970 there were only 260 women members of sport organizations in only three sports. By 1999 these numbers had risen to 5,000 members in organizations that represented twenty-five sports, compared to 16,750 men in organizations representing thirty-one sports. This increased participation at home has produced increased participation in regional and international events. For example, no Honduran women participated in the 1973 Central American Sport Games, but in the sixth games in 1997, 134 Honduran women athletes formed 31 percent of the total Honduran delegation and gained almost half the medals won by Honduras. Similarly, in the growing physical fitness industry, women form the majority of users of fitness centers and hold positions as professors of physical education, trainers, organization leaders, and referees, although still at a percentage far below that of men.

Edeltraud Minar

Bibliography

Galeano, Jorge. *Historia del Baloncesto en Honduras.* Tegucigalpa, Honduras: Comité Olímpico.

Minar, Edeltraud. (1966) *Historia de la Natación Hondureña.* Tegucigalpa, Honduras: Comité Olímpico.

———. (1996) *Historia del Atletismo* (Cuadernos de Documentación No. 6). Tegucigalpa, Honduras: CIDDE.

HORSEBACK RIDING

Equestrian competition offers one of the few sporting arenas in which women and men compete equally, with the horse leveling the playing field. Although women were long excluded from organized horse sports, which, based on the traditions of battle and work, remained exclusively male-oriented for centuries, they fought vigorously for acceptance and eventually came to dominate many equestrian disciplines in excellence and sheer numbers. Through the years, society's changing view of the horse has also furthered the progress of women and riding: the animal's role changed from that of a man's instrument of work

A group of women ride sidesaddle, a style of riding once required for women, but now only a minor sport. (Kit Houghton)

and war to one of a more woman-friendly domesticated companion for recreation and amusement. In modern times, more than 80 percent of people involved in equestrian activities are female.

In significant ways, women possess advantages over men in equestrian pursuits. Their wider hips place their center of gravity securely in the saddle. Unable to rely on the physical strength natural to most men, they use in its place techniques integral to successful riding—balance, finesse, and, most important, communication. Horses, which are passive herd animals, respond best to communication through a soft touch, a soothing voice, and an overall gentle manner. Female equestrians seem to excel at this type of communication, making the equine–human connection a true partnership. Their sensitivity and intuition put the horse at ease and free it to be more receptive and cooperative to the demands of training and performance. Similarly, a woman receives back from her horse unconditional affec-

tion, an outlet for her teaching and nurturing impulses, and a means of enjoying outdoor exercise and connection with the natural world. Finally, the female–horse relationship appeals to some women's fantasy of "taming the wild beast," while amazingly at the same time fulfilling for them the little girl's dream of grooming, braiding, dressing up, and showing off horse and rider. All of these powerful themes underlie women's interactions with horses.

History and myth provide a rich account of women and horses, who have maintained a colorful relationship since the horse's domestication 6,000 years ago. Greek myth tells of the famous nation of fierce woman warriors called Amazons, who founded the first cavalry, rode astride, and flourished in a society completely lacking men; Celtic myth alludes to a horse goddess named Epona. The recorded history of women and horses dates back as far as 61 CE, when Boadicea, the widow of a king in East Anglia and a superb chariot driver, led an uprising in London against the conquering Romans. By the late 1300s, an unmistakably female addition to equestrian history began to appear around Britain—the ladies' sidesaddle, introduced by King Richard II's wife, Anne of Bohemia, and designed for women to ride with both legs on one side of the saddle.

Up until the introduction of the sidesaddle, women either wore a split skirt and rode astride or sat *pillion*, on a pillow behind the man's saddle. When the sidesaddle first made its appearance in the Middle Ages, it was used only by the wealthy, and most women paid little attention and continued to ride astride. A notable example was Joan of Arc, a saint, warrior, and great horsewoman who, riding astride, led French armies to victory over England in the 1400s. In the fifteenth and early sixteenth centuries, European ladies were encouraged to ride and hunt, but gradually a shift in the social acceptability of these activities for women began to develop. By the late sixteenth and early seventeenth centuries, riding astride was deemed improper for ladies, and hunting and cross-country riding were not considered safe or respectable. The "women's saddle," or sidesaddle, took hold, and fashion soon followed. Women in Europe and the newly forming United States were forced by society's dictates to don tightly fitted vests, layers upon layers of petticoats, long skirts, high-collared blouses, and other adornments that made riding dangerous, impractical, and sometimes impossible.

Notable women riders of the eighteenth century were Mary Queen of Scots, Marie Antoinette, and the Marquise of Salisbury, who became the first woman Master of Foxhounds for the Hatfield Hunt in 1775. The perils of riding on such an unstable saddle did not deter upper-class women in the United States and Europe from dressing up and meeting for casual rides. The outings gave them an opportunity to bond, socialize, and escape the confines of society for a little while. The horse came to symbolize, for them, freedom.

In 1830, a Frenchman named Jules Pellier developed a new sidesaddle, outfitted with a leaping horn that allowed women to wrap one leg on the pommel of the saddle. With this technology, the sidesaddle became infinitely more secure and revolutionized the possibilities of safe hunting and riding for women. Unfortunately, the saddle was introduced at the height of women's unacceptability in hunts and other equestrian pastimes; the saddle did not come into use in Britain, the world's hub of organized equestrian activities, for another thirty years.

By the late 1800s in the United States, ranch life on the western frontier necessitated that women ride astride, and increasingly more of their sisters across the Atlantic followed suit, albeit with significantly more controversy and opposition. The women remained persistent, and fashions began to change to accommodate riding astride in the early 1900s. By 1938, virtually all women had reverted to this safer method of horsemanship. The sidesaddle disappeared from public life for several decades, until a renewed interest in the technique led to the founding in 1974 of the U.S. Sidesaddle Association, which boasted more than 2,000 members in 1999. The World Sidesaddle Federation was founded in 1980. In the late 1990s, many large horse shows in America and Europe offered flat and jumping classes for sidesaddle competitors, with year-end awards presented to champions on regional and national levels.

The Industrial Revolution made workhorses virtually obsolete, and cavalry forces were gradually mechanized between 1900 and 1950, so the well-trained but jobless equines were newly categorized as sporting companions for recreation. As such, they became much more accessible to women and all amateur-level horsemen. Women's battle for acceptance in horse sports had not ended with the disappearance of the sidesaddle, however.

Female participation in hunting, racing, and Olympic equestrian competition, which began in 1912, would not be seen for many years. The 1930s saw women and horses through a sheen of glamour in movies like *National Velvet, Black Beauty,* and *My Friend Flicka.* The real-world glamour of competing in national or Olympic competition was not achieved by women until 1952, when the first female equestrian, dressage rider Marjorie Haines of the United States, was permitted to ride in the Games.

SHOW JUMPING

Show jumping is an exhilarating sport of power, speed, and grace, in which riders and horses are judged on their ability to jump a course of tight turns and obstacles without knocking anything

JANE CLARK, ORGANIZATION LEADER

Jane Clark of Cooperstown, New York has been an incredible force in the world of equestrian sports. An avid and successful rider as a child and adult, and an invaluable presence as an owner, breeder, and sponsor of top hunter, jumper, and driving horses, Clark served for five years as first vice president of the AHSA, beginning in 1986. In 1991, she was elected unanimously as the president of the Association-not only the first female president in the organization's eighty-five year history but also the youngest. As president, she saw the Association safely through some hard times, including an insurance fraud scandal and a controversy over horses and heat at the Olympic Games in Atlanta. In 1996 Clark again made history by being the first woman elected to the FEI Bureau and Executive Committee, a group that directed international policies and issues concerning equestrian sports. She also served on the Board of Directors of the USET, the U.S. Olympic Committee, and the American Horse Council, in addition to running several charitable foundations, historical associations, and the National Baseball Hall of Fame.

down or exceeding time limits. After each rider has completed one round, all competitors who finished *clean*, or without time or jumping faults, are invited back individually for a *jump-off*, a shortened course that stresses speed. The competitor that finishes the class with the fewest penalties, in the fastest time, is the winner.

One of the three Olympic equestrian disciplines, along with three-day eventing and dressage, show jumping is popular around the world, with a heavy concentration of interest in the locales of its origin, Western Europe and the United States. Jumper classes range from preliminary level up to the highest difficulty, called Grand Prix. In Grand Prix show jumping contests, riders and horses are asked to compete in fourteen to sixteen jumps ranging in height from 1.4 meters (4.5 feet) to over 1.8 meters (6 feet). The obstacles might also be water jumps, high vertical fences, combination jumps, or *oxers*, which test the horse's ability to jump a distance of 1.5 to 1.8 meters (5 to 6 feet) long as well as high. A specialty class at show jumping events is the *puissance*, in which a large wall jump is constructed, competitors attempt it, and it is increased in height continually until nobody is able to clear it without incurring a penalty. The first woman to win the puissance was Caroline Bradley of Britain, who took the title in 1974. Her mark did not last long, and the puissance height record in 1999 was 2.35 meters (7 feet, 8.5 inches).

Women competed in Olympic show jumping on equal terms with men in 1956, and by the early 1960s, the United States had started to produce successful women show jumping riders like Kathy Kusner and Mary Mairs (Chapot). Both women gave strong performances in the 1964 Olympic Games in Tokyo and the 1968 Olympics in Mexico. Kusner became the only woman to be on three Olympic teams when she rode at the 1972 Olympics in Munich. Later she became a successful professional racing jockey. In 1984 Leslie Burr (Howard) and Melanie Smith, both from the United States, became the first female members of a gold-medal-winning team in Olympic show jumping at the Games in Los Angeles. Smith added the historic medal to her trophy case, which already included honors for her triumphant ride to become the first female winner of the show jumping World Cup, in Gothenburg, Sweden, in 1982. The 1984 Olympics marked the tail end of an era (1975–1985) when female riders from the United States dominated the sport of show jumping.

In the 1990s show jumping arenas around the world teemed with female riders at every level. Leslie Burr-Howard and Anne Kursinski made up one-half of the 1996 silver-medal-winning U.S. team at the Olympic Games in Atlanta. The American Horse Shows Association's (AHSA) National Junior Jumper Championships are consistently topped by some bold-riding female

Lulu Rochford and her mount, Ladybird V, jump a fence during training prior to the selections for the British national show jumping team in 1949. (Hulton-Deutsch Collection/Corbis)

teens, and there appears to be no slowing in the growth of the sport for women.

DRESSAGE

Although the definition of dressage, French for "training," is nothing more than the development of the horse's three natural gaits—the walk, trot, and canter—the definition belies a complex and demanding task. Many years of careful, day-by-day training must go into coaching a dressage horse as it develops the physical strength and mental understanding for its task.

In competitive dressage, horse and rider perform a prescribed test in an enclosed, flat arena, performing the movements called for in the test at the markers or "letters" that are placed on the border of the ring. Tests highlight the degree of training that should be in evidence at a particular level, such as the collection or extension of the stride, lateral movements, or movements off the track. Horses are moved progressively through levels, beginning with training level, then moved on to first, second, third, fourth, and fifth levels,

and if it demonstrates sufficient ability, the horse begins competing in the levels of Prix St. Georges—Intermédiaire I, Intermédiaire II, and finally, Grand Prix. The latter four levels are the international levels, or Fédération Equestre Internationale (FEI) levels, and Grand Prix is the highest-caliber level contested at major competitions, including the Olympics.

In Grand Prix dressage competition, riders are scored by five judges situated around the arena, who mark the quality and correctness of each competitor's movements on a scale of 1 to 10. There is a maximum score possible for the test, but no dressage rider has ever received a perfect score. The contest is comprised of two parts, the preset, 8-minute Grand Prix test, and the specialized *freestyle*, or *Kur*, which is individually choreographed by each competitor and set to music. Some of the movements that horses perform in both sections include the *piaffe*, or trotting in place; the elegant *passage*, trotting with a suspension between each step; extended gaits; and pirouettes.

Women have won more Olympic medals in dressage than in any other equestrian sport. The first woman to be awarded an Olympic medal in dressage was Lis Hartel, a Danish rider, who, along with her horse Jubilee, won the individual silver medal at the 1952 Olympic Games in Helsinki, Finland. She repeated the feat four years later at the Olympic Games in Stockholm. Her accomplishments were all the more amazing not only because she was one of the female pioneers of Olympic equestrian sports but also because she was paralyzed from the knees down.

In 1956, Germany sent an all-woman dressage squad to the Olympic Games in Stockholm, Sweden. The team won the silver medal, and their outstanding rider, Liselott Linsenhoff, won the individual bronze. Sixteen years later in Munich, Germany, she became the first woman to win an individual Olympic gold medal in dressage on her horse Piaffe. Concurrent with Linsenhoff's career were the exploits of British dressage rider Lorna Johnstone, one of the first British women to compete in Olympic dressage, at Stockholm. She won the national dressage championships in the United Kingdom thirteen times and then proceeded to Olympic competition in Munich, where, at the age of seventy, she placed twelfth—

the highest of anyone on her team—and set a record at the time as the oldest Olympic competitor in history.

Olympic dressage from 1972 to 1984 was dominated by women and continued to draw a high percentage of female competitors. Four of the top five riders in the 1996 Olympic dressage contests were women, including the gold and silver medal winners. In 1999 the U.S. Dressage Federation reported a membership of 28,000, with numbers on an upward trend every year and women constituting 95 percent of membership.

THREE-DAY EVENTING

One of the three Olympic equestrian disciplines, three-day eventing, also called combined training, is the complete test of horse and rider. Based on the traditions of the cavalry, the sport tests competitors in three defined areas: dressage, speed and endurance, and stadium jumping. In the course of competition, however, competitors must also exhibit the bravery, fitness, obedience, athleticism, and ability to keep going after a grueling ride of the kind that was so necessary for cavalry horse-and-rider pairs.

Day one of the contest is reserved for the dressage phase, which emphasizes obedience and athleticism, though at a lower level than in pure dressage competition. The second day is the four-phase endurance test. The cross-country phase tests the horse's endurance and ability to jump fixed obstacles similar to those that might be found on a cross-country ride of the cavalry, such as water jumps, ditches, and fallen trees. The height of the obstacles must not exceed 1.2 meters (3.9 feet) in height or 3.0 meters (9.8 feet) in width. Before the cross-country test, the horse and rider must complete three other phases: two sets of roads and tracks—a few miles of trotting and slow cantering to warm up—and one phase of steeplechase—high-speed jumping over brush fences. The goal in all three phases is to complete the tests within the time allowed and without jumping penalties. The third day features the stadium jumping phase, which tests the competitors' fitness to continue after the previous day of

LINDA ALLEN, AMERICAN COURSE DESIGNER

Linda Allen of Salinas, California, is the world's premiere show jumping course designer, a career that seemed destined to evolve out of her varied and successful equestrian experiences as a rider, judge, trainer, and international competitor.

Allen began showing saddle seat on a half-Arabian mare before moving onto American Saddlebreds and competing as well in the hunter and jumper rings in the northern California area. The hunters and jumpers held the most appeal and became Allen's main occupation; she immersed herself in the horse business, training and competing around the United States and Canada. Success in the jumper ring provided a chance for her to ride for the U.S. Equestrian Team abroad and the opportunity to meet the British course designer, Pamela Carruthers.

A few years later, after injury precluded further time in the saddle, Allen found herself on yet another learning situation, this time in the world of course design. She continued to work with Carruthers whenever possible, learning to design courses that were safe and educational for the horses. By the mid-1980s, Allen was designing for some of the most important horse shows in the United States, including the Washington International Horse Show in Landover, Maryland.

Allen has since established herself as a predominant international course designer in a field dominated by men. Her achievements reached new heights at the 1996 Olympic Games in Atlanta, where her challenging show jumping courses were praised uniformly by competitors, trainers, and spectators. She continued to design for major international shows, like the Devon Horse Show in Pennsylvania, the USET Festival of Champions in New Jersey, the Los Angeles National Horse Show, the Pennsylvania National Horse Show, and the World Cup Show Jumping Finals. Allen was also active as a judge and on the panels of several vital AHSA committees.

all-out riding. The stadium jumping phase is very similar to show jumping, only with lower fences and no jump-off. The goal is not to test the natural jumping ability of the horse but simply to prove that it is fit and well-prepared. The competitor with the least number of penalty points over the three days is the winner.

Eventing riders and horses compete at five different levels in the United States based on experience: novice, training, preliminary, intermediate, and advanced (Olympic level). Human and equine competitors must advance gradually through these ranks to ensure their readiness for the demands of the rigorous tests of fitness and control. In the United States, this process is overseen by the U.S. Combined Training Association (USCTA), which in 1999 had 12,000 members, 65 percent of whom were female, and American Horse Shows Association, the national equestrian federation, which had 70,000 members, 85 percent of them female.

Some major three-day eventing competitions saw women ride to success early on. Perhaps the most prestigious event in the world, the United Kingdom's Badminton, was first run in 1949; five women participated, one of whom finished fifth. The first woman to win the event was Margaret Hough, who took top honors in 1954 riding her horse, Bambi. For three consecutive record-setting years from 1957 to 1959, Sheila Wilcox rode to victory at Badminton. Other newsmakers in the sport of eventing were British rider Mary Gordon Watson, the first female winner of the eventing world championships in 1970, and Princess Anne, who competed at the top level in the 1970s and brought public attention to the sport before switching full time to steeplechase.

Of the three Olympic equestrian disciplines, Olympic-level three-day eventing barred women as competitors for the longest time, mostly because of the sport's military origins and strenuous nature. No woman competed in an Olympic three-day event until 1964 in Tokyo, when American rider Helen du Pont participated on her horse, Mr. Wister. They finished thirty-third, and, following their lead, women soon began thronging to the sport.

The first woman to win a team gold medal was British rider Jane Bullen at the 1968 Mexico City Olympics. In 1979 American Torrance Watkins Fleischmann took the individual bronze at the alternative Olympics. In 1984, of the forty-eight competitors in the Olympic three-day event, eighteen were female. American Karen Stives, riding Ben Arthur, became the first woman to win an individual silver medal, and Virginia Holgate of Britain took the bronze. The tradition of female excellence in three-day eventing has grown, with women taking a front-seat role in the 1996 Olympics. Sally Clark of New Zealand won the silver medal on her horse, Squirrel Hill, and Kerry Millikin of the United States took the individual bronze on her talented mount, Out and About. Mara De Puy of the United States finished sixth, on Hopper, and two other women, Jill Henneberg, on Nirvana II and Karen O'Connor, on Biko, rounded out the silver-medal-winning U.S. team.

OTHER EQUESTRIAN DISCIPLINES

With the exception of racing, polo, and rodeo, women participated in equestrian activities at a disproportionately high percentage compared to the world population. In the last quarter of the twentieth century women also featured prominently in other horse riding events.

Hunter Seat Riding

Hunter seat riding, based on the hunting traditions of Europe, poses a whole new set of challenges for horse and rider. The goal for success is not being the fastest or jumping the highest, but rather displaying correct form, balance, control, and seamless transitions, both jumping and "on the flat." The vast majority of riders and horse people in the hunter ring, whether professional, amateur, or "backyard" enthusiasts, are female. Many successful Grand Prix jumper riders, like Leslie Burr-Howard, began their professional careers in the hunter arena before moving on. A review of the results of the prestigious AHSA Hunter Seat Equitation Medal and ASPCA/Maclay Championship reveals a majority of female winners and female trainers like the United State's Missy Clark, whose students dominate year after year.

Stock Seat (Western)

A style of horsemanship developed to meet the needs of Western frontiersmen and cattle ranchers, stock seat riding has nonetheless grown to be an acceptable and popular sport for women. Women compete in all recognized Western horsemanship classes: reining, in which competitors perform set patterns and movements like sliding stops, circles, and roll-backs; working cow horse, which asks competitors to separate and control a single cow from a herd; stock seat equitation, which tests riders' position, control, and balance; as well as cutting, team penning, barrel racing, and to a much lesser extent, rodeo. Women have kept pace with men as winners of the AHSA's National Stock Seat Equitation Championships and also represented 58 percent of the membership of the Western-oriented American Quarter Horse Association.

Racing

Women's participation in horse racing, whether flat, harness, or steeplechase, was a long time in coming. However, starting with Queen Anne of Britain, who inaugurated the famous races at Ascot in 1711, women have long been enthusiasts of the sport. The first woman recorded as a competitor in a horse race was Mrs. Alicia Thornton of Britain, who in 1804 drew a huge crowd of spectators to the track to witness her controversial and groundbreaking ride. Though she led throughout the race, her horse went lame in the final quarter and she did not finish. In 1969 the first race allowing a female jockey was run in the United States. British racing authorities were forced to follow suit in 1972. Since then there have been several high-profile female jockeys, including Princess Anne in steeplechase and Americans Julie Krone and Kathy Kusner in flat racing.

Endurance

The equestrian discipline of endurance challenges competitors to complete a long and arduous trail ride within a set amount of time. Riders must gauge carefully their horse's fitness and set a pace that will allow them to finish. Each horse's condition is carefully monitored at specific checkpoints, and equines appearing in any way unfit to go on are removed from competition. Arabian horses, which are world-famous for their hardiness and stamina, are the most popular breed for endurance competitions. A friendly though competitive group, endurance riders welcomed women into their sport early on and indeed boasted two women as the top competitors in the discipline: Valerie and Danielle Kanavy, a mother-and-daughter team who won just about every major endurance championship and continually emerged on top at national and world competitions.

Saddle Seat

Riders of American Saddlebreds and Morgans are the usual competitors in saddle seat riding and equitation contests. They ride on a small, flat saddle and keep their stirrups very long as they guide their horses through patterns and gait changes, including special gaits exclusive to the American Saddlebred breed. As in most horse sports, women dominate. In the history of the AHSA's National Saddle Seat Equitation Championship, only a handful of boys have won the competition; the biannual Saddle Seat World Cup crowns a winning team and individual, the majority of whom have been young women from the United States and South Africa.

Mary A. Conti

Bibliography

Bein, Lorri. (1997) "Jane Clark's Lasting Legacy." *Horseshow Magazine* 1, LXI: 30–31.

Midkiff, Mary D. (1996) *Fitness, Performance and the Female Equestrian.* New York: Howell Book House.

Newsum, Gillian. (1988) *Women and Horses.* Hampshire, UK: The Sportsman's Press.

Owen, Rosamund. (1984) *Art of Side-Saddle Riding.* London: Trematon Press.

HORSE RACING

The history of women in horse racing has been one of struggle against male domination of the sport and, paradoxically, of resistance to women's participation by owners and other women influential in turf affairs. In most sports, women are seen as being at a physical disadvantage if pitted against male adversaries, but equestrian events are a major exception. In show jumping, eventing, and dressage, women have proved the equals of male riders. Yet in horse racing, including flat, jumps, and harness racing, they have not, save in a minority of cases, made the grade against masculine opposition at the elite level, nor were they allowed to try for many years.

HISTORY

Instances of races for women riders can be found in the eighteenth and nineteenth centuries, but they were one-off events, of interest more for their novelty than for actual racing. When Alicia Thornton of Great Britain, riding sidesaddle, beat leading jockey Frank Buckle in a race at York in 1805, thousands flocked to see "the jockey in petticoats," though it should be noted that his horse carried 13 stones 6 pounds and hers 4 stones less. (A stone equals 14 pounds.)

In one area of racing women did compete regularly against men. This was in point-to-point racing, which emerged in the late nineteenth century as an amateur version of the steeplechasing

organized by hunt clubs. When the rules of this branch of the sport were formalized by the Masters of Hounds Committee in 1913, women were not prohibited from riding against males; indeed, several had already done so under the aegis of particular hunts. It can be speculated that an acceptance of women in the hunting field led to an enlightened policy in point-to-point racing. This policy, however, did not last. During the 1920s women-only races began to develop, and in 1929 new rules promulgated by the Master of Hounds Committee rendered women ineligible to ride at point-to-point meetings except in races confined to their own gender. Since then, parallel events for men and women have been the norm, with only a few open races. Nevertheless, for a decade and a half the point-to-point authorities were well ahead of their counterparts in flat and National Hunt racing in terms of gender equality. Unfortunately, they were brought back into

---

SUFFRAGETTES SEEK VOTE BY TORCHING RACE TRACKS

The women's suffrage movement in Britain targeted horse racing in 1913 because the turf was considered a bastion of male power and privilege and the sport of politicians. Campaigning for votes for women, the suffrage activists initially aimed to draw attention to their cause by peaceful protest but an increasingly militant faction embarked on a series of more violent demonstrations. In April 1913 two arson attacks took place at Scottish racetracks. On the first occasion a grandstand at Ayr, Scotland's premier course, was destroyed by a fire that caused an estimated £3,500 in damage. Although the culprits were not caught, women's suffrage literature was found in the vicinity. The second incident was an attempt to set fire to the paddock and grandstand at Kelso racecourse near the English border. It failed but five women were arrested, and three were subsequently imprisoned for the attack. On other occasions, fire raising (arson) in England led to the destruction of the grandstands at Birmingham and Hurst Park and an unsuccessful attempt on Cardiff racecourse in Wales. Two women were sentenced to three years imprisonment for the Hurst Park incident.

One of the most famous episodes in women's suffrage history, however, occurred at the English Derby meeting in June 1913. As the runners approached a wide bend in the course, Emily Davison, who had already served a prison term for her suffrage activities, ran on to the track and was knocked down, dying some days later from a fractured skull. Whether this was a political gesture or an accident is unclear. It is said she was attempting to bring down Amner, a horse belonging to King George V, in order to publicize the cause. But Amner's jockey, having seen the look of horror on her face before the collision, believed it was a tragic accident. Some race participants thought that it was sheer coincidence that she brought down the king's horse because it would have been very difficult to select a specific runner from among the field; others were convinced that she was merely crossing the track and failed to see the last of the horses because of the bend. But the incident lives on in folklore as an example of the bravery and determination of a woman who believed firmly in female equality.

the pack rather than setting a lead for others to follow.

REMOVING THE BARRIERS

As in many sections of society, it took equal opportunity legislation and legal action to force the breakthrough. First to drop the barrier was the United States after court action was taken in 1968 in Maryland by Kathy Kusner, an Olympic equestrian, to secure her riding license. By the early 1970s the United States had more than sixty registered female jockeys. In Britain the Jockey Club, for centuries a male fortress, did not allow women to race on the flat until 1972, compete against male amateurs until 1974, or compete against male professionals until 1976, when forced to do so by the Sex Discrimination Act. In Australia federal legislation in 1979 forced all the country's racing authorities to accept female riders.

The first woman to ride against men was the American Diane Crump at Hialeah race track in Florida on 7 February 1969—Kathy Kusner had injured her leg at a Madison Square Garden horse show and was unable to claim that distinction. The first to win—possibly the first female to beat men in a professional sports event—was Barbara Jo Rubin aboard Cohesion at Charles Town, West Virginia, later that month. Cheryl White became the first female African-American jockey to win a thoroughbred race when she piloted Jetolara to victory at Waterford Park, West Virginia, in September 1971. Harness driver Bea Farber was the first woman to win a title at a major track and the first to break the thousand-win barrier.

Other women on the historical honor board include New Zealander Linda Jones, the first woman to win against men in Australia when Pay The Purple was adjudged first in a three-way photo finish in the Labor Day Cup at Doomben on 7 May 1979, and the Australian Wehr sisters Carlene, Ramona, and Leonie who finished first, second, and third in the Stuart Handicap at Alice Springs in July 1982. In Britain Meriel Tufnell won the Goya Stakes, the first flat race for women at Kempton on 6 May 1972; and Karen Wiltshire was the first to beat male professionals in 1978.

JOCKEYS AND DRIVERS

Opposition to women riders came from several quarters: conservative administrators who raised

Solna Joel stands proudly beside her mount, Filus, after racing to victory in the annual Newmarket Town Plate in 1948. (Hulton-Deutsch Collection/Corbis)

the economic smoke screen of the costs of providing separate changing facilities; chivalrous traditionalists who feared for the safety of women riders, especially over the jumps; jockeys' wives who worried about sexual impropriety; and many male jockeys, particularly the journeymen, who openly argued that women would be dangerous as they did not have the strength to control fractious horses but covertly feared more competition in an already oversupplied labor market. Some jockeys were verbally hostile: Nick James, the president of the American Jockeys Guild, reckoned "jockettes," as he disparagingly labeled them, would "make a mockery of thoroughbred racing"; British steeplechase rider Steve Smith Eccles felt that "women jockeys are a pain. Jumping is a man's game. They are not built like us. Most of them are as strong as half a disprin." The champion jockey Lester Piggott was even more dismissive of their efforts on the flat, merely noting that "their bottoms are the wrong shape."

In the United States male riders collectively instigated boycotts of races but stopped when they were fined by racing authorities and threatened with court action. Others, both in the United States and Europe, adopted overly aggressive tactics such as bumping and deliberate obstruction, though in the interests of racing the stewards clamped down on such behavior. Moreover, once male jockeys realized that women were serious about their riding, they desisted from "dirty tricks." In the words of Gay Kellaway, the first female to win at Royal Ascot, "although in 1987 some still did not like being beaten by a woman, it had become accepted." Similarly women drivers were accepted in harness racing once they had demonstrated competence and caution.

OPPORTUNITY AND VICTORY

Given the opportunity, the better women riders can hold their own against male opposition. In 1982 Beverley Buckingham was champion jockey in Tasmania, Australia; in the United States Blyth Miller was leading steeplechase rider twice in the early 1990s; and in Britain "Queen of the Sands" Alex Greaves, the only woman to ride out her apprenticeship claim (a weight allowance given to trainee riders who have won less than a specified number of races), has one of the best all-weather track riding records, though she still finds it difficult to secure regular mounts on the conventional courses. Indeed, the vast majority of her rides have come via trainer David Nicolls, to whom she is married.

Like many other good riders, Greaves has found that legislation is not enough to overcome discrimination ingrained by years of tradition in a conservative industry. Many owners and trainers are still reluctant to offer women mounts. Female jockeys are caught in a vicious circle of nondevelopment: Without rides they cannot demonstrate their ability to win, but without a winning record they cannot get the opportunities. Of course, this applies to aspiring male riders as well, but they do not have to contend with the additional prejudice. Female drivers in harness racing have faced similar resistance.

A few women riders have gained the respect of their male competitors. Leading American jockey Angel Cordero concedes that Julie Krone, winner of nearly 2,000 races in her first decade as a professional, "don't ride like a girl, . . . she can ride with any jockey in the country." Although some women have used their sexuality to secure mounts, in the saddle the successful ones have had to be tough and ruthless and see themselves as such. Mary Bacon, one of America's pioneering female riders, said that her success came down to the fact that she could be "vicious," and Julie Krone physically fought with several male jockeys. Author Lynn Haney, who wrote on the pioneer female American jockeys in the early 1970s, argued that they had to consciously reject the traditional role assigned to women and "exercise all the prerogatives that are usually considered the male domain—warrior, breadwinner, decisionmaker."

HEALTH ISSUES

Many of the tribulations of being a jockey are nondiscriminatory. Getting weight off is an occupational necessity for all jockeys, male or female. Obviously Canadian Miriam McTague, who shed more than 84 pounds, almost half her body weight, to become a jockey was a special case, but all flat-race riders, apart from those blessed with natural lightness, have to severely curtail how much they eat. Even riders with no apparent weight problems have often found themselves trying to sweat off that additional pound because an ability to ride at a lower weight increases the chances of employment in a competitive profession where there are always far more jockeys chasing mounts than there are rides available.

Unlike their predecessors, modern jockeys have the benefit of access to scientific knowledge on nutrition, but theirs is still a life of fierce selfdiscipline. At the same time as existing on a starvation diet of tea and toast for breakfast, no lunch (though perhaps a bar of chocolate for energy), and a light supper, they have to keep fit and strong enough to control a thousand pounds of horseflesh. Bulimic behavior and excessive use of laxative pills are not uncommon for either gender. For jump jockeys, poundage is less of a problem, perhaps reflecting the hunting origins of the sport, as most weights carried are above the minimum 9-stone 7-pound mark, often the top weight in flat-racing. In harness racing handicapping is by yards, not pounds, reflecting the lesser importance of the driver's weight.

Riding is a dangerous profession. For those who ride over hurdles and especially jumps, falls are an accepted part of the business. In the 1990s the fall rate for jump and hurdle jockeys was roughly one in fourteen mounts, with about one in eighty rides resulting in an injury sufficient to keep the rider from riding without medical clearance. Falls are rarer on the flat: only one in three hundred mounts leads to a fall. But almost one in two of these results in serious injury: whereas a jump jockey knows that most falls happen when the horse meets obstacles deliberately placed in its path and can be mentally prepared to take action, flat racing has no such advance warning system to allow riders to prepare themselves for damage limitation, and when a horse slips over at high speed, often in the midst of other half-ton creatures, the consequences can be severe. Mary Bacon was hospitalized with serious injuries three times in her early career. Julie Krone broke her back but returned to the saddle. Unable to return was Barbara Jo Rubin, the first woman to win against men, who quit after having her pelvis broken, her third major accident in four years of professional riding. Before being forced to retire by the Jockey Club doctor, Gee Armytage, perhaps the best British female jump jockey, broke her knee once, her wrists and arms twice, her elbows three times, her collar bone four times, and finally her back. Colleague Sharon Murgatroyd was paralyzed in 1991. Another steeplechase rider, Jayne Thompson, was killed in a fall in 1986.

IN THE STABLES

These days more than half the work force in the stables is female. Replacing stable lads with stablehands is economically viable as well as politically correct. Trainers appreciate (and exploit) their female workers who love horses and who are prepared to work long hours at menial tasks for little money simply to be with them. It is generally acknowledged that in some respects girls make better grooms than boys because girls are generally quieter, more reliable, and less likely to abuse a horse. Trainers also find them less militant. Susan Gallier, who worked as a stablehand in the 1980s in both France and Britain, felt that the girls received preferential treatment as they were paid the same rate as the boys but were rarely asked to deal with a rampant colt or un-

block a stinking drain. That said, boys were also more likely to be called on to ride trial gallops, an aspect of the job that provides valuable experience for the budding jockey. This is because many trainers adhere to the view that the very qualities that make women such good exercise riders, lightness and gentleness of touch, work against them as jockeys, whose full control of mounts is vital.

A prohibition on women training racehorses had more to do with authority structures in the sport than the perceived physical demands of the job. In 1938 when New Zealand horsewoman Mrs. A. "Granny" McDonald trained Catalogue to win the Melbourne Cup, she was responsible for the horse's preparation, supervised the gallops, and planned its warm-up races. Yet under the prevailing system, it was her husband's name that went into the record books as the winning trainer. During times of emergency, many women have run their husband's stables but should they actually take them over as widows, then racing propriety demanded that the license be held by their head lad. Similarly, when Norah Wilmot inherited her father's training enterprise in 1931, she was not allowed to hold the license, despite having been his assistant for twenty years. Not all racing authorities were as rigid. In the 1960s, when Sydney-based Betty Lane found she could not get a license there, she left the metropolitan area and went to a country track where the Western Districts Racing Association allowed her to train. In Britain, after two decades of fruitless campaigning, Florence Nagle had to take the Jockey Club to the Court of Appeal in 1966 to gain the right to train under her own name. She was seventy-two at the time, hardly with a career to look forward to, but argued that "this was a matter of principle. I am a feminist. I believe in equal rights for women. Things should be decided by ability, not sex." Her actions paved the way for women such as Jenny Pitman, who became the first female to officially train a Grand National winner when Corbiere triumphed in 1983.

Even after these barriers had been breached, the belief that married women could not operate independently of their partners was still held in the racing establishment. Gai Waterhouse, daughter of the Australian trainer Tommy Smith, had her own training license revoked following the warning-off of her bookmaker husband for his involvement in a "ring in" (the fraudulent substitution of one horse for another) scandal. Like Nagle, she had to go to court to rectify the situation.

OWNERSHIP AND OFFICIALDOM

There were instances of women owning and racing horses in Britain before 1800, but their numbers were small in relation to their male counterparts. Even in the late nineteenth century, few women owned racehorses and some preferred to do so under assumed male names, such as the Duchess of Montrose, who raced as "Mr. Manton," and the actress Lily Langtry, who adopted her assumed name from her island home—"Mr. Jersey." The reason for this is unclear, because their identity remained an open secret. Moreover it was unnecessary by the turn of the twentieth century because the Jockey Club did allow females to register colors.

The key to successful racehorse ownership is to have plenty of money, and wealthy women have often fared well. The women of the British royal family, Queen Victoria excepted, have been turf enthusiasts, owning many successful horses and, in the case of Princess Anne, have taken part in racing as an amateur jockey. Although her sojourn on the turf cost over £3 million, statistically Dorothy Paget, granddaughter of wealthy American politician William C. Whitney, had a successful career in racing with 1,532 winners, among them seven Cheltenham Gold Cups (five in succession with Golden Miller), two Champion Hurdles, a Grand National (also with Golden Miller), and a wartime Derby in 1943 with Straight Deal. In 1940–1941 and again in 1951–1952 she was leading National Hunt owner. Yet in Britain, female owners, even those of the right social class, were still kept out of the Jockey Club by its voting system till 1977.

Undoubtedly there has been a male-imposed glass ceiling in racing administration, but historically many women have also been reluctant to enter an industry in which, certainly at the racetrack level, irregular hours are the norm. Nevertheless, in recent years some have made it to the top, including Sue Ellen, who as of 1999 ran the Epsom racecourse in England, home to the Derby. From 1949 to 1973 Mirabel Topham ran Aintree, the Liverpool course that is home to the famous Grand National Steeplechase, but she did own the place, her family, on the male side, having been involved with the track as clerks of the course and managers for almost a century.

Officialdom in racing—judges, starters, and stewards—has remained very much a male preserve until recent decades. Those women who have made the grade in these lines of work, such as Connie Dallis, one of only a handful of harness racing judges, have had a lifetime associated with the sport and gained acceptance through perseverance, knowledge, and an acceptance of the sport's traditions.

SPECTATORS

Women as spectators also faced social rules concerning their behavior and presence. Early race meetings were often community holidays to which all were welcome; and women did attend, though there was strict social demarcation of the classes. Originally confined to carriages and private grandstands, wealthy women benefited from the advent of enclosed racecourses and race clubs in the last quarter of the nineteenth century, which allowed them to appear in public but separate from the mass of spectators, including their working-class sisters. As with the lawns and flowers, they were there to be decorative.

While denied career opportunities in racing, women have always been prized as accessories to the sport. In the musical *My Fair Lady*, Eliza Dolittle's transformation from flower seller to lady included a visit to one of the most fashionable gatherings of the English social calendar, the races at Ascot, where she was paraded in a failed effort to pass her off as a woman of quality when she used street language spoken in a perfect upper-class accent. The superficial aspect of female participation in racing can still be seen in the outrageous hats, flashy outfits, and high-heeled shoes of many women racegoers, for whom dressing up is the main attraction of a day at the races.

REPORTING

As in most aspects of the sport, female media representatives have been a rarity in racing. In Britain eyebrows were raised in 1938 when the *Daily Mail* appointed Rita Cannon as a racing correspondent. By 1984 there was greater acceptance of Pohla Smith when she became the sole racing writer for United Press International, though this was only a decade or so after women were first allowed into the press box for the Kentucky Derby.

GAMBLING

Most men attend race meetings with a view to gambling rather than glamour, but for respectable women it was socially unacceptable to be seen gambling in the nineteenth century, a time when they were expected to be custodians of family values and high moral standards. Politicians and others in authority were anxious to prevent working-class women from squandering the housekeeping money, and in the Australian state of Victoria, women were even forbidden by law in 1906 from placing bets with on-course bookmakers. The advent of the totalizator (pari-mutuel in some countries) has made it both easier and more acceptable for women to gamble. Under this system of betting, the aggregate pool of bets, less operating costs and a deduction to plough back into racing, is divided among all winning betters, unlike wagers with bookmakers, which are at predetermined odds. Bets are placed with impersonal counter staff, and small amounts, well below the minimum allowed by bookmakers, can be wagered. A survey of racegoers in Britain in the 1990s showed that women tend to risk smaller amounts than men. Until the mid-twentieth century, off-course betting was illegal in most countries, and even when it was legalized, the unrefined atmosphere of the betting shops was not attractive to female gamblers.

Female bookmakers existed in the nineteenth century, most of them operating illegally off the courses. The first to achieve respectability was Helen Vernet. Following a serious illness that affected her lungs, her doctor advised her to spend more time in the open air: she opted to go racing several times a week. While doing so she became aware that many women wished to bet in small amounts that other bookmakers were reluctant to accept. During the 1918 racing season, Mrs. Vernet let it be known among her friends that she would accept bets of 5 or 10 shillings handed to her in writing. Though this was illegal, her clientele increased. The professional bookmakers objected and had her warned off by racecourse officials. Arthur Bendir, however, who had established the bookmaking firm of Ladbrokes in 1902, saw the economic potential and publicity value of employing her as the first licensed female bookmaker on British racecourses. He was proved right, and during her career with Ladbrokes, which began in 1919, she never earned less than £20,000 a year from her commissions and her shrewd gambling. In 1928 she purchased a partnership in the firm. Marika Hurry took out a bookmaker's license in Melbourne, Australia, in the 1980s, but few others seem to have followed Helen Vernet's lead. Perhaps in the interaction that is required in placing bets and negotiating odds, most gamblers have preferred the more brash personalities of male "bookies."

Where women have made their mark in taking bets has been in the betting shops, legalized in Britain from 1961, and as totalizator operatives. When this device was introduced in Britain in 1929 to cater to the small-scale racecourse punter, most of the face-to-face contact was still with men, but recent years have witnessed the deliberate cultivation of an image based on the "tote ladies." In France, Japan, and North America there is also significant female employment behind the "mutuel" counters.

CONCLUSION

Women's exclusion from racing has been partly attributable to the prejudices of female members of the leisured classes, many of whom were wealthy enough to own racehorses and gain access to the inner circles. The Honorable Mrs. George Lambton, although acknowledging the prowess of women in stable management and their equal ability to men, strongly disapproved of the possibility of women trainers: "once the door was open and women allowed into the sacred precincts of the weighing room on the official footing as trainers, what is to stop them from becoming jockeys too?" Even after equal opportunity legislation forced change in the sport, some women still doubted its wisdom. Dorothy Laird, Honorable Secretary of the Lady Jockeys Association of Great Britain (founded on her suggestion in 1972), was convinced by visits to injured jockeys that jump racing was no place for women. Trainer Auriol Sinclair supported this view and stated that "I wouldn't put up a woman however good she was because I don't think they are built for the falls." And racing terminology has continued to undermine the efforts of women to be treated equally: the term "gentleman rider" has disappeared from the racing lexicon, but women in racing—be they jockeys, spectators, or totalizator operators—are still patronizingly referred to as "ladies."

Wray Vamplew and Joyce Kay

Bibliography

Alcok, Anne.(1978) *They're Off: The Story of the First Girl Jump Jockeys*. London: J.A. Allen.

Armytage, Gee. (1989) *Gee: The Diary of a National Hunt Jockey*. London: Queen Anne Press.

Bland, Ernest. (1950) *Flat-Racing Since 1900*. London: Andrew Dakers.

Fox, Kate. (1997) *The Racing Tribe*. Oxford: Social Issues Research Centre.

Gallier, Susan. (1988) *One of the Lads*. London: Stanley Paul.

Haney, Lynn. (1973) *The Lady Is a Jock*. New York: Dodd, Mead.

Hargreaves, Jennifer. (1994) *Sporting Females: Critical Issues in the History and Sociology of Women's Sports*. London: Routledge.

Hill, Christopher R. (1988) *Horse Power: The Politics of the Turf*. Manchester: Manchester University Press.

Munting, Roger. (1996) *An Economic and Social History of Gambling in Britain and the USA*. Manchester: Manchester University Press.

Pollard, Jack. (1988) *Australian Horse Racing*. Sydney: Angus & Robertson.

Ramsden, Caroline. (1973) *Ladies in Racing*. London: Stanley Paul.

Sharpe, Graham. (1994) *The William Hill Book of Racing Quotations*. London: Stanley Paul.

Smyly, Patricia. (1979) *Encyclopaedia of Steeplechasing*. London: Robert Hale.

Tanner, Michael, and Gerry Cranham. (1992) *Great Jockeys of the Flat*. London: Guiness.

HUNGARY

Hungary is a central European country with a population of approximately 10.2 million people. Women have always had an important, yet unrecognized role in the country's political, religious, and cultural life, of which there is a 1,000-year written history. This included participation in sports considered exclusively masculine in many other places.

HISTORY

Before the Hungarians settled in the Carpathian Basin, male-dominated families were characteristic. Aristocratic women, however, had power through their dowries. During the creation of the new state within the basin (during the life of Géza I, 972–997, and István I, 997–1038), these women retained much of their power. In the second half of the thirteenth century, they participated in running and jumping events as recreational pastimes. In a decree of 1263, it can be read that Jolanta, the daughter of the royal falcon keeper, defeated her own daughter in running and jumping. Wives of aristocratic noblemen had other forms of sport: hunting with falcons and different forms of ball games. Mary, wife of King Sigismund (reigned 1387–1437) was depicted in a fresco playing a ball game with her husband.

Hungarian students who studied at medieval Italian universities (e.g., Padua, Bologna) popularized ball games in Hungary, where they were played at court and in noblemen's castles. The sports of the peasantry took place in the form of folk games played during religious festivals such as Whitsuntide, weddings, and harvest festivals.

During the 150 years of Turkish occupation in the sixteenth and seventeenth centuries, the so-called fighting woman became the ideal in Hungary. Poems and songs were written about women, such as Ilona Zrinyi, who defended their castles in heroic battles. Zsuzsanna Lórántffy advanced the case of women's sports by acting as a patron for Johannes Amos Comenius, author of a book in which he urged physical education for girls.

In the eighteenth century, Turkish occupation was replaced by the Hapsburg reign. From Vienna, Queen Maria Theresa issued the "Ratio Educationis" (1777), which became the basis of Hungarian national education. Under Austrian rule, according to this law, physical education became available for girls of the lower social classes, although it is unlikely that girls participated regularly in physical education. In 1833, the wife of Clair Ignotius, a French officer, founded the Gymnastics School of Pest, where girls studied German and Swedish gymnastics.

Riding and fencing—and toward the end of the nineteenth century, skating and tennis—became more important for aristocratic women. The fashion magazines of the age often depicted women participating in some kind of sport. In 1830 the first swimming pool was opened, and on certain days it was open only for women. Long-distance "Danube swimming" often had female participants. One of the best known of them was Klára Petzke, who won an international swimming competition on 5 August 1895 in Vienna.

After the 1867 agreement with Austria that created the dual monarchy of Austria-Hungary, the spread of modern sports accelerated. Middle-class women's participation in sports became more common. Their ideal was Elisabeth, wife of Emperor Franz Joseph, who was well known for her brilliant riding and love for such sports as fencing and gymnastics. When she was in Hungary in Gödöllo, she had gymnastics equipment fitted in her room.

Typical sports for middle-class and aristocratic women were tennis and skating. The first Hungarian championship was won by Paulina Pálffy in tennis in 1894. An artificial pond was built in a park in Budapest, where skating became a very popular winter pastime and women formed the majority of the Budapest Skating Club. In addition, fencing and hiking became very popular among women. Cycling started to spread among women at the beginning of the 1880s. In 1883, Viktor Silberer, a publisher from Vienna, introduced his Zeppelin in Hungary and took a woman, Ilka Pálmay, for a flight.

In general, however, there was societal opposition to the participation of women in sports, as evidenced by an article published in the late nineteenth century. In 1889 the magazine *Herkules* published an article that stated: "Prejudices have to disappear. It should not be a shocking thing if we see a woman skating, riding, fencing, playing ball games. It is no longer fashionable to be nervous, impatient, capricious. We will never reach a healthy Hungary that way." Similarly, Elek Matolay, leader of the National Hungarian Gymnastics Club, wrote in his book *History of Gymnastics:* "Gymnastics for women does not differ from that of men, only the exercises have to be adapted to their body. Women also need skills, health, outdoor activity, just like boys."

Hungarian swimmer Krisztina Egerszegi swims the breaststroke leg of the women's 400-meter medley at the 1992 Olympic Games. (TempSport)

THE TWENTIETH CENTURY

In the early twentieth century, a wider range of women became acquainted with different types of sports in physical education classes and through the support of the Social Democratic party and the People's Catholic party. The first secondary school for women was founded in 1896 in Budapest. The first political organization for women, the Union of Feminists, published the magazine *Woman and Society,* in which they fought for total equality in sports. Several other political organizations were formed, including the Camp for Christian Women. It was led by the Catholic Margit Schlachta, who became the first female member of the Hungarian parliament in 1920. Catholic principles dominated in this organization's view of sports and physical education. The group advocated sports activity for women, but only at a moderate level that did not disturb family life. On the other hand, Catholics supported the activity of *Levente,* a paramilitary youth organization. After the World War I and Hungary's loss of two-thirds of its territory, military training became especially important. After 1939, taking part in the activities of the *Levente* became compulsory for women.

As elsewhere, social and economic differences led to variations in sport participation. Tennis, golf, yachting, motor sports, horse riding and racing, and archery remained sports for the aristocrats. Ball games, track and field, gymnastics, swimming, and fencing were carried out within the framework of middle-class sports clubs like the National Gymnastics Club and the Hungarian Athletics Club, which sponsored sports for both men and women.

As more Hungarian women began to take part in sports, they were increasingly successful in international competition, with the greatest success in figure skating. Lili Kronberger won world championship titles in 1910 and 1911, and Opika Méray Horváth followed in 1912, 1913, and 1914. With the appearance of the modern Olympic Games and European and world championships, the achievements of female athletes became front-page and feature-article news. The first Hungarian woman to participate in the Olympic Games was Gizella Tary, who placed sixth in fencing in 1924. The first Olympic medal (a bronze) for women was won by Emilía Rotter in Lake Placid in 1932, in pairs figure skating. The first two Olympic gold medals were won by Ibolya Csák in the high jump and by Ilona Elek in the foils, both in Berlin in 1936.

After World War II, women's sports became highly politicized. As in other communist nations, sport success was expected to prove the superiority of that political ideology. Carefully trained and encouraged to compete for national and political honor, Hungarian women did well for their country. The Olympic Games of 1952 and 1956 were a case in point. The gymnast Ágnes Keleti became the most successful Hungarian woman Olympic champion ever, with ten medals, five of them gold. The swimmers were also very successful. Among the non-Olympic sports, table tennis was the most important. Although women were rarely allowed to advance in politics, in sports they were supported wherever they promised to do well in international competition, for example, in kayaking and canoeing, fencing, basketball, handball, and volleyball.

Ordinary married women, however, had little time to spend on sports because the two–wage-earner family was the norm. Most were employed outside the home as well as carrying out their domestic duties.

After the end of communism in 1989, life became financially more difficult, and the average family had less opportunity to participate in sports. Elite female athletes continued to be successful and became media stars, mirroring the practices of the West. The most notable of these new champions were Krisztina Egerszegi, who won five gold medals in Olympic swimming (200-meter backstroke in Seoul, 1988; 100- and 200-meter backstroke and 400-meter medley in Barcelona, 1992; and 200-meter backstroke in Atlanta, 1996), and Rita Kõbán, who won two in kayaking (kayak four in Barcelona, 1992; and kayak single in Atlanta, 1996). In 1992 tennis star Monica Seles, born of a Hungarian family in Yugoslavia and living in the United States, was elected Hungarian Sportwoman of the Year. Egerszegi was the runner-up.

If chess is considered a sport, which it is in Hungary, then the Polgár family must be mentioned. László Polgár consciously prepared his daughters (Zsuzsa, Judit, and Zsófia) for championships. With their father's help, the Polgár girls have become chess superstars. Competing at the international level, the sisters were chess-Olympic champions in 1988 and 1990. All three of the Polgár sisters qualified as International Masters, which includes males and females. Zsuzsa was the women's world champion in 1996, and Judit was first in the women's rankings from 1989–1997.

CURRENT SITUATION

After the collapse of the socialist sport model and the disintegration of the "socialist welfare system," the public sector withdrew support from recreational activities and a "sports for all" philosophy. It was replaced by the private sector in sports and health, and the cost of participation precluded the involvement of the great majority of women and men. The revival of a voluntary sector to support sports activities has been slow to emerge. Physical education, however, continues to be a part of the curriculum required for all students in elementary and secondary schools.

Katalin Szikora

Bibliography

Földesiné-Szabó, Gyöngyi. (1988) *Tévhitek a nöi sportban.* Budapest: TF Közlemények, 3.

Levelekiné, R. Matild, ed. (1963) *A nö és a sport.* Budapest: TTT.

Polgár, László. (1989) *Nevelj zsenit!* Budapest: Interart.

Sas, Judit. (1984) *Nöies nök és férfaik.* Budapest: Akadémiai.

Siklóssy, László. (1929) *A magyar sport ezer éve 1–3.* Budapest: OTT.

HUNTING

The word *hunting* refers to a complex mixture of actions and attitudes, and to some extent its usage is always specific to each culture and context. The definition used here is that employed by British historian John MacKenzie: "the pursuit, driving, ambushing, and trapping of wild animals of all species with the intention of killing them for meat, other animal products, or purely for sport."

HISTORY

Humans have inhabited the earth for more than 2 million years, and during virtually all of that time, they have been hunters. Only during a tiny fragment of that time—roughly the past 12,000 years—have some humans lived as nonhunters. By the mid-twentieth century, anthropologists ventured the suggestion that it was the activity of hunting that made us human in the first place, making this suggestion because the hunter–forager pattern of survival has been so persistent throughout human cultural history, and hunting has been so decisive in shaping societies and defining human interactions with the world of nonhuman nature. This suggestion was flawed in that it erroneously assumed hunting to be an exclusively male activity. In fact, many women can and do hunt. They probably hunted in great numbers before history began to be written. Women hunters, though their ranks significantly diminished with the development of predominantly patriarchal, agrarian societies, are far from absent from the historical record.

Hunting does not correlate in any simple fashion with a diet based on meat. Procuring meat may or may not be a prime motivation for a hunter. At the same time, gathering—the female-dominated activity usually juxtaposed to male hunting—most often yields animal as well as veg-

A 1950s female hunter with her dog. (Picture Network International, Ltd.)

etable resources for human consumption. The key distinction, then, between hunting and gathering has less to do with the kinds of protein they provide than that former involves armed pursuit, the latter collecting. A further distinction is that while the products of gathering almost always account for the bulk (generally around 70 percent) of the diet in hunter–gatherer societies, hunting is always more highly valued by those societies in terms of its ritual and symbolic significance.

HUNTING AND HUMAN CULTURAL EVOLUTION

According to the framers of the hunting hypothesis, it was with the hunting adaptation that the genus *Homo* evolved the complex set of behaviors that made us truly human: intelligence, erect posture (bipedalism), language, the spirit of cooperation, tool manufacture and use, and the sexual division of labor. This last development was of particular importance. Early man would never have been able to concentrate his time and energies on the business of evolving had early woman

---

CYRENE AND THE LION

And Hypseus cherished his fair-armed daughter, Cyrene; she cared not for pacing to and fro before the loom, nor for merry banquets with stay-at-home maidens of her own age; but, contending with brazen darts and with the fachion, she would slay the fierce beasts of prey, thus in very deed assuring deep and perfect rest for her father's kine, while she spent on her eyelids but a scanty store of slumber which is so sweet a bed-fellow when dawn draweth near. Once did Apollo, the far-darting god of the wide quiver, find her without spears, wrestling alone with a monstrous lion; and forthwith he called Cheiron from out his halls and spake to him in this wise: "Son of Philyra, leave thy hallowed cave and look with wonder at a woman's spirit and mighty power. See what a contest she is waging with un-daunted head, this maiden with a heart which no toil can subdue, and a mind that no fear can overwhelm. From what mortal being was she born? From what race hath she been reft, that she should be dwelling in the hollows of the shadowy mountains? And she is putting to the test a strength that is inexhaustible. Is it right to lay an ennobling hand upon her? aye, and, by consorting with her, to cull the honey-sweet flower of love?"

PINDAR
(5th century BCE), Pythian Ode 9, 17ff. In Telesikrates of Kyrene: The Odes of Pindar, including the Principal Fragments, *introduced and translated by Sir John Sandys. London: William Heinemann; Cambridge, MA: Harvard University Press, second and revised edition, 1919, p. 17ff.*

---

not been content, as Desmond Morris put it, to "stay put and mind the babies while the males went hunting." Men roved far afield to hunt and to invent culture and adventure, while women gathered foodstuffs close to home and eventually managed to originate horticulture. In the evolutionary scheme of things, women's work was assumed to be physically and intellectually less challenging because, as one proponent of the "man the hunter" view succinctly put it: "Plants stand still, but animals move." The opposition of male hunting to female gathering was further supported by biological differences between the sexes: women are not only the childbearers, they are also generally smaller and weaker than men, and thereby are less suited to the rigors of hunting.

Feminist anthropologists readily countered that this line of reasoning assumed, absurdly, that women were not active participants in the process of human evolution. They constructed the so-called gathering hypothesis to account for the ways in which women's foraging might have been the primary force behind human cultural evolution. In its own way, this thesis turned out to be as oversimplified and flawed as the one it sought to refute. Like the hunting hypothesis, it accepted not only that males and females are destined to different social roles by virtue of their sexual anatomy, but also that women had never hunted in significant numbers.

Indeed, there are compelling reasons why some women would have chosen not to hunt in prehistoric times: Hunting large animals with such primitive tools as spears is a high-risk activity, and women of childbearing age were too important to the community to place in such danger. In addition, infants and toddlers would interfere with their mothers' hunting effectiveness. However, there is no evidence for the assumption that most prehistoric women did not hunt. Indeed, it is far more likely that at times when they were not hampered by late-term pregnancy or childcare—or whenever they could get someone else to look after their young children—they were important participants in the group activity that hunting large animals represented. This likelihood is borne out by ethnographic evidence of women's active hunting in such modern hunter–forager cultures as the Tiwi Aborigines of Australia, the Mbuti Pygmies of Central Africa, the Philippine Agta peoples, and several North American tribes. In these cases, those men and women who are skilled at hunting, hunt; those who are not perform other essential tasks, among them child care.

One argument that was formerly invoked against prehistoric women's hunting was that there was no evidence they had the tools for the job. It is true that in most contemporary hunter–forager cultures (that is, those presumed to be closest in structure to what prehistoric societies must have been like), tools that can double as weapons are made and used by males only. Hence, the hunting tools that survive from Paleolithic times—axes and clubs, arrow tips, spear points—have been assumed to have been men's tools. Yet not only is there no objective reason to presume that women did not also make and use these tools, evidence has recently come to light of intricately woven nets and snares dating back to around 27,000 BCE. Because women are widely credited with the invention of weaving, these archaeological finds support the view that women of the Upper Paleolithic used these implements to engage in group hunting. Modern tribal people still find hunting with nets to be an efficient—and generally quite safe—method for capturing animals ranging from birds and small game to larger prey like deer and elk. The first clear archaeological evidence of gender or social-class stratification only occurs in grave contents dating to between the sixth and fourth millennia BCE. Assuming, then, that prehistoric cultures were on the whole more egalitarian than modern ones, women's displacement from the hunting fraternity appears to be largely a product of relatively recent historical developments, having to do with social forces set in motion by the rise of agrarianism and urbanization.

WOMEN HUNTERS IN WESTERN HISTORY

There is some material evidence for women's participation in hunting in various parts of the ancient world. Egyptian paintings dating to the second millennium BCE depict women and men hunting waterfowl from boats, using nets and boomerang-like instruments. Women were also shown accompanying men hunting large game from chariots. In the fourth century BCE, the Greek

A female hunter with her kill. (Daniel O. Todd/Corbis)

historian Xenophon, who erected on his Spartan estate a temple to the goddess Artemis where annually he staged hunting games in her honor, wrote: "All men who have loved hunting have been good; and not men only, but those women also to whom the goddess has given this blessing." Scholars are divided on the question of how much women actually participated in hunting in the Graeco-Roman world. However, the likelihood that at least some women did hunt is strengthened not only by statements such as this one, but also by the fact that women's hunting plays a key role in myths such as those of Atalanta's participation in the Calydonian boar hunt and Dido's romance with Aeneas. And the goddess of the hunt, Artemis (Roman Diana), was widely recognized as a women's goddess, presiding over childbirth as well as the world of nonhuman nature.

Since patriarchal gender distinctions and hierarchical class stratification were firmly in place in the ancient civilizations of Greece and Rome, hunting can be assumed to have been largely a prerogative of aristocratic women. This pattern persisted through much of European history. For example, Charlemagne's wife, Hildegarde, and their six daughters were all avid hunters, particularly fond of chasing wild boar and aurochs (huge, wild European cattle, now extinct). In succeeding centuries down through the Renaissance, queens and consorts dominated the ranks of female hunters: Elizabeth I of England (1533–1603), Mary Queen of Scots (1542–1587), France's Catherine de Medici (1519–1589), and Sweden's Queen Christina (1626–1689) were among those especially noted for their passion for the sport.

In the medieval period, perhaps because they were not preoccupied with marriage and family concerns, women belonging to religious orders joined aristocrats in the ranks of female hunters and falconers. Henry III of England (1207–1272) made special provisions for "the Reverend and Pious Ladye Mabel de Boxham," abbess of Barking, to chase hare and deer on his estates. Dame Juliana Berners, a fifteenth-century abbess, is credited with writing *The Boke of St. Albans* (1486), the first treatise written in English about hawking, hunting, and fishing.

NINETEENTH- AND TWENTIETH-CENTURY DEVELOPMENTS

Were aristocrats and royalty the only women who hunted? Or were they the only ones whose exploits were deemed worthy of recording in the vast body of primary literature about hunting? Over the course of European history, hunting came to be perceived ever more strictly as a man's activity—indeed, as the definitive masculine rite of passage, in some ways equivalent to military service. Thus, by the nineteenth and early twentieth centuries, white hunters were among the most prominent characters in the cast of colonizers in Africa and Asia, first in the name of imperialistic conquest and later in the name of adventure. Not a few of these adventurers were upper-class women, whose big-game hunting sometimes took the form of pure sport, sometimes of science in the collection of specimens for increasingly popular natural history museums in Great Britain and the United States. Whether for sport or science, trophies—some from animals now threatened or endangered—were taken in huge numbers, and as a number of scholars have demonstrated, this subduing of nature was directly related to the subduing of native human populations, whose own right to hunt was sharply restricted or denied.

Yet the too-ready equation of hunting with an imperialist cultural elite is challenged by at least two historical cases from the same period. English fox hunting was one arena in which women made particularly impressive strides during the nineteenth century, becoming generally regarded as the equals of men in the field by the century's end. This was a particularly remarkable feat, given that women rode sidesaddle: the cross-saddle was not deemed acceptable for horsewomen until the 1930s. While practiced elsewhere, fox hunting as a cultural institution is in some ways unique to the English countryside, in that it is an event in which, although class distinctions are not forgotten, the classes are brought together as a community. The equal opportunity spirit of the hunt is amply illustrated by the fact that the two most renowned huntswomen of the nineteenth century were the Empress Elizabeth of Austria (1837–1898) and a Liverpudlian prostitute nicknamed "Skittles" (Catherine Walters, 1839–1920). Women continue to the present day to play a prominent role in fox hunting.

The other case in which women's hunting took a more egalitarian shape was in North America. Pioneer women needed to be as adept with firearms as their menfolk, and it has been argued that from Jamestown onward, hunting (by both sexes) played a crucial role in the taming of the American wilderness. Although much of this hunting must have been for survival rather than for sport, those two categories are not so readily distinguishable in actual practice. American women of the nineteenth and early twentieth centuries, when the U.S. population was still largely rural, appear to have enjoyed venturing afield in substantial numbers with their brothers and husbands. Women hunters appear frequently in hunting-related advertising and in outdoor publications of the period. As Steve Grooms in *Gray's*

Sporting Journal noted, "Annie Oakley was not a freak. She was exceptional because she shot so well, but she was one of many women of her time who enjoyed target shooting and hunting." It seems to have been only around the time of World War II that hunting came to be defined as a male-only activity and American girls and women were actively discouraged from taking part. That has begun to change, apparently due to several factors: the feminist movement, women's health and fitness concerns, and the increase in women's freedom and disposable income of their own. During the 1990s, the number of American women hunters, across social classes, roughly doubled, from around 1 million to well over 2 million, and the trend appears to be toward more women hunters in the future.

WOMEN, HUNTING, AND ENVIRONMENTALISM

If one grants that hunting plays a conspicuous role in wildlife conservation—and not everyone does, including the women who make up approximately 80 percent of the animal rights movement—the question still remains: Why would women wish to engage in an activity so frequently identified with the cultivation of masculinity? The answer appears to give the lie to conventional gender stereotypes. Surveys repeatedly show that women hunt for approximately the same reasons as men, including to put food on the table, demonstrate skill, get exercise, and get away from it all to commune with nature. And women derive about the same levels of satisfaction as do men from these activities.

Women do not seem as prone to cite competition or the procuring of trophies as high motivations for participating in hunting. They are more inclined than males to actively seek instruction in firearms use and safety, as well as in other aspects of their chosen sport, be it archery or black-powder riflery, wingshooting, or waterfowling. To date, they have a considerably better track record than male hunters when it comes to ethical behavior in the field. Part of the explanation for this may be that women typically take up hunting as adults, when their value systems are firmly in place, and not to be macho or prove their masculinity.

CONCLUSION

Given the changing demographics of American society—the rise of female single-headed households, the shift to a largely urban population, the decline in the numbers of men who are introducing their sons to hunting, the fact that nearly 90 percent of the male hunting population is middle-aged or older—some experts in the field have declared women to be the future of hunting. Whether or not this turns out to be the case, the increased participation of women hunters lends a decidedly new (though in some ways very old) look to the hunting community.

Mary Zeiss Stange

See also Animal Rights, Fishing, Shooting

Bibliography

Anderson, J. K. (1985) *Hunting in the Ancient World.* Berkeley: University of California Press.

Ardrey, Robert. (1976) *The Hunting Hypothesis: A Personal Conclusion Concerning the Evolutionary Nature of Man.* New York: Atheneum.

Buxton, Meriel. (1989) *Ladies of the Chase.* North Pomfret, U.K.: Trafalgar Square.

Dalhberg, Frances. (1981) *Woman the Gatherer.* New Haven, CT: Yale University Press.

Ehrenberg, Margaret. (1989) *Women in Prehistory.* Norman: University of Oklahoma Press.

Grooms, Steve. (1997) "Upland Women." *Gray's Sporting Journal* (August): 36–41.

Ingold, Tim. (1987) *The Appropriation of Nature: Essays of Human Ecology and Social Relations.* Iowa City: University of Iowa Press.

Kellert, Stephen, and Joyce K. Berry. (1987) "Attitudes, Knowledge, and Behaviors Toward Wildlife as Affected by Gender." *Wildlife Society Bulletin* 15, 3: 363–367.

Lee, Richard, and Irven DeVore, eds. (1968) *Man the Hunter.* Chicago: Aldine Publishing Company.

MacKenzie, John M. (1988) *The Empire of Nature: Hunting, Conservation and British Imperialism.* Manchester: Manchester University Press.

Morris, Desmond. (1967) *The Naked Ape.* New York: McGraw-Hill.

Morrow, Laurie, and Steve Smith (1996). *Shooting Sports for Women.* New York: St. Martin's Press.

Pringle, Heather. (1998) "New Women of the Ice Age." *Discover* (April): 62–69.

Rosaldo, Michelle. (1980) "The Use and Abuse of Anthropology: Reflections on Feminism and Cross-Cultural Understanding." *Signs: Journal of Women in Culture and Society* 5, 3: 389–417.

Stange, Mary Zeiss. (1997) *Woman the Hunter.* Boston: Beacon Press.

Tabet, Paola. (1982) "Hands, Tools, Weapons." *Feminist Issues* (Fall): 3–62.

Tanner, Nancy, and Adrienne Zihlman. (1976) "Women in Evolution, Part I: Innovation and Selection in Human Origins." *Signs: Journal of Women in Culture and Society* 1, 3: 585–608.

I

IAIDO

Iaido is a Japanese martial art that has been transformed from a military skill to a modern sport, practiced for recreation and in competition. One aspect of this transformation is the involvement of women. Iaido consists exclusively of solo *kata*, or forms. All forms emphasize etiquette in the respectful handling of the sword, properly drawing, cutting, and returning the sword to the scabbard. The rules and conventions of the sport are the same for women as they are for men.

HISTORY

Iaido originated in the *katana* (long sword) techniques of the samurai of Japan, which were codified beginning around 1390. When the Tokugawa Shogunate (1603–1867) unified the country after a long period of civil conflict, edicts were issued to transform the samurai from warriors to refined individuals, able to serve in the government. Skills included martial arts, reading, writing, administration, and finer arts, such as calligraphy and painting.

Peace changed the reasons for martial study. Hayashizaki Jinsuke Shigenobu (1546–1621) is the legendary founder of iaido. He holds this place not only because he codified a system of *batto jutsu* (solo sword-drawing techniques), which he called Shimmei Muso Ryu, but also because he promulgated the idea that practicing sword forms with meditative intent could make one a better person, and so benefit society. (The well-known connection between Zen and the martial arts had been established as far back as the fourteenth century.)

Following the Tokugawa Shogunate, the Meiji Restoration (1868–1911) saw "sportification" of combative sword forms (*kenjutsu*) into kendo, still widely practiced today by both men and women in Japan and throughout the world. Meanwhile

Deborah Klens-Bigman practicing an iaido swordcut. (Suzanne Langenwalter)

the *batto jutsu* forms evolved from Hayashizaki through successive headmasters, who introduced more philosophical refinements. The term "iaido," meaning, essentially, "way of presence in the moment," was first used to describe the sword-drawing art in 1932.

RULES AND PLAY

Though only samurai men traditionally practiced long sword, men and women from all walks of life around the world now study iaido. There is no difference in the standard of training for men and women. Participants wear the same style of practice clothing and follow the same curriculum. The uniform consists of *keikogi* (a loose-fitting top), *hakama* (wide-legged, pleated trousers), and an *obi* (belt). Depending on the style, the uniform may be white, dark blue, or black. Except for optional knee pads, no protective gear is worn, or considered necessary. *Iaito,* unsharpened practice swords, are mostly used, though some practitioners use "live" (that is, sharp) swords with the permission of their teachers.

Throughout iaido training, emphasis is placed on Zen mindfulness and a sense of calm concentration. All forms emphasize etiquette in the respectful handling of the sword and the proper drawing, cutting, and returning of the sword to the scabbard. The most practiced styles of iaido are the Muso Shinden Ryu and the Muso Jikiden Eishin Ryu, presumed to be branches of the original style of *batto jutsu* founded by Hayashizaki. Both styles contain three sets of kata: a beginner's set, a middle level set, and *oku* (secret) forms for high-level students. The names of the sets are the same for both styles. The beginner's set, the Omori Ryu, consists of twelve kata, eleven beginning from the *seiza* (kneeling position), and one starting from a standing position. These forms acquaint students with the basics of properly drawing, cutting, and sheathing the sword. The kneeling position provides the student with a stable base, thus building strength and control in the lower body. The middle set, Hasegawa Eishin Ryu, consists of ten kata, nine originating with the practitioner sitting in *tatehiza*, a position with one knee raised, and the tenth in *seiza*. The imaginary opponents in these forms are in much closer proximity to the student than in the first set, requiring close-in stabbing and cutting movements. The footwork is more intricate, featuring weight shifts, sliding back and forth along the floor on the knees, and stepping toward and away from the imaginary opponent. The high-level set, called Okuiai (secret *iai*) consists of both standing and *tatehiza* forms.

Kata at this level look surprisingly simple, like natural movement, but the simplicity is deceptive; a student may study for ten years or longer before beginning to comprehend and technically be able to handle these forms.

In addition, the All-Japan Kendo Federation has developed ten kata drawn from various styles, called the Zenkenrenmei or Seiteigata forms. Affiliated kendo federations around the world practice these forms and hold standard ranking examinations for them. The popularity of practicing these forms varies among kendo players. For example, in Eastern Canada and the United States, there is a great deal of interest in Zenkenrenmei; whereas in parts of Japan, it seems less important.

Like other modern *do,* or martial arts forms, rankings exist, though progress through the ranks is slower than in other martial arts. In the United States, there are informal *kyu* (level) ranks, followed by *dan* (black belt) rankings. In general, it takes three years of consistent practice to reach first *dan,* meaning that the student understands the Omori Ryu set of forms. No distinction is made between men and women in testing for rank. Teaching on a formal level ideally does not take place until fifth *dan* or higher, meaning fifteen years or more of study, and deep understanding of all three sets of forms.

CURRENT ISSUES

Since women did not study iaido in significant numbers until the 1970s, most of the senior teachers are men. As in many other Japanese art forms, however, women are becoming increasingly visible as students and teachers. In the United States, iaido has become popular only in the 1990s, so most women are still beginning and intermediate students.

Various kendo organizations have sponsored forms competition in iaido, and competition for ranking in Zenkenrenmei is intense in some U.S. kendo *dojo,* or practice halls. In these cases, there may sometimes be a distinction between men's and women's competition, as there is in modern kendo.

Iaido has been criticized for emphasizing meditation and self-improvement over combat efficiency. The criticism is partially justified due to unskilled teachers who do not know proper technique. The best training consists of good form, good technique, and good mental presence.

SUMMARY

Iaido remains mostly a noncompetitive martial art with solo kata practice as the principal activity. Originally practiced almost exclusively by men, women are participating in increasing numbers. Rules of etiquette and qualification for rank are the same for women as for men. Forms competition in iaido has also become more popular, though Zen mindfulness through proper technique remains the ultimate goal of practice.

Deborah Klens-Bigman

See also Kendo

Bibliography

Draeger, Donn F., and Robert W. Smith. (1980) *Comprehensive Asian Fighting Arts.* Tokyo: Kodansha International.

Taylor, Kimberly, and Goyo Ohmi. (1997) "The Omori ryu: A History and Explanation." *Journal of Asian Martial Arts.* 6, 1: 80–103.

Warner, Gordon, and Donn F. Draeger. (1982) *Japanese Swordsmanship: Technique and Practice.* New York and Tokyo: Weatherhill.

IMMUNITY

The immune system, which is designed to protect the body from the devastating effects of illness and injury, is enhanced during exercise. At the same time, exercise also appears to have a short-term negative effect on the immune system; immune cells are reduced in number and/or activity during the few hours following exercise. Moderate regular exercise or training has a positive impact on the natural killer cells, but does not seem to influence others parts of the immune system. Considerable scientific evidence demonstrates that exercise changes the immune system for the better; however, whether these changes routinely help protect the body against disease is less clear. The available evidence suggests that exercise affects the immune systems of men and women in the same way.

ANTIBODIES: THE "KILLERS" WITHIN US

People are continually exposed to substances that can be harmful. Fortunately the human body is quite well protected. Physical barriers (such as skin and mucous) and behavioral changes (such as avoiding toxic substances and people who are ill) are the first lines of defense. Substances that get past these defenses (usually bacteria, viruses, and other microorganisms) encounter a highly complex system called the immune system. The immune system is composed of cells and substances in the blood stream and lymphatic system that provide protection from infection, disease, and cancer.

The immune system is made up of two general types of cells: specific and nonspecific. Non-specific cells are the first ones deployed to fight invaders. They are activated immediately upon entry of the foreign material and attack all invaders. In contrast, specific cells may take several days to develop and go into action.

Nonspecific phagocyte cells (cells that engulf foreign materials) include monocytes, neutrophils, and macrophages. These phagocytes ingest and destroy foreign and unwanted cells and particles. Natural killer (NK) cells are nonspecific cells that attack, bind to, and kill invading foreign cells, including cancer cells and those infected by viruses.

The antigen-antibody response is the basis of acquired or specific immunity. Antigens may be viruses, parasites, bacteria, or toxic substances released by microorganisms. When an antigen invades the body, it provokes an immune response—the development and production of antibodies that respond to the specific invading antigen.

B cells produce and release antibodies into the blood stream. These antibodies bind to the antigen and neutralize its harmful effects. T-killer cells, produced in response to an antigen invasion, are specialized killers of virus-infected, cancerous, and other foreign cells. They bind to the target cell and release a toxic chemical to kill the invader. Upon the first invasion of a substance, the body's production of B and T-killer cells is relatively slow. The immune system must identify the invader, or antigen, and design B and T-killer cells that are specific to that antigen. If the antigen invades again, rapid production of the antigen specific B and T-killer cells occurs because the body has the earlier version to copy rather than having to start from scratch. Thus, people's bodies have many different types of B and T-killer cells—one for every invader the body has ever had. B and T-cells are as permanent as any change in the body. They may deteriorate with age, but should be ready for the next invasion of that antigen.

Immunoglobulins, T-helper cells, and certain proteins are also important in the immune response. These are apparently unaffected by exercise.

EXERCISE AND IMMUNE FUNCTION

Determining the effects of exercise on immune function is no simple matter. Hormones released, intensity and duration of the exercise, and fitness level of the individual probably modify the impact of exercise on immune function. Researchers have examined various components of the immune system during and after a variety of exercise tasks, making any general interpretation of results difficult. Study design further complicates the situation. Some studies use a small number of subjects; others use large numbers of subjects but rely on surveys of self-reported symptoms of illness rather than clinical observations. Nevertheless, despite such limitations, some trends are apparent. These trends are based on data from men, but the few studies using women show that the immune system response to exercise is similar in men and women.

An important component of the exercise-immune relationship is the type of exercise. Acute exercise is a single exercise session and the immediate postexercise recovery period (for example, jogging three miles and the few hours following that exercise). Chronic exercise is regular exercise training (for example, jogging three miles four times weekly for twelve weeks or longer).

ACUTE EXERCISE AND IMMUNE FUNCTION

During acute exercise of moderate intensity and duration, immune cells (B cells, T-killer cells, and NK cells) increase in concentration. Soon after an exercise session, the levels decrease and return to pre-exercise levels within a few hours. This increase during exercise may be due to loss of fluid (specifically, plasma volume in the blood system) through sweating rather than increased production of immune cells.

Higher-intensity and/or longer-duration exercise also promotes an increase in immune cells.

During the recovery from exercise (thirty minutes to two hours), the number of lymphocytes and NK cells increases, then gradually returns to normal or pre-exercise levels. This period is followed by an immunosuppression period: the lymphocyte count drops below pre-exercise levels for six hours or longer. This immunosuppression may continue for twenty-four hours following extremely rigorous exercise.

In a study of young girls (age ten to twelve), researchers compared the responses of highly trained gymnasts and untrained (but normally active) girls. Both groups ran on the treadmill for twenty minutes, achieving a heart rate of 170–180 beats per minute. There were no differences in immune responses between the two groups.

No one has been able to pinpoint the reason for these changes, but several suggestions have been made. Changes may be related to the stress hormones released during exercise (epinephrine and cortisol) or the higher body temperatures during exercise. Muscle injury caused by extreme exercise releases an enzyme (CPK) that may suppress the immune system so that an autoimmune response is not triggered. Glutamine (the energy source for lymphocytes) may be shifted to the muscle cell, thus limiting the energy available for immune cell activity.

While the changes observed may have little effect on the body's defense against disease, some experts suggest that it is wise to avoid people who are in the contagious stage of an illness during the first few hours following a particularly long or hard workout or competition. Several survey studies of marathon runners suggest that the risk of upper respiratory tract infection (the common

ACTIVITY AND IMMUNITY POSSIBLY RELATED

The effect of physical activity on the human immune system has not yet been fully studied. Based on existing evidence, experts say that physical activity can be both beneficial and harmful to the immune system. Regular, moderate exercise seems to enhance the immune system and makes humans more resistant to infection. However, intense, strenuous activity may weaken the immune system and make individuals more susceptible to infection for a few hours after the activity ends.

cold) is greatest in the few hours following competing in a marathon. Researchers used surveys to collect information on cold symptoms of individuals who completed the race and those who trained for the same race, but did not run in the event for reasons other than illness. Those who ran and finished had significantly more cold symptoms than those who did not compete—suggesting that the immune system is weakened for a week or two following exhaustive exercise.

CHRONIC EXERCISE AND IMMUNE FUNCTION

Determining the effects of chronic exercise on the immune system is difficult because it is hard to separate the effects of fitness level from the effects of the training or exercise itself. In addition, the immune system may be influenced by the psychological stress of training.

Chronic exercise or physical training promotes many beneficial physiological changes—for example, reduced resting heart rate, improved blood fat levels, and stronger muscles—and psychological changes such as improved self-esteem and reduced anxiety and depression. In healthy individuals, regular moderate exercise also seems to enhance natural killer cell activity and immunoglobulin level. However, there is no convincing evidence of changes in any other portion of the immune system. Thus, the immune system appears to have a small but positive response to moderate training.

David Nieman has suggested that the impact of exercise on the immune system follows a J curve. According to his proposal, sedentary individuals have average risk of illness, those who engage in moderate training have a reduced risk of illness, and people who participate in intensive, exhaustive exercise have a higher than normal risk of illness.

Evidence that repeated exhaustive training and the psychological stress of hard training impair immune function comes from studies showing increases in illness in athletes who consistently train hard.

AGING, EXERCISE, AND IMMUNE FUNCTION

The immune system is particularly sensitive to aging and shows a progressive deterioration with age. Elderly individuals are more susceptible to autoimmune disorders and cancers than younger people. Some evidence suggests that regular exercise can enhance the immune system of elderly women.

Two studies of elderly women showed improved immune function (T-cell and NK cells) in subjects who participated in a walking program. The walking program included forty-five-minute walks five days a week at a moderate intensity for fifteen weeks. At the end of the study, women walkers had higher NK cell activity than women who did not walk. In a similar study, elderly women walkers showed improved immune function at six weeks (as evidenced by fewer cold symptoms), but at fifteen weeks their immune systems were no different than those of other women, suggesting a temporary effect (researchers do not know why). In another study, highly conditioned elderly women had fewer cold symptoms than moderately conditioned women or inactive women and moderately conditioned women had fewer symptoms than inactive women.

The evidence suggests that elderly women benefit from exercise, but it's unclear how much exercise is necessary before their immune systems benefit. It may be that in the elderly long-term training is necessary for changes in the immune system to provide protection from illness and disease.

PRACTICAL IMPLICATIONS

The impact of changes in the immune system resulting from exercise and training is somewhat uncertain. Although changes in cell number and activity are apparent, it is not clear that this will provide protection from illness and/or disease. Using the available evidence, experts have proposed the following guidelines to reduce the risk of illness following exercise and competition. First, individuals should control lifestyle factors that influence the immune system: eat well, keep psychological stress to a minimum, avoid chronic fatigue, minimize nontraining stress, and reduce intensity or duration of exercise in high environmental temperatures. Second, athletes should take a number of specific actions: (1) Train and compete wisely: space hard workouts and race events as far apart as possible, avoid overtraining.

(2) Avoid sick people after an event: be careful particularly during the first few hours when the immune cell count and activity is below baseline level. (3) Get adequate sleep and rest: fatigue contributes to negative immune responses. (4) After an illness that involves the immune system, wait six months before training hard: this allows the immune system to recover fully before adding the exercise stress. (5) Reduce workout intensity and duration during the infectious stage of an illness or when signs or symptoms of infection are observed: workouts may intensify the infection by further weakening the immune system. (6) Get a flu shot to enhance immune function and supplement acquired immunity.

Carol L. Christensen

Bibliography

MacKinnon, Laurel T. (1992) *Exercise and Immunology.* Champaign, IL: Human Kinetics.

Nieman, David C. (1998) *The Exercise-Health Connection.* Champaign, IL: Human Kinetics.

INDONESIA

Indonesia is the largest nation in Southeast Asia with a population of more than 200 million people. Indonesians inhabit some 13,667 islands covering a total area of 1,904,569 square kilometers (1,180,832 square miles) from the Malay Peninsula in the west to New Guinea in the east. The nation is divided into twenty-seven provinces, with 87 percent of the population of Muslim faith, 9 percent Christian, 2 percent Hindu, and a modest number of Buddhists. With its many languages, regions, and cultures, Indonesia is a highly diverse nation. Religion and politics have been the two governing forces in women's sports, and despite some improvement, both continue to constrain participation.

HISTORY

Indonesia gained independence in 1950, but its approach to sports reflects its history as a Dutch colony. The government has tried to eliminate some of the more obvious restrictions of racial and class discrimination, under which, for example, local inhabitants were barred from sports clubs and swimming pools. Even before independence, however, competitive sport played a role in unifying the nation. The national games, or PON (Pekan Olahraga Nasional), an event introduced in 1948 and held every four years, has provided opportunities for athletes from all parts of the far-flung nation to compete.

Indeed, since independence, political leaders have viewed sports participation as a means to unify the people. In 1962 the Ministry for Sports was established under the first president, Sukarno. During his term of office (1950–1966), he used sport extensively as a tool to manipulate policy, foreign and domestic. After generations of being kept from sport, the participation of girls and women dramatically increased during this period.

TRADITIONAL CONSTRAINTS ON COMPETITIVE SPORT

Religious prohibitions prevent many Muslims from taking part in competitive sports. Because Islam is the dominant religion in Indonesia, women have participated very little in elite sport competition. Women's involvement in sports was limited further with the New Order government of Suharto and his promotion of the national ideology of "pancasila." Pancasila was a practical guide for life and politics, which tried to bring diverse social groups together in harmony. Pancasila comprises five principles: belief in God, national unity, humanitarianism, people's sovereignty, and social justice and prosperity. Under this ideology, women were considered guardian mothers, who functioned as auxiliaries of their husbands and did all domestic work. This "Dharma Wanita" (Duty of Women) doctrine established by the government implied that activity outside the home was inappropriate for women, particularly if it caused them to neglect their so-called primary duties. This limitation presumably included participation in competitive sports. Schools continued to teach physical education, and girls were expected to participate in three classes per week. However, participation in tradi-

INDONESIA'S BEST

W omen's sport in Indonesia during the 1990s has been dominated by the exploits of two world class athletes, Susi Susanti, in badminton, and Yayuk Basuki, in professional tennis.

Born in 1971 in Tasikmalaya, in West Java, Susi Susanti is Chinese. At fourteen she joined the sports school in Ragunan, Jakarta. Susanti represented her nation in the Uber Cup from 1986 until her retirement in 1998. She became the All-England Badminton champion in 1990, the first Indonesian to achieve that honor. In 1992, Susanti beat Bang Soo-Hyun of South Korea in the singles tournament in the Barcelona Olympics. Susanti, a six-time World Grand Prix champion between 1990 and 1996, was awarded the Service Star of the First Order, Indonesia's highest medal of merit.

Born in 1970, twenty-eight-year-old Yayuk Basuki was raised in a family of five children in Yogyakarta and has been ranked consistently in the top fifty of the WTA tour. Like Susi Susanti, she attended the Ragunan Sport Centre, from which she graduated in 1989. Basuki won the Sportswoman of the Year trophy in 1986, 1989, and 1990. In 1991 she won her first WTA tournament at Pattaya City and reached the third round at Wimbledon. In the same year, Basuki was named best female athlete of the year in Indonesia. She competed at the Barcelona Olympic Games the following year. She had a breakthrough in 1997, reaching the Wimbledon quarterfinals and joining the top twenty for the first time.

tional activities such as *pencak silat,* the traditional combat sport and martial art, declined at that time. In the early 1970s, the directorate of sport in the Ministry of Education and culture promoted physical fitness and active recreation, and some of the traditional activities were revived. A Sports for All ideology was introduced by the government in 1981, with the aim of encouraging mass participation.

INTERNATIONAL COMPETITION

Women take part in many sports in Indonesia, including weightlifting, water skiing, table tennis, swimming, tennis, diving, cycling, shooting, and judo. Badminton has become the most successful international sport for Indonesia, and the leading players tend to be of Chinese descent. In 1975 the national women's badminton team won the Uber Cup (the equivalent of the Thomas Cup for men), and in 1980, the second world badminton championship was held in Jakarta. These events marked a reemergence and a consequent improvement in the standards of international performance. Players such as Wiharja Verawaty, Imelda Wigoena, Ivana Lie, Teresia Widiastuty,

and Ruth Damayanti led the way. In Kuala Lumpur, Malaysia, in 1982, Verawaty Fajirin was the runner-up in the world cup, and in Jakarta, three years later, Lie matched this feat. In Guangzhou in 1989 eighteen-year-old Susi Susanti, destined to become the most illustrious player of her generation, was the first Indonesian to win this title. The following year, when the tournament was held jointly in Bandung and Jakarta, Sarwendah Kusumawardani came in second.

BARRIERS TO SUCCESS

The political, social, and economic turmoil in Indonesia in the late 1990s had a negative impact on the development of women's sport. Swimmers, for example, were withdrawn from their overseas training schedules to save money. Religion and economic status were significant barriers to success with athletes in individual sports.

Several Indonesian women athletes have also been involved in more isolated controversies. Minarti Timur, an international badminton player, was banned for eighteen months for using a performance-enhancing substance in January 1991. The first sexual harassment case in Indone-

Indonesian badminton competitor Susi Susanti. (Stephen J. Line)

total of sixty-six were females. In 1980 Indonesia joined the boycott of the Moscow Games, but many more women took part in the following years. In 1988, Lilies Handayani, Nurfitriyani Saiman (Lantang), and Kusuma Wardhani won a team silver medal in archery, the first Indonesian medal ever, in the Olympics. The archers also won the bronze team medal in the world championships in 1995. Women were well represented at the Olympics of 1992; of the forty-eight competitors who went to Barcelona, nineteen were women. They competed in table tennis, judo, archery, tae kwon do, badminton, and tennis. Susanti, a badminton player, became Indonesia's first Olympic gold medalist, when she beat Bang Soo-Hyun of South Korea in the finals of the singles tournament at Barcelona. The Olympic experience of 1996 was a disappointment for the women's badminton team. Although women again won medals, Susanti (bronze) and Mia Audina (silver) did not manage to match the performances of 1992. Of ninety-four athletes sent to Atlanta, thirty-five were female.

MOST RENOWNED COMPETITORS OF THE 1990S

Women's sports in Indonesia during the 1990s were dominated by two world-class athletes: Susanti, probably the most famous and most successful badminton player in the history of the game; and Yayuk Basuki, a professional tennis player with the Women's Tennis Association (WTA).

Susanti was born in 1971 in Tasikmalaya, in West Java. At age fourteen, she joined a government sponsored sports school in Ragunan, Jakarta. Susanti has been nicknamed "Srikandi," after the only Indonesian shadow puppet that depicts a female character, who is a fighter. She represented her nation in the Uber Cup from 1986 until her retirement in 1998, and was the All-England Badminton champion in 1990, the first Indonesian to achieve that honor. As a prize for her 1992 Olympic performance, she received a house from the government. Susanti, a six-time world Grand Prix champion between 1990 and 1996, was awarded the Service Star of the First Order, Indonesia's highest medal of merit.

As a tennis player, Basuki has been ranked consistently in the top fifty of the WTA tour. Born

sian sport occurred in 1993. It involved the archer and Olympic medalist Lilies Handayani. The head of the Archery Association was subsequently asked to resign by KONI (the national sports council). And in 1994, thirteen-year-old swimmer Catherine Surya was stripped of the medals she won at the thirteenth national games the previous year, when it was discovered she had taken an anabolic steroid. Cash rewards promised by provincial governments to swimmers may have influenced her coach to provide drugs, although there was no evidence that the coach took bribes.

OLYMPIC PARTICIPATION

Indonesia first participated in the Olympic Games in Helsinki in 1952. Between 1952 and 1976 only nine Indonesian Olympians out of the in 1970, Basuki began playing at age eight, when her athletic abilities were recognized. Like Susanti, she attended the Ragunan Sport Centre, from which she graduated in 1989. Basuki won the Sportswoman of the Year trophy in 1986, 1989, and 1990. In 1991 Basuki first made the top fifty list, and reached the third round at Wimbledon. In the same year, Basuki was named best female athlete of the year in Indonesia. She competed at the Barcelona Olympic Games the following year. In 1997 she reached the Wimbledon quarterfinals and joined the top twenty for the first time.

Indonesia still confronts considerable economic and political turmoil, a situation that interferes with sports at all levels. However, Indonesian women have undeniably made considerable progress since independence.

Nicholas G. Aplin

Bibliography

Cribb, Robert B., and Colin Brown. (1995) *Modern Indonesia: A History Since 1945.* London: Longman.

Moolenizjer, Nichlaas J., and Sieswanpo. (1980) "Sport and Physical Education in Indonesia." In *Sport and PE Around the World*, edited by W. Johnston. Indianapolis, IN: Monograph No. 5, Phi Epsilon Kappa Fraternity, 314–338.

Mulder, N. (1996) *Inside Indonesian Society: Cultural Change in Java.* Singapore: Pepin.

Saraswati Sunindyo. (1993) "Gender Discourse on Television." In *Culture and Society in New Order Indonesia*, edited by V. M. Hooker. Singapore: Oxford University Press, 134–148.

Sfeir, L. (1985) "The Status of Muslim Women in Sport: Conflict Between Cultural Tradition and Modernization." *International Review for Sociology of Sport* 20, 4: 283–305.

Suryadinata, L. (1981) *Eminent Indonesian Chinese.* Singapore: Gunung Agung.

INJURY

The incidence of athletic injury continues to rise. Though modified equipment and improved training techniques can reduce the risk of injury, the National Institute of Arthritis and Musculoskeletal and Skin Diseases (NIAMS) estimates that 17 million sport-related injuries occur every year within the United States. International rates vary among countries but are also generally rising. As a given sport becomes more popular, rates of injury are likely to increase. Women's participation in sport has increased significantly since the passage of Title IX in 1972, within and outside the United States, which in turn has created an increase in athletic injury among women. As a result, issues regarding risk factors and postinjury concerns specific to women have become critical areas for research.

Women do seem to have an increased risk for certain sports-related injuries due to anatomical differences between men and women. Additional types of injuries have been identified as frequently occurring among women; that these may or may not be related to unique mental states and social conditions makes their identification and discussion of their causes controversial.

PHYSICAL INJURY

A majority of the injuries that female athletes incur are considered sport-related as opposed to being solely attributable to gender. Many high-risk sports such as soccer, basketball, and ice hockey have historically been dominated by men. That women and girls have greater opportunity to engage in contact sports, which have a relatively high incidence of athletic injury, has undoubtedly influenced injury prevalence rates.

Knee and Ankle Injuries

A distinct anatomical difference between men and women related to ankle and knee injuries involves the Q-angle. This angle is formed by the intersection of two imaginary lines on the upper leg. The first line bisects the thigh region (femur) and the second line begins at the patella (kneecap) and progresses straight up toward the head. Because women have wider hips to accommodate childbirth, this angle is wider in women than in men. Wide hips force the patellofemoral region to compensate for the body's misalignment, which can result in one of two conditions, muscle laxity or tightness. Laxity is best described as resembling an overused rubber band that has lost its strength.

Tightness, in contrast, refers to inflexibility or stiffness. Laxity and tightness are related in that they tend to occur in opposing muscle regions. For example, if a particular muscle region is lax, such as the thigh muscle, or quadriceps, then complimentary regions such as the hamstrings tend to be tight to compensate for laxity. This, in turn, results in an imbalance.

The Q-angle also affects the knee and the ankle region due to a phenomenon termed the kinetic chain reaction. This kinetic chain reaction occurs where the wide Q-angle from the hip causes stress on the knee. This, in turn, causes a reverse stress on the ankle, and both stresses may increase the risk of injury in those areas. Common injuries to those areas include knee ligament strains and tears, ankle sprains, and fractures.

Rotator Cuff Injuries

The rotator cuff is the ball and socket joint in the shoulder. Compared to men, women tend to have increased laxity and decreased strength in their shoulders, which increases their susceptibility to injury in that area. Another anatomical difference between men and women is the carrying angle. This angle is formed by the intersection of lines that bisect the upper arm and lower arm at the elbow joint and corresponds to the width of the hips.

Carrying angle refers to a woman's ability to carry objects at her side allowing the arm to swing naturally while clearing the width of the hips. Because the carrying angle limits one's ability to execute an overhand throwing motion, it influences body mechanics. As a result, women are more likely to have a sidearm swing, which places greater strain on the joint and associated muscle groups. When the athlete uses the involved muscles, for example, as in the case of a softball pitcher, she may find herself at increased risk for shoulder dislocations or overuse injuries.

Lumbar Spine Injuries

Sex differences in the number of lumbar spine injuries are not as clearly attributable to anatomy as are the arm and leg injuries. Injuries of the spinal region are very common in such sports as ballet, gymnastics, and figure skating. Typically, a greater number of women than men participate in sports where athletes exceed the normal range and limits of flexibility in the back. Therefore, women may have a higher incidence of lumbar spine injuries than do men because they are more likely to choose these sports, not because of their gender.

Foot Pain

It has been suggested that women are more susceptible than men for developing foot-related disorders such as bunions, corns, and calluses on the heel, called retrocalcaneal bursitis. Many of these problems are due to the design of women's shoes, including athletic footwear. Women's shoes are typically designed so that the shoe narrows to the tip. This design is contrary to the natural shape of the foot, and as a result may cause a significant amount of pain and discomfort as well as lead to blisters, corns, and calluses.

PSYCHOLOGICAL PROBLEMS

Unlike anatomical differences, psychological differences between men and women are not as ea-

---

ANTERIOR CRUCIATE LIGAMENT TEARS

According to *Women's Sports & Fitness*, girls and women are from two to eight times more likely to suffer anterior cruciate ligament (ACL) tears than are boys and men. Surveys of high school and college athletes show that in basketball the ratio is 6:1, in gymnastics 3:1, and in soccer 2:1. Experts believe this variance is due to anatomical differences in bone and joint size and strength which make females more susceptible. Fortunately, ACL injuries are now routinely treated by surgery followed by physical therapy which is 95 percent successful.

sily distinguished and at times can be very controversial. In general, the field of psychology is host to constant debates about the relative contributions of nature and nurture: genetic predisposition or environmental processes. Current thought is that the interaction of the two explains more of the variance in human nature than either of the two alone. Thus, the following discussion of psychological factors associated with an increased risk for athletic injury applies to men and women.

Personality

Initial studies of the relationship between injury and psychological factors focused on the athletic personality. Many of the early findings have not been replicated, and in some cases they were reversed. Although distinct personality differences quite likely contribute to a person's injury susceptibility, no definite statement can be made at this time. Research with the most promise involved multidimensional aspects of personality (for example, optimism, hardiness, and coping) that are thought to regulate resiliency to stress, negative feelings, and subsequent coping. Recent efforts have begun to look instead at alternative environmental explanations for injury vulnerability.

Life-Event Stress

How the stress of life events might affect athletic interest has received considerable attention in the psychology literature. The relationship between stress and injury is viewed as very similar to the relationship between stress and illness. Early attempts to link life-event stress examined the impact of positive and negative experiences upon one's health. Researchers have focused predominantly upon negative life events and their relation to injury/illness vulnerability. Most probably, stress and injury can be explained through a complex interaction of psychological and physiological variables involving cognitive, emotional, and behavioral pathways. In general, stress influences thought, emotion, behavior, and physiology, which in turn have reciprocal effects.

An athlete may be more vulnerable to injury because of immediate responses to stress such as an inability to concentrate or identify visual cues (that is, peripheral narrowing) as well as behav-ioral disruptions (for example, sleeping disturbance and alcohol use). Long-term effects of stress may increase the athlete's vulnerability through the effects of the nervous system on the immune system (immunosuppression), and on the skeletal muscle system (impaired recovery), which in turn can create a variety of health problems and increase injury susceptibility. For example, given the same exercise stimulus, high- and low-stress athletes exhibit different stress hormone responses, with different manifestations: high-stress athletes are more likely to have trouble paying attention and identifying visual cues (peripheral narrowing).

COPING WITH SPORT INJURY

Several important factors influence how well one copes after being injured. Severity of injury, team status (for example, starter versus nonstarter), time of season, coping resources, and social support available to the athlete are only few of the potentially influential factors. Logically, it would seem that injury severity and its probable effect on the athlete (that is, prognosis for recovery) would most affect the athlete's response to injury. This is not always the case. Thus, health care professionals need to be familiar with models of emotional response to injury.

Efforts to understand how athletes respond to injury have also evaluated thought processes. These models suggest that how an athlete thinks, feels, and acts after an injury are determined by an interaction of individual and situational factors. This approach emphasizes the athlete's appraisal of injury, where her response is largely influenced by the perceived threat compared to her coping resources. For example, consider an athlete who tears her anterior cruciate ligament (ACL) in the middle of her competitive season. She responds to the knee injury by comparing her perceived ability to cope to the demands that lie in front of her (surgery, rehabilitation, pain). Individual characteristics (for example, optimism) and situational factors (for example, social support) work together to mediate the response to injury. No definitive evidence exists to suggest that men and women cope differently with athletic injury. What has been suggested, however, is that gender differences exist in social support, with women reporting greater social support than men. Such support tends to buffer the stress response.

STRATEGIES FOR INJURY PREVENTION

To identify athletes who may be at an increased risk for injury, coaches and health care professionals can use preseason screenings to evaluate various important areas, including physical and psychological risk factors.

Physical Examinations

Because of the anatomical differences that place women at risk, it is imperative to conduct a thorough examination of the upper and lower extremities: shoulder and patellofemoral region and ankle. The examiner should note laxity, inflexibility, and weak muscle regions of the body that are of particular importance for the athlete's sport. For example, physicians or athletic trainers should examine the knees, ankles, shoulders, and hands for volleyball players; knees, ankles, shoulders, spine, wrists, and elbows for gymnasts; and knees, ankles, elbows, and shoulders for softball players. If they find deficits in any areas, they should set up a rehabilitation program designed specifically to strengthen those areas. For example, Jenny McConnell developed a series of widely acclaimed exercises created specifically to strengthen the patellofemoral region.

To deal with foot problems and women's tendency to develop them, the simplest approach is education. Active women need to increase their knowledge about footwear needs. They should learn how to identify their support needs and how to choose appropriate footwear. Most shoe manufacturers tend to offer various styles with a particular design (that is, for a wide foot) that may not be suitable for everyone. Representatives from a reputable women's athletic footwear supplier may be one avenue to gain access to this information either by offering a workshop or by making a referral to a local expert in the area.

Psychological Screenings

Much as coaches and other professionals would identify physiological risk factors through a preseason screening, they might also use a psychological survey to identify at-risk individuals. A word of caution: use of the majority of psychological questionnaires is restricted to those who are familiar with them, their administration, and the interpretation of the results. One useful strategy would be to find a trained professional, such as a sport psychologist or athlete counselor, who understands the unique concerns of athletes. Such a person could assist in finding the best method of identifying at-risk individuals, as well as developing specific interventions aimed at decreasing risk for injury (for example, stress management). Studies have shown promising results on the efficacy of psychological interventions to prevent athletic injury.

POST-INJURY INTERVENTIONS

Beyond targeting at-risk individuals before the competitive season, various strategies can help an athlete's recovery from an athletic injury once it has occurred. Compared to medication and surgery, which depend largely upon the specific injury characteristics, psychological interventions

COMMON INJURIES

Here are the most common injuries women sustain in popular recreational sports.

Tennis: elbow and shoulder strains
Golf: lower back, neck, wrist, and elbow strains
Running: heel pain and low back strain

Softball: leg, groin and shoulder strains
Volleyball: ankle and shoulder strains
Soccer: ankle sprains and knee ligament tears
Basketball: ankle, calf and knee strains; knee ligament tears

STUDY ON INJURIES AND HIGH SCHOOL ATHLETES

In September 1999 the National Athletic Trainers' Association (NATA) released findings of a three-year study of injuries among high school athletes. The study focused on injuries sustained in ten high school sports in a sample of 246 high schools across the United States from 1995 to 1997. Included in the study were girls softball, field hockey, soccer, basketball, and volleyball. The study found more injuries occurred during practice than during actual games. The only sport that did not conform to this pattern was soccer, for both boys and girls. Other conclusions relevant to girls were that knee injuries are most frequent in girls soccer, surgery is most often needed for girls soccer injuries, and surgery is least often needed for girls field hockey injuries. The NATA recommended that the study findings be used to develop injury prevention initiatives for high school sports programs.

can be more widely applied to injured athletes. Hence, the focus of this section is restricted to various psychological postinjury interventions. Many studies have looked at psychological interventions designed to facilitate injury rehabilitation and recovery, but few empirical papers have documented the effect of those interventions. One notable exception is the use of a cognitive-behavioral intervention (called stress inoculation training, SIT) with postsurgical athletes. Compared with controls who received only physical therapy, athletes who received SIT in conjunction with physical therapy experienced significantly less pain and anxiety during rehabilitation. They also required fewer days to return to physical functioning as defined by specific criteria. Goal setting, relaxation, and imagery also appear to be useful in the rehabilitation process.

CONCLUSION

As the number of female athletes continues to rise, it will become increasingly more important to address specific concerns that women face regarding injury risk, prevention, and treatment. Historically, women's issues in sport, as well as in the general fields of medicine and psychology, have not been a significant focus of attention. As a result, our knowledge of women and sport injury is in its preliminary stage. Given the increased awareness of the issue, it is only a matter of time until knowledge about sport injury among women begins to advance, as have other areas that involve women's unique concerns within medicine and psychology.

R. Renee Newcomer

See also Athletic Training

Bibliography

Agostini, Rosemary, and Sid Titus. (1994) *Medical and Orthopedic Issues of Active and Athletic Women.* St. Louis, MO: Mosby.

Arendt, Elizabeth A. (1996) "Common Musculoskeletal Injuries in Women." *Physician and Sportsmedicine* 24, 7: 39–42.

Brewer, Britton W., Daryn E. Linder, and Craig M. Phelps. (1995) "Situational Correlates of Emotional Adjustment to Athletic Injury." *Clinical Journal of Sport Medicine* 5, 4: 241–245.

Brewer, Britton W. (Guest Editor). (1998) "Special Issue: Theoretical, Empirical, and Applied Issues in the Psychology of Sport Injury." *Journal of Applied Sport Psychology* 10, 1.

Carver, Charles S., and Michael F. Scheier. (1994) "Situational Coping and Coping Dispositions in a Stressful Transaction." *Journal of Personality and Social Psychology* 66: 184–195.

Crocker, Peter R., and Thomas R. Graham. (1995) "Coping by Competitive Athletes with Performance Stress: Gender Differences and Relationships with Affect." *The Sport Psychologist* 9: 325–338.

Endler, Norman S., and James D. Parker. (1994) "Assessment of Multidimensional Coping: Task, Emotion, and Avoidance Strategies." *Psychological Assessment* 6, 1: 50–60.

Heil, John. (1993) *Psychology of Sport Injury.* Champaign, IL: Human Kinetics Publishers.

Hutchinson, Mark R., and Mary L. Ireland. (1995) "Knee Injuries in Female Athletes." *Sports Medicine* 19, 4: 288–302.

Ireland, Mary L., Michael Gaudette, and Scott Croo. (1997) "ACL Injuries in the Female Athlete." *Journal of Sport Rehabilitation* 6, 2: 97–110.

Kerr, Gretchen, and Judy Goss. (1996) "The Effects of a Stress Management Program on Injuries and Stress Levels." *Journal of Applied Sport Psychology* 8, 1: 109–117.

Klarica, A. (1996) "Coming Back from Injuries and Setbacks." *Women in Sport* 2, 2: 64–65.

Lazarus, Richard S., and Susan Folkman. (1984) *Stress, Appraisal, and Coping.* New York: Springer.

Love, Phyllis A. (1993) "Sports Medicine Strand." *Women in Sport and Physical Activity Journal* 2, 2: 87–92.

McConnell, Jenny. (1993) *McConnell Patellofemoral Treatment Plan.* Marina del Ray, CA: McConnell Seminars.

Nixon, Howard L., II. (1996) "Explaining Pain and Injury Attitudes and Experiences in Sport in Terms of Gender, Race, and Sports Status Factors." *Journal of Sport and Social Issues* 20, 1: 33–44.

O'Brien, M. (1995) "Women and Sport." *Sports Exercise and Injury* 1, 3: 131–137.

Pargman, David. (1993) *Psychological Bases of Sport Injuries.* Morgantown, WV: Fitness Information Technology, Inc.

Perna, Frank M., and Sharon L. McDowell. (1995) "Role of Psychological Stress in Cortisol Recovery from Exhaustive Exercise Among Elite Athletes." *International Journal of Behavioral Medicine* 3, 1: 13–26.

Ross, Michael J., and R. Scott Berger. (1996) "Effects of Stress Inoculation Training on Athletes' Postsurgical Pain and Rehabilitation After Orthopedic Injury." *Journal of Consulting and Clinical Psychology* 64, 2: 406–410.

Schnirring, Lisa. (1997) "What's New in Treating Active Women." *Physician and Sportsmedicine* 25, 7: 91–92.

Singer, Robert N., and Paula J. Johnson. (1987) "Strategies to Cope with Pain Associated with Sport-related Injuries." *Athletic Training* 22, 2: 100–103.

Williams, Jean M., and Mark B. Andersen. (1998) "Psychosocial Antecedents of Sport Injury: Review and Critique of the Stress and Injury Model." *Journal of Applied Sport Psychology* 10, 1: 5–25.

Additional information was provided by Frank Perna and Joni Roh.

INNEBANDY

Innebandy is arguably the most popular sport in Sweden, yet it is almost unknown in the United States where it originally developed from a game called unihok in the 1950s. The reason for the sport's quick growth in popularity in Sweden is likely due to that country's well-organized sport club program that has long characterized athletic and leisure pursuit participation. The game of innebandy is also relatively easy for new players to master and the equipment is minimal, making it an attractive choice for club and youth team sponsorship. Innebandy is very similar to what North Americans know as floor hockey, but instead of a puck, a whiffle ball is used, creating a much faster-paced game. Like floor hockey, innebandy players use sticks that are very similar to ice hockey sticks.

Two women play innebandy, a Swedish game similar to floor hockey, but played with a whiffle ball. (Elisabeth Hedman Photograph)

Whereas floor hockey in North America remains a recreational game played primarily in school physical education classes, innebandy is played at the recreational level and at the competitive level—including international competition between high-level national teams throughout Scandinavia and Europe. In Finland the game is called "salibandy" and in Switzerland it is called "unihockey." International play is regulated by the International Floorball Federation, which was founded in 1986. In 1999 the first national-teams competition outside of Europe was played in Singapore where the Europeans were joined by teams from the host country, Australia, and Japan.

A more extensive look at the history of innebandy traverses the seas and oceans between Europe, Scandinavia, and North America several times; and first references date back to the early 1500s. An activity called bandy was perhaps the original game. It was played on ice with sticks and a softball-sized ball. Bandy is still popular in Scandinavian countries and is thought to have led to the development of ice hockey in North America. It is thought that floor hockey developed from ice hockey as a way to practice ice hockey during the off-season. Originally, floor hockey was played indoors with either a puck or a lightweight plastic ball. When the sport was adopted by Swedish visitors to the United States in the 1950s, a whiffle ball became standard (since the Swedish bandy used a ball rather than a puck). Though the sport is known by a variety of names throughout Scandinavia and Europe, the name of floorball achieved dominance with the founding in 1986 of the International Floorball Federation, the governing body for world floorball.

RULES AND PLAY

Because the sport is relatively new, many changes have occurred in the rules development, equipment, and rink and goal sizes. Today, the international rink is 40 by 20 meters (44 by 22 yards) with a goal on either end measuring 160 by 115 centimeters (5.2 by 3.8 feet). In recreational play, the rink dimensions can vary, but they generally adhere to the rule of length equals two-times-width. A team consists of six players, one of whom is a goalkeeper. As in many similar sports, the object is to score more goals than the opposing team. In innebandy, there are three 20-minute periods.

Perhaps a major difference between ice hockey, bandy, floor hockey, and innebandy is the level of participation by women. Innebandy is the only sport among these that has supported national-level teams and international competition by women from its beginning. Women's and men's national teams followed similar paths with the first major competition, the European Cup held in 1993 in Finland for women and in Sweden for men. In 1994 the first European championships were held for men, followed in 1995 by the first women's European championship. The first world championship for men was held in 1996 in Sweden and the first world championship for women was held in 1997 in Finland. The championships are held every year, in even years for men and in odd years for women.

Linda S. Stanley

Bibliography

International Floorball Federation. (1998) *The International Floorball.* Sweden: IFF.

Olsson, C., and P. Persson. (1996) *Innebandy.* Stockholm, Sweden: Raben & Sjogren.

INTERCOLLEGIATE ATHLETICS

Intercollegiate athletics refers to sporting competitions in which a team representing one college or university plays another such team. Various forms of interschool athletic contests exist in many countries. Highly commercialized, professionalized, and institutionalized intercollegiate athletics is, however, a unique and visible phenomenon of higher education in the United States. This entry focuses on the history of intercollegiate athletics for women in the United States.

HISTORY

The origin of women's intercollegiate athletics is completely different from that of the men's. Men's athletics began with spontaneous, student-initiated extracurricular activities. College athletics for women, in contrast, had its roots in traditional physical education programs designed solely for female students in women's colleges and coeducational institutions.

A dominant nineteenth-century medical view was that women, from puberty to menopause, would be periodically weakened by menstruation, and that they would break down physically and mentally if they had to assume any other work beyond domestic duties. It was believed that girls would suffer from education because it would consume the energies that otherwise were the vital force for achieving the state of "true womanhood." Such a male-created image of "frail" women justified male resistance to women's right to higher education as well as other opportunities traditionally dominated by men, often in the name of protecting the "weaker sex."

Progressive thinkers and educators believed not only that women should have the same right to higher education as men but also that they possessed the same capacity for succeeding. Those who established women's colleges or were associated with women in coeducational institutions insisted that physical fitness was essential for women to be successful at intellectual endeavors. Physical education, thus, was incorporated as an integral part of the women's experience of higher learning, especially after its introduction at Vassar College in 1865. By the 1890s, physical education programs existed in all eastern women's colleges and most universities throughout the country as well as in the women's colleges of Oxford and Cambridge in Britain. From the very beginning, women physical educators took firm control of physical education for women in British and American colleges and universities. They not only taught their students sport skills but also determined for them the "appropriate" sport behaviors and the "acceptable" values for young women.

The last decade of the nineteenth century saw a significant change in college physical education programs—the relatively dull routine of gymnastic exercises was giving way to more exciting games and sports. By the turn of the century, nearly every institution of higher education had a sport program for women. In the United States, popular physical activities and sports included

archery, bowling, boating, track and field, horseback riding, skating, swimming, golf, and tennis. In Great Britain, cricket, field hockey, and rowing were popular. As women's physical activities came to emphasize team games rather than individual sports, basketball became the most popular team sport for American female collegians. The first officially recorded intercollegiate athletic contest for women was a basketball game between Stanford University and the University of California at Berkeley in 1896. Basketball continues to dominate women's intercollegiate athletics today.

Basketball, originally invented in 1891 by James Naismith (1861–1939) as a winter game for his students at the YMCA Training School in Springfield, Massachusetts, became the storm center of philosophical conflict between men's and women's college athletics. When Senda Berenson (1868–1954) introduced basketball to her students at Smith College in 1892, she modified the game for women to limit physical exertion and maintain a high standard of sportsmanship. The modified game had little acceptance beyond Smith College and other women's colleges in the northeast region of the United States. Lacking a uniform set of rules for women nationwide, many teams assumed the men's game as the standard and approached it with the same stress on winning. Concerned about the intense increase in competitiveness and an "unwomanly" performance, female physical educators warned of the danger of women blindly imitating the men's game.

To unify the women's game and to keep control of women's physical education, a Women's Basketball Committee was formed in 1899, the first national organization to regulate sports for college women. In Britain, where field hockey continued to be more popular than netball (the British version of Naismith's game), an All-England Women's Field Hockey Association was formed in 1895.

"EVERY GIRL IN A SPORT"

The formation of the Women's Basketball Committee symbolized the beginning of a collective effort of American female physical educators to control women's athletics. The game of basketball provided them with an effective channel into the whole world of women's sports. Twenty years after Berenson adapted the men's game, not only had basketball become the most popular team sport for women, but more than half of women's teams were still playing the men's game or different versions of women's basketball. Thus, with the growth of women's basketball came increased concern among women leaders over the direction of women's athletics. It became apparent, toward the end of the 1910s, that most women leaders favored intramural sports over intercollegiate athletic contests. They soon consolidated themselves for a crusade against varsity competition for women. The catalyst for the women leaders' decision to take firm control of women's athletics was a series of actions taken by the Amateur Athletic Union (AAU) of the United States in 1922.

During the first three decades of the modern Olympic Games, women were excluded from participating in track and field. When a petition for the inclusion of women in track and field for the 1920 Games was rejected by the International Olympic Committee (IOC), the newly formed Fédération Sportive Feminine Internationale (FSFI) decided in 1922 to hold its own "Jeux Olympiques" for women in Paris. Responding to the invitation of the FSFI, a U.S. team was formed and sent to Paris under the auspices of the AAU. The AAU's decision to send a women's team to the Paris Games met strong opposition from women physical educators who were reluctant to give up control of women's athletics. Reacting to the AAU's action, the Committee on Women's Athletics (CWA) of the American Physical Education Association (APEA) passed a resolution that prohibited any women's athletic affiliation with the AAU. The fight between the CWA and the AAU intensified when the AAU announced its jurisdiction over American women's track and field after the highly successful 1922 "Women's Olympics" in Paris. In the middle of the CWA–AAU conflict, a new organization was formed and soon joined the fight.

The National Amateur Athletic Federation (NAAF) was formed in 1922 to promote sport and games for everyone and to address dissatisfaction with the United States Olympic programs. In April 1923, a Women's Division of the NAAF was established under the leadership of Lou Henry Hoover, wife of future president Herbert Hoover,

Teammates from Arizona State University run side by side in the women's 10,000-meter race at the 1990 Pac-10 Track and Field Championships. (Kevin R. Morris)

who advocated sex-separate organizations due to "fundamental differences" between athletics for men and women. A major outcome of the first conference of the Women's Division was the philosophy of antivarsity, anti-Olympic competition, known as "the Platform." It stressed that women's sport should be "play for play's sake" and controlled by women. It condemned the participation of American women in international competitions and emphasized that sport should serve the masses rather than the privileged few.

By publishing and distributing antivarsity and anti-Olympic materials, the CWA and the Women's Division promoted an alternative recreational model of athletics in the form of Play Days, thus excluding themselves from the world of competitive sports. This anticompetitive philosophy was dominant during the 1920s and 1930s when "Play Days," "Sports Days," and "telegraphic meets" replaced most intercollegiate contests. During "telegraphic meets," students competed on their own campus in swimming or track and field, then telegraphed the results to their opponents, who had done the same on their campuses.

The essence of the Play Day was the focus on participation over competition, best known by the slogan "a sport for every girl and every girl in a sport." The Play Day usually consisted of female students from a number of schools gathering together for a day of sport activities. While basketball was usually the most popular event, many other sports were also available, such as archery, baseball or softball, field hockey, soccer, swimming, track and field, tennis, and volleyball. A unique part of the Play Day was that individual schools would not compete against one another under school colors. Rather, teams composed of players from various schools would play. Consequently, winning became less important for the participating institutions. What was emphasized was the social interaction among the players of the various institutions. It was believed that social values could be derived from such competition.

The women physical education leaders often denied that they were opposed to competition, only to the "wrong type" of competition. Nevertheless, most intercollegiate contests were eliminated by the end of 1920s. A prevalent belief among women physical educators at the time was that there was hardly any kind of intercollegiate contest that did not stimulate an excessive desire for winning. For more than a decade, Play Days dominated the sporting scene for college women. They eventually gave way to "Sports Days," a somewhat more competitive model of interinstitutional sport competition that recognized teams as representatives of individual schools.

THE RETURN OF INTERCOLLEGIATE COMPETITION

Anticompetitive attitudes dominated women's physical education during the years between the two World Wars. Toward the end of that period, and especially after World War II, the demand for highly competitive women's athletics increased, and the number of varsity teams grew. As early as 1936, Gladys Palmer of Ohio State University (OSU) had called for the formation of a "National Women's Sport Association." In 1941 Palmer and her colleagues at OSU organized the first Women's National Intercollegiate Golf Tournament, despite strong opposition from the women leaders in the National Section on Women's Athletics (NSWA) of the American Association for Health, Physical Education, and Recreation (AAHPER). This group opposed "national tour-

naments of any sorts" and "any organization to increase competition." The tournament was a success and became an annual event after World War II.

Indirectly, the war stimulated the growth of intercollegiate athletics for men and women. Especially important was the change in society's attitudes toward women in general and their participation in sports in particular. Female physical educators responded to this change.

The Women's National Collegiate Golf Tournament was resumed after the war in 1946. Increasing numbers of women physical educators began to favor varsity competition, and disagreements emerged regarding the directions of women's athletics. By the end of the 1950s, there was very little support for a total ban on intercollegiate competition. In 1957 the first national governing body for women's collegiate athletics, the National Joint Committee for Extramural Sports for College Women (NJCESCW), was formed to set guidelines and standards for women's intercollegiate competition.

SOCIAL CHANGE AND WOMEN'S ATHLETICS

American society changed even more dramatically in the 1960s. With the civil rights and women's movements exerting their influence on almost every aspect of American life, the demand for equality in women's athletics also gained momentum. In 1963 the Division for Girls and Women's Sports (DGWS, formerly the NSWA) revised its policies and procedures for competition in girls' and women's sports and recognized the needs of highly skilled women athletes. In the following year, the NJCESCW decided to dissolve itself and recommended that the DGWS assume its functions in 1965. Realizing the increase in competitive opportunities and the need for leadership in the development and control of intercollegiate athletics for women, the DGWS established the Commission on Intercollegiate Athletics for Women (CIAW) in 1966.

While American physical educators edged slowly toward higher levels of intercollegiate competition for women, their British counterparts tended to lag behind. British students maintained more control over their sports than their American sisters had, and there was little enthusiasm for duplicating the American system of nationally organized and highly competitive intercollegiate sports.

MEN'S INVASION
IN WOMEN'S SEPARATE SPHERE

The 1960s also saw the emergence and growth of the National Collegiate Athletic Association's (NCAA) interest in women's athletics. While traditionally a men's organization, the NCAA's newfound interest was not accidental. For decades, the NCAA fought, with little success, against the AAU for power in U.S. amateur athletics. Ironically, the consecutive U.S. defeats by the Soviets in the 1956 and 1960 Olympic Games not only hurt the image of the United States in Cold War politics but also became a major source of renewed battle for power between the NCAA and AAU. As NCAA institutions provided most of the male medal winners in the Olympics, it was only natural to expect that a greater emphasis on women's intercollegiate sports might bring an additional harvest of Olympic medals. Dissatisfied with the poor management and performance of the 1960 U.S. Olympic team, especially of its women, the NCAA saw women's intercollegiate athletics not only as a means to challenge the dominating Soviet women, but also as a way to wrest control of amateur athletics from the AAU. Furthermore, if colleges were to produce the best athletes for the American team, then the NCAA wanted control of the U.S. Olympic Committee. The NCAA demanded that the organization be restructured, and orchestrated the "federation movement" to challenge AAU's power in amateur sports.

The NCAA's muted but vital interest in women's sports soon became a threat to the traditional separate sphere of women's athletics. To ward off any male invasion while responding to the call for more opportunities for highly skilled women athletes to compete, the women physical education leaders in the DGWS formed the Commission on Intercollegiate Athletics for Women (CIAW) in 1966 to organize national championships. Only a year later, the NCAA established a committee to study the feasibility of controlling and supervising women's intercollegiate athletics. Thus, women physical educators and the men in the NCAA were pursuing their interest in women's intercollegiate athletics, but from different perspectives and with different goals.

During its existence from 1966 to 1972, the CIAW established standards and controlled competitions of women's intercollegiate athletics through sanctioning regional tournaments, promoted the formation and growth of governing bodies of women physical educators at local, state, and regional levels, and held national championships in seven different sports. Realizing their limited power and resources as a commission to manage the increasing needs and expanding problems of collegiate athletics, female physical education leaders formed the Association for Intercollegiate Athletics for Women (AIAW) in 1971. In June 1972, the AIAW officially replaced the CIAW.

THE AIAW ERA

The creation of the AIAW was a major milestone in the development of women's intercollegiate athletics. It became the first institutional membership organization—rather than one composed of individual professionals—to govern intercollegiate athletics for women at the national level. With a professional staff, the AIAW was better prepared than its predecessors, financially as well as administratively, to promote and regulate women's collegiate athletics.

The mission of the AIAW was to provide governance and leadership dedicated to the assurance of standards of excellence and educational soundness in women's intercollegiate athletics. While sharing the common goal of promoting high level athletic competition, the AIAW distinguished itself as the advocate of an "educational model" different from the big-time "commercial model" championed by the NCAA. When it became operational in 1972, one of AIAW's most distinctive features was its policy prohibiting athletic scholarships for women student-athletes. This policy was hailed by the AIAW leaders as one of the organization's greatest strengths. The turn of events in the following months, however, soon forced the AIAW leaders to reexamine the feasibility and legality of their rules.

Weeks after the AIAW became operational, Congress passed Title IX of the Education Amendments of 1972, prohibiting sex discrimination in educational institutions receiving federal financial aid. The essence of Title IX was to provide inclusion and equal opportunities for men and women in all educational activities, including intercollegiate athletics. Ironically, while Title IX seemed to threaten the tradition of men's college athletics, it assumed the male model to be the ideal. Moving toward equality thus meant moving the women's "educational model" toward the men's "commercial model." It also cast dark clouds over the separate sphere of women's collegiate athletics. Conversely, the thought of true equality upset many male sports administrators who feared they might be forced to share their budgets with programs for women. Like a double-edged sword, Title IX granted millions of women the opportunities in school and college athletics traditionally afforded only to men. At the same time, the new law was interpreted to demand equality with men and their male model. The court of law as well as most feminists soon used the men's model to judge women's parity in sport. Such perceptions of the law created an "obligation" for the NCAA to provide equal opportunities for women. It also brought legal and social challenges to the AIAW's policies designed to protect the so-called "educational model" of women's athletics.

Within seven months of the passage of Title IX, the NCAA at its 1973 convention changed its "male only" policy to allow women to participate in NCAA contests. In the meantime, a group of women student-athletes and coaches from two Florida colleges filed a lawsuit challenging the antiathletic-scholarship policy of the AIAW. While the women leaders saw their antiathletic-scholarship policy as a core element of their educational model, some women coaches and administrators, and many women athletes at the grassroots level, saw the AIAW stance as women's discrimination against women. They believed that if men were given scholarships based on their athletic talents, women should also receive them. The AIAW policy created a legal problem for the colleges. A school would have to choose to treat its male and female student-athletes equally or follow the different rules of the NCAA and the AIAW. Foreseeing an unfavorable legal climate and, more importantly, the inevitable loss of AIAW membership should they accept the court challenge, the DGWS/AIAW revised its scholar-

ship statement by removing its discriminatory aspects. In the end, the fear of losing membership outweighed the AIAW's philosophical commitment. To maintain its power and control of women's intercollegiate athletics, the AIAW sacrificed a major part of its educational model.

The impact of Title IX on intercollegiate athletics was pervasive even before the full implementation of its regulations. Although not a legal mandate, merger of men's and women's athletic departments soon became a trend on college campuses. The years after the passage of Title IX saw an acceleration of department mergers under a single administrative structure, most of them under the control of the former men's athletic directors. Under Title IX, department merger became the only logical choice for individual institutions to deal with the reality of the time. Legally it avoided potential litigation due to different rules for men's and women's programs. Financially it helped to shrink the "double" budgets of athletics in an inflation-ridden economy. Thus, the control of women's sports by women, at least at the institutional level, rapidly disintegrated. In fact, mergers of men's and women's programs became a prevailing trend at all levels of amateur athletics in the United States. The AIAW, however, to keep women's athletics under the control of women, distinguished itself as an organization that consistently advocated, and sought to implement, "separate-but-equal" as the guiding principle to determine the governance of intercollegiate athletics.

At the national level, the NCAA tried to co-opt the AIAW even before the AIAW became officially operational. Following the passage of Title IX, the NCAA first opposed applying Title IX to athletics. After failing at that, it decided to work with the AIAW to find mutually acceptable rules and tried again to form an alliance with the women's organization. By the fall of 1978, efforts of the NCAA and AIAW to reconcile their differences had failed, and each organization proceeded to establish its own national championship for women—NAIA in 1980, and NCAA in 1980 for Division II and III, and in 1981 for Division I. In addition to national championships, the NCAA also adopted a "Governance Plan," apparently designed to appease women. It not only guaranteed minimum representation of women in NCAA decision-making organs but equal championship travel reimbursement for male and female participants.

The impact on the AIAW of the NCAA's entry into women's athletics was immediate and substantial. It soon became clear that the AIAW would have difficulty surviving. Before the end of 1981, the AIAW had significant losses of member institutions and membership dues, championship participants, television revenues, and commercial sponsors. Foreseeing the worsening of the situation, the AIAW leadership decided to discontinue the operation of the association. On 30 June 1982, the AIAW officially ceased all activities save one: an antitrust lawsuit against the NCAA. Eight months later, the AIAW lost its lawsuit at the U.S. District Court level. Finally, in May 1984, the U.S. Court of Appeals for the District of Columbia Circuit rejected the AIAW's arguments, thus closing the final chapter of the legal dispute between the AIAW and the NCAA as well as ending the decade-long existence of the AIAW. With the demise of the AIAW, women lost most of their power and control of women's intercollegiate athletics.

The AIAW v. NCAA antitrust lawsuit had a profound implication in intercollegiate athletics for men and women. From a broader perspective, the AIAW's defeat in court can be seen as the dramatization of the fate of its sex-separate philosophy in the larger society. The battlefield was tilted against the AIAW when Title IX of the Education Amendments Act was enacted in 1972. The law, however, was not the cause of the fall of the AIAW. The antisex-discrimination legislation simply created a legal environment in which the sex-separate philosophy of the AIAW could not survive.

Although the AIAW was a victim of Title IX and the men's organizations' entry into the "separate sphere" of women's athletics, its demise should not be confused with the fate of intercollegiate athletics for women. Title IX meant greater opportunity for women's participation in sports. The victim was the sex-separate philosophy that insisted that women's athletics be controlled by women. It is doubtful that the NCAA cared more about equal opportunity for women than its power and control in U.S. amateur sports. It is, however, equally doubtful that the AIAW leaders cared more about the welfare of those they controlled than their own power and control over women's intercollegiate athletics. This desire for power and control by the men and women was actually the real obstacle that prevented reconciliation of different rules and possible affiliation

NCAA-SPONSORED SPORTS

Twenty-four women's sports are sponsored by the NCAA in the United States.

Archery	Rifle
Badminton	Rowing
Basketball	Skiing
Bowling	Soccer
Cross Country	Softball
Equestrian	Squash
Fencing	Swimming
Field Hockey	Swimming, Synchronized
Golf	Tennis
Gymnastics	Track
Ice Hockey	Volleyball
Lacrosse	Water Polo

between the AIAW and NCAA. The AIAW leaders wanted nothing less than equal representation on decision-making positions in any combined organizations. The NCAA maintained that it was unrealistic for men to accept an equal share of power with women. The AIAW's stance was idealistically correct but practically unwise. The position of the NCAA, on the other hand, was no more than a reflection of the men's attitude toward the AIAW. Backed by its experience, stability, and above all, abundant financial resources, the NCAA never saw the financially and administratively dependent AIAW as an equal. After all, the NCAA's attitude toward the AIAW was probably representative of attitudes toward women in most other areas of American society.

During its eleven-year existence, the AIAW experienced a rapid growth in membership and services and provided invaluable intercollegiate athletic opportunities for women. In 1971–1972, the charter year of the association, the AIAW had only 278 members and conducted merely seven national championships. By 1980–1981, the AIAW had a membership of 961 universities and colleges, making it the largest membership organization in the history of intercollegiate athletics. The AIAW also sponsored forty-one national championships in nineteen sports, a formidable feat compared to the forty-three championships offered for men by the NCAA.

The accomplishments of the AIAW, however, should not be considered as mainly the result of the so-called educational model, because the history of the AIAW's growth was rather the antithesis of that model. Toward the end of the 1970s, AIAW's educational model, with few exceptions, had actually been replaced by a commercial one. In less than six years, the AIAW changed itself from an organization of idealism to one whose policies were largely determined by its commercial potentials. The only significant difference between the AIAW and the NCAA by the turn of the decade was not their philosophical commitments but the degrees of success in their commercial endeavors. When the NCAA began to offer national championships with financial incentives for women, a substantial number of schools abandoned the commercially unsuccessful AIAW in favor of the commercially successful NCAA.

THE 1980S AND 1990S: NCAA, NAIA, AND NJCAA

The traditionally sex-separate control of women's intercollegiate athletics ended when the AIAW ceased operation in June 1982. Since then, intercollegiate athletics for women has been administered by three organizations—the NCAA, the NAIA, and the National Junior Collegiate Athletic Association (NJCAA). While the NAIA and NJCAA provided indispensable services to men and women student-athletes at predominantly four-year private institutions and two-year colleges, respectively, the NCAA remained the primary governing body of college athletics for men and women. In 1981–1982, the inaugural year of its women's program, the NCAA offered twenty-nine national championships for women in twelve sports. More than 4,000 student-athletes and 619 teams competed in the championships. The NCAA women's program grew significantly in the next fifteen years. In 1996–1997, more than 10,000 participants and close to 1,400 teams took part in thirty-six national championships in fourteen sports. Together with the programs offered by the NAIA and NJCAA, there were sixty-six national championships for women. The major contributor to the abundant athletic opportunity for college women was undoubtedly the continuing implementation of Title IX. Unfortunately, the pressure of Title IX compliance had not only added to the financial burdens of many already debt-ridden athletic departments but resulted in the dismantling of certain "minor sports" in men's programs.

CONCLUSION

Resistance to the growth of women's intercollegiate athletics, especially from the traditional male establishment of college athletics, remains strong. Despite the improvement in participation opportunities and expenditures on women's programs, the gap in operating expenses between men's and women's programs has changed little among NCAA-member institutions in the 1990s. Women are still underrepresented in administrative positions, and coaching positions are more male-dominated in percentage terms, than they were in 1972. The goal of gender equity in intercollegiate athletics is far from achieved.

Ying Wu

Bibliography

Cahn, Susan K. (1994) *Coming on Strong: Gender and Sexuality in Twentieth-Century Women's Sport.* Cambridge, MA: Harvard University Press.

Costa, D. Margaret, and Sharon R. Guthrie, eds. (1994) *Women and Sport: Interdisciplinary Perspectives.* Champaign, IL: Human Kinetics.

Emery, Lynne. (1982) "The First Intercollegiate Contest of Women: Basketball, April 4, 1896." In *Her Story in Sport: A Historical Anthology of Women In Sports,* edited by Reet Howell. West Point, NY: Leisure Press, 417–423.

Fletcher, Sheila. (1984) *Women First: The Female Tradition in English Physical Education.* Reprint, London, and Atlantic Highlands, NJ: Athlone Press, 1993.

Guttmann, Allen. (1991) *Women's Sports: A History.* New York: Columbia University Press.

Hult, Joan S., and Marianna Trekell, eds. (1991) *A Century of Women's Basketball: From Frailty to Final Four.* Reston, VA: American Alliance for Health, Physical Education, Recreation and Dance.

Lucas, John A., and Ronald A. Smith. (1978) *Saga of American Sport.* Philadelphia: Lea & Febiger.

McCrone, Kathleen E. (1988) *Playing the Game: Sport and the Physical Emancipation of English Women, 1870–1914.* Lexington: University of Kentucky Press.

NCAA Annual Reports. (1981–1997). Overland Park, KS: National Collegiate Athletic Association.

NCAA Gender-Equity Study: Summary of Results. (1997) Overland Park, KS: National Collegiate Athletic Association.

Sefton, Alice Allene. (1941) *The Women's Division National Amateur Athletic Federation: Sixteen Years of Progress in Athletics for Girls and Women, 1923–1939.* Stanford, CA: Stanford University Press.

Smith, Ronald A. (1988) *Sports and Freedom: The Rise of Big-Time College Athletics.* New York: Oxford University Press.

Solomon, Barbara Miller. (1985) *In the Company of Educated Women: A History of Women and Higher Education in America.* New Haven, CT: Yale University Press.

Swanson, Richard A., and Betty Spears. (1995) *History of Sport and Physical Education in the United States.* Dubuque, IA: Brown & Benchmark.

Vertinsky, Patricia. (1994) *The Eternally Wounded Women: Women, Exercise and Doctors in the Late Nineteenth Century.* Manchester, U.K.: Manchester University Press.

Wu, Ying. (1997) "The Demise of the AIAW and Women's Control of Intercollegiate Athletics for Women: The Sex Separate Policy in the Reality of the NCAA, Cold War, and Title IX." Ph.D. diss., Pennsylvania State University.

Yarbrough, Roy E. (1986) "Perceptions of Three Black Leaders of the National Intramural-Recreational Sports Association: The Formative Years, 1950–1975." Ed.D. diss., University of North Carolina at Greensboro.

INTERNATIONAL ASSOCIATION OF PHYSICAL EDUCATION AND SPORT FOR GIRLS AND WOMEN

The International Association of Physical Education and Sport for Girls and Women (IAPESGW) grew out of the efforts of women working in the field of physical education. What they sought was a way to meet together and find better ways of learning from, and cooperating with, each other.

The association, which was founded in 1949, has its roots in earlier women's athletics groups. In 1947 the International Committee of the National Association of Directors of Physical Education for College Women in the United States of America held a congress. In 1949 Copenhagen was the site of the First Congress of Physical Education. These two events spurred the establishment of IAPESGW and helped focus its mission on bringing together women of many countries working in the field of physical education and sport; strengthening international contacts; discussing mutual problems; promoting the exchange of people and ideas among member countries and of research into problems affecting physical education and sport for girls and women; and cooperating with other organizations that provide services to women.

Dorothy Ainsworth, a founder of IAPESGW, linked physical education and sports activities with the changing role of girls and women in society. She declared that "we need to think of ways in which physical education will help to strengthen the qualities the girl will need if [she] is to be of the greatest value and most content in the world of today. She will need strength of body and character. . . . She must learn to control herself and to be able to adjust to others. These things do not just occur, they are the result of wise leadership. We are trying through physical education to help the girl to become a useful, happy and well-balanced person."

Over the years, the number of member nations in IAPESGW grew from twenty-three in 1949 to fifty-six in 1982. Today IAPESGW has members on every continent and counts among them developed and developing countries. It hosts scientific congresses every four years.

Some themes of former congresses illustrate the range of issues that IAPESGW deals with: "Physical Education of the Youth of Today," in 1965; "Traditional and Modern Forms of Physical Education," 1969; "Sports for All," 1973; "Better Teaching and Coaching," 1977; and in 1981, "New Dimensions in Sport—A Challenge for Women." The 1997 congress was held in Lahti, Finland, and Alexandria, Egypt, hosts the 2001 congress. The fiftieth anniversary of IAPESGW was celebrated at a conference in July 1999 at Smith College in Northampton, Massachusetts.

IAPESGW participates in the International Council for Sports Sciences and Physical Education (ICSSPE) and has been active as one of five members of the International Committee for Sport Pedagogy. IAPESGW will play an important role in developing and implementing an International Charter for Physical Education, discussed at the ICSSPE World Summit of Physical Education in 1999 in Berlin. The association is also supporting an international audit, conducted by the International Society for Comparative Physical Education and Sport, of the role of physical education in schools.

IAPESGW is a member of the International Working Group on Women and Sport, as part of an ongoing effort to monitor and promote implementation of the 1994 Brighton Declaration and the 1998 Windhoek Call for Action on Women and Sport. The Association works with other international and regional agencies and organizations to promote physical activity and sports, including the Commonwealth Secretariat, the new Association of African Women In Sport (AWISA), the Association of Arab Women in Sport, the Foundation for Olympic and Sport Education, UNESCO, and the World Federation of Sporting Goods Industries. IAPESGW also helps secure money for women from less developed countries to attend conferences and training and regional events.

Margaret Talbot

Bibliography

Tollich, Helene. (1984) "The History of IAPESGW." *Sport Science Periodical.* 32–36.

INTERNATIONAL COUNCIL FOR HEALTH, PHYSICAL EDUCATION, RECREATION, SPORT AND DANCE

The International Council for Health, Physical Education, and Recreation (ICHPER) was founded in 1958 in Rome. In 1995 its name was changed to the International Council for Health, Physical Education, Recreation, Sport, and Dance (ICHPER-SD), reflecting a growing awareness of the relationship between these activities. Its membership is comprised of professionals in the areas of health, physical education, and recreation. Although the organization was not founded strictly for women, one of its goals was to promote fitness and sports for girls and women. In fact, ICHPER-SD was the first international organization to have as one of its foci the promotion of fitness and sport for girls and women worldwide.

From the mid-1970s on, ICHPER-SD, in collaboration with the National Association for Girls and Women in Sport (NAGWS), has promoted opportunities globally for women as teachers, coaches, and administrators. Through the NAGWS Latin American Commission for Girls and Women in Sport, the two groups designed and developed programs to promote interest in sport, physical education, and fitness for children in the Caribbean and Central and South America. In 1984 UNESCO sponsored an ICHPER-SD publication titled, "The Role of Girls and Women in Developing Physical Education and Sport Programs."

ICHPER-SD was part of an extensive coalition that sponsored the first Asian Women in Sport conference in Manila in 1996, on the theme of "Lessons in Leadership: From Competence to Confidence." In 1997 in Manila, "Connecting Sport Science and Volleyball" was cosponsored by USA Volleyball Member Relations and Human Resources Division, ICHPER-SD Women and Sport Commission, Women's Sports Foundation—Philippines, Philippines Sports Commission, and Philippine Volleyball Association. In 1999 in Cairo, the ICHPER-SD World Congress Leadership Development Seminar, "Lessons in Leadership: From Competence to Confidence," was based on the Asian model devised with ICHPER-SD Girls and Women in Sport leadership.

The ICHPER-SD Commission on Girls and Women in Sport continues to play a prominent role in the development and promotion of girls and women in sport by conducting workshops, seminars, and congresses on girls and women in sport throughout the world. The conferences described above represent its most recent focus on promoting quality sport and fitness programs for girls and women in Asia and the Middle East.

Doris R. Corbett
Darlene A. Kluka

INTERNATIONAL OLYMPIC COMMITTEE (IOC)

The goal of the Olympic Games is to bring the world's best athletes together to compete against each other in a spirit of peaceful cooperation. The Games are organized by the International Olympic Committee (IOC) in cooperation with the National Olympic Committees of participating countries and the International Sports Federations of the various sports. For many centuries, sports activities were regarded as primarily the province of men. Since the 1960s pressure has been brought to bear on national, regional, and international organizations to extend women's rights in general. As this worldwide movement for equal rights has grown, so too has a movement for complete and equitable participation for women in Olympic sports. The IOC, however, has steadily resisted the creation of a women's sports commission within its purview. The committee remains a male entity, with only a small number of female members.

In 1973 several delegates to the IOC-sponsored Olympic Congress in Varna, Bulgaria, pressed for the creation of women's sports commission within the IOC. They included the few women at the time who held senior positions in sports associations such as Lia Manoliu, vice-president of the Romanian Olympic Committee. The Varna Congress, however, simply declared that "The IOC, the International Federations and the National Olympic Committees should consider the inclusion of women in their memberships and commissions." Eight years later, at an Olympic Congress in Baden-Baden, Germany, IOC president Lord Killanin acknowledged that no progress had been made in admitting women into decision-making positions at the IOC. Killanin also repeated his objection to establishing a special commission for women's sports within the IOC.

RESOLUTIONS OF INTERNATIONAL OLYMPIC COMMITTEE—WORLD CONFERENCE ON WOMEN AND SPORT (1996)

Resolution

The Conference,

Congratulating the International Olympic Committee (IOC) on its initiative to stage a World Conference on Women and Sport with representatives of many countries and non- and inter-governmental organizations;

Welcoming the initiative of the IOC to establish a working group on Women and Sport looking forward to hearing continued positive recommendations therefrom;

Also welcoming the evidence of cooperation between sectors of the sports community asnd government, both at national and international level, in promoting issues relative to women in sport;

Looking forward to the staging of similar events at appropriate intervals to further promote the advancement of women;

Recalling that the aim of the Olympic Movement is to build a peaceful and better world through sport and the Olympic ideal, without discrimination of any kind;

Recognizing that the Olympic ideal cannot be fully realized without, and until there is, equality for women within the Olympic Movement;

1. Calls upon the IOC, the International Federations (Ifs) and the National Olympic Committees (NOCs) to take into consideration the issue of gender equality in all their policies, programmes and procedures, and to recognize the special needs of women so that they may play a full and active part in sport;

2. Recommends, that all women involved in sport be provided equal opportunities for professional and personal advancement, whether as athletes, coaches, or administrators, and the Ifs and the NOCs create special committees or working groups composed of at least 10% women to design and implement a plan of action with a view to promoting women in sport;

3. Requests the commissions dealing specifically with the issue of women in sport be set up at national and international level;

4. Recommends the establishment by NOCs of athletes' commissions including women, as a way of training women as leaders;

5. Encourages the IOC to continue working toward the goal of attaining an equal number of events for women and for men on the Olympic programme;

6. Suggests, that within Olympic Solidarity a special fund can be earned for the promotion of women's sports at all levels as well as for the training of women administrators, technical officials, and coaches with emphasis on developing nations;

7. Requests, that the IOC organize each year, and on the five continents, a training course for women in one of the following areas: coaching, technical activity, administration, or media/journalism;

8. Proposes, that one of the criteria assessment of cities bidding to host the Olympic Games be their demonstrated ability to serve the needs of women in sport;

9. Endorses and encourages the increased production of research and statistical data on subjects relating to women and sport and the dissemination thereof to all parties involved in the sports movement, including success stories on advancements made in the sport for women and girls;

10. Urges the IOC to discontinue the current process of gender verification during the Olympic Games;

11. Calls upon the national and international sport federations to facilitate and promote sport for women with disabilities, in light of the fact that women with disabilities face a double challenge in the world of sport;

12. Encourages the IOC, in its relations with non- and inter-governmental international organizations, especially those that have as their focus girls and women, to cooperate in efforts that have as their aim the creation of global programmes of physical education in schools and in the community in order to promote health and quality of life;

13. Recommends, that the IOC advise governments of its technical assistance to developing countries;

14. Requests, that the IOC direct its working group on Women and Sport to consider issues specific to the needs of women and children in sport, taking into account the importance of family sport in the development of young female athletes;

15. Recommends, that the IOC working group on Women and Sport be given the status of an IOC commission;

16. Encourages the IOC to continue to develop educational material to assist in advancing opportunities for women in sport;

17. Recommends, that the IOC identify a theme for the 1996–2000 quadrennial: "Olympiad for Women."

At the meeting of the IOC's Executive Board in Atlanta in December 1994, President Juan Antonio Samaranch emphasized that they had to "devote efforts to the development of women's sport and the gender structure of its decision-making levels. It is our job," he said, "to enhance women's access to positions of responsibility in the management of sport at the national and world level."

Four women were sent on behalf of the IOC to represent the Olympic Movement at the Fourth World Conference on Women in Beijing in 1995: DeFrantz of the IOC Executive Board, Lu Shengrong, Sophia Raddock, and Gunilla Lindberg. In December 1995, the IOC president created the working group on women and sport to advise him and the Executive Board on all matters relating to women. Chaired by DeFrantz, it had members from the IOC, the international federations, and National Olympic Committees, (NOCs) including athletic representatives and independent members.

IOC WORLD CONFERENCE ON WOMEN AND SPORT

On 14–16 October 1996 in the Olympic Museum Auditorium in Lausanne, Switzerland, the IOC convened the World Conference on Women and Sport, with more than 220 participants from ninety-six countries attending. Several initiatives were undertaken as a result of the conference. The conference recommended that the IOC Working Group on Women and Sport, chaired by DeFrantz be given the status of an IOC commission. Conference participants also recognized that the

Olympic ideal cannot be fully realized without equality for women within the Olympic Movement.

The conference also recommended that all women involved in sport be provided equal opportunities for professional and personal advancement, whether as athletes, coaches, or administrators, and that the International Federations (IFs) and the NOCs create special committees or working groups composed of at least 10 percent women to design and implement a plan of action with a view to promoting women in sport.

Another request by participants was that the IOC organize each year, and on the five continents, a training course for women in one of the following areas: coaching, technical activity, administration, or media/journalism. They also called upon the national and international sport federations to facilitate and promote sport for women with disabilities, in light of the fact that women with disabilities face a double challenge in the world of sport.

The conference also encouraged the IOC, in its relations with non- and intergovernmental international organizations, especially those that have as their focus girls and women, to cooperate in efforts that have as their aim the creation of global programs of physical education in schools and in the community to promote health and quality of life. The group requested that the IOC direct its working group on women and sport to consider issues specific to the needs of women and children in sport, taking into account the importance of family support in the development of young female athletes.

WOMEN DECISION MAKERS IN THE IOC

Between 1981 and 1994, the IOC added sixty-four new members, of whom seven were women. The IOC subsequently added five more female members, making for twelve women members out of a total of 118 members by 1998: Flor Isava (Venezuela), Pirjo Häggman (Finland), Mary Alison Glen-Haig (Great Britain), Princess Nora (Liechtenstein), Anita DeFrantz (United States), H.R.H. the Princess Royal, Princess Anne (Great Britain), Carol Anne Letheren (Canada), Vera Caslavska (Czech Republic), Gunilla Lindberg (Sweden), Lu Shengrong (China), H.R.H. the Infanta Dona Pilar de Borbón (Spain), Nawal El Moutawakel (Morocco), and Irena Szewinska (Poland). In 1997, DeFrantz was the first woman elected a vice-president of the IOC. In January 1999, Häggman resigned as part of the scandal involving payments to IOC members by representatives of cities seeking to host the Olympic Games. News reports suggested that Häggman's (now) ex-husband had received jobs and consulting fees from officials in Quebec and Salt Lake City and that Häggman herself may have received rent-free accommodations. In addition to these IOC positions, twenty-six other positions on IOC commissions and working groups were held by women.

In addition to the movement to add more women to the IOC and IOC bodies, women have been active in seeking more decision-making authority on the NOCs. At the end of 1998, women served as the president, vice-president, or secretary-general of NOCs of thirty-three nations: Angola, Antigua and Barbuda, Aruba, Austria, Azerbaijan, Canada, Cook Islands, Fiji, Ghana, Great Britain, Grenada, Hong Kong, Iran, Korea, Mauritania, Namibia, Pakistan, Philippines, Poland, Saint Vincent and the Grenadines, Slovakia, Swaziland, Sweden, Syria, Switzerland, Tonga, Trinidad and Tobago, United States, Uzbekistan, Venezuela, Virgin Islands, British Virgin Islands, and Zambia. Finally, women served in senior positions in nine international sport federations: archery, badminton, equestrian, field hockey, rowing, tennis, netball, orienteering, and squash, although the last three are not yet Olympic sports.

The Editors

See also Olympics

INTERNATIONAL WOMEN'S GAMES

The International Women's Games were first staged on 20 August 1922, in Paris, by the Fédération Sportive Féminine Internationale (FSFI), which had been founded on 31 October 1921 by Alice Milliat, president of the Fédération des Sociétés Féminines Sportives de France (established 1917). Eleven events comprised these first Jeux Olympiques Féminins (Women's Olympic Games): 60- and 100-meter sprints, 300- and 1000-meter races, the 100-yard hurdles, a 440-yard relay, high and long jumps, a standing long jump, the shot put, and the javelin. Twenty thousand spectators filled the stadium. Led by Mary Lines,

Maj Jakobsson, Sweden, running at the Women's World Games in Prague, 1930. (Agne Holmstrom)

who won three gold medals and one silver medal, the British team of sixteen women narrowly defeated the thirteen American women, who had sailed to Paris over the objections of the women's division of the National Amateur Athletic Federation (NAAF). Coverage of the games in the French press was very positive.

Neither Sigfrid Edström, president of the International Amateur Athletic Federation (IAAF), nor Pierre de Coubertin, president of the International Olympic Committee (IOC), was happy about the prospect of "Women's Olympics." Edström, however, who negotiated on behalf of the IAAF and the IOC, reluctantly agreed to grant official IAAF recognition to the FSFI, and to request that the IOC add track and field to the program of the 1928 Olympics. In return, the FSFI ceased to use the word "Olympic."

The second International Women's Games took place in Göteburg, Sweden, in August 1926. The program, extended to three days, was basically the same as in Paris except that the 100-meter race was shortened to 100 yards and the 300-meter race was shortened to 250 meters, and there were new contests for the discus and for walkers (1000 meters). Ninety-two women from fifteen countries competed. France's Marguerite Radideau ran the 100-yard dash in 11.8 seconds, but the sensation of the Games was Japan's lone representative, nineteen-year-old Hitomi Kinue, who was first in both long jumps, second in the discus, and third in the 100-yard race.

The acceptance of five women's track-and-field events at the 1928 Olympic Games might have signaled the end of the FSFI, but the IOC voted in 1929 not to repeat its experiment with female athletes. The FSFI's response to this setback was to invite 214 women to Prague's Letna Stadium for the third International Women's Games in September 1930.

The track-and-field program was expanded to twelve events and there were new competitions in basketball, team handball, and "hazena" (a sport similar to team handball). Germany, which had not been represented in Paris or Göteburg, had the strongest team, but the brightest star of these games was Poland's Stanislawa Walasiewicz, subsequently known in the United States as Stella Walsh. She won gold medals in the 60-, 100-, and 200-meter races.

Women's World Games in Cothenburg, Sweden, 1926. Halina Konopacka of Poland throws the discus. (Agne Holmstrom)

At an Olympic Congress in Berlin in 1930, the IOC once again reversed itself and restored women's track and field to the program for the 1932 Olympics. The FSFI went ahead, nonetheless, with the Fourth Women's Games, which took place in London's White City Stadium in August 1934. Team handball was dropped, but the track-and-field program was expanded to include the pentathlon. The 800-meter race, which was dropped from the Olympics after 1928, was contested in London just as it had been in Prague. The German team, strongest of the nineteen present, overwhelmed its opponents and tallied more points than the next three teams combined. Women from the United States competed only in basketball; they lost the final game to the French.

In 1934, the number of spectators dwindled to only four to five thousand, a small fraction of the crowd present in 1922. To this disappointment was added a second. On 12 October 1936, Edström informed Milliat that the IAAF considered the FSFI-sponsored games scheduled for Vienna in 1938 to be merely European championships. After these championships, the FSFI disbanded, but Milliat had achieved her most important goal; women's track and field remained an Olympic sport.

Allen Guttmann

Bibliography

Guttmann, Allen. (1991) *Women's Sports.* New York: Columbia University Press.

Leigh, Mary H., and Thérèse M. Bonin. (1977) "The Pioneering Role of Madame Alice Milliat and the FSFI." *Journal of Sport History* 4:72–83.

INTERNATIONAL WORKING GROUP ON WOMEN AND SPORT

The International Working Group on Women and Sport (IWGWS) was formed to help implement the Brighton Declaration of 1994 and the Windhoek Call for Action of 1998. It is an informal and flexible organization whose membership is composed of representatives from key governmental and nongovernmental women's sports organizations around the world. Its broad mission is to promote and facilitate the development of sport and physical education opportunities for girls and women around the world. The group promoted the implementation of the Brighton Declaration and development plans for women's sport programs. It serves as a contact point for the exchange of information about the development of women's sport opportunities, ensures that women's sport is a topic addressed in international forums. It helped organize the 2002 World Conference on Women and Sport in Canada.

Membership in the IWGWS is informal, with no elections and no rigid selection criteria. Rather, members are asked to serve because they have skills, abilities, or knowledge such as a familiarity with political or international women's sports or the ability to develop strategic plans that will help the IWGWS achieve its goals. In selecting members, the group also seeks members from a number of nations to ensure that all major regions of the world are represented. The Secretariat in 1999 was housed at the Department of Canadian Heritage (Sport Canada) in Hull, Quebec.

The Editors

See also Brighton Declaration; Windhoek Call for Action

INTRAMURAL SPORTS

Intramural sports are extracurricular athletic competitions that take place within the "muralis" (walls) of an educational institution, with students as the main participants. Toward the end of the twentieth century, intramural sports were the most popular participant-oriented extracurricular activities on college campuses. While today's men and women students generally have equal opportunities to participate in the activities, the origins of intramural sports were distinctively different for the opposite sexes. The prototypes for such sports developed in the nineteenth century in England's public schools (for boys) and in American women's colleges.

ORIGINS: "SPORT FOR THE GOOD OF ALL"

Two events in the 1890s had great impact on the development of intramural sports for women. In 1892 Senda Berenson (1868–1954) of Smith College adapted, for her female students, the game of

A dozen University of California-Los Angeles basketball players prepare for the annual intramural championship. (Underwood & Underwood/ Corbis)

basketball, invented only months earlier by James Naismith (1861–1939) at the nearby Springfield YMCA Training School. Basketball soon became the most popular team sport played by collegiate women. Berenson's contribution to intramural sports, however, was more than the devising of women's basketball. Her belief in "sport for the good of all" was evidenced by the rules she devised for women's basketball. To eliminate the roughness common in the men's game, Berenson prohibited ball snatching; to prevent the best player from dominating the play, she prohibited dribbling and divided the court into three sections, in each of which two players were stationed. Male spectators were barred from the gymnasium. As Berenson noted: "The aim in athletics for women should above all things be health—physical health and moral health." Ber-

enson's basketball game, with its carefully limited competition, epitomized the philosophy of intramural sports in the years to come.

No less important than Berenson's rules for women's basketball was the first "Field Day" of track and field competition at Vassar College in 1895. Although the event attracted the attention of many national newspapers, the competition was kept within the "separate sphere" of women. At Vassar as at Smith, men were restricted from viewing the activities. The sex-separate approach at these schools was no accident but a reflection of the philosophy that was intended to keep women's sports morally pure and out of men's control.

By the first decade of the twentieth century, men's intercollegiate athletics, but not women's, had grown into a national phenomenon and become an important part of the entertainment industry. While men's athletics became increasingly competitive (and violent), women's sports on college campuses were moving fast in the opposite direction. To preserve women's sports from the corruption that characterized many of the men's programs, female physical education leaders set out to create a model that would ensure "a game for every girl and every girl in a game." Intramural sports were preferred over intercollegiate contests because they were much less competitive. Intramurals soon became the dominant form of athletics for women.

The specific form taken by these intramurals was the "Play Day." Play Day emphasized socialization and participation over competition and winning. The day-long event usually brought together female students from at least three schools for a day of sport activities. Basketball usually dominated in popularity, but many other sports were also available, such as archery, baseball, field hockey, soccer, swimming, tennis, track and field, and volleyball. What distinguished Play Day from similar events was that individual schools did not compete as school teams. Rather, they formed teams using players from various schools. Because no one school could then claim victory, winning became less important, and instead, social interaction between players became the primary focus. The Play Day system also tended to discourage intensive team training or coaching. Teams were more like pick-up teams of children's games than like intercollegiate varsity squads.

SUBSEQUENT HISTORY

The noncompetitive Play Day dominated college women physical educators' philosophy during the years between the two World Wars. During the war years, women everywhere were encouraged to be physically fit, but the emphasis was on calisthenics rather than sports. After the wars, the organization of intramural sports reached a new level when the National Intramural Association (NIA) was formed. Gathered at New Orleans's Dillard University in 1950, twenty men and

COLLEGE FIELD DAY AT VASSAR

On 9 November 1895, America's first college field day for women took place at Vassar College in Poughkeepsie, New York. Held on a designated athletic circle of the college green, the curious event at the women's college attracted some four hundred spectators and the attention of many newspapers. The newspaper reporters, however, must have been women, or, unlikely, well-disguised men, for men were not allowed to view the activities.

It was a well-organized occasion by the Athletic Association of the college. A total of twenty-two women representing all classes were listed as competitors for the five track and field events. The first event was the 100-yard dash, won by Miss Elizabeth Forbes Vassar in 16 seconds. In the running broad jump, Miss Baker took first place with a distance of 11 feet and 5 inches. Miss Thallon of Brooklyn captured the 120-yard hurdle crown with a time of 25 seconds. Thallon would later return to Vassar in 1906 to teach Latin and serve as a judge for many future field days. In the running high jump, Miss Brownell was the sole competitor and cleared the bar at 48 inches. Brownell did not receive first place, however, for she had graduated in 1895 and was competing as a postgraduate. Miss Haight won the final event, the 220-yard dash, with a time of 36.25 seconds.

It was such a rainy day that on one occasion the cartridges for the starter's pistol grew so damp they would not go off. Despite the effort to keep the event within the "separate sphere" of women, the first field day at Vassar was truly an antithesis against the frail image of the Victorian woman. "Lady-like" behavior was apparently not the theme of the day. According to a *New York Tribune* report: "There was not false modesty as [the girls] entered the field. . . . One girl stopped to pull up her stockings. Another girded up her waist band. They were there to win."

women intramural directors from eleven traditionally black colleges created a national governing body to promote intramural sports and encourage professional growth in ways hitherto untried by traditional physical education and athletic departments. The all-black association soon became racially integrated by inviting white intramural directors to its annual conference in 1952. Racial integration, however, was accompanied by gender separation within the NIA. In 1960 the organization formally eliminated women from its membership. It would take more than a decade, and an intense debate within the membership, for the NIA to revise its constitution to accept women as members. The timely revision of the membership policy barely prevented the organization from inevitable legal challenges that would follow the passage of Title IX, the sex-discrimination law passed by the Congress in 1972. The NIA extended its scope of interest and control in 1975 when its membership voted to change the name of the organization to the National Intramural-Recreational Sports Association (NIRSA).

In the late 1970s and early 1980s, while men and women in intercollegiate athletics intensified their battle over control of intercollegiate sports, relative gender harmony reigned in intramural sports. In 1987 the NIRSA elected Mary Daniels of Ohio State University its president, the first female chief in the history of the organization. While the implementation of Title IX regulations was a continuous financial and political issue in intercollegiate athletics, the law that promoted gender equity was readily accepted within intramural programs.

CONCLUSION

In the 1990s, financial support increased for the expansion of traditional intramural programs. In addition, coeducational activities enjoyed increasing popularity, which was generally not the case in intercollegiate athletics. At the national level, the NIRSA grew into a full-fledged organization with nearly twenty employees, more than half of whom were women. Women also had 50 percent representation on the board of directors, the policy-making body of the NIRSA. An association with more than 3,000 individual and institutional members, the NIRSA operated in 1997 with a budget of $1.7 million while expecting continuing growth in membership.

Ying Wu

Bibliography

Ainsworth, Dorothy S. (1930) *The History of Physical Education in College for Women.* New York: A. S. Barnes.

"Athletic Girls of Vassar." (1985) *New York Tribune* (10 November): 3.

Berenson Papers. "Speeches and Notes." Smith College Archives, Northampton, MA.

Costa, D. Margaret, and Sharon R. Guthrie, eds. (1994) *Women and Sport: Interdisciplinary Perspectives.* Champaign, IL: Human Kinetics.

"A Field Day at Vassar." (1895) *New York Times* (10 November): 2.

Guttmann, Allen. (1991) *Women's Sports.* New York: Columbia University Press.

Lee, Mabel. (1983) *A History of Physical Education and Sports in the U.S.A.* New York: John Wiley & Sons.

Lucas, John A., and Ronald A. Smith. (1978) *Saga of American Sport.* Philadelphia: Lea & Febiger.

Means, Louis E. (1963) *Intramurals: Their Organization and Administration.* Englewood Cliffs, NJ: Prentice-Hall.

Mitchell, Elmer D. (1939) *Intramural Sports.* New York: A.S. Barnes.

National Intramural-Recreational Sports Association. (1999) *Nirsa History.* <http://www.nirsa.org>.

Sefton, Alice Allene. (1941) *The Women's Division National Amateur Athletic Federation: Sixteen Years of Progress in Athletics for Girls and Women, 1923–1939.* Stanford, CA: Stanford University Press.

Solomon, Barbara Miller. (1985) *In the Company of Educated Women: A History of Women and Higher Education in America.* New Haven, CT: Yale University Press.

Spears, Betty. (1991) "Senda Berenson Abbott: New Woman, New Sport." In *A Century of Women's Basketball: From Frailty to Final Four,* edited by Joan S. Hult and Marianna Trekell. Reston, VA: AAH-PERD, 19–36.

Swanson, Richard A., and Betty Spears. (1995) *History of Sport and Physical Education in the United States.* Dubuque, IA: Brown & Benchmark.

Tricard, Louise Mead. (1996) *American Women's Track and Field: A History, 1895 through 1980.* Jefferson, NC: McFarland.

IRAN

Iran is a West Asian nation with a population of 65 million. The country's official and most widely spoken language is Persian, and Islam is the religion of the vast majority of the population. In traditional Iranian society, sport and physical education were the exclusive domain of men. Given the strict sexual segregation of urban Muslim society, women were not even allowed to enter the traditional Iranian gymnasiums as spectators.

The first to introduce physical education for girls were Christian missionaries in the nineteenth century, who included it in the curricula of their schools. However, since these schools catered mostly to Iran's non-Muslim minorities, their impact remained limited. The few Muslim women who graduated from these schools were among the first Iranians to demand access to physical education for all women.

After the constitutional revolution of 1906, physical education for women became part of the modernization agenda as a means to help reform and regenerate Iranian society. In the 1930s physical education became compulsory in public girls' schools, and in 1935 a new state-sponsored Ladies' Center made the development of physical education programs for women one of its main goals. In 1939 the first national championships were held in track and field and swimming.

Conservatives opposed women's sports and girl's physical education, mostly because the wearing of sportswear in view of men violates the traditional Islamic dress code (*hijab*), which requires that a woman cover her body with the exception of her face, hands, and feet in the presence of unrelated men. However, under the rule of the Pahlavi dynasty, which sought to westernize Iranian life, an ever-increasing number of women belonging to

Shooting is one sport Iranian women compete in internationally as they can do so wearing the hijab (traditional Islamic clothing). (Stephen Shaver/Corbis)

the nondevout upper and middle classes were involved in many sports. Female members of the royal family acted as patrons of the state-sponsored Women's Sport Organization of Iran.

Many of the Islamic revolutionaries who opposed the Shah's regime in the 1970s considered women's sports an aspect of the degenerate western culture that the ruling classes wanted to force on Iran's Muslim society. After the proponents of an Islamic state consolidated their hold on the country in the wake of the 1979 revolution, most competitive sports for women were stopped in 1981 when the *hijab* became compulsory. A Directorate of Women's Sports Affairs was established within the national Physical Education Administration in 1980, although it did not become really active until 1985. The Directorate's mission statement says: "In the Islamic system, sport serves as one of the best means of helping women better to fulfill their holy duties of motherhood in order to raise healthy children and educate the future generation for the community. Sport also allows them to participate in important social activities." In accord with this general mission, women's sports is seen by the government as helping to "develop and preserve" women's physical and mental health, making women more perceptive, enhancing their spiritual and moral well-being, and occupying leisure time.

It was only after the death of Ayatollah Khomeini in 1989 that women's sports were revived, when the daughter of President Ali-Akbar Hashemi Rafsanjani, Fa'ezeh Hashemi, took a personal interest in women's sports. Hashemi convened the First Islamic Countries' Sports Solidarity Congress for Women in Tehran. The congress led to the founding of an organization that held "Islamic Countries' Women Sports Solidarity Games" in 1993 and 1997 and that has become the major women's sports organization in the Muslim world. At these games women from predominantly Muslim countries competed in the total absence of men. In addition to organizing the games, it supports and encourages women's sports, collects information about Muslim women athletes, and produces reports and books.

Under Hashemi's leadership, the state has allocated more money for women's sports, and sports halls and swimming pools have been set aside for women. At these facilities, women compete according to international rules and standards, but men are not allowed to be present. Women in Iran participate in twenty-five different disciplines including such individual sports as handball, tennis, karate, and equestrian, and team sports such as basketball and hockey. Programs are also available for disabled women athletes. In addition, young women may attend special sports high schools, study physical education in fourteen universities, and obtain advanced degrees so as to be able to teach physical education to other women. Moreover, as most women's sports must be conducted without men present, Iranian women are active in all aspects of sports including training, coaching, and administration. Women hold three of the eleven seats on the National Olympic Committee (NOC). The dress codes imposed on Iranian women by the state mean that internationally Iranian women have been able to compete only in shooting and rowing, and Iranian women did compete in shooting at the 1992 Barcelona and 1996 Atlanta Olympics.

Despite these advances, women's sport participation remains controversial in Iran and in the spring of 1996 became a major political issue when Hashemi advocated allowing women to ride bicycles in one of Tehran's parks. Muslim conservatives objected, but Hashemi's election to the Iranian parliament in 1996 and her nomination to the vice-presidency of the NOC allowed her to stand firm. On the other side of the argument, Iranian feminists consider current policies inadequate and demand further concessions, such as the right to attend men's soccer games.

H. E. Chehabi
(with the assistance of the General Office
of Women Sport Affairs, Islamic Republic of Iran)

See also Islamic Countries' Women's Sports Solidarity Council and Games

IRELAND

Ireland is a small island on the western tip of the European land mass. It is split between the Republic of Ireland, which covers twenty-six southern counties, and Northern Ireland, which occupies the six northeastern counties. The partition of Ireland took place as a result of the 1921 Anglo-Irish Treaty, which created the southern Irish Free State as an independent nation (becoming the Irish Republic in 1948). Northern Ireland continued to be a part of the United Kingdom. The population of the Republic stands at 3 million and that of Northern Ireland at 1.75 million. The majority of the Republic's population is Catholic (97%), while Northern Ireland is divided between Protestant (60%) and Catholic (40%).

The nature of sectarian division and the history of partition in Ireland has led to an intense period of civil disobedience and violence since the late 1960s. The modern troubles in Northern Ireland have cost in excess of 3,000 lives, and few aspects of life have remained unaffected. Irish nationalism prompted the revival or creation of non-British sports, including camogie, the national game for women.

SPORTING PAST

The sporting history of Ireland has been profoundly affected by the presence of conflict between the nationalist and unionist strands of belief. In the prefamine period (prior to 1846), Irish sporting events were based around fairs and festivals held on saints' days. At such events physical activities included folk football, a form of hurling, strength demonstrations, and dancing competitions. In accordance with the nature of Irish society at this time, the majority of those taking part in these events were male, although some evidence suggests that women participated. The famine of 1846–1851 led to the deaths of some 2 million Irish people, and a similar number immigrated to distant shores, an important part of the Irish diaspora that, among many other things, spread Irish sport around the world. In the wake of the postfamine chaos, however, such activities as sport became unimportant. Sporting events were also seen as frivolous by the church, and were often outlawed by the British authorities that occupied Ireland at that time.

During the 1880s modern codified sports spread the short distance across the Irish Sea from Britain, and found favor in Ireland among the social elites. The most popular sports were soccer, rugby, hockey, and cricket. As a result of their faithful following among the British army stationed in Ireland, they were given the generic title "garrison games" by Irish nationalists. The nationalists resented the presence of the British in Ireland, and opposed the detrimental influence that British pastimes had on native Irish culture. In 1884 the Gaelic Athletic Association (GAA) was founded as part of a general reawakening of Irish nationalist sentiment.

THE EMERGENCE OF WOMEN'S SPORT

The GAA was absolutely central in the success of political nationalism in Ireland but, more important in the context of sport, it was the key element in preserving an identifiable native culture. In its earliest years, the GAA was solely interested in male sport. This changed in 1905, with the foundation of Cumann Camógaíochta, the Camogie

HISTORY AND INCREASING OPPORTUNITIES

For most the twentieth century, camogie, the female version of the Irish national game of hurling, was the primary sport for girls and women, as a well as a powerful symbol of Irish tradition and national identity. In the 1990s as Ireland became a more secular and global nation, sports opportunities for women increased, and champion distance runner Sonia O'Sullivan and champion swimmer Michelle Smith became national celebrities.

Association of Ireland. Based on the male game of hurling, camogie is a fast and forceful ball-and-stick game played by two teams of fifteen players each. Camogie was the single most important women's team sport in Ireland until the 1980s.

As the most important sporting body in independent Ireland after 1921, the GAA was to play a central role in the evolution of school sport. As such, camogie became a key game within the school system for girls. In Northern Ireland, the school system promoted either camogie in Catholic schools or hockey and netball in Protestant schools.

ELITE SPORTS

Although many women played sport throughout the twentieth century, their participation was largely restricted to school-level activities. In 1924 the fist Olympic team to represent the Irish Free State included only two women: Hilda Wallis and Phoebe Blair-White. Both took part in the lawn tennis competition, Wallis finishing fifth in the mixed doubles, Blair-White failing to get past the first round in either the women's singles or the mixed doubles. Marguerite Dockrell competed for Ireland in swimming at the 1928 Games, and Dorothy Dermody in fencing at the London Games in 1948. It was not until the Melbourne Games of 1956 that an Irish woman competed in the premier track and field competitions of the Olympics. The numbers of women competing for Ireland at the Olympics have always been low, a statistic that reflects the difficulties for women in the sporting arena in Ireland. It was not until the 1984 Olympics in Los Angeles that the number of women in the Irish squad crept into double figures, with an unprecedented thirteen Irish women traveling to the Games.

The very nature of Irish society has posed the largest problem for women's sport in Ireland. Women have traditionally played a secondary role in a patriarchal society that was, until the 1990s, dominated by the teachings of the Catholic Church.

THE RISE OF WOMEN'S SPORT

In the late 1980s and through the 1990s, Ireland, and in particular the Irish Republic, has undergone an intense period of secularization and modernization. The election of Mary Robinson to the office of president of the Irish Republic in 1990 (the first woman to hold major office in Irish history) signaled radical changes in Irish life and, most important, the place of women. Robinson's period in office saw referendums that changed the laws governing divorce and abortion in Ireland, greater employment prospects and equality for women, and the development of a more secular notion of women's function within society. Such radical changes have been reflected in the sporting life of Ireland. Camogie has continued to be popular, but it is now accompanied by a rapid growth in women's Gaelic football (organized on an official basis since 1974). In Ireland the Ministry of Youth and Sport, and in Northern Ireland the Sports Council for Northern Ireland, have been far more rigorous in their promotion of sport for women.

Most symbolically, Irish women have had sporting role models in recent years. In track and field, Sonia O'Sullivan's success at a variety of European and international competitions at the 5,000-and 10,000-meter distance made her one of the biggest sporting commodities in Ireland in the 1990s. Even bigger than O'Sullivan was Michelle Smith who was the first Irish woman to win a medal at the Olympic Games. In 1996 at Atlanta she won three gold medals and one bronze in swimming. The toast of Ireland, she rose quickly to stardom. Her victories, indeed her career performances, have come under intense scrutiny since Atlanta, and in 1998 she was banned from competition for four years for tampering with a urine sample.

Despite Smith's downfall, women's sport in Ireland is in the best shape it has ever been. Its success and popularity reflect the fundamental changes that have taken place in Ireland during the twentieth century.

Mike Cronin

See also Camogie; United Kingdom

Bibliography

Cronin, Mike. (1999) *Sport and Nationalism in Ireland: Gaelic Games, Soccer and Transformations in Irish National Identity since 1884.* Dublin: Four Courts Press.

Hayes, Liam, Vincent Hogan, and David Walsh. (1995) *Heroes of Irish Sporting Life.* Dublin: Medmedia.

Healy, Paul. (1998) *Gaelic Games and the Gaelic Athletic Association*. Cork: Mercier Press.

Houlihan, Barrie. (1997) *Sport, Policy and Politics. A Comparative Analysis*. London: Routledge.

Naughton, Lindi, and Johnny Watterson. (1992) *Irish Olympians*. Dublin: Blackwater.

of Isabelle's performances was cherished by the guilds.

Marijke den Hollander

Bibliography

Renson, Roland. (1977) "Kings Shooting and Shooting Kings." *Newsletter of the Association for the Anthropological Study of Play* 4, 2: 14–18.

ISABELLE OF THE NETHERLANDS

(1566–1633)
RENAISSANCE ARCHER

Archduchess Isabelle, daughter of Philip II of Spain, reigned over the Spanish Netherlands (southern Netherlands, now Belgium) together with her husband, Albert. In keeping with her father's effort to counter the rise of Protestant reform, she participated several times in the archery contests that were an important part of the Catholic culture of the Spanish Netherlands. She was not the first female ruler to compete with bow and arrows. Aristocratic women in the Spanish Netherlands were often skilled archers who participated in hunting parties.

Isabelle appeared as the guest of the all-male archery guilds that were a mainstay of local tradition. On 15 May 1615, during a crossbow contest organized on the occasion of the yearly procession in Brussels, the archduchess shot at the popinjay, the wooden bird fixed atop a tall mast. The Flemish artist Anton Sallaert captured Isabelle's victory in one of his paintings.

During the annual festive popinjay contest, in contrast to the weekly matches of the guild members, the emphasis was on chance rather than on skill. The title of "king" was awarded to the person lucky enough to knock down the popinjay. On 5 August 1618, Isabelle participated in the annual archery match to establish "king" of the year of the Saint Joris guild of Ghent. Of this event an anonymous painting was made, which was ascribed to Lucas Horenbault. The memory

ISLAMIC COUNTRIES' WOMEN'S SPORTS SOLIDARITY COUNCIL AND GAMES

The Islamic Countries' Women's Sports Solidarity Council supports Islamic religious beliefs and law, and, at the same time, provides an opportunity for Muslim women to participate in regional and international sports competition. In 1993, the council hosted the first Islamic Countries' Women's Sports Solidarity Games, known less formally as the Islamic Women's Games. The Games, in effect, represent a compromise between two conflicting sets of beliefs. Female athletes from Western nations wanted women included on the all-male teams from Islamic nations in international and Olympic competition. The religious beliefs of Muslim nations, however, restrict women's participation in sports. In a paper entitled "Comparative Survey on Athletes Participating in the first Islamic Countries' Women's Sports Solidarity Games," Shokoh Navabinejad, a member of the National Olympic Committee of Iran, put the political, religious, and cultural questions in perspective:

> Following the victory of the Islamic Revolution in 1978 which brought about a change in the System of the Country, an independent Women's Sports Organization had to be established due to the governing Islamic Values. This organization was directed by women and accordingly made use of female experts, coaches and referees whose main goal was to develop "Sports for all" amongst women nationwide. However, as far as the competitive sports are concerned, our women athletes, observing the Islamic principles, are not in a position to compete in the international competitions in view of the circumstances under which these events are held, which are contradictory to the Islamic Criterion.

Many in the Islamic world believe it difficult, perhaps impossible, to maintain the proper dignity and the obligations of their religion and still have Muslim women participate in international and Olympic sports events. Under Islamic law, male and female athletes may not participate together, a rule that severely restricts Muslim nations' ability to participate in international events. It was, therefore, the goal of Fa'ezeh Hashemi, the daughter of former Iranian President Ali-Abar Hashemi Rafsanjani, to create an atmosphere that promoted women's sports within the structures of Muslim life. Hashemi's involvement was based on her conviction that sports play a key role in life today; serve as a means to achieve political, cultural, and economic progress; and constitute an important part of the social infrastructure. Additionally, in accordance with Islamic values, she argues that any action that may help reach perfection in belief and action is valuable and that Muslims demand a sound atmosphere in which to promote women's sports based on Islamic and humanitarian precepts.

With these ideas in mind and also with the desire to respect the objectives of the international Olympic movement, the first Islamic Countries' Women's Sports Solidarity Congress (ICWSSC) was held in October 1991 in Tehran. According to congress organizers, the main objective was to strengthen and reinforce solidarity among Islamic countries. Stressing they were "ever guarding the Islamic values," more than forty delegates met to develop a program for women's sports. They rep-

resented the countries of Malaysia, Cameroon, Egypt, United Arab Emirates, Kuwait, Bahrain, Afghanistan, Benin, Bangladesh, Nigeria, Fiji, The Gambia, Sudan, Lebanon, Pakistan, Azerbaijan, Libya, Burkina Faso, Brunei, and Indonesia. The participants identified three primary goals. First, to establish and strengthen solidarity among the women of Islamic countries. Second, to develop and expand competitive sport within the framework of Islamic life. And, third, to spread sports culture among youth. During the Congress, representatives exchanged views on the necessity and importance of women's sports in Islamic culture. They also discussed the effects of sports on the physical and psychological health of women; the effects of sports on women's health in the family; women, sports, and the economy; and violence in sports and its harmful effects on women.

Congress representatives emphasized the importance and benefits of women's sport in Islamic culture, the need "to purify sports communities from the current corruption," and their desire to unify Muslim women through sports. Participants planned the next congress for the spring of 1992, with the first Islamic Countries' Women Sports Solidarity Games to be held in February 1993. Fa'ezeh Hashemi was unanimously elected as the president of the congress.

WESTERN REACTIONS

Meanwhile, on the international front, the controversy over Islamic women's participation in international sports competition intensified in 1992 when two Frenchwomen, Linda Weil-Curiel, an attorney, and Annie Susier, a women's rights activist, discovered that thirty-five of the participating countries in the 1992 Barcelona Olympic Games had no women members in their delegations. Many of these nations were Muslim. Curiel and Susier formed the Atlanta Plus to lobby the International Olympic Committee (IOC) to ban those nations without women members from participating in the Atlanta Games in 1996.

Atlanta Plus petitioned the IOC to fight "gender apartheid" and to enforce its own Olympic Charter, which declares that "all forms of discrimination with respect to a country or a person, whether for reasons of race, religion, politics, sex or any other are incompatible with the Olympic Movement." The organization emphasized that

THE HIJAB: THE MUSLIM WOMEN'S COVERING

Wearing the hijab has been controversial for centuries, and as Muslim women in many countries continue to participate in sports it will continue to provoke debate. The *hijab* refers to the covering of the head and the body, and the word is also used to refer to particular garments as well as to the modest behavior, manners, and speech expected of a respectable, devout Muslim woman. Not all Muslim women wear the hijab, but when they do it has a significant influence on their level of physical activity and involvement in sports.

The wearing of the hijab is based on the following text: "O Prophet, tell your wives and daughters and the believing women to draw their outer garments around them when they go out or are among men. That is better in order that they may be known to be Muslims and not annoyed" (Qu-r'an 33:59). This requirement is supported by the Hadith, or Traditions, of the Prophet Muhammad: "When a girl reaches the menstrual age, it is not proper that anything should remain exposed except this and this. He pointed to the face and hands." Proponents argue that the hijab is a statement of modesty, not of male oppression, as it is sometimes perceived to be by non-Muslims. The hijab itself varies enormously from region to region. Sometimes the entire body, including the face, is covered with an enveloping garment. In other places, simple headscarves constitute the hijab.

Islam is not the only religion to maintain that a woman's body, especially her head, ought to be covered. Some Orthodox Jewish women wear wigs and other headcoverings, and some Catholics expect women to wear a headcovering in church. When it comes to girls' and women's participation in physical education and sports, however, Islamic restrictions on clothing can be extremely significant and present complications for school officials in countries—including the United States, Britain, and France—where there are significant Muslim communities. It would be impossible to participate in most sports wearing the hijab of some regions. Nonetheless, some Islamic countries have provided ways for women to participate in sports by banning men from training and competitions, since the rule of the hijab is designed to avoid the male gaze. In addition, women are also able to participate in quite a number of sports—including horse-riding sports, archery, and shooting—wearing certain forms of the hijab that do not restrict their movements.

---

this was an issue of human rights, not simply "a cultural/religious issue nor a women's only issue." While pressing for the inclusion of Muslim women on previously male-only teams, Atlanta Plus also registered its disapproval of the notion of games for women only.

THE FIRST GAMES

On 13 February 1993, Fa'ezeh Hashemi welcomed more than 400 participants and guests from Azerbaijan, Bahrain, Bangladesh, Iran, Kyrgyzstan, Malaysia, Maldives, Pakistan, Syria, Tajikistan, and Turkmenistan to the opening ceremonies of the first Islamic Countries' Women's Sports Solidarity Games in Tehran. Events included badminton, volleyball, basketball, handball, table tennis, shooting, track and field, and swimming. Team sizes and participation varied from country to country. For example, Azerbaijan, the country with the most delegates, brought 118 athletes and Bahrain brought only one.

In his speech during the opening ceremonies of the games, Iranian President Rafsanjani addressed the political controversy surrounding Muslim women and international sports competitions: "The problem lies in the current manner of the practice of sports in the World and Regional competitions. We value all those who have a respect for purity and continence and for restrictions thereby applied by our religion on women as well as men in view of *fatwa* [Islamic legal opinion] and the realities of creation."

To assure compliance with Islamic law, the female athletes wore full *hijab* dress (traditional Muslim attire, the full-length black dress and veil) in the presence of men at all times. For some women from less traditional Muslim nations, this was a new experience. Except for the opening ceremony, men were banned from the Games Village. Hijab was worn by the torch carrier and by all women during the opening and closing ceremonies and during any press conferences and interviews. During competition in track and field, swimming, basketball, badminton, handball, and table tennis, with no men present, the women wore more modern sports uniforms, and armed guards patrolled outside to prevent men from entering. Men were allowed to watch the shooting competition because all the participants were wearing full hijab. All coaches, officials, technicians, and executive personnel present during the competition were women. Dame Mary Alison Hague of England, a representative of the International Olympic Committee (IOC) observed the overall competition, and Mary Benaham, a basketball delegate from Ireland, observed the basketball games. They reported that the games met international standards. Male coaches were housed on segregated floors in the games hotel, had their own elevator, and were not allowed to share transportation with the female athletes. Photography during the competition was prohibited, although an all-female crew made a documentary film of the competition. When the games were over, only women throughout Iran viewed it. The competition ended with Kyrgyzstan placing first; Iran, second; and Azerbaijan, third in terms of total medals won. One indication of the success of these games on the international level was that IOC President Juan Antonio Samaranch asked Fa'ezeh Hashemi to become vice-president of the Iranian Olympic Committee.

PREPARATION FOR THE NEXT GAMES

The study, conducted by Shokoh Navabinejad, of athletes who participated in the games provides an overall view of Muslim women athletes. In all, some 300 of the participating athletes filled out a comprehensive questionnaire made available in Russian, English, and Arabic. In 1994, during the fifth General Assembly of ICWSSC, the sports development committee discussed and evaluated some of their major activities. Under the directorship of Shokoh Navabinejad of Iran, and with the participation of women delegates from Bahrain, Bangladesh, Iran, Azerbaijan, Cameroon, Kuwait, Morocco, and men from Tanzania and Bangladesh, the committee reviewed a research questionnaire developed to survey the status of women's sports in Islamic countries. The committee also reviewed an assessment of the need for women referees and coaches, and discussed the establishment of training classes. The survey showed that 54 percent of the athletes were from the Central Asian Republics (the former Soviet Republics) and another 37 percent were from Iran.

Navabinejad also wrote a "Comparative Survey on Athletes Participating in the First Islamic Countries' Women's Sports Solidarity Games," based on a survey of over 300 athletes who participated in the first games. The survey compared the athletes of the Central Asian Republics, who won the most medals in the events, with the athletes of Iran and the other countries. She found that the winners had started their athletic careers at an earlier age, spent twice the time training as had the other athletes, and had greater experience representing their respective national teams.

Navabinejad made several suggestions to develop long-term planning for women's sports programs in Islamic countries. She noted that schools are the primary site for discovering talented children and young adults with potential for competitive sports. Talented girls should be offered the regular training necessary to develop their potential. To further promote the competitive performances of national teams, weekly training sessions, which averaged about five hours a week but topped twelve in the Central Asian Republics, should be increased, and new opportunities created for female athletes to take part in national and international competitions.

The sixth executive board meeting of ICWSSC was held in Kuwait on 10 June 1997. Hashemi commented that the ICWSSC was broadening its activities. She acknowledged Iran's contribution to the promotion of Islamic women in sports, but urged that making the movement a truly international one would be a great success. "An international movement shall be more successful and better when its activities extend to all its member countries and so organizing this session in Kuwait is considered as a turning point in the council's activities which will be recorded in Muslim's Women's Sport's history."

The executive board also reviewed the work of the training committee of ICWSSC on training coaches and referees and established guidelines for their certification. Participants in the training programs must be "women who believe in Islam," have passed health exams, be nominated from a sports organization in a concerned country, and have active experience in their repective sports. For those candidates without a B.A. or a higher degree in physical education, a curriculum was designed to offer instruction in both the practice and basic theory of coaching principles. It included sixty hours of practical training sessions and course work in first aid, general physiology and anatomy, and sports hygiene.

Following the first Islamic Women's Games, the Islamic women's sports movement experienced some growth. On 21–28 July 1994 the first Muslim Student Games were held in Tehran under similar ground rules. While there were athletic events for both men and women, all female participation took place when men were not present. The second Islamic Women's Games were scheduled for 1997 and were to be hosted by Pakistan. To prepare for those games, a smaller competition was held in Islamabad in 1996 with 320 participating athletes from eleven nations. Pakistanis, however, voiced strong opposition to the competition, and to women's participation in sports in Pakistan. As a result, at the executive board meeting of the ICWSSC in Kuwait, it was decided that the second Islamic Countries' Women's Sports Games would once again be held in Tehran, this time in December 1997.

THE SECOND GAMES

Participants in the second Islamic Women's Games competed in twelve different sports: badminton, basketball, tennis, gymnastics, table tennis, shooting, track and field, swimming, volleyball, handball, karate, and chess. Due to the change in venue and a lack of appropriate facilities, the planned competitions in hockey and squash were canceled. Juan Antonio Samaranch issued the following statement about the upcoming games: "I do appreciate the precious initiative of the Islamic Republic of Iran in founding the Islamic Countries' Women's Sports Games. The IOC and all its members admire the high values of this movement and will never forget it." More-

over, Anita DeFrantz, the vice-president of the IOC, noted that: "The second Islamic Countries' Women's Sport Games are very important for women who might otherwise never have the opportunity to compete at elite level sports. This event is a major step toward Olympic Competition. . . . These competitions, initiated by Mrs. Hashemi, have been providing a proper ground for achieving new experiences in sports by young girls and women."

In his remarks during the opening ceremony, the head of Iran's Expediency Council, Hashemi Rafsanjani, pointed to Iran's program of women's sports as an example to other Islamic nations searching for a moderate and healthy way to integrate women's sports: "We haven't had to keep away a half of society from the benefits of sports, and the role of sport in the physical and mental health of family, and the education of children." Fa'ezeh Hashemi also stressed that one-fourth of the women in the world live in Muslim countries.

The games began with a total of 748 participating athletes representing twenty-five countries. A total of 290 referees officiated in the twelve different sports. At the conclusion of the games on 19 December 1997, Iran led the competition with 58 gold medals, 55 silver, and 37 bronze. Kazakh-

Table 1. Results of the Second ICWSG

Country	Gold	Silver	Bronze
Iran	58	55	37
Kazakhstan	35	5	9
Indonesia	19	13	—
Kyrgyzstan	13	10	5
Syria	10	29	25
Azerbaijan	7	13	32
Turkmenistan	6	11	41
Pakistan	3	14	9
Sudan	2	—	—
Bosnia	1	1	—
Jordan	1	1	—
Bangladesh	—	2	1
Tajikistan	—	—	—

Source: Secretariat of Islamic Countries' Women's Sports Solidarity Council

stan finished second with 35 gold medals, 5 silver, and 9 bronze. Indonesia finished third with 19 gold medals and 13 silver.

The Islamic Women's Games have afforded Muslim women the opportunity to participate in sports in a manner consistent with Islamic law and have also provided a venue for participation in sports at the international level. The ICWSSC has emerged as the primary women's sports organization in the world and plans to continue the Games and increase sports opportunities for women in accordance with the tenets of Islamic law. By Western standards, Muslim women athletes may appear severely limited; within their own culture, they are experiencing much greater freedom in a world from which they were once barred.

Daniel Bell
Mickey Friedman

Bibliography

The First Meeting. (1993) Tehran, Iran: The Organizing Committee of the first Islamic Countries' Women's Sports Games.

ISRAEL

Israel is a Middle Eastern nation founded in 1948 with a population of just over five million. It is the only nation with a predominantly Jewish population. Equality between men and women was one of the founding principles of the state, but the gap between principle and reality is substantial when it comes to participation in sports, with women's participation lagging substantially behind men's.

HISTORY

For generations, the Jewish tradition tended to emphasize intellectual rather than physical development. Interest in sports among Jews took place mainly in Western Europe and was influenced by European social movements. A majority of immigrants who settled in Israel, came from Eastern Europe, where Jews had little involvement in sports, and where Jewish culture was more in line with the traditional emphasis on the

mind rather than the body. Women's sports were of even less importance than those of men.

Compounding this is the broader structure of Israeli society. In contrast to the Western image of social equality, Israeli society is characterized by traditional family structures, in which gender-specific roles are established and reinforced in accord with national ethnic and religious values. Thus, the norms that favor a family role for women often limit the opportunities for sports careers for women. The low social status of female athletes compared to male athletes means that they do not regularly receive financial support. In addition, women's sports suffer from a lack of suitable coaches and professionals.

Despite these general limitations on women's participation, several women athletes have made it to the elite level in Israel. In the Asia Games and the Asian championships, in which Israel participated between 1954 and 1974, women won eleven out of Israel's total of eighteen gold medals. And out of the fourteen Israeli athletes who had finished eighth or better in their events, two were women—Esther Ruth Sahamorov and Yael Arad. They are considered the best female Israeli athletes since the founding of the State of Israel. Sahamorov was a sprinter, hurdler, and long jumper, and she won several medals including two golds (hurdles and pentathlon) in the Asian Games held in Bangkok in 1970 and golds in the 100-meter sprint and 200-meter hurdles in the 1974 Asian Games in Teheran. At the Munich Olympic Games in 1972, she failed to reach the finals in the 100-meter race by a thousandth of a second and did not participate in the semifinals, following the murder of eleven Israeli athletes, including her coach, Amizur Shapira. In the Montreal Olympics in 1976, Sahamarov achieved the best performance of an Israeli athlete to date when she qualified for the 100-meter final and finished in sixth place. Yael Arad, the national champion in judo, was the first Israeli athlete to win an Olympic medal when she took the silver at the 1992 Games in Barcelona.

The fact that Israel is an immigrant state and received Jewish athletes from the worldwide Jewish diaspora is significant. The influx of new talent has at times raised the competitive level of the national teams considerably. Two women worthy of mention are Angelica Rosiano of Romania and

YAEL ARAD, ISRAELI SILVER MEDALIST

The only Israeli athlete to win an Olympic medal, Yael Arad, won a silver medal in the half-middleweight judo division at the 1992 Olympics in Barcelona. Arad defeated the German world champion, Frauke Eickoff, in the semi-finals and then lost the final in a 2-1 split decision to former world champion, Catherine Fleury of France.

Ágnes Keleti of Hungary. They came to Israel after having had successful careers in Europe, and they trained newer generations of athletes in table tennis and gymnastics from the 1950s on.

THE FUTURE

The international success of Sahamarov and Arad stands out against the background of general discrimination against women athletes in Israel. Their success has forced Israeli leaders to realize that the situation must be changed. In 1994 the Sports Association (which is under the Ministry of Education) established a division for the Advancement of Women in Sports. The head of this division is the well-known swimmer Shlomit Tur. This division has established several goals: develop appropriate leadership and enrichment programs for female athletes; form a committee to provide medical, physiological, and psychological services; encourage more scientific research and more media coverage of women's sports; develop international ties; and encourage the development of physical education for women.

The extra attention given to women's sports in the 1990s led to several accomplishments. The number of women who participate in competitive sports increased from 17 percent in 1995 to 24 percent in 1997. The government developed several programs of competitive training for women. Legal changes helped promote further change and established criteria for equality. For example, a court has ruled that women must be represented in the directorate of the state-run gambling foundation, and financial allocations must be distributed equally among male and female teams. By 1998, 15 percent of the members of the Israeli Olympic Committee were women, as opposed to 5 percent in the previous year. Research studies in the unique aspects of women's sports are receiving greater support in 2000 than in the past, and many efforts have been made to afford women's sports more media coverage. These new initiatives taken together contribute to the hope that women's sport participation in Israel will someday reach the level of participation in Western nations.

Haim Kaufman

Bibliography

Bar-Eli, M., A. Spiegel, and M. Yaaron. (1998) "Israeli Women in the Olympic and Maccabiah Games 1932–1992: Patterns of Stability and Change." *Movement* 4, 3:295–318.

Bernstein, A. (1997) "Survey of Women in Sports in the Media." *Physical Education and Sport* 5:15–16.

Hanegby, R. (1997) "Short-lived Career of Women Tennis Players in Israel." *Physical Education and Sports* 6:25–26.

Kaufman, H. (1996) "The National Ideas of the Term Jewish Muscles." *Movement* 3, 3:261–282.

Tel-Aviv University. (1994) "Women in Sports in Israel." Symposium in Memory of Captain Itzhak Hochman. Tel Aviv, Israel: The Unit of Sports and Physical Education.

Toor, S. (1997) "Women in Competitive Sports—The Central Theme in the Olympic Academy." *Physical Education and Sports* 5:14–15.

Unit for the Advancement of Women in Sports. (1998) *Women in Sports in Israel.* Netanya, Israel: Wingate Institute.

Unit of Competitive Sports. (1993) *Women in Competitive Sports and the World.* Netanya, Israel: Wingate Institute.

———. (1995) "Women in Competitive Sports. *Congress of Competitive Sports (November 1994),* edited by B. Dagon. Netanya, Israel: Wingate Institute.

ITALY

Italy is located in southern Europe and has a population of about 57.5 million; it became a nation in 1861 through the unification of what had been politically distinct city-states. Formal sports began to develop in the middle of the nineteenth century following unification, but it was not until the 1980s that women began generally to participate in sports. A variety of factors limited, and in some ways continue to limit, sports participation by women. These include the traditional "male" orientation of Italian society; the influence of the Roman Catholic Church; a rigid class structure, which limited sports participation to the upper classes; and a continuing tension between the "progressive" central and northern regions and the "traditional" south. Despite these obstacles, women have competed in sports since the 1980s in ever-increasing numbers. Their role in the management of sports, however, remains very restricted.

THE PIONEERING AGE: NATIONHOOD TO WORLD WAR I

After the Kingdom of Italy was established in 1861, the government required gymnastics in the schools. However, only a limited number of pupils in the well-off northwestern regions of Italy actually participated. The rest of the nation lacked schools, teachers, suitable equipment, and gymnasiums. In Turin, then the national capital, the Società di Ginnastica Torinese (Society of Gymnastics of Turin) set up summer courses in 1861 to train male teachers.

In those years, gymnastics was commonly seen as a form of military training in accord with the German model for physical education. Accordingly, gymnastics for girls and women was frowned upon, both by the middle class who associated it with "masculinity," and the lower classes who believed it would cause harm to a girls' physical and moral well-being. Only the wealthiest aristocratic girls practised gymnastics and some other sports. In doing so, they were well within the bounds of what was considered acceptable for upper-class women in Europe.

In 1867 the first course for female teachers was offered at the Società di Ginnastica Torinese, but it had little impact because through the 1870s gymnastics in the schools was practiced mostly by boys. Only with the enactment of the De Sanctis' Law in 1878 was gymnastics made compulsory in all schools for both boys and girls of all social classes.

In the 1890s the physiologist Angelo Mosso (1846–1910), following the British model, advocated participation in sports and games for both men and women. He argued that women's health could be improved through participation in sports such as tennis, croquet, and Swedish gymnastics. Unfortunately, Mosso did not win the support of many of his contemporaries, and female sports did not develop across Italian society.

The principal locus of women's sports in the 1890s was the sports clubs that drew an upper-middle class membership. The first female gymnastics unit within a sports club was founded in Siena in 1881 and the second in Rome in 1890. Later in Milan, the Female Mediolanum (1897) and the Insubria Female Society (1898) were founded. They also were directed by women. In 1908 the first national championship in women's gymnastics was held in Milan, contested by eighteen sports societies from northern and central Italy. In the rural southern regions, male dominance and a more traditional world view excluded most women from the new sports culture.

In the more modern north, "male" sports were practiced by a small number of daring women, who were sometimes admired and sometimes satirized by contemporary commentators. World War I interrupted the development of sport in general.

FEMALE ATHLETICISM DURING THE FASCIST REGIME

After World War I, European women, who had worked hard in traditionally male jobs as substitutes for men engaged in the conflict, became increasingly aware of their rights. Influenced by the wind of freedom that modernism was spreading throughout Italy, feminism developed in opposition to Italy's traditionally male-dominated ethos. In 1919 ten thousand women competed at a gymnastics contest in Venice. And in 1921 at a sports exhibition in Rome, women participated in sports commonly classified as masculine such as shooting, javelin, and shot put.

At that time Benito Mussolini (1883–1945), founder of the fascist movement, was planning his rise to power. He came to power in 1923 and remained in power until 1943. The fascist ideology and government took control of the physical and moral education of students and workers by enrolling them in numerous state physical education and sport organizations. The goal was to rebuild Italian character by enabling people to adopt a more social and collective behavior through sports and gymnastic exhibitions. Its final goal was shaping the "New Italian."

The fascist commitment to eugenics led party members to reject the traditional Roman Catholic opposition to women's sports and to include female sport activities in their program. But, to maintain government control, in 1928 the Federazione Italiana d'Atletica Femminile (Italian Federation of Women's Athletics), which was founded in Milan in 1923, was abolished by the Carta dello Sport (Sport Charter). In its place, the government-controlled Comitato Olimpico Nazionale Italiano (CONI; Italian National Olympic Committee) was given the task of managing sport in Italy. The CONI leadership deemphasized the development of women's sports because women's sports were considered to be secondary in importance. Thus, in the 1930s only a few sports—such as basketball, swimming, skiing, skating, tennis, and track and field—were considered suitable for women.

The development of women's sports was further hindered by the hostility of the Church and by lingering perceptions of some people who were afraid of a possible "masculinization" of Italian girls. The idea that sports could be dangerous with regard to female reproductive organs—possibly causing female sterility—also persisted despite the support given to women's participation by most physicians.

From 1929 through membership in the Opera Nazionale Balilla (ONB; National Ballet Organization), young girls were able to participate in nonstressful, unexciting exercises focusing on eugenic, aesthetic, and moral development. Their teachers came from the Academy of Orvieto, which was established for the training of female physical education teachers. Beginning in 1931,

female university students could join Gruppi Universitari Fascisti (Fascist university groups) and could participate in intercollegiate championships.

For working women there was the Opera Nazionale Dopolavoro (OND; National After-hours Organization), founded in 1937, which provided an institutional setting for various physical activities and paramilitary gymnastics exhibitions. The frequency of these public exhibitions increased considerably after 1937, when OND, ONB, and other bodies joined the militarized Gioventù Italiana del Littorio (Italian Youth Organization).

The regime offered a special treatment to a number of selected and talented girls, who were trained to perform internationally and to bring acclaim to the Italian nation and fascist ideology and government. Some of them, such as the pilot Carina Massone Negrone (1911–1994), the skier Celina Seghi (1920–), the skaters Adriana Rianda (1920–) and Ada Spoto (1921–), and especially the track and field athletes Carla Testoni (1915–) and Ondina Valla (1916–) did well in international competitions.

WOMEN'S SPORT AFTER WORLD WAR II

After the fall of fascism and the end of World War II, Italian women were given the right to vote for the first time. The new constitution proclaimed full equality in duties and rights between sexes, but women's rights "on paper" were not realized in practice.

In these years, the Ministry of Education of the newly constituted Italian Republic resumed control of physical education in primary and secondary schools. At the university level, in 1946, the Centro Universitario Sportivo Italiano (Italian University Sport Center) was established, and national and international university sport championships were held regularly. CONI started collaborating with the schools in 1950, and some sports were officially added to the educational curriculum.

In 1952 the fascist academies for physical education teacher training—renamed the Instituto Superiore di Educazione Fisica (ISEF; Higher Institute of Physical Education)—reopened in Rome for both sexes. In 1958 physical education and sports in the schools were reorganized again. Within a few years, ten officially recognized ISEFs opened in the country. Furthermore, from 1968 the Ministry of Education and CONI started organizing the Giochi della Gioventù (Youth Games) for all pupils. In 1983 they inaugurated Campionati Studenteschi (Student Championships) for high school students as well.

Women's participation in postwar physical education and sports increased very slowly, together with the economic development of the nation and the gradual emancipation of Italian women from purely domestic roles. In spite of fascism, and at the same time because of fascism, women had learned that they had bodies that could compete in serious athletic competition as well as bear children.

Within the school system, from the second half of the 1940s to the 1980s, women's involvement in sports increased quite slowly. Physical education (at least two hours per week) was compulsory but strictly separated by gender. Only female teachers could teach girls, and different programs were prescribed for them than for boys. The content of these programs was still influenced by the earlier ones and involved basic and applied gymnastics and relatively little sport. The high school programs finally unified in 1990, and mixed classes were taught by both male and female physical education teachers.

In comparison with the schools, the postwar sports world was more open to women, but the recruitment of women was still hindered by old ideas that emphasized the domestic role for women. Despite the efforts of CONI and local societies, in the second half of the 1940s and in the 1950s only a few women were involved in serious sporting activities and even fewer competed at the international level. In 1959 0.5 percent of Italian women practiced sport; out of every 100 athletes, fewer than ten were women.

In the 1960s, despite economic development and compulsory education that had been extended from five to eight years, women's participation in sports hardly increased as the traditional beliefs about the role of women continued to limit sports participation by girls. Nonetheless, by having practiced sports in high school and by having competed in the annual Youth Games, a few pioneering women maintained sporting habits beyond their school years. In the 1970s the post-1968 feminist movement stimulated the de-

Since the 1980s, Italian women have become world-class competitors in several sports. Here, Anna Rita Sidoti crosses the finish line to take first place in the 10-kilometer walk at the World University Games in 1995. (AP Photos)

velopment of women's sports. More aware of their rights and reassured about their identity, women participated significantly more for the first time.

The 1980s was the breakthrough decade for women's sports in Italy. Women's participation increased notably, especially in such northern and central regions as Val d'Aosta, Friuli Venezia Giulia, Trentino Alto Adige, Emilia Romagna, and Marche. In southern Italy, women's participation was only about half that of the national female average. Still, statistics from 1981 revealed that women in the south were entering sports participation more rapidly than were men in the south.

A survey in the mid-1980s indicated that 14 percent of the female population was involved in sports. In 1988, out of 1,056,699 young people practicing sports within the federations affiliated with CONI, 39.7 percent were girls. The unknown number of young and older women practicing physical activities outside of CONI, and the recognized sports clubs were not included in these statistics. Girls enrolled in federations were especially active in gymnastics and volleyball, and more women participated in these sports than men did. Women also participated in significant numbers in swimming, fencing, hockey, softball, and skiing.

By the late 1980s, women formed about 30 percent of the membership of sport federations. In addition the breadth of women's participation increased as sports traditionally popular among men attracted women as well. Some women won world championships in automobile racing, bicycling, judo, swimming, archery, sailing, surfing, and wind surfing. By participating in regional, national, and international contests, and by appearing on television and in newspapers, women athletes became role models who inspired others to take up sports. Sara Simeoni, winner of the high jump at the 1980 Olympics, was the best-known of these international champions.

THE CONTEMPORARY SITUATION

In the last decade of the twentieth century, the Italian population remained stable and its average age increased. As these trends were expected to continue well into the twenty-first century, the Italian government looked for ways to improve the quality of life for its older citizens. One method of reaching this goal was to encourage healthy life habits, including participation in physical activities. In 1997 the Ministry of Educa-

tion and CONI jointly began an effort to involve all Italian students—from kindergarten through high school—in an extended program of physical and sports education. The resulting Sport per Tutti (Sports for All) program was a large-scale effort involving all citizens in sports and various non-competitive physical activities. This initiative was undertaken in concert with other nations throughout the European Union.

In Italy most organized sporting activities are managed by the Ministry of Education and by CONI (through thirty-nine national federations, eighteen associated sports, 11,000 local sports clubs, twenty regional, and ninety-four provincial agencies). This co-leadership is a peculiarly Italian phenomenon that seems useful in promoting the diffusion of sporting activities throughout the nation. Survey information from 1995 suggested that thirty-four million Italians (61.8 percent of the population aged three years and over) practiced at least some physical activity and that the modernization of the nation had lowered the gap in participation between people in the north and the south. The 1995 statistics also showed that the level-of-participation gap between men and women had been greatly reduced. In a population of 26,823,000 men and 28,478,000 women, 33 percent of men and 36.8 percent of women were active in at least some physical activity.

This growth in participation has also been reflected in the successes of Italian women in international competitions in many sports. From the 1960s on, Italian women haved performed well and won Olympic medals in track and field, fencing, and equestrian events. And at the Barcelona Olympic Games in 1992, the Italian fencer Gio-

A WOMAN COACHES MEN'S SOCCER

In June, 1999 Carolina Morace was picked as head coach of the Viterbo, an Italian men's professional soccer team. The first woman to coach a men's team in Italy, she had been a star player herself, scoring 105 goals in 151 international matches. After retiring in 1998 at age 34, Morace became a television sports commentator. Some accused the team of selecting her to generate publicity, but the team owner, Luciano Gaucci, said she was selected because of her experience and abilities and that her tenure with the team was entirely dependent on the team's success on the field.

vanna Trillini, and the women's fencing team won gold medals, and Emanuela Pierantozzi took a silver in judo. At the Atlanta Olympics in 1996, the cyclists Antonella Bellutti and Paola Pezzo won gold medals, as did the women's fencing team, and Italian women won silver and bronze medals in canoeing, fencing, and judo.

At the Winter Olympics in Albertville in 1992, skier Debora Compagnoni won a gold medal. Stefania Belmondo won one gold and one silver medal, and the women's cross-country relay team took the bronze in the 5-kilometer event. This success was improved upon at the 1994 Winter Games in Lillehammer, when the Italian female athletes triumphed: Manuela Di Centa, nicknamed "the Queen of Lillehammer," won two gold medals and two silver medals in Nordic skiing. Debora Compagnoni won her second Olympic gold medal, and Gerda Weissensteiner took the gold in the singles luge. Italian women also won four bronze medals: one for Stefania Belmondo in Nordic skiing, two for Isolde Kostner in Alpine skiing, and one for the women's 5-kilometer cross-country relay team.

Italian women became national athletic heroes in 1998. At the Olympics in Nagano, Compagnoni, after winning her third Olympic gold medal, became one of the most successful skiers of all time, replacing the male skier Alberto Tomba as a national hero. And Franca Fiacconi won the prestigious New York City Marathon in 1998.

It is worth noting that these accomplishments took place during a major economic recession, which one would expect to have a negative impact on the development of sports. In fact, unemployment across Europe, especially among young people and women, was at its highest level in Italy. Even so, most Italian women found it important to exercise and keep fit and healthy. In 1999 a survey indicated that 36.8 percent practiced some form of outdoor activity, such as running, cycling, swimming, or jogging.

Nonetheless, men in Italy have continued to enjoy more opportunity to be involved in sports than women. One particular area of concern is sports administration: of seventeen CONI executives, forty-three members of the National Council, and three Italian members of the International Olympic Committee, none was a woman. Many consider this absence of representation to be especially disgraceful given the international achievements of Italy's women athletes.

Gigliola Gori

Bibliography

Bonetta, Gaetano. (1990) *Corpo e nazione: L'educazione ginnastica, igienica e sessuale nell'Italia liberale.* Milan: Franco Angeli.

CONI, ed. (1987) *I numeri dello sport-Atlante della pratica sportiva in Italia.* Florence: Le Monnier.

———. (1995) *Lo sport in movimento-Evoluzione della pratica sportiva in Italia.* Bologna: Editori Calderini.

De Grazia, Victoria. (1981) *The Culture of Consent: Mass Organization of Leisure in Fascist Italy.* Cambridge: Cambridge University Press.

———. (1993) *Le donne nel regime fascista.* Venice: Marsilio Editori.

De Juliis, Tonino, and Mario Pescante. (1990) *L'educazione fisica e lo sport nella scuola italiana.* Florence: Le Monnier.

Ferrara, Patrizia. (1992) *L'Italia in palestra-Storia, documenti e immagini della ginnastica dal 1833 al 1973.* Rome: La Meridiana.

Frasca, Rosella Isidori. (1983) *E il Duce le volle sportive.* Bologna: Patron Editore.

Giuntini, Sergio. (1992) "La donna e lo sport in Lombardia durante il fascismo." In *Donna lombarda 1860–1945,* edited by Torcellan, Gigli, and Marchetti. Milan: Franco Angeli.

Gori, Gigliola. (1996) *L'atleta e la nazione-Saggi di storia dello sport.* Rimini: Panozzo Editore.

———. (1991) "Women and Sport between the Nineteenth and Twentieth Century: The Hard Take off of a Discriminated Italian Minority." In *Sport and Cultural Minorities.* Helsinki: The Finnish Society for Research in Sport and Physical Education, 133–144.

———. (1996) "Female Sport in Italy: A Contraversial Symbol of the Facist Ideology." In *Sport as Symbol; Symbols in Sport,* edited by F. van der Merwe. Sankt Augustin, Germany: Academia Verlag, 71–80.

Martini, Marco. (1994) "Sesso debole? Un secolo di smentite." In *Lo Sport Italiano,* 1, no. 8–9. Rome: CONI.

Motti, Lucia, and Marilena Rossi Caponeri, eds. (1996) *Accademiste a Orvieto-Donne ed educazione fisica nell'Italia fascista 1932–1943.* Perugia: Quattroemme.

Salvini, Alessandro. (1982) *Identità femminile e sport.* Florence: La Nuova Italia.

J

JAMAICA

Jamaica is an island nation in the Caribbean Sea with a population of 2.5 million. A former British colony, the Jamaican sport experience has continued to reflect British influence, but since the 1980s it has also been strongly influenced by the United States sport culture. Jamaica has a highly developed educational system, and women have enjoyed a relatively high status. They comprise 46 percent of the workforce and have a literacy rate higher than that of men. Both sport participation in school and their high social status have made women's sports an important activity in Jamaica. Despite the small population, Jamaican women are among the elite athletes of the world in netball and track. In the 1990s basketball emerged as a major sport for women as well.

MAJOR SPORTS IN JAMAICA

Netball is a variant of basketball. It was invented in England in the early twentieth century and then exported to British colonies around the world. It is most popular in Australia and New Zealand, but it has also caught on in the former British Caribbean colonies of Jamaica, Barbados, and Trinidad. In the 1990s the Jamaican team, led by Connie Francis, emerged as one of five best in the world and the best in the Caribbean. Its climb to the top of the sport was halted only by its failure to defeat Australia, one of the two top teams in the world.

In the 1990s, basketball became a strong contender as the most popular sport. Basketball, the fastest growing sport in Jamaica (and around the world), has been drawing girls and young women away from netball. The move to basketball began when cable television brought men's professional National Basketball Association games to all of Jamaica and made Michael Jordan a hero on the island.

Sandra Farmer-Patrick of Jamaica competes in the women's 400-meter hurdles at the Olympic Games. (TempSport)

ELITE COMPETITION

Jamaica is best known in the international sport world for its women's track team. The anchor of the team in the 1980s and 1990s was Merlene Ottey, who won nearly forty medals in international competitions and has represented Jamaica in five consecutive Olympics. At the 1996 Olympics in Atlanta, the Jamaican women won medals in four events and finished in the top seven in three others. Deon Hemmings, considered Jamaica's best female track athlete in the late 1990s, won the gold medal in the 400-meter hurdles, and her teammate Debbie Ann Parris finished fourth. Ottey took the silver medals (at the age of thirty-six) in the 100- and 200-meter dashes, and the 4 ×100-meter relay team won the bronze medal. In addition, Dione Rose and Michelle Freeman finished fifth and sixth in the 100-meter hurdles, Sallie Richards finished seventh in the 400-meter run, and the 4 ×100-meter relay team finished fourth. Two years later at the Goodwill Games, the Jamaican women continued their success with gold and silver in the 400-meter run, silver and bronze in the 100-meter hurdles, and gold in the 4 ×100-meter relay. The team has been a source of considerable pride in Jamaica, and the team's success has been phenomenal given the small size and population of the nation. On the international track and field circuit, Jamaica is known as "the sprint factory of the Caribbean."

Although track holds a secure position, men's sports may start to eclipse women's sports. Basketball is more popular with men, and men's high school basketball receives much attention. In addition, the men's soccer (association football) team improved in the 1990s, and it played at the highest level of international competition, drawing much media coverage. Nevertheless, Jamaican women continue to have many opportunities in sports.

The Editors

See also Netball; Ottey, Merlene

Bibliography

The Jamzone!SportsZone. (1999) <http://www .geocities.com/The/Tropics/Cabana/4929 /trackfiled.htm>.

JAPAN

Japan is an island nation in East Asia with a population of about 127 million. It is a modern nation, and its economy is one of the strongest in the world. In many ways, however, Japanese society remains traditional in that it adheres to ancient Japanese customs and beliefs. This unique marriage of the traditional and the modern has influenced women's participation in sports. In the past women's participation was quite limited, but beginning in the 1990s, many women began to participate in sport recreationally. Japanese women have been successful in many international sports. Still, women's full participation remains limited.

HISTORY

During the Meiji Restoration (a period of political centralization under imperial rule from the 1860s to 1912), participation in sports was considered unseemly for women. A woman's place in Japanese society was governed by the principle of *ryosaikenbo*, which meant that a woman was to be a helpful wife to her husband and a wise mother to her children. The principle of *ryosaikenbo* was supported by Japanese civil law, which afforded women a lower status than their husbands and stated of a wife that "she requires her husband's agreement in all important matters." Because wives could not own family property, their role in the Japanese economy was severely restricted.

Under these circumstances, women's participation in sports was acceptable only if it was consistent with *ryosaikenbo*, a requirement that had the practical effect of banning women from partaking in most sports and even from watching some. It was not until 1877 that women were allowed to see all of the sumo wrestling matches (women spectators had been partially allowed since 1872, being banned from the first day only).

The formal Japanese education system now in existence was established by the Education Order of 1872, and since then, most women's sports in Japan have been pursued and developed at all levels of the education system. However, change came slowly and not without resistance. Newspapers criticized girls' sports as being indulgent and not useful in preparing them for marriage. Parents objected to their daughters performing gymnastics.

What slowly created the opportunity for girls and women to participate in sports was the acceptance of modern dress styles. In the nineteenth century, the dress style required of women was a particularly limiting factor in sports participation. When *kazokujogakko* (women's secondary schools for the peerage) were opened in 1886, educators noted that the kimono (traditional Japanese woman's costume) did not encourage participation in gymnastics. One educator proclaimed that "since women's standard clothes were the most inconvenient on account of tying up both the upper and lower limbs by both sleeves and skirt, gymnastics was made very difficult. There-fore . . . our school students must wear Western style clothes during our school times." In 1899 German educator E. Balz (1849–1913) promoted similar ideas when he spoke at the general meeting for Japanese Women's Hygiene in Women's Higher Normal Schools. He emphasized the need to make Japanese women's clothes less restrictive.

Bloomers were introduced to Japan by Akuri Inokuchi, who had graduated from the Boston Normal School of Gymnastics in 1902. She then made a tour of gymnastics programs in girls' schools on the east coast of the United States. On returning to Japan in 1903, Inokuchi suggested that bloomers would be the best school uniform and sportswear for girls. She asserted that bloomers allowed women to move more freely, were better suited to sports than the traditional kimono, and would not undermine elegance if the skirt was put on over the bloomers. In 1905 the report of the Japanese Investigation Committee for Gymnastics and Games concurred with her opinion.

Schools did not adopt these ideas instantly. But as a result of her influence, they were partly adopted in the two existing women's Higher Normal Schools in Tokyo and Nara. Tokuyo Nikaido (1880–1941) was also an influential figure in the development of women's sports. She introduced another style of women's school sportswear, the tunic, from England, where she had lived from 1913 to 1915.

By the early twentieth century, school clothing for girls and young women had been transformed, making it easier for them to participate in physical education. For example, the students at Nara Women's Higher Normal School (Nara Women's University after 1949) played baseball and danced around the maypole in the English-style tunic. They also played tennis and threw the discus in bloomers. Earlier, the Tokyo Women's Higher Normal School had adopted similar improvements in sportswear. In general, it was in the twentieth century that women's clothes were fully redesigned in the elite secondary schools. Western-style games, gymnastics, dance, and appropriate clothing for them evolved concurrently.

Champion Japanese women wrestlers, 1926. (Bettmann/Corbis)

The first sports taught in the schools were gymnastics and modern dance, and they were imported from either northern Europe or the United States. The Delsarte system (an expressionistic gymnastics invented by François Delsarte of France, 1811–1871) had been introduced into the Women's Secondary Missionary School in Yokohama by the middle of the Meiji Restoration period. Jinzo Naruse, (1858–1919), a founder of the Japan Women's University, explained the usefulness of the Delsarte system for women in his 1896 book, *Women's Education*: "I believe that it is very helpful for girls to learn the polite attitude, behavior, and appearance."

Inokuchi had encouraged Swedish exercise for girls. But she was later criticized by Toyo Hujimura (1876–1955). Because the German Naturliches-Turnen approach emphasized a more natural approach to physical activity, Hujimura thought it was more appropriate than the Swedish exercises. The Regulation Act for Women's Upper Secondary Schools was enacted in 1895, and gymnastics and games were included in the curriculum in 1903. The games included the marching game *hagoita* (a traditional girls' game played with a shuttlecock and flat boards), croquet, and lawn tennis. In the Taisho era (1912–1926), a so-called democratic movement in post–World War I Japan, education for women was encouraged, and women's gymnastics and games were more widely accepted. Some games were also played as extracurricular activities including volleyball, track and field, swimming, basketball, tennis, and table tennis.

ORGANIZATION AND COMPETITION

On 27 May 1922, the first Women's Federal Athletic Meeting for Women's Higher Normal Schools was held at the Tokyo Women's Higher Normal School. This athletic meeting was essentially the first opportunity that women had to participate in a well-organized national athletic competition in Japan (which was supported by the Tokyo YMCA). In 1924 the Japan Association of Women's Physical Education was formed, followed by the Japan Women's Sport Federation (JWSF) in 1926. This federation would become a member of the Fédération Sportive Féminine Internationale (FSFI) by 1930. In 1924 the first meeting of the Women's Olympic Games of Japan was held in Osaka. Also held in 1924 was the Meijijingu Athletic Meeting, where women competed in track and field, basketball, volleyball, and tennis. This tournament continued annually until its fourteenth meeting in 1943. However, formal participation was limited to students of upper secondary schools.

Other efforts to improve women's sports also took place before World War II, but these focused on traditional sports activities. For example, educator Hiro Miura (1898–1992) had sought to improve the qualifications of women's physical educators and instructors in the Taisho era. She wanted to improve women's health and strength through modern dance and the new forms of aesthetic gymnastics invented by Isadora Duncan (1878–1927), Rudolf Laban (1879–1958), Jacques Dalcroze (1865–1950), R. Bode (1881-1970), B. M. Mensendieck (1864–1959), and Mary Wigman (1886-1973). These people contrived new expressionistic gymnastics, rhythmical dance, new aesthetic gymnastics, or calisthenics based on the anatomical physiology of women. Miura's ideas and practice continued into the war (1936–1941), and she gave lectures to school teachers after 1945.

EARLY ELITE ATHLETES

In 1926 Kinue Hitomi (1908–1931) participated in the International Women's Games held in Goteberg, Sweden. She was the only Japanese woman at the Games and the first Japanese woman to succeed in international sports competition. Remarkably, she won gold medals in the long jump and the standing long jump and silver medals in the discus and the 100-yard dash. In 1928 Hitomi also won a silver medal in the 800-meter event in the Olympic Games in Amsterdam. The swimmer Hideko Maehata succeeded Hitomi as Japan's leading female athlete, winning Olympic silver medals in the 200-meter breaststroke both in Los Angeles in 1932 and in Berlin in 1936. Because of extensive media attention, she became a celebrity.

Maehata's success was soon eclipsed by the coming war and the need to devote resources to building the national defense. *Kyudo* (Japanese traditional archery) and *naginata* (Japanese halberd) were added to the physical education curriculum in women's normal schools, upper secondary schools, and training schools, while *kendo* (Japanese fencing) and *judo* were required for men in 1936. These martial arts formed *budo*, the tradi-

A JAPANESE WOMAN'S PLACE IS IN THE HOME

Women's full and equal participation in sports has been limited by the traditional Japanese value system and the notion of *ryosaikenbo*, the belief that a woman's primary duties are as wife and mother. Supported by the legal code in the past, *ryosaikenbo* has weakened since World War II, but many women still do not participate in sports because family duties continue to come first.

tional sports that were supposed to train both mind and body as well as promote self-defense and national defense. *Kyudo* and *naginata* were added because it became important to develop women's physical strength to aid national defense.

POSTWAR DEVELOPMENTS

Following World War II, the civil laws of Japan were revised in accordance with the new constitution that reflected a democratic ideology and provided for equal status for men and women. Five years after the war ended, the percentage of women attending upper secondary schools was 36.7 percent. This increased to 55.9 percent in 1960, 82.7 percent in 1970, 95.4 percent in 1980, and 97.0 percent in 1995. And the percentage of women in the workforce slowly increased from 36.9 percent to 50 percent from 1950 to 1995. During this same period, the number of female athletes, sports instructors, and sports educators also began to increase, most coming from the upper class and so able to be independent of conventional domestic roles.

Despite the war's devastating effects on Japan, it did raise people's awareness of women's sports to a new level. They were viewed both as a way of improving national morale and as a means of rebuilding Japan's reputation around the world. While great athletes such as track star Kinue Hitomi had already demonstrated individual dedication to sports, this era brought an emphasis on sports for the benefit of the nation. Women's sports in Japan diversified and flourished following the Tokyo Olympic Games of 1964. By 1970 there were female rugby players, bodybuilders, yachtswomen, boxers, karate experts, and ice hockey players. After the first Tokyo International Women's Marathon was held in 1979, women's marathons sponsored by newspapers became the most popular sporting event for Japanese women, and marathoners such as Akemi Masuda and Yuko Arimori became national celebrities. The first Japanese women's mountaineering team climbed Mount Everest in 1975. In 1977 another famous sportswoman, the professional golfer Hisako Higuchi, won the United States Open, the first Japanese woman to do so. By the 1990s both men and women played most sports recreationally.

JAPAN IN THE OLYMPICS

The Olympic Games saw growing numbers of Japanese women participating and winning medals. The Japanese women's volleyball team won a gold medal in 1964, and it was credited with raising the status both of women athletes and the sport of volleyball. At the 1992 Barcelona Olympic Games, Kyoko Iwasaki won the gold medal in the 200-meter breaststroke at the age of fourteen, making her the youngest gold medalist in this swimming event. In winter sports, Seiko Hashimoto was chosen to represent the Japanese Olympic competitors in 1994, the first time a woman had been so honored in Japanese history. She was also selected as the captain of all Japanese participants for the Olympic Games. Until Hashimoto, a woman had never been chosen for this position in Japan. The 1998 Nagano Winter Olympic Games also produced many young women who won medals, including the skier Tae Satoya, who won a gold medal in the freestyle mogul, becoming the first ever Japanese Olympic medalist in this event.

CONCLUSION

The twentieth century brought great progress for Japanese women's sports. But despite this progress, women still find it difficult to continue with sports once they finish school. After graduation, many women no longer have the opportunity to participate in organized sports unless they go to private clubs, gyms, tennis schools, or swimming schools, where the cost of admission and tuition is high. Married women also find it difficult to continue with sports because they still have the primary responsibility for raising children. By the 1990s local government organizations became more responsible for promoting life-long sports and activity at the local and community levels due to the enactment of the "Lifelong Learning Promotion Law" in 1990. In this development lies the possibility of greater opportunities for women to take part in sports.

Keiko Ikeda

Bibliography

Clarke, Gill, and Barbara Humberstone, eds. (1997) *Researching Women and Sport.* Houndmill and London: Macmillan.

Esashi, Shogo. (1992). *Josei-Supotsu-no-Syakaigaku* (Sociology of Women's Sport). Tokyo: Fumaido Publishing Co.

Foster, John. (1977) *The Influence of Rudolph Laban*. London: Lepus Books.

Guttmann, Allen. (1991) *Women's Sports: A History*. New York: Columbia University Press.

Hanna, Judith Lynn. (1988) *Dance, Sex and Gender: Sign of Identity, Dominance, Defiance and Desire*. Chicago and London: University of Chicago Press.

Hargreaves, Jennifer. (1994) *Sporting Females: Critical Issues in the History and Sociology of Women's Sports*. London and New York: Routledge.

Harumi, Koshimizu, ed. (1981) *Kindai-Nihon-Joshi-Taiikushi* (Modern Japanese History of Women's Physical Education). Tokyo: Sports and Physical Education Publishing Co.

Hitomi, Kinue. (1929) *Supaiku-no-Ato* (Traces of Her Spikes). Tokyo: Heibonsha.

Inokuchi, Akuri. (1906) *Taiiku-no-Riron-Oyobi-Jissai* (Theory and Practice of Physical Education). Tokyo: Kokko.

Kaminuma, Hachiro. (1959) *Kindai-Nihon-Joshi-Taiikushi-Josetu* (Introduction to Japanese History of Women's Physical Education). Tokyo: Fumaido Publishing Co.

Mainichi-communications, ed. (1986) *Encyclopedia of the Meiji-era's News*, vols. 1–3. Tokyo: Mainichi-communications.

Naruse, Jinzo. ([1896] 1983) *Joshi-Kyoiku* (Women's Education). Reprint, Tokyo: Nihontosho Center Co.

JOYCE, JOAN

(1940–)

U.S. FAST-PITCH SOFTBALL PLAYER

The best fast-pitch softball pitcher of all time, Joan Joyce exploited a slingshot technique to deliver a variety of pitches, including screwballs, rises, drops, curves, and knuckleballs, often at speeds in excess of 160 kilometers (100 miles) per hour. She led her teams to thirteen national amateur, one international amateur, and four professional championship titles.

Joan Joyce. (AP Photos)

Joyce was born on 1 August 1940 in Waterbury, Connecticut, where, with the encouragement of her parents, she was able to develop her sport interest. When she was fourteen, she joined the Brakettes, a women's softball team sponsored by the Raybestos Company. Her pitching debut took place during 1957 when she was moved from first base to the mound to replace the legendary Bertha Tickey who was injured. Joyce pitched a no-hitter and won the Amateur Softball Association (ASA) National Championship for the Brakettes.

Joyce played most of her softball with the Brakettes, leading them to twelve national titles. During a three-year stint in the mid-1960s with the Orange Lionettes in California, she added another national title to the tally. Her international career was sponsored by the ASA, which nominated the national champion to represent the United States at the World Championships conducted by the International Softball Federation. Fittingly, she led the United States to its first victory. The Raybestos Brakettes won the third world championship on their home diamond at Stratford, Connecticut.

In a ten-minute exhibition against American Baseball Hall of Fame legend Ted Williams, she allowed only one base hit and one foul from forty pitches. With such speed and variety, Joyce accumulated an outstanding set of personal statistics, including a 507–33 win-loss record and a winning percentage of .904, 105 no-hitters, 33 perfect games, and the most strike-outs in a game (40 in 19 innings in the pre-tie-breaker era). In addition, she had a very competitive lifetime batting average of .327.

Joyce shared her love and knowledge of softball. In 1974 she coached Brooklyn College to eight consecutive victories after the team won only two of its first seven games. With John Anquillare she coauthored *Winning Softball* (1975). An appearance on a television sports comedy show led to a meeting with other prominent sportswomen including Billie Jean King, with whom she established the International Women's Professional Softball Association in 1976, which ended her amateur career. The professional association lasted only four years, with Joyce's team, the Connecticut Falcons, taking all four league titles. As a pro, Joyce had an amazing record: 101 victories, 15 losses, 34 no-hitters, and 8 perfect games.

Since softball was not the only sport at which Joyce excelled, she has been compared to Mildred "Babe" Didrikson. Three months after taking up ten-pin bowling, Joyce had a 180 average. While she was a student in California, she was selected for the national basketball team. And at the age of thirty-seven (when many golfer's careers are ending), she lowered her golf handicap enough to qualify for the Ladies' Professional Golf Association (LPGA) tour. She was a consistent, if not a big, winner, but did not perform especially well in the major tournaments. She was also a teaching golf pro in Florida. The ASA recognized her outstanding achievements and inducted her into the National Softball Hall of Fame in 1983.

Lynn Embrey

Bibliography

Boutilier, Mary A., and Lucinda SanGiovanni. (1983) *The Sporting Woman.* Champaign, IL: Human Kinetics.

Condon, Robert J. (1991) *Great Women Athletes of the Twentieth Century.* Jefferson, NC: McFarland.

Dickson, Paul. (1994) *The Worth Book of Softball: A Celebration of America's True National Pastime.* New York: Facts on File.

Hollander, Phyllis. (1978) *100 Greatest Women in Sports.* New York: Grossett & Dunlap.

Joyce, Joan, and John Anquillare. (1975) *Winning Softball.* Chicago: Henry Regnery.

JOY, NANCY

(1915–1997)

ENGLISH CRICKETER, AUTHOR, AND SCHOLAR

Nancy Joy was well known in cricket circles as the author of *Maiden Over: A Short History of Women's Cricket and a Diary of the 1948–49 Test Tour to Australia.* Born on 22 July 1915, Joy grew up in a cricket-loving family. Her father, F. D. H. Joy was a school headmaster and the family home, Bentley, was in Hampshire. She was educated at Downe House, Newbury, and then Somerville College, Oxford, where she achieved second-class honors in philosophy, politics, and economics.

At Oxford, Joy was a cricket blue (an award offered to someone who represents his or her university in sport) and after World War II, vice-captained the South (England) cricket team and also played for Middlesex. Her reputation as a solid, reliable batswoman resulted in her being selected for the English team that toured Australia and New Zealand in 1948–1949. Although she did not play in any of the Tests (a match between two countries lasting five days for men, four for women), her average for the tour was a respectable thirty runs and her highest score was ninety-one runs.

On her return, Joy wrote *Maiden Over.* Although it was not the first book on women's cricket, it was considered significant in that it was the first book about women actively playing, and it proved entertaining and informative. The "over" in the title is the term used for the set of six balls delivered by the bowler from one end of the pitch. A "maiden over" occurs when no runs are scored during that set of six. Published in 1950 and reprinted in 1996, the book generated new interest in the women's game.

Described by her friend and colleague Netta Rheinberg (team manager for the 1948–1949 tour and coauthor of *Fair Play* with English captain Rachael Heyhoe-Flint) as a woman of substance, Joy contributed to the game in many other ways. She

The cover of Nancy Joy's history of women's cricket. (Amanda Weaver)

served as Honorary Assistant Secretary to the Women's Cricket Association and was the first chairman of the press and publicity subcommittee. She also assisted the Hampshire women's cricket club with coaching and sponsorship. In 1950, she became Rheinberg's editorial partner in the takeover from Marjorie Pollard of the magazine *Women's Cricket* and wrote many of its editorials over the following four years.

Joy was a woman of strong personality and high intellect and her interests extended beyond sport. While she continued to follow the game and attend matches, she branched out in other areas. After working for a time as a personnel officer with J. Lyons and Co., she took up a position with Southampton University where she was given a doctorate in literature and where she pursued research in the fields of mental health, un-

employment, and industrial therapy. She also became increasingly interested in theology and in 1988 her *Letters to An Atheist* was published. She became a lay reader in the diocese of Winchester and wrote her third book, *Commit Yourself*, in 1993.

Another passion was archaeology. Joy traveled to areas such as the Middle East on many occasions. In middle age, she met and married George Wansbrough. They had no children and, suffering from poor health, he died early in the marriage. Joy died suddenly in her home at Winchester, aged eighty-two. Through *Maiden Over*, she left a lasting legacy to women's sport in a time when women, especially cricketers, struggled for recognition and support.

Amanda Weaver

Bibliography

Hayhoe-Flint, Rachael, and Netta Rheinberg. (1976) *Fair Play, The Story of Women's Cricket.* Sydney, Australia: Angus and Robertson.

Joy, Nancy. (1950) *Maiden Over, A Short History of Women's Cricket and a Diary of the 1948–49 Test Tour to Australia.* London: Sporting Handbooks Limited.

JOYNER-KERSEE, JACKIE

(1962–)

U.S. TRACK AND FIELD ATHLETE

Many experts regard Jacqueline Joyner-Kersee as the greatest female athlete of all time because of her success in multiple Olympic events, including the grueling two-day heptathlon. She set several heptathlon world records and won three Olympic gold medals, one silver medal, and two bronze medals in track and field. Her grandmother had predicted her greatness at birth, deliberately naming her after the wife of then-President John Kennedy. "Someday," she declared, "this girl will be the first lady of something."

Jackie Joyner-Kersee competes in the high jump at one of the seven events in the heptathlon at the 1990 Goodwill Games. (Karl Weatherly)

Joyner-Kersee was born on 3 March 1962, one of four children in a poor neighborhood in East St. Louis, Illinois. Her father was a construction and railroad worker and her mother a practical nurse. With encouragement from her family, Joyner-Kersee worked hard in school and excelled in athletics. In addition to studying modern dance at a neighborhood recreation center, she also participated in a track program. Despite coping with asthma, she became a proficient runner and jumper by the time she was a teenager. Aware of her abilities in many different track events, a coach suggested that she train for the five-event pentathlon. When she was told that this event offered the best Olympic opportunities for women, she began training for the competition, which then included the 80-meter hurdles, the shot put, the high jump, the long jump, and the 200-meter run. (The 100-meter hurdles later replaced the 80-meter event, and eventually the 200-meter run became the 800-meter.)

In addition to winning the National Junior pentathlon title for four years in a row (between the ages of fourteen through seventeen), Joyner-Kersee also played on her high school basketball and volleyball teams, and excelled at these sports too. She was ranked as the best female basketball player in the state.

Her high grades (she graduated tenth in her class) and her sports achievements earned her a basketball scholarship to the University of California at Los Angeles (UCLA), where she studied communications and history and earned a history degree in 1985. She played on the university's basketball team and in her senior year she was named an all-American. Here, too, the track and field coach, Bob Kersee (who later became her husband) urged her to train in several track and field events, rather than in any single event.

In 1984, a year after she represented the United States at the world championships in Finland, she competed in the heptathlon in the Los Angeles Olympics. This event replaced the pentathlon, and it contained seven events over two days; the 200-meter sprint had been reinstated and the javelin throw added. Although a pulled muscle hampered her efforts, Joyner-Kersee led the event for the first six events, and if she had jumped 3 centimeters further in the long jump or shaved .33 seconds off her 800-meter run, she would have won the gold medal.

Free of injury, Joyner-Kersee shattered the world heptathlon record in 1986, earning 7,148 points in the Goodwill Games, held in Moscow. Joyner-Kersee was the first woman to score over 7,000 points and, she was also the first American woman to set a world record in the event. That same year, she received the Sullivan Award, the nation's highest honor for an amateur athlete. In 1987, the Associated Press named her the Athlete of the Year, and in 1986 and 1987 she was the recipient of the Jesse Owens Award, becoming the first athlete to win this award two times.

In 1987, she won the heptathlon and the long jump at the national championships, and she tied a world record in the Pan-American Games with her jump of 24 feet 5 inches. Winning both events again at the World Track and Field Competitions in Rome, she earned 4,256 heptathlon points the first day, the highest first-day total ever achieved.

In 1988, she set the American record for the long jump and the 60-meter hurdles, and she tied the 100-meter hurdles record of 12.61 seconds. During the 1988 Olympics in Seoul, South Korea, she twisted her knee in the long jump, but set another Olympic record with her jump the following day. With a jump of 23 feet 10 inches, she earned a gold medal in that event. Her Olympic record 7,291 points in the heptathlon earned her another gold.

At the 1992 Olympic Games in Barcelona she again won the gold medal in the heptathlon, and also won a bronze medal in the long jump. Four years later, at the Atlanta Olympics, after withdrawing from the heptathlon competition because of an injury, Joyner-Kersee settled for a bronze medal in the long jump. She is the only woman to have won multi-event titles at two Olympics, and no other man or woman has done so at three Olympics.

Although her Olympic career had come to a close, the awards did not cease. In 1992, the Women's Sports Foundation named her as the Amateur Athlete of the Year, and she was the only athlete to have garnered this title three times. The International Amateur Athletic Federation (IAAF) named her the Female Athlete of the Year in 1994.

Using her athletic achievements and the subsequent media exposure, Joyner-Kersee committed herself to being a role model for young women. Her sense of dedication, discipline, and sportsmanship had been evident throughout her years of competition, and she strove to bring these values to minority women. The community in which she grew up remained important to her, and she worked to keep open the recreation center she frequented as a child. She created the Jackie Joyner-Kersee Community Foundation to develop leadership, educational, and recreational programs for urban youths across the country. She is also a popular motivational speaker and the president and founder of a sports marketing business, JJK & Associates.

Kelly Boyer Sagert

Bibliography

Condon, Robert J. (1991) *Great Women Athletes of the Twentieth Century*. Jefferson, NC: McFarland.

Harrington, Geri. (1995) *Jackie Joyner-Kersee*. Broomall, PA: Chelsea House.

Joyner-Kersee, Jackie, and Sonja Steptoe. (1997) *A Kind of Grace: The Autobiography of the World's Greatest Female Athlete*. New York: Warner Books.

Toomey, Bill, and Barry King. (1988) *The Olympic Challenge 1988*. Costa Mesa, CA: HDL Publishing.

Wallechinsky, David. (1988) *The Complete Book of the Olympics*. New York: Penguin Books.

JUDGING *see* Officiating

JUDO AND JUJUTSU

Judo and jujutsu are related Japanese martial arts forms, both of which are based on grappling, holds, and locks. Jujutsu refers to a variety of unarmed martial arts systems that developed under the Japanese samurai, and it continues to be practiced in various forms and in international competition. Judo, which means "gentle way," is a codified sport that was developed at the beginning of the twentieth century.

Judo is best known because of its status as an Olympic sport. The women who won gold medals in judo competitions at the Olympic Games in Atlanta in 1996 and in the jujutsu world championships in Paris in November 1996 received titles strictly equal to those of the men's division. Among these women, Tamura Ryoko of Japan, Marie-Claire Restoux of France, and Yael Arad of Israel are so well known in their own countries that their fame is no longer restricted to the judo world.

By the 1990s, judo and jujutsu had their own national and international organizations. Sports rules allowed everybody to distinguish one from the other. This has not always been the case, particularly in Western countries where even specialist circles were as confused as the general public about the difference between the two practices. Thus, some clarification is in order.

Jujutsu (in the Japanese language *jutsu* refers to technique) as a generic term is used to describe a variety of systems of fighting while minimally armed. The jutsu forms developed from the tenth century onward were meant for use on the battlefield. As the warrior became less important in Japanese society, jujutsu was adapted for the needs of common people. By the nineteenth century jujutsu was designed for urban purposes and thus focused on techniques useful in the altercations that took place in civil life.

In 1882 Kano Jigoro (1860–1938) reshaped traditional martial arts for educational purposes. He originated judo—from the words *ju*, meaning gentle in the sense of to give way or to yield, and *do*, meaning "way"—as a method of physical, intellectual, and spiritual education. Kano called his school the Kodokan Institute. He reoriented the throws, locks, strangles, and other blows of old jujutsu forms, and got rid of all the dangerous gestures. By imposing mutual grappling, he narrowed the distance between opponents and then reduced the violence of the fights. Physical exercise and self-defense situations were considered as means to improve one's health and mind.

SOCIAL AND CULTURAL DIMENSIONS

Various factors can explain the evolution of the place of women in jujutsu and in judo, i.e. the social status of women in society, the way these physical activities were introduced in various countries, and the way they permeated in their host cultures. History tells us about the specificity of these practices, their typical values, and the so-

Sun Fu Ming of China defeats Estela Rodriguez of Cuba in the finals of the women's heavyweight judo events at the 1996 Atlanta Olympic Games. (Dimitri Lundt)

ciability patterns that govern relationships between martial artists. The place occupied by women appears to obey two opposite models. According to different periods and societies, women's attitudes and behavior either seem to be dictated by masculine patterns, or they reveal strong opposition to a minority status and a quest for identity recognition.

Concerning women's participation in judo and jujutsu in modern times, two different periods are obvious. From the beginning of the century to the 1960s, women have had nothing more than a minor role in the world of Japanese martial arts. Apart from rare exceptions, they had little autonomy. From the 1960s onward, a shift occurred in the social attitudes toward women. Modernized sport-oriented judo became a field for women who demanded equal rights and access to judo contests.

During the Meiji Restoration (1868–1912), the evolution of Japanese society in general and its educative system in particular stressed discipline, ethics, courage, and patriotism. were highly valued. *Bushido*, the honor code of the warrior, was the common moral basis of the new army. The general history of martial arts demonstrates how far the practice is linked to dominant images of masculinity and how deeply institutionalized discrimination is anchored. In Japan, the art of fighting was a man's privilege.

DEVELOPMENT OF JUJUTSU IN THE WEST

In the early days of this century, Japanese hand-to-hand techniques became famous worldwide, first during the Boxer Rising (1900). Shortly after, in 1905, the amazing victory of Japan over Russia reinforced the myth of Nipponese invincibility. The efficiency of the Japanese army during hand-to-hand fights puzzled observers, leading to the perception of jujutsu as a "secret weapon." Demonstrations of jujutsu in the West by Nipponese teachers led to the establishment of jujutsu schools. Factors such as the popularity of Japan and the interest in Oriental arts may also be cited to explain the appeal of the Japanese method in Western countries. Early twentieth-century "gurus" of physical culture such as Eugene Sandow shrewdly marketed the martial art form, and jujutsu rapidly caught on in the early twentieth century.

Whether real or imagined, jujutsu's reputation as an efficient fighting method remained its most remarkable characteristic and was to be the dynamo of its development. Because it appealed to the British aristocracy, jujutsu became fashionable among the elite classes of English-speaking countries, the very groups who appropriated sports and physical activities and turned them into symbols of status.

DEVELOPMENT OF WOMEN'S PARTICIPATION IN JUJUTSU

The gap was wide between the image of invincibility displayed by the Japanese army and the daily exercises in jujutsu classes at physical culture schools in London, New York, Chicago, and Paris. Nonetheless, the Japanese method rehabilitated the use of a fair force; used with anatomical precision, this useful and aesthetic strength was more attractive than toughness and rash brutality. It was meant to be used by the weak against the brutal aggressor. It was thus also bound to appeal to the "new woman" fighting for her rights in the early days of the century.

Yet very few women were then involved in martial arts, constrained as they were by the rules of decorum. Physical contact, proper clothing, and respectable attitudes had to be adapted to class behavior. Women's exercise was closely de-fined by medical experts who attempted to ban sporting activities that allegedly jeopardized female reproductive functions. Whereas professional manuals for soldiers or policemen explicitly displayed techniques, those written for women muted violent illustrations and emphasized health and mild physical exercise.

Although rare, there are examples of the emergence and the appeal of jujutsu among women that correspond to achievements of women's autonomy at the turn of the century. During the first wave of feminism, English suffragettes readily exploited the utilitarian side of jujutsu. During street fights with the police, they gave the Japanese method political connotations. In London in 1912, after a demonstration march from Tottenham Court Road to Marble Arch, they scurried to a prearranged refuge in the gymnasium of Mrs. Edith Garrud, the first British woman jujutsu instructor. When the policemen who were chasing demonstrators arrived, they were silently working on the mats in their jujutsu uniforms. In this context, the Japanese method was designed to counteract the myth of female frailty.

The approaches adopted varied with the motives and origins of participants. In a 1912 preface to a French manual entitled *Défendez-vous Mesdames*, the Countess of Abzac begged modern women to acquire strength and freedom. From their male counterparts, Abzac asked for forbearance: "Gentlemen, be reassured! By learning how to defend herself, a woman does not refuse to give of herself."

DEVELOPMENT OF WOMEN'S PARTICIPATION IN JUDO

Kano began to exert every effort to internationalize his method. Traveling and sending his leading disciples abroad, Kano organized the spread of judo. By the late nineteenth century, as Japan modernized and the traditional feudal order declined, judo superseded jujutsu worldwide. With Kano's theories, the Japanese combat method acquired new scientific and educative dimensions. Women were also concerned by these changes but, in traditional martial arts settings, their practice was under the control of a *sensei*, or teacher, devoted to Nipponese conceptions. It was not before the late 1940s that women's judo started to become established and that women gained black-belt status. In the Kodokan archives, the first enrollment of a woman dates back to 1893. However, it was not until November 1926, that a women's section (*joshi bu*) was formally opened. The first woman to be awarded a black belt, in January 1933, was Osaki Katsuko. About 1949, Ruth Gardner from Chicago became the first non-Japanese female student to study at the Kodokan Institute in Tokyo. Miss Collet, from France, was the second.

While developing judo for women, Kano adopted the conception of the feminine body dictated by contemporary science and eugenic theories. Physical exercises for women were designed to make them healthy and attractive, to help them get ready for motherhood. Kano did not want to overtax female bodies. Judo teacher Fukuda Keiko wrote in *Born for the Mat, a Kokokan Textbook for Women, Judo* (1973), that women's practice was similar to men's as far as *randori* (free exercise), *kata* (formal pre-arranged techniques), and lectures were concerned. She adds: "but in *randori* and *kata*, women's physical and emotional differences were considered especially in relationship to future mothers. Professor Kano conferred with experts and judo medical science research personnel to make sure that the course of instruction and methods taught were right for women."

During the early 1960s, Phyllis Harper voiced the leading conception of judo in the United States. In an article entitled "Women's Judo Develops Femininity," she affirmed that "judo should be ladylike and should embody and exemplify the essence of the gentle way." The Nipponese example reinforced the beliefs of those who thought strength was meant for men and aesthetics for women. Most of the time, women were taught by male instructors until some women became judo teachers. It may be assumed that, in the United States, the stress put on femininity, as it appears in Harper's text, may have turned radical feminists away from judo. In Australia in 1968, Patricia Harrington and Betty Huxley founded the first women's judo federation for the purpose of propagating Kodokan *joshi* judo. In California, Fukuda Keiko was very instrumental in teaching a Kodokan-oriented women's judo.

Women had to fight for the right to fight. If, in the early 1950s, female judo players were allowed to compete in some countries (including France and Morocco), these isolated attempts were regu-

larly ignored or ridiculed. Up to then, women took part in classing contests, but were denied the right to compete and obtain official titles. A new orientation appeared in the 1960s when tournaments were organized for female judo players in West Germany, Switzerland, Austria, and later Italy and Great Britain. Judo as a sport no longer was a territory of virility to be conquered. On the contrary, female champions claimed equality as a right. Why should their participation be limited to technical tournaments or kata exhibitions? Female judo players of the 1970s refused to be considered as a minority. Like men, they demanded access to competitive meetings on equal footing.

One of the first pioneers of women's competition, Rusty Kanokogi, defied the rules of separatism. Pushing back her short hair, she entered the 1961 New York State YMCA championships. The world of judo, a traditionally male bastion, blatantly displayed its conservatism and took away the medal she had won. In order to prevent any recurrence of female participation, the word "male" was surreptitiously added to the titles of all future championships. The example of Kanokogi's judo career underscored the constraints imposed on women in the 1960s, by the prejudices of a male-dominated sport.

WOMEN IN MODERN JUDO AND JUJUTSU

Attitudes evolved according to economic and social changes, but also with the number of medals obtained by women in international events. The rise of women's judo reflected the general tendency in the 1970s in favor of women's rights. It also reflected internal changes in the sport itself. The master-disciple relationship and the classing system called for a hierarchy in which the roles of each were clearly defined. The frame of reference was altered by an increasing emphasis on sport. The international culture of sport gradually replaced the Oriental ethic of an educative martial art. Progressively, the egalitarian perspectives of coaches replaced the gender-biased views of the sensei. To these internal evolutions must be added the effects of a consumer society which greatly influenced the motivation of top judo players.

The International Olympic Committee's decision to include judo contests for men in the program of Tokyo's Olympic Games in 1964 set the stage for women's high-level competition. The European Judo Union organized an experimental competition in 1974 in Genoa, Italy. In 1975—the international year of the woman–the first European judo championships for women took place in Munich, Germany. The first world championships in New York in 1980, in which Rusty Kanokogi played a prominent part as an organizer, and the 1982 Paris championships cleared the way for the establishment of women's judo as an exhibition sport at the 1988 Seoul Olympics. It became a full Olympic event at the Barcelona Games in 1992.

In various countries, the number of players has significantly increased since female judo champions obtained world and Olympic titles. Statistics vary, but in 1996 women accounted for roughly 20 percent of most color belts and about 10 percent of black belts. There were also many female referees in both men's and women's tournaments. In June 1998 the International Judo Federation invited thirty-four female referees from around the world to Germany for the first-ever referee symposium for women.

The statues of some female judo players stand next to the best soccer players in the world at Madame Tussaud's in London and in the Paris Wax Museum. One century after Mrs. Garrud and the Countess d'Abzac, the world and Olympic titles of Ingrid Berghams from Belgium, Cecile Nowak from France, and Driulis Gonzales from Cuba underscored the equality of male and female judo players. This evolution was possible, mostly, because of pioneers who had the courage to fight traditions. They initiated a chain reaction that compelled international judo to revise its models.

The modernization of Kano's method sparked the rebirth of jujutsu. As sport-oriented judo abandoned its utilitarian dimension, modern jujutsu adapted to the needs of society to fill the gap. Led by Italy, jujutsu was organized on an international basis. An International Jujutsu Federation was founded, and in 1986 the first World Cup of jujutsu was held. The example of modern judo was followed and women were immediately allowed to take part in contests in the fighting system (free combat) or in the duo-system (technical exhibition).

Finally, it must be said that the place occupied by women in the 1990s was still linked to internal factors, in particular, individual commitments

and dependencies upon Japanese traditional methods. As a proof of cultural reluctance, the first Japanese national championships for women were not held until 1978. The real causes of this development were numerous. Women's desire to have access to equal treatment joined the interests of judo leaders who were eager to manage female victories and new membership. Thus, the changes in women's participation occurred within the tensions that characterized a method of education marked both by its original culture and by the culture of modern international sports.

Michel Brousse

Bibliography

Amateur Athletic Union. (1963) *1963 Official AAU Judo Handbook*. New York, AAU.

Atkinson, Linda. (1983) *Women in the Martial Arts: A New Spirit Rising*. New York, Dodd, Mead & Co.

Brousse, Michel. (1996) *Le Judo, son Histoire, ses Succès*. Paris, Liber.

Cherpillod, Armand. (1907) *Meine Selbsthilfe, Dschiu-Dschitsu für Damen*. Neuenburg, Attinger.

Corcoran, John, and Emil Farkas. (1988) *Martial Arts, Traditions, History, People*. New York, Gallery Books.

Draeger, Donn F. (1983) *The Martial Arts and Ways of Japan*. New York, Weatherhill.

Fukuda, Keiko. (1973) *Born for the Mat, a Kodokan Textbook for Women, Judo*. San Francisco, Private edition.

Gardner, Ruth B. (1971) *Judo for the Gentle Woman*. Rutland, VT: Charles E. Tuttle Co.

Hancock, H. Irving. (1906) *Le Jiu-Jitsu et la Femme: Entraînement Physique au Féminin* (translation of *Physical Training for Women by Japanese Methods* [1904]). Paris, Berger-Levrault.

Harrington, Patricia. (1992) *Judo, a Pictorial Manual*. Rutland, VT: Charles Tuttle Co.

Kodokan. (1961) *Judo by the Kodokan*. Osaka, Nunoi Shobo Co.

Pherdac, Charles. (1912) *Défendez-vous Mesdames, Manuel de Défense Féminine*. Paris, Rueff.

Smith, Robert. (1958) *A Complete Guide to Judo*. Tokyo, Charles E. Tuttle Co.

Watts, Emily. (1906) *The Fine Art of Jiu-Jitsu*. London: William Heinemann.

K

KALLIO, ELIN

(1859–1927)

FINNISH TEACHER AND FOUNDER OF GYMNASTICS MOVEMENT

Elin Kallio had a distinguished career as a teacher of gymnastics, but she is best remembered for her other lifework as the founder and developer of the independent women's gymnastics movement in Finland. Born Elin Waenerberg into the family of a high-ranking official, she was educated at a school for girls and acquired her physical educator's training in 1875 and 1876 at the only institute in the country that trained female gymnastics teachers.

In 1876, in Helsinki, she and her cousin founded the first women's gymnastics club in a Nordic nation. From 1879 to 1881, she studied for a degree at the Swedish Royal Gymnastic Central Institute in Stockholm. From 1884 to 1926, Kallio taught at the Finnish-language girls' school in Helsinki, which from 1886 also served as a preparatory school for teachers. Even with her health failing in the last year of her life, she continued teaching junior classes.

The Gymnastic Institute of the University of Helsinki was opened for women in 1894. Kallio taught there for a year, and then quit on grounds of principle. For lack of a university program in Finland, Kallio and many other female gymnastics teachers had studied for their degrees in Stockholm and became advocates of the Swedish gymnastic system—and thus suspect to the Finnish men's gymnastic establishment. In response to this attitude, Kallio and others established an independent Finnish Women's Gymnastic Federation in 1896. Henceforth, Finnish women would decide independently the direction of their gymnastic movement. Kallio served as the president of the federation until 1917.

Elin Kallio. (S VoLi, Helsinki)

Her principal field of responsibility was the education of gymnastics instructors. Federation courses for instructors began in 1907, and by 1909 were organized into a special institute. The Federation's primary goal was to train instructors for the women's sections of workers' sports clubs and sports clubs in rural regions. "Mama Kallio" was the heart and soul of these courses.

Kallio's writing was as innovative as her teaching and organizational work. Her first book *Gymnastiktabeller* (Gymnastic Programs) was published in 1886. *Naisvoimistelun käsikirja* (Handbook of Women's Gymnastics) was published in 1901 and later in several new editions. In 1903, she wrote *Kansan lasten leikkikirja*, a collection on children's games to be used by the temperance movement. *Komentoharjoituksia* (Exercises in Commanding), published in 1909, was a handbook for her course for instructors.

Kallio overcame many hurdles by sheer strength of personality. In her pioneering work for women's gymnastics she had to beg for permits and licenses, curry the favor of bank directors, and constantly employ her sharp pen and tongue in her fight against the male authorities. Widowed after a marriage of ten years, with no children, she dedicated the rest of her life to her work. As Finland entered the twenty-first century, an independent women's gymnastic movement of tens of thousands of members bore witness to the success of Mama Kallio's lifework.

Leena Laine

Bibliography

Kurvinen, Heli. (1959) "Elin Kallio, Suomen Naisvoimistelun Äiti." *Suomen Naisten Liikuntakasvatusliiton Julkaisu no. 34.* Helsinki: SNLL.

Lewis, Madalynne, S. (1970) "A Philosophy of Finnish Women´s Physical Education as Represented in Selected Writings of Elin Kallio, Elli Björkstén and Hilma Jalkanen." Ph.D. diss., University of Southern California.

KARATE

Karate is a weapon-less martial art and combat sport whose modern form was developed in twentieth-century Japan. Though many believe that karate is practiced mainly for self-defense—and know it chiefly through dramatic displays such as smashing bricks or boards—few realize that it takes years of practice to master karate techniques well enough to be able to defend oneself from serious physical threat. Although karate was developed as a means of self-defense by people who were forbidden to carry weapons by their conquerors, it has evolved into a sport that women and men of all ages practice for physical, mental, and spiritual fulfillment. Karate in its many forms is one of the most widely practiced of the martial arts.

HISTORY

Karate was originally developed on Okinawa, a small island situated near China and Japan, which throughout much of its history had been the target of invaders. These invaders, who included the Japanese, frequently confiscated and banned the use of weapons by native Okinawans. The Okinawans therefore developed a system of fighting using their arms and legs, as well as everyday farm tools. Thus was born karate, or "empty handed" fighting. Women and men would practice their skills alone in the forests or fields using sickles or bamboo polls. Eventually, even a harmless-looking farm woman reaping her crops became a force to contend with.

By the mid-nineteenth century, when the Japanese assimilation of Okinawa was complete, martial arts and weapons were again permitted on the island. The Japanese were impressed by what they saw of the Okinawan empty-handed fighting techniques, known *Okinawa-te*, and it soon spread throughout Japan under its new name: *karate-jutsu*. In the twentieth century, when Gichin Funakoshi (1868–1957), a karate instructor from Okinawa, taught Okinawa-te in Japan, it acquired the name *karate*. It was in Japan that Funakoshi refined the art, borrowing influences from judo and removing the more violent moves.

Sport karate became increasingly popular and widespread in the 1940s and early 1950s, when American and British servicemen stationed in East Asia took it up, then brought it back to their countries. Throughout the 1950s and 1960s, attempts were made to consolidate the many styles of karate that had emerged. Despite the different styles, and the rivalries that grew among karate schools, sport karate grew in popularity, with tournaments drawing karate practitioners from around the world. It was not until the mid-1960s that women began to compete in tournaments in the United States.

Little information is available concerning the early period of women's involvement in American sport karate. The scarcity of information stems from the lack of attention given to the various stages of development in women's karate, as well as from the low level of interest generated among its members. Tournament promoters also showed little interest because the profits from the small number of entrants rarely paid the costs of the trophies.

DEFINING A SPORT BY ITS GOALS

Like other martial arts, karate can be understood two ways: in its historical tradition and as a modern sport. The basic distinction between traditional karate and the modern sport karate is the concept of competition. In traditional karate, the competition is with oneself and the goal of competition with opponents is to learn and improve. In modern karate, the goal of competition with opponents is to win matches and tournaments. The goal is winning, which in traditional karate is not a goal at all.

Still, the 1960s and 1970s were not without their determined female karate practitioners, including Ruby Paglinawan, who in 1964 fought three male opponents in a tournament, and Janet Walgren, who garnered victories from coast to coast. In 1973, a few women who had achieved black-belt status were employed as chief referees for female competition at various events around the country.

While competition was originally limited primarily to men, today women compete in sparring and kata tournaments. There are even some mixed kata competitions, and occasionally mixed sparring between men and women.

RULES AND PLAY

Unlike *aikido*, *judo*, and *jujutsu*, karate is not a grappling art. Students learn to deliver powerful, economical kicks and strikes, and to block oncoming attacks using their arms and legs. The emphasis is on developing strong, perfect, accurate techniques—an element of the art that grew out of the need to stop an attacker with a single blow.

But karate emphasizes more than just simple, straightforward blows. It is a complex system of techniques that use just about every part of the body. Choosing what part of the hand with which to throw a simple strike, for example, becomes an exercise in and of itself. Should you strike your opponent with the knuckle of your middle finger? The tips of your forefinger and middle finger? The side of your hand? The area between your thumb and index finger? Maybe you should forget striking with your hand, and opt for the top of your wrist.

Karate runs the gamut from full-force fighting to noncombative styles that focus on traditional forms and techniques. It can be aggressive and loud, characterized by hard, explosive bursts of techniques, combined with deep abdominal shouts. And it can be soft, as demonstrated through its forms, which are simply prearranged combinations of strikes, blocks, and kicks.

There are three types of training. In full-contact karate, well-padded students strike and kick each other with full force. A milder version of full-contact karate involves training students to control their techniques to the point where a strike or kick either stops just short of hitting the opponent or taps the opponent lightly. The third type of training involves teaching students traditional forms and techniques.

TECHNIQUES

As in all martial arts, balance is essential, and starts with the stance. Many karate stances distribute weight evenly, as in the traditional "sumo" stance in which the feet are spread wide and the knees are bent. Other stances, including the "cat" stance, place greater weight on the back leg, allowing the front leg ample opportunity to strike out. Then there are stances that favor the weight on the front leg to allow the student to kick straight out with the back leg.

But legs are not just for kicking; they are just as useful for jamming or sweeping to the side an opponent's attacking leg. As with hand techniques, foot techniques use all parts of the leg, including the ball of the foot, side edge of the foot, heel, instep, sole, toes, and the knee.

Basic blocks are performed to defend against punches aimed at the head, midsection, or lower body. In blocking a punch, new students generally use their hand or forearm. Later, they will extend their repertoire of blocks to incorporate both arms, then their feet and legs.

Women are usually surprised that they do not require tremendous upper body strength to throw

Sara Keays of Bath defends herself against the "roundhouse kick" of opponent Jane Lowe of Mansfield during a warm up at the European Karate Championships in 1970. (Hulton-Deutsch Collection/Corbis)

a powerful punch. In karate, much of that strength comes from the hips. A punch begins at the hip, then shoots forward creating a whiplash affect that forces the arm to project itself straight out. More muscular individuals often throw ineffective punches because of their bulky upper body and their tight hips.

Just as punches are generally linear, strikes are usually circular. They can be delivered with the elbow or the knee, as well as the back of the fist, bottom of the fist, side edge of the hand, and ridge part of the hand. When a strike or a punch is thrown properly, the student can hear her uniform snap, signaling that the technique had ample power and speed.

Karate kicks are almost tailor-made for women. As with punches and strikes, kicks begin in the hips. This, combined with most women's inherent flexibility, makes for high, powerful kicks that are effective against even a large opponent.

STYLES

Karate contains a variety of styles distinguishable only by minor differences. Some styles advocate low, deep traditional stances that are aesthetically pleasing, but of little practical value when fight-ing; other styles utilize high, mobile stances that are ideal for sparring but are not as dramatic. Some styles emphasize soft moves designed to simply block an attack. Other "hard" styles utilize blocks that not only stop a strike but injure the attacking limb as well.

Many styles incorporate low and high stances, as well as hard and soft moves. One such style is *Goju-ryu*, an Okinawan style that means "hard-soft." Other popular Okinawan styles of karate are *Isshin-ryu*, *Shorin-ryu*, and *Uechi-ryu*. Goju-ryu combines hard and soft moves with circular techniques and deep abdominal breathing to create a style that is symmetrical and graceful, yet powerful and well-suited for fighting. Fast, light moves typify Shorin-ryu. To keep this quick pace, the Shorin student uses high stances and prefers hand techniques over kicks. When she does throw a kick, it is usually below the opponent's waist. Isshin-ryu combines elements of Shorin-ryu and Goju-ryu to create a street-smart fighting art. Its notable features include unique body shifting movements, high stances, and no-nonsense techniques, including below-the-waist kicks, and snap punches and kicks. For aggressive karate students, Uechi-ryu offers tough conditioning methods to make the body impervious to kicks and punches. In sparring, this style emphasizes strong grabbing techniques, coupled with takedowns, as well as hard kicks to the legs and midsection.

Japanese karate styles include a version of Okinawan Goju-ryu that goes by the same name. Similar to the Okinawan version, Japanese Goju-ryu emphasizes dramatic breathing methods, timing, and speed as well as quick continuous punches and strikes. *Shito-ryu* is a fairly hard style but does incorporate soft techniques borrowed from Goju-ryu. The style also stresses the art of weaponry. *Shotokan* emphasizes low, deep stances for balance as well as direct linear attacks. Shotokan fighters are recognized by their low kicks, foot sweeps, low stances, and hip power—a trademark of Japanese karate in general and Shotokan karate in particular. *Wado-ryu* rejects hard physical conditioning in favor of spiritual development. Students still learn all the basics—punches, kicks, blocks, and strikes—as well as sparring and forms, but emphasis is on body shifting, and thus avoiding the full brunt of an attack.

CONCLUSION

Since karate schools are not licensed, there are no hard and firm statistics on the number of men and women karate practitioners. However, there does appear to be a trend toward female-only martial arts schools in which teaching methods are tailored to the concerns of women.

Karate is currently not an Olympic sport. It became an international medal sport for the first time, however, at the 1999 Pan-American Games in Winnipeg, Canada, where there was a women's division.

Monica McCabe Cardoza

Bibliography

Black Belt Magazine. (1999) North Hollywood, CA: Rainbow Publications.

Corcoran, John, and Emil Farkas. (1983) *Martial Arts: Traditions, History, People.* New York: Gallery Books.

Higaonna, Morio. (1985) *Traditional Karatedo: Fundamental Techniques.* Tokyo: Minato Research and Publishing Co.

McCabe Cardoza, Monica. (1996) *A Woman's Guide to Martial Arts: How to Choose a Discipline and Get Started.* New York: Overlook Press.

Ribner, Susan, and Richard Chin. (1978) *The Martial Arts.* New York: Harper & Row.

Yamaguchi, Gosei. (1972) *The Fundamentals of Goju-Ryu Karate.* Burbank, CA.: Ohara Publications.

Information was also provided by the National Women's Martial Arts Federation (Detroit) and the USA National Karate-do Federation (Seattle).

KELETI, ÁGNES

(1921–)

HUNGARIAN GYMNAST

With ten Olympic gold medals, Ágnes Keleti was Hungary's greatest gymnast. Her athletic career was played out in pre- and post-World War II Europe, and it was affected by the Nazi persecution of Jews and Cold War politics.

Keleti was born Ágnes Klein in Budapest on 9 June 1921. She first became interested in gym-

Ágnes Keleti performing on the balance beam. (Katalik Szikora)

nastics shortly before World War II, and her training began at the Jewish VAC Club of Budapest. She quickly became a top gymnast, but her career was interrupted by World War II. During the war, her father was removed to Auschwitz, where he was killed by the Nazis. Keleti and the rest of her family survived by finding refuge in a "Swedish House" administered by Swedish diplomat Raoul Wallenberg, who became famous after the war for his role in assisting Jews to avoid deportation to Nazi concentration camps.

After World War II, Keleti returned to gymnastics and won her first Hungarian championship in 1946, on the uneven parallel bars. In 1947, she dominated the Central European Gymnastics Championships. She initially earned her living as a fur worker, but she was later a demonstrator at the Faculty of Gymnastics of the Budapest School for Physical Culture. Keleti was also an accomplished musician and played the cello professionally.

After serving as an alternate in 1948, Keleti competed in both the 1952 and 1956 Olympic Games, where she won 10 medals, including five gold. Keleti won four medals at the 1952 Olympics in Helsinki, including an individual gold in the floor exercises. At the 1954 World Gymnastics Championships, she won the uneven parallel bars, for her only individual world title, and also was on the winning Hungarian team in the team portable apparatus event.

Her greatest gymnastics effort came at the 1956 Melbourne Olympics when she won six medals, including four gold. In the individual apparatus finals, she won the balance beam, floor exercises, and the uneven parallel bars. A poor performance in the horse vault, where she finished twenty-third, cost her the all-around individual gold, as she finished second to the Soviet Union's Larisa Latynina. Keleti also won gold as part of the Hungarian team in the portable apparatus event.

Politics again interceded in her career. On 4 November 1956, Soviet tanks entered Budapest to quell an uprising there. Keleti defected when she was in Melbourne. She stayed in Australia and then settled in Israel, where she taught physical education at the Orde Wingate Institute and later became the national women's gymnastics coach.

Bill Mallon

Bibliography

Kamper, Erich, and Bill Mallon. (1992) *The Golden Book of the Olympic Games*. Milan: Vallardi & Associati.

Matthews, Peter, Ian Buchanan, and Bill Mallon. (1993) *The Guinness International Who's Who of Sport*. London: Guinness.

Mezö, Ferenc. (1955) *Golden Book of Hungarian Olympic Champions*. Budapest: Sport lap—És Könyvkiadö.

Postal, Bernard, Jesse Silver, and Roy Silver. (1955) *Encyclopedia of Jews in Sports*. New York: Bloch.

KENDO

Kendo is a Japanese martial art in which attack and parrying exercises are carried out with bamboo practice swords called *shinai* while the com-

batants wear heavy protective gear and helmets. The word "kendo" means literally "The Way of the Sword." In modern times, the traditional fighting systems or schools (*ryuu*) of Japanese swordsmanship (*kenjutsu*) have been developed into uniform systems of practice; some, including kendo, have taken on aspects of the organized form of modern sports. Kendo nonetheless continues to hold to its traditional focus on spiritual and character development through the practice. Kendo is one of the most popular sports in Japan and has spread to all parts of the world. Since the first women's kendo championship in 1962, women have developed a strong presence in international kendo and compete at the highest levels.

HISTORY

Modern martial arts sports in Japan such as kendo were a product of the martial culture that emerged in Japan as a result of the long period of civil war from 1467 to 1568. The warfare ended with the unification of Japan under the rule of the feudal lord Ieyasu Tokugawa, and the nation entered a long period of internal peace. During this period, the martial arts that had been useful in war were transformed into peacetime activities, and different systems of practice were developed. Various types of wooden and bamboo practice swords and protective armor were developed; due to differences in ideology and technique, there was much variation in style. With peace, the military class was free to engage in other pursuits in addition to swordsmanship, and self-study through Buddhism, Confucianism, and Shintoism were combined with training in the martial arts (generally called *budo*, or the martial way). Thus training in swordsmanship now had the dual purpose of physical and spiritual development. In the following Meiji period (1868–1912), interest in traditional budo, kenjutsu, and the other budo revived.

In 1879, the Tokyo Metropolitan Police (TMP) cited the usefulness of kenjutsu in suppressing insurrection. The TMP was particularly significant in the development of modern kendo: to create a curriculum of instruction, the TMP drew upon the various ryuu and developed a uniform system of compulsory forms, or *kata*. After the TMP had instituted its system, a new group, the Dai Nippon

Butokukai, was formed in 1895. This group expanded on the kata, instituted ranks, and by 1906 created a school for martial arts teachers. By 1908, the Bujutsu Semmon Gakko (martial arts specialty school) was able to receive accreditation by the Ministry of Education. Kendo was added as an elective to the school curriculum in 1911, becoming a regular subject in 1917. Kendo training continued in the public education curriculum until Japan's surrender, ending World War II. A ban on martial activities, implemented by the American occupation authorities, ended in 1952, and kendo once again appeared as a core subject in the national education curriculum. This time, girls' kendo was also included.

The first all-Japan women's kendo championship was held in 1962. In 1994, in the ninth world Kendo championships in Paris, women's demonstration matches were held, and in the tenth of this series held in Kyoto in 1997, a women's championship was conducted alongside the men's tournament.

A well-recognized activity in Japan, kendo also enjoys great popularity internationally. There are kendo clubs all over the world. Since the advent of the modern era the participation of women in kendo has increased steadily, and women have developed a significant presence in what once was a male-dominated activity. In the late 1990s, seven women in Japan held the high rank of seventh *dan* (seventh-degree "black belt" equivalent rank). Women serve as team members, teachers, and club organizational managers in all strata of the kendo community. Kendo activities are not limited to separated practice (*keiko*) and competitions (*taikai*), but rather, keiko often combines men, women, and sometimes children, together in a single practice.

RULES AND PLAY

The practice of kendo incorporates a bamboo practice sword (*shinai*, or literally, bamboo sword) and protective armor (collectively termed *bogu*; literally, protective equipment). The development and use of this equipment cannot be underestimated in the development of modern kendo, as it has enabled unrestricted, full-contact combat. For safety purposes, set target areas are identified within the limits of the protective armor. Also, by defining exact targets, precise ex-

Kendo. (Jerome Prevost; TempSport/Corbis)

ecution of techniques, a thoughtful approach to the opponent, and skillful sword handling are developed.

Traditional dress consisting of a tunic (*keiko-gi*), fashioned after the protective jacket of an Edo period (1603–1868) fireman's coat, and the traditional loose, bloused trousers (*hakama*) is still the customary outfit of both men and women. For the study and demonstration of the kata, wooden or steel swords are utilized. Although modern materials and manufacturing techniques have been implemented in some cases, the equipment in kendo remains faithful to those traditional accoutrements that have been developed since ancient times.

Kendo techniques (*waza*) are executed by swinging the shinai in an arcing motion or by thrusting with correct body posture in coordination with body movement (*tai-sabaki*), a foot strike (*fumi-komi*), and spirit, which is manifest in the form of a sharp call when striking (*ki-ai*). This concept is distilled into the phrase "*Ki-Ken-Tai-Ichi*," literally, "spirit, sword, and body, as one." The culmination of these elements in one decisive blow to the opponent's target area (*datotsu-bui*) results in a successful strike (*yuko-datotsu*). The datotsu-bui are identified as the crown of the helmet (*men*), the right and left arm gauntlets above the wrists (*kote*), the right and left side of the torso armor (*doh*), and a thrust to the throat armor plate at the base of the helmet's chin area (*tsuki*). The various techniques fall into two distinct groups: preemptive attacks (*shikake-waza*) and attacks based on the opponent's advance (*oji-kaeshi-waza*).

In kendo matches (*shiai*), two opponents are judged by three referees (*shimpan*) on a court measuring approximately 9 × 11 meters. The match is timed, the length varying with the age of the contestants and the level of competition. Regulation matches for adult championships are five minutes long. The shimpan declare strikes as valid by raising flags that correspond to the colored markers worn by the players. Matches are won (*shobu-ari*) when a player successfully executes two yuko-datotsu or if one yuko-datotsu has been scored when the time period is over. Ties may be left unsettled (*hikiwake*) or may be resolved by an extension (*enchou*) of time. Various forms of tournaments are conducted including individual, team, and "winner-stays" type arrangements. Husband and wife tournaments, family team tournaments, and mother-and-child competitions as well enjoy great popularity. Consistent with kendo's origins, matches follow a pattern of formal etiquette that is observed by all involved. Salutations and mutual respect are fundamental.

Although there is no exclusivity in the world of kendo, many clubs and regional organizations choose to gain entry to a national kendo federation for support and to be able to conduct tournaments and activities at the national level. These national federations can, in turn, apply for membership to the International Kendo Federation. Membership to this organization is required for participation in the world championships and other international activities of the federation.

SUMMARY

The Way of the Sword has, in modern times, been transformed from a life-taking skill to a healthy forum of self-improvement, social exchange, cooperation, and intense competition for both men and women. From its early roots in mortal combat, Japanese swordsmanship has undergone extensive modification and development. However, the dual path of physical and spiritual development lives on today in the form of modern kendo.

M. I. Komoto

Bibliography

All Japan Kendo Federation. (1996) *Japanese-English Dictionary of Kendo.* Japan: All Japan Kendo Federation.

Draeger, Donn F. (1974) *Modern Bujutsu & Budo.* New York: John Weatherhill.

Hurst, G. Cameron, III. (1998) *Armed Martial Arts of Japan: Swordsmanship and Archery.* New Haven, CT: Yale University Press.

Nakano, Yasoji, and Nariyaki Sato. (1973) *Fundamental Kendo.* Tokyo: Japan Publications.

Ozawa, Hiroshi. (1997) *Kendo: The Definitive Guide.* New York: Kodansha America.

Sasamori, Junzo, and Gordon Warner. (1989) *This is Kendo.* Tokyo: Charles Tuttle Co.

Skoss, Diane, ed. (1997) *Koryu Bujutsu.* Berkeley Heights, NJ: Koryu Books.

———. (1999) *Sword & Spirit.* Berkeley Heights, NJ: Koryu Books.

KENYA

Kenya is located in East Africa and has a population of 29 million. A British colony from 1920 until 1963, Kenya has since independence suffered periods of economic and political instability. This has made it difficult to develop a central and well-funded sports program aimed at girls and young women. In Kenya, as in other African nations with multi-ethnic populations, efforts to create a central sports structure and programs have also been stymied by the same ethnic rivalries that hamper development of political and economic cohesion. Beyond these factors, development of women's sports has been slowed by the traditionally superior position afforded men in Kenyan society. Following independence the government looked to male sports—and especially to long-distance running—as a means of gaining international attention. Much effort was devoted to developing and promoting world-class male athletes and less attention was given to sports in general.

HISTORY

At the time of independence, the sports education system for boys and girls was based on the British system, with women participating in basketball, cricket, field hockey, and volleyball. After independence, sport opportunities opened up for men but changed little for women, despite expansion of the educational system. By the 1990s, some 500 schools offered physical education for girls and young women, compared to only about 150 in the 1960s. Even with this growth, physical education programs remained biased in favor of boys and were run mainly by male coaches.

The generally inferior position of women in Kenyan society has also hindered the growth of women's sports in rural communities. Girls are dominated by their fathers and women by their husbands. Women are expected to care for the family and home, and in rural regions, work on the farm or herd domestic livestock on land near the home. Twenty percent fewer women than men are literate, and the average woman bears six children. In this setting, it is not surprising that it was male sports that developed after independence, with a focus at the international level on male distance runners, many of whom were from the Kalenjin-speaking ethnic groups.

Many of these distance runners came from the mountainous western region where people were used to traveling long distances over difficult terrain by foot. Kenyan runners excelled in international and Olympic competitions in races of 1,500, 5,000, and 10,000 meters, the 3,000-meter steeplechase, and the marathon. Runners such as Kip Keino, Naftali Temu, and Amos Biwatt became international stars in the late 1960s, and John Kagwe and Joseph Chebet were the best of six or seven world-class Kenyan marathoners in the 1990s. These athletes and others who followed benefited from training in the United States and Europe, contracts with meet organizers who sought the best athletes to draw large audiences, and world-level coaching—all of which were unavailable to female athletes in Kenya.

EMERGENCE AND DEVELOPMENT OF WOMEN'S SPORT

It was not until the 1980s that women's sport began to be treated as a serious endeavor. When it did begin to develop, as with men, the focus was on long-distance running, the sport that had and would continue to bring attention to Kenya as a

Teala Loroupe (right) celebrates her bronze medal performance in the 10,000-meter race at the world championships in Spain. (Reuters Newmedia Inc/Corbis)

nation. Fewer resources were devoted by the government to promoting most other sports, although support was given to shorter-distance track events, and by the late 1980s Kenyan women were successfully competing in these events on a regional level. The government began to actively promote running for girls and young women and regularly scheduled races to identify boys and girls with potential to be world-class distance runners. Those who seemed especially talented were selected for special training that usually required them to live away from their communities and families and also placed them under the guidance of European coaches and trainers. Young women from rural communities and ethnic groups in which men dominated saw participation in running as a means of escaping poverty and making a fuller life for themselves. European coaches and promoters encouraged the sport establishment to help develop runners; they viewed Kenyans as having natural talent as distance runners.

In the 1990s, the new attention given to women's distance running began to show results when the 1996 Kenyan Olympic team included ten women, nine of them distance runners: Naomi Mugeo (1,500 meters); Lydia Cheromei, Pauline

Konga, and Rose Cheruiyot (5,000 meters); Sally Barsosio and Tegla Loroupe (10,000 meters); Salina Chirchir, Joyce Chepchumba, and Angeline Kanana (marathon). The tenth Olympian was Jennifer Mukonyo, the only Kenyan archer on the team. At the Olympics in Atlanta, Pauline Konga took the silver medal in the 5,000-meter run, thus becoming the first female Kenyan athlete to earn an Olympic medal. At the world track and field championships in Athens in the following year, Sally Barsosio continued the tradition when she won the 10,000-meter run.

Like Kenyan men, Kenyan women have come to the front in the marathon in the 1990s. A leading Kenyan woman marathoner of the 1990s was Tegla Loroupe. Standing 4 feet and 11 inches tall and weighing 84 pounds, she took the 1998 Rotterdam Marathon with the time of 2 hours 20:47, beating by nineteen seconds the world record, which had been held by the Norwegian marathoner Ingrid Kristiansen for the previous thirteen years. Loroupe also won the prestigious New York Marathon twice (1994, 1995) and the 10,000-meter run at the 1994 and 1998 Goodwill Games. Injuries and illness hampered her efforts in the late 1990s. Another leading marathoner is Joyce Chepchumba, who set a new world record of 2 hours 23:22 at the 1999 London marathon, where women and men run separate races.

Beyond running, women's sports still receive much less attention than do men's sports. Soccer (association football), cricket, and rugby, all holdovers from the British era, are Kenya's major team sports, but women are involved primarily as spectators. Basketball, the fastest growing team sport in the 1990s, has attracted both men and women. The national men's and women's teams have been supported by the government; businesses back amateur and semiprofessional teams; and basketball is now a part of the school curriculum. In 1998, the women's national team performed credibly in the world championships in Australia, and the Kenyan league title was taken by the women's team sponsored by Kenya Railways. As with long-distance running, both Kenyan men and women players see basketball as a means of escaping poverty. The best players strive for the opportunity to play in leagues in Europe, Canada, and Asia.

At the close of the twentieth century, more women than ever were participating in sports in Kenya, although their level of participation is still far lower than that of men. This is largely due to a continuing bias across Kenyan society that favors men and male activities and limits participation by women in the public sector. Nonetheless, talented and dedicated female athletes are recognized in the highly visible sports of distance running and basketball. Athletes such as Tegla Loroupe see themselves as role models for future generations.

Gherardo Bonini
David Levinson

Bibliography

Alessandrini, Guido. (1998) "Dossier Kenya." In *Jogging la Grande Corsa*, ATFS Annuals 1981–1998; 47–53.

Gambaccini, Peter. (1998) "Simply Smashing." *Runner's World* (July): 76–78.

Manners, John. (1998) "A World of their Own." *Runner's World* (June): 92–99.

Noden, Merrell. (1998) "Tegla Loroupe Aims to Lower her Marathon Best and Elevate Kenyan Women." *Sports Illustrated/CNN* (31 October). http://www.cnnsi.com.

KERRIGAN, NANCY

(1969–)

U.S. FIGURE SKATER

When her international figure-skating career made her a celebrity, Nancy Kerrigan had been following the paths of such earlier figure skaters as Sonja Henie, Peggy Fleming, and Dorothy Hamill. However, her story differs from the stories of these other skaters in two important ways. First, despite considerable success on the ice, she never won a major international championship. Second, she gained much media attention as the victim in one of the most outrageous incidents in the history of women's sport. Her celebrity also demonstrates the power of media in shaping the presentation and perception of modern sports.

Kerrigan was born in Woburn, Massachusetts, on 13 October 1969 to Brenda and Dan Kerrigan. Her parents supported her interest in skating. Her father worked extra jobs to pay for lessons and ice time, and took out loans as well. In order to support her daughter, her mother, though legally blind, attended many of Kerrigan's competitions. Kerrigan began skating at age six but was not a finalist in a national competition until age twenty, a relatively late age for skaters of her generation.

In subsequent years, she improved steadily and in 1992 won the bronze medal at the Olympics and the silver at the world championships. Her prospects to capture the next world championship seemed bright, but in 1993 she performed a long and listless program that placed her fifth in the world championships. Moving on, she began preparing for the 1994 Lillehammer Olympics. While leaving the practice rink in Detroit where the national championships were being held on 6 January 1994, Kerrigan was clubbed across the leg by an assailant with a metal pipe. The assault did not cause serious injury, but the bruising that resulted forced her to withdraw from the championships and miss several weeks of practice for the Olympics.

With Kerrigan absent, Tonya Harding won the national championship and was placed on the U.S. Olympic Team, as was Kerrigan. The police investigation revealed that the assailant was hired by Jeff Gillooley, the ex-husband of Tonya Harding, Kerrigan's main American rival. Gillooley and his accomplices were arrested. Harding was also accused of participating in the planning of the assault, a charge she denied, although later she did admit that she took part in the cover-up of the incident. As a result, she was fined $100,000, required to perform community service, and banned from competition for life by the U.S. Figure Skating Association.

The assault created a media frenzy that built on already considerable efforts to promote the Kerrigan-Harding rivalry. Kerrigan had been portrayed as the tall, dark-haired, elegant skater who had benefited from the best coaching and most expensive costumes. Harding had been portrayed as the short, blond, athletic skater who was self-taught, made her own costumes, and practiced in public rinks. These portrayals were not entirely accurate, but they spiked viewer interest in the already popular sport of figure skating. The assault

Nancy Kerrigan shows her graceful style as she performs a forward outside spiral during her skating routine at the 1992 Winter Olympic Games. (Neal Preston)

and Harding's possible involvement only added to the sensationalism, and at the Olympics every move by each athlete was carefully recorded and interpreted. In the actual competition, Harding seemed rattled, skated poorly, and finished seventh, while Kerrigan maintained her composure and won the silver medal, finishing a fraction of a point behind the Ukraine's Oksana Baiul. The competition had the sixth-largest television audience in history.

The combination of the assault, the attention it brought to Kerrigan, her composure in the Olympics, and the worldwide media coverage of the competition made Kerrigan a celebrity. She returned home to victory parades and offers of millions of dollars in product endorsement contracts. She retired from amateur competition and participated in traveling ice shows and a world tour of Olympic champions. In September 1995, she married her manager, Jerry Solomon, and in December 1996, she gave birth to their son Matthew. In addition to her professional skating and advertising work, she used her celebrity to promote several social causes, including the Massachusetts Children's Trust Fund.

Janet Luehring-Lindquist
Marijke den Hollander

Bibliography

Coffey, Wayne R. (1994) *Dreams of Gold: The Nancy Kerrigan Story.* New York: St. Martin's Paperbacks.

Edelson, Paula. (1998). *Nancy Kerrigan.* Philadelphia: Chelsea House Publishers.

Morrissette, Mikki. (1994) *Nancy Kerrigan: Heart of a Champion.* New York: Bantam Books.

Spence, Jim. (1995) *Nancy Kerrigan, Courageous Skater.* Vero Beach, FL: Rourke Press.

KING, BILLIE JEAN

(1943–)

U.S. TENNIS PLAYER

An outspoken advocate of equal rights for women, Billie Jean King created a forum for her views as one of the top female tennis players of the 1960s and 1970s. In a career that spanned nearly three decades, she won sixty-seven Women's Tennis Association (WTA) singles titles including thirty-nine Grand Slam singles titles and ranks fifth on the all-time victory list with 695. She held a record twenty Wimbledon titles.

King was the first woman in any sport to earn more than $100,000 in a single season of competition ($117,000 in 1971), and was the driving force behind the creation of a women's professional tennis tour in 1971. Through her efforts to promote women's professional sports and opportunities for female athletes, King became one of the most important symbols for women's sports and the women's movement in the 1970s and 1980s.

Born Billie Jean Moffitt on 22 November 1943 in Long Beach, California, King became involved in sports as a youngster. She played baseball with her father and brother, and played football with her neighborhood friends. At age ten, she played on a championship girls' softball team. King enrolled in the free tennis lessons offered by city recreation coach Clyde Walker on the municipal courts at Houghton Park in Long Beach. For the next five years, King worked diligently to improve her game. She won her first title, the Southern California Championship, in 1958. When she was sixteen, King began taking lessons from tennis great Alice Marble. After lessons with Marble, Billie Jean's national ranking jumped from nineteenth to fourth.

In 1960, King reached the finals of the national girls' eighteen-and-under championship. The following year, she and Karen Hantze, both seventeen years old, became the youngest pair ever to win the women's doubles title at Wimbledon. In 1962, King returned to Wimbledon, and before 18,000 spectators on Centre Court, she defeated top-ranked Margaret Smith of Australia, 1–6, 6–3, 7–5, in the second round. The victory vaulted King into the world of world-class singles tennis.

TOP-RANKED PLAYER

By December 1965, three months after marrying Larry King, she was ranked number one in the world. She held that rank five times between 1966 and 1972, and was in the top ten a total of seventeen years (beginning in 1960). King also ranked number one in doubles for a record twelve years, eight of those years with partner Rosie Casals. Her aggressive serve-and-volley style of play served her well on the fast grass courts of Wimbledon, and as a doubles player where her quick reflexes and creative shot-making made her a formidable foe.

After defending her Wimbledon doubles title with Hantze in 1962, King teamed with Maria Bueno (1965), Rosie Casals (1967–1968, 1970–1971, 1973), Betty Stove (1972), and Martina Navratilova (1979) to win ten women's doubles titles at Wimbledon. She won the women's singles title at the All-England Championships six times (1966–1968, 1972–1973, 1975) and captured four mixed doubles championships with Owen Davidson (1967, 1971, 1973, 1974). In 1973, King scored "the triple" at

Wimbledon—winning the singles, doubles, and mixed-doubles championships.

King found an equal amount of success on her home soil. She won thirty U.S. singles and doubles championships, both amateur and professional, including the U.S. Open singles four times (1969, 1971, 1972, 1974), doubles five times (1964, 1967, 1974, 1978, 1980), and mixed doubles four times (1967, 1971, 1973, 1976). In eight years of Federation Cup play for the United States, King won all twenty-seven of her doubles matches.

CHAMPION OF TENNIS FOR WOMEN

From her position as the top female tennis player in the world, King worked to promote professional women's tennis. In 1970, she spearheaded a group of women players to form the Virginia Slims women's professional tennis circuit. Perhaps King drew the greatest attention of her career for her victory in the "Battle of the Sexes" over the fifty-five-year-old former tennis champion Bobby Riggs. Riggs, long known for his gamesmanship in the tennis world, had criticized the quality of women's play and had defeated Australian champion Margaret Court in the first "Battle of the Sexes." In 1973, King accepted his challenge to compete in a five-set match. With much pomp and promotion, they met before 30,472 spectators at the Houston Astrodome, the largest paid attendance in tennis history. King won easily in three sets (6–4, 6–3, 6–3), and the match not only brought attention to tennis and women's tennis but also became a symbol of a woman's right to participate in sports and to test her athletic and physical potential.

Billie Jean King founded the Women's Tennis Association (WTA), the players' union, in 1973

and served as its president from June 1973 to September 1975 and from September 1980 to September 1981. In 1974, she began a new magazine, *womenSports* (forerunner to *Women's Sports and Fitness*); and in 1974, she was one of the founding members of the Women's Sports Foundation.

Billie Jean King's efforts to establish professional tennis for women spilled over into the women's rights movement in the 1970s. As a public figure, King was outspoken in her beliefs of equal opportunity and successfully used her number-one ranking on the tennis court to draw attention to the issues of the era. In 1990, *Life* magazine named Billie Jean King one of the 100 Most Important Americans of the Twentieth Century. Only three other athletes—Babe Ruth, Jackie Robinson, and Muhammad Ali—made the list. Citing King's efforts to promote and support the women's sports movement in America, *Life* declared her the "winningest woman for equal rights."

Despite her successes in the public arena, her private life was less than smooth. In 1981, King was sued for palimony by one-time personal assistant Marilyn Barnett. King publicly admitted to the affair and won the lawsuit, but lost a number of commercial endorsements as a result.

King retired from competitive tennis in 1984 to focus her time and energy as the chief executive officer of World Team Tennis. However, she returned to the courts as a participant of the 1995 and 1996 Virginia Slims Legends Tour to benefit the National AIDS Fund, and she captained the U.S. team for the 1995 and 1996 Federation Cup and the 1996 U.S. Olympic tennis team.

Her awards include the *Sports Illustrated* Sportswoman of the Year in 1972, and the Associated Press Female Athlete of the Year in 1967

INCREDIBLE ATHLETE GIVES BACK

In 1999, *Real Sports* selected Bille Jean King as the "Woman of the Millennium." In a lengthy article about her life, career, and contributions to equality and women's sports, the magazine cited King's accomplishments as an athlete, coach, entrepreneur, administrator, role model, and philanthropist. Many leaders in the sports world agree that King has had and continues to have a major impact on the sports world, including Richard Lapchick, founder of the Center for the Study of Sports and Society at Northeastern University, who commented that "She changed the nature of sport in America."

KORBUT, OLGA

(1955–)
SOVIET GYMNAST

Olga Korbut has been called many things, including the "first of the pixies," "a circus act," and "queen of the gymnasts." Despite the wide range of opinions that the public and other gymnasts have expressed about her, no one disputes that Olga Korbut changed women's gymnastics forever.

Korbut was born 16 May 1955 in Grodno, Belarus. She had not been a strong student in school, but her teacher noticed her agility during physical exercises and recommended that Korbut enroll in one of the gymnastics schools run by the State Sport Committee. At the age of eleven, Korbut began her gymnastics training at the State Sport School in Grodno, under the supervision of Renald Knysh. He was an innovator in the world of gymnastics. His students were some of the boldest and bravest, perfecting moves that many people considered death-defying. Knysh was always on the lookout for gymnasts who would be willing to try out his newest innovations and in Olga Korbut, only eleven years old and fearless, he found the perfect pupil.

Korbut began gaining attention from the gymnastics community in the Soviet Union when she took fifth place in the 1969 national championships. The following year, Korbut earned first place on the vault at the nationals; and she was named a reserve member of the Soviet national team. Later that year, Korbut became ill and suffered an injury that kept her out of training for several months. The experience made an impression on her, and when she returned to gymnastics, she trained more seriously than ever.

The breakthrough year came two years later in 1972 when Korbut placed third all-around at the national championships in Kiev and then took first at an international tournament in Reja. Just before the 1972 Olympic Games in Munich, she garnered the Soviet Union Cup, the highest prize for gymnastics in the Soviet Union. She was named an alternate for the Soviet Union Olympic

Billie Jean King returns a ball to Margaret Court of Australia at Wimbledon in 1970. Her achievements on and off the court made her one of the leaders of the women's sports movement. (Bettmann/Corbis)

and 1973. She was inducted into the International Women's Sports Hall of Fame in 1980 and the International Tennis Hall of Fame in 1987. She was given the 1995 Sarah Palfrey Danzig Award, U.S. tennis's highest honor for sportsmanship and contributions to the game, and the 1997 Women's Sports Foundation's Flo Hyman Award.

Janet Woolum

Bibliography

"100 Most Important Americans of the Twentieth Century." (1990) *Life Magazine* (Fall): 28.

King, Billie Jean, with Kim Chapin. (1975) *Billie Jean*. London: W. H. Allen.

——, with Frank Deford. (1982) *The Autobiography of Billie Jean King*. New York: Granada Publishing.

——, with Cynthia Starr. (1988) *We Have Come a Long Way: The Story of Women's Tennis*. New York: McGraw-Hill.

Team, and took the place of an injured team member. At the age of seventeen, Korbut walked into the Olympic Sportshalle in Munich and into history.

On the first day of competition, Korbut performed flawlessly. She executed elements no one had ever seen before, including a backward somersault on the uneven parallel bars. The international audience was astounded. The Soviet team earned the gold medal in the team competition. The media was captivated by Korbut's playful attitude, wide smiles, bright eyes, and yarn-tied pigtails. Korbut's picture accompanied the story of the Soviet team victory in newspapers around the world.

On the second day, Korbut competed individually for the all-around title. She was in second place at the start of the day, but a costly mistake on the uneven parallel bars knocked her down to seventh place. Just as she had expressed her happiness and excitement on the first day, Korbut showed her frustration and disappointment on the second. She came away from the parallel bars crying, and the media continued to focus on her story.

On the third day, Korbut bounced back from her failure in the all-around competition to demonstrate the "Korbut loop" on the uneven parallel bars and the "Korbut somersault" on the balance beam. Spectators gasped and marveled at her daring, dangerous movements; judges rated her highly; and Korbut came away with the silver in the uneven parallel bars and the gold in the balance beam and floor exercise. The media loved the three-day drama of Korbut's remarkable success, frustrating failure, and amazing rebound. Even though Korbut was not the top-rated gymnast on her own team, the media attention made her one of the most popular and best-known athletes of the 1972 Games.

In 1972, the Associated Press named her the Female Athlete of the Year, and ABC's Wide World of Sports named her Athlete of the Year. In towns all across the United States, girls took up gymnastics by the thousands. Gymnastics centers credited Korbut with precipitating a completely unexpected interest in the sport, with many of their new pupils showing up for practice wearing yarn-tied pigtails and dreaming of being "just like Olga."

Showing her athletic style, Olga Korbut performs a split handstand on the balance beam during the individual events competition at the 1972 Olympic Games in Munich. (Bettmann/Corbis)

A NEW DIRECTION FOR WOMEN'S GYMNASTICS

Women's gymnastics had historically been a sport dominated by "athletic ballerinas," physically mature women with long, lean bodies and strong, compact muscles developed within a feminine form. Women competed well into their twenties and thirties. For example, the first Olympic Women's Gymnastics champion, Maria Gorokhovskaya, won the gold at the Olympics in Helsinki when she was thirty-one years old and Larisa Latynina won her first Olympic medal at the age of twenty-one and continued competing until she was thirty-two, when she retired from the sport to coach for the Soviet Union's State Sport Committee. Similarly, Hungary's Agnes Keleti won her first Olympic medal at age thirty-one and her last at thirty-five. But Korbut's appearance on the scene of international gymnastics rang in a new era for the sport, a time of younger, smaller, more agile competitors.

Standing under five feet tall and weighing about ninety pounds, Korbut could execute moves differently than her more mature competitors, whose bodies were taller, heavier, and more curvaceous. Gymnastics had traditionally been competition of purity of form and style, where physically mature women performed each element—from the simplest to the most difficult—with expressiveness and grace. Critics of Korbut said that her emphasis on difficulty threatened the femininity and lyricism that made women's gymnastics so unique and beautiful.

The debate over purity of form versus athletic difficulty continued for several years, but the trend started by Korbut was clear. Gymnasts continued to be younger and smaller—so young, in fact, that Shannon Miller of the United States was considered an "old timer" in 1996, when she was only twenty-one years old. Korbut herself would suffer from this "infantilization" of women's gymnastics at the 1976 Olympics, when at the age of twenty-one, she was overshadowed by fourteen-year-old Nadia Comaneci from Yugoslavia, who captured massive media attention by becoming the youngest Olympic gymnastics champion ever. Although Korbut won two medals in 1972, the media virtually ignored her, focusing instead on the younger Comaneci.

The trend toward youth and smallness had far-reaching consequences for the girls who aspired to be Olympians. Gymnastics officials in the United States noticed a higher rate of compulsive dieting, eating disorders, and malnutrition among teenage girls. Because of these poor eating habits, girls suffered injuries more often, and injuries became more severe. In an attempt to discourage women from taking up unhealthy habits to keep their bodies small and light, the International Olympic Committee (IOC) raised the age limit for women gymnasts to sixteen, beginning with the 2000 Olympics in Sydney, Australia.

Korbut retired from competition in 1976 and became a coach for the Belarus State Sport Committee. In 1982, she was named to the International Sports Hall of Fame. She married singer Leonid Bortkevich and later had a son, Richard. In 1987, the Chernobyl nuclear disaster exposed Belarus to dangerous fallout radiation, and Korbut experienced thyroid problems and exhaustion as a result. She decided to use her celebrity status to call attention to the problems of the Belarussians, and in 1990, she became the spokeswoman for the Emergency Help for Children Foundation. In 1991, she moved with her family to Atlanta, Georgia, to teach gymnastics and raise funds and awareness for the Foundation.

Looking back on her spectacular rise to fame, Korbut lamented having been so young and unprepared for the experience at the time it happened. She was happy to have influenced so many girls to take up gymnastics, but in an interview with *Sports Illustrated*, she stated that she believed there should be different classifications for girl gymnasts and women gymnasts. She also hoped that women would be able to compete for a long time, rather than feeling they were "finished" when their bodies matured. She said that gymnastics should be appreciated for its beauty, not just for its dangerous elements.

Despite the debate and controversy, it is undeniable that Olga Korbut influenced women's gymnastics more than any other gymnast before her. Her exuberance, skill, and fearlessness made her an international star and role model for girls around the world and changed the sport of women's gymnastics.

Wendy Painter

Bibliography

Findling, John E., and Kimberly D. Pelle. (1996) *Historical Dictionary of the Modern Olympic Movement.* Westport, CT: Greenwood Press.

Johnson, Anne Janette. (1996) *Great Women in Sports.* Detroit: Visible Ink Press.

Markel, Robert, ed. (1997) *The Women's Sports Encyclopedia.* New York: Henry Holt.

Suponev, Michael. (1975) *Olga Korbut: A Biographical Portrait.* Garden City, NY: Doubleday.

KORFBALL

Korfball is a coed sport that combines elements of basketball, netball, and handball. It was invented in 1902 by school teacher Nico Broekhuysen

(1877–1958) as a safe, noncontact game that boys and girls could play together. The new sport caught on and quickly gained a following. In the 1990s, korfball was the fourth most popular team sport—behind soccer (association football), volleyball, and field hockey—in the Netherlands, where 640 clubs had 100,000 players. In the large competitive league system players range in age from six to fifty-plus. There are no professional players in korfball, although players in the highest Dutch league receive an allowance for expenses. Korfball is played in other countries, although not as a major sport. Women and men are in theory equal competitors; in reality, women are generally assigned positions where they have less chance to score.

HISTORY

Broekhuysen developed korfball while he was attending a handicraft course in Nääs, Sweden. One of a group of progressive educators, he was looking for low-cost, open-air games that boys and girls could play together. While attending the course, he became acquainted with "ringboll." The non-Scandinavian participants labeled this game "basketball" although there was no basket. The goals were constructed of two long poles with rings of band iron on top. Inspired by his experiences with ringboll, Broekhuysen developed a game he called korfball, *"korf"* being the Dutch word for basket. He had two poles constructed that had detachable, bottomless cane baskets on top. He then established a set of basic rules and started to play the game after school hours with the boys and girls of the highest grades of his school.

The new game was played outdoors on a court divided into three sections, with a pole (a korf attached at the top) erected in each of the two outer zones about 5 meters from the baseline. Each team had twelve players, six male and six female. Two of each sex took up their positions in each of the three zones. Other educators immediately became interested in the new game, and soon korfball clubs began to be established. In 1903, the Dutch Korfball Association was established (now called Koninklijke Nederlandse Korfbal Vereniging, or KNKV) with Broekhuysen as its first president.

Korfball was exported to countries that were under Dutch colonial control (Indonesia, Surinam, and the Dutch Antilles) at the time, but the Dutch made little effort to promote the game internationally. In 1920, the Dutch Korfball Association demonstrated korfball at the Antwerp Olympic Games. As a result, the Belgian Korfball Association was established in 1921. The first international match between Belgium and the Netherlands took place in 1923, and has continued to be an annual event. In 1924, the International Korfball Bureau was founded and in 1933 became officially known as the International Korfball Federation (IKF). The international organization, however, remained inactive for a long period because of a lack of funds.

After World War II, the Dutch began to promote korfball in other countries. In 1946, korfball was introduced into Great Britain. Demonstration tours were conducted in Austria, Denmark, and Switzerland, but these countries did not adopt the game. In the 1960s, korfball was successfully launched in the Federal Republic of Germany. In 1967, the first European Cup Tournament in outdoor korfball for national champion clubs was organized. (There is also an annual European Cup

ENCOURAGING SEXUAL EQUALITY

Korfball was developed as an alternative to highly competitive masculine sports. It is perhaps the only sport that from the beginning was meant to have coed teams and to encourage sexual equality in sports. Although winning remains the objective, physical aggression is discouraged, and cooperation, especially between opposite-sex players, is encouraged. However, as the game has become more popular and more international, it has not reached its initial goals: studies show that men control the sport and that men more often occupy the scoring positions on the court.

Dutch girls and boy enjoy korfball as "Puppies" (age 6-8), 1978. (P. Wolsink)

Tournament for indoor korfball.) In the 1970s, korfball became well established in France, Spain, Papua New Guinea, and Luxembourg, mostly because it was promoted by enthusiastic teachers.

In 1976, the KNKV was invited by two United States physical education professors who were both originally from the Netherlands, Dr. Jan Broekhoff (Oregon State University, Eugene) and Dr. Nicolaas Moolenijzer (University of New Mexico, Albuquerque) to make a longer demonstration tour at universities in the United States. The initiative was a consequence of Title IX of the Education Amendments of 1972, stipulating equal sport opportunities for males and females. In 1978, the U.S. Korfball Federation (USKF) was established. In 1979—three years after the first trip—a second trip was made with demonstrations in Illinois, Wisconsin, California, and Oregon. By that time Broekhoff was the president of the USKF, and Moolenijzer, the secretary. The American tours represented major growth for the sport and prompted the IKF to invest in the international expansion of korfball. In 1979, the federation's international coach, Adri Zwaanswijk, embarked on a six-month world tour to promote korfball as a coed sport and a passport to coeducation. He gave workshops and courses in fifteen countries.

On the occasion of its seventy-fifth anniversary in 1978, the KNKV organized the first world championship, which included six European teams as well representatives from Papua New Guinea and the United States. The world championship takes place every four years and korfball has been on the program of the World Games since 1985. The 1990s saw the rapid expansion of korfball in Eastern Europe, following periods of dramatic political and economic change. In 1993, korfball was officially recognized by the International Olympic Committee (IOC). In 1998, Portugal hosted the first European indoor korfball championship. In most of these international competitions the Dutch team was victorious. Belgium has been its biggest rival. In the late-1990s, Taiwan, Portugal, and the Czech Republic made substantial progress in competitive strength.

Korfball today is an international sport, and is played in Finland, Portugal, France, the Czech Republic, Armenia, India, South Africa, the United States, Australia, New Zealand, and Taiwan. The IKF comprises thirty-four national korfball federations, and is a member of the General Association of International Sports Federations (GAISF) as well as the International World Games Association (IWGA).

Although it is now an international sport, korfball is nevertheless still a small sport. The Netherlands has 100,000 players, but this figure is not matched by the sum of all players in all other IKF countries. That it has attained only this modest popularity is probably due to its leading proponent, the Netherlands, being a small country that does not have a strong position in the grand scheme of international cultural exchange compared to strong exporters of sports, such as the United States, England, Germany, and Japan.

RULES AND PLAY

Korfball was originally played outdoors on a three-zone court with four players (two male and two female) of each side per zone. In 1990, however, the middle (connecting) zone was abolished. This was the result of the growing popularity of indoor korfball, which was introduced in the 1950s and played in two zones (each side having two players in each zone), and also with a view to the internationalization of korfball due to the fact that two-zone korfball is a faster, more spectacular game (faster change of offensive actions to one of the two korfs), an important promotional consideration.

The Dutch outdoor leagues start in autumn and continue in spring. The indoor season, which is much more popular with spectators, television broadcasters, and most players, runs from November until the end of March. The high point of the korfball year is the annual indoor championship final, which annually attracts 9,000 spectators to the Ahoy Sport Palace in Rotterdam.

Indoor korfball is played on a court of 40 × 20 meters, with the outdoor court as large as 60 × 30 meters. A post 3.5 meters high with a korf on top is placed 6.7 meters (10 meters, outdoors) from the baseline of each of the two halves. Korfball is played with a ball about the same size and weight as a soccer ball and made of leather.

Four players from each team (two male, two female) play in each half, as the offense and defense. Each time two goals are scored (two by either team or one by each) the players change zones, so that the attackers become defenders and vice versa. During the 1997–1998 Dutch indoor league season, the average number of scores per match was 39.7, meaning about twenty changes per match. This aspect of the game requires players to master both offensive and defensive skills. Players may not run or dribble with the ball.

The objective in offense is to develop passing and running combinations to create a shooting opportunity. Shooting when defended is not permitted. An attacker is defended when his or her personal opponent is nearer to the post, is within arm's length, and is actively trying to block the ball. This aspect of the game limits the advantage that would otherwise accrue to taller players since they are not allowed to jump-shoot over their opponent if they are in a defended position.

Korfball is characterized by players moving around the court in pairs, each consisting of an offensive player with a personal opponent. Rapid changes of speed and direction, combined with good teamwork and passing, are required for the attacker to break free from the opposing player and receive the ball to shoot. Goals can be scored through shots from a distance (22 meters is not exceptional) or from close range when an attacker

A championship level korfball match in Rotterdam, the Netherlands. (Wim Timmer)

has passed the defense player by using feints and moving quickly. The defenders attempt to remain close to their opponents and to be alert to opportunities to intercept passes or to capture the rebound following a shot. Korfball restricts physical contact as it is meant to be a noncontact sport. The emphasis is on skill and speed, not on power or aggression.

WOMEN, KORFBALL, AND EQUALITY IN SPORTS

The mixed-gender teams of korfball, plus its proponents' claim that korfball is a passport to co-education, has opened doors for the introduction of korfball. But the question remains as to whether korfball can really be seen as a means of facilitating the blending of men's and women's sports cultures. Do both sexes have equal status and power within korfball? Potentially, male and female competitors are equals. In reality, they are not.

Korfball has the potential to be played on a highly competitive level with equal chances for success and status for men and women. The same cannot be said for the related games of team handball or basketball. The difference lies in the specific combination of the spatial structure and the number of players in a section of the court and the consequences for defense tactics. In handball and basketball the position of the goal at the end of the playing field, combined with a relatively large number of players, leads to a system of zone defense or to a combination of zone and person-to-person defense. If these sports were played with mixed sides, male players would more easily penetrate the defense through their physically smaller and weaker female opponents.

In korfball, on the other hand, two elements of the game promote equity. First, because the position of the korf makes it possible to attack from all directions and the small number of defenders (only four) tactically excludes the option of a zone defense, the person-to-person defense system is essential. Consequently, every player in the attack zone has a single person defending him or her. Second, the rules require two males and two females in each section, from both sides, and players are allowed to guard or attack only opponents of the same sex. These features of the game tend to cancel any gender-based differences in height, strength, or speed. Since there is generally no reason to assume that female players are technically or tactically less competent than their male teammates, the role division (e.g., who is the scoring player and who does the supportive work) can be arranged independently of the gender factor.

Tactically, in assigning positions to players, teams also consider the issue of which player must be supported in order to score by determining who of the four in the offense section has the best chances to score on his or her defender. In this lies the potential for sex equity within korfball. However, a team in which female players have the same or a higher status (according to successful score tries) is unusual. In the 1997–1998 season, this was the case for only three out of sixteen teams in the highest Dutch league.

The view that korfball still suffers from traditional ideas about the division of roles and power also emerges when looking at the positions that men and women hold in the formal power structures of the korfball organizations. Males are still overrepresented as referees as well as in administrative positions, and there is no formal mechanism in place to change this situation despite the fact that half the players are women.

Bart Crum

Bibliography

Bottenburg, Maarten van. (1992) "The Differential Popularization of Sports in Continental Europe." *The Netherlands' Journal of Social Science* 28, 1: 3–30.

Crum, Bart. (1988) "A Critical Analysis of Korfball as a 'Non-Sexist Sport.'" *International Review for the Sociology of Sport* 23, 3: 233–240.

Summerfield, Karen, and Anita White. (1989) "Korfball: A Model of Egalitarianism?" *Sociology of Sport Journal* 6: 144–151.

KRISTIANSEN, INGRID

(1956–)

NORWEGIAN DISTANCE RUNNER

Ingrid Kristiansen was one of the premier distance runners of the 1980s and the only runner, male or female, to have held the world record for the 5,000-meter, the 10,000-meter, and the marathon races. Her world-record marathon time of 2:21:06 for a marathon in which women do not compete alongside men, set in London in 1985, stood until broken in the London marathon of 1999.

Ingrid Kristiansen was born in Trondheim, Norway, on 21 March 1956. Her family were avid cross-country skiers, and she excelled at the sport. Among the top skiers in Norway by her late teens, she competed in the 1976 Olympics and in the 1978 world championships. After graduating from college she went to work as a researcher and with little time for skiing, she switched to running as a form of exercise. After she abandoned her skis, she continued to wear gloves whenever she competed, and white gloves became her trademark. In 1981, she married Arve Kristiansen, an engineer and marathon runner and they later had a son and daughter, with Kristiansen returning to training and competition shortly after the birth of her children.

Once she reached her peak in the mid-1980s, she dominated the decade's 5,000-meter and

Ingrid Kristiansen of Norway being applauded after breaking the women's world record and winning the 1985 London Marathon. (Hulton-Deutsch Collection/Corbis)

10,000-meter races. In 1984, she was the first woman to run the former distance in under fifteen minutes (14:58:89). Her world record of 14:37:33 lasted for eight years. In 1985, she became the first woman to race the 10,000-meter in less than thirty-one minutes (30:59:42). Her 10,000-meter world record, set in 1986, lasted for seven years. Although she won most of the prestigious city-sponsored marathons, including London (four times), Boston (twice), Houston, Chicago, and New York, her career as a marathoner was overshadowed by that of her countrywoman Greta Waitz (who won thirteen major marathons).

Kristiansen's one "failure" was her inability to win an Olympic medal. Like nearly everyone else at the 1984 Olympics, she assumed that Joan Benoit's marathon pace was too fast for the heat and humidity of Los Angeles. By the time Kristiansen realized her mistake, it was too late. She finished in fourth place. For the 1988 Olympics in Seoul, she concentrated on the 10,000-meter race, for which she was a clear favorite after her victories in the European (1986) and the world championships (1987). She led the pack until a foot injury forced her to drop out.

In 1993, China's Wang Junxia lowered Kristiansen's 10,000-meter world record by nearly 48 seconds, but this extraordinary achievement has been called into question by observers noting that many of China's female athletes have tested positive for banned substances. Her marathon record finally gave way to the latest generation of Kenyan marathon runners in the late 1990s.

Allen Guttmann

Bibliography

Lawson, Gerald. (1997) *World Record Breakers in Track and Field Athletics.* Champaign, IL: Human Kinetics.

KRONE, JULIE

(1963–)

U.S. JOCKEY

Throughout her career, Julie Krone battled negative attitudes about women in horse racing. When she decided at age fifteen to become a jockey, she never realized that some people emphatically thought women "did not belong" in the sport. Though the prejudice against women's participation persists, Krone's success in the 1980s and 1990s paved the way for more women to compete as jockeys and, most important, to compete in high stakes races.

Julieanne Louise Krone was born in Benton Harbor, Michigan, on 24 July 1963. She grew up on a farm near Eau Claire, Michigan, with her family and numerous pets, farm animals, and horses. By the age of four, Krone was riding horses every day. She rode constantly, learning important lessons the hard way. Although Krone became an outstanding dressage rider, she preferred the speed of a racing horse. While watching the Belmont Stakes on television in 1978, she decided that she was going to be a jockey.

During her spring vacation in 1979, Krone worked at Churchill Downs as a "hotwalker"— someone who walks horses to cool them down after a race. Krone convinced her mother to allow her to return to Louisville the next summer, when she worked as a groom and exercise rider. The summer after that, Krone worked as an amateur rider on the Michigan fair circuit, gaining practical experience in over sixty races.

Julie Krone, the only woman to win a Triple Crown race, rides at the Belmont Racetrack in New York. (Jerry Cooke)

When she returned home for her senior year of high school, Krone was consumed by her dream of being a jockey. Deciding to quit school, she moved to Tampa, Florida, to live with her grandparents. There, she worked as a groom and exercise rider while she earned her jockey's license. In 1981, she became an apprentice jockey and began riding in races.

Once the meet (the racing season) at Tampa Bay Downs ended, Krone sought to race at other tracks. It was difficult to find trainers willing to let "a girl" race their horses because horse racing had been a male-dominated sport since its inception. Owners and trainers did not believe that women had the physical size or stamina to control a horse for an entire race. They had denied jockey licenses to women until a female jockey sued for a license in the 1960s and won, and no female jockey ever gained national attention for more than a few races. Krone quickly came to realize that she was being judged more harshly because she was fe-

male. Although other jockeys assaulted her on and off the track with disparaging words and even with physical attacks, she never backed down.

Krone faced other obstacles along the way. In 1982, at Pimlico Park in Maryland, track officials found marijuana in her car and suspended her from racing for sixty days. It was torture for Krone to be away from racing for so long, but she stated later that the punishment was one of the best things to ever happen to her. In the winter of 1982, Krone was thrown from a horse and broke her back. Although she was not paralyzed, she required several months to recover from the injury, the first of many falls. Over the years, she suffered broken bones, crushed joints, and bruised muscles and organs. Her injuries required more than twenty steel pins to help heal broken bones in her arms, legs, and ankles. After each injury, Krone recovered and returned to the track much more quickly than her doctors expected, testimony to her determination as well as to her physical condition. It seemed that no matter what the injury, nothing could keep Krone from racing.

Thanks to her persistence and dedication, Krone had her share of successes. In 1987, her wins at Monmouth Park and the Meadowlands made her the first woman to win a riding title at any of the major American tracks. On 6 March 1988, she won her 1,205th race, surpassing the record set by Patricia Cooksey for the most wins by a female jockey. In 1988, Krone became the first woman to compete in the Breeder's Cup. In 1989, she became the first jockey in Meadowlands history to win six races in one day. She is, in fact, still only one of four jockeys to ever win six races in one day. By riding in the Belmont Stakes in 1991, and winning it in 1993, she became the first female jockey ever to ride in and win one of the Triple Crown Races.

Krone married sports journalist and producer Matt Muzikar in 1995. She was so obsessed by her career that she rode a full card even on her wedding day. On April 8, 1999, Krone formally retired from racing, at the age of thirty-five and having won more than $80 million in purses.

Wendy Painter

Bibliography

Callahan, Dorothy. (1990) *Julie Krone: A Winning Jockey*. Minneapolis, MN: Dillon Press.

Gutman, Bill. (1996) *Overcoming the Odds: Julie Krone*. Austin, TX: Steck-Vaughn Publishers.

Johnson, Anne Janette. (1996) *Great Women in Sports*. Detroit: Visible Ink Press.

Krone, Julie, and Nancy Ann Richardson. (1995) *Riding for My Life*. Boston: Little, Brown.

Savage, Jeff. (1996) *Julie Krone: Unstoppable Jockey*. Minneapolis, MN: Lerner Publications.

Woolum, Janet. (1992) *Outstanding Women Athletes*. Phoenix, AZ: Oryx Press.

L

LACROSSE

Lacrosse is a team sport played on a field with sticks and a ball, with the goal of hurling the ball into the other team's goal. It was developed by Native Americans in Canada, taken over by the European colonists, popularized at elite schools, and taken up by women in Great Britain in 1886.

While much has been written about men's lacrosse and the Native American origin of the game, little has been written about the women's game. This lack of information has led to two widespread misconceptions. The first is that women's lacrosse is played like men's lacrosse. The second is that its origins are closely linked to the indigenous game of *baggataway*. In reality, although it initially bore some similarity to the men's game (e.g., number of players on the field, names of playing positions, shape of sticks/crosses), women's lacrosse is connected to the men's game and to the indigenous sport only in roundabout ways. In the 1990s, English-speaking countries dominated the game, but women of many nations now compete internationally. Each country has its own women's lacrosse governing body, but the game at the international level is overseen by the International Federation of Women's Lacrosse Associations (IFWLA).

HISTORY

The origins of the women's game can be found on the playing fields of the public (private) schools in Great Britain. The earliest recognized start date for lacrosse in England is 1886, when the game was played at Ladybarn House, a Manchester co-educational preparatory school. Details on the rules and nature of these early games are sketchy. Evidence suggests that the first formalized game of women's field lacrosse was played at St. Leonards School for Girls, St. Andrews, Scotland, in 1890.

Lacrosse players from north and south England playing a match in the 1920s. (Hulton-Deutsch Collection/Corbis)

Louisa Lumsden, a retired headmistress at the school, introduced lacrosse at St. Leonards. She had vacationed in New Hampshire, in the United States, and had in 1884 viewed a lacrosse match between the Canghuawaya Indians and a club team from Montreal, Canada. Taken with the beauty and grace of the game, Lumsden wrote to her successor, Frances Jane Dove, about introducing the game at St. Leonards.

These beliefs are reflected in what little is known about the early rules of the game. Unlike men's lacrosse, from the beginning the women's version deliberately emphasized throwing, catching, and running skills. Moreover, bodily contact was not allowed; the notions of etiquette and player safety were central to the game.

The development of women's lacrosse reflected the changing attitudes about physical activity for girls and women. Victorian views required that they remain graceful and feminine and not display aggressive or overly physical traits when engaged in vigorous activity. Under the guidance of women such as Frances Jane Dove, lacrosse was promoted with these elements in mind.

Women's lacrosse spread across Britain as former St. Leonards teachers and students moved on to teach at other schools and colleges. Frances Jane Dove founded Wycombe Abbey in 1896 and introduced lacrosse to the school. By 1903 the game was taught at the leading physical training colleges for women. Lacrosse enjoyed enormous growth around the turn of the century as it spread through the British educational system, and by 1912 the Ladies Lacrosse Association (LLA), later the All England Women's Lacrosse Association (AEWLA), was formed to govern the rapidly increasing numbers of club teams.

At about the same time as the LLA's founding, international play between Scotland, England, and Wales began. When the game began at St. Leonards, competition was limited to interhouse teams of eight players each. By 1895 the number of players increased to ten per side, then to twelve by 1913, the year of the first Scottish trials (i.e., trials used to select regional, territorial, or national team members).

The Scottish Lacrosse Association (SLA) was formed in 1920 and organized the first club tournament in 1925. By 1931 membership numbers had grown to include eleven clubs and/or colleges and five pre-university schools. By the 1990s membership in the SLA consisted of eight clubs/university teams as well as seven schools (reasons for this decline are not clear). Numerous clubs and schools not affiliated with the association were also playing women's field lacrosse (e.g., company-, town-, territorial-, regional-, or community-based teams). Scotland has fielded a team at every World Cup (1982, 1986, 1989, 1993, 1997), as well as an under-nineteen squad at the first world junior championship in 1995.

Wales shares a comparable lacrosse history. Although the Welsh began competing against England and Scotland in 1912, it was not until the late 1920s that enough clubs had been formed for serious competition. By that time, the game was played at approximately ten schools, as well as a few clubs and colleges. Women's field lacrosse enjoyed reasonable success until the end of World War II, when membership numbers declined. Although drawing from a very small population base, Wales has consistently fielded a team at all international competitions and has toured extensively through the United States, Australia, Canada, and Japan.

DEVELOPMENT OUTSIDE GREAT BRITAIN

Women's lacrosse began to spread beyond the borders of these nations fairly quickly. Australia was also an early participant in the game, which was introduced there in the early part of the twentieth century by women teaching in secondary schools in major cities. Many early proponents were either born in England and then emigrated down under or were educated in England and introduced there to the "games culture" of the British school system. The game enjoyed moderate success during the early years, and the first women's association was formed in 1936. Within four years the Victorian Women's Lacrosse Association (VWLA) was affiliated with the United States Women's Lacrosse Association (USWLA) and the AEWLA. As in Wales, World War II seriously affected the women's game, putting it on hold until 1961. In 1962 the Australian Women's Lacrosse Council (AWLC) was formed and interstate competition began, initially between Victoria and South Australia. Western Australia joined the AWLC in 1964, with Tasmania joining in 1978. Despite its geographic isolation, Australia hosted its first international tour in 1969 and a team traveled to the United States in 1972. In 1989 Australia hosted the third World Cup. Australia has been a perennial medal winner at all World Cups, capturing the world championship in 1986 and the junior world championship in 1995.

Although many view lacrosse as a game with Canadian roots, women's lacrosse was virtually unknown in Canada through the first half of the twentieth century. The few reports of women playing lacrosse often indicate that the girls played box lacrosse (i.e., played indoors in a manner similar to ice hockey with six players per team, goalkeeper, two defensive players, and three forwards on the floor at a time). As in the United States, attempts to introduce the game were made and were initially successful. But for unknown reasons, following brief periods of popularity, women's lacrosse simply disappeared. Organized women's field lacrosse began in Canada in 1982 when the Canadian Lacrosse Association (CLA), the national governing body for all lacrosse in Canada, was notified by the IFWLA of plans to hold the first World Cup tournament. Courtney Solenberger, a Philadelphian and former U.S. player, was recruited to coach the Canadian team, which consisted of a group of female box lacrosse players. After only two weeks of practice, the Canadian team headed to Nottingham, England, where it surprised the women's lacrosse world by placing third in the World Cup tournament. This unforeseen success led to the subsequent formation of a women's field lacrosse committee within the CLA, and by 1983, provincial teams were competing for a national championship. Under the guidance of Carol Patterson, a former teacher and native of Baltimore, Maryland, and Jenny Kyle, originally from England, women's lacrosse flourished during the mid-1980s. However, played predominantly as club sport, the game's popularity faltered during the late 1980s and early 1990s because Canada's large size and small population base made it difficult to sustain membership numbers. However, by the mid-1990s women's lacrosse was revitalized with the development of high school and university leagues in Ontario.

England, Scotland, Wales, the United States, Canada, and Australia are longstanding members of the women's lacrosse community. In the late 1980s and early 1990s these nations were joined by the Czech Republic, Japan, and Sweden. Early Czech initiatives on lacrosse date to the mid-1960s, when a youth club developed "Czech lakrosse" based on drawings of an aboriginal form of the game. This version, which allows contact, is played with players on each side using a tennis ball and a one-handed aluminum stick that resembles a squash racquet rather than the crosses used elsewhere. Enjoyed by women and men, Czech lakrosse has grown substantially since its inception, and general enthusiasm for the sport led to the introduction of the women's field lacrosse game in the late 1980s. International coaching tours, followed up by visits from former college and university players, helped develop field lacrosse, albeit on a limited basis. By 1990 the Czech Women's Lacrosse Association (CWLA) became the eighth member of the IFWLA, and they appeared in their first World Cup in 1993 in Edinburgh, Scotland.

Japan also made its first World Cup appearance in Edinburgh. Lacrosse in Japan started in approximately 1986 when representatives from colleges in the United States were invited to Japan to give lacrosse clinics and camps to male and female university students. The Japan Lacrosse Association (JLA) was formed in 1986 to manage the explosive growth lacrosse enjoyed there. A student league was formed two years later and was responsible, along with the JLA, for several international tours and the establishment of the International Lacrosse Friendship Games. The IFWLA world coaching tour also made its first trip to Japan in 1989 and has continued to visit the country annually.

Several other countries, such as Sweden, New Zealand, Holland, France, India, and South Africa, have expressed an interest in developing the women's game in their country. The IFWLA has undertaken several coaching and demonstration tours to these nations to get the game started. However, all these initiatives were still developing as of 1999.

Formed in 1972, the IFWLA is made up of representatives from each member country. Its basic

INCREASING POPULARITY

Lacrosse is one of the most rapidly growing sports for young women in the United States. In 1999 130 college programs were affiliated with the NCAA, 370 high school teams, and 150 college and high school clubs. Once popular mainly in the east, lacrosse has spread to colleges and universities in the west, although the best collegiate teams are still in the east (University of Maryland, Princeton, Virginia, Dartmouth, North Carolina, and Georgetown, among others).

aims include promoting international understanding through the development of women's field lacrosse; development of rules to facilitate international competition; and promotion of international tours and competitions. In carrying out these aims, the IFWLA tries to provide a common standard of play. The international association has also been instrumental in introducing and developing the game in other nations via its coaching tours and by securing equipment that some countries cannot afford. Many of the development tours, especially to Japan and the Czech Republic, were instituted and/or lead by Jackie Pitts, former IFWLA president and later IFWLA vice president for development and promotion. Other individuals, such as Lanetta Ware, IFWLA president as of 1999, have also been instrumental in promoting game playing and officiating.

RULES AND PLAY

Women's field lacrosse, although once similar to the men's game, has evolved into a fast, free-flowing, and highly technical sport with its own rules. Unlike the men's game, there is no off-side and players (twelve per side) may go anywhere on the field (with the exception of the goalkeeper). The field is a minimum of 92 meters (100 yards) long, with no boundaries other than natural obstacles. The game consists of two 25-minute halves.

The game is played with player-to-player marking and at times closely resembles basketball and soccer with its use of spaces, cutting, and feinting. The three strategic zones on the field are attack, mid-field, and defense. The attack zone is composed of three "homes"—first, second, and third players whose primary responsibility is to go to the goal and score. They are supported by the left and right attack wings. These players also play the mid-field and serve as connectors for the defense, carrying or passing the ball from the defensive to the offensive ends of the field. The attack wings also work in conjunction with the left and right defense wings, who also serve as mid-field connectors and support the third woman, cover point, and point. These latter three positions are the primary defenders and mark the opposition's three homes. Finally, there is the goalkeeper, who is the first and last player on the team—first in initiating attack sequences and last in stopping opponent's efforts.

This version of lacrosse allows for stick-to-stick contact, and players wear minimal protection

PLAYER SAFETY IN LACROSSE

Women's field lacrosse has traditionally emphasized speed, skill, and grace in the absence of physical contact. Although the nature of the game has evolved—with more physical play and increasing congestion around the goal area—the game has remained relatively safe, and leg injuries are more common than injuries to face or body. Threats of lawsuits, however, as well as changing attitudes about how the game should be played, have led the sport's governing bodies to consider rule changes to increase player safety. The most radical suggestion has been to introduce a hard-shell helmet combined with a face mask, similar to that worn by goalkeepers, for all players in addition to the already mandatory mouth guard. The helmet was tried in Massachusetts and Australia, but although it prevented injuries to eyes and face, its use also resulted in a more physically aggressive style of play. Anecdotal evidence suggests that players feel invincible when wearing such equipment.

Special eye goggles have also been recommended. Goggles are highly effective when combined with a mouthguard, and a rule change implementing mandatory goggle and mouthguard use would effectively minimize or eliminate facial, ocular, nasal, and oral injuries. Women's lacrosse associations have instituted other rule changes (the 11-meter fan, free space to goal and restraining) in an effort to reduce player injury. The primary aim of these changes is to reduce congestion close to the goal, the area of the field where injuries occur most frequently.

(gloves, mouth guards, and eye protection), some of which is mandatory under national or international rules. Only the goalkeeper wears a helmet (for obvious reasons). Women's lacrosse rules, from the beginning, have been predicated on player safety. Body contact and rough or dangerous checking is not permitted. Players may not shoot or pass in a dangerous fashion. Defensive and offensive players are responsible for playing the game in a safe manner and keeping their bodies and crosses under control at all times. Restrictions on contact and emphasis on control demand that players develop solid technical skills. The result is a highly skilled, fast-moving, exciting sport.

Historically, women's field lacrosse has been based on a mix of speed, skill, and grace, with little physical contact. Although the nature of the game has changed over time (e.g., eleven-on-twelve attacks, increased congestion around the goal area, increased physical play), the game has remained relatively safe, with leg injuries the most frequent type recorded. Despite this record, threats of lawsuits and changing attitudes about how the game should be played have led the sport's governing bodies to consider significant rule changes to ensure player safety. The most radical suggestion has been to outfit all players with a hard-shell helmet combined with a face mask, similar to that worn by goalkeepers. This type of protective equipment was tried in Massachusetts and part of Australia, but players gave it a mixed reception. The helmet–face mask combination did prevent eye and face injuries, but its use also resulted in a more physically aggressive style of play. Players seemed to have adopted an air of invincibility when wearing such equipment. Anecdotal evidence from these leagues coincides with game legislators' views that the helmet–face mask combination, while preventing some injuries, would not necessarily make the game safer.

Goggles, an alternative form of eye–face protection, have been developed, approved, and recommended for women's field lacrosse. These goggles afford substantive protection to the eye and nose area and either eliminate injury or greatly reduce its severity. When combined with a mouth guard, this type of protection is seen as highly effective. The problem is that the use of eye goggles is optional, while use of a mouth guard is mandatory in all countries. A rule change implementing mandatory goggle and mouth guard use would effectively minimize or eliminate injuries to the face, eyes, and mouth.

Although they have not acted on enforcing mandatory ocular–facial protection, women's lacrosse associations, such as the USWLA and the IFWLA, have instituted other rule changes (e.g., 11-meter [36-foot] fan, free space to goal, shooting space, restraining lines) to reduce player injury. These initiatives are designed to reduce congestion close to the goal, the area of the field where injuries occur most frequently. The ongoing challenge for the game's legislators, then, is to implement means of ensuring optimal player safety while maintaining the integrity of the sport.

Women's field lacrosse has grown steadily since its inception in the late 1800s. This growth, as well as its diffusion to other nations, has been contingent upon the efforts of educators and players who were, and continue to be, willing to invest their energies in teaching this sport to others. National associations and the IFWLA have also supported this diffusion and development.

Susan L. Forbes

Bibliography

All England Women's Lacrosse Association. (1987) *Souvenir Brochure: Lacrosse 1912–1987*. London: All England Women's Lacrosse Association.

Avery, Gillian. (1991) *The Best Type of Girl: A History of Girls' Independent Schools*. London: Andre Deustch.

Brasch, Rudolph. (1970) *How Did Sports Begin? A Look at the Origins of Man at Play*. New York: David McKay.

Bryan, Sandy. (1988) "Czech Lakrosse." *United States Women's Lacrosse Association Newsletter* (November–December).

Crawford, Ray. (1987) "Moral and Manly: Girls and Games in the Prestigious Church Secondary Schools of Melbourne, 1901–1914." In *From "Fair Sex" to Feminism: Sport and the Socialization of Women in the Industrial and Post-Industrial Eras*, edited by J. A. Mangan and R. J. Parks. London: Frank Cass, 182–207.

Dunn, Katherine. (1998) "Area Coaches Stand on Pro Side in Debate over Restraining Line." *The Baltimore Sun* (6 March).

Forbes, Susan L., and Lori A. Livingston. (1994) "From Frances Jane Dove to Rosabelle Sinclair and Beyond: The Introduction of Women's Field Lacrosse to North America." In *Proceedings of the 10th Commonwealth and International Scientific Congress,* edited by F. O. Bell and G. H. Van Gyn. Victoria, British Columbia: University of Victoria, 83–86.

Frayne, Trent, and Peter Gzowski. (1965) *Great Canadian Sport Stories.* Toronto: Canadian Centennial Publishing.

Fritz, D. T. (1992) "A Special Relationship: Women's Lacrosse in the U.S. Owes Its Existence to the U.K." *Lacrosse* 16, 2: 70.

Green, Tina Sloan, and Agnes Bixler Kurtz. (1989) *Modern Women's Lacrosse.* Hanover, NH: ABK Publications.

Hawthorne, Peel. (1993) "Seeing Eye to Eye on Protection." *Women's Lacrosse* (April/May): 1.

Howell, Nancy, and Maxwell L. Howell. (1969) *Sport and Games in Canadian Life: 1700 to Present.* Toronto: Macmillan of Canada.

International Federation of Women's Lacrosse Associations. (1991) *Handbook.* Scarborough, Ontario: J. Stanga.

"The Lacrosse Match, 1896." (1897) *Wycombe Abbey Gazette* 1, 1: 7.

Livingston, Lori A., and Susan L. Forbes. (1996) "Eye Injuries in Women's Lacrosse: Strict Rule Enforcement and Mandatory Eyewear Required." *The Journal of Trauma, Injury, Infection and Critical Care* 40, 1: 144–145.

Lumsden, Louisa. (1933) *Yellow Leaves: Memories of a Long Life.* Edinburgh: William Blackwood & Sons.

McCrone, Kathleen. (1987) " 'Play up! Play up! And Play the Game!' Sport at the Late Victorian Girls' Public Schools." In *From "Fair Sex" to Feminism: Sport and the Socialization of Women in the Industrial and Post-Industrial Eras,* edited by J. A. Mangan and R. J. Parks. London: Frank Cass, 97–129.

Metcalfe, Alan. (1987) *Canada Learns to Play: The Emergence of Organized Sport, 1807–1914.* Toronto: MacMillan of Canada.

"Moose Jaw Girls Play Lacrosse: So This Is a Man's World—Come Again!" (1950) *Moose Jaw Times-Herald* (May 19).

Morrow, Don. (1982) "The Canadian Image Abroad: The Great Lacrosse Tours of 1876 and 1883." In *Proceedings: Fifth Canadian Symposium on the History of Sport and Physical Education.* Toronto: University of Toronto Press, 11–23.

Roxborough, Henry. (1966) *One Hundred-Not Out: The Story of Nineteenth Century Canadian Sport.* Toronto: Ryerson Press.

"The Shield" (1890) *St. Leonards School Gazette* 1, 12: 131.

Stewart, Eileen. (1976) "Girls Lacrosse: Yesterday & Today!" *Lacrosse: The Canadian Game* 2, 1: 3.

Vennum, Thomas Jr. (1994) *American Indian Lacrosse: Little Brother of War.* Washington, DC: Smithsonian Institute.

LATIN AMERICAN MULTISPORT FESTIVALS

A number of international multisport festivals in the Americas preceded and followed the first Pan American Games. The South American Games were held as early as 1917. The Central American Games of 1921 in Guatemala City, Guatemala, and the South American Games the next year in Rio de Janeiro, Brazil, were included in independence centennial celebrations of Central America and Brazil, respectively. With the encouragement of Count Henri Baillet-Latour, vice president (and soon to be president) of the International Olympic Committee (IOC), and further planning in Paris during the 1924 Olympics, Mexico City, Mexico, organized the first regional games in the Americas recognized by the IOC in 1926. Only Mexico, Cuba, and Guatemala participated, in seven sports. A women's program of swimming, tennis, and volleyball had been proposed, but no women were included in the teams of the three countries.

This festival, known since 1938 as the Central American and Caribbean Games, has grown immensely in participation and number of sports and has been repeated on a regular four-year basis. The region of eligible countries includes Mexico, Central America, the Caribbean, and the northern tier of South American nations. Women began to participate in the second edition of the games, in 1930 in Havana, but only tennis was offered and all competitors were Cuban. The next games, in San Salvador, El Salvador, in 1935, included tennis (three countries only) and volleyball (two countries) for women. In Panama in 1938, the women's program added basketball, fencing, swimming, and diving (exhibition by a single Cuban woman). The 1946 games in Barranquilla, Colombia, added track and field as well as softball. In Guatemala in 1950, women's fencing and volleyball were not included, and softball was not offered for men or women. The 1954 games in Mexico returned fencing and volleyball to the women's program. In Caracas, Venezuela, in 1959, synchronized swimming was an exhibition sport. In 1962, in Kingston, Jamaica, basketball was dropped from the women's program, but it was reinstated in 1966, in San Juan, Puerto Rico. In 1970, in Panama, 400-meter and 800-meter races were added to women's track, this being the first appearance of races longer than 200 meters. That year Cuban women began to dominate the track and field events. Gymnastics was added, and nearly all of the first six places in all events went to Cubans. In 1974 the games were in Santo Domingo, Dominican Republic, and softball returned to the women's program. In 1978 in Medellín, Colombia, a 1500-meter race was added to the track events. María Colón of Cuba won the javelin (she won again in 1982 and 1986, dropping to second place in 1990). Synchronized swimming was a new medal sport. In Havana in 1982, the 3000-meter run, 400-meter hurdles, table tennis, shooting, and archery were new events for women. In 1986 the games were in Santiago, Dominican Republic, and even longer races were added for women: 10,000 meters, and a marathon. Also, field hockey, judo, and rowing were added to the women's program. Sylvia Poll of Costa Rica won gold medals in eight individual swimming events and two more in the relays, setting Central American and Caribbean records in all ten. Mexico hosted the 1990 games. New sports for women were badminton and bowling (both also new for men), canoeing, cycling, racquetball, Tae kwon do, and sailing. Also new in 1990 was equestrian sport, which mixes men and women in the competitions. In 1993 the Central American and Caribbean Games were in Ponce, Puerto Rico, and in 1998 in Maracaibo, Venezuela.

A smaller regional sport festival began in 1973, when Guatemala organized the first Central American Games. These games were intended to be repeated every four years, but difficulties arose at times and the games have been hosted on a somewhat irregular basis. At the end of the 1990s, the five original Central American republics, (Guatemala, El Salvador, Honduras, Nicaragua, Costa Rica) Belize, and Panama were eligible to participate. Women were included from the first, participating in 1973 in track (races through 1500 meters) and field, basketball, equestrian sport,

fencing, swimming, tennis, and volleyball. Marfa del Milagro Parfs of Costa Rica was the sensation of the 1973 games, winning thirteen gold medals and one silver medal in swimming. By the third games, held again in Guatemala in 1986, the women's program included the additional sports of bowling, gymnastics, softball, and table tennis. Women also participated in the exhibition sports of badminton and sailing in 1986. The 1990 Central American Games were in Tegucigalpa, Honduras; 1994, San Salvador; and 1998, San Pedro Sula, Honduras.

As the geographic area of eligible countries for international multisport festivals diminishes, the overall importance of the festivals, costs of participation, and general level of competition decrease. Thus, the numbers of participating countries and athletes and the overall proficiency of performances decrease from the Olympics, through the Pan-American, Central American and Caribbean, and finally the Central American Games.

Richard V. McGehee

See also Pan American Games

Bibliography

Ferreiro Toledano, Abraham. (1986) *Centroamérica y el caribe a través de sus juegos.* Mexico, D.F.: Artes Gráficas Rivera.

McGhee, R.V. (1994) "Los Juegos de las Américas: Four Inter-American Multisport Competitions." In *Sport in the Global Village,* edited by R.C. Wilcox. Morgantown, WV: Fitness Information Technology, Chapter 26.

Montesinos, Enrique, and Sigfredo Barros (1984) *Centroamericanos y del Caribe: Los más antiguos juegos deportivos regionales del mundo.* La Habana, Cuba: Editorial Científico-Técnica.

LATVIA

The republic of Latvia is a small nation with a population of 2.4 million on the eastern coast of the Baltic Sea in northeastern Europe. For much of its history Latvia was dominated by Germany or Russia, and it was part of the Soviet Union from 1945 until it became an independent nation in 1991. Although there was a tradition of Latvian sports such as pushing the disc and rowing, organized sports did not begin until the middle of the nineteenth century, and they were much influenced by Germany, Great Britain, and Sweden. Interest in sports was also influenced by Latvia's northern location, which favored participation in indoor sports and winter snow and ice sports.

As was the case in most nations, organized men's sports appeared first. The Rigaer Rowing Club was founded in 1852, the Riga Gymnastics Society in 1862 (although most members were Germans), and the Cyclists' Society in 1898. Women's participation in organized sports began in the twentieth century and grew in the 1920s and 1930s when Latvia was free of German and Russian control and sports were actively promoted throughout the nation. At the international level, Latvian women athletes were active in the field events of discus, shot put, and javelin, as well as in distance walking and airplane racing. Two Latvian women were contestants at the 1928 Summer Olympics and three participated in the 1936 Winter Olympics. In European and international competitions, Latvian women were highly regarded in the shot put and javelin, and Latvia was known as the "country of javelin throwers." The best-known Latvian woman athlete was Lavize Puce, who competed as a javelin thrower from the 1930s into the 1950s.

At the local level, women participated in organized sports such as basketball, ice skating, and swimming in large numbers, and by 1938 some 9,000 women were members of sports clubs. The YMCA established facilities in Latvia for women athletes. Other sports that drew women enthusiasts were cycling, downhill skiing, snow shoe racing, volleyball, and gymnastics.

Following World War II, when Latvia was part of the Soviet Union, Latvian athletes, including women, competed at the international level as part of the Soviet team formed from athletes from all the constituent republics of the Soviet Union. After the end of the Soviet Union, Latvian women competed on the Latvian Olympic teams. While the number of women team members has ranged from only one to thirteen, seven Latvian women have won Olympic gold medals: Inese Jaunzeme (1956, javelin), Tatjana Veinberga (1964, volleyball), Uljana Semonova (1976, 1980, basketball), Tamara Dauniene (1976, basketball), Natalija Las-

conova (1988, team gymnastics), Vera Zozula (1980, luge), and Elvira Ozolina (1960, javelin). Of these, Semonova was the best known internationally—as the 6-foot-10-inch center of the Soviet basketball team and the leading scorer in the 1976 and 1980 Olympics.

Sports at the local level during the Soviet era remained an important part of daily life for men and women, although reliable information for this period is not available. In 1997, members of sports clubs and associations in Latvia included 14,023 women and 28,257 men.

In 1991 the Latvian Association of Women's Sports was founded to increase and broaden the role of women in sports and in social and political life. Its specific goals were to train more women coaches, to organize fitness programs for women, to disseminate information about women's sports, and to encourage women to become more active in leadership roles in Latvian politics and business. In 1999, the association had 250 members and was located in Riga, Latvia. Its president was Astra Mille, a Latvian journalist. Latvian women's sports achievements are noted in the Latvian Sports Museum and the Latvian Olympic Museum.

Astra Mille
David Levinson

Bibliography

Crike, Vilis, and Gunars Gubins. (1970) *The History of Latvia Sports*. Rockville, MD: American Latvian Association.

Kise, Anna. (1965) *Physical Culture and Sports in Latvia*. Riga, Latvia.

LATYNINA, LARISSA SEMYENOVNA

(1934–)

SOVIET GYMNAST

Larissa Latynina has been called the "gymnast of the century" because she is the only gymnast, male or female, ever to have won the all-around title four times in international open competition, twice at the Olympic Games (1956, 1960), and twice at the world championships (1958, 1962). A recipient of the Olympic Order, presented by the International Olympic Committee, and a member of the International Gymnastics Hall of Fame, Latynina was also the only gymnast to win a gold medal in each of the four modern events for women in world championship and Olympic competition.

Born on 27 December 1934 in Kherson, Ukraine, Latynina developed a love of ballet early in her life. At age thirteen she saw a gymnastics competition and knew immediately that she could combine the grace and skill of a ballerina with the daring of the gymnast, and she chose to follow sport rather than dance. After high school, Latynina moved to Kiev to study physical education at the Physical Culture Institute. There, she met Alexander Misakov, who would coach her for the greater part of her career. They became good friends and worked very well together, often requiring little talk. They seemed to have a special intuition about each other. He required extensive training on the balance beam during each practice, knowing well that this event is often the Achilles heel of the all-arounder. His goal was to develop stability and consistency. In addition, she continued her training at the ballet bar and also attended training sessions under some of the best Ukrainian ballet masters.

Latynina dominated women's gymnastics for twelve years, from 1952 until 1964. At the 1956 world championships in Melbourne, she won every individual gold medal with the exception of floor exercise (silver). She thus became one of only two women in the twentieth century to narrowly miss a sweep of all events in their quest for a world all-around title. (Vera Caslavska nearly achieved a similar sweep at the 1968 Olympic Games in Mexico City, losing the gold for the balance beam by less than one point.) In addition to these achievements, Latynina won four golds in floor exercise—three in the Olympic Games (Melbourne, 1956; Rome, 1960; Tokyo, 1964) and the fourth at the world championships in Prague, Czechoslovakia, in 1962.

Latynina's approach to gymnastics was traditional. She was concerned about the expanding

Larissa Latynina performs on the balance beam at the 1956 Olympics in Melbourne. (AP Photos)

use of acrobatics in the floor exercise event, preferring a more classical, balletic approach. In an interview, she stated, "After all, a woman should remain a woman." The title of her book, *What Is This Little Girl's Name?*, reveals her attitude. Despite this attitude, she prepared the acrobatic Olga Korbut for her debut at the Munich Olympics in 1972. Latynina coached the Soviet team from 1967 to 1977 but was replaced as senior coach because of her views favoring beauty of performance over acrobatics and tumbling. She was said to be "out of touch." She coached for a decade more in Moscow and was appointed chief organizer for the Moscow Olympics in 1980, strongly defending the women she coached on the Soviet team who had been accused of taking performance-enhancing drugs.

After retirement, Latynina enjoyed swimming in the summer, skiing in the winter, and tennis with her husband, Yuri Feldman. The latter was a cyclist and former champion in the Soviet Union. Their daughter, Tanya, like her mother, studied ballet.

A. B. Frederick

Bibliography

Chaikovsky, Anatoli. (1963) "Laurels Crown Diligence of Larissa Latynina" (translated by Mildred Prchal from *Sportovani Gymnasticka*, a Czech gymnastics publication). In *The Modern Gymnast* (September): 29.

Götzt, Andreas, and Eckhard Herholz. (1992) *Das Turnjahrhundert der Deutschen*. Berlin: Edition OST.

Gutman, Dan. (1996) *Gymnastics*. New York: Viking.

Lessa, Christina. (1997) *Gymnastics Balancing Acts*. New York: Universe Publishing.

Marshall, Nancy Thies, and Pam Vredevelt. (1988) *Women Who Compete*. Old Tappan, NJ: F.H. Revell Co.

Melik-Karamov, Vitaly. (1980) "Latynina Discusses Olympic Women." *Gymnast* (September): 57.

Moran, Lyn. (1978) *The Young Gymnasts*. New York: K.S. Giniger.

Ryan, Joan. (1995) *Little Girls in Pretty Boxes*. New York: Doubleday.

Simons, Minot, II. (1995) *Women's Gymnastics: A History*. Carmel, CA: Welwyn Publishing.

Straus, Hal. (1978) *Gymnastics Guide*. Mountain View, CA: World Publications.

Silken Laumann acknowledges the crowd after winning the first heat at the 1996 Summer Olympics in Atlanta, Georgia. (AP Photos)

LAUMANN, SILKEN SUZETTE

(1964–)

CANADIAN ROWER

Silken Laumann is the greatest female rower ever produced by Canada. Her brilliant career has lacked only an individual sculling gold medal, but her failure to win gold at the 1992 Olympics may have been her finest moment in sport.

Laumann was born on 14 November 1964, in Missisauga, Ontario. She began her sport career as a runner but at age seventeen turned to rowing along with her older sister, Danielle. They quickly advanced to the Canadian national team and, in 1984 at Los Angeles, California, teamed to win a bronze medal in the Olympic double sculls. After Danielle retired from the sport, Laumann continued with other partners and began to scull a single as well. In 1985, she finished fourth at the world championships in the single sculls. After a single sculls gold medal at the 1987 Pan-American Games, she returned to the doubles for the 1988 Olympics at Seoul, finishing seventh with Kay Worthington.

After the 1988 Olympics, Laumann focused almost exclusively on the single sculls. She finished seventh at the 1989 world championships and moved up to finish second in 1990, before winning the singles world championship in 1991. She dominated women's sculling in that year, also winning international titles at Lucerne, Switzerland, San Diego, California, and Hazelwinkel, Belgium; as part of the World Cup competition.

With the 1992 Barcelona Olympics on the horizon, Laumann was the heavy favorite to win the gold medal in single sculls. But shortly before the Barcelona Olympics, training at a lake in Essen, Germany, on 16 May 1992, her scull collided with another scull, and the impact drove a piece of the splashboard into her leg. She sustained an open tibia fracture, with concurrent nerve damage, which permanently weakened her leg. She also lost skin and soft tissue that required multiple operations. She noted that "the muscles on the outside of my right leg were peeled back and hanging down to the ankle . . . the doctors thought I would never row again." Her gold medal plans seemed doomed, but she refused to quit. Pushing herself through rehabilitation, she was determined to compete at Barcelona, Spain, even if she was at less than her previous dominant self. "I will not forget getting back into the shell. I love the sport so much, but I didn't fully realize it until I got out there. I just sat in the boat for a time, pushed off the dock, then started to cry. It was wonderful."

Laumann did not win the single sculls at Barcelona, but she did finish third behind her archrival, Romania's Elisabeta Lipa. Many observers agreed with Olympic chronicler Bud Greenspan when he said: "Canada won four gold medals and one bronze medal in rowing at Lake Banyoles. Let the word go out that on this day the bronze medal shone as brightly in the Barcelona sun as any of the gold."

Laumann's career did not end at Barcelona. Still with nerve and muscle damage to her injured leg, she finished second at the world championship in 1995 in the singles and repeated that finish for an Olympic silver medal at Atlanta, Georgia, in 1996 before retiring.

Bill Mallon

Bibliography

Canadian Team Handbook/Guide De L'Équipe Canadienne.

Greenspan, Bud. (1992) *16 Days of Glory: Barcelona 1992.* New York: Cappy Productions.

Quinn, Hal. (1992) "Reviving the Dream." *Maclean's* (27 July):44–45.

Wallechinsky, David. (1996) *Sports Illustrated Presents the Complete Book of the Summer Olympics.* New York: Little, Brown.

LAW

The law's unique contribution to women in sport lies in its providing them opportunities equal to men in participation, employment, and enjoyment. Equal opportunity is achieved through the application of laws of individual nations and the results of court decisions implementing these laws. The most profound international influence in the expansion of opportunities for women were the United Nations General Assembly resolution, *The Convention on the Elimination of All Forms of Discrimination Against Women and the Declaration* and *Platform for Action* of the Fourth World Conference on Women in September 1995 in Beijing, China. By 1999 the UN resolution had been ratified by over two-thirds of the organization's member countries. Although neither document was legally binding, both inspired the creation of binding legislation throughout the world.

INTERNATIONAL FOCUS

Under international human rights law, women and men are vested with fundamental freedoms and human rights without regard to characteristics such as sex and race. Regardless of cultural particularities, religious tenets, and levels of development, women all over the world are entitled to enjoy human rights. There are three main reasons for calling attention to women's human rights: 1) To inform women that they have human rights and are entitled to enjoy them. . . . 2) To expose and combat rights violations that are based on sex or gender. . . . 3) To shape a new human rights practice, that fully addresses the human rights of women.

The UN resolution applies to intentional discrimination and acts that have a discriminatory effect. A committee was established to monitor international compliance. Nations ratifying the resolution were required to submit to the secretary-general of the United Nations a report on the legislative, judicial, administrative or other measures they had adopted to implement the Convention within a year after its entry into force and then at least every four years thereafter.

The Beijing Declaration stated that "women's rights are human rights . . . and the Declaration reaffirms the Vienna concept that the human rights of women and of the girl child are an inalienable, integral and indivisible part of all human rights and fundamental freedoms." The declaration also reaffirmed a commitment to:

the equal rights and inherent human dignity of women and men and other purposes and principles enshrined in the Charter of the United Nations, to the Universal Declaration of Human Rights and other international human rights instruments, in particular the Convention on the Elimination of All Forms of Discrimination against Women and the Convention on the Rights of the Child, as well as the Declaration on the Elimination of Violence against Women and the Declaration on the Right to Development.

It should be noted that the key area of concern for women throughout the world in the 1990s was violence against women. Another area of concern was women's capacity to inherit real and personal property. In many countries women were allowed to inherit only one-half that of their male siblings. Culture and tradition influenced decisions on the position of women throughout the world.

The role and value of sport and physical activity for women differed throughout the world, as did each country's view of women in competitive athletics. Historically, nations had seen sport and physical activity as a male domain; only a few had seen them as important to females. Among those favoring sport and physical activity for all were nations that still generally restricted competitive athletics to men. Few, if any, countries of the world enforced equity in competitive athletics.

Within the *Platform for Action* of the Beijing Conference, sport and physical activity were described in the two statements that follow, each taken from different points in its statements of objectives:

Develop Non-Discriminatory Education and Training in response to Education and the Training of Women:

Provide accessible recreational and sports facilities and establish and strengthen gender-sensitive programmes for girls and women of all ages in education and community institutions and support the advancement of women in all areas of athletics and physical activity, including coaching, training and administration, and as participants at the national, regional and international levels.

Strengthen Preventive Programmes that Promote Women's Health:

Create and support programmes in the educational system, in the workplace and in the community to make opportunities to participate in sport, physical activity and recreation available to girls and women of all ages on the same basis as they are made available to men and boys.

The United Nations General Assembly resolution and the Beijing *Platform for Action* served as the cornerstone for the rights of women to participate in, be employed in, and enjoy sport and physical activity.

UNITED STATES

Although, as of 1999, the United States had not ratified the UN resolution on the elimination of discrimination against women, it had experienced more litigation over equal opportunity for women than any other country in the world. Increasingly this litigation was occurring in sport, particularly competitive athletics.

In the 1990s in the United States, sport was used with increasing frequency as a vehicle for achieving gender equity in various social realms. Litigation among secondary and collegiate women wishing to participate in sport was phenomenal, in terms of its frequency and its success. Litigation on pay and other issues for coaches of women's sports teams also occurred. The volume of litigation on women's issues in sport in the United States far exceeded the attention to equity in other countries, and it was expected to encourage other nations to choose sport as the vehicle for obtaining women's rights.

The primary laws influencing gender equity in sport in the United States were the equal protection clause of the Fourteenth Amendment to the U.S. Constitution; Title IX of the Education Amendments of 1972; the Civil Rights Acts of 1987 and 1991; and a legal theory, "disparate impact," that evolved from the results of employment litigation. The Civil Rights Act of 1991 had a profound impact on the results of litigation because it provided attorney fees and punitive damage awards, awards that did not exist before the act.

The equal protection clause of the Fourteenth Amendment states: "No state shall make or enforce any law which shall . . . deny to any person within its jurisdiction the equal protection of the law." "An equal protection challenge must show that groups of people are being treated differently without justification. An equal protection challenge in scholastic and collegiate sport is a complaint by a group of people (women) that they are being treated different from others (men) in athletics and that no justification exists to warrant the difference in treatment." Many cases paved the way for equity for women in sport in the United States, including *Brenden v. Independent School District* (1972, 1973), *Hollander v. Connecticut Interscholastic Athletic Conference, Inc.* (1971, 1972), *Reed v. Nebraska* (1972), *Haas v. South Bend Community School Corporation* (1972), *Morris v. Michigan State Board of Education* (1973), *Gilpin v. Kansas State High School Association* (1974), *National Organization for Women v. Little League Baseball, Inc.* (1974), *Darrin v. Gould* (1975), *Magill v. Avonworth Baseball Conference, et al.* (1975), *Fortin v. Darlington Little League, Inc.* (1975), *Carnes v. Tennessee Secondary School Athletic Association* (1976), *Bednar v. Nebraska School Activities Association* (1976), *Leffel, et al. v. Wisconsin Interscholastic Athletic Association* (1978), *Israel v. West Virginia Secondary School Activities Commission* (1989), *Libby v. South Inter-Conference Association* (1990), and *Habetz v. Louisiana High School Athletic Association* (1990). All involved instances in which women either tried to play on existing men's teams or requested separate teams for women. During the period, *Bucha* (1982) challenged the types of events used in women's swim competitions, while *Rittacco* (1973) and *Yellow Springs Exempted Village School District*

(1981) questioned laws denying competition for women. Title IX of the Education Amendments of 1972, which played a significant role in creating a climate for equity in the United States, states that:

> No person in the United States shall, on the basis of sex, be excluded from participation in, be denied the benefit of, or be subject to discrimination under any education program or activity receiving federal financial assistance. (20 USC section 1681).

Under Title IX the U.S. government implemented an administrative body that monitored and investigated complaints. This administrative body not only created guidelines to explain and monitor Title IX but also promoted an atmosphere of sensitivity to complaints. Title IX and its guidelines were a useful adjunct to legal complaints filed under the Fourteenth Amendment.

Disparate impact, a theory that evolved from the results of litigation in employment, involved practices that appear to be neutral in their treatment of groups but fall more harshly on one group. Methods of analysis used in evaluating incidents of discrimination were statistics, history, procedures, and specific instances. These were used to identify patterns and practices of discrimination. For example, in athletics, opportunities for participation must reflect the male/female enrollment ratio for the school or college. If 14 percent of the male school population participates in competitive sport, 14 percent of the female school population will be expected to participate in competitive sport. While the figures do not have to be identical, they are expected to be within a 3 percent range.

GENDER EQUALITY AT GOLF CLUBS

In a landmark 1999 decision, a jury in Massachusetts found that nine women had been discriminated against by the Haverhill Golf and Country Club and awarded the women $1.9 million in damages. The women claimed that the club denied them full membership and also denied them equal access to the golf course. The decision is expected to have ramifications at private country clubs across the United States, some of which have similar policies or traditions which deny women equal memberships and access to facilities. Although these clubs are private facilities, they come under the purview of equal access laws for public facilities because courts have ruled that if they provide access to individuals beyond their members, they are public facilities.

SPORT AND GENERAL EQUALITY

The link between women's participation in sport and equality in professions and at the polls is indicated by this editorial from the *New York Times* of 18 November 1876 which comments on women's performance in a walking race and alludes to a recent Supreme Court decision banning women from the Bar (legal profession): *The acclaim with which the victor was carried off the ground signalized the downfall of an ancient prejudice. . . . Obviously, those who have aspirations above babytending, dishwashing, and writing for magazines will refuse to accept walking matches in lieu of possible forensic honors. Let such be encouraged, however, by what has been encouraged. The world moves—is moving. To day it is the walking match; next it will be the coveted Bar. After that, who shall tell how soon the ballot will come?*

CASE LAW CREATED CHANGE

Among the leading cases in sex discrimination in athletics were *Ridgway, Haffer, Blair, Cohen, Roberts, Favia, Cook, Boucher, Pederson, Beasley, Horner,* and *Adams.*

Ridgway v. Montana High School Athletic Association (1988) was a class action suit brought on behalf of all the young women in Montana high schools against the High School Athletic Association (HSAA). It alleged violation of Title IX, the Fourteenth Amendment, and the constitution of Montana. The plaintiffs claimed discrimination in the number of sports offered; seasons of play; length of seasons; practice and game schedules; and access to facilities, equipment, coaching, trainers, transportation, school band, uniforms, publicity, and general support. The court fashioned an agreement that provided equal opportunity for all Montana women and appointed a facilitator to oversee the change.

Haffer v. Temple University (1987), a class action suit, focused on three claims: the extent to which Temple University afforded women students fewer "opportunities to compete" in intercollegiate athletics, the disparity in resources allocated to the men's and women's programs, and the disparity in the allocation of financial aid to male and female students. Discrimination in violation of the Fourteenth Amendment and the Pennsylvania Equal Rights Amendment was found in opportunities to compete, expenditures, recruiting, coaching, travel and per diem allowance, uniforms, equipment, supplies, housing and dining facilities, and publicity.

In *Blair v. Washington State University* (1987), the trial court excluded football in the equity calculation. The plaintiff appealed the decision; the Supreme Court of Washington reversed the decision, requiring that football be included in all calculations for finance and participation. *Blair* defined the role of football in equity considerations.

Cohen v. Brown University (1997, 1996, 1995, 1993, 1992), a class action suit against the university, its president, and its athletic director for discrimination against women in collegiate athletics, was brought in response to the demotion of the women's gymnastics and volleyball teams from varsity to donor or club status. A preliminary injunction restoring the volleyball and gymnastics teams to varsity status was issued by the United States District Court of the District of Rhode Island. Also, Brown was prohibited from eliminating or reducing the funding of women's sports. The United States Court of Appeals, First Circuit, affirmed the district court's decision (*Cohen v. Brown*, 1993). The district court, after a lengthy bench trial, found Brown to be in violation of Title IX and ordered the university to submit a comprehensive plan for compliance within 120 days (*Cohen v. Brown*, 1995). When the court determined that Brown's compliance plan was inadequate, it was forced to formulate a plan based on

Brown's objectives. The remedial order required Brown to make women's gymnastics, fencing, skiing, and water polo varsity sports. On 21 November 1996, the United States Court of Appeals upheld the district court's ruling; Brown University had violated Title IX by discriminating against females in demoting the volleyball and gymnastics teams to club status. Brown University's petition for writ of *certiorari* to the United States Supreme Court was denied (*Brown University, et al. v. Cohen, et al.,* 1997).

Roberts v. Colorado State Board of Agriculture (1993[1], 1993[2], 1993[3]) was triggered by the elimination of the women's softball and baseball teams at Colorado State University in June 1992. By using "equity by enrollment" figures of the undergraduate population for a fourteen-year period beginning in the 1980–1981 school year, plaintiffs demonstrated that "average disparity between enrollment and athletic participation rates for women was 14.1%" (1993[1], 1512). Also, Colorado State failed to show a history and continuing practice of program expansion for women; no new teams had been added in the past twelve years. Colorado State appealed. The Court of Appeals, Tenth Circuit, affirmed the trial court's decision; Colorado State's writ of *certiorari* to the U.S. Supreme Court was denied.

In *Favia,* female athletes were successful in reinstating an eliminated sport, while *Cook* (1992, 1993) and, later, *Bryant* (1997) were successful in raising Colgate University's women's ice hockey team from club to varsity status. Like Brown, Colgate had been an all-male school until the 1970s. In the short span of a little over twenty years the male/female ratio had become nearly 50/50. Enrollment for the 1990–1991 school year was 53 percent male and 47 percent female. The issue, however, was financial, the difference between $238,561.00 and $4,600.00.

In *Boucher, et al. v. Syracuse University* (1996), members of the women's lacrosse and softball teams were successful against Syracuse University in their quest for a broader selection of sports and higher levels of competition.

Pederson, et al. v. Louisiana State University (1996) was a case that fine-tuned gender equity; issues were damage awards and the finding of an intent to discriminate. To award damages, the court had to find that harm was intended. The court "held that the violations are not intentional. Rather they are a result of arrogant ignorance, confusion regarding the practical requirements of the law, and a remarkably outdated view of women and athletics which created the byproduct of resistance to change" (918).

At Alabama State University, Beasley, a recruited female athlete, was never given a scholarship and for a long period of time the medical problems she sustained as an athlete were not covered by the institution. Beasley not only won her case, *Beasley v. Alabama State University, et al.* (1997), she was allowed to bring punitive damages against the university.

Among scholastic women successfully achieving gender equity were twelve female high school slow-pitch softball players who brought a cause of action against the Kentucky High School Athletic Association (KHSAA) in *Horner v. Kentucky* (1994). After failure in the lower court, they were successful in the United States Court of Appeals, Sixth Circuit.

Adams v. Baker, et al. (1996) was Tiffany Adams's successful bid for a spot on the wrestling team. The court said the United School District No. 626, Valley Center, Kansas, either had to establish a wrestling team for women or permit females on the existing team.

In June 1997 the National Women's Law Center filed a sex discrimination suit against twenty-five National Collegiate Athletic Association (NCAA) member institutions, stating that female athletes received a disproportionate small amount of finances.

Two acts in the 1990s that strengthened U.S. laws were the Equity in Athletics Disclosure Act (1994) and the Fair Play Act (1997). The Equity Act requires that colleges and universities collect and disclose information concerning gender equity in intercollegiate athletics. The Fair Play Act requires the U.S. government to publish financial and other information about sports.

In the 1990s women achieved success in participation, employment, and enjoyment of sport and physical activity. It was expected that the United Nations resolutions on women's equity and rights and the Beijing Declaration would extend that success to all women in all nations in the twenty-first century.

Annie Clement

Bibliography

Clement, Annie. (1998) *Law in Sport and Physical Activity*. Tallahassee, FL: Sport and Law Press.

Lockwood, Carol Elizabeth, et al., eds. (1998) *The International Human Rights of Women*. Chicago: American Bar Association.

Naughton, Jim. (1997) "Bias Complaint Forces Colleges to Confront Tension Between Title IX and NCAA rules." *The Chronicle of Higher Education* (20 June): A39–A40.

Schuler, Margaret A., and Dorothy Q. Thomas, eds. (1997) *Women's Human Rights*. Washington, DC: Women, Law and Development International.

LEE, MABEL

(1886–1985)

U.S. EDUCATOR

Mabel Lee was the director of physical education for women at the University of Nebraska for twenty-eight years. Her long and meaningful life was a testimony to her efforts to promote the inclusion of quality daily physical activity and sport in the lives of all human beings.

Lee was born in Iowa on 18 August 1886. Despite the fact that few females were afforded formal education in the 1800s, her mother and father dedicated themselves to providing educational opportunities for four daughters. Fascinated with the human body and its ability to move gracefully, forcefully, and flexibly, Lee discovered the Boston Normal School of Gymnastics, a school where she could study health and physical activity. Her father, however, believing that attending such a school so far from home was ridiculous, prompted her to enroll in and graduate from Coe College. After completing a degree in psychology and philosophy, Lee was determined to pursue her dream of earning a degree in health and physical education.

The Boston Normal School of Gymnastics, headed by Amy Morris Homans, was combined with Wellesley College, a prestigious women's college. Wellesley's prestige and location gave Lee much opportunity: some of the greatest philosophers in the fields of health and physical education—including Harvard University professors—resided in the nearby Boston area.

Having completed the degree at Wellesley College, Lee became a woman on a mission, using her energy, enthusiasm, intelligence, determination, drive, and passion to devise and advocate physical activity programs for women. As a teacher, she touched the lives of students at Coe College, Beloit College, Oregon State University, and the University of Nebraska at Lincoln. It was in Lincoln that Lee was able to blossom and flourish, providing outstanding leadership as director of physical education for women from 1924 to 1952.

Lee was a significant force for change within her profession. Her charismatic personality, dedication to excellence, and visionary leadership helped her to enlist others in her crusade for the promotion of lifetime physical activity. She became the first woman president of the American Physical Education Association (APEA) and the first woman president of the American Academy of Physical Education (AAPE), where she was also named a fellow. She was also involved in the establishment of the National Association of Physical Education for College Women (NAPECW) and was its president.

Once retired from the University of Nebraska, Lee wrote many books that influenced the thinking of the profession: *Memories of a Bloomer Girl* (1977), *Memories Beyond Bloomers* (1978), and *History of Physical Education and Sport in the USA* (1983). She was also honored with a Fulbright Professorship to Iraq; she received honorary doctorates from Coe College, George Williams College, and Beloit College; and the University of Nebraska's women's physical education building was named after her. Her life is probably best summarized by an honor bestowed upon her by the President's Council for Physical Fitness and Sport in 1982. Mabel Lee, whose mission was to teach the importance of physical activity and fitness in the lives of all, was acknowledged as one of five women in the United States who had significantly impacted the lives of women in physical education and sport. Mabel Lee died on 3 December 1985 at the age of ninety-nine.

Darlene A. Kluka

Bibliography

Coe College Web site. "Mabel Lee Biography." <http://www.coe.edu>. 1998.

Ulrich, Celeste. (1986) "Mabel Lee." *Journal of Physical Education, Recreation, and Dance* 3: 24–26.

LENGLEN, SUZANNE

(1899–1938)

FRENCH TENNIS PLAYER

Suzanne Lenglen, the great French tennis champion, was one of the "titans of the twenties," the athletes who smashed records, broke barriers, changed movement patterns, and altered perceptions of what the human body and spirit could achieve during the "Golden Age" of sports. Her career spanned much of this golden age.

Born in Compiègne, France, she became the first recorded child prodigy in tennis. Lenglen was trained at the tennis club in Nice by her father, who was her first and only coach. He was a severe taskmaster, and he perfected his daughter's skills with a rigorous training program and fashioned her game according to that of male tennis players. Lenglen's style of play, which included an overhand serve, a volley, and an approach shot in which she hit the ball on the rise, proved successful. In 1913, at the age of fifteen, she won the women's club championship at Nice and a year later won the world hard court championship at Saint-Cloud, a suburb of Paris, in singles and doubles and took second in the mixed doubles.

Lenglen's first appearance at Wimbledon was delayed by World War I. In 1919 the French champion arrived at Wimbledon to challenge the forty-year-old, seven-time champion Dorothea Lambert Chambers. With a victory over Chambers, Lenglen's career was launched. She became the first foreign-born female singles champion at Wimbledon, where she introduced an entirely new game to the world of tennis as she enthralled the British press.

After this victory, Lenglen created a public persona with a flamboyant style of dress, which

Suzanne Lenglen, c. 1920. (Corbis)

included a short silk skirt, a bandeau of brightly colored silk, bracelets, and a white fur coat. After she adopted the freer style of clothing, other tennis players followed her lead and discarded corsets and other restrictive clothing. An equally flamboyant style of play and living made Lenglen a media star, one of the first to forge a link between sport and show business. She was probably the first athlete, and certainly the first female athlete, to understand the power of the media and how to use the media for self-promotion.

After winning all three titles (singles, doubles, and mixed doubles) at the world hard court championship in Saint-Cloud in 1920, she won all three titles at Wimbledon that same year. After Wimbledon, she won the gold medal in the 1920 Olympic Games at Antwerp, where she introduced herself as "The Great Lenglen." Repeated victories at Saint-Cloud and Wimbledon the next year confirmed that Lenglen was indeed the champion of the world.

To prove that she was indeed the world champion, Lenglen was enticed to enter the American championship at Forest Hills in 1921. Suffering from an attack of the flu, Lenglen defaulted against the American champion, Molla Mallory. This default badly tarnished Lenglen's reputation, and her claim of being world champion was

SHE SHOWED HER ANKLES AT WIMBLEDON

Suzanne Lenglen shocked many English tennis fans at Wimbledon in 1919 when she appeared in a calf-length dress, with garters holding her stockings above the knee and sipping brandy from a flask between sets. Lenglen's clothing, initially seen as outrageous, became chic, however, and her bandeau, worn around her hair to keep it off her face, became a fashion accessory adopted by women both on and off the tennis court. Elizabeth Ryan, winner of nineteen Wimbledon doubles titles, said, "All women tennis players should go down on their knees in thankfulness to Suzanne for delivering them from the tyranny of corsets."

questioned because some people believed that she defaulted to avoid defeat.

She continued to dominate tennis, however, winning three more world hard-court titles (1922–1924), defeating Mallory at Wimbledon in 1922, and then winning again in 1923 for the fifth time. She withdrew from Wimbledon in 1924 due to illness but reclaimed her position by winning at Saint-Cloud and Wimbledon in 1925. By the end of that summer, she dominated tennis as no athlete had dominated a sport at that time.

Lenglen's career culminated early in 1926 with a challenge from Helen Wills, who had replaced Mallory as the American champion. The "Match of the Century," as it came to be known, was Lenglen's greatest triumph. She returned to the Côte d'Azur to play at the Carlton Club in Nice before thousands of spectators, who included the best sportswriters of the day, princes, and grand dukes. Lenglen won the match. This was the last time the two ever met in singles competition.

The match with Wills was the climax of Lenglen's career, after which all else would seem anticlimactic. Later in the same year, she was accused of insulting Queen Mary by appearing late for a match. She withdrew from the tournament, claiming illness, never to play at Wimbledon again. Later that year Lenglen signed a contract with C. C. ("Cash and Carry") Pyle to play in the United States and became the first professional tennis player, man or woman. She began her professional career in October in Madison Square

Garden, defeating Mary K. Browne, whom Pyle had also signed as part of his touring team. The tour ended early in 1927, and Lenglen returned to France, where she continued to play professional tennis for a few more months. Lenglen wanted to compete, and to do so she needed amateur status as there were few, if any, opportunities to compete professionally. The French tennis federation refused to reinstate her amateur status, although they did so with a male French player. In 1929 she sold sports clothes in a Parisian dress house. Although she was something of a celebrity, she needed the money.

From 1933 to 1938, she directed a government-sponsored tennis school in Paris. In 1938 she became very ill with pernicious anemia and died during the Wimbledon fortnight as Helen Wills Moody prepared to win her eighth singles title.

In a seven-year period from 1919 to 1926, Lenglen did not lose a match except for the one default at Forest Hills, and she lost only two sets in singles. She won eighty-nine of ninety-two matches in three categories at Wimbledon. She also won fifteen world hard-court championships, fifteen French national championships, six Wimbledon singles titles, and two Olympic gold medals. Her legacy extends beyond her records, however. Lenglen's transformation of cultural perceptions of movement, sport, and the female athlete; her challenges to accepted standards of behavior; and her alteration of the style of play in tennis seemed to have dissipated with her death. It would be twenty years before Gussie Moran shocked Wimbledon audiences with lace panties in 1949. It would be 1968, almost forty years, before tennis became a viable professional sport. And it would be forty years before Billie Jean King confronted society with a shocking lifestyle and dazzled the world with a serve-and-volley style of play and a victory in "The Battle of the Sexes" in 1973. None of these were not without precedent, however—Suzanne Lenglen had foreshadowed these in the 1920s.

Susan J. Bandy

Bibliography

Anet, Claude. (1927) *Suzanne Lenglen.* Paris: Simon Kra.

Clerci, Giovanni. (1984) *Suzanne Lenglen: La Diva du Tennis.* Paris: Rochevignes.

Danzig, Allison, and Peter Brandwein, eds. (1948) *Sport's Golden Age.* New York: Harper and Brothers.

Engelmann, Larry. (1988) *The Goddess and the American Girl.* New York: Oxford University Press.

Gardiner, A. G. (1926) *Certain People of Importance.* London: Jonathon Cape.

Pileggi, Sarah. (1982) "The Lady in the White Dress." *Sport s Illustrated* 57: 63–79.

Skene, Don. (1953) "Wills and Lenglen and Money." In *The Greatest Sport Stories from the Chicago Tribune,* edited by Arch Ward. New York: A.S. Barnes.

LESBIANISM

Lesbians—women who choose to have social, emotional, and sexual relationships with other women—are doubly disadvantaged in sport, first as women and second as members of a stigmatized sexual minority. Although there is evidence of extensive lesbian sport participation as players, physical educators, coaches, officials, and administrators, there is also a long history of discrimination and harassment of lesbians, and women suspected of being lesbian, at all levels of sport.

HISTORY

Contemporary forms of prejudice against lesbians in Western countries had their beginnings in the early 1900s; by the 1920s, sexologists had firmly established that homosexuality and lesbianism were deviant, and this psychiatric label persisted up to the 1970s, when American gay and lesbian activists succeeded in demedicalizing sexual preference. Until the early twentieth century, intimate friendships between women had been accepted rather than pathologized; thus, the close bonds that developed between sportswomen had rarely been cause for concern. Since that time, however, single-sex contexts such as women's colleges and women's sports, especially team sports traditionally played by men, have been suspected of attracting and/or producing lesbians. Under these conditions, sport has come to represent pleasure and danger for lesbians. While sports provide a welcoming place where one might expect to find lesbians, it is also a place where lesbians are the frequent targets of intense homophobia (the irrational fear and hatred of lesbian, gay, and bisexual people, manifested in ostracism, harassment, or violence).

Throughout most of the twentieth century, sport in Western countries was viewed as an appropriate means of socializing boys into "normal" heterosexual manhood. In contrast, critics of female sports, including doctors and educators, were concerned about the threat to normal, healthy womanhood posed by girls' and women's sporting participation. Although most of the early medical concerns about the alleged dangers to the female reproductive system have been dismissed, the general apprehension about links between sport and sexually nonconforming girls and women ("tomboys" and "butch" women) persisted. For example, the 1990s preoccupation among psychiatrists and parents with "gender-identity disorder" demonstrated yet again the important links between sports and the social construction of heterosexual femininity. For a girl, "excessive" interest in sports was one of the "disordered" behaviors that demonstrated failure to accept her appropriate feminine identity. Needless to say, a boy's preoccupation with sports was not seen as cause for concern.

THE "OVERREPRESENTATION" THEORY

There has been considerable debate in sport circles about the theory that lesbians are overrepresented, especially in team sports and nontraditional activities such as martial arts. There is little conclusive evidence to support or refute the claim; however, it is possible to identify a number of factors that have contributed to this perception.

First, sportswomen of all sexual orientations often present and conduct themselves in ways that do not meet conventional standards of female heterosexuality ("femininity"). Thus, they present a challenge to the prevailing stereotypes of women as passive, dependent, and sexually appealing to men, as well as posing a threat to the male monopoly of sports. Since sports promote personality characteristics conventionally defined as masculine—risk taking, dominance, and aggression, for example—conservative critics also view female sport participation as a potential threat to power relations between the sexes, which rely in large part on rigid sex roles and emphasized sex differences (e.g., "boys will be boys"). For these reasons, women in sport are likely to be labeled lesbian in an attempt to discourage sexual nonconformity and to discredit women's sport.

Related to this pattern of challenging heterosexual femininity is the theory that the independent or nonconforming spirit that prompts girls and women to play sports also functions in relation to sexuality, leading women to choose to live as lesbians. However, this idea of an independent personality trait does not explain why many lesbians lead otherwise conventional lives and/or show no interest in sport, nor does it take into account the debate about sexual orientation as an innate characteristic rather than a matter of choice.

Regarding the relationship between sport and women's autonomy, however, there is ample evidence to show that heterosexist norms of "feminine" behavior, clothing, and appearance can limit girls and women, figuratively and literally, while physical strength and athletic competence enhance confidence and self-esteem. In short, regardless of motivation, sports offers physical, social, and psychological benefits to girls and women of all sexual orientations. For women who suffer the combined impact of sexism and homophobia, perhaps in addition to racism and classism, the benefits of sport are particularly important.

Second, for many decades, lesbians, even those with limited sporting ability, have found women's recreational sports a welcoming place for physical activity and social interaction. Out-door team sports such as softball or soccer attract large numbers of lesbians as players and spectators. In some communities, given the general trend for other leisure pursuits to be open to both sexes, team sport may be one of the few remaining single-sex social activities. And, free from the constraints imposed by male partners, lesbians may have more discretionary leisure time for sport than many heterosexual women. Hence, lesbians may, in fact, be in the majority in some women's sport leagues.

Third, even a small number of visible lesbians in a particular sport is often construed, according to homophobic ways of thinking, as a lesbian "takeover." If approximately 10 percent of the female population were lesbian (a generally accepted statistic), and if this proportion of sportswomen were openly lesbian, their presence would be difficult to discount, particularly in sports that attract extensive media coverage, such as the Ladies Professional Golf Association (LPGA). However, most lesbians in sport—players, coaches, physical educators, administrators—keep their sexual identities hidden because of justifiable fears of ostracism, harassment, or violence.

LESBIANS IN MAINSTREAM SPORTS

Lesbians in mainstream sports have long been an invisible presence. The chilly climate produced by homophobia makes it difficult or even dangerous for lesbians to be open about their sexual identities in sports, as in many other social settings. Since there is a longstanding homophobic perception that sports either "masculinize" women or attract women who are "masculine" (meaning lesbian) at the outset, female athletes of all sexual orientations come under scrutiny because of their presumed lesbianism. Hence, lesbian athletes are likely to keep their identities hidden and remain "in the closet," heterosexual women may disassociate themselves from their lesbian teammates, and both groups may expend time and energy keeping up the appearance of heterosexuality.

This apologetic approach to maintaining an acceptable image of women's sport was particularly evident in the 1960s and 1970s as female sporting participation in schools, universities, and communities increased. Even supportive commentators drew attention to the conventional beauty of prominent female athletes to establish their heterosexual credentials, rather than challenging the homophobia behind most criticisms of women in sport as well as the double standard that required female (but not male) athletes to pay attention to their appearance. By the 1980s and 1990s, an era marked by the growing commercialization and commodification of sport and athletes, there was added pressure on all women in professional and high-performance sport to present themselves as heterosexually attractive and to dispel rumors of lesbianism to maintain corporate sponsorship and popularity with fans.

STAYING "IN THE CLOSET"

Since the 1920s and 1930s, the so-called Golden Age of women's sport, lesbian players have experienced pressure from peers, coaches, and administrators to stay "in the closet" (to keep their sexual identities hidden) for the good of the team—a sport variation on the 1990s American military code for gays and lesbians, "don't ask, don't tell." This practice blames lesbians for the alleged threat they pose, while it exonerates those who express the homophobic view that visible lesbians damage the image of women's sport. At the same time, pressure to stay "in the closet" makes lesbians in sport particularly vulnerable to harassment and discrimination, since the code of silence prevents them from reporting incidents to the authorities. Some coaches expressly state that they do not allow "it" (lesbianism) on their teams, a position that forces women who are lesbian to present themselves as heterosexual, to hide all aspects of their private lives, and to live in fear of exposure. The hyperfeminine dress code enforced by many coaches (long hair, makeup, tight-fitting uniforms) is yet another attempt to promote a heterosexual image for women's sport.

For lesbians who are professional or elite athletes, the consequences of disclosure include lost sponsorships or elimination from teams, as well as the obvious vulnerability to censure, harassment, or violence experienced by all women who are in the public eye. In the 1980s and 1990s, some prominent sportswomen, including tennis champion Martina Navratilova and LPGA golfer Muffin Spencer-Devlin, "came out" publicly and proudly as lesbian, and their positive examples encouraged lesbians in all levels of sport. Although many lesbian sports figures who remained in the closet were recognized by their lesbian fans, this alone did not lead to heightened awareness and acceptance in the nonlesbian community. Thus, it remains important that women in school and community sports and recreation, not just elite athletes, be able to lead openly lesbian lives and serve as positive examples to girls and women.

In the highly competitive context of American intercollegiate sport, women experience some of the same pressures as professional sportswomen to emphasize their heterosexual credentials. For lesbians holding athletic scholarships, the stakes are particularly high since disclosure can mean elimination from the team and the end of a university career. Homophobia is pervasive in the recruitment process in intercollegiate sport, as evident, for example, in the practice of "reverse recruitment," whereby coaches or athletic directors circulate rumors of widespread lesbianism in other university athletics departments to persuade (homophobic) parents to place their daughter in that university's program. In a variation on this practice, (usually)

DISCRIMINATION AGAINST SEXUAL ORIENTATION

Research with college and professional coaches and athletes indicates discrimination and homophobia confront women athletes if they are openly identified as lesbian. They may be avoided by recruiters, denied scholarships, have limited coaching opportunities, or have trouble recruiting players. For professionals, they may lose or not be offered product endorsement contracts. Thus, some athletes who are lesbians choose to conceal their sexual orientation to avoid mistreatment and discrimination.

male university athletic directors canvass their colleagues regarding the sexual preference of female candidates for coaching or administrative positions to eliminate lesbian applicants.

Despite the homophobic perception of the lesbian monopoly of sport, the number of lesbian athletes, coaches, or administrators who are visible and influential as leaders remains very small. In fact, internalized homophobia leads some lesbians in sport leadership—coaches, administrators, physical educators—not only to stay in the closet themselves but also to act in harassing or discriminatory ways toward other lesbians in an apparent attempt to suppress all evidence of the lesbian presence in sport. Common rationales include keeping "politics" out of sport, and keeping one's private life private; however, homophobic discrimination is a public and a political issue and, as such, it needs to be addressed at all levels.

Lesbian physical education teachers and coaches working with children and adolescents often face the threat of job loss when administrators and parents discover their identities, because of the homophobic perception of lesbians as "inappropriate" role models or, worse, sexual predators (despite clear empirical evidence that a pedophile is most probably male and heterosexual). This chilly climate in youth sports forces many women to present themselves as heterosexual, to curtail any discussions of sexuality or homophobia, and to avoid political activities that may mark them as lesbian and/or feminist (since these two identities are often equated by homophobic critics).

SPORT BY AND FOR LESBIANS

In the face of the chilly homophobic climate in mainstream sports since the 1950s, lesbians have established an alternative network of recreational sporting clubs and leagues in major urban centers, as well as in some smaller communities, throughout North America, Australia, and the United Kingdom. By the 1980s, there were lesbian organizations serving a wide variety of sporting interests, including softball, soccer, rugby, basketball, volleyball, ice hockey, golf, swimming, hiking, camping, and canoeing. In the United States and Canada, softball became one of the favorite lesbian team sports, and, for many decades, women's leagues served as an informal meeting place for lesbians. There was significant growth, too, in the

number of mixed gay (male) and lesbian sport clubs and leagues, and many of these sent teams to the Gay Games, an international gay/lesbian/bisexual sport and cultural festival held every four years since 1982 and organized on the principles of inclusion, participation, and personal best.

Many lesbian leagues established in the 1970s and 1980s operated on feminist principles of inclusion and open participation, welcoming women of any sexual orientation or ability level on the understanding that all participants would support the goal of a lesbian-friendly climate. Some clubs also included in their goals changing the value system of mainstream sport: emphasizing participation and fun over winning; making rule changes to encourage less skilled players; and organizing child care, car pools, and social events to promote fun and friendship. However, since most participants had been socialized in and through mainstream sports, organizers of these clubs often had difficulties reconciling the needs and expectations of competitive players with those of less athletic women who just wanted to enjoy the game. Furthermore, it could not be assumed that all lesbians were politicized or identified with feminism as a political agenda, even when they signed up with a feminist league. Many lesbian and gay athletes uncritically espoused the values of mainstream sports and simply wanted to replicate these in lesbian/gay sport associations. The resulting tensions presented an ongoing challenge to organizers of lesbian clubs and leagues and, on a larger scale, to Gay Games organizing committees.

CONCLUSION

Lesbians in mainstream sports face the combined negative effects of sexism and homophobia. Protection offered by antidiscrimination policies is by no means widespread, and athletic departments and sport organizations generally lag behind other sectors of society in developing and applying policies and procedures to ensure the safety, security, and welfare of lesbian athletes. Only a small minority of progressive men and women in leadership positions in sports have addressed this serious problem. The development of sports by and for lesbians at the community level and the 1992 establishment of the quadrennial Gay Games at the international level represent creative lesbian and gay initiatives aimed at countering the homophobia of mainstream sports.

Helen Jefferson Lenskyj

See also Gay Games; Homophobia

Bibliography

Birrell, Susan, and Diana Richter. (1987) "Is a Diamond Forever? Feminist Transformations of Sport." *Women's Studies International Forum* 10, 4: 369–379.

Cahn, Susan. (1993) *Coming On Strong: Gender and Sexuality in Twentieth Century Women's Sport*. New York: Free Press.

Griffin, Pat. (1998) *Strong Women, Deep Closets*. Champaign, IL: Human Kinetics.

Krane, Vikki. (1996) "Lesbians in Sport: Towards Acknowledgement, Understanding and Theory." *Journal of Sport and Exercise Psychology* 18, 3: 237–246.

Krane, Vikki, ed. (1997) *Women in Sport and Physical Activity Journal* 6, 2 (special issue on "Lesbians in Sport").

Lenskyj, Helen. (1994) "Sexuality and Femininity in Sport Contexts: Issues and Alternatives." *Journal of Sport and Social Issues* 18, 4: 356–376.

Palzkill, Bergid. (1990) "Between Gymshoes and High Heels: The Development of a Lesbian Identity and Existence in Top Class Sport." *International Review for the Sociology of Sport* 5, 3: 221–233.

Rogers, Susan Fox, ed. (1995) *SportsDykes*. New York: St. Martin's Press.

Woods, Sharon, and Karen Harbeck. (1992) "Living in Two Worlds: The Identity Management Strategies Used by Lesbian Physical Educators." In *Coming Out of the Classroom Closet*, edited by Karen Harbeck. New York: Harrington Park Press, 141–165.

Zipter, Yvonne. (1988) *Diamonds Are a Dyke's Best Friend*. Ithaca, NY: Firebrand.

LIEBERMAN-CLINE, NANCY

(1958–)

U.S. BASKETBALL PLAYER

Beginning in the early 1970s, Nancy Lieberman-Cline was a major force in the amateur and pro-

Nancy Lieberman drives down the court at Madison Square Garden. (Bettmann/Corbis)

fessional game of basketball and continued to be active in the promotion of women's sports and opportunities for women in the sporting world. In 1976, Lieberman-Cline, nicknamed "Lady Magic," was the youngest member of the U.S. Olympic women's basketball team and ten years later she was the first woman to play in a men's professional basketball league.

Lieberman-Cline was born on 1 July 1958 in Brooklyn, New York. Until her sophomore year of high school she played basketball with the boys. She then joined the Rockaway Seahorses, one of the best teams in New York, and also played for an Amateur Athletic Union team. While a junior in high school, she competed for the United States in the Pan American Games.

After high school, she earned a starting spot as guard for the Old Dominion University (ODU) basketball team. She led Old Dominion to Association of Intercollegiate Athletics for Women (AIAW) national championships (1979, 1980) and earned the ODU Outstanding Female Athlete of the Year award in 1977–1980. She earned the Broderick Award for two years (1979, 1980) and Kodak All-American honors for three consecutive years (1978–1980). Because of her stellar performance on and off the court, she is the only two-time recipient of the NAGWS Wade Trophy (1977, 1978). In 1975 she was the youngest member of the gold medal U.S. Pan-American Games team. Winning a silver medal in the 1976 Olympic Games in Montreal made her the youngest basketball player (male or female) in Olympic history to earn a medal. Although she made the 1980 Olympic team, her attempt for the gold was stopped by the U.S. boycott of the Game.

As a professional, Lieberman-Cline played for the Women's American Basketball Association in 1980 with the Dallas Diamonds. She became their leading scorer and led them to a league championship in 1984. She was the first woman to play in a men's professional league with the Springfield Fame of the United States Basketball League (1986–1988). During that time, her earnings–from salary, endorsements, personal appearances, movie and videos, and ownership in sporting goods stores—exceeded the million-dollar mark. In 1987 she joined the Harlem Globetrotters and the Washington Generals for their 1987–1988 world tour. Here she met her husband-to-be, a Washington General standout, Tim Cline, in 1988. Soon thereafter, Lieberman-Cline wanted to try once more for the Olympic team for the 1992 Games. Although she played with them through 1991, she did not make the final cut. In 1992, she announced her retirement from basketball as the first woman to earn $1 million as a basketball player.

Lieberman-Cline also established herself as one of the first women basketball stars in print and broadcast media. She wrote a column for several years on women's issues in the *Dallas Morning News* as well as a bimonthly column in *USA Today*. She also coauthored a text in 1996, *Basketball for Women: Becoming a Complete Player*. One of the first women color-commentary broadcasters for ESPN for collegiate games, she was also an analyst for NBC Sports during the 1988, 1992, and 1996 Olympic Games and was a broadcaster for ESPN2, Fox Sports Network, and ABC.

She was inducted into the Basketball Hall of Fame in Springfield, Massachusetts, in 1996, making her the youngest woman in the hall. After the U.S. women took the gold at the 1996 Olympic Games, Lieberman-Cline decided to return to professional play, this time with the Women's National Basketball Association (WNBA). In 1997, she became one of the oldest players in the league as a member of the Phoenix Mercury. Retiring a second time, Lieberman-Cline accepted the position of head coach and general manager of the newly established expansion team of the WNBA, the Detroit Shock, in 1998. Stretching beyond basketball, Lieberman-Cline, a longtime member of the Women's Sports Foundation, became its first president for the new millennium.

Darlene A. Kluka

Bibliography

Lieberman-Cline, Nancy, Robin Roberts, Kevin Warneke, and Pat Head Summitt. *Basketball for Women: Becoming a Complete Player.* Champaign, IL: Human Kinetics.

LIECHTENSTEIN

Liechtenstein is a small nation with a population of 31,000 in the Alps in central Europe. Throughout its history, the nation has been much influenced by the neighboring nations of Switzerland and Austria, although Liechtensteiners view themselves as a distinct cultural group. Due to its location in the mountains, Alpine skiing is the major sport and the only one at which Liechtensteiners have been victorious at the international

Hanni Wenzel of Liechtenstein speeds around a slalom pole at the 1980 Olympics at Lake Placid. (AP Photos)

level. Liechtensteiners also enjoy tennis, ice skating, swimming, and hiking, but these are mainly recreational activities. Liechtenstein came to the attention of the skiing world in 1974 when Hanni Wenzel (1956–) won the world championship in the slalom.

Wenzel was born in Germany and had lived in Liechtenstein since her family moved there in 1957. She was granted citizenship after the 1974 championship and went on to become the first Liechtensteiner to win a medal at the Olympics, taking a bronze medal in the slalom in 1976. In 1980 at Lake Placid, she added to this with gold medals in the slalom and giant slalom and a silver in the downhill. From 1974 to 1984 she won thirty-three races and was World Cup champion in 1978 and 1980. Her sister Petra skied for Liechtenstein at the 1980 Olympics but did not win any medals, while her brother Andreas took the silver medal at the 1980 Olympics and was also World Cup champion that year. To round out the family history, it should be noted that their father won the Alpine combined title at the World Student Games in 1954. Liechtenstein has not enjoyed similar success since the Wenzels, although in 1984 Ursula Konzett took the bronze medal in the slalom at the Sarajevo Olympics.

The Editors

LIFEGUARDING

Lifeguarding (known also as lifesaving) is the name given to the general activity of watching swimmers, cautioning them against dangerous behavior, and rescuing them when they become caught in a hazardous situation. Lifeguarding began as a service job, but today lifeguarding competitions are held internationally to encourage guards to maintain high levels of skill and fitness.

Although women have been lifeguards since the mid-nineteenth century, only in the early decades of the twentieth century were they able to participate in substantial numbers. They continue to strive to be treated as equals despite media portrayals (such as *Baywatch*—the world's most popular television program in the 1990s) that at times present them in a negative light.

HISTORY

Lifeguarding has a truly international history. Although swimming has been part of a number of cultures for centuries, it was not until the late eighteenth century that concerted efforts were made to organize individuals to rescue swimmers in distress. Women lifesavers have a vital history as trained professionals.

In 1774 the Royal Humane Society was founded in England, based upon the work of the Society for the Recovery of the Apparently Drowned, which had been established in 1767 in Amsterdam. The British association was interested primarily in the resuscitation of swimmers and recovered sailors, not in swimming rescue techniques. Lifesaving reached North America in 1780 when the Humane Society of Philadelphia positioned signs by the harbor to inform people where lifesaving equipment was located. The Massachusetts Humane Society (1785), which was fashioned after the Royal Humane Society, built shelters on the beach to provide sanctuary for shipwrecked sailors.

The United States Volunteer Life Saving Corps was set up in 1870 by Edwin D. Ayers. It was incorporated in 1890 in New York State, with Wilbert E. Longfellow as the general superintendent. The United States Coast Guard Life Saving Service was established in 1871. In Great Britain, the Royal Life Saving Society (1891) was founded to supplement the work of the Royal Humane Society. In 1894 the Royal Life Saving Society was brought to Australia. The Surf Bather's Association of New South Wales was created in Sydney, Australia; this later became the present-day Surf Life Saving Association of Australia. The precursor to this national organization was the Bondi Surf Bather's Life Saving Club, which was founded in 1906.

In the latter decades of the nineteenth century, lifesaving emerged as part of a variety of organizations throughout the world; in Europe, women participated in the activity. In Germany, the *Arbeiterschwimmbund* (Workers' Swimming Federation), established in 1893, allowed women to teach swimming and, later on, lifesaving. The

Women compete in the 1995 New South Wales Lifesaving Championships off Australia's Gold Coast. (Paul A. Souders/Corbis)

Deutsche Lebens-Rettungs-Gesellschaft (German Lifesaving Society) was established in 1913. In the Scandinavian countries, particularly Sweden, women have participated in lifesaving since the mid-nineteenth century. Sweden established a women's lifesaving championship in 1921. Lifesaving was instituted in the Netherlands in the late nineteenth century, and women established their own association (Hollandsche Dames Zwem Club), which assisted in the founding of the national association. In other nations, however, lifeguarding remained largely a male preserve.

WOMEN AS LIFEGUARDS

Women's participation in lifesaving was limited until the first decades of the twentieth century primarily because of perceptions of gender differences and the belief that women were physically inferior. Women were subject to social restrictions; at some beaches they were restricted to segregated bathing huts. Also common was the conviction that women lacked the physical strength to conduct water rescues.

Between 1890 and 1920, social attitudes began to change, and women were encouraged to swim as well as to participate in other sports that had previously been considered unsuitable. The transformation in social attitudes toward women's

swimming was apparent in the change in women's bathing costumes. Previously, modesty had been the ruling principle in women's swimming attire; the skirts and other weighty elements of the suits made swimming itself difficult. This changed early in the twentieth century, when functional suits were introduced, although not without social opposition.

Women in many parts of the world are still restricted from participating as lifeguards because social attitudes there have not changed and many belong to religions that prevent them from wearing swimming attire.

UNITED STATES

Wilbert Longfellow was appointed commodore of the United States Volunteer Life Saving Corps in 1909, and he became a key figure in lifesaving in general and women's involvement in particular. In 1914 he moved to a newly created program at the American Red Cross to begin what he called "the waterproofing of America." He began immediately to develop a variety of new lifesaving methods. The Young Men's Christian Association (YMCA) also became involved with lifesaving and opened its first aquatic school in Boston in 1916.

Longfellow began the World's Life Saving Alliance in 1913, following a series of visits to girls' camps, to give women who were interested in lifesaving the chance to demonstrate their skills. Women were allowed to take the Red Cross tests and join the Life Saving Corps beginning in 1920. At first women had a separate corps from the men, as well as different proficiency tests. Within a year, however, the same lifesaving tests were required of men and women.

The corps still remained separate, however, and women were not given the same responsibilities as men. The women's corps was not expected to perform actual lifeguard work. Women lifesavers were supposed to be of service in women's camps and places where the attendance of men was restricted. The World's Life Saving Alliance for Women and the Red Cross Life Saving Corps for Women were merged shortly thereafter, and by 1925 nearly 16,000 lifesaving certificates had been issued to women.

Nevertheless, women did in fact save swimmers in distress. In the 1920s and 1930s the *Red*

THE FIRST TEST FOR THE "WOMEN'S LIFE SAVING CORPS" (1920)

1. Swim twenty yards, dressed in skirt, blouse and shoes which shall be fastened in the customary way. Without resting, other than floating, she must remove the skirt, blouse and shoes, and continue to swim for eighty yards before touching the shore.
2. Swim several strokes on surface, then surface dive in from six to eight feet of water, and retrieve a ten-pound object, landing same on bank. The object should be carried on the upper side of the body.
3. Carry living subject ten yards by each of the following methods: Breast stroke, cross shoulder, head carry, two-point carry.
4. Break wrist-hold, front-strangle hold, back-strangle hold in deep water and land patient by swimming fifteen feet.
5. Float one minute in any posture and tread water thirty seconds.
6. Land a patient properly from pool, or surf or open water, as if unconscious.
7. Demonstrate the Schafer prone pressure method of resuscitation and be a subject for demonstration by another.

Women's Life Saving Corps of the American Red Cross. ARC 1003. Washington, D.C.; The American National Red Cross, 1920. In Mays, Appendix B, The History of the Water Safety Program of the American National Red Cross, *279.*

Cross Courier, the official newspaper of the American Red Cross, devoted a number of stories to the work of young women who had performed aquatic rescues. In 1939 the American Red Cross issued the millionth lifesaving certificate. The recipient was a woman, Carol Hawes, and Commodore Longfellow himself presented her certificate. Since the 1940s women have continued as equal partners in lifesaving organizations in the United States.

CANADA

Lifesaving began in Canada under the auspices of the Royal Life Saving Society of England. The first of these branches was established in Ontario in 1908. In late 1894 Arthur Lewis Cochrane was appointed honorary representative of the Swimmer's Life Saving Society of London in Canada. He moved to Toronto and became an instructor at Upper Canada College. In 1895 he started the Upper Canada Life Saving Corps. The original girls'-school affiliate of the Royal Life Saving Society (RLSS) was the Young Women's Christian Guild Pool, founded in 1911. Mary Beaton, the first woman in Scotland to obtain the diploma (the highest award granted by the RLSS),

was the instructor at the YWCA pool. In 1911 Cochrane's daughters Honora and Dorothy became the first women to achieve lifesaving's Award of Merit in Canada.

Women remained active members of lifesaving organizations in Canada, particularly during World War II. When the Water Safety Service of the Canadian Red Cross Society was established in 1944, women were included from the start.

AUSTRALIA

Surf lifesaving has been an important activity for men in Australia since the early part of the twentieth century. Women were restricted to a support role, such as ladies fund-raising committees. They also prepared refreshments for the patrols and for surf carnivals. Although women had demonstrated their lifesaving capabilities by the early 1930s, they were not allowed to join the beach patrols or enter surf competitions. They were occasionally featured in competitions against other women in demonstrations at local surf carnivals.

Although women were needed to monitor the beaches during World War II, they were returned to their support role at the end of the war. Finally, in 1980, the National Surf Life Saving Council granted women the right to test for their surf bronze medallions, which signified their qualifications as lifeguards and gave them the opportunity to become active lifesavers. Henceforth they would be allowed to do their share of beach patrols and compete at surf carnivals. Women won approximately one-third of the bronze medallions in the 1980–81 surf season. Their opportunities to succeed at surf carnivals were limited, however, because they were forced to compete in the same categories as men.

BARRIERS TO WOMEN'S INVOLVEMENT

Women have made progress in their quest to provide lifesaving services throughout the world. They have, however, been hindered by notions of difference and inferiority. In the United States, questions about appropriate female behavior, activities, and dress limited women's full participation as lifesavers until the 1930s. In Canada, women's traditional role as nurturer and protector of the young was reinforced by lifesaving pioneer A. L. Cochrane, who claimed that it was "good that the women should do lifesaving as the youth of the community are so very much under their protection and direction." In Australia, the close connection of surf lifesaving with notions of masculinity restricted women's entrance into lifesaving until the 1990s.

LIFESAVING COMPETITIONS

The inclusion of women in lifeguarding as a competitive activity began in 1925 in Canada, with the competition for the Cochrane Cup, a lifesaving trophy. The first winner was Willard Hall, a group sponsored by the Women's Christian Temperance Union. Although the University of Toronto's men had actually earned more points, they relinquished their place to the women's group because of their remarkable performance. The next year Willard Hall won the cup unconditionally—followed by the YWCA, the University of Toronto men, and a boy's camp.

International competition began about thirty years later. Spurred by Melbourne's selection as the site of the 1956 Olympics, professional lifeguards from the host country invited their counterparts from around the world to participate in an international lifeguarding competition. Although only male lifesavers from Great Britain,

Ceylon, New Zealand, Australia, California, and Hawaii attended, the event was enormously popular and drew more than 100,000 spectators.

Since the 1960s, lifesaving competitions have expanded. These competitions are designed to encourage lifeguards to maintain high levels of fitness and to enhance skill development. Since the late 1970s, women have competed throughout the world in competitions sponsored at the local, national, and international levels. Some of the local and national sponsors include the Dublin (Ireland) Lifesaving and Lifeguard Club, the University of Tsukuba (Japan) Lifesaving Club, the Surf Life Saving Association of Great Britain, Surf Life Saving Australia, the Lifesaving Society of Canada, the German Lifesaving Federation, and the United States Lifesaving Association. International competitions are sponsored by the International Life Saving Federation.

Some of the events contested in lifesaving competitions include surf swimming, beach sprints, surf ski paddling, board paddling, team events (such as the taplin relay and belt race), the Iron Man and Iron Woman event (which includes a combination of skills and requires excellent technical ability as well as a high level of physical fitness), and still water/pool events. In the United States, an All-Women Lifeguard Tournament, sponsored by the National Park Service, has been held since the mid-1990s.

Lifeguarding has become mandatory at virtually all public swimming venues, and the need for trained lifeguards continues to increase. Women are now guarding swimmers everywhere, from the crowded beaches of New York City to small-town swimming pools. Their participation is and will continue to be necessary for the future of recreational swimming.

Alison M. Wrynn

See also Surf Lifesaving

Bibliography

Baker, Richard D. (1980) "The Lifesaving Movement." In *Lifeguarding Simplified: The Management Principles and Techniques of Lifeguarding.* New York: A.S. Barnes.

Berridge, Mavis E. (1966) "The Development of the Red Cross Water Safety Service and the Royal Life Saving Society in Canada." Unpublished master's thesis, Madison: University of Wisconsin.

Booth, Douglas. (1994) "Swimming, Surfing and Surf-Lifesaving." In *Sport in Australia: A Social History*, by Wray Vamplew and Brian Stoddart. Cambridge: Cambridge University Press.

Mays, Margaret A. (1973) "The History of the Water Safety Program of the American National Red Cross." Unpublished doctoral dissertation, Springfield, Mass: Springfield College.

Rosen, Gaye. (1982) "Women and Sport in Australia: Surf Life Saving as a Case Study." In *Proceedings of the Sports Science—Section 34 Fifty-second A.N.Z.A.A.S. Congress*, Macquarie University, 36–49.

Silvia, Charles E. (1965) *Lifesaving and Water Safety Today*. New York: Association Press.

LINES, MARY

(1893–?)

ENGLISH RUNNER

Regarded as the best female athlete of her era, Mary Lines was not only a world-class runner but also a tenacious organizer of women's athletics. Lines was born in England on 3 December 1893. While still a young woman, she began to fight for emancipation of women through sport. During World War I, she ran a series of exhibition races in England against Violette Guénaud Morris (1895–1944) of France to raise money for the establishment of a women's athletics syndicate. After the war she was influenced by the ideals of women's sport advocate Alice Milliat and continued her activities. She overcame frequent injuries and the opposition of conservative authorities to become co-founder and recognized leader of the Women's Amateur Athletic Association (WAAA), the British self-governing body of women's athletics.

In the autumn of 1922, the governing body of British athletics, the Amateur Athletic Association (AAA), refused without apparent justification the WAAA's official request of affiliation. Lines fearlessly led the WAAA to an autonomous way of life, with independent championships and regulations. The groups were not reconciled until just a few years before the outbreak of World War II.

Lines's brilliant racing career reached its apogee from 1921 to 1925, when she competed at the international level in the 60- to 880-yard dashes and in the 120-yard hurdles. In 1921 she won four events at the international women's match between France and England. At the first women's games in Paris in 1922, she won the 100-yard meter race and the long jump, and ran the first leg for Great Britain's winning effort in 400-yard relay. Her 100-yard run in the relay was later classified by the Fédération Sportive Féminine Internationale as the world record for the 100-yard dash.

Gherardo Bonini

Bibliography

Cowe, Eric. (1985) *International Women's Athletics from 1890 to 1940*. Bingley, UK: Cowe.

Lovesey, Peter. (1980) *The Official Centenary History of the AAA*. London: Guinness Superbooks.

Serra, Luciano. (1969) *Storia dell'atletica europea 1793–1968*. Rome: Edizioni di Atletica Leggera.

LING GYMNASTICS

The Swedish gymnastics teacher and poet Per Henrik Ling (1776–1839) developed Ling gymnastics (also called Swedish gymnastics) at the beginning of the nineteenth century. The system became widespread throughout the world, especially in schools and military training, and was particularly important in the physical education of girls.

Ling got his inspiration from many sources: he lived in Copenhagen, Denmark, from 1799 to 1804, where he went to lectures on German Romanticism, went to fencing lessons, and got to know the gymnastics institute run by the Dane Franz Nachtegall. Ling then worked as a fencing master at Lund University in Sweden, where he began to develop his special system of rational and systematic physical exercises. He tried to make gymnastics scientific on the basis of anatomy and physiology, and he divided gymnastics into four areas: military, medicinal, educational, and aesthetic. In 1813 Ling became head of the newly established Kungliga Gymnastiska Centralinstitutet (GCI, or Royal Gymnastics Central

Institute; since 1993, the Gymnastics and Sports College) in Stockholm, where gymnastics teachers have since been trained. It was not until 1864 that women were allowed to take the one-year course at GCI and thus become qualified as gymnastics teachers (in 1871 the course became a two-year course).

In many countries, gymnastics for girls in school began around the middle of the nineteenth century. Interest in the physical education of girls was based on a recognition of their poor state of health, and the teaching was in the beginning done by men. Ling's system was in harmony with the nineteenth-century quest for scientific and rational explanations, one of the manifestations of which was a new concern for the health and hygiene of the general population.

The collective, form-developing exercises of the system promoted virtues such as clean living, order, and precision. The exercises were meant to be adapted to the body of the individual, and their effect was measured by the harmonious development of the body, not, as in sport, by winning or losing competitions. The perception of the body in Swedish gymnastics was based on the idea of a universal body, a male body; women were perceived as weaker and frailer men. The system was thus based on a "one-sex" perception of the body, which in many ways did not correspond with the perception of the time of male and female gender differences as biologically based or with the scientific construction of what was specifically *feminine*.

The fact that the system became so widespread around the world was mainly due to the very well-trained Swedish gymnastics mistresses, who went abroad in large numbers and argued that women were those best suited to teach and train girls and women. In this way, the Swedish women created a platform for a new, real profession for women. One of the striking pioneers was Madame M. Bergman-Österberg, who went to London in 1881 and was instrumental in the introduction of Swedish gymnastics into the London Board Schools; in 1885 she established training courses for women in physical education, first at Hampstead Physical Training College and later at Dartford College in England.

Swedish gymnastics, which in many places supplanted other national systems, was often criticized, then and later, as being boring drills. But Swedish gymnastics promoted virtues in line with the norms of the time for what was appropriate for women, and the female teachers understood how to keep a balance between social respectability and emancipation. The exercises helped in the development of a harmonious body and gave the girls and women a better understanding of hygiene and health as a qualification for becoming mothers and homemakers in a modern society.

The universal nature of the system also made it possible to adapt it to the needs of different classes, or, perhaps it should be said, to the perceived need of society to *civilize* these classes. For instance, the collective exercises, under the command of the teacher, were effective in inculcating middle-class virtues in the uneducated and training them in physical discipline and control. In addition to this, for the girls of the educated classes (the middle and upper class), the system was a physical and hygienic supplement to the more challenging exercises in various games.

Else Trangbaek

Bibliography

Festskrift ved GCI-GIH's 175-årsjubileum [*The Festschrift of GCI-GIH's 175th jubilee*]. (1998). Stockholm: Gymnatik och Idrottshögskolan.

Ljunggren, Jens. (1999) *Kroppens Bilding: Linggymnastikens manlighedhetsprojekt 1790–1914. Bulilding the Human Body: The Manliness Element of Ling Gymnastics Building 1790–1914.* Stockholm: Gymnatik och Idrottshögskolan.

Trangbæk, Else. (1987) *Mellem leg og displin: Gymnastikken i Danmark i 1800 tallet, Duo 1987* [*Between Games and Discipline: The Development of Gymnastics in Denmark in the Nineteenth Century*]. Auning, Denmark: DUO.

———. (1997) "Gender in Modern Society: Femininity, Gymnastics and Sport." *The International Journal of the History of Sport* 14 (December) (special issue on "The Nordic World").

LITERATURE

In no society, not even in ancient Sparta, have women participated in sports to the same degree that men have, but there has never been a time when women were wholly excluded from sports. Before the twentieth century, however, women's athletic achievements almost never stimulated the imagination of poets, dramatists, or writers of prose fiction. Two major exceptions to this generalization—Atalanta and Brunhilde—were both entirely the products of male fantasy.

ATALANTA AND BRUNHILDE

Although the legend was originally Greek, Atalanta's story, which appeared in many different versions, was best told by the first-century BCE Roman poet Ovid in Books VIII and X of his *Metamorphoses*. Abandoned as an infant and reared by a she-bear, Atalanta was physically the match for any man she met. Armed with a spear, she joined the hero Meleager in his hunt for the white-tusked Calydonian boar on Mount Parnassus. She was in at the kill. Atalanta was also famous as a wrestler. She vanquished Peleus, the father of the hero Achilles. Yet she was most famous for a lost contest she should have won. Reluctant to marry and confident of her swiftness, she promised to accept the first suitor to outrun her. She defeated a number of haplessly enamored challengers, who paid for their passion with their lives, before she encountered Melanion, who had received three golden apples from Aphrodite, the goddess of love. Whenever Atalanta surged to the lead, Melanion tossed one of the apples into her path, a stratagem that tempted her to pause. She gathered the apples and lost the race.

Brunhilde's fate was similar. She, too, having promised to marry the man who outperformed her athletically, was defeated by a trick. The story is part of the Nibelungenlied saga. Gunther and his friend Siegfried voyage to Iceland so that Gunther can challenge Brunhilde in three stipulated feats of strength. He loses heart when he observes that it takes three men to carry her spear. His spirits droop even further when he watches twelve men trying to lift one of the stones that she hefts with ease. Fortunately for Gunther, his powerful friend Siegfried, rendered invisible by a magic cap, gives him a helping hand. Siegfried intervenes again after Gunther's marriage to subdue an intransigent Brunhilde, whom the unlucky bridegroom had failed to bring to bed.

Women like Atalanta and Brunhilde were definitely not the stuff of medieval fantasy, but Re-

THE

GIRL'S BOOK OF DIVERSIONS;

OR,

OCCUPATION FOR PLAY HOURS.

BY MISS LESLIE.

" The sports of children satisfy the child."—GOLDSMITH.

LONDON:
PRINTED FOR THOMAS TEGG AND SON, CHEAPSIDE;
TEGG, WISE, AND TEGG, DUBLIN ; GRIFFIN AND CO., GLASGOW ;
AND J. AND S. A. TEGG, SYDNEY, AUSTRALIA.

1835.

The title page from the popular British games book published in 1835. (Osborne Collection of Toronto Library)

naissance writers such as Lodovico Ariosto and Edmund Spenser created the doughty maidens Bradamonte and Britomart. As women warriors, they had at least the physical potential for athletic achievement. In the nineteenth century, Atalanta reappeared in poems by Walter Savage Landor, William Morris, and Algernon Charles Swinburne, while Brunhilde returned to sing the music of Richard Wagner. Poems like Swinburne's *Atalanta in Calydon* (1860) and operas like Wagner's *Ring of the Nibelungs* presaged the female athlete as a theme for twentieth-century literature.

JUNIOR FICTION

In addition to the world of popular culture, where characters like Wonder Woman and the "Baywatch" lifeguards on television occasionally indulge in sports competition, young athletes have regularly appeared as the heroines of juvenile fiction. In 1895 the American journalist Abbie Carter Goodloe published "Revenge," in which a group of fictional college women humiliate an initially scornful young man by besting him at golf, tennis, and a number of other sports. Equally typical of the juvenile-fiction genre are three anonymous stories published in 1921–1922 in the British journal *Football and Sports Library:* "Meg Foster Footballer," "Captain Meg," and "Football Island." Trained by the militant Mrs. Trooper, "the strongest woman in the world," a team of young working-class women triumph over their opponents on the soccer (association football) field. When molested by thuggish men, they prove that they can defend their virtue as well as their goal. Enid Bagnold's enormously popular novel *National Velvet* (1935) dramatizes young Velvet Brown's passion for horses (encouraged by her mother, who swam the English Channel when she was young). Disguised as a boy, Velvet rides her piebald horse to victory in the Grand National Steeplechase. More recent British and American juvenile fiction—including Stephanie Grant's "Posting Up" (1995) and Rebecca Rule's *Lindy Lowe at Bat* (1995)—continue to assert the right of girls to play whatever sport they choose and to portray them as bold and skillful athletes.

ADULT FICTION

Serious fiction by major authors has also made a place in sports for girls and women. But many of these sporting women are limited to minor roles. Jordan Baker figures briefly as a dishonest golfer in F. Scott Fitzgerald's *The Great Gatsby* (1925). When the character is the heroine, her sport participation is often peripheral, which is the case for fiction as different as Edith Wharton's *Age of In-*

FEMALE PROPONENTS OF "MANLINESS" IN CHILDREN'S LITERATURE

There is a consensus that "muscular Christianity" originated with the best-selling novels of Thomas Hughes (*Tom Brown's Schooldays*, 1857) and the Reverend Charles Kingsley (*Westward Ho!*, 1855). One of their heroes' oft-mentioned virtues, usually developed on school playing fields and/or in confrontations with bigger bullies, was the concept of "manliness." Yet it is not generally realized that other authors preached a similar gospel long before the 1850s; or indeed that many of these unacknowledged writers were women.

One of the earliest was Dorothy Kilner, who wrote many children's books, often under the pseudonym of "M.P.," i.e. Mary Pelham. In her popular *The Life and Perambulations of a Mouse*, first published in 1783, several pages are devoted to fighting in a just cause; and after her Christian hero Tomkins vanquishes the ubiquitous bullies, "he passed through school as much respected as any boy." Kilner even had two heroes named Tom Brown: in *First Going to School* (1804) and *The Good Child's Delight* (1819). In Maria Edgeworth's novel *Frank* (1801), the young hero is ed-

ucated to be "manly" throughout and "to excel his companions in bodily strength and agility." And little Hugh, in Harriet Martineau's *The Crofton Boys* (1841) proves his "spirit" in a struggle with some bigger, older boys. Catherine Sinclair introduces young Harry in *Holiday House* (1844), who delights in cricket and football and becomes "a great favorite among the boys." Charles Maitland, in Frances Catherine Barnard's *The Schoolfellows, or Holidays at the Hall* (1845), proves himself by saving another boy from drowning.

Although Kingsley's seafaring heroes were preceded most significantly in the novels of Frederick Marryat in the 1840s, an even earlier nautical example was given by Mary Belson in her *The Adventures of Thomas Two-Shoes* (1818), in which young Christian Thomas sails to Madeira, Jamaica, and Tunis.

"Manliness" was also commonly stressed in the numerous works of non-fiction by female authors which appeared before 1857, such as Louisa Lovechild's *Sport of Youth* (1835). One wonders if Hughes and Kingsley read these books as boys and were influenced by them?

nocence (1920), in which May Welland is an archer, and Philip Roth's *Goodbye, Columbus* (1959), in which Brenda Patimkin swims and plays tennis. In other literary works, the female athlete is the heroine and sports are thematically central. While such works are hardly ubiquitous in nineteenth- and twentieth-century literature, they have certainly become common.

John Betjeman, postwar England's most popular poet, was enthralled by female athletes "full of pent-up strength" ("Pot-Pourri from a Surrey Garden"), "strongly adorable" ("A Subaltern's Love-Song"), striding on "the strongest legs in Pontefract" ("The Licorice Fields at Pentefract"), or standing "in strong, athletic pose" ("The Olympic Girl"). It is not always clear exactly what Betjeman's heroines do in the way of sports, but other writers have imagined women participating in a wide range of graphically dramatized sports.

In Grant Allen's popular novel *Miss Cayley's Adventures* (1899), the impressively competent heroine is a graduate of Girton College, Cambridge, who rows while at school, wins a trans-Alpine bicycle race against male competition, and shoots a tiger while spending time in India. The fateful huntress-heroine of Ernest Hemingway's "The Short Happy Life of Francis Macomber" (1936) "accidentally" shoots her husband on safari after he proves himself to be a coward. The heroine of *The High Cost of Living* (1978), by Marge Piercy, is a karate expert. "Claire-la-Magnifique," a 1980 short story by the French writer Guy Lagorce is about a female fencer who uses her foil against a would-be rapist. Sara Vogan's 1981 novel *Shelly's Leg* (1981) and Pat Griffin's "Diamonds, Dykes, and Double Plays" (1994) are about softball players. Rita Mae Brown set *Sudden Death* (1983) in the fiercely competitive world of women's professional tennis. Lesbian marathoners finish their races and embrace their lovers in Sara Maitland's "The Loveliness of the Long-Distance Runner" (1983) and Jenifer Levin's "Her Marathon" (1994).

Since 1983 *Aethlon*, a journal devoted entirely to sports literature, has published a number of poems and short stories, mostly by unknown athlete-writers, that focus upon the experience of women engaged in sports.

In *Le Paradis à l'ombre des épées* (The Paradise in the Shade of the Swords, 1920), Henry de Montherlant created a pair of runners who bring the ad-olescent hero to the startled realization that athletic women are sexually attractive. "The bodies of women represented by contemporary painters and sculptors, those of the nude women whom I had seen, even the professional models considered to be 'jolies femmes,' were horrible." They are disfigured by "pads of fat." When the hero encounters the runners, "Mademoiselle V" and "Mademoiselle de Plé Meur," he understands "that a woman's body can be beautiful—if it is trained."

Dominique, the heroine of Montherlant's *Le Songe* (*The Dream*, 1922), is obsessed by "the ideal of the Amazon." She is "a strong girl, with broad shoulders, a helmet of hair, and heroic hands that hurled the javelin across the field." Standing before a mirror, she is positively narcissistic: "Without changing her pose, she contracted her muscles across the length of her body. . . . Her entire body was like a thing of delicately hammered metal. . . . The lateral ridges of her abdomen flexed, mounted, slid smoothly one above the other beneath her breasts." When she races, she feels an inexpressible ecstasy: "Intoxicating, intoxicating, intoxicating sensation of calling upon oneself and feeling oneself respond!" Unfortunately, for all her sensuality, Dominique fails to evoke a sexual response from the novel's ascetic hero.

Erotic athleticism is more successful in a 1928 novel by Kasimir Edschmid. Gagaly Madosdy, the sophisticated female protagonist of *Sport um Gagaly* (Sport Around Gagaly), is described as "an Athena in tennis shoes." She is the hero's "sporting and feminine ideal." Physically stunning, she has legs that are "perfectly beautiful, muscular, curved and firm, but nonetheless graceful." The hero, who excels in a number of different sports, is also attracted by a younger athlete whose "steel-slim body" seems to be made "of thin bronze" (94, 136, 304). Unable to choose between the mature and the adolescent versions of female perfection, the hero decides to marry the younger woman and, apparently, to continue his affair with the older one. Neither of the women is bothered by this because they, in the meantime, seem to have fallen in love with one another.

Although she is less known than Montherlant and Edschmid, Jenifer Levin has written a comparably memorable novel. Dorey Thomas, the heroine of *Water Dancer* (1982), is a swimmer who seeks to overcome a psychic trauma by feats of nearly incredible endurance. She enters the lives of David "Sarge" Olssen and his wife Ilana, two older swimmers who have grown apart because they are haunted by a ghost of their own. Their son drowned in an effort to swim the strait that challenges Dorey. Although the older couple are initially distrustful and even resentful of Dorey, they agree to train her.

In the course of the novel, there are tense evocations of physical effort: "Below the waist she was numb. Above the waist torn to shreds." There are also exquisite scenes of sensuality. Both of the Olssens are sexually attracted to Dorey. When Sarge helps Dorey bathe, he tells her, "You'll be . . . the strongest lady on earth," a thought that pleases her and excites him. When Ilana massages Dorey, she comments, "All those muscles and you're still very soft, that's remarkable." Dorey responds to their sexual interest in her and all three act upon their impulses. Although the reader expects the result to be catastrophic, it is quite the opposite. Their love of the young swimmer brings the older couple closer to one another and Dorey—empowered by their love and their faith in her—achieves her athletic goal. The three of them overcome their ghosts. Or, as Dorey puts it, they have finally "put Humpty-Dumpty together again."

Allen Guttmann

Bibliography

Bagnold, Enid. (1935) *National Velvet*. New York: William Morrow.

Bandy, Susan, and Anne S. Darden, eds. (1999) *Crossing Boundaries: An International Anthology of Women's Experiences in Sport*. Champaign, IL: Human Kinetics.

Betjeman, John. (1958) *Collected Poems*. London: John Murray.

Brown, Rita Mae. (1983) *Sudden Death*. New York: Bantam Books.

Edschmid, Kasimir. (1928) *Sport um Gagaly*. Berlin: Paul Zsolnay.

Goodloe, Abbie Carter. (1895) "Revenge." Reprinted in Sandoz (below), 278–292.

Grant, Stephanie. (1990) "Posting-Up." Reprinted in Sandoz (below), 31–67.

Griffin, Pat. (1994) "Diamonds, Dykes, and Double Plays." Reprinted in Sandoz (below), 197–210.

Hermingway, Ernest 1938. *Short Stories*. New York: Random House.

Lagorce, Guy. (1980) *Les Heroiques*. Paris: Julliard.

Levin, Jenifer. (1982) *Water Dancer*. New York: Poseidon Press.

——. (1993) *The Sea of Light*. New York: Dutton.

——. (1994) "Her Marathon." Reprinted in Sandoz (below), 293–311.

Maitland, Sara. (1983). "The Loveliness of the Long-Distance Runner." Reprinted in Sandoz (below), 159–169.

Montherlant, Henry de. (1922) *Le Songe*. Paris: Gallimard.

——. (1954) *Les Olympiques*. Paris: Gallimard.

Piercy, Marge. (1978) *The High Cost of Living*. New York: Harper & Row.

Sandoz, Joli, ed. (1997) *A Whole Other Ball Game*. New York: Noonday Press.

Vogan, Sara. (1981) *In Shelly's Knee*. New York: Knopf, 1981.

LITHUANIA

Lithuania is one of the Baltic nations of northern Europe and has a population of 3.7 million. Formerly a republic of the Soviet Union, it became an independent nation again in 1991.

Formal education in Lithuania was established in 1397 with the founding of the Episcopal College in Vilnius. Physical education was introduced in 1773, adopting gymnastics programs from Sweden. Lithuania came under Russian control in 1795, and in 1803 the Russian government banned physical education in the schools. While Lithuanians formed their own schools (called *daraktori*), they did not teach physical education, and in 1831, after a Lithuanian revolt, Lithuanian schools were closed. Little is known about women's participation in sports during this period, although it is likely that few women participated, as suggested by the regulations of Russian sports clubs. These stated that "women and military men of lower rank are not accepted."

In the early twentieth century, interest in sports increased, partly in reaction to concerns about the health of children and partly as part of the Sokol (pan-Slavic movement) gymnastics program in Eastern Europe. In 1919 the first physical education program, based on German and Swedish gymnastics, was established in a primary school. The first women's wrestling championship took place in Kaunas botanical garden on 18 July 1912.

After Lithuania declared independence in 1918, many young people who were engaged in sports elsewhere in the Russian Empire returned to Lithuania; among them were J. Janaviciute-Kripiene and Elena Kubiliunaite-Garbaciauskiene. The sports movement began to grow in Lithuania, and many women took an active part in the Lithuanian Physical Education Association (LPEA). In October 1921, a track and field competition took place in a badly prepared sports ground in Azuolynas park. Women participated in this competition for the first time and ran the 100-meter race. Kubiliunaite-Garbaciauskiene was among the founders of the LPEA, and LPEA women were the first to play basketball. In 1922 the LPEA became the champions of Lithuania. Many women from the LPEA were well-known athletes in Lithuania, and later they became the members of Lithuanian national teams.

On 17 March 1923, Ona Sulginas and J. Sulginiene helped to found a women's amateur sports club. Track and field athletics, shooting, and basketball were cultivated, and competitions were organized from time to time. In 1923 there were fifty-four members in this club. The club itself was supported by Danute Slezeviciene and Ona Stulginskiene, who were wives of Lithuanian authorities. In 1924 the club joined the Lithuanian Sports League. On 19 February 1924, the Kaunas tennis club was established. B. Navickiene took an active part in helping to organize its activity. The club represented Lithuania in international competitions.

Until 1933 only military men could take part in riding competitions, but from 1933 on, civilians participated as well. L. Pavilciute took part in these competitions on 15 May 1933. In table tennis, the Lithuanian national women's team participated for the first time at the world championship in Prague on 12–18 March 1936. The first European women's basketball championship took place in 1938 in Rome, where the Lithuanian national team won the silver medal. In 1939 the women's chess championship was organized in Lithuania for the first time. E. Raclauskaite became the winner. Later she represented Lithuania in the world women's chess championship in Buenos Aires, Argentina, in 1939.

World War II and other political events in 1939 changed the Lithuanian state and society. Lithuanian physical education was reorganized according to the Soviet model. During the postwar period, Lithuania's name was made famous by such basketball players as Ona Butautiene, Jurate Daktaraite, and Genovaite Sviderskaite and by Birute Kalediene in track and field athletics. Daktaraite played on the Soviet Union's basketball team when it won the world championship in 1959 and the European championship in 1960. In table tennis, Aldona Skaruliene was European champion in 1970; Asta Giedraityte accomplished the same feat in 1974; and Laima Balaisyte won the world championship, also in 1974. Angele Jankunaite-Rupsiene played on the Soviet Union's women's basketball team, which won the gold medal in the Moscow Olympics in 1980.

In the years of independence since 1991, Lithuanian women athletes have achieved great results. Dalia Gudzineviciute won silver and bronze medals in the European shooting championship of 1992, and the Lithuanian national women's basketball team won the European championship in 1997.

K. Kardelis
S. Kavaliauskas
R. Mazeikiene

Bibliography

Lietuvos kuno kulturos ir sporto istorija. (1996) Vilnius.

Lithuanian Central Archive. Unpublished manuscripts.

Lithuanian State Department of Physical Education and Sport. Unpublished manuscripts.

LONG DISTANCE FLYING

Humans had long dreamed of being able to soar like birds. By the early twentieth century airplanes, though still cumbersome mechanical beasts, offered hope that powered flight might eventually become practical. It did, and in a sad irony, the use of reconnaissance and fighter planes during World War I, for espionage or battle, greatly advanced aeronautical design and performance. Women aviators did not fly as military pilots, but the end of the war heralded an era in which they began to take to the skies, breaking records and achieving public acclaim.

Long-distance flying is, as sport or recreation, essentially endurance flying. Pilots try to break records by going the longest distance in the least amount of time in a particular craft. When aviators first began testing the limits of distance, women were at something of a disadvantage, lacking as they did the flight experience of the male military pilots. The sport itself, however, posed no barriers, because it relied on endurance and stamina rather than muscle and strength. Women went on to compete and broke a substantial number of records.

HISTORY

World War I had proved the practicality and reliability of airplanes. The next question was whether aircraft could safely fly vast distances. If intercontinental travel was to become a practical form of transportation, aircraft manufacturers and pilots had to prove that machines and their operators could endure the strain of marathon journeys.

Male aviators were best placed for this type of sporting competition. During World War I only men had been accepted into air forces, with women fliers officially grounded. Although several females had received pilot's licenses (the first was France's Raymonde de Laroche in 1910), they were restricted to training and support roles for the duration of the conflict. Moreover, after the war, highly credentialed male pilots were trying to establish careers in civil aviation, often by working for fledgling airmail and passenger services. With a glut of trained pilots, competition for positions was tough: it was little wonder that female aviators, who had had less opportunity to hone their flying talents, were at a distinct disadvantage in the pilot job market.

Male pilots took up the challenge of long-distance flying with zeal. Pilots attempted and completed an array of epic flights during the two decades after the war. Some took part in specially organized races in quest of substantial money prize (which was often put up by newspapers seeking exclusive coverage of a contest); others chased fame and fortune by trying to break officially recognized distance records. Typically, aviators compared their performances with those of previous competitors in terms of overall distance traveled or time taken to traverse a particular route.

Women who wanted to fly long distances, however, faced several obstacles, one of which was the question of whether such an activity was indeed suitable for females. At the same time, questions were raised about their stamina and capacity to withstand long and grueling flights. Pioneering women pilots ignored both issues, and by the end of the 1920s female aviators had gained a measure of acceptance at the typically male-dominated flying clubs in Europe, North America, and Australia. Flying authorities even began to officially record and publish the accomplishments of women pilots.

Aviation, however, was a very expensive activity, whether as a leisure pursuit or as a sport, so it was generally women of financial means who took to the skies. For women pilots, then, flying was not only an adventure but also a display of their elite social status. By the 1930s owning a plane was a fashion statement, with respected women's magazines promoting the idea that women could establish a sense of self-reliance by taking to the skies. Yet these magazines were cautious, as was the daily press, about women's role in high-performance flying—particularly their suitability for long-distance aviation.

Nevertheless, many women went on to become pilots who crossed vast territories. Some of these pilots even became household names. Amy Johnson of England was the first woman to fly solo from London to Australia in 1930. The trip took nineteen days, but it was an exceptional feat: Johnson was a relatively inexperienced pilot, yet her flight took only four days longer than that of the record holder, the Australian Bert Hinkler, two years earlier. By the mid-1930s another female pilot, the New Zealander Jean Batten, had received international acclaim after breaking several aviation records, including a solo flight from England to Australia in just five and three-quarter days.

In 1932 Amelia Earhart further established her reputation as an outstanding pilot by becoming the first person after Charles Lindbergh to fly the Atlantic solo. Four years later, the Briton Beryl Markham became the first woman to fly nonstop from England to the United States and the first pilot to make this east–west crossing solo. Outstanding women aviators from France, Germany, and the Soviet Union also set numerous flying records in their own regions.

The media spotlight on long-distance air racing was transitory—for male and female pilots. After World War II, intercontinental flights became commonplace, which eliminated much of the rationale for competitive distance aviation. But there were still some flying records to chase, particularly for women. In 1964, Americans Geraldine Mock and Joan Merriam Smith made separate bids to become the first woman to fly solo around the world (a feat that had not been attempted since 1937, when the flight of Earhart and navigator Fred Noonan ended in tragedy and mystery). Both pilots made the trip successfully, with Mock completing the journey slightly before Smith.

Soon after, their achievement was eclipsed by British aviator Sheila Scott, who between 1965 and 1972 became the most renowned female pilot of the post–World War II era. At a time when jet planes were becoming commonplace, Scott revived some pioneer spirit of early aviation by breaking numerous long-distance records for light aircraft. She is best remembered as the first person to fly solo in a light plane, equator to equator, over the North Pole. In 1980, Briton Judith Chisholm flew from England to Australia to commemorate Amy Johnson's flight of fifty years earlier. In the process she cut Scott's 1966 time by half. But Chisolm's journey was subject to little fanfare: her Cessna Turbo plane was well equipped to make the journey.

WOMEN AS FLIERS

Four major reasons help to explain why women were able to fly to prominence during the 1920s and 1930s. First, distance aviation did not require pilots to have particular body height, particular body shape, or physical strength. This meant that people with a variety of body types—men and women—could take to the skies with ease. Pro-

Members of the "99 Club" of aviatrices pose in Los Angeles in 1933. (Bettmann/Corbis)

spective pilots needed to develop advanced motor skills, not bulging biceps or muscular thighs. Second, by comparison with other forms of motor sport, which were conducted on closed racing circuits, flying-club officials couldn't keep as close a watch over female athletes in the sky. Hence, women who set out to break distance or endurance records could, if they chose, do so without a lot of fanfare—although fanfare was precisely what many of them sought. Third, even though pioneer female aviators commonly received huge public welcomes at airfields around the world, they were generally quick to reassure inquirers of their femininity. As Amy Johnson once put it, they were not a bit of the masculine type. In other words, most prominent female pilots, while determined to prove they could fly as well as or better than men, seemed reluctant to make their quest part of a concerted effort to transform the traditional gender order. Most noticeably Jean Batten, who established world distance aviation records in the mid-1930s, displayed feminine sophistication in dress, style, and manners. She even pretended that strict bladder training enabled her to fly nine hours without the need to urinate: in reality, she had a rather cumbersome, yet highly necessary, toilet facility installed in the plane. Fourth, the popular press, though usually receptive of the achievements of female pilots (particularly from a nationalistic perspective), consistently reminded readers—either through interviews or photographic shoots—that these fliers were emphatically feminine, even glamorous, sportswomen. Female pilots who failed to live up to this expectation were lampooned as tomboys, and thus labeled deviant women.

Daryl Adair

Bibliography

Adair, Daryl. (1995) " 'Wings Across the World': The Heyday of Competitive Long Distance Flying in Australia, 1919–1934." *Sporting Heritage,* 1: 73–90.

Babington-Smith, Constance. (1967) *Amy Johnson.* London: Collins.

Cadogan, Mary. (1992) *Women with Wings.* London: Macmillan.

Lovell, Mary. S. (1987) *Straight on Till Morning.* New York: St Martin's Press.

———. (1989) *The Sound of Wings.* London: Hutchinson.

Mackersey, Ian. (1990) *Jean Batten: The Garbo of the Skies.* Auckland, New Zealand: MacDonald.

Moolman, Valerie. (1981) *Women Aloft.* Alexandria, VA: Time-Life Books.

Thomas, J. (1988) "Amy Johnson's Triumph, Australia 1930." *Australian Historical Studies* 23, 90 (April): 72–84.

Jeannie Longo-Ciprelli waits for the start of her individual time trial at the 1996 Olympic Games, an event in which she won the silver medal. (Mike King)

LONGO-CIPRELLI, JEANNIE

(1958–)

FRENCH CYCLIST

Jeannie Longo-Ciprelli was one of the twentieth century's most successful female competitive cyclists. Over a period of more than fifteen years, she shaped, raised the status of, and ruled the international cycling scene like no other women, winning everything that could be won in women's competitive cycling. She was a multiple French champion, world champion, and Olympic gold medal winner.

Jeannie Longo-Ciprelli was born in Saint-Gervais, France, on 31 October 1958. Her sports career actually began in a sport that has nothing to do with cycling. Alpine skiing fascinated this woman from the Savoy Alps. She competed in this sport together with her older sisters Maryse and Raphaelle. Competing in a giant slalom at the age of ten, she suffered a complicated break of her lower leg, and it took a full two years before she was nominated again for the regional team. Although achieving good results and times, she could no longer compete at a level to qualify for the French national team. Her best result was in the 1982 French slalom championship, where she finished fifth.

Her interest in cycling was awakened by her husband-to-be and coach Patrice Ciprelli, who was a member of the same Alpine skiing club. Upon learning that the 1980 women's world road cycling championships were being held in her region, she decided to get a cycling license. In 1979 she won her first French road race championship, a victory that marked the beginning of her successful cycling career, which included the full range of cycling events. She was the road race world champion in 1985, 1986, 1987, 1989, and 1995; the individual pursuit world champion in 1986, 1988, and 1989; points champion in 1989; and time trial champion in 1996 and 1997. At home, she was the French road race champion from 1979 to 1989, 1992, and 1995; individual pursuit champion from 1980 to 1989, 1992, and 1994; and points champion in 1988 and 1989. She set the hour world record of 48.159 kilometers (29.925 miles) in 1996 and won the women's Tour de France in 1987, 1988, and 1989; the Tour of Texas in 1984 and 1985; and the Tour of Colombia in 1987 and 1988.

Longo-Ciprelli retired briefly but came back to win the silver medal in the individual road race and the silver medal in the individual pursuit at the 1992 Olympic Games in Barcelona. She was the Olympic champion in the individual road race at the 1996 Olympic Games in Atlanta. In addition, she was also successful in time trials on both track and road, both in one-day races and in multistage races.

Heike Kuhn

Bibliography

Bombrun, Hervé. (1998) "Jeannie Longo: 'La piste, c'est la guerre des nerfs.' " *Vélo Magazine* (June): 30.

Comte, Gilles. (1996) "La Longo enfin . . . ?" *Vélo Magazine* (September): 36–37.

Droussent, Claude. (1989) "La dame de fer." *Vélo Magazine* (November): 28–30.

Fourny, André-Arnoud. (1989) "Jeannie Longo: Reponse á tout." *Vélo Magazine* (June): 30–32.

———. (1989) "Dix Ans de regne . . ." *Vélo Magazine* (November): 24–27.

———. (1989) "Un faux depart?" *Vélo Magazine* (November): 31.

———. (1991) "Jeannie Longo: 'Je croyais avoir tout vu.' " *Vélo Magazine* (September): 30–31.

Le Gars, Philippe. (1992) "Longo aux yeux." *Vélo Magazine* (April): 26–31.

LOPEZ, NANCY

(1957–)

U.S. GOLFER

Nancy Lopez was inducted into the Ladies Professional Golf Association (LPGA) Hall of Fame in 1987, when she was thirty and into the World Golf Hall of Fame in 1989. Entry into the LPGA Hall of Fame is limited to women who have been members in good standing for ten consecutive years and have won at least thirty official events, including two major championships. It took Lopez only ten years to accomplish what it has taken some athletes thirty or more years in professional golf to do. As a Mexican-American athlete, Lopez has proved an important role model to young women; as the mother of three daughters, she has demonstrated that a sporting career need not be sacrificed for family life.

Nancy Lopez was born on 6 January 1957, in Torrance, California. By the time she was eight, her father had moved the family to Roswell, New Mexico, and had started teaching her to play golf. Lopez was twelve when she won the New Mexico Women's Amateur (1969). She followed that by winning the (USGA) Junior Girls championship at age fifteen in 1972 and again in 1974. She also captured the Western Junior three times, and in 1975, at age eighteen, she won the Mexican Amateur. The same year, she entered the U.S. Women's Amateur and finished in a tie for second place. In 1976 she won the (AIAW) National Championship, playing for Tulsa University, and was named All-American and Tulsa University Female Athlete of the Year; she also played for the U.S. Curtis Cup and World Amateur teams. At only twenty years of age, Lopez dropped out of Tulsa University, turned professional, and hit the LPGA tour with a flurry, finishing second in four of her first six events. In 1978, she won consecutive tournaments in late February and early March, and finished second the next week. In May 1978, she won in Baltimore, New Jersey, and New York, and two weeks later claimed the LPGA Championship in Ohio. By June 25, she had accumulated five victories in a row. Named the

Nancy Lopez crouches down after missing a birdie putt by less than an inch on the green of the 8th hole at the LPGA tournament in Lake Lanier, Georgia, in 1988. (Bettmann)

1978 Rolex Rookie of the Year and the Rolex Player of the Year, she was also awarded the prestigious LPGA Vare trophy (given for the lowest scoring average on the tour), breaking the mark of 72 for the first time in women's golf (71.76). Lopez won a total of nine times that year. In her second full year on the tour, she reaped eight victories, was named LPGA Player of the Year, and again was awarded the Vare trophy.

From 1978 through 1993, Lopez won tournaments in fifteen out of sixteen years, including times when she was pregnant. Her family commitments did not interrupt her stellar performances. In fact, her commitment to her dual roles as golfer and mother of three daughters was a great attraction to fans. Lopez was proud of her Mexican American heritage and of putting her daughters (Ashley, born in 1983; Erinn, in 1986; and Torri, in 1991) first in her thoughts. Always smiling, never hiding from autograph seekers, and playing with determination and feeling, Lopez brought women's golf into the living room and made it a game for all women—homemakers, executives, and aspiring young female professionals.

Lopez's popularity with fans and sponsors alike is credited for much of the surge in interest in the LPGA throughout the 1980s. Following Title IX legislation and enforcement in the late 1970s, the public looked to Lopez as a role model for young girls who saw a professional sport as a possible career. Her marriage to professional baseball player Ray Knight only contributed to the widespread acceptance of the female athlete as an equal partner in the emerging sports business.

Lopez continued to bring energy to women's professional golf through the 1990s. In 1998 she made a gallant run at the one title eluding her, the U.S. Open. Shooting four rounds in the 60s, she set yet another benchmark in LPGA history and played herself into the final day's contention. Media coverage and viewing exceeded that for the British Open, a testimony to her attraction of the fans. By 1998 Lopez had cut back on the number of annual tour events she entered to spend more time with her family, including a stepson, Brooks. She started several ventures for women in golf, including the development of the Nancy Lopez Golf Company and a new line of clubs designed for women. She also continued to pursue the U.S. Open.

Nancy Lopez was named the *Golf* magazine Golfer of the Decade for the years 1978–1987 and was awarded the 1992 Flo Hyman Award by the Women's Sports Foundation. Probably most characteristic of her game, she received the USGA's 1998 Bob Jones Award, which recognizes distinguished sportsmanship in the game of golf. Her many philanthropic activities included raising money for scholarships for her alma mater and a hospice center in Albany, Georgia; building a Habitat For Humanity House and a community softball field for girls; and organizing a pro-am tournament to raise money for AIM for the Handicapped, a worldwide program that benefits children and adults with special ambulatory and communication needs. In the words of the former USGA president Judy Bell, "Nancy Lopez embodies the highest ideals of sportsmanship, generosity, and grace, and she exemplifies these compelling qualities in the actual arena where the stakes are highest and the pressure is the greatest."

Debra Ann Ballinger

Bibliography

Holmes, John. "Lopez Receives USGA's Bob Jones Award." <http://www.golf.com/news/>. 1998.

"The Lopez Record." <http://www.golf.com/golf-digest/profiles/lopezc0897.htm>. August 1997.

LPGA. "Lopez Puts Lean Years Behind Her." <http://www.golf.com/tour/lpga/rochester/press/ap061897.htm>. 1998.

LPGA. "Nancy Lopez." <http://www.lpga.com/tour/bios/Lopez.html>. 1998.

"Nancy Lopez Golf: Defining the Women's Game." <http://www.nancylopezgolf.com>. 1999.

Sirak, Ron. (1998) "Lopez to Develop Club Line with Palmer." <http://www.golf.com/women/index.html>. 1998.

"World Golf Hall of Fame Inductees." <http://www.golfweb.com/library/ap/hallinductees 980516.html>. 1998.

Donna Lopiano, speaking on behalf of the Women's Sports Foundation. (AP Photos)

LOPIANO, DONNA

(1946–)

U.S. SOFTBALL PLAYER, COACH, ATHLETIC ADMINISTRATOR, AND ATHLETIC EQUITY ACTIVIST

Donna Lopiano is considered one of the most influential women in athletics for her work in seeking equity for all. Through her work, she has increased women's access to sports and thus expanded the opportunities for girls and women in sport.

Lopiano was born in Stamford, Connecticut, and grew up there during the 1960s. She was involved in athletics from an early age, but because she was a girl, she was denied opportunities to compete. The experience of being barred from Little League Baseball because of her gender motivated Lopiano toward a career aimed at helping end inequities in athletics.

From the age of fifteen, Lopiano competed on the Raybestos Brakettes, a nationally recognized women's amateur softball team. She was a three-time most valuable player of the American Softball Association national tournament, nine-time American Softball Association All-American, and six-time American Softball Association Champion in her nine years of competition with the Brakettes. Lopiano was recognized for her softball talent when she was inducted into the National Softball Hall of Fame in 1983.

In 1968 Lopiano graduated from Southern Connecticut State University with a degree in physical education. While in college, she played softball, basketball, field hockey, and volleyball. Her master's and doctoral degrees are from the University of Southern California.

Lopiano has been a teacher, coach, and an administrator. As a coach, she has led programs of men's and women's volleyball, women's basketball, field hockey, and softball. Her first administrative position, at the age of twenty-five, was at Brooklyn College, as an assistant athletic director and coach. She went on to become the director of women's athletics at the University of Texas for fifteen years. During this time she saw the budget increase from $57,000 to more than $4 million and Texas win eighteen National Collegiate Athletic Association women's titles.

In 1992 Lopiano was named the executive director of the Women's Sports Foundation, an organization dedicated to increasing opportunities for girls and women in sports and fitness through education, advocacy, recognition, and grants. As executive director, she worked to increase opportunities for girls and women by lobbying for increased funding and protecting Title IX legislation.

Shawn Ladda

Bibliography

Johnson, Anne (1996). *Great Women in Sports.* Detroit, MI: Visible Ink Press.

Women's Sports Foundation (1998). <http://www.womenssportsfoundation.org>.

LUGE

Luge (from French, meaning "sled") is a minor winter sport confined primarily to the Alpine region of Europe. Humans have been using sleds for transport in snowy climates for transportation and probably recreation for thousands of years, but luge as a sport emerged only in the middle of the nineteenth century in the Alps when British tourists began racing down icy courses on sleds. The sport then developed in Switzerland and by the end of the century was popular in Germany

Sylke Otto, German luge gold medalist at 2000 Winter Goodwill Games. (Corbis/AFP)

and Austria as well. The invention of the flexible sled in the 1960s, which allowed lugers to control the sled through their body movements, was the final step in the emergence of luge as an international sport.

Luge is a precise, fast, and dangerous sport in which athletes speed down a curved, ice-covered track while lying in a supine position on their sled. Lugers steer the sled through body movements, and even the slightest error can cause a loss of the hundredths of seconds that will be the difference between victory and defeat.

Women began competing in the 1950s, and a women's singles race was included when luge became an Olympic sport at the 1964 Winter Olympics in Innsbruck, Austria. The first women's gold medalist was Ortrun Enderlein of East Germany, which marked the beginning of Germany's domination of the sport, followed by Austria and Italy. In the 1990s the sport grew to include competitors from twenty-five nations and two major annual competitions: the World Cup circuit and the world championships. Luge is also an Olympic sport, and in Olympic years the Olympic competition serves as the world championship.

At competitions, each nation is allowed to race in men's and women's singles events and in the doubles event with either a same-sex or mixed-sex team. The rules and regulations for men and women are about the same, although women compete on a slightly smaller track (800 to 1,050 meters [2,625 to 3,445 feet]) than do men (1,000 meters to 1,300 meters [3,281 to 4,265 feet]).

The Editors

Bibliography

Farber, Mike. (1998) "Bobsled and Luge." *Sports Illustrated* 88, 5 (9 February): 124.

Layden, Tim. (1998) "Born to Luge." *Sports Illustrated* 88, 5 (9 February).

M

MACCABIAH GAMES

The Maccabiah Games are held every four years in Israel, generally in the year following the Olympic Games. During their seven decades of existence, the Maccabiah Games have grown into one of the largest Olympic-style gatherings of the twentieth century. Although obviously influenced by the Olympic movement, the Maccabiah Games have a distinct mission: to serve as a vehicle for Jewish national ideals. Indeed, the stated aim of the Games is to attract the largest possible number of Jewish athletes, officials, spectators, and tourists to Israel from around the world. Women have played a prominent role in the success of the Maccabiah Games since, in contrast to the Olympic movement, the Maccabiah ideology has from its inception actively encouraged women to take part, emphasizing participation rather than performance.

HISTORY

In 1911 Fritz Abraham, a German Zionist who was strongly influenced by English sports, authored an intriguing article in the *Jüdische Turnzeitung,* the journal of the rapidly expanding Jewish gymnastic and sports movement (Jüdische Turnerschaft und Sportbewegung—later Maccabi), in which he proposed holding a gathering of Jewish gymnasts and sportsmen in an Olympic-style competition. "If we believe at all in the victory of our national idea," he wrote, "then we also should hope to organize a Jewish-national Olympiad." He further stated that

> The world will perhaps become aware of how many outstanding athletes there are among us. Jews still help to build the fame of foreign nations while they fail to recognize their own nationality. . . . If we could only show how many Jewish nationalists participated in sports during the years 1903–1909, then perhaps in 1913 an athletic meet-

ing at the 11th Zionist Congress might offer the promise of our own all-Jewish Olympic Games.

Although World War I scuttled Abraham's idea, by 1924 Gustav Spiegler, an Austrian Maccabi leader, resurrected it with a new twist. In a column in *Der Makkabi,* he suggested that "Before we go to the world Olympics, we should first establish a personal selection process and that is what the Jewish Olympic festival should be all about." He added later that the Games should be held in Eretz Israel—the Jewish homeland in Palestine—and that they should also include a seminar-style academy where Jewish scholars would lecture. His proposal contained two revolutionary notions: first, that Eretz Israel participate in the world Olympic movement; second, that a parallel Jewish "Olympic" festival be established.

The first Maccabiah Games were held in 1932 in Tel Aviv. Since that time, the Games have not repudiated their nationalistic overtone. While they have worked toward Zionist recognition of the role of sport in national aspirations, they have at the same time placed the participation of women in a context different from either the Olympic Games or other regional sports festivals.

PHILOSOPHICAL FOUNDATION

Zionist doctrine aimed to create a broad national community and to implement a modern revolution through a movement that prided itself upon its association with youth. As part of this objective, Zionism sought to redefine the role of women in Jewish society and, consequently, to create a new body image for Jewish women. To combat anti-Semitic stereotypes, Zionists wished to create a "new Jewish man and woman," cleansed by physical toil and baptized by robust physical activity.

The philosophical foundation of the Maccabiah Games reflected this Zionist strategy of the inclusion of women and the redefinition of their roles. Thus, since the inception of the Maccabiah Games, the number of women who have participated, as well as the number of women's events, have always surpassed those of the Olympics. Sports such as tennis, basketball, table tennis, and water polo for women, for example, appeared on the program of the second Maccabiah Games in 1935. The Winter Games in 1933 and 1935 introduced more events for women than did their Lake Placid or Garmisch-Partenkirchen counterparts. One of the most memorable milestones for women at the Maccabiah Games took place in 1965, when Debbie Marcus was the first woman to light the flame at Maccabiah Stadium in Ramat Gan, on the outskirts of Tel Aviv.

In the first Maccabiah Games, U.S. athlete Sybil Koff won almost all the track and field events. Koff repeated this performance in the second Maccabiah Games, but the most celebrated athlete of the 1935 festival was another American, Lillian Copeland. The 1928 and 1932 Olympic champion in shot put and discus, Copeland refused to participate in the 1936 Olympics in Nazi Germany. Later, several female athletes who participated in the Maccabiah Games went on to win Olympic medals, among them the American Marylin Ramenofsky (in swimming) and the Israeli Yael Arad (in judo).

THE GAMES SINCE 1948

The establishment of the state of Israel gave new impetus to the participation of women in the Games. Starting in 1950, the Games included an ever-increasing number of female athletes from all over the world. Events such as chess, judo, karate, lawn bowling, squash, ten-pin bowling, softball, field hockey, badminton, golf, and even bridge and backgammon were added to subsequent festivals. The addition of Masters Maccabiah (for people over the age of 35) and Junior Maccabiah (for youth) and regional games gave more opportunities for women to shape the emerging image of the Games. After the collapse of the Soviet Union in the early 1990s, a multitude of Olympic-caliber Jewish female athletes from Eastern and Central Europe joined the Maccabiah ranks, such as the famed Polgar sisters from Hungary, who were among the most celebrated chess players in the world.

George Eisen

Bibliography

Eisen, George. (1979) "Maccabiah Games: A History of the Jewish Olympics." Ph.D. diss., University of Maryland.

Maccabi USA/Sports for Israel. (1999) <http://www.maccabiusa.com>.

Wein, Chaim. (1983) *Hamacabbiot B'Eretz Israel*. Ramat Gan, Israel: Maccabi World Union.

MACEDONIA *see* Yugoslavia

MAGAZINES

Magazines, like other types of media, help form and reinforce popular perceptions of women's sport. The precursors of modern magazines appeared in the seventeenth century as learned journals. Magazines with a more popular orientation emerged in the eighteenth century. References to women's sport have been traced to the earliest days of mass-circulation magazines. Despite the growth in girls' and women's sports, no widely circulated magazine covers general sports for women.

HISTORY

In the late nineteenth and early twentieth centuries, several general-interest magazines, as well as more narrowly focused women's publications, exhibited a rising level of interest in athletic women. Stories, photographs, and illustrations depicted women engaged in a variety of recreational physical activities. Typically, articles and images during this period concentrated on affluent women engaged in such socially acceptable sports as tennis, golf, skiing, archery, and swimming.

A notable exception to the genteel image of sportswomen presented by most general-interest magazines was the coverage of women athletes in the *National Police Gazette*. Founded in 1845, the *Gazette* was a sensationalistic weekly tabloid that mixed crime reporting, sexual titillation, and sport news. The *Gazette* became one of few publications that regularly featured women engaged in weightlifting, boxing, and other sports that did not fit the prevailing perceptions of acceptable femininity. Although the *Gazette* clearly used women as sexual objects to promote sales in its nonsports reporting, the reporting of women's sport was much less lascivious. Captions of the photographs and illustrations depicting female athletes sometimes made references to their physical appearance, but, in general, the photographs, captions, and stories about female athletes were presented in a straightforward way.

Throughout the twentieth century, there have been several magazines devoted exclusively to women's sport and related physical activities. *La Femme Sportive*, a bimonthly, was published in France from 1912 until at least the 1930s as the official publication of the Fédération des Sociétés Sportives de France, a women's athletic organization founded by Alice Milliat. Milliat organized a series of international women's sport competitions in the 1920s and 1930s and was the prime mover behind the addition of women's track and field to the Olympic Games. Milliat's magazine reflected her multisport, international interests. *Deutsche Turnzeitung für Frauen*, edited by Martha Thurm and published from 1900 to 1915, was a German monthly focusing on Turnen-style gymnastics. An Australian magazine called *Sportswoman* was published in Melbourne during the 1930s.

The United States has produced the greatest number of women's sport magazines. Perhaps the earliest was *Woman's Physical Development*, founded in 1900 in the United States by Bernarr MacFadden, the leading physical culturalist of the era. MacFadden changed the title to *Beauty and Health: Women's Physical Development* in 1903. The magazine openly and straightforwardly promoted the ideal of women's strength and vigorous physical exercise. In 1906 the magazine was absorbed by MacFadden's magazine *Physical Culture*, written for a male and female audience, which continued to offer a steady number of articles about women.

Another early-twentieth-century American women's sport magazine was Constance M. K. Applebee's *Sportswoman*. Applebee was a British physical educator who popularized women's field hockey in American colleges. She coached and taught at Bryn Mawr College from 1904 to 1967 and published *Sportswoman* from 1924 until 1936. The magazine provided news and training information about several sports.

The number of women's sports and fitness magazines increased in the 1990s, reflecting the growing interest and participation of women in sports. (Karen Christensen)

Woman Athletic, a publication of the Illinois Women's Athletic Club in Chicago was another early source of women's sport information. *Woman Athletic* began in 1912 and continued into the 1930s. Reflecting the interests of the club's wealthy membership, the magazine published stories and photographs about society, fashion, and sports. The sports coverage, especially the photography, was wide ranging and included equestrian sports, skiing, swimming, ice hockey, weight training, boxing, basketball, sled dog racing, bowling, archery, sailing, track and field, and golf.

A single-sport magazine, *Woman Bowler*, founded in 1936, was the publication of the Women's International Bowling Congress. It lasted nearly sixty years. The magazine ceased publication in 1994 and then survived for a couple of more years as an annual called *WB for the Woman Who Bowls*.

THE MODERN ERA

The oldest general interest women's sport magazine is *Women's Sports and Fitness*, founded by tennis star Billie Jean King and her husband, tennis promoter Larry King. Launched in 1974 as a monthly titled *womenSports*, the magazine has undergone a series of title and ownership changes. The Kings sold the magazine in 1976 to Charter Publishing Company. Billie Jean King's name continued to appear on the masthead as the publisher through 1978.

Douglas Latimer took over as publisher in 1979. He changed the title to *Women's Sports*, and the magazine became the membership publication of the Women's Sports Foundation, establishing a relationship that continued in one form or another into the 1990s. In mid-1984 Latimer instituted another title change, renaming the magazine *Women's Sports and Fitness*. The new title reflected an editorial move away from predominantly sport coverage to a greater emphasis on personal fitness and appearance.

Through the late 1980s and into the 1990s, under the ownership of World Publications, Inc., and later Women's Sports and Fitness, Inc., the trend toward an emphasis on fitness, featuring an abundance of photographs of Lycra-clad models and aerobics instructors, continued. The shift in editorial policy culminated in 1998 when Condé Nast, a major publisher of fourteen other women's magazines, bought *Women's Sports and Fitness* for a reported $5 million.

Condé Nast's purchase of *Women's Sports and Fitness* marked the end of its own effort to independently establish a genuine women's sports magazine. The company, in January 1996, had announced plans to develop a magazine offering serious coverage of women athletes, events, and issues. The debut issue of *Condé Nast Sports for Women* in 1997 held to the promise, but Condé Nast, apparently concerned about an initial lack of advertiser and reader enthusiasm, quickly reduced the emphasis on sport. When the company bought *Women's Sports and Fitness* in 1998, it com-

bined its new magazine with the older one under the title *Women's Sports and Fitness*. Despite its title, the hybrid bimonthly was essentially a fitness magazine. Among the features promoted on the cover of the July/August 1998 issue was "Hot Summer Fun! 52 Ideas to Get You Off That Beach Towel," "First Lady of Fitness: Tipper Gore Wants You to Get in Shape," and "Getting a World-Class Butt."

Condé Nast was not the only company to express an interest in reaching female readers with a sport title in the late 1990s. *Sports Illustrated* tested two trial issues of *Sports Illustrated Women/Sport* in 1997. In early 1999 the company published another issue with plans to put out quarterly issues during the remainder of the year. *Sports Illustrated*'s interest in a women's publication was rather ironic given the magazine's history as a frequent target of feminist criticism due to its poor coverage of women's athletics.

A number of scholarly studies have documented that *Sports Illustrated* underreports women's sports and reinforces sexist stereotypes. A 1994 study examined *Sports Illustrated* covers from 1957 through 1989. They found that only 4.4 percent of the athletes on the covers were females and that women on the cover were more likely than men to be presented in nonactive sport poses. Another analysis published in 1979 studied the magazine during four six-year periods from 1956 to 1976 and reported that stories about women fluctuated from 3.2 percent to 6.8 percent. A 1988 study analyzed *Sports Illustrated*'s content before, during, and after the passage of Title IX in the United States to determine whether the legis-

WOMEN'S SPORTS MAGAZINES

In the 1990s several new women's sports magazines were launched in the United States, all targeted at physically active women who are not professional athletes. In order to attract readers and advertisers, the magazines have tried a variety of editorial content approaches. Some have emphasized women's sports with a focus on competitions, training, and female athletes. Others have emphasized physical activity, beauty, fashion, and celebrities. And others have attempted to combine both types of content. It is not yet clear which, if any, approach will prove to be the most successful.

lation had led to a reduction in negative stereotypes associated with women's sport participation. That research concluded that although coverage of women had become more frequent after Title IX, it tended to focus on "sex-appropriate" sports such as tennis, rather than "sex-inappropriate" sports like rugby.

To many critics, the most pernicious example of *Sports Illustrated*'s treatment of women has nothing to do with women athletes, but rather concerns the models who appear in the magazine's annual swimsuit issue. Marketed to a male audience, the swimsuit issue features models in bathing suits photographed in a variety of exotic locales. The popularity of the swimsuit issue among male consumers has spawned a variety of marketing spin-offs such as calendars, videos, and special television programs. *Sports Illustrated*'s success has prompted *Sport* and *Inside Sports,* two other mainstream men's sports magazines, to develop their own swimsuit issues. Some scholars have argued that the swimsuit issue is an example of how sport and sport media are used as mechanisms of continued male domination of women.

Magazines like *Women's Sports and Fitness, Sports Illustrated,* and Australia's *Women in Sport,* which began in 1995, represent multisport publications. Throughout the 1980s and 1990s, however, several sport-specific magazines and newsletters emerged. Examples include *Golf for Women, Coaching Women's Basketball, Women's Soccer World, Wahine* (surfing), and *FastPitch World* (softball). These publications do not seek to attract a mass, general audience, but rather rely on the interest and commitment of readers attracted to a particular sport. Other publications seeking a particular niche also appeared in the 1990s. *Girljock* was aimed at a predominantly lesbian readership. *Women's Sports Market Report,* as the title implied, was a newsletter intended for those interested in the business of women's sport.

The proliferation of so-called niche publications was one of the most discernable trends in women's sport media in the 1990s. Another was the appearance of Internet-based magazines, or webzines, devoted to women's sport. As was true of paper-based media, most webzines focused on a specific sport. A particularly well-produced example of the genre was *Full Court Press: The Women's Basketball Journal* (www.fullcourt.com), a webzine launched in 1996.

By mid-1998 there was no magazine offering real coverage of multiple women's sports. The lack of such a magazine, however, created a vacuum that Amy Love sought to fill with the creation of a new publication. Love, in October 1997, announced plans for a December 1998 launch of *Amy Love's Real Sports.* The December 1998 launch took place as scheduled. It was followed by a special spring 1999 issue. The publication plan called for a bimonthly magazine covering many sports, supplemented by a website (www.real-sports.com).

One of the contradictions of sport in the late 1990s was that as girls' and women's sport grew and prospered as a spectator and participant phenomenon, there was no widely circulated, well-established magazine that reflected its increasing mass appeal.

Wayne Wilson

See also Advertising; Beauty; Marketing; Media; Sexuality

Bibliography

Creedon, Pamela, ed. (1994) *Women, Media, and Sport: Challenging Gender Values.* Thousand Oaks, CA: Sage Publications.

Davis, Laurel. (1997) *The Swimsuit Issue and Sport: Hegemonic Masculinity in Sports Illustrated.* Albany, NY: State University of New York Press.

Duncan, Margaret. (1993) "Beyond Analyses of Sport Media Texts: An Argument for Formal Analyses of Institutional Structures." *Sociology of Sport Journal* 10, 4: 353–372.

Kane, Mary Jo. (1988) "Media Coverage of the Female Athlete Before, During and After Title IX: *Sports Illustrated* Revisited." *Journal of Sport Management* 2, 2: 87–89.

Reid, Leonard, and Lawrence Soley. (1979) "*Sports Illustrated's* Coverage of Women in Sports." *Journalism Quarterly* 56, 4: 861–863.

Salwen, Michael, and Natalie Wood. (1994) "Depictions of Female Athletes on *Sports Illustrated* Covers, 1957–1989." *Journal of Sport Behavior* 17, 2: 98–107.

Todd, Jan, Joe Roark, and Terry Todd. (1991) "A Briefly Annotated Bibliography of English Language Serial Publications in the Field of Physical Culture." *Iron Game History* 1, 4/5: 25–40.

MALAWI

Malawi is located in southeastern Africa and has a population of about 11.5 million. Women in Malawi have traditionally been assigned the role of mother, and in the world of work they are largely found in such caretaker and support positions as nurse, secretary, and teacher. Women have not played a full role in Malawi society; in the 1990s they comprised only 40 percent of the work force, had an illiteracy rate of 63 percent (compared to 36 percent for men), and had an average of 6.7 children. Given these conditions, it is not surprising that women in Malawi have not traditionally been active participants in sports. That situation is beginning to change, however. In the late 1990s, some women embraced the Brighton Declaration supporting the development of women's sports and have subsequently worked to increase sports opportunities for women in Malawi. In addition, the Olympic and Commonwealth Games Association have become active in training women as coaches and administrators. Nonetheless, many men continue to resist the involvement of their wives and daughters in sports.

PHYSICAL EDUCATION

Both girls and boys are required to take physical education classes for eight years in primary school. Thus, girls regularly participate in track and field, gymnastics, netball, soccer (association football), basketball, and the traditional sport of mahanaim between the ages of six and thirteen. Surveys show that in the period 1996–1998 about 90 percent of girls participated in physical education, a 10 percent increase over the previous two years. However, physical education is not required in secondary schools, where the number of girls who participate drops to only 50 percent, mostly on an informal basis in soccer, netball, basketball, tennis, cricket, and mahanaim. This situation may change in the future, since in 1998 the government began offering a diploma course in physical education at Domasi College of Education and also began developing a physical education curriculum for secondary schools. At the college level, women's participation continues to decrease, with

only about 40 percent participating. The decrease seems due in large part to a continuing perception that sports are for men and not for women.

The major exception to this pattern is cricket, which since 1997 has been actively promoted as a sport for women as well as men. Cricket is taught in schools across the nation, and twenty of the forty-eight cricket coaches in Malawi are women, teaching cricket to both boys and girls in the schools. Although these coaches teach at Level One (lower grades), women are also being trained for higher-level positions.

RECREATION

Participation in sports for recreation is not a common activity for women in Malawi. Although 60 percent of women in cities play sports recreationally, only about 15 percent of rural women do so, and Malawi is a largely rural nation. However, in both groups, the level of participation increased from 1994–1996 to 1996–1998, but at a much slower rate in rural areas. Across the nation, netball, basketball, volleyball, and traditional dances are the most popular sports activities.

ELITE SPORTS

The identification, support, and training of female athletes for national, regional, and international competition are only beginning in Malawi. Similarly, training opportunities for women in sports administration and coaching have been limited; although they increased in the 1990s, men still hold most administrative and coaching positions. One major problem facing sports development programs is the reality that many women who participated in sports as girls drop out when they reach adulthood, in part because of limited training opportunities and in part because of traditional attitudes about sex roles that discourage women from remaining involved in sports.

In the 1990s the development of elite athletes focused on track, represented by athletes such as Ruth Kenani in the 100-meter sprint; Catherine Chikwakwa, Julian Chikwasa, and Dolla Mkandawire in the 400-meter run; and Agnes Chikwawa in the 3000-meter run. The latter has drawn the most attention, and her training for the African Games and the 2000 Olympics has been supported by the Olympic and Commonwealth Games Association. In 1998 she was sent to Kenya to train for these events. An important event promoting sports is the annual Olympic Day, when women compete in volleyball, basketball, running, soccer, and sack-and-bottle races.

Advocates of women's sports recognize that three developments must take place for women's sports to develop fully in Malawi. First, traditional attitudes about women's role in society must change. Second, a plan must be put forth for the development of women's sports. Third, financial support must be forthcoming from the government and the private sector to implement the plan.

Irene M. Kadammanja

Information provided by Albert Ndalama, Issac Phiri, Moses Seunda, John Chamba, and A. T. Mlogeni.

MALLORY, MOLLA

(1884–1959)

NORWEGIAN TENNIS PLAYER

Molla Bjurstedt Mallory was the dominant female tennis player in the United States between 1915 and 1923. Born in Oslo, Norway, on 6 March 1884, and christened Anna Margrethe Bjurstedt, she took up the game in 1903 and soon established herself as Norway's top player, winning the women's singles title eleven times. She studied in Germany and France, won a bronze medal in the 1912 Summer Olympics in Stockholm, and came to the United States in 1914.

Mallory began playing competitive tennis as soon as she arrived in the United States, won the first four tournaments she entered, and by 1915 was the top-ranked female player. According to *The Outlook* (2 June 1915), she played "with a fire and dash that betrays the Viking blood in her veins." She was the national women's singles champion eight times (1915–1918, 1920–22, and 1926), doubles champion twice (1916–1917), and mixed doubles champion three times (1917, 1922–1923), although she never won a major international title. Mallory's most celebrated match was her victory over Suzanne Lenglen in the semi-

Molla Mallory. (UPI/Corbis/Bettmann)

finals of the 1921 U.S. national tournament, when Lenglen, losing badly, defaulted after the first game of the second set.

Known for her spirited play and her outgoing and friendly attitude toward other players, Mallory competed until 1929, when a knee injury forced her retirement.

In 1919 she married Franklin Mallory, a stock broker. He died in 1934, and she worked in the federal government's Office of Censorship during World War II, where her language abilities were valuable. After the war, she worked as a salesperson for Lord & Taylor, a department store in New York City. She was elected to the International Tennis Hall of Fame in 1958 and died in Stockholm after a long illness on 22 November 1959.

John E. Findling

Bibliography

Bjurstedt, Molla. (1916) *Tennis for Women*. New York: Doubleday, Page.

Collins, Bud, and Zander Hollander. (1980) *Bud Collins' Modern Encyclopedia of Tennis*. Garden City, NY: Dolphin.

Grimsley, Will. (1971) *Tennis: Its History, People and Events.* Englewood Cliffs, NJ: Prentice-Hall.

MANAGEMENT

Sport management includes the functions of planning, organizing, leading, marketing, and evaluating within an organization whose primary objective is to provide sport- or fitness-related activities, products, and/or services. The two primary areas of sport management are management in the spectator sport industry, which focuses on consumer entertainment, and management in the fitness industry, which concentrates on consumer participation in sport activities.

Historically, most sport managers worked on a volunteer basis. In the last half-century, however, the sport industry has grown into a $200 billion industry, which resulted in many more full-time paid positions. While men have filled the majority of sport management positions, both paid and volunteer, the number of female sport managers increases yearly.

As the number of females participating in sport increases, so too does the number of sport teams, leagues, and organizations, as well as the demand for sport equipment and clothing. All of these translate into additional career opportunities in sport management.

Sport management has also become an academic field of study, which has opened more doors for women. The percentage of female students in undergraduate and graduate sport management programs is 25 percent and 35 percent, respectively. Although these percentages have remained constant for the past seven years, the overall number of women in sport management programs has increased due to the explosion of programs offered throughout the United States and around the world.

HISTORY

For women, the first step toward sport management was establishing their own sport clubs, events, governing bodies, and organizations. This was followed by women's movement into the leadership ranks of coed sport organizations. Finally, women broke barriers to enter positions within male-dominated sport properties and positions.

In the ancient Olympic Games in 776 BCE, the earliest record of sport management, women could not participate either on or off the field. This situation continued throughout history, and eventually women started to establish their own organizations and events. Most often female athletes took on the role of sport managers and organized associations and events that increased opportunities and exposure for female athletes. Although women were rarely recognized as sport managers, many female pioneers did in fact pave the way for women to have careers in sport management.

SPORT CLUBS AND EVENTS

Of sport clubs and events formed exclusively for women by women, the Ladies Club for Outdoor Sports was one of the first. It was organized by thirty women from New York in 1877 with an all-female membership that participated in tennis, archery, and other sports. In 1880 a group of women from New Orleans organized the Pearl Archery Club, one of the first sports clubs for women in the southern United States. In 1903, Chicago-area women formed the Chicago Sports Club. This sports facility accommodated gymnastics, swimming, and bowling, and members participated in tournaments in fencing, basketball, bowling, water polo, and swimming.

Women from the coed Philadelphia Cricket Club organized the first national tennis tournament for women in 1887, when they invited women from outside their own club to participate. The United States Lawn Tennis Association (USLTA) opened membership to women in 1889 and soon took over sponsorship of the national tournament.

SPORT ORGANIZATIONS

As more women began to take part in sports in the early twentieth century, women established and administered various women's sport organizations. The first referenced sport organization created for and run by women was the Woman's National Bowling Association (WNBA), now the Women's International Bowling Congress. The

WNBA was created in 1916 by forty women from eleven midwestern and northeastern cities. By the late twentieth century it was the largest sport organization for women in the world. Next came the Women's Swimming Association of New York, formed in 1917 by area swimmers. When women first began competitive swimming, members from this association made up the Olympic teams.

Then, in 1921, after years of fighting with international sport federations for acceptance of female athletes and women's international competitions, Alice Milliat of France organized the Fédération Sportive Féminine Internationale (FSFI) to regulate women's sports and to stage a separate Women's Olympic Games. Over twelve years (1922–1934) the FSFI conducted four successful Women's Olympic Games, the first of which took place in Paris in 1922 in front of twenty thousand spectators. These Games, organized and administered entirely by women, were so successful that the International Olympic Committee (IOC) and the International Amateur Athletic Federation (IAAF) were forced to include women's track and field events in the Olympic Games beginning in 1928.

In 1944, Hope Seignious, Betty Hicks, and Ellen Griffin funded and incorporated the Women's Professional Golf Association (WPGA).

Five years later, the Ladies Professional Golf Association (LPGA) was formed in 1949 by Mildred "Babe" Didrikson and Patty Berg with the sponsorship of Wilson Sporting Goods. The LPGA became an officially chartered organization in 1950.

In intercollegiate competition for women, the Commission on Intercollegiate Athletics for Women (CIAW) was the first governing body of its type. Formed in 1967, the CIAW served as a platform to establish intercollegiate competitions for women, as well as national collegiate championships for golf, tennis, gymnastics, track and field, and other sports. In 1971 the CIAW changed its name to the Association of Intercollegiate Athletics for Women (AIAW). This association continued to govern women's college athletics as an independent group outside college physical education departments until 1981, when the National Collegiate Athletic Association (NCAA) took over control of both male and female intercollegiate competition.

From the 1970s through the 1990s, the tennis player Billie Jean King of the United States served as the most prominent leader and role model for women in sport management. Beginning in 1970, King, along with Gladys Heldman, publisher of *World Tennis* magazine, and other female tennis players, organized the Virginia Slims Tennis Tournament in Houston, Texas. This was the first tour-

A FEW OF THE TOP 100 INFLUENTIAL PEOPLE IN SPORTS

In its December 14, 1998, issue *The Sporting News* published its annual list of the 100 most influential people in sports. The list is dominated by men and most are team owners, league executives, media executives, and player agents. Only six women made the top 100:

46 Anita DeFrantz, Vice-President of the International Olympic Committee
71 Sara Levinson, President of National Football League Properties
88 Donna Lopiano, Executive Director of the Women's Sports Foundation

90 Se Ri Pak, Professional Golfer
96 Val Ackerman, President of the Women's National Basketball Association
98 Sandra Ortiz-Del Valle, Teacher and Coach in New York City who has won a lawsuit against the National Basketball Association for refusing to appoint her a referee

While women are scarce on the list so too are representatives of other groups. Only eleven athletes are listed, and six are lumped together as number 50 (Michael Jordan is number 4), and only eleven non-whites are listed.

nament for women professional tennis players to be held separately from male players.

In 1973 King founded the Women's Tennis Association (WTA) and served as president until 1975 and again from 1980 to 1981. In 1974 King, along with Joan Joyce, helped to establish the International Women's Professional Softball Association (IWPSA) and in the same year was one of the founding members of the Women's Sports Foundation (WSF).

King then broadened her involvement. In 1981 she founded *womenSports*, a magazine that was a forerunner to *Women's Sports and Fitness*. After retiring from competitive tennis in 1984, King became the first female commissioner in professional sport history, governing Team Tennis. Team Tennis is the first professional sport league in which women compete on a completely equal basis with men. King continues to serve as commissioner of Team Tennis and remains an active proponent of women in sport both on and off the field. Aside from King, Mildred "Babe" Didrikson, Anita DeFrantz, and Donna Lopiano also stand out as leaders in women's sport management.

ORGANIZATIONS FOR LEADERSHIP

In the 1990s, a number of women's professional sport organizations, as well as committees within organizations, were dedicated to promoting and increasing the number of women in leadership and employment positions. These organizations served as resources for women interested in sport careers, as well as giving women already in the industry a chance to meet and share experiences.

The Association of Women in Sport Media (AWSM) is a professional organization whose aim is promoting and helping women pursue careers in sport media. AWSM offers a job bank for members, a scholarship program, a job fair, and an annual convention. The membership is about seven hundred.

The National Association for Girls and Women in Sport (NAGWS) is a nonprofit educational organization designed to serve the needs of administrators, teachers, coaches, leaders, and participants of sports programs for girls and women. The group has about 4,850 members.

The National Association of Collegiate Women's Athletic Administrators (NACWAA) supports programs and furthers the development of women athletic administrators in collegiate sports programs. NACWAA has an annual conference, telephone hotline to answer questions, and a week-long leadership institute. The membership stands at about eight hundred.

The Women's Basketball Coaches Association (WBCA) promotes women's basketball by bringing together coaches at all levels to develop a reputable identity for the sport of women's basketball and to foster and promote the development of the game in all of its aspects as an amateur sport for women and girls. Its membership is five thousand.

Women in Sports and Events (WISE) is an organization created by women, for women. WISE provides professional access and guidance, presents and explores career-related issues, and offers a forum for problem solving and enrichment for women in the sport industry and other major event markets. Membership is about seven hundred.

The Women's Sport Foundation (WSF) is a membership organization that provides opportunities and support for women in sport. Some of their member services include a resource center that serves as a clearinghouse for information on women's sports, a speakers' bureau, an annual college scholarship guide, various awards and scholarships, and grants for travel, training, and leadership. The membership stands at about 250,000 associate members and 4,000 voting members.

Several publications are dedicated directly to helping women enter sport management. One is the *Women's Sports Wire* (WSW). The WSW was founded in 1995, the first and only national clearinghouse for women's sport news and information. The clearinghouse publishes two editions, a business edition and an employment edition (*WS Job Wire*). The *WS Job Wire* delivers up-to-date job listings in a variety of areas from sales and marketing to coaching.

Beginning in the late 1970s, women began pressing hard for equal representation in sport organizations that represent both male and female athletes. Targeted organizations included the National Collegiate Athletic Association (NCAA), national Olympic committees, and the International Olympic Committee (IOC). The following examples highlight the progress as well as the time that it has taken for women to enter the sport world as men's equals, both on and off the field.

COLLEGIATE SPORTS

With the increased attention and money in women's sport, men are finding the coaching and management positions in women's sport more attractive. In 1972 more than 90 percent of the coaches of women's teams were women. Today women hold only 47.7 percent of women's college coaching positions and a mere 1 percent of men's college teams. In another study, the WSF found that in 1995–1996 women filled fewer than 2 percent of full-time head and assistant head collegiate coaching positions for men's teams, yet men filled 45 percent of full-time head positions and 33 percent of full-time assistant head coaching positions for women's teams.

In sport management employment opportunities within collegiate athletic programs, women have lost markedly in terms of top management positions. In 1972 more than 90 percent of women's collegiate athletic programs were headed by women. Yet, in 1996 women held only 35.9 percent of all administrative jobs related to women's collegiate athletic programs with 23.8 percent of the women's programs having no female involved in the administration. Similarly, in a 1993 study of 402 NCAA Division I-A top, middle, and first-line administrators, 83 percent were male. In 1997, of the 305 athletic directors at Division I schools, 5.2 percent were women. Among 111 schools playing Division I-A football, only 7 (6.3 percent) had female athletic directors. In total there were 137 (13.8 percent) female athletic directors with the majority (82) in Division III. Of the universities employing full-time sport information directors, only 11.9 percent were female. Much of the decline in number of female athletic directors is due to the merging of male and female athletic departments after the passage of Title IX, when male athletic directors assumed responsibility over both departments.

These discouraging statistics notwithstanding, recent years have seen important efforts and accomplishments toward increasing the prominence of women administrators in collegiate programs. During the 1981 NCAA convention, legislation was passed mandating that every member institution identify a primary woman administrator who is the highest-ranking female administrator involved with the member institution's intercollegiate athletics program. Referred to as senior woman administrators, these officials participate in decisions about budgeting or other issues regarding student athlete welfare; help to develop and implement gender equity action plans as needed; and represent the needs and interests of women within the intercollegiate athletics department, campus, and community. At the conference level, the senior woman administrator should attend conference meetings and review general issues related to athletics, particularly issues related to women. Nationally, the administrator should represent her institution at the NCAA national convention, serve on NCAA committees, and act as a peer reviewer for athletic certification.

Some women have achieved high positions within organizations. In 1982 Patty Viverito was hired as the first woman commissioner of the Gateway Football Conference, and in 1988 Phyllis Holmes was appointed president of the National Association of Intercollegiate Athletics (NAIA). Holmes was the first woman to serve as president of any national coed sport organization. In 1991 the NCAA elected Judy Sweet as its first female president. Also in 1991, Barbara Hedges was named athletic director for the University of Washington, making her the first female athletic director of a NCAA Division I school that includes football.

More recently, the restructuring of NCAA governance offers women more opportunities to take part in management councils within the association's administrative structure. In 1987 the NCAA also created a Committee on Women's Athletics to study and address concerns of female athletes and collegiate administrators. The committee identified as its primary focus enhancing women's involvement in intercollegiate athletics, specifically in the areas of coaching, athletics administration, officiating, and support services. To address problems in these areas, in 1988 the committee initiated the NCAA Women's Enhancement Program, the purpose of which is to increase both the number of qualified women and the number of opportunities for them to work in the field. The program includes postgraduate scholarships for women studying sport administration, internships at the NCAA national office to provide on-the-job experiences for women who want to work in intercollegiate athletics, and a resume bank for women seeking careers in intercollegiate athletics.

Statistics suggest that the internship program is indeed achieving its goal. Between 1988 and 1998, forty-eight women participated in the NCAA internship program. Of these women, 94 percent subsequently accepted positions in the sport industry, 2 percent enrolled in graduate school, and 4 percent were seeking employment. The committee also studied the senior woman administrator position.

OLYMPIC SPORTS

Women's employment and volunteer leadership positions in the Olympics has shown a slow but steady increase in the number of women represented at all levels from the national governing bodies to the International Olympic Committee (IOC). Although the modern Olympic Games were conceived in 1894, the first two women (Flor Isava-Fonseca of Venezuela and Pirjo Haeggman of Finland) were not appointed to the IOC until 1981. Anita DeFrantz became the first woman from the United States to sit on the IOC in 1986 and in 1997 was elected to serve as the first female vice president of the IOC. As of August 1998, twelve out of the 118 IOC members were women, representing 10 percent of the IOC membership. A woman has filled one of the most influential positions within the IOC, the secretary-general, for more than twenty-five years, beginning with Monique Berlioux in 1971. Additionally, in 1996, four women (10 percent) served as presidents of international federations, five (12.5 percent) as secretary-generals (executive directors) of international federations, and six (3 percent) as national Olympic committee presidents.

In July 1996, the IOC adopted a proposal to ensure continued promotion of women within sport and its technical and administrative structures. In brief, the proposal stated that by the end of the year 2000 women should hold at least 10 percent of the offices in all of the national Olympic committees' decision-making structures and by the end of the year 2005, that proportion should have increased to 20 percent. Additionally, the IOC challenged international federations, national federations, and all other sport organizations belonging to the Olympic movement to meet the standards set out for the national committees.

The United States offers a good example of the status of women in the administration of Olympic sports. In 1997 twenty-four out of 107 (22 percent) United States Olympic Committee (USOC) board of directors were female; one out of six (16 percent) of the USOC executive officers (vice presidents) were female; seven out of forty-one (17 percent) national governing board executive directors were female; and eleven out of forty-one (27 percent) national governing board presidents were female. Overall, in 1997 the number of women in national governing body (NGB) positions increased by 5 percent and the number of female NGB presidents more than doubled, from 12.5 to 27 percent. Of the 519 USOC employees, 295 (57 percent) were female with 47 of 137 (34 percent) serving in the capacity of an official/manager; and 57 out of 103 (53 percent) holding professional positions. The remainder served in administrative support/clerical/laborer positions (191 out of 351, or 54 percent). For the four-year period 1997–2000, among 355 positions on twenty USOC committees, women filled 104 (up 37 percent from the four-year period 1993–1996). One reason cited for the increased participation of women in Olympic-related positions is Project Gold, a program implemented by the USOC in 1996 to increase the participation of minorities and women in governance positions within the Olympic family.

Internationally, numerous efforts are also underway to increase the number of women in leadership roles within sport. The first true effort dates back to the second Conference of European Ministers of Sport in 1978, where a motion was made for greater involvement of women in sport. As a result, a number of recommendations were adopted in 1980 at the third Conference of European Ministers of Sport to facilitate employment in executive posts of more women who were currently or who had been involved in sport, so that policy might benefit from their experience at all levels. It was further suggested that governments ask governing bodies to consider introducing special steps to ensure that women hold decision-making sport positions at local, national, and international levels. In 1989 the first European conference to focus exclusively on women's positions of leadership in sport took place. Entitled "Women in Sport—Taking the Lead," the conference met to study ways to encourage women to become more active and to ultimately increase the number of women in advisory, decision-making, and administrative bodies. In 1995 the group studied the percentages of female executive board members in sport federations to evaluate women's progress in sport management positions. The results showed that in gymnastics, 28 percent of board members were women; 12 percent in swimming; 9 percent in handball; 8 percent in tennis; and 3 percent in soccer. Most federations indicated that they were trying to increase these percentages through courses, mentoring programs, and publicity campaigns.

The first international conference on women in sport was held in Brighton, England, in May 1994. At that conference, delegates endorsed the document known as the Brighton Declaration on Women in Sport. The aim of this declaration was to increase the involvement and leadership of women in sport. The conference also agreed to develop an international strategy for women in sport that would encompass all continents and share model programs among nations. This conference was followed by the proposal approved by the IOC in July 1996 to increase the number of women in sport leadership positions. The IOC also held the first seminar on leadership for women in sport in Suva, Fiji, in May 1996, followed by the World Conference on Women in Sport in Lausanne, Switzerland. Some of the more important recommendations from the world conference included a call for equal opportunities for women's professional and personal advancement, whether as athletes, coaches, or administrators at all levels of the Olympic movement; a recommendation to designate Olympic Solidarity funds for the training of women administrators with emphasis on developing countries; and the establishment by national Olympic committees of athletes' commissions that include women, as a way of training women as leaders.

WOMEN IN MALE PROFESSIONAL SPORTS

Aside from a few women who either inherited teams or worked alongside their husbands, women did not begin to break into the manage-

Marilyn Carlson, chair of the committee that brought the 1992 Super Bowl to Minneapolis. (Layne Kennedy/Corbis)

ment ranks of such male-only sport organizations as the National Football League (NFL), major league baseball, the National Basketball Association (NBA), and the National Hockey League (NHL) until the 1980s. The first female owner of any male professional sport team was Helen Britton, who inherited the St. Louis Cardinals baseball club of the National League in 1911. She remained an owner until 1917. The second female owner was Effa Manley, who co-owned with her husband the Newark Eagles, a Negro League baseball club in the 1930s and 1940s. In 1978 Georgia Frontiere, owner of the St. Louis Rams, became the first female team owner in the NFL after her husband died. More recently, Denise DeBartolo-York became the chairperson of the DeBartolo Corporation, which owns and operates the San Francisco 49ers. In addition, a few other

Table 1. Females in Executive Sport Positions

Pro League	Number of Female Team/ League Execs*	Percent of Total Execs	Percent of Female TV Audience
MLB	11 of 190	5.8%	44%
NBA	19 of 203	9.4%	40%
NFL	10 of 171	5.8%	40%
NHL	13 of 187	6.9%	41%

(Bachman 1997)

*Refers to women in CEO, CFO, COO, president, or vice president positions.

Table 2. Female Representation in the Sports Industry

INDUSTRY SEGMENT	MALE	FEMALE
Major league team	79.1%	20.9%
League office	66.7%	33.3%
College/university	75.0%	25.0%
Marketing agency	75.0%	25.0%
Minor league team	91.9%	8.1%
Arena/venue	78.9%	21.1%
Broadcast/media	86.5%	13.5%

(Barbano, ed. 1997)

women are partial owners of teams. These include Marge Schott, who in 1985 became an owner of the Cincinnati Reds, and Linda Alvarado, who invested in the Colorado Rockies, a major league baseball team, in 1993.

Aside from female owners, the first woman to serve as president of a male professional sport team was Susan O'Malley. In 1986 O'Malley started with the Washington Bullets basketball team (now the Wizards) as director of advertising. She subsequently became director of marketing in 1987 and then interim executive vice president in 1988. In 1991 she was named president of the Washington Bullets, making her the first and only female president in the NBA. In 1998 O'Malley was named president of Washington Sport and Entertainment, which incorporates Bullets presidency with responsibilities over the business operations of the Washington Capitals, a hockey team, the WNBA Washington Mystics, MCI Center, Ticket-Master, and Centre Management Group.

Other notable women leaders include Ellen Robinson, who from 1996 to 1998 served as president of Ascent Sports, which controls the business operations of the NBA Denver Nuggets and NHL Colorado Avalanche teams. In August 1998, Wendy Selig-Prieb was named president and CEO of the Milwaukee Brewers. Selig-Prieb was promoted from vice president and general counsel, a position she held since 1990, after her father Bud Selig was appointed commissioner of major league baseball. Other noteworthy names within the world of professional male sports include

Sara Levinson, the highest-ranking female working for the NFL as the president of NFL Properties; Bernadette Mansur, the highest-ranking female working for the NHL as vice president of communications; and Paula Hanson, senior vice president of Team Operations, as the highest-ranking female in the NBA. Major league baseball (MLB) has four female vice presidents, one of whom is Leslie Sullivan, vice president of broadcasting, who has worked for the league since 1985.

OTHER SPORT-RELATED CAREERS

Women are also making progress in the fields of sport medicine, media/communications, facility management, and sport manufacturing, though few employment statistics are available to document this trend. Of the twelve thousand active members of the National Athletic Trainers Association (NATA), 43 percent are women. Women also account for 43 percent of all university and college athletic trainers who are members of NATA. Only 4 percent of female members work in professional sports. Efforts, however, are being made to increase the number of female athletic trainers at all levels. For example, NATA established the women in athletic training committee in 1995. Since then the committee has developed and completed a survey soliciting concerns from female and male members and produced a sexual harassment brochure. Similarly, the Professional Baseball Athletic Trainer Society (PBATS), a membership association of athletic trainers in professional baseball, implemented an intern program open to both sexes in 1996; in 1997 four women participated in the program.

The first professional sport umpire was Bernice Gera, who in 1972 was hired by the New York–Pennsylvania Class A League. Gera umpired just one game before quitting in frustration over a bad call and the unjust treatment received from her umpiring partner. In 1997 the NBA stepped forward and hired two women referees, Dee Kantner and Violet Palmer.

Women are also making some inroads in the health and fitness industry. Among sixteen health and fitness companies that have twenty-five or more clubs, five list women as principals or primary media contacts. And although women remain sparse in the executive management levels of sporting goods companies, the numbers continue to increase. Three of Nike's twenty-nine executives are women (10.3 percent), which is an all-time industry record. Serving as role models are such women as Kathy Davenport, vice president and general manager for Lady Foot Locker; Mary Ann Domuracki, chief executive officer for Danskin; Marilyn Oshman, chair of Oshman's Sporting Goods; and Helen Rockey, president and chief executive officer for Brooks Sports.

The first female sportswriter was Mary Garber, who in 1944 was hired by the *Winston-Salem Journal*. A number of female reporters were hired during World War II. In 1998 there were approximately twenty female newspaper sport editors in the United States, of whom Cathy Henkel is recognized as the first. Henkel was hired as a sportswriter by the *Seattle Times* in 1987 and promoted to sport editor soon after.

Television has had so few female sportscasters that most of the pioneers are still in the business. In 1991 *Sports Illustrated* reported that fewer than fifty women worked as sportscasters at the 630 network affiliate stations around the country. Beginning in 1965, Olympic swimmer Donna de Varona became the first female sport commentator on network television after retiring from amateur competition. In 1987 Gayle Sierens was the first woman broadcaster to do play-by-play for an NFL game. Eight years later, in 1995, Suzyn Waldman became the first woman to broadcast a network play-by-play baseball game. Overall, much of the credit for opening up opportunities for female sportscasters goes to the sport network

ESPN. The first female broadcaster the cable network hired was Gayle Gardner in 1983.

SCOUTS AND AGENTS

Of all sport management positions, the most difficult by far for women to enter are those that deal with the player-versus-business side of professional sports (scouting and athlete representation). A few women, however, have broken the barrier, beginning with Mrs. Roy Largent, who in 1943 was employed, along with her husband, as a scout for the Chicago White Sox. The first female agent to represent NFL players was Ellen Zavian. Much of Zavian's work now is with female athletes since she is the executive director of the Women's Players Association. Linda Bodgan, daughter of the Buffalo Bills' owner Ralph Wilson, serves not only as the Bills' corporate vice president but also does some scouting work. Although most top-ranking women in sport franchises do not make direct player decisions, the decisions made by men do affect the financial, legal, or marketing departments, which often involves the women on the business side of sport.

CONCLUSION

Historically, most female sport managers who were not associated by family (wife, daughter, daughter-in-law) rose from the playing and coaching ranks. "Long ago, the issue more than gender was, if you hadn't played the game, could you know how to evaluate the talent, could you know how to market the game, could you know how to sell the sizzle?" said Wendy Selig-Prieb, president of the Milwaukee Brewers.

More recently, however, the trend has been to hire women from outside the sport industry, particularly from radio and television advertising and from publishing. Sara Levinson, who was president of MTV before heading NFL Properties, is one example. Consequently, women have their largest presence in professional sports in public relations and marketing. Women in sport management continue to face obstacles that female executives face in other businesses. Typically, if a male is leaving a position, he refers his friend, generally another male. This cycle further compounds the perception that since few women work in sport management, few qualified women are available. For those who do succeed in landing a traditional male position, the standards are often higher; women must prove themselves much more than men. Through the efforts of numerous organizations and early pioneers—and with recognition by men that even if women may not play a particular sport, they may enjoy and understand it—more and more women are being hired into the ranks of professional sports.

Lisa Delpy

See also Administration; Coaching; Intercollegiate Athletics; Marketing; Ownership; Physical Education; Unionism

Bibliography

Acosta, R. Vivian, and Linda J. Carpenter. (1996) "Women in Intercollegiate Sport: A Longitudinal Study—Nineteen Year Update, 1977–1996." Unpublished manuscript, Brooklyn College.

Bachman, Rachel. (1997) "Women in the Front Office." *The Oregonian* (9 November): C1.

Barbano, Sharon, ed. (1997) "Sobering Statistics." *Women's Sports Market Report* 2, 3 (September/October).

British Sports Council. *The Brighton Declaration on Women in Sport.* (1994) London: British Sports Council.

Council of Europe. (1996) *Sports Information Bulletin,* no. 8 (42). Brussels: Sports for All Clearinghouse.

Fasting, Kari. (1995) "European Women in Sport: Monitoring the Implementation of the Recommendations Adopted by the 1991 ESC in Oslo." Farson, Sweden: Swedish Sports Confederation.

Ferdon, Eleanore Johnstone, and Mary Rose Main. (1995) *Off and Running: Exploring Sport Careers.* New York: Girl Scouts of the USA.

Hums, Mary A., Carol A. Barr, and Gudron Doll-Tepper. (1998) "Roles and Status of Women in Sport Management." *Journal of the International Council for Health, Physical Education, Recreation, Sport and Dance* 34, 2 (Winter).

Hums, Mary A., Carol P. O'Bryant, and Linda Tremble. (1996) "Strategies for Increasing Minorities and Women in Sport Management and Physical Education Teacher Preparation Programs: Common Recruitment and Retention Themes." *Women's Sport and Physical Activity Journal* 5, 2.

Kidane, Fekrou. (1995) "Women in the Olympic Movement." *Olympic Review.* Lausanne, Switzerland: International Olympic Committee.

Lucas, John A. (1992) *Future of the Olympic Games.* Champaign, IL: Human Kinetics.

Mullin, Bernard, Stephen Hardy, and William Sutton. (1993) *Sport Marketing.* Champaign, IL: Human Kinetics.

NCAA. (1998) *Women's Enhancement Program.* <http://www.ncaa.org/programs>.

Oglesby, Carol A. (1998) *Encyclopedia of Women and Sports in America.* Phoenix, AZ: Oryx Press.

Women's Sports Foundation. (1997) *Gender Equity Report Card.* East Meadow, NY: Women's Sports Foundation.

Woolum, Janet (1992). *Outstanding Women Athletes: Who They Are and How They Influenced Sports In America.* Phoenix, AZ: Oryx Press.

MARATHON AND DISTANCE RUNNING

The marathon footrace is a modern event. There was no marathon in ancient Greece; the event was created for the first modern Olympic Games in 1896 in commemoration of the runner who carried the news of victory (over the invading Persians) from Marathon to Athens in 490 BCE. Men were the only official participants in the first marathons held in Greece as trials for the 1896 Games in Athens. Marathon courses at first were variable, ranging from 22 to 25 miles. Because they were thought too weak, women were for much of the twentieth century banned from competing in marathons. Women first competed in the Olympic marathon in 1984, when Joan Benoit of Maine won the race, thereby bringing much attention to women marathoners in the United States. Women now routinely compete in marathons, and some of the best-known women athletes of the late twentieth century, such as Grete Waitz, Joan Benoit, Ingrid Kristiansen, Rosa Mota, and Tegla Loroupe, are marathon runners.

EARLY HISTORY AND LIMITS ON WOMEN

The British administrators of the 1908 London Olympic Games decided that the Princess of Wales should start the race in the presence of the royal grandchildren. To accommodate them, the starting line was pushed back to the lawn at

Windsor Castle. The marathon runners ran 26.2 miles to the finish line at White City Stadium. This distance was eventually accepted as the official marathon distance throughout the world.

Quite probably the title of the first woman marathoner goes to Great Britain's Violet Piercy, who ran a 3:40:22 time at the Polytechnic Harriers' 26.2-mile marathon course, the official marathon distance, on 3 October 1926. Piercy's run was an act of mental as well as physical courage in an age when women deferred to men, and male opinion held that women could not run long distances. On 9 December 1963, two women began the Culver City Marathon, the most important marathon in the western United States, and one of them, Merry Lepper, finished in 3:37:03. If the course had been certified, this would have been a world record for women.

Until 1979 the Amateur Athletic Union (AAU) controlled track and field and long-distance running in the United States. The AAU staged the United States Olympic Trials and decided who would participate in international competitions. Since the longest race for women in the Olympics was the 800-meter, the AAU had no real reason to support long-distance running for women. Instead, the U.S. athletic bureaucracy neglected women's long-distance running and held to the notion that such events would damage women's health.

Women were not unwelcome in the marathons. They would run alongside men over the same course but presumably in their own race. In the early 1960s, when entrants in the Boston Athletic Association Marathon numbered fewer than one thousand, children and dogs often ran alongside the competitors for a bit; like them, a woman runner would be considered a particularly enthusiastic spectator, carried away by the excitement of the race. As long as she was not an official entrant and as long as her finishing time was not recorded, the woman runner posed no threat and encountered few problems. Roberta Gibb Bingay jumped into the field and became the first woman ever to run in and finish the Boston Marathon on 19 April 1966. She had trained for this event and ran with the official entrants, but she wore no number and achieved no official time.

When Kathrine Switzer challenged the proscription against women in 1967, she ran with a number and tried for an official time in the Boston Marathon. She appreciated the difference between running alongside the marathon for 26.2 miles and running as an official entrant. Switzer, a journalism student at Syracuse University, entered the 1967 Boston Marathon by sending in an application for "K. V. Switzer" and having a male runner, her coach and teammate Arnold Briggs, present her health certificate and collect her number. Switzer was an AAU member who had occasionally run in the half-mile and mile for the Lynchburg College men's track team. She knew that the 1.5-mile cross country was the longest distance race the AAU had for women. She called media attention to the problem by demanding sanction and equality as a woman marathoner in one of the most prestigious international events. After her 1967 Boston run, Switzer insisted that running long distance was as natural for women as for men. She also explained that her marathon was in part an expression of feminist beliefs.

Many women saw marathon running as a symbol of causes higher than athletic competition. Kathrine Switzer first ran the Boston Marathon the year after the founding of the National Organization for Women (NOW) in June 1966. NOW aimed to oppose sexual discrimination in all areas by relying on women's resources and women's potential to effect change. The movement toward greater athletic opportunities for women derived strength from their need for vocational opportunity. The forces that created NOW would later expand to provide sanction and a pool of potential athletes for the women's marathon in the United States.

THE EMERGENCE OF WOMEN'S MARATHONS

The women's marathon progressed in Europe, where private sports clubs gave women more support in training for longer distances. Dale Greig of Great Britain ran a 3:27:45 women's record marathon on 23 May 1964, and Mildred Sampson of New Zealand lowered that record to 3:19:33 on 21 July later that year. Just after Switzer's famous run at Boston, Maureen Wilton of Canada ran 3:15:22 on 6 May 1967. In West Germany, Dr. Ernst van Aaken actively encouraged women to run long distances. With his coaching, Anni Pede-Erdkamp ran 3:07:26, a new world record, on 16 September 1967.

The rule that forbade women to run in the Boston Marathon was put to a real test in 1967 when trainer Jock Semple—in street clothes—entered the field of runners to try and pull Kathrine Switzer (261) out of the race. (Corbis/Bettmann)

Nina Kuscsik and Sara Mae Berman ran the Boston Marathon unofficially for the first time in 1969. Berman won Boston unofficially in 1969, 1970, and 1971. She also won the first United States marathon open to women, in Atlantic City on 25 October 1970. Six women Road Runners Club of America (RRCA) members were allowed to enter because the marathon was a "closed" competition sponsored by the RRCA. Sara Mae Berman had drawn up the plans for the RRCA women's auxiliary that began in 1965, the same year as the RRCA's first National Women's Cross-Country Championships. Berman, age thirty-two and the mother of three, was introduced to running by her husband, an aerospace engineer. Kuscsik was about thirty, a registered nurse, and also the mother of three. She had been an enthusiastic sport participant in roller skating, speed skating, and bicycle racing.

By 1970 women were actively pursuing equal rights at most major races. The New York City Marathon accepted women as official runners since it began in 1970. At the 1970 Bay-to-Breakers, a San Francisco race of approximately eight miles and fourteen hundred participants, about a dozen women carried placards reading, "AAU Unfair to Women" and "Who Says Women Can't Run?" Such pressure from runners convinced the 1971 AAU Convention to allow women to compete in races up to ten miles and to approve the marathon for a few women. On 23 May 1971 Frances K. Conley won the first Bay-to-Breakers women's division since the race began in 1912. Cheryl Bridges set an American record of 2:49:40 at Culver City on 5 December 1971. On 17 April 1972 Nina Kuscsik became the first woman to win the woman's division of the Boston Marathon officially.

The first American women to run the marathon learned about the sport from men. Kuscsik and Berman apparently were influenced by their husbands, Switzer had a male track coach, and Gibb Bingay trained with her husband-to-be, a member of the Tufts University track team.

Women also participated in Road Runners Club of America functions; the races were open to women, and there were Age Group Competitions, race-day officiating, and even parties that provided a milieu in which women could receive information on training and racing. Thus many learned of the benefits of running: that they would feel better with regular exercise and that their endurance would be enhanced. Some women were attracted to running as an efficient method of weight control.

Printed information for runners had long been available. Browning Ross had encouraged women's running in his periodical *Long Distance Log*. Robert Anderson's *Runner's World* featured columns specifically for women runners by author/runner Pat Tarnawsky and physician/runner Joan Ullyot. Ullyot's book, *Women's Running*, was released by World Publications in 1976; in its sixth printing by late 1977, *Women's Running* encouraged recreational running for its health benefits but assumed that jogging would progress to serious competition.

The association of running with such values as health, fitness, and even feminism attracted women to marathoning. Long-distance running became part of the feminist attitude toward health care, which emphasized women's assertion of control over their own bodies. The marathon became an opportunity for women to explore their physical limits of endurance and speed.

The first National AAU Marathon Championship for women was held in San Mateo, California, on 10 February 1974; there were forty-four finishers, twenty-one under 3:30:00. The first International Women's Marathon, organized by physician and women's running advocate Ernst van Aaken, took place on 22 September 1974 in Waldniel, West Germany. There were forty-five entrants, nine from the United States. Jacqueline Hansen, winner of the 1973 Boston Marathon, was the first woman in the world under 2:40:00, with a 2:38:19 at the Nike-Oregon Track Club Marathon on 12 October 1975. Hansen continued her career in long distance both as a competitor and as an activist fighting for a women's Olympic marathon. The 1975 New York City Marathon had thirty-six women finishers, fourteen under 3:30:00. By 1976 there were about 800 competitive women marathoners worldwide and about thirty-nine women who had run the marathon in less than three hours.

THE OLYMPICS

On 2 October 1976, fifty-three women representing nine countries assembled at the starting line of the second unofficial International Women's Marathon championship in Waldniel, West Germany. Seven runners finished under 2:55:00. According to marathon historians and statisticians David E. Martin and Roger W. H. Gynn, "The quality and international scope of these results served to crystallize in the minds of many a desire to have a women's Olympic marathon" (p. 325). While other sports had professional levels or world championships, the ultimate level of competition

THE PROBLEM WITH WOMEN'S MARATHON RECORDS

One controversy that continues to plague women's marathon running concerns what rules govern the establishment of women's marathon records. The general view is that the record may be set in any sanctioned marathon. The purist view is that the true women's marathon record is the one established in a women's only marathon. Underlying the purist viewpoint is the argument that in mixed marathons women runners benefit from the faster pace of the elite male runners, and women are not competing just against other women. Some observers point out that certain elite women marathoners who are paced by male runners have an unfair advantage over other women. For example, Tegla Laroupe's 1998 record set in the Rotterdam marathon has been questioned by sportwriters who point out that she was paced by men and also that the men aided her by bringing her drinks from the aid stations.

Franca Fiacconi of Italy crosses the finish line to win the women's division of the 1998 New York City Marathon with a time of 2:25:17. (Corbis/AFP)

for the marathon is the Olympic Games. Adding a new event to the Olympic Games involves the highest level of the international sports bureaucracy, the International Olympic Committee (IOC). To be added to the Olympic program, a women's event would have to be widely practiced in twenty-five countries and on two continents. Women's long-distance running would have to develop a wide participant base in order to meet this requirement.

The world had to notice the women's marathon after the extraordinary performances of Grete Waitz. Although Waitz was known only as a track runner, the administrators of the 1978 New York City Marathon invited her to the event, where she set a world record of 2:32:30. Returning to the New York City Marathon in 1979, she ran 2:27:33, becoming the first woman to break 2:30 for the marathon. In the 1980 New York City Marathon, Waitz set another world record of 2:25:42.

The presentation in upscale periodicals of information about running helped create an economically desirable constituency for women's running as well as a didactic tradition in which women learned from other women. In the 1970s, social emphases on both a healthful lifestyle and a slender appearance led to the association of fitness with attractiveness. Popular culture picked up and exploited the connection between fitness and feminist imperatives. While opportunity to compete in the marathon was now theoretically open to any woman, the pool for this event was identified as middle-class, college-educated women, and their appeal to the corporate world as consumers hastened the acceptance of the women's marathon.

Avon Products, Inc., an international cosmetics firm, noticed that women's sports were a suitably feminist advertising vehicle for cosmetics. William Corbett, Avon's public relations director, met Kathrine Switzer through the Women's Sports Foundation and asked her to suggest a running program for Avon; she responded with a detailed proposal for a series of women's races, a championship, and related advertising themes. The first Avon Marathon—International Women's Championship was held in Atlanta, Georgia, on 19 March 1978. Twenty-nine states were represented among the competitors, and seven countries besides the United States: Brazil, Canada, Hungary, Japan, the Netherlands, New Zealand, and West Germany. The prestige of Avon cosmetics overseas probably influenced many women to accept long-distance running as a pastime. The presence of marathoners of many nationalities was of importance to meeting the IOC participation requirements.

The Avon International Running Circuit held events in five countries—Australia, Japan, United Kingdom, United States, and West Germany—during the 1978–1979 season. On 22 September 1979, under the direction of Dr. Ernst von Aaken and Kathrine Switzer, the second Avon International Women's Marathon was held in Waldniel, West Germany. The third Avon International Women's Marathon was held 30 August 1980 in London. The field of approximately 200 included women from twenty-seven countries and five continents. The Avon International Women's Marathon held in Ottawa, Canada, on 23 August 1981 had 631 entrants. By 1982 the Avon International Running Circuit was holding races in Brazil, Canada, Chile, France, Hong Kong, and the Netherlands. In 1983 Argentina, Belgium, Italy, Mexico, New Zealand, Spain, and Thailand joined the Avon circuit. By that time, other corporations were, like Avon, genuinely interested in training runners and developing opportunities for competition as well as using running as a promotional activity.

In 1979 a grant from Blue Ribbon Sports (Nike) started the International Runners' Committee (IRC), an advocacy group for elite athletes. The executive board of the IRC comprised fifteen runners, representing all continents; among them were marathoners Jacqueline Hansen Sturak, Doris Brown-Heritage, Nina Kuscsik, Leal-Ann Reinhart, and Joan Ullyot of the United States, Eleanora Mendonca of Brazil, and Sarolta Monspart of Hungary. Jacqueline Hansen Sturak eventually succeeded Joe Henderson as the IRC's executive director. While the Avon Running Circuit ensured a popular base of participation in the sport, the International Runners' Committee worked to secure a place for the elite women. As their first objective, the IRC aimed for a full program of distance races for women in the 1984 Los Angeles Olympic Games. The IRC did not plan to stage races or govern the sport; rather, they intended to communicate the needs of the athletes to the sport bureaucracy. The IRC hoped to increase opportunities for competition and to improve running administration.

The International Amateur Athletics Federation (IAAF) was the highest level of administration for track and field sports; the IOC deferred to the IAAF in specific track and field matters. At their August 1979 meeting in Montreal, the IAAF women's committee recommended recognition of women's 5,000- and 10,000-meter records. In November 1979 IAAF president Adrian Paulen issued a message to the competitors in the Tokyo International Women's Marathon, supporting an Olympic marathon for women and indicating he would lobby the IOC on behalf of the event for the 1984 Games. In Lausanne, Switzerland, on 16 April 1980, Paulen and Secretary-General John Holt presented several new women's track events, including the marathon, to the IOC program committee. Official acceptance of a women's marathon came at the next IOC meeting in 1981, when on 23 February the executive board of the IOC approved a women's Olympic marathon, beginning with the 1984 Games. Joan Benoit of the United States was the first winner of an Olympic marathon for women.

THE 1990S

In 1985, Ingrid Kristiansen of Norway set a world record for women at the London marathon. Kristiansen's record, 2:21:06, stood until 1998. During the 1990s, runners from Africa, particularly from Kenya and Ethiopia, emerged as the elite women marathoners in the great international races such as the Boston Marathon, the New York City Marathon, and the Olympic Marathon. In 1999 the world marathon record for women in a race alongside men was 2:20:47, set by Tegla Loroupe of Kenya in the 1998 Rotterdam Marathon. Once the domain of young, mostly white, upwardly-mobile professionals, marathon fields were now more representational of the whole of society; the sport crosses ethnic as well as class boundaries. Like many other women's races, the marathon became an expression of feminism and an assertion of women's solidarity and physical strength.

Pamela Cooper

Bibliography

Cooper, Pamela. (1998) *The American Marathon.* Syracuse, NY: Syracuse University Press.

Guttmann, Allen. (1991) *Women's Sports: A History.* New York: Columbia University Press.

Martin, David, and Roger W. H. Gynn. (1979) *The Marathon Footrace: Performers and Performances.* Springfield, IL: Charles C. Thomas.

Quercetani, Roberto L. (1990) *Athletics: A History of Modern Track and Field Athletics, 1860–1990.* Milan: Vilardi and Associates.

MARBLE, ALICE
(1913–1990)
U.S. TENNIS PLAYER

One of the first women to use a serve-and-volley approach, Alice Marble won an impressive list of titles with her aggressive tennis game. Alice Marble was born on 28 September 1913. At age thirteen, her life revolved around baseball. She became the mascot for her hometown minor-league team, the San Francisco Seals. When she was fifteen, her brother gave her a tennis racquet and advised her to take up a more feminine game. She flatly refused to play the "sissy game" and took

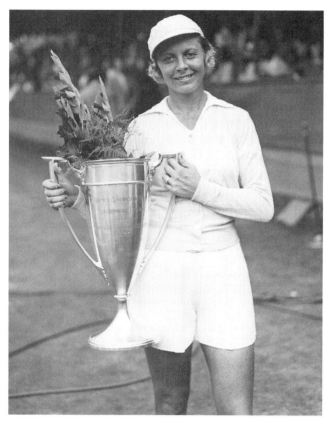

Alice Marble of San Francisco poses with the Women's National Singles Championship cup. (Bettmann/Corbis)

the racquet to Golden Gate Park, only to demonstrate its uselessness. Within a week, however, she was hooked on the sport. From that time forward, tennis dominated her life.

In 1934 Marble's tennis career took an unexpected plunge. After playing a record number of games in record-breaking heat at a tournament at Forest Hills, New York, she suffered heat exhaustion and was ill for several weeks. Shortly thereafter, she collapsed during a French tournament and was diagnosed with tuberculosis; she was told she could never play tennis again. While convalescing, Marble discovered that her doctors had been too harsh in their prognosis. She slowly recovered her health through a program of diet, exercise, and tennis practice.

Two years later, in 1936, she began her comeback with a string of singles and doubles victories. In 1938 she won the U.S. women's singles, women's doubles, and mixed doubles titles as well as the Wimbledon ladies' doubles and mixed doubles titles. Her streak continued into 1939,

when she won the Wimbledon ladies' singles title despite a badly torn stomach muscle. She also won the ladies' doubles and mixed doubles titles at Wimbledon that year, winning an unusual "All-England tennis triple crown." She was named Associated Press Female Athlete of the Year in 1938 and 1939.

In 1941 Marble turned professional and began a U.S. tour with other tennis stars. When she discovered that she was being paid less than one-third of the top male player's salary, she threatened to walk off the tour. The tour sponsor capitulated and offered her a revised contract with the same terms as her male counterpart.

Marble was so deeply affected by World War II that she attempted to enlist in the armed forces. However, her severe illnesses in 1934 had made her unfit for duty. At the request of President Franklin D. Roosevelt, she co-chaired a physical fitness program for the Office of Civil Defense. During her work with the program, she met Joseph Crowley, an army pilot, whom she married in 1942. In early 1945, Crowley's plane was shot down over Germany. Marble's sense of loss was dissipated by an unusual opportunity to avenge her husband's death. She became a spy for army intelligence and successfully completed her mission to gather information about Nazi escape plans at the end of the war.

Marble ignored prejudices and stereotypes and respected people for their accomplishments. She openly defended homosexual players and nonwhite players who were shunned by other members of the tennis community. In a letter published in *World Tennis* magazine, she contested the exclusion of Althea Gibson and other black players from U.S. Lawn Tennis Association (USLTA) tournaments. Her argument that all players should be judged on their playing ability was heard; Gibson played her first USLTA tournament in 1951, thus breaking the "color barrier" that had existed since the USLTA's inception.

Marble took a break from competitive tennis in the early 1950s but returned as a coach in the early 1960s. She was inducted into the Tennis Hall of Fame in 1964. When she died on 13 December 1990, Marble was praised as a woman whose courage and determination had overcome many obstacles.

Wendy Painter

Bibliography

Collins, Bud, and Zander Hollander. (1994) *Bud Collins' Modern Encyclopedia of Tennis.* Detroit: Gale Research.

Marble, Alice, with Dale Leatherman. (1991) *Courting Danger: My Adventures in World-Class Tennis, Golden-Age Hollywood, and High-Stakes Spying.* New York, NY: St. Martin's Press.

MARKETING

Marketing involves selling a product or image; in sport marketing, this may be directly related to sport or it may involve sport in an attempt to sell something else. Sport marketing, then, has two functions: the first is the marketing of sport products and services (athletes, events, teams); the second is the marketing of other consumer and industrial products or services through the use of sport (for example, marketing a particular cosmetic through the image of an attractive athlete). Women have been and continue to be used in both.

HISTORY

Women were first associated with sport marketing between 1893 and 1924 in a way that represents the second kind of marketing. This involved using illustrations of women in physically active poses (for example, holding a tennis racket or golf club or skiing, snowshoeing, fishing, boating, cycling, or swimming). These images appeared on the covers of American magazines (*Ladies Home Journal, Good Housekeeping, Redbook*) and in advertisements for such companies as Coca-Cola, Palmolive, Ford, and Kelloggs, and were used to promote the sale of the magazine or the advertised product. They also supported the idea that all types of women could engage in sports, therefore increasing women's interest in sports, although this may not have been their aim.

Beginning with World War I, companies sponsored women factory workers in Europe and the United States to form competitive teams in industrial leagues. The Haines Hosiery team was one of the most successful. This again illustrates the second definition of sport marketing.

In 1943, during World War II, the All-American Girls Professional Baseball League (AAGPBL) was formed. The AAGPBL lasted for a decade with more than six hundred women taking the field and over a million fans watching. Although the league had little competition—the war made it the only game in town—various sport marketing techniques were used to encourage attendance. Wrigley, the major sponsor, even enrolled the players in charm school to learn to encourage a more feminine manner, and required the players to wear short skirts during games. This type of marketing represented the first definition of sport marketing.

INTERCOLLEGIATE ATHLETIC SPONSORSHIP

One of the first examples of corporate sponsorship for women at the intercollegiate level took place in the early 1950s. Wayland Baptist College, in Wayland, Texas—one of the first schools to offer full scholarships for women's basketball—accepted in-kind transportation assistance from a man named Hutcherson and hence came the name the Hutcherson Flying Queens.

One of the most significant sponsors of women's collegiate basketball has been the Kodak Corporation. In 1973 Kodak began its relationship with women's basketball by sponsoring the Poconos Invitational Girls' Basketball Camps in Pennsylvania. This subsequently led to the company's relationship with the Association of Intercollegiate Athletics for Women (AIAW), the All-American Women's College Basketball Team, and today with the Women's Basketball Coaches Association (WBCA). The goal for Kodak was to get the AIAW to use Kodak film for their events and promotional materials.

Another early supporter of women's collegiate athletics was Sara Lee, who in 1991 initiated the National Collegiate Athletic Association (NCAA) Women of the Year dinner, which it sponsored for two years.

PROFESSIONAL SPORTS SPONSORSHIP AND MARKETING

One of the first true sponsorship deals negotiated to support women's professional sports took place in 1949 when Wilson Sporting Goods agreed to sponsor the formation of the Ladies Professional

Golf Association (LPGA). Wilson's involvement not only provided the necessary prize money but also lent credibility to women's sport and increased media attention.

In 1970, with the support of Virginia Slims, Billie Jean King, Gladys Heldman (publisher of *World Tennis* magazine), and other players were able to organize the first separate, all-female tournament for women professional tennis players. In 1991 the Virginia Slims Tennis Tournament paid $24 million in prize money.

Tambrands, Inc., was another company that supported women's sports. In the early 1980s Tambrands sponsored the U.S. swimming and synchronized swimming teams and in 1989 began to sponsor the Women's Sports Foundation's Grants for Girls program. Interestingly some women's sport organizations (for example, WTA) actually refused sponsorship of Tambrands; they believed the company's association with menstruation might not be a positive marketing strategy, especially when targeting both male and female audiences.

Another early supporter of women's sports was Avon. In 1980 Kathrine Switzer created the Avon Women's Sports Program to provide opportunities in tennis and running for over a million athletes. At times her budget reached $7 million with a full-time staff of fourteen people.

ATHLETE ENDORSEMENTS

Women athletes have a very hard time landing endorsements. Not only must they perform at the highest level in their sport, they must also have model beauty off the court to be considered for an endorsement. Mia Hamm, perhaps the best female soccer player in the world, is one example; she receives approximately $1 million annually in endorsement contracts. Sexual preference also plays an important factor in securing endorsement opportunities. Although Martina Navratilova has been called the greatest tennis player ever, her open lesbianism may have reduced her potential for endorsement contracts.

One of the greatest female athletes, Babe Didrikson, was also one of the finest female sport marketers. Following her spectacular showing at the 1932 Olympic Games, where she won three track and field medals, she capitalized on her fame and traveled across the United States performing exhibitions of her athletic skill in a wide range of sports. Thousands of fans paid to see her on tour, and companies also lined up for her endorsement. In fact, Didrikson lost her amateur status when she allowed her name to be used in an automobile advertisement after the Olympic Games. Even before 1932 Didrikson was sponsored by Employers Casualty Company in Dallas to play on the company's Amateur Athletic Union (AAU)-sanctioned basketball team and to compete in AAU track and field meets. It was not only her athletic talent that made Didrikson a marketing phenomenon but also her flamboyant and provocative character.

In 1940, one of Didrikson's close golf friends, Patty Berg, signed an endorsement contract with the Wilson Sporting Goods Company at a salary of approximately $7,500 a year. In addition to playing in exhibitions around the country, Berg made appearances at summer camps for girls and offered golf clinics and schools.

CELEBRITY CLOTHING ENDORSEMENTS

Marketers of sports clothing believe that women, more so than men, make their footwear and clothing purchase decisions on the basis of fit and performance-related features. Nonetheless, some manufacturers have followed the male model and hired celebrity athletes to endorse their products. Some female athletes who have endorsed athletic footwear for women are professional basketball players Sheryl Swoopes (Nike Air Swoopes IV), Nikki McCray (Fila Nikki), and Jennifer Azzi (Reebok 3D Quotient); tennis player Serena Williams (Puma Cell Factor); and skateboarder Cara Beth Burnside (Vans Cara Beth).

More recently, Sheryl Swoopes, a leading basketball player, received acclaim for being the first female athlete to have a Nike athletic shoe—"Air Swoopes"—designed and named for her. Overall, opportunities for endorsements have dramatically increased since the start of the Women's National Basketball Association (WNBA). One of the most visible WNBA players is Rebecca Lobo. In addition to endorsement contracts with a shoe and ball manufacturer and a bank and automobile manufacturer, Lobo will be the first player associated with the WNBA Barbie, of which over one million units will be shipped. In addition, she was the first to have her image placed on Huffy backboards.

THE FUTURE OF WOMEN AND SPORT MARKETING

Considering that 80 percent of a household's purchasing decisions are made by women and that more and more women are playing and watching sports, advertising and marketing executives are likely to realize soon that women's sport marketing is a good investment. The International Events Group, a company that tracks and analyzes corporate sponsorship, estimates that women's sports accounted for $600 million of the $4.5 billion that corporations dedicated to sport sponsorships in 1997. This is more than double the $285 million spent on women's sport in 1992.

Though the value of women's sport will likely increase in time, it is still much lower than that of men's sports. Official sponsorship packages for the 1999 FIFA Women's World Cup sold in the $2–$4 million range, compared to the $30–$40 million range for the 1998 FIFA Men's World Cup.

The University of Texas at Austin was the first intercollegiate program to understand the differences between the men's and women's games, and as a result they created a marketing strategy for women's basketball. With this strategy, the Lady Longhorns increased the average attendance to 6,000–8,000 spectators a game and are selling 4,800 season tickets at prices ranging from $60–$70 each. Research on who attends women's basketball games at the University of Texas showed that the most likely spectator, who also watches men's athletics events, is the baseball fan, not the fan of men's football or basketball. In fact, there was less than a 5 percent overlap between

The importance of physical appearance for female athletes in winning endorsement contracts has a prime example in Russian tennis player Anna Kournikova, who became one of the most sought-after female athletes for endorsement deals in spite of the fact that she had not won a major tournament as of the year 2000. (AFP/Corbis)

those who purchased tickets and made contributions to men's sports and those who did the same for women's sports.

Research also showed that the demographics of the women's sport spectators included a majority of people who were young professionals with daughters, or older, retired persons with high levels of disposable income. Spectators of women's sports also tend to be more consumer conscientious and responsive to cause-related marketing, especially when that marketing strikes a personal chord. Some of the more common issues that concern women include battered women, sexual abuse and harassment of women, and women's health problems, such as breast and ovarian cancers and osteoporosis. For example, General Motors donated $.50 to the National Alliance of Breast Cancer Organizations for every WNBA ticket sold, and Sudafed donated $.50 to women athletes for every Sudafed purchase. Likewise, the LPGA has designated the Komen Breast Cancer Fund as its official charity, and Reebok has provided assistance for battered women's programs.

Some women's sports advocates and marketing experts believe that women's sports could benefit from recent public sentiment against perceived greed among elite athletes and the high prices of men's sports. For the marketer, the issue is one of positioning these new products for different audiences. According to Donna Lopiano, executive director of the Women's Sports Foundation, women's sport should appeal to a more diverse set of values such as victory, effort, speed, and excitement, while also portraying athletes as serious, articulate, talented, and community-minded.

There are several examples of women working in the area of sports marketing who take into consideration the needs and uniqueness of female athletes. One of these individuals is Ellen Zavian, the executive director of the women's player association. Zavian was the first female agent to represent NFL players; she later utilized those skills to assist the women's soccer team in negotiating the pregnancy leave and child-care clause in their contract. Sylvia Allen, president of Allen Consulting, Inc., has been involved with sport marketing for over twenty-five years and specializes in developing strategic alliances and tailoring sport marketing programs and event sponsorship to best meet client needs. Another female pioneer in the sport marketing field is Barbara Paddock, vice president and director of sport marketing for Chase Manhattan Bank. Paddock oversees a seventeen-member staff with a budget of approximately $5 million for the Bank's major sponsorships—many of which assist women's sport. Chase is a corporate partner with the WTA Tour and in 1988 extended its support of women's tennis to the grassroots level by creating the Chase Tennis Camps for Girls. Sharon Barbano, formerly with Reebok and currently the editor and publisher of *The Women's Sports Marketing Report* is another example of this new trend. *The Women's Sports Marketing Report* is a bi-monthly publication covering women's sport industry news, developments, trends and strategies for marketing executives, agencies, media, and corporate sponsors. There are also organizations designed just for women in sport marketing, such as Women in Sports and Events (WISE) and the National Association of Collegiate Women Athletic Administrators (NACWAA) that serve to disseminate knowledge and to network.

Another important factor in the marketing of women's sport is media coverage. Men's sports have historically dominated all media coverage of sports and hence command a great marketing advantage. Media coverage not only allows the public to identify with players and teams, it also raises the importance of the sport in the public's eyes. If women's sports are never seen, heard, or read about, no one will take notice or care about them.

The 1996 Olympic Games, however, set four new benchmarks for women and sports: the highest participation level of women in the history of the Olympic Games; the magnitude of media coverage of women's performances; the public perception that the talents of male and female athletes are equally valued; and the popularity of women's team sports among the media and the

MARKETING FEMALE ATHLETES IS BIG BUSINESS

The marketing of female athletes and individuals in related professions such as sports management and journalism is a complex task and in the 1990s required the skills of marketing and career planning professionals. These marketing firms provide a wide range of services including career guidance, resume preparation, interview training, job searches, the arrangement of internships, salary negotiation, the creation of networking opportunities, the scheduling of public appearances, event management and promotion, and the negotiation of endorsement contracts.

public. Prior Olympic Games media coverage featured sports that conformed to the traditional feminine image of appropriate physical activity for women—gymnastics, running, diving, swimming, and equestrian events—but in 1996 women's team sports were highlighted as well.

"Overall sports coverage is becoming more inclusive. The sheer magnitude of the electronic and print media coverage of the 1996 Games brought influential and inspirational female athletes and role models to girls and women all over the world and will help to promote global gender equity in sport," states Wendy Hillard, television commentator and former president of the Women's Sports Foundation. In fact, one of the main reasons for the success of the WNBA is the television coverage it has received.

Nevertheless, more than 80 percent of all sport coverage goes to men's sports. When women do receive coverage, they are not always portrayed in the same athletic manner as men; rather, they are shown in a more feminine, nonphysical manner. Progress is being made, however, with an increase in the number of females writing and reporting on sport and holding editorial positions in which they decide what to cover.

Marketing women in sport is not easy, yet the statistics show that women are interested in sport, are watching it, and hold significant purchasing power. Experts believe that this combination should soon catch the attention of media, advertisers, and other marketing professionals.

Lisa Delpy

See also Advertising; Beauty; Magazines; Management; Media; Sexuality; Sportswear Industry

Bibliography

Lopiano, Donna. (1998) *Women's Participation in Sports: Trends and Changes.* East Meadow, NY: Women's Sports Foundation.

Miller, Ernestine. (1992) *Sports Woman Day Book.* New York: Harry N. Abrams.

Ogelsby, Carol, ed. (1998) *Women and Sport in America.* Phoenix, AZ: Oryx Press.

Women's Sports Foundation. *Women's Sports Media Coverage.* East Meadow, NY: Women's Sports Foundation.

MARKHAM, BERYL

(1902–1986)

ENGLISH AVIATOR

Beryl Markham is remembered for a single, yet most significant, feat: in 1936 she became the first woman to fly nonstop from England to the United States, and the first pilot to make this crossing solo. Born in Leicestershire, England, in 1902, Beryl Markham was raised in Kenya from the age of four by her English father. She received her education at local European schools, and her father taught her how to ride, train, and breed horses. At the age of eighteen she became the first woman in Africa to be awarded a license to train race horses.

Markham was drawn to the challenge of learning to fly airplanes. By 1931 she had earned a commercial pilot's license, which she used to transport mail and passengers around East Africa. She was eager, at a time when long-distance aviation was still novel, to set sporting records. After Markham made her famous solo crossing of the Atlantic, she became an instant celebrity and was honored with a ticker-tape parade in New York.

Beryl Markham, English society sportswoman and aviatrix, in the cockpit. (Bettmann/Corbis)

Her autobiographical novel, *West with the Night* (1942), focused on life in Africa and the trials and tribulations of flying planes over that vast continent. The book reached thirteen best-seller lists and by the late 1990s had sold well over a million copies.

While Markham was an achiever in public, her private life rarely flourished. She married and divorced three times. In 1928 she gave birth to a son, who was raised by her mother-in-law. He died in a car accident in 1970, together with his two daughters. Markham had rarely spent time with any of these kin. She spent her final years living alone in a bungalow provided by the Jockey Club of Kenya.

Daryl Adair

Bibliography

Cadogan, Mary. (1992) *Women with Wings: Female Flyers in Fact and Fiction.* London: Macmillan.

Lovell, Mary S. (1987) *Straight On till Morning: the Biography of Beryl Markham.* New York: St. Martin's Press.

Markham, Beryl. (1989 [1942]) *West with the Night.* London: Virago.

MARTIAL ARTS *see* Aikido, Iaido, Judo and Jujutsu, Karate, Kendo, Taekwondo, Tai Chi, Wushu

MAYER, HELENE

(1910–1953)

GERMAN FENCER

Helene Mayer was a patriotic German whose blue eyes and blond braids gave her the look of the ideal Aryan woman. Any claim to that status was, however, disputed after Adolf Hitler and the National Socialist (Nazi) Party came to power in January 1933. Her father, a prominent physician, was a Jew. What she thought of her Jewish ancestry is

unknown. There is no evidence that she considered it an important aspect of her identity.

From childhood, Mayer was physically active. She had ballet lessons when she was seven, and she was fascinated by sports, especially horseback riding, swimming, and skiing. Once she began to fence, however, that sport became her passion. Her hometown of Offenbach, a center of the sport, was an ideal place to train. As a 14-year-old, Mayer placed second in the national championship. From 1925 to 1930, she won the German championship in the foils competitions. She became internationally famous in 1928 when she won Olympic gold in Amsterdam. Four years later, at Los Angeles, she was fifth.

Mayer decided to study for a diplomatic career with a grant from the German government and in 1933 enrolled at Scripps College in Claremont, California. National socialist racial politics, however, caused Mayer to be expelled from the Offenbach Fencing Club and lose financial support from the German state. Despite her concerns about events in Germany, she finished her B.A. degree in 1934 and went on to complete a master's degree. She then took a position teaching at Mills College in Oakland, California. She did, however, continue her training in fencing, winning the American championship a total of eight times (1934, 1935, 1937, 1938, 1939, 1941, 1942, and 1946).

In an effort to blunt the international boycott movement that threatened the 1936 Olympics, which were to be held in Berlin, the Nazi regime decided in the fall of 1935, after considerable hesitation, to invite Mayer to compete on the German fencing team. She agreed to return to Germany on the condition that she enjoy the right of full citizenship. This was granted.

The German media were instructed not to publicize these negotiations nor to headline her success at the Games, which was considerable. Mayer won the silver medal in foils. At the victory ceremony, she raised her right arm in the Nazi salute, a gesture that greatly intensified the still-unfinished debate about the morality of her participation in what some have called "the Nazi Olympics." It may be assumed that Mayer's decision to compete was connected with her love of Germany as well as with her love of sport, but it may also imply her lack of identification with the

Jewish community and her political naivete. One should not forget, however, that many Jewish athletes from other countries participated in the Olympic Games of 1936.

After the Games, Mayer chose to reside in the United States, which probably saved her life. In the early 1950s, after World War II (and after the Nazi extermination of most European Jews), Mayer returned to Germany and married an engineer. By this time Mayer was already ill with cancer, and she died in 1953 at the age of 43.

Gertrud Pfister

Bibliography

Niewerth, Toni, and Gertrud Pfister. (n.d.) "Jewish Women in Gymnastics and Sport in Germany until 1938." In *One Hundred Years of "Muscular Judaism": A Century of Sport in Jewish History and Culture.*

Pfister, Gertrud, and Toni Niewerth. (1999) "Jewish Women in Gymnastics and Sport in Germany." *Journal of Sport History,* 9: 287–326.

MEDIA

Mass media is a term for all widely disseminated nonprint media (television, radio, and movies) and print media (newspapers, magazines, and books). They provide several services, among which the timely reporting of current events and entertainment of the masses seem to be the most vital. It is evident that responsibility for content is inherent in the very nature of the media's job and that the selection process is critical, as the mass media has become one of the most powerful institutional forces for shaping values and attitudes in modern culture. It is not only the depicting of an event but the interpretation of that event that makes it crucial for the shaping of perceptions, attitudes, and values about culture.

Media is covered here in two articles. The first article, by Joan Chandler, discusses the history and social context of media coverage of women's sports, focusing on the United States. The second article, by Ilse Harmann-Tews and Bettina Rulofs, discusses international media coverage of women's sports, focusing on the way men and women are represented in the media.

HISTORY AND SOCIAL CONTEXT

By the time females anywhere in the world had become visible in more than a few, largely upper-class, amateur sports, the content, form, ambience, and audience expectation of sporting events had already been established. The sport industry, dominated worldwide by males, grew up with the media industry; when female athletes were able to attract media attention, they had of necessity to work within the model of sport designed by and for males. Yet females had at the same time to demonstrate that they had lost none of the "feminine" qualities that would make them attractive mates and worthy mothers.

Without media coverage, sport events remain of local, even personal, interest. Although media attention can fan existing flames of interest, media exposure cannot by itself create an audience. The relationship of media to female athletes has therefore been, and remains, complex. Female athletes worldwide, amateur or professional, must confront a developed media mode of coverage, in addition to the specific cultural images that women of particular nationalities and classes are expected to embody. At the 1996 Atlanta Olympic Games, for example, the Iranian flag-carrier was a woman who marched with her head covered. She was the sole female Iranian competitor because Muslim women can compete in only four Olympic sports. All others require clothing deemed immodest.

In essence, media cannot portray sporting events that do not exist. Similarly, profit-conscious media will not portray events that are thought unlikely to have an audience. The cultural constraints that have hindered female participation in sport are the same constraints that have determined the nature of female athletes' media exposure.

EARLY PRINT COVERAGE

From newspapers' early days, some women's sporting events were reported. Newspapers were probably first published in Germany in 1609, in England in 1622, and in France in 1631. These early papers did not necessarily appear regularly, but by 1711, approximately 44,000 copies of British newspapers were published every week; by 1776, fifty-three newspapers were published in London alone. These eighteenth-century newspapers and weeklies occasionally recorded women's sporting events, such as "smock races," boxing, cricket, archery, and horse racing.

Between 1855 and 1875, European newspapers became much cheaper, and their circulation was increased with the spread of literacy during the latter part of the nineteenth and early twentieth centuries. But societal strictures on women's public competitions were by then overt; when the cycling craze took off in the 1880s and 1890s, women began to race—and were castigated for it in the press. While the French allowed women to race on cycling tracks, the British did not. Although publicity attended a French women's 12-kilometer race in 1903 and the German women's track and field races in 1904, not all the comments were laudatory. All the women had to run in costumes covering their arms and legs; the question was, however, should they be running competitively in public at all.

In the United States, sport magazines such as *American Turf Register and Sporting Magazine* (first issued in 1829), the *National Police Gazette* (1845), and *Field and Stream* (1873) whetted Americans' appetites for sport news. From their inception, newspapers reported sport events, although it was not until 1883 that Joseph Pulitzer organized a separate sport department at *New York World*. William Randolph Hearst at the *New York Journal* was responsible for printing the first newspaper sport section in 1895. Sport reports increased newspaper circulation, but although some women reporters covered sport and women in Philadelphia even organized a Women's Sportswriters Association in 1929, to all intents and purposes women's sport in the United States was invisible. On 1 June 1900, for instance, the *New York Times* had one sport page. The most space was devoted to horse racing (including results from Toronto, Canada, and Epsom, England) and professional baseball; men's tennis, rowing, boxing, polo, and chess also were included. While the newspaper found space for the election of the Princeton and Harvard track team captains, the only women's sport mentioned was amateur golf.

On 1 June 1950, this sport coverage had expanded to four pages and included three photographs, all of males. By now, coverage was international, and male sports included horse and car racing, cricket, golf, tennis, basketball, bowling, polo, lacrosse, soccer (association football), track, and boxing; college football schedules and NFL signings were noted. Women still fared badly; only a Long Island Women's Golf Association tournament and female results in the French tennis championships were reported. Yet plenty of women's sport was going on. It simply was not noticed by the media. Magazine and newspaper editors in the United States assumed that their readers, male and female, were satisfied to read about men's sport.

RADIO AND TELEVISION

By 1950 newspapers in Britain and the United States had two rivals—radio and television—for sport coverage. Radio brought an immediacy to sport reporting that newspaper accounts lacked, but it made little difference to coverage of women's sport. Television became popular after World War II; in 1948, 172,000 sets were sold in the United States, and sport provided roughly one-third of the programming. Worldwide, the growth of television was phenomenal; between 1980 and 1990 the number of TV sets in China rose from about 630,000 to 118 million. By 1988 one TV set was sold in India every five minutes. But while television was new technologically, what it transmitted followed what viewers had become familiar with in earlier media: men's sports.

In those parts of the world where radio and television broadcasting was dependent on advertising for its profits, sport was used to draw in consumers. But programmers in the early years still assumed that consumers of sport were male. Not all radio and TV broadcasting was based on the commercial model. The British Broadcasting Corporation began its life depending on fees paid by owners of radios; commercial competition did not start in Britain until 1954. Except for the traditional upper-class sports, however, British radio and TV did not have much to do with women's athletics. In the Soviet Union and other communist countries, where the media was entirely state-financed and state-controlled, women's athletics were showcased, but there was little public support. In his history of spectator sport in the Soviet Union, Edelman scarcely mentions female athletes, because "Women's sports, actively supported by the government as political window dressing, had little public following among women or men."

What little attention was paid in the media to women's sport before the last quarter of the twentieth century was heavily dependent on social class. Both in Europe and America, upper- and middle-class women were imbued with the amateur code. Edith Wharton's fictional portrayal of a female archery contest in the 1870s demonstrates the qualities female athletes were thought to epitomize. May Archer, in Wharton's *The Age of Innocence* (1920), competes not for acclaim or money but for an inconsequential piece of jewelry; dressed in an attractive special costume, expensive to launder, May serenely shoots her arrows and is gracious to those she vanquishes, for to have won is less important than to have competed.

While upper- and middle-class women could safely play some sports, lower-class women were hampered by lack of time and money and by societal prejudice against public displays of the female body, save in traditionally sanctioned ladylike situations. In the United States, however, some industries sponsored sporting clubs for female as well as male employees. One of them gave Mildred "Babe" Didrikson her opportunity to turn her passion for sport into a profession. She starred as a basketball player and was spectacular in track and field, but not even her Olympic medals were enough to open a career as a professional. She took up golf seriously because she could see little future in sports that the media either did not report or reported only every four years. She hoped to be able to excel at amateur golf to make her name, before using the game as a profession, but the United States Golf Association quickly banned her. One of the women who managed Texas women's golf protested the reason for Didrikson's exclusion: "The fact that she was poor and had no clothes did not mean she had to be ruled a professional." USGA, however, was not about to surrender its carefully cultivated, upper-crust public image. Class prejudice changed slowly. The tennis player Billie Jean King, who grew up in the 1950s, was left out of a group photo at the Southern California junior

championships because her family could not afford proper tennis clothing.

CLASS AND COVERAGE

Class also determined, at least in Britain and America, the development of the fan base for female sport on which media coverage depended. In Britain, girls who attended private schools from the mid-nineteenth century onward were made to feel that sports prowess was nearly as important for them as for their brothers. Females continued playing a variety of sports in college and as adults. In the United States, however, college curricula were changed during the 1920s and 1930s to provide completely different athletic experiences for men and women. The men's athletic department, defined since the late nineteenth century as the advertising arm of the college, had little or nothing to do with physical education as such and was to all intents and purposes a professional sports program. Partly in revulsion against this debasement of the amateur ideal, women's collegiate programs became increasingly attenuated, emphasizing participation for all and cooperation rather than competition. Schools, public and private, reflected the same values; media followed suit, by ignoring most women's sport.

Before World War II, American college educators, through their professional associations, even did their best to sabotage one of the few opportunities for female athletes to gain media attention: the Olympic Games. Not that Pierre de Coubertin, founder of the modern Games, had ever intended women to compete; he did not believe maidenly modesty and public displays of athleticism were compatible. At the 1896 Olympics, no women competed. In 1900 women's golf and tennis were included, but only archery was allowed in 1904. Gradually, women's events were added, but track and field, introduced in 1928, was curtailed before the 1932 Games because both the British and American press made much of some women's apparent exhaustion in the 800-meter race. Ironically, Babe Didrikson won two gold medals in 1932, but the press coverage she received was not wholly flattering; she was not the beauty queen that reporters expected female athletes to be.

Besides class, ethnicity affected media coverage in the United States. Black athletes, male or female, were not regularly covered by the mainstream press, but black females during the 1920s to the 1940s did get coverage in the black press. A history of hard work by black women had created a more robust physical ideal than the one dominant among middle-class white women. Accordingly, black colleges encouraged females to work at their athletics, while white female students were being confined to "play-days." It was from these black colleges that American Olympic athletes such as Alice Coachman, Wilma Rudolph, and Wyomia Tyus emerged. Most black females, however, were constrained athletically by poverty and overwork, like their lower-class white counterparts; college was for the fortunate few.

It is fair to say that until the 1970s, media coverage of female athletes was not merely sparse but reflected dominant images of the ideal woman, even in countries such as Germany, where women were encouraged to become physically fit. Germany's most widely read newspaper, the *Bild-Zeitung*, even in the 1990s, still favored sexually attractive losers over homely winners. From this perspective, women are designed for motherhood, and their primary task is to attract a mate. Sport could not, by definition, remain at the center of a woman's life; whatever she did athletically must appear easy and must not make her either too lean or too muscular. From the media's point of view, men played sports, while women merely "played at" them.

Coverage of women's sport was driven as much by world events as by cultural and social norms. Hitler seized on the Olympic Games for his own political purposes; as the Cold War developed, the Olympics became the site of a contest for global superiority. Medal counts are unisex; and as television coverage began to add to the print coverage already devoted to the Olympics, nations set in place programs to develop young athletes, both male and female, to ensure themselves a place on the international stage. For most competitors, male or female, the Olympics are still a private affair, as relatively few sports receive much coverage, and few athletes appear more than briefly in print or on the screen. But during the 1950s and 1960s, females worldwide began to get access to training, to facilities, and to international competition on a new scale, while medal ceremonies and other rituals focused on women as well as men. Fewer women than men still compete in both Summer and Winter Games; but during the 1980s and 1990s increasing numbers of viewers who would not normally have watched sport were drawn into Olympic telecasts. Some of them provided a growing audience for national and international championships in sports they had hitherto ignored.

COVERAGE TODAY

Media coverage of female sport worldwide today is vastly different from that of 1950, or even of 1970. As socially acceptable roles for women changed, so did media coverage for their sports. The changes, however, have not been without cost, and some would claim that the changes have been more apparent than real, in that a female's role in sport is still ambivalent.

MAGAZINES CHOOSE GREATEST ATHLETES OF THE CENTURY

To mark the end of the twentieth century, ESPN organized a panel of experts to select and rank the greatest athletes of the century. The list was limited to athletes from North America, and five women made it: track and field athlete and golfer Babe Didrikson (#10); tennis player Martina Navratilova (#19); track and field athlete Jackie Joyner-Kersee (#23); sprinter Wilma Rudolph (#41); and tennis player Chris Evert (#50). Four of these also appeared on the *Real Sports* list of the five top women athletes of the twentieth century. *Real Sports* did not pick Chris Evert but picked former Romanian gymnast, Nadia Comaneci, instead. The magazine also selected Billie Jean King as the woman of the millennium. *Sports Illustrated for Women* also selected Didrikson, Joyner-Kersee, Navratilova, and King, along with Norwegian figure skater Sonja Henie.

In the first place, the amateur ideal has disappeared from all sport now covered by the media. In the United States, amateurism's last institutional gasp was represented by the Association for Intercollegiate Athletics for Women (AIAW). Formed in 1971, the AIAW intended to prepare women for the highest levels of competition, using the best coaches and facilities. But the AIAW also intended to provide a women's model for collegiate athletics; competing, not necessarily winning, was to be the name of the game. The AIAW did secure an NBC contract to broadcast basketball championships, and gained some other TV exposure. Yet, naive and lacking a power base, the AIAW was swallowed up by the National Collegiate Athletic Association (NCAA) in 1982; female college athletes now play according to rules designed predominantly for men, by men, and in a commercialized sport world dominated by men.

The NCAA simply epitomizes the facts of life for the female athletes worldwide whom the media now covers. The qualities that were once defined as masculine—aggression, physicality, power, speed, and the will to win at all costs—are now those of any competitor in world-class competition in any sport. Women figure skaters must now be able to leap as well as glide; in a quasi-commercial for the Nagano Games, the oldest female luger nonchalantly reeled off her injuries as a mark of her durability. Unisex clothing often disguises gender—one skier hurtling down a slope looks much like another. Media covers winners, and what it takes to win was defined long before female competitors were brought onto TV.

The desire to win is, of course, no new phenomenon. Historically, some competitors went to extraordinary lengths, even in local contests, before record books were invented. But the tangible and intangible rewards for winning, as well as the apparatus of coaching, trials, and national and international championships that money generated by television has made possible have created a climate that can turn the lowliest contest into a matter of life and death. For females, media coverage now hinges on learning that lesson early.

Disregard for bodily injury is an inevitable concomitant of a desire to win at all costs. For female athletes, both training and performance-enhancing drugs may have more serious long-term effects than for their male counterparts.

Chamique Holdsclaw of the University of Tennesee basketball team accepts the ESPY Award for Female Athlete of the Year in 1999 at the nationally televised ESPY Awards show. (AP Photos)

Little boys do not become champions in sporting competitions open to adult males because they can never be strong enough. Little girls, however, may be better at gymnastics and figure skating than adult women, simply because they are more flexible and lighter. Although miniature skaters like Tara Lipinski are not as erotically attractive as mature skaters like Katarina Witt, they have the charm of childhood and attract more spectators than any other winter athletes, male or female. The intensive training required of these young female athletes, however, can disturb the menstrual cycle, leading to low estrogen production and loss of bone density during the very period of life when females should be building it. In the past, females were held back from sport competition by faulty medical strictures; now, winning seems more important than health.

Yet it is paradoxical that while the male definition of sport is now accepted by female athletes worldwide, media coverage of female athletes is still largely dominated by traditional concepts of what a female athlete should look like and how she should behave. Dennis Rodman has made millions by intentionally developing a crass, bad-boy image, which fits nicely into sterotypes of nouveau-riche, bad male athletes. Such opportunities are not open to women; Tonya Harding's failure to look like a "lady" nullified the attention given to her athletic skills. The late Florence Griffith-Joyner deliberately cultivated a fashion-model appearance, which might have garnered attention even had she not won, but which enhanced the endorsement offers her three Olympic gold medals produced. When Chris Evert retired from tennis in 1989, *Sports Illustrated* described her retirement as a move to become a full-time wife, even though she remains active in the sport and works as a television analyst. In countries that have long-standing traditions of upper-class sporting competition, such as horseback riding, in which men and women compete on an equal footing, it is not assumed that athletic women may be lesbians. In the United States, however, such fear has always dogged sponsors, making it even more necessary for female athletes seeking endorsements to dress conventionally, behave decorously, and be seen, if possible, with husbands and children.

As advertising now rules newspapers, radio, and television throughout most of the world to the point that even noncommercial media must watch their ratings, sports events must have a fan base if they are to retain media attention. Just as men's soccer leagues struggled in the United States because the American educational system promotes football, so women's professional leagues have found it hard to bring in an audience because few women played sports seriously. Title IX, however, part of the 1972 Education Amendments Act, forbade discrimination on the basis of sex in activities receiving federal funding. After a slow start, U.S. educational institutions have found themselves not merely supporting girls' and women's athletics, but actively promoting them.

A female fan base of experienced players has steadily grown, and while several women's professional basketball leagues, for instance, sputtered and died, in 1997 the National Basketball Association underwrote and marketed the Women's National Basketball Association (WNBA), organizing TV coverage of live games played in NBA arenas. This league has a female fan base and showcases American players, many of whom gained their professional experience in Europe, where prejudice against women's sport has traditionally been lower.

Yet the WNBA still faces problems. One WNBA veteran player, Sue Hicks, worried in an interview that the players' love of basketball itself, which entrances fans, could quickly turn into the take-it-all-for-granted attitude of male professionals and lead to a style of play that puts an individual player's career before the welfare of the team. In addition, basketball epitomizes one of the fundamental problems of women's team sport, for if the aim of professional sport is that of the Olympic motto, "Faster, higher, stronger," few sports will ever be played as well by women as by men.

It is true that in some countries and in some time periods, specific sports have had masculine or feminine connotations. The Olympic sport of synchronized swimming remains a female domain. The tennis player John McEnroe made the point that in the United States tennis was long regarded as a "sissy sport"; it did not require the ability to withstand pain while inflicting it on one's opponent, an American hallmark of masculinity. The very nature of some sports makes it possible for men and women to play them differently, which may lead to fans regarding the women's game as more attractive. When a men's singles match was about to begin at Wimbledon following a women's match, for instance, one spectator was heard remarking to another, "Oh, now it's just going to be serve, volley, and into the net. Time for tea." Some tennis connoisseurs watching the Billie Jean King–Bobby Riggs match in 1973 saw two hucksters desecrating the traditions that had given them their fame. But such fans were in a tiny minority; this so-called Battle of the Sexes had less to do with female athleticism than with the temper of the times.

CONCLUSION

The WNBA serves as a useful example of the problem within women's professional sport. If women's professional basketball loses the qualities that make it worth watching in its own right, then those who labeled it "inferior" may appear to be correct, and NBA support and TV contracts will wither and die. If, however, the WNBA can go on playing the game that girls grew up playing (which many still play as adults), their fan base is assured. As societal roles change, audiences will also change, and media coverage will follow. It remains to be seen to what extent females will be able to carve out for themselves their own sporting domain and find appropriate media coverage for it, or whether new generations will find a unisex model of sports entirely acceptable.

Joan M. Chandler

Bibliography

Cahn, Susan. (1994) *Coming on Strong: Gender and Sexuality in Twentieth Century Women's Sport*. New York: Free Press.

Cayleff, Susan. (1995) *Babe: The Life and Legend of Babe Didrikson Zaharias*. Urbana: University of Illinois Press.

Costa, Margaret, and Sharon Guthrie, eds. (1994) *Women and Sport: Interdisciplinary Perspectives*. Champaign, IL: Human Kinetics.

Creedon, Pamela. (1994) *Women, Media and Sport: Challenging Gender Values*. Thousand Oaks, CA: Sage Publications.

Edelman, Robert. (1993) *Serious Fun: A History of Spectator Sports in the U.S.S.R.* New York: Oxford University Press.

Guttmann, Allen. (1986) *Sports Spectators*. New York: Columbia University Press.

———. (1991) *Women's Sports: A History*. New York: Columbia University Press.

Hult, Joan, and Marianna Trekell. (1991) *A Century of Women's Basketball: From Frailty to Final Four*. Reston, VA: American Alliance for Health, Physical Education, Recreation and Dance.

Klein, Marie-Luise. (1986) *Frauensport in der Tagerpresse*. Bochum: Brockmeyer.

Klein, Marie-Luise, and Gertrud Pfister. (1985) *Goldmädel, Rennmiezen und Turnküken: Die Fran in der Sportberichterstattung der Bild-Zeitung*. Berlin: Bartels and Wernitz.

Oriard, Michael. (1993) *Reading Football: How the Popular Press Created an American Spectacle*. Chapel Hill: University of North Carolina Press.

Ryan, Joan. (1995) *Little Girls in Pretty Boxes: The Making and Breaking of Elite Gymnasts and Figure Skaters*. New York: Warner.

INTERNATIONAL MEDIA COVERAGE OF WOMEN'S SPORTS

Media and sport have undergone tremendous changes over the past twenty years and have evolved a symbiotic relationship. Media uses sport to sell newspapers and magazines, to boost television ratings, and to attract sponsors; at the same time, sport uses media coverage to attract people to sport by creating interest and demand. A number of authors have argued that, perhaps more than any other social institution, sport perpetuates male superiority and female inferiority. Essentially, this argument is based on the notion that sport represents a potent medium through which biological or physical differences interface with social and cultural interpretations of gender role expectations. The media's role in this process of constructing hierarchies will be the focus of this article, which suggests that gender difference is translated into gender hierarchy through the depiction of females athletes not only as "other than" but as "less than" their male counterparts. The article offers an overview of the international research concentrating on the representation of female and male athletes in sports media, covering studies on televised sports, newsprint, and magazines.

A survey of the representation of women athletes constructed by the media demonstrates two general themes: first, the amount of coverage reveals the underrepresentation of women athletes in the sport media; second, the type of coverage indicates various patterns of trivialization, marginalization, and sexualization of women athletes.

UNDERREPRESENTATION AND STEREOTYPING OF WOMEN'S INVOLVEMENT IN SPORT

Studies dealing with the quantitative coverage of men's and women's sport agree in one finding: the amount of coverage of women's sport remains far below the coverage of men's sport. Marie-Luise Klein (1986) analyzed the sport coverage of four German daily newspapers in the course of one year and found that 4 to 6 percent of the articles dealt with female athletes, compared to 87 to 95 percent covering men's sport. Margaret Carlisle Duncan and Michael A. Messner (1994) investigated six weeks of televised late-night sport news on three Los Angeles network affiliates and found that 5 percent of the air time was devoted to women's sport and 94 percent to the sporting activities of men. The near-invisibility of women athletes on televised sport news was accompanied by an almost total absence of interviews with women athletes and coaches. Moreover, there is a tendency to focus on a gag feature when devoting time to a report on women's sport. This lack of serious treatment of female athletes in sport news (e.g., nuns playing volleyball at a church celebration) is amplified by the fact that news about male athletes generally deals with up-to-date important sport events.

The overall data show that the coverage of women's involvement in sport is dramatically lower than the coverage of men's involvement in sport and does not reflect the (rising) participation rates of females in sport. This lack of coverage creates the impression that females are nonexistent in the sporting world. Media coverage is a symbolic representation of society and reflects dominant values or norms. By not reporting on women's sports, by not incorporating female athletes in the news, sport media symbolically annihilate their position in society and the role they play in sport.

Yet the general underrepresentation of female athletes in media is not as one-dimensional as these figures suggest. Although women's sport is notoriously underreported, there are some sports that are predominantly covered as female sporting activities. Catriona T. Higgs and Karen H. Weiller (1994) analyzed the television coverage of the 1992 Summer Olympic Games, focusing on segments that featured same-sport activities for men and women. They found that of the three sports covered most of the time (basketball, track and field, and gymnastics), most of the air time for basketball and track and field dealt with males (74 percent and 63 percent), whereas 84 percent of the entire air time for gymnastics dealt with women's gymnastics. These results indicate that media coverage emphasizes the representation of women and men in "gender-appropriate" sports, thus reinforcing the stereotyping of sporting activities of men and women.

TRIVIALIZATION AND MARGINALIZATION OF WOMEN'S SPORT

When women athletes are represented in the media, their involvement and accomplishments are often trivialized and portrayed as less than those of "real" athletes. One prominent feature of devaluing female athletes in media is the use of condescending descriptions. Women athletes are more often depicted by their forenames than are men athletes, and they are more often referred to as "girls" and "young ladies," whereas men are only seldom depicted as "boys" but are referred to as "men," "young men," or "young fellas." Furthermore, descriptions of female athletes also involve infantilizing attributes, such as "Cinderella" or "Turnküken" (literally, "gymnastics chicks"). The naming reinforces a basic element of social structure–that of gender division as well as the asymmetry that is associated with it. As S. Eitzen and M. Baca Zinn note (1989), this process can be interpreted as "the deathletization of women."

Another way of depicting the inappropriateness of women in sport is the notion of family or other commitments outside sport. Female athletes are shown and referred to more often in these contexts than male athletes, for example, as mother, girlfriend, teenager in school, daughter, or wife. This presentation of female athletes identifies women athletes as social beings who do not or cannot devote their life completely to sport but are "naturally" involved in social commitments.

Although overt discrimination against women as athletes has decreased in the media, there are still some clear signs of direct devaluation of women in sport media, especially in the coverage of female athletes who enter traditionally male sports. Biitta Pirinen (1997) studied Finnish newspaper coverage of female athletes who were for the first time contesting in traditionally male sports, such as boxing, ski jumping, hammer throwing, triple jump, and pole vault. Although she found promoting discourses about the female newcomers that concentrated on the power and strength of the athletes, she also found discourses that overtly depicted the women as inappropriate and ridiculous in these sports: for example, "The jumps had a comic appearance about them, with the girls' bodies and the poles almost equally stiff in the jump" (p. 244).

With regard to televised sport, disparities between men's and women's representation are usually manifested in the construction of an event and the quality of the production itself. Men's contests are often presented as dramatic spectacles of great importance and as fierce competition, whereas women's events are presented as recreational activities that often serve as an opening presentation for the men's game and that may be interrupted by references or even interviews with players of the men's game. The effect of trivializing women's events is exacerbated by the quality of the production, which is generally less technically sophisticated and less dramatic when reporting on women's contests, with far fewer on-screen graphics and slow-motion pictures and less visual editing.

SEXUALIZATION OF WOMEN ATHLETES AND EMPHASIS OF SEX-DIFFERENCES

Another indication of the social construction of gender differences and hierarchies in sport is the emphasis on women's physical appearance, as well as the presentation of female athletes as desirable sex objects. Descriptions of the outward appearance, which stand in no direct relation to the sporting performance, are often found in media portrayals of female athletes. The description of women as sex objects is a common way of dealing with women in media. Yet it seems that the body-centered system of sports supplies journalists with abundant ideas for presenting women in sexualized contexts.

An important means of constructing differences between male and female athletes is sport photography. Photos suggest reality, and the spectator of a photo believes the content of the photo to be authentic. Duncan (1990) deciphers sport photographs to present female athletes as weak and dependent on men. For example, weakness and deference are created when female athletes are photographed from above eye-level, which allows the spectator to look down on them, whereas male athletes are very seldom pictured from above. Duncan also reveals that the photos of female athletes may be compared with photos of soft-core pornography. The focus of the camera on certain parts of the female athlete's body (like breasts, hips, legs, etc.) and the use of a compliant expression on her face are photographic techniques that are found in pornographic magazines as well.

Andrea Bachmann (1998) revealed in a study about the coverage of the 1996 Summer Olympic Games in Austrian daily newspapers and sport magazines that sexist descriptions—one example was the term *Pinup*—were frequently used to refer to female competitors. Female athletes who were engaged in summer sports, such as surfing and beach volleyball, were often presented in an erotic way. While men were presented in spectacular scenes, managing the various thrills of the rough sea, the female surfers were depicted frequently in nonsporting positions, such as preparing their boards on the beach, thus allowing intimate glances at the females' bodies. In contrast, coverage of men's sport contains far fewer references to outward appearance; references to appearance if any, emphasize qualities related to the athletes' performances, such as strength and stamina.

Physical size or muscularity is an essential indicator of strength and an essential symbol of male power. Because sport is ultimately about physical activity and because males run faster, jump higher, and throw farther than females, sport offers an arena for reproducing male power and dominance through the physicality of the body. By emphasizing the sexual differences between female and male athletes, mass media convey the message that men are more appropriate for sports than women. This means that media naturalize stereotyped pictures of men and women, which imply that men are strong, aggressive, cool-headed, and have stamina, whereas women are weak, sociable, and emotional. Christy Halbert and Melissa Latimer (1994) analyzed references to the difference of physical competence between female and male athletes in the live commentary on the "Battle of the Champions" in 1992, the coed tennis competition between Martina Navratilova and Jimmy Connors, won by Connors in two sets (7–5; 6–2). The physical competence of Navratilova and her ability to win were questioned throughout the whole match, even in phases where the outcome of the match was unclear. The character portraits of Navratilova and Connors were also different: "While only a few references were made about Connors' emotions, the commentators pointed out Navratilova's feelings and emotional vulnerabilities seventeen times throughout the match" (p. 304).

The above example reveals that media establish a patriarchal order in sport that is based on the natural order of physical superiority of men. Media's tendency to maintain men's magnificence in sport is documented in an impressive way by an analysis of the reporters' comments in situations of success or failure. In their study of live commentary on the U.S. men's and women's basketball championships in 1989 and 1993, Duncan and Messner discovered differences in the attribution of successes and failures of male and female players. "Men appeared to succeed through a combination of talent, instinct, intelligence, size, strength, quickness, hard work, and risk-taking. Women also apparently succeeded through talent, enterprise, hard work, and intelligence. But commonly cited with these attributes were emotion, luck, togetherness, and family" (p. 21). Although Duncan and Messner found greater respect for women's athletic competence and less ambivalence about their strength in 1993 than in 1989, there was still a difference in treatment of women and men in the commentary on failures. If female players failed to complete a successful shot, commentators repeatedly referred to this failure and attributed it directly to the female players' poor skills. If male players failed to play well, the commentators did not mention the fault at all or attributed it to factors beyond the male players' control, for example, to the outstanding sporting competence of the players' opponents or to the outer conditions of the game: "It was a tough ball to catch, though, 'cause the backboard was causing some problems" (p. 21).

A severe phenomenon of depicting women athletes' "otherness" is the questioning of their femininity. Outstanding efforts of female athletes are now and then questioned in sport media by referring to their "abnormal" appearance and suggesting anomalies concerning hormones and chromosomes. At other times, women's outstanding physical abilities might receive a less direct "she plays like a man," which further illustrates the hierarchy of sport: an extraordinary performance by a woman can only be explained through questioning her female biology or by comparing her to men; such a performance just cannot be "female."

AMBIVALENCE IN WOMEN'S SPORT COVERAGE

Ambivalence is the term initially used by Duncan and Cynthia A. Hasbrook (1988) to explain how media portrayals of women athletes contain contradictory messages. Their findings indicate that verbal and visual depictions of female athletes often combined positive and flattering portrayals with subtly negative suggestions that trivialized or undermined their sport performance.

Recalling some of the results of Duncan and Messner regarding the construction of an event and the quality of the production, one may easily characterize these disparities between women's and men's coverage as manifestation of ambivalence. By employing nonprofessional production techniques in television coverage of women's sports, while presenting men's games with professional technique, selling them as dramatic events and shedding a clear-cut and positive light on them, media reinforce male hegemony in sport.

In the commentaries of the live telecasts of the 1986 NCAA women's and men's basketball championships, Duncan and Hasbrook (1988) found additional evidence of the ambivalence conveyed with women's sport coverage. As teamwork is of utmost importance for success in any team sports, commentaries on team competencies are highly valued in contrast to commentaries on individual skills. Duncan and Hasbrook found that attributes describing team competence were dominant in the men's game, whereas such attributes were only seldom found in the women's games reportage. Here, attributes describing individual skills of the women outnumbered the attributes of team competence. In this case, women's teamwork was disparaged simply by lack of commentary. Instead of focusing on the all-important teamwork aspects of the game, commentators tended to discuss its aesthetic aspects.

Another example of ambivalent messages in women's sport coverage are conflicting descriptions of female athletes' sporting abilities. Various studies have come to the conclusion that attributes of strength and power dominate in the commentary of men's sports, whereas in the commentary of women's sporting events, weakness descriptors intermingle with strength descriptors in such a way that the messages are contradictory. Thus a strength descriptor might, for example, be directly followed by an attribute of weakness: "She powered through the pick and roll only to throw up a weak shot" (Higgs and Weiller, p. 238). The crux of such an ambivalent remark about a female player's athletic competence is that it is a subtle form of devaluing women's abilities. Probably most spectators would not perceive it as discriminatory, because the reporter does not say directly that women are not appropriate for sports. But these techniques of producing ambivalence and incongruity in the commentary of women's sport create an unattractive and vague image of women in sport.

CONCLUSION: MEASURING PROGRESS

Researchers have all indicated that male athletes receive a disproportionate amount of coverage when compared with female athletes. One wonders whether there has been any change and progress over the past decades, given the fact that a rising number of women have been participating in sport and entering top-level sport competition. Comparing data is difficult, and caution is needed in interpreting previous research that is not designed for immediate and direct comparison. However, some studies do suggest trends of change–some for worse, some for better.

One of the long-standing criticisms of media accounts of women's sport concerns the amount of coverage. Those few longitudinal studies that allow a comparison produce inconsistent results regarding changes in quantitative coverage. A longitudinal study of six British national newspapers comes up with a surprising result: although there was a dramatic increase in the quantity of general sport newsprint over the decade of 1984 to 1994, the proportion of coverage for women decreased. In contrast, women were featured in increasing numbers between 1964 and 1987 in *Sports Illustrated*, though women in "sex-appropriate" sports were featured significantly more often than female athletes in "sex-inappropriate" sports. A comparison by Duncan and Messner of televised late-night sport news in the United States between 1989 and 1993 concludes that there was almost no change in the underreporting of women's sports. While their study identified some notable improvements in the quality of production, they noted that quality remained uneven. Instances of verbal infantilization of women athletes by using their first names, though decreasing, were still significant. Tennis commentators who tended to downplay women's athletic successes systematically in the 1989 study tended to express greater respect for their abilities and strength five years later. Overall, however, comments and explanations of women's suc-

cesses and failures still reflected gender asymmetries.

The above examples demonstrate that media representations of women in sport can be seen as ideological sites for the production and reproduction of relations of gender that undermine women's participation in sport. Although a few studies give hints for a positive change in the presentation of women in sport media, it can be concluded that the social construction of women's sport by the media still demands change.

Ilse Hartmann-Tews
Bettina Rulofs

Bibliography

Bachmann, Andrea. (1998) " 'Wie eine Katze schmiegt sie sich an, an die Hochsprunglatte:' Geschlechterdifferenz in der Sportbrichterstattung. Eine inhaltsanalytisch-semiotische Untersuchung zum Frauen- und Männersport am Beispiel der Olympischen Spiele 1996 in Atlanta und der Schi-WM 1996 in der Sierra Nevada." Ph.D. thesis, University of Salzburg.

Daddario, Gina. (1998) *Women's Sport and Spectacle: Gendered Television Coverage and the Olympic Games*. Westport, CT and London: Praeger.

Duncan, Margaret Carlisle. (1990) "Sports Photographs and Sexual Difference: Images of Women and Men in the 1984 and 1988 Olympic Games." *Sociology of Sport Journal* 7, 1: 22–43.

Duncan, Margaret Carlisle, and Cynthia A. Hasbrook. (1988) "Denial of Power in Televised Women's Sports." *Sociology of Sport Journal* 5: 1–21.

Duncan, Margaret Carlisle, and Michael A. Messner. (1994) *Gender Stereotyping in Televised Sports: A Follow-up to the 1989 Study*. Los Angeles: Amateur Athletic Foundation of Los Angeles.

Eitzen, S., and M. Baca Zinn. (1989) "The Deathletization of Women: The Naming and Gender Making of Collegiate Sport Teams." *Sociology of Sport Journal* 6, 4: 362–370.

Flatten, Kay, and Hilary Matheson. (1997) "Gender Politics in Sport Newsprint: A Longitudinal Study of Six British National Newspapers." In IASI-10 Proceedings. (Paris, 10–12 June): 326–332.

Halbert, Christy, and Melissa Latimer. (1994) "'Battling' Gendered Language: An Analysis of the Language Used by Sports Commentators in a Televised Coed Tennis Competition." *Sociology of Sport Journal* 11: 298–308.

Higgs, Catriona T., and Karen H. Weiller. (1994) "Gender Bias and the 1992 Summer Olympic Games: An Analysis of Television Coverage." *Journal of Sport and Social Issues* 18, 3 (1994): 234–248.

Kane, Mary Jo. (1988) "Media Coverage of the Female Athlete before, during and after Title IX: Sports Illustrated Revisited." *Journal of Sport Management* 2: 87–99.

Kane, Mary Jo, and Janet B. Parks. (1992) "The Social Construction of Gender Difference and Hierarchy in Sport Journalism: Few New Twists on Very Old Themes." *Women in Sport and Physical Activity Journal* 1, 1 (1992): 49–83.

Klein, Marie-Luise. (1986) *Frauensport in der Tagerpresse.* Bochum: Brockmeyer.

Messner, Michael. (1994) "Sports and Male Domination: The Female Athlete as Contested Ideological Terrain." In *Women, Sport and Culture,* edited by Susan Birrell and Cheryl Cole. Champaign, IL: Human Kinetics, 65–80.

Pirinen, Riitta. (1997) "Catching Up with Men? Finnish Newspaper Coverage of Women's Entry into Traditionally Male Sports." *International Review for the Sociology of Sport* 32, 3: 239–250.

MEDICINE

As long as there have been athletes, there have been people who attended to their medical needs. These people were often coaches or trainers trying to keep their athletes competing at optimal condition. As sport and participation in sport grew, a complex industry developed, one committed to keeping elite, amateur, and fitness athletes healthy and competitive. This article provides a brief history of how medical opinion has discouraged or encouraged women's participation in sports. The different practitioners involved in the care of active patients and the percentage of these practitioners and patients who are women will also be examined.

ADVICE ON PHYSICAL ACTIVITY THROUGH THE AGES

Traditional medicine has historically turned to the physician as the primary provider of medical care, and doctors have been making recommendations regarding physical activity for preventing and treating medical illness since Hippocrates. Hippocrates recommended moderate exercises, stating, "all parts of the body which have a func-

tion if used in moderation and exercised in labors in which each is accustomed, become thereby healthy, well-developed and age more slowly. If unused and left idle, they become liable to disease and defective in growth, and age quickly." The medical profession thought that exercise was especially beneficial for children and regularly prescribed exercise as early as the 1400s.

Medical opinion in the past has most often mirrored prevailing public sentiment rather than relied on scientific data. Although physicians encouraged moderate activity for children and men, they at the same time helped to reinforce the cultural belief that physical activity was dangerous for women. During the Victorian era, when weakness and frailty were considered normal and desirable in women, the medical community issued warnings about "over-taxing" the delicate female. The ovaries and uterus were determined to be the source of most medical and emotional problems and were blamed for innate frailty.

In 1849 Dr. Hollick wrote, "The uterus, it must be remembered, is the controlling organ of the female body, being the most excitable of all, and so is ultimately connected, by the ramifications of its numerous nerves, with every other part." Dr. M. E. Dirix agreed, stating, "Thus women are treated for diseases of the stomach, liver, kidneys, heart, lungs, etc.; yet, in most instances, these diseases will be found on due investigation, to be, in reality, no diseases at all, but merely the sympathetic reactions of the symptoms of one disease, namely, a disease of the womb."

Because the reproductive organs were regarded as the controlling force in women, menses was of particular concern. Dr. W. C. Taylor warned, "We cannot too emphatically urge the importance of regarding these monthly returns as periods of ill health, as days when the ordinary occupations are to be suspended or modified." Scott Hall agreed, stating, "All heavy exercise should be omitted during the menstrual week . . . a girl should not only retire earlier at this time, but ought to stay out of school from one to three days as the case may be." Dr. Howard Kelly echoed the commonly held medical view, explaining that while it was reasonable for a girl to play sports, she "must consider a regularly recurring interval when her nervous force is so taxed by the demands of her economy that the excessive effort demanded by the game places her at a disadvantage for the moment, beside exposing her to the risk of lasting ill effects, even so great as life-long invalidism." He admitted that "some strong vigorous girls do sometimes play tennis, basket-ball, and hockey at such times with impunity, but no girl can risk the strain of a match game without danger of suffering from it sooner or later."

There were some dissenting opinions, primarily from women doctors. Dr. Mary Putnam Jacobi lamented, "It is considered natural and almost laudable to break down under all conceivable varieties of strain. . . . Women who expect to go to bed every menstrual period expect to collapse if by chance they find themselves on their feet for a few hours during such a crisis. Constantly considering their nerves, urged to consider them by well-intentioned but short-sighted advisors, they pretty soon become nothing but a bundle of nerves." Dr. Elizabeth Garrett Anderson argued that female invalidism was exaggerated by male doctors. She pointed out that in the working classes, women engaged in strenuous work that continued during menstruation.

In fact, only in the upper class could a woman afford the luxury of invalidism. In the factories, in the fields of the American South, and on its western frontiers, women were required to perform strenuous physical activity to survive. Dr. Sylvanus Stall attempted to explain this by stating, "At war, at work, or at play, the white man is superior to the savage, and his culture has continually improved his condition. But with woman the rule is reversed. Her squaw sister will endure effort, exposure and hardship which would kill the white woman. Education which has resulted in developing and strengthening the physical nature of man has been perverted through folly and fashion to render woman weaker and weaker."

EDUCATION AND FITNESS

In the early 1900s, the women's suffrage movement arose and progressed, and women began to take advantage of new-found freedoms. They started enrolling in colleges and universities in larger numbers than ever before. The medical community and college administrators were concerned that these female students would be unable to endure the stress of college life, so they instituted physical fitness programs. In order to avoid medical complications, these programs were designed so they were not too strenuous. Dr. John Shoemaker wrote that "the prime object of physical education for the female sex is the promotion of health and grace . . . the possession by it of great strength is not desirable, nor possible." These programs focused on fresh air, cooperation, hygiene, and posture.

Women's physical activity increased with the invention of the bicycle in the early 1900s. A national craze for bicycling developed, and women were swept up with the trend. The medical community was concerned that bicycle seats would be harmful to a woman's reproductive organs. Nevertheless, in spite of these warnings, women continued to cycle and have healthy babies, proving medical fears unfounded.

With the advent of World War I and World War II, there was a drain of manpower to the armed forces. Women went to work in factories out of necessity, and cultural beliefs supported this trend as patriotic. Accordingly, medical opinion shifted with the prevailing societal views. The work was very strenuous, but women persevered. Indeed, instead of breaking down, they flourished with the new freedoms. To provide relief from the long hours and physically demanding work, companies, with the backing of the medical community, organized sport teams. Women participated in sports in facilities void of men who had left for the war, and women's professional leagues were even started.

Having become physically fit out of necessity, women in the 1940s realized that it was possible to be physically active without ill effect. Fitness programs designed specifically to meet the demands and challenges of the "period of peace and reconstruction" were advocated. In *Conditioning Exercises for Girls and Women,* the totally fit woman was described as one who "possesses endurance, strength, and stamina. Her body is sound; it is free from infection and remediable physical defects. . . . She has developed, also, motor skills for purposes of utility, safety, and recreation in leisure time." Although jobs and gyms were now once again filled with men returning from the war, it was no longer possible to close the door that gave women access to the world of activity.

CHANGING VIEWS

The 1960s became a decade of change in which social and cultural values were questioned, including the role of women. In his book on physical fitness, Thomas Cureton states, "Our program for physical fitness applies equally to men and women" and further cautions that "the woman who is really concerned about her physical being must overcome the erroneous psychological attitude that there is something unfeminine about exercising the muscles." While previous generations of physicians had warned about the risk of exercise during menstruation, it was now suggested that exercise might help ameliorate subjective responses to menstruation.

By the 1970s, the opportunities and glorification of sport participation for men was entrenched in society. However, there were limited opportunities for women to compete in sports, especially at high levels. This all changed dramatically with the advent of Title IX of the Education Amendments Act in 1972. Title IX prohibited discrimination in educational institutions that receive federal funds. Sport participation by women rapidly increased as more opportunities became available. The medical profession, while generally supportive of the trend toward more sport participation by women, was concerned that women might be predisposed toward injury. There was particular concern that the breasts and genitals would be at risk. However, research quickly proved that these injuries were among the least common in women athletes. Injuries seemed to be more sport specific than gender specific, although various aspects of women's physiology do make them more vulnerable in some areas.

As it had been with previous generations of doctors, menstruation continued to be of concern. Some women were asked not to swim while menstruating for fear that they would contaminate the water. But by this time, a scientific model had become the norm, and research was conducted to see if menstruation actually affected pool water. It was discovered that it did not affect the water any more than the regular bacterial flora from a person's skin or mouth. Thus, in this instance, scientific data helped dispel cultural bias.

Through the last few decades, society has continued to place more value on athletes and athletic competition. The medical community now recommends physical activity for both men and women. Exercise has been shown to improve cardiovascular status and diabetes and to prevent hypertension, lower cholesterol, and improve the quality of life. It is used as part of a comprehensive treatment plan to maintain fitness and wellness. The National Institute of Health consensus statement on health and physical activity recommended that all people in the United States increase their regular physical activity to a level appropriate to their capacities, needs, and interests. It recommended that all children and adults set a long-term goal to accumulate at least thirty minutes or more of moderate-intensity activity on most, or preferably all, days of the week.

Physical activity recommendations have also changed dramatically for the pregnant woman. Medical advice used to warn about the dangers of excessive physical activity, especially during pregnancy. As recently as the 1980s, the official recommendation of the American College of Obstetrics and Gynecology was that a pregnant woman's heart rate should not exceed 140 beats per minute during exercise. The latest recommendations are more individualized and take into account a woman's pre-pregnancy fitness regimen as well as her pregnancy history. Many women keep on exercising right up to their due date without adverse complications.

SPORTS MEDICINE TODAY

Sports medicine is a relatively new field and is still in the process of evolving. It can be defined as the medicine of exercise, concerned with the total medical care of the exercising individual. It is a unique field in medicine because exercise can be both the cause and the treatment for different conditions. It is concerned with injury prevention, diagnosis, treatment, and rehabilitation, as well as with enhancing performance. Sports medicine deals with all individuals who exercise, many of whom have special needs. Disabled athletes, pediatric and adolescent athletes, and female athletes all have concerns that merit particular attention.

Initially, orthopedic doctors were the sports medicine doctors. They were the most completely trained physicians in musculoskeletal pathology.

Like most surgical subspecialties, this one included—and still includes—very few women. Only 2.3 percent of active, board-certified orthopedic surgeons are women. With an average age of forty-two, female orthopedic surgeons tend to be much younger than their male counterparts. In fact, 46 percent of female orthopedic surgeons are under age forty. More and more women are entering orthopedic surgery residencies, and it is expected that these numbers will rise.

With an increasing body of knowledge in orthopedic surgery and the increasing interest of doctors and patients in sports medicine, orthopedic sports medicine fellowships were developed. These provide orthopedic surgeons with extra training and experience in the field of surgical sports medicine. Only 15 percent of female orthopedic surgeons who undertake fellowships choose sports medicine.

In response to the growing number of sports orthopedists, the American Orthopedic Society for Sports Medicine was founded in 1972. The society promotes and supports education and research in sports medicine, and it also supports programs designed to advance knowledge in the recognition, treatment, rehabilitation, and prevention of athletic injuries. Less than 1 percent (0.25%) of the members are female.

Other physicians also consider themselves sports medicine specialists. Many problems that athletes develop are not musculoskeletal in nature. Athletes may have problems like asthma, diabetes, or common upper respiratory infections that are more appropriately treated by a primary care physician (family practice, internal medicine, pediatrics). Because of their sport participation, these athletes may need special treatment plans or consideration. With the growth of managed care, primary care physicians are often the first and only physicians to treat many athletes. It has been estimated that up to 25 percent of routine office visits to a family practitioner involve musculoskeletal complaints, such as pulled muscles, sprains, and the like.

Given the rise in interest and the complexity of nonsurgical problems of the athlete, primary care sports medicine fellowships were developed. These offer extra training for primary care doctors in both nonsurgical musculoskeletal problems and the medical concerns of athletes. Both allopathic (M.D.) and osteopathic (D.O.) physicians have formed specialty societies to provide a forum for these sports medicine doctors. They are the American Medical Society for Sports Medicine (AMSSM) and the American Osteopathic Academy of Sports Medicine (AOASM). While roughly one-third of primary care doctors are women, only 7 percent of the membership of both these sports medicine societies are women.

Physical therapists are another group of medical professionals that are involved in the care of the active person. Their primary concern is timely

MEDICINE AND WOMEN IN SPORTS

In the late twentieth century medical science played a major role in enhancing the opportunities for women to participate in sports, primarily by providing evidence that physical activity and sports are beneficial to women. It was not always that way. Earlier in the century medical evidence and opinion were often used to limit women's participation. The arguments were often connected to female reproductive functions as in this report of the 1925 Pedagogic Conference of the International Olympic Committee: "The differences which appear in the nervous, skeletal and muscular systems are all necessary adjuncts of the great work of Parturition and anything that might hinder or make this more difficult must be heavily deprecated. . . . It seems to me, therefore, that if those sports and games which are suitable for men be modified and reduced so that they cannot in any way injure the woman, and if we can create organizations which will enforce these modified regulations stringently, we will have gone a long way toward achieving our objectives."

rehabilitation and return to activity for the injured athlete. The American Physical Therapy Association (APTA) has more than 75,000 members. Physical therapy has traditionally been dominated by women, and this is reflected in today's membership. Of APTA members, 82 percent are women. A sport section was started twenty-five years ago for those with a sport focus. While most general physical therapists are women, the trend is reversed when it comes to the sport physical therapist. In this group, 75 percent of the sport section members are male. Even in a primarily female profession, women are still underrepresented when it comes to sports.

Athletic trainers care for the athlete on a routine basis. They are hired primarily by schools and charged with the prevention, treatment, and rehabilitation of athletic injuries. They diagnose and treat many injuries that are not serious enough to be brought to the attention of the physician but can often have profound implications on an athlete's ability to play. The National Association of Athletic Trainers (NATA) members are 43 percent women. Women have made great progress in this profession, caring for elite professional and collegiate athletes of both sexes.

An organization that encompasses sports medicine professionals of all disciplines is the American College of Sports Medicine (ACSM). It attempts to promote and integrate scientific research, education, and practical implications of sports medicine and exercise science to maintain and enhance physical performance, fitness, health, and quality of life. Because membership is open to everyone from the physician to the fitness instructor, it may be more representative of women's involvement in sports medicine as a whole. The ACSM membership is 38 percent female.

Thus, while the numbers of women who participate in sports both recreationally and competitively has risen tremendously in the last quarter of the century, the numbers of women who care for athletes have not matched that growth. Professions that are traditionally male tend to be even more overrepresented when it comes to sports medicine. Even professions that are typically female, such as physical therapy, have disproportionate numbers of male sports therapists. As participation by women in sport continues to rise, this will, it is hoped, translate to an increased number of female health professionals caring for athletes.

CONCLUSION

Medical opinion has been used throughout the ages as reinforcement of culturally held beliefs about women exercising. Initially, this was unsupported by any scientific data. As women began to exercise more and more, it was discovered that exercise offered the same benefits to women as to men. Today, the medical community needs to continue to research issues that are of particular concern to women. The medical community can and should be an ally to the exercising woman.

Kimberly G. Harmon

See also Aging; Amenorrhea; Anemia; Athletic Training; Biomechanics; Body Composition; Breast Health; Eating Disorders; Immunity; Injury; Menstrual Cycle; Nutrition; Osteoporosis; Pain; Performance; Reproduction; Endurance; Stress and Stress Management

Bibliography

Brukner, Peter, and Karim Khan. (1993) *Clinical Sports Medicine.* Sydney: McGraw-Hill.

Cureton, Thomas. (1965) *Physical Fitness and Dynamic Health.* New York: Dial Press.

Duggan, Anne, Mary Ella Montague, and Abbie Rutledge. (1945) *Conditioning Exercises for Girls and Women.* South Brunswick and New York: A.S. Barnes.

Enrenreich, Barbara, and Dierdre English. (1978) *For Her Own Good.* Garden City, NY: Anchor Book/Doubleday.

Latimer, Caroline. (1909) *Girl and Woman.* New York: D. Appleton.

Lutter, Judy. (1994) "History of Women in Sports: Societal Issues." *Clinics in Sports Medicine.* Philadelphia: W. B. Saunders. 13(2); 263–278.

Ryan, Allan, and Fred Allman. (1974) *Sports Medicine.* New York: Academic Press.

Shoemaker, John. (1908) *Health and Beauty.* Philadelphia: F. A. Davis.

Whiteside, Patricia. (1980) "Men's and Women's Injuries in Comparable Sports." *Physician and Sportsmedicine* 8(3); 130–137.

MENSENDIECK, BESS M.

(1864–1957)

DUTCH-AMERICAN PHYSICAL CULTURE PROPONENT

Bess M. Mensendieck was one of the early proponents of women's physical culture and emancipation through the body. She created schools and published to a wide audience in the United States and many European countries. She was born of American and Swiss descent as Elisabeth Marguerite Eltrich van Wagel in the Netherlands on 1 July 1864 and died in 1957 in New York.

Beginning in 1884, Mensendieck was trained as a sculptor in Paris, studied music, and specialized in singing. She took up medical studies in Paris and worked with Professor G.B. Duchenne on electrical muscle stimulation. Mensendieck continued her medical studies in Munich, where she was married for two years to Carl Caspar Christian Mensendieck, a German medical doctor who was running a fresh air sanatorium. Finally, Mensendieck finished her medical studies in Switzerland.

Primarily in Germany, from 1900 on, Mensendieck started to teach her "system" for female teachers of physical culture. In 1906 Mensendieck published her first major book, *Körperkultur des Weibes: Praktisch hygienische und praktisch ästhetische Winke* (Physical culture for women: Practical hygienic and practical aesthetic advice). In 1910 she opened her Central Institute for Mensendieck Gymnastics in Berlin. Her ideas were popular and by 1912 her book had reached its fifth edition.

During World War I and for three years after, Mensendieck lived in New York City. There she published her *Standards of Female Beauty* (1919). After returning to Germany, Mensendieck published her third book, *Funktionelles Frauenturnen* (Functional gymnastics for women), in 1923 and her fourth, *Functioneele Lichaams-Oefeningen voor de Vrouw en het Kind* (Functional gymnastics for women and children), in 1924.

Upon her return to Germany, Mensendieck found that her system had changed considerably in her absence. She spent until 1929 fighting unauthorized variations of her system, and eventually she created the International League for the True Mensendieck System, which proclaimed itself the only authorized system. Mensendieck was running her courses primarily in the Netherlands, Germany, and Denmark, but she had pupils in at least thirteen countries. She promoted her system in a series of books: *Bewegungsprobleme: Die Gestaltung schöner Arme* (Movement problem: The creation of beautiful arms), 1927; *Anmut der Bewegung im täglichen Leben* (Graceful movement in daily life), 1929; *It's Up To You*, 1931; and *Look Better—Feel Better: The World Renowned Mensendieck System of Functional Movements for a Youthful Body and Vibrant Health*, 1954.

Mensendieck's system can best be understood in light of her early artistic and medical training. She aspired to recreate women from the aesthetic perspective of Greek antiquity. She realized that through slow exercise, including isometrics, a woman can train her body, much like a sculptor creates a beautiful figure. The teachers she trained were in high demand by the medical profession because they directly addressed muscle weakness. Mensendieck taught anatomy in great detail, and many of her exercises have become basics in the bodybuilding movement. For Mensendieck, a beautiful body should be able to make beautiful and graceful movements, so the beauty of the body and the beauty of motion were one. She demanded intellectual progress from her students, and she aimed to shape the body in a natural and efficient way—not in a way that men might consider pleasing. Though she directed her teaching exclusively toward women, many of her books were also bought by men (perhaps because the women posing for the exercises were nude).

One variation on her system was promulgated by the German Mensendieck Society, which combined the exercises with music and rhythmical movements. Mensendieck considered this approach degrading. She argued that women should not be restricted to rhythmic gymnastics and dance but should have a system that was intellectually, physically, and aesthetically demanding—

in other words, just like a program for men. Mensendieck also disapproved of the work of Jaques-Dalcroze, as she felt that the body should not be sculpted by external rhythms but only by its own "physiological rhythm." She considered herself most strongly influenced by Genevieve Stebbins. Mensendieck argued for her form of "functional gymnastics" on the grounds that only functionality could lead to aesthetics. Because she stressed not only beauty and health but also women's responsibility for their own fate, Mensendieck's work was considered by many contemporaries as the beginning of the women's emancipation movement in physical education and gymnastics.

Arnd Krüger
Claudia Meimbresse

Bibliography

Mensendieck, Bess M. (1906) *Körperkultur des Weibes: Praktisch hygienische und praktisch ästhetische Winke* (Physical culture for women: Practical hygienic and practical aesthetic advice). Munich, Germany: Bruckmann.

————. (1919) *Standards of Female Beauty, Based on Conscious Muscle Education: Ideals of Physical Beauty Passed through Thought and Fixed in Form.* New York: Schob & Wieser.

————. (1923) *Funktionelles Frauenturnen* (Functional gymnastics for women). Munich, Germany: Bruckmann.

————. (1923) "Mein System" (My system) in *Künstlerische Körperschulung* (Artistic training of the body), edited by L. Pallat and F. Hilker. Breslau, Germany: Hirt.

————. (1924) *Functioneele Lichaams-Oefeningen voor de Vrouw en het Kind* (Functional gymnastics for women and children). Amsterdam, Netherlands: H.J. Paris.

————. (1927) *Bewegungsprobleme: Die Gestaltung schöner Arme* (Movement problems: The creation of beautiful arms). Munich, Germany: Bruckmann.

————. (1929) *Anmut der Bewegung im täglichen Leben* (Graceful movement in daily life). Munich, Germany: Bruckmann.

————. (1931) *It's Up to You.* New York: A. Meusser.

————. (1954) *Look Better—Feel Better: The World-Renowned Mensendieck System of Functional Movements for a Youthful Body and Vibrant Health.* New York: Harper.

Mensendieck-Gymnastic. Vierteljährliches Mitteilungsblatt des Bundes für reine Mensendieck Gymmnastik e.V (Quarterly journal of the Association of Pure Mensendieck Gymnastics). Berlin, Germany: Bund für Reine Mensendieck Gymnastik (Only one volume published, in 1932).

————. (1937) *The Mensendieck System of Functional Exercises for Educating the Musculature According to the Mechanical Laws That Underlie Its Operation, and for Improving the Muscle-Automatism That Are Used for Performing Everyday Movements.* Portland, ME: Southworth-Authoesen.

MENSTRUAL CYCLE

The menstrual period is a cyclic event that is present throughout the reproductive years of most women. The cycle halts while a woman is pregnant or is using a hormonal method of contraception, and for many women, menstruation also ceases while they are breastfeeding. The hormonal fluctuations that occur during the menstrual cycle are related to sport and athletic performance in several ways. These hormonal changes might be expected to influence and be influenced by exercise. In addition, some problems associated with the menstrual cycle, such as severe cramps or heavy bleeding, might at times affect an athlete's performance.

Menstruation is a biological occurrence, but it nevertheless has cultural implications in most societies. The meanings associated with menstruation and customs regarding the role and status of menstruating women influence women's participation in sport. No cross-cultural research has been done on menstruation and sport, but research on menstruation in general suggests that in many cultures women's lives are restricted during menstruation.

Some of these restrictions involve prohibitions on contact with men, which reflect a belief that menstruating women are, from a religious perspective, polluting or impure and therefore will cause harm to men. Others restrictions are on women's activities, including seclusion in "menstrual huts." All of these affect women's participation in sports in some societies.

DEFINITIONS

Menarche is the time of a woman's first menstrual bleeding, and menopause is the time of her last

ADVICE FOR STRONG WOMEN (1883)

*A Nineteenth-Century Woman Offers Exercise
as a Cure for Menstrual Pain*

Menstruation should be entirely devoid of suffering. A woman should have no cognizance of this function, save by the discharge. Could this be the rule, instead of the prevalent exception, the capacity of strength and endurance either for work or pleasure would be increased one hundredfold. The nation not only needs strong men but strong women, strong in physical as well as mental development. This strength is required for prosecuting a persistent warfare against prevailing and existing wrongs, as well as for transmitting health and vigour to the coming generation.

A *woman in perfect health* need take no especial care and make no change in her manner of life at this period. But under our artificial habits of life, such a woman is the exception rather than the rule, and in most cases some attention must be paid to the recurrence of the menses.

Many young ladies in attendance upon school feel a need of some indulgence at that time and are often granted respite from duty. Women following any regular occupation have learned to plan a day of lighter work at the recurrence of the period. Yet on the contrary some have found that congestion and pain are relieved by occupation sufficient to interest the mind, with exercise adapted to increase the circulation.

ALICE B. STOCKHAM
(1883) Tokology: A Book For Every Woman. Chicago: Sanitary Publishing.

menstrual period. The average age of menarche in the United States is twelve. Menarche is considered delayed if it occurs after the age of sixteen. The average age of menopause is fifty-one. Many women experience irregular menstrual periods during the year after menarche and for about five years before menopause.

The typical menstrual cycle lasts twenty-eight days, with fourteen days between the first day of menstrual bleeding and ovulation, and another fourteen days from ovulation until the next menses. The first half of the cycle is considered the follicular phase, and the second half, the luteal phase. A woman's estrogen levels are low in the early follicular phase and highest at ovulation. The ovaries produce progesterone only after ovulation, during the luteal phase. Just before the onset of the menstrual period, estrogen and progesterone levels fall dramatically.

Researchers have found it difficult to design and interpret studies that involve different phases of the menstrual cycle because of the natural variations in menstrual cycle length, as well as variable definitions of menstrual cycle components. A normal menstrual cycle may last anywhere from twenty-six to thirty-five days, with the length of the follicular phase varying the most of the different phases. Studies use different definitions of "early," "mid," and "late" follicular, "menstrual," and "ovulatory" phases, and these definitions confuse the interpretation of study findings.

MENSTRUAL DYSFUNCTION

Female athletes seem to be prone to particular types of menstrual dysfunction that fall along a spectrum; these kinds of dysfunction occur more frequently in female athletes than in nonathletes.

Amenorrhea is the most extreme abnormality and usually refers to the absence of menstrual bleeding for six months or for a length of time equal to the sum of the three previous menstrual cycles. The International Olympic Committee (IOC) has defined amenorrhea as a condition in which a woman has had no more than one menstrual period in a year. Physicians classify a woman as amenorrheic if she has never had a menstrual period (primary amenorrhea), or if she has had one or more periods and then stopped menstruating (secondary amenorrhea). When medical professionals believe that exercise is the primary cause for amenorrhea in an athlete, the diagnosis is "exercise-associated" or "athletic" amenorrhea.

Oligomenorrhea refers to menstrual cycles longer than thirty-five days and is usually, but not always, associated with failure to ovulate. A luteal phase defect or inadequate luteal phase is the most subtle, and difficult to diagnose, abnormality of the menstrual cycle. In a luteal phase defect, ovulation occurs, but inadequate amounts of progesterone are produced after ovulation. Researchers do not know how common luteal phase defects are in athletes or in the general population, largely because the diagnosis requires a biopsy of the lining of the uterus or the drawing of multiple blood samples.

EFFECT OF MENSTRUAL CYCLE PHASE ON EXERCISE PERFORMANCE

Many female athletes believe that the phase of their menstrual cycle can affect their performance. Whether this is true or not, women have won medals and set records in all phases of the menstrual cycle. Very few scientific studies have focused on the influence of the phase of the menstrual cycle on athletic performance. Of those that have, most have shown little if any difference in maximal and less-than-maximal exercise performance in different phases of the menstrual cycle. Researchers have looked at various factors. They include oxygen uptake, the body's use of carbohydrate and fat, heart rate, respiratory exchange ratio, how much exertion the athlete feels she is putting out, how long it takes her to become completely fatigued, plasma lactate levels, and acute fluid replacement after exercise-induced dehydration.

Some studies show that the body may use slightly more energy during the luteal phase as compared to the follicular phase. Some investigators have proposed that strength-training sessions may be more effective if women plan them according to the phases of the menstrual cycle, with more frequent sessions in the follicular than in the luteal phase. However, none of the factors measured have been shown to translate into an actual change in exercise performance between phases of the menstrual cycle.

Similarly, investigators have not been able to show that amenorrheic athletes have reduced or less effective exercise performance compared to athletes with normal menstrual cycles. Some minor differences in measurable factors such as blood antioxidants may occur between these two groups, but these differences have not been shown to affect performance. One indirect effect on athletes with long-standing amenorrhea and low estrogen levels is bone loss that may result in musculoskeletal injuries and decreased performance.

EFFECT OF EXERCISE ON THE MENSTRUAL CYCLE

A spectrum of menstrual abnormalities seems to occur more frequently in female athletes. Some groups of female athletes have been shown to have delayed menarche. Ballet dancers, gymnasts, and young competitive runners seem to be at highest risk of this abnormality, but a young athlete may be at risk in any sport begun at an early age in which exercise is vigorous and low body weight is desirable.

Since the 1970s, investigators have recognized that certain groups of athletes, notably long-distance runners, gymnasts, and ballet dancers, have a higher incidence of amenorrhea, or absence of menstrual periods. Cyclists, rowers, swimmers, recreational weight lifters, and competitive body builders may also be at increased risk. Recently, as researchers have recognized the association of amenorrhea in some athletes with bone loss and with disordered eating, they have developed the concept of the female athlete triad (amenorrhea, osteoporosis, and disordered eating).

Female athletes also seem to have a higher incidence of more subtle abnormalities in the menstrual cycle, including oligomenorrhea and a luteal phase defect. At least one study suggests that these athletes may also be at increased risk for bone loss.

Evidence suggests that vigorous exercise alone, without weight loss, may induce luteal phase abnormalities or slight menstrual irregularity in some women. However, vigorous exercise is probably not sufficient by itself to delay menarche or lead predictably to amenorrhea. Most women will not develop amenorrhea from exercise alone; they generally also have low body weight and poor nutrition with caloric deficiency, and they also experience high levels of emotional stress.

MENSTRUAL CYCLE DISORDERS AND THE ATHLETE

Common problems associated with the menstrual cycle include dysmenorrhea, premenstrual syndrome, and heavy menstrual periods. Dysmenorrhea refers to crampy lower abdominal or back pain that occurs just before and with the onset of menstrual bleeding. Some athletes feel that exercise worsens their menstrual cramps; others believe that regular exercise diminishes the severity of symptoms. Most women have some dysmenorrhea, but it is mild enough so that they can control it successfully with ibuprofen or similar pain medications. When dysmenorrhea is severe, an athlete may be incapacitated, and her performance interrupted in cycles. In this case the athlete should be evaluated by a physician. Oral contraceptive pills can sometimes dramatically relieve dysmenorrhea.

Regular exercise may also alleviate some of the negative effects of the menstrual cycle. The normal hormonal changes associated with ovulation can result in a combination of premenstrual symptoms that include abdominal bloating, irritability, crying spells, fatigue, appetite changes, breast tenderness, and the sensation of fluid retention. Regular physical exercise has shown to diminish these physical symptoms in some women. However, as many as 10 percent of women report that these symptoms are severe enough to interfere with their usual activities; some of these women would be considered to have premenstrual syndrome. During the premenstrual phase of the cycle, severely affected women athletes may not perform as well as they would at other times.

A competitive athlete who experiences heavy or prolonged vaginal bleeding may also find it affects her performance. The heavy bleeding may itself be inconvenient at the time of competition. If the problem is persistent, it may result in anemia and fatigue. An athlete's performance may improve when this problem is recognized and corrected.

ORAL CONTRACEPTIVE PILLS

Many athletes are prescribed oral contraceptive pills at some time during their careers. Oral contraceptives are used for many things in addition to birth control. In the athlete, they may be prescribed to normalize menstrual bleeding, treat dysmenorrhea, or provide estrogen replacement for the amenorrheic athlete. The large selection of specific oral contraceptive pills on the market makes it difficult to examine their effect on exercise performance. The contraceptives may cause subtle changes in some variables, but studies do not show any consistent effect of oral contraceptives on exercise performance.

CONCLUSIONS

Female athletes can benefit from knowledge about the menstrual cycle and its interactions with exercise. An alteration of the menstrual cycle may be the first tangible sign of overtraining or poor nutrition and should signal athletes and trainers to reevaluate training programs. Early identification of disorders of menstrual function and treatment by health care providers may optimize an athlete's performance.

Lorna A. Marshall

See also Amenorrhea; Medicine; Reproduction

Bibliography

Buckley, Thomas, and Alma Gotleib, eds. (1988) *Blood Magic: The Anthropology of Menstruation.* Berkeley: University of California Press.

LeBrun, C. M. (1994) "The Effect of the Phase of the Menstrual Cycle and the Birth Control Pill on Athletic Performance." *Clinical Sports Medicine* 13: 419–441.

Marshall, Lorna A. (1994) "Clinical Evaluation of Amenorrhea in Active and Athletic Women." *Clinical Sports Medicine* 13: 371–387.

Speroff, L., R. H. Glass, and N. G. Kase. (1994) *Clinical Gynecologic Endocrinology and Infertility.* 5th ed. Baltimore: Williams & Wilkins.

Yeager, K. K., F. Agostini, A. Nattiv, and B. Drinkwater. (1993) "The Female Athlete Triad: Disordered Eating, Amenorrhea, Osteoporosis" (commentary). *Medicine & Science in Sports & Exercise* 25: 775.

MENTAL CONDITIONING

Mental conditioning and training are the processes by which an athlete prepares herself psychologically for performance or competition. Mental training techniques help athletes acquire physical skills, but they also aid in developing mental discipline and work habits, concentration, and techniques to manage stress and anxiety.

HISTORY

Mental conditioning and training for performance situations are practices that extend far back into history, perhaps prehistory. One can observe wild and domestic members of the cat family "dreaming" about the hunt, perhaps rehearsing the next day's chase. Modern athletes at rest may spontaneously visualize their events or be awakened from sleep by muscle spasms that mimic an actual performance. People have used mental training to achieve many goals and states, from the spiritual to the pragmatic. Those engaged in physical activity, from children at play to experienced athletes, use mental practice techniques to prepare themselves for their next stage of accomplishment. Two six-year-olds pretending they are world badminton champions as they hit back and forth in the yard have something in common with advanced athletes who integrate regular mental conditioning techniques into their training schedules.

FIVE COMPETENCIES NEEDED IN SPORT

The Psychology of Sport describes five forms of competence, all of which are important to the athlete's constructive development in sport and in life. The first of these is called *physical competence*, which includes the athlete's ability to control her body, as well as her physical skills. The second is *intellectual competence*, or the ability to solve problems with the mind. The third is management of feelings, termed *emotional competence. Social competence*, or the ability to deal with other people, is the fourth. The fifth is *spiritual* or *existential competence*, a person's realization of values and purpose in life.

The sport world today is biased toward the belief that mental training techniques are used exclusively to develop physical skills. The scope, in fact, is much broader. The techniques may be used for advancement in all five of the crucial areas of development. Mental training techniques do indeed help in acquiring physical skills, but they also help in developing mental discipline and work habits, concentration, and ways to manage stress and anxiety. Athletes can use them to rehearse for major meets and competitions, to overcome balks and errors, and to learn from setbacks or lost matches or games. They can also use them to increase their knowledge about sport and about life in general. All of these areas of competence go into the making of a top athlete.

DO-IT-YOURSELF TECHNIQUES

Professionals who teach mental conditioning techniques—such as coaches, sport psychologists, and psychologists—are merely using specifications and detailed programs to apply ancient practices. Most modern applications, too, have some scientific support from studies that show that they generally do have the desired effect. The field has expanded enormously since some of the first articles were published on mental practice in sport in Germany in the 1930s and in North America in the 1960s. It is, however, quite possible for athletes, or parents and their children, or coaches to practice some techniques on their own without professional aid. Most top athletes use mental practice naturally. The basic premise is that relaxation followed by mental rehearsal will expand one's feeling for sport skills, as well as the ability to execute them. The athlete merely needs to place herself in the center of her visualizations in which she is an active and successful agent of her sport. Ten very simple techniques follow that an athlete may do on her own.

1. Relaxation followed by visualization (of the desired states): The individual may sit in a chair or lie down, play music, and dream of future goals. She may imagine how it feels to acquire a new skill, to be good enough to compete with the best, and to travel and become part of the culture of world sport.

2. Positive thinking or positive self talk: Most people have heard of the old Émile Coué (1857–1926) advice, to look in a mirror each morning and repeat three times "Every day in every way I am getting better and better." An athlete might choose one skill to work on over and over in her mind's eye. She would talk positively to herself each time. For example, "You can do it."

3. The use of tapes: An athlete may use tapes while relaxing for the purpose of increasing relaxation. These may be commercial relaxation tapes (available at most specialty stores) or tapes of her own voice citing the desired skills, dreams, and goals of the future.

4. Focused visualizations: The athlete may use organized images of whole games, routines, or specific executions perfectly done. She may use her mind's eye again to visualize perfect and smoothly executed shots or plays. She may watch herself react to a difficult call or umpire's error with renewed determination on the next play, as opposed to becoming upset.

5. Strategy review sessions: The athlete is practicing mentally when reviewing a game, strategy, goal, or other event with a coach, team, or other athletes. Many wise coaches set apart time, not for the pep talk, but for the mental training, discipline, and knowledge the athlete can acquire in group learning sessions.

6. Mirror feedback: An athlete may do full length mirror training (as do ballet dancers). This allows one to practice a movement or skill repeatedly with immediate visual feedback. It may be done in slow motion. It may be done in the privacy of one's own room at any time of day in any kind of weather.

7. Study of videos: The athlete may use videos of her own performance, perhaps taken by parents, coach, or friends, to see and understand not just the errors made but, more important, to see and feel again the successes and the skills being acquired. The videos of outstanding athletes in the same sport are invaluable. By watching and studying Olympic and world champions, the athlete can learn from the more advanced athlete's endurance, skill, and inspirational style.

8. Keeping a diary: The athlete may wish to keep a sports diary in which she records her emotional journey in sport. Enjoyable and difficult events may be recorded. Challenges and progress are noted day by day or week by week.

9. Pools and trampolines and other media: The athlete may enter another medium, for example, a pool or a trampoline. Through this new medium, the athlete can again imagine and repeat movements and skills in a changed tempo, thus increasing psychomotor skills and coordination.

10. Books: The athlete can read autobiographies and biographies (available at all age levels) to learn from the experiences and perspectives of outstanding athletes in the sport.

RESEARCH SUPPORT

Although many of the common aides discussed have been used for years by athletes, one of the first systematic reviews of research on mental practice in sport was the 1967 report by Alan Richardson. This was followed by a 1971 review by Dorothy Mohr and further updates by Deborah Feltz and Daniel Landers, and Feltz, Landers, and Betsy Becker, who used the advanced technique of meta-analysis to summarize the results across available studies. These authors conclude there is a scientific basis for the use of mental practice in sport skill training. Mental practice is a valuable adjunct or support for the training of athletes.

Another line of research support for mental conditioning or training comes from the well-established field of behavioral medicine as practiced by experimental clinical psychologists. Psychologists have long addressed the issue of changing behavior via the application of psychological techniques. Many dysfunctional behaviors and symptoms can be modified by applying behavioral techniques. Major contributions in this area are reported by Albert Bandura, Albert Ellis, Daniel Kirchenbaum, Richard Suinn, and Michael Mahoney, et al. The stress, anxiety, blocks, and compulsions experienced by people in everyday life are readily extrapolated to the extreme situations faced by many athletes as they try to overcome their hurdles, staleness, and the stress in sport. The eating disorders, substance abuse problems, sexual dysfunctions, and depressions found in athletes are also found in the general population. It is amazing that it took so long for the fields of sport and psychological intervention to converge.

But converge they have. Most of the authors named above have applied their findings from clinical, behavioral, and health psychology to sport. At the same time, professionals from human kinetics, physical education, and sport have expanded their fields so that mental training techniques have become a research field and a field of application.

A CAUTION

One problem that should have been foreseen lies in the overuse of mental training techniques. This may occur when enthusiasts try to impose the techniques on children who have little interest in them because they wish to run, jump, and experiment on their own. This has also occurred when personnel have scheduled long hours of mental training into the already overloaded schedules of advanced athletes. It is important for professionals to realize that after brief introductions to the techniques available, it is the athlete who must decide readiness for their adoption. The athlete is encouraged to experiment with them as long as she is motivated to do so.

PROFESSIONAL TECHNIQUES

The following are categories of technique used by professionals to overcome dysfunctional thought, behavior, and emotion that may block the development of the athlete. They are used with the intent of assisting the athlete toward maximum potential. There is much overlap with the do-it-yourself techniques already described.

1. Competence training. On a broad level, all mental training aims to increase the experience of inner control on the part of the athlete. Bandura's (1991) work on self-efficacy, William Morgan's pioneering work on effort sense, and this author's work on competence motivation focus upon the acquisition of feelings of mastery, agency, and personal control.

2. Relaxation and meditation. Relaxation is a technique often used to ready the athlete for various mental training techniques. Hundreds of commercial tapes on relaxation are available. There are several varieties of relaxation, explained by their titles. Some of these are relaxation tension contrasts, progressive muscle relaxation without tensing, and differential relaxation. Meditation was pioneered in North America by Herbert Benson in his best-selling book, *The Relaxation Response*. His breakthrough and the emerging interest in Asian meditation techniques applied to sport resulted in a number of highly readable books on such topics as the inner athlete, golf in the kingdom, and inner tennis. At the time of his writing, the "Zen" flavor of these books was quite foreign to the achievement-oriented American culture.

3. Positive thinking. Most forms of psychotherapy try to change negative thinking to positive thinking in the client. This is true of most cognitive therapies, including Aaron Beck's cognitive therapy for depressed people or

THE FIVE FORMS OF COMPETENCE

In order to be successful at sports, some experts say that an athlete must develop five forms of competence: physical, intellectual, emotional, social, and spiritual. Mental conditioning techniques used by athletes to prepare for competition can enhance all five forms of competence, but are most often employed to enhance physical performance.

Ellis' rational emotive therapy. A forerunner of these techniques was Maxwell Maltz's work, which he described in *Psycho-Cybernetics*. In sport, a range of specific techniques to encourage positive thoughts are used. Discriminant cue analysis trains the athlete to analyze the difference between positive and negative outcomes and to learn the cues for positive outcomes. Thought-stopping techniques refer to the interruption of dysfunctional thoughts and behaviors for the purpose of substituting positive ones. Paper-tracing rehearsals and "walk-through" techniques are additional methods of magnifying the positive.

4. Affective control. Some sport psychology techniques are specifically addressed to the control of overly aroused emotions or the stimulation of motivations and feelings if the athlete is under-aroused. Whatever the problem, too much or too little motivation or energy, it is clear the athlete prefers to be in control for maximum performance potential. David Roland's *The Confident Performer* gives the performer ready advice, while the work of Rainer Martens and associates on anxiety in sport reviews the research support for this approach.

5. Cognitive-behavioral techniques. These are direct applications from cognitive and behavioral psychology to sport training. An overview of the use of cognitive psychology in sport is supplied by Morgan and an example of behavioral analyses applied to sport is provided in Gary Martin's *Sport Psychology Consulting; Guidelines from Behavioral Analysis*.

6. Autogenic training, self-hypnosis, and bio-feedback. Each a separate technique or set of techniques, the three share an attempt to enable the athlete to gain control over the involuntary nervous system by homeostatic self-regulation. Autogenic training (Johannes Schultz and Wolfgang Luthe) is done without equipment and is a form of relaxation followed by muscle control training. Biofeedback (Gary Schwartz and Jackson Beatty) has been a very promising technique relying on physiological feedback from equipment. The

purchase of equipment may be burdensome and too expensive for many athletes. Self-hypnosis (Brian Alman and Peter Lambrou) is a time-honored set of techniques and disciplines using relaxation, imagery and self-talk to gain self-regulation.

7. Visual motor behavioral rehearsal (VMBR). This technique was developed by Suinn in working with Olympic caliber skiers. He used relaxation, ski course simulation, and simulated movement. Suinn has written a popular training manual.

8. Attentional control training. Robert Nideffer has developed one of the most erudite and complex methods for the analysis of athlete focusing styles. He measures several variations in attentional styles needed across and within sports (for example, broad attention needed in basketball to know where other players are, and narrow attention needed in the act of striking a golf ball, when the athlete must shut out distractions). Nideffer's system educates the athlete regarding attentional styles needed in specific sports and helps the athlete to adjust or correct as needed.

9. Religious and spiritual training. This emphasis should not be overlooked in sport. Arguably one of the most successful movements for behavioral change has come from twelve-step programs (growing out of the techniques of Alcoholics Anonymous). While there are no studies yet on the efficacy of twelve-step programs applied to sport behavior, many athletes have participated in these programs for many different purposes. These programs will likely become more popular in the future when applied directly to sport.

CONCLUSION

Around the professionalization of the field of mental conditioning and the complexities and details of many techniques, a field of academic investigation has developed. Yet many of these techniques have been around for centuries and can be practiced in simple ways by anyone who wants to enhance her mental condition. Thus some sportswomen find that they prefer to experiment on their own or perhaps with the help of coaches or other athletes. Others prefer to work with people with a professional background or to rely on techniques that have been evaluated through scientific research.

Dorcas Susan Butt

Bibliography

Alman, Brian M., and Peter T. Lambrou. (1995) *Self-Hypnosis: The Complete Manual for Health and Self-Change.* London: Souvenir Press.

Bandura, Albert. (1986) *Social Foundations of Thought and Action: A Social Cognitive Theory.* Englewood Cliffs, NJ: Prentice-Hall.

———. (1991) "Perceived Self-Efficacy in the Exercise of Personal Agency." *Journal of Applied Sport Psychology* 2: 128–163.

Beck, Aaron T. (1991) "Cognitive Therapy: A Thirty-Year Retrospective." *American Psychologist* 46: 368–375.

Benson, Herbert. (1975) *The Relaxation Response.* New York: Morrow.

Butt, Dorcas Susan. (1987) *The Psychology of Sport: The Behavior, Motivation, Personality and Performance of Athletes.* New York: Van Nostrand.

Cox, Richard H. (1998) *Sport Psychology: Concepts and Applications.* 4th ed. Boston: McGraw-Hill.

Ellis, Albert E. (1987) "The Impossibility of Achieving Consistently Good Mental Health." *American Psychologist* 42: 364–375.

Feltz, Deborah L., and Daniel M. Landers. (1983) "The Effects of Mental Practice on Motor Skill Learning and Performance: A Meta-Analysis." *Journal of Sport Psychology* 5: 25–57.

Feltz, Deborah L., Daniel M. Landers, and Betsy J. Becker. (1988) "A Revised Meta-Analysis of the Mental Practice Literature on Motor Skill Learning." In *Enhancing Human Performance: Issues, Theories, and Techniques,* edited by D. Drucklman and J. Swets. Washington, DC: National Academy Press, 1–65.

Owens, DeDe, and Daniel S. Kirschenbaum. (1998) *Smart Golf: How to Simplify and Score Your Mental Game.* San Francisco: Jossey-Bass.

Mahoney, Michael J., Tyler J. Gabriel, and T. Scott Perkins. (1987) "Psychological Skills and Exceptional Athletic Performance." *The Sport Psychologist* 1: 181–199.

Maltz, Maxwell. (1966) *Psycho-Cybernetics.* New York: Simon & Schuster.

Martens, Rainer, Robin S. Vealey, and Damon Burton. (1990) *Competitive Anxiety in Sport.* Champaign, IL: Human Kinetics.

Martin, Gary L. (1997) *Sport Psychology Consulting: Guidelines from Behavioral Analysis.* Winnipeg, Manitoba: Sport Science Press.

Mohr, Dorothy. (1971) "Mental Practice." In *Encyclopedia of Sports Sciences and Medicine.* New York: Macmillan, 52–55.

Moran, Aiden P. (1996) *The Psychology of Concentration in Sport Performance: A Cognitive Analysis.* Hove, UK: Psychology Press.

Morgan, William P. (1981) "Psychophysiology of Self-Awareness during Vigorous Physical Activity." *Journal of Sports Medicine and Physical Fitness* 52: 385–427.

Nideffer, Robert M. (1989) *Attention Control Training for Sport.* Los Gatos, CA: Enhanced Performance Services.

Richardson, Alan. (1967a). "Mental Practice: A Review and Discussion" (Part 1). *Research Quarterly* 38: 95–107.

———. (1967b). "Mental Practice: A Review and Discussion" (Part 2). *Research Quarterly* 38: 263–273.

Roland, David. (1997). *The Confident Performer.* London: Nick Hern Books.

Schultz, Johannes, and Wolfgang Luthe. (1959) *Autogenic Training: A Psycho Physiological Approach in Psychotherapy.* New York: Grune and Stratten.

Schwartz, Gary E., and Jackson Beatty. (1977) *Biofeedback: Theory and Research.* New York: Academic Press.

Suinn, Richard M. (1986). *Seven Steps to Peak Performance.* Toronto, Ontario: Luber.

Williams, Jean M., ed. (1993) *Applied Sport Psychology: Personal Growth to Peak Performance.* 2d ed. Mountain View, CA: Mayfield.

MEXICO

Mexico is in southern North America and has a population of 94 million. Mexico has a long history of sport. Women's participation in sports in Mexico is something of a paradox. On the one hand, women participated in two indigenous sports activities—the Mesoamerican ball game and Tarahumara running—that have drawn considerable attention from scholars and journalists. But, on the other hand, women in Mexico have been largely excluded from sports since the Spanish conquest began in 1520. To a large extent, this exclusion reflects the Spanish value system, which placed men in positions of power and relegated women to activities in the home. Even in the late 1990s, this ideology remained potent in Mexico; women form only 28 percent of the workforce, are allowed an abortion only if their life is at risk, and have an illiteracy rate almost twice that of men. In accord with this pattern, sport participation by women remains low in comparison to many other nations.

INDIGENOUS SPORTS

In the sport world, Mexico is perhaps best known for its indigenous Mesoamerican ball game, which began about 3,500 years ago but, repressed by the Spanish colonists, had largely disappeared by the end of the sixteenth century. Consequently, not a great deal is known about the game, and what is known comes primarily from the archaeological study of hundreds of ball court sites from as far south as Nicaragua to as far north as southern Arizona in the United States. The game was played on stone or earth courts with a rubber ball, which participants sought to knock through an elevated hoop using their feet, legs, and torsos but probably not their hands. The game was played for ritual purposes (to encourage fertility) and for recreation, and games were evidently the object of heavy betting. The games were taken so seriously that in games played at the highest levels of competition, before the rulers of ancient Mexican societies on elaborate stone courts, the losers might be sacrificed to the gods. One of the many unanswered questions about the Mesoamerican ball game is whether or not women participated. Some experts believe that there is a strong possibility that women participated in some form of the game. This view is supported by the discovery of small figurines with feminine features and special clothes, such as hand protectors, loin cloths, and short boots, that are associated with the sport. In addition, the arms of the figurines are protected with some kind of material, probably quilted, similar to those seen in representations of male players. From these artifacts, researchers infer that male and female players probably dressed similarly. Additional evidence from written sources suggests that there might have been separate games for men, women, and mixed competitions, and also that some women were so

Young women exercise in an aerobics class on the Plaza Principal in the historic district of San Miguel de Allende, Mexico. (Macduff Everton/Corbis)

skilled that their achievements were noted. There is also some archaeological evidence—again in the form of figurines—that women were spectators and perhaps gamblers at ball games.

Another indigenous sport, and one that survives into the late twentieth century, is the cross-country racing known as *carreras de arihueta* of the Tarahumara Indians in the state of Chihuahua in northwestern Mexico. The region is mountainous, and Tarahumara men and women are known throughout Mexico as long-distance runners. Some outsiders have attributed Tarahumara running endurance to genetic factors, although research suggests that it is actually "practice" in the form of long-distance travel on foot up and down hills and mountains that accounts for the Tarahumaras' ability. For example, studies have shown that Tarahumara children raised in schools outside the mountains have no greater endurance than do children in the general Mexican population. Men and women race, although not against one another. The races take place during the day and night, and they are accompanied by much ritual and heavy betting on the outcome. In the men's races, the men kick a ball as they race, using a long pole to move the ball from thickets or rocks. The women, depending on their community, use either a ball and a forked stick to move it along, or, more commonly, a hoop made of fiber and a stick to move it along. Tarahumara

UNKNOWN MEXICO (1902)

A Description of Mexican Women's Involvement in Games

Races are also run by women, and the betting and excitement that prevail on these occasions run as high as at the men's races, though on a smaller scale. Instead of tossing the ball with their toes, they use a large wooden fork, with two or three prongs, to pitch it forward. Sometimes they have a ring of twisted strips of yucca leaves instead of the ball, but more often two interlocked rings which they throw ahead with a stick curved at the end. This game, which is called *rowémala* (*rowé* signifies a ring), must be very ancient, for rings of this kind have sometimes been found in ancient cliff-dwellings. It is certainly a strange sight to see these sturdy amazons race heavily along with astonishing perseverance, when creeks and water-holes come in their way, simply lifting their skirts *à la Diane* and making short work of the crossing.

CARL LUMHOLTZ
(1902) Unknown Mexico: A Record of Five Years' Exploration of the Western Sierra Madre. *New York: Charles Scribner's Sons.*

races are team sports in which one player kicks or hurls the ball or hoop out in front and then the first team player to reach it does the same; the pattern continues until the race is finished. The rules for the women's races are about the same as for the men's, although the course is usually shorter and the women's race is accompanied by less ritual preparation. For example, women do not wear the rattling belts that are of ritual importance to the men. Also, it is claimed that, unlike the men, women do not cheat.

FROM COLONIAL TIMES TO THE 1990s

During the period of Spanish colonial rule, the Spanish introduced sports such as fencing, fighting with lances, foot races, and horseback racing that were useful for training Spanish soldiers. Native Mexicans were usually barred from participating in these activities. After independence, foot racing and horseback racing were retained as sports, as were *charrería* (rodeo), and bullfighting, although none of these involved women to any significant degree.

Sport in the modern sense emerged in Mexico at the end of the nineteenth and the beginning of the twentieth century, primarily as a form of recreation, although some sports such as rodeo and bullfighting also served as forms of mass entertainment. By the close of nineteenth century, soccer (association football), track and field, and basketball were being played in Mexico, although there is no evidence that they were being played on an organized basis.

During the Porfiriato era (1884–1911), the children of wealthy families who were educated overseas brought back new sports, such as basketball, from the United States and stimulated interest in existing sports such as soccer and track and field. In 1902 sport in Mexico received a boost when officials of the Young Men's Christian Association in the United States established a facility with a regulation-size basketball court, tennis court, and a rudimentary gym. The first women's basketball teams were formed in 1904 at the Conservatory and the Escuela Normal in Mexico City, with the first women's championship in Mexico City in 1922. This was ten years after the first sport competitions were held for men.

With women's participation in sports limited, relatively few Mexican women have participated in international sport competitions. The first woman to compete in the Olympic Games was Eugenia Escudero, in fencing at the 1932 Olympics. Over the next six Olympics, a total of only twenty-three women competed. In preparation for the 1968 Olympics, hosted by Mexico City, sports in general were promoted and considerable resources devoted to training athletes for the Games. Forty-two women were on the Mexican team, and they competed in swimming, fencing, and volleyball, with Pilar Roldán winning a silver in the foil in fencing and Maritere Ramírez a bronze in the 800-meter freestyle swim competition. At the 1968 Games, Enriqueta Basilio became the first woman to light the Olympic flame.

The combination of economic problems and the political turmoil following the 1968 Games led to a general collapse of support for sports, and women's sports at the highest level declined as well, with twenty-two women on the 1972 Olympic team, only five on the 1976 team, ten in 1980, twenty-one in 1984, eleven in 1988, twenty-four in 1992, and twenty-seven in 1996. In addition to the older sports, women added diving, rowing, and tennis to their roster of Olympic sports. The women's soccer team qualified as one of the sixteen teams in the 1999 Women's World Cup, but half the team was composed of Mexican-American women from the United States. The team did not make it out of the first round.

> *Charlotte Bradley Rues*
> *Colette Soto Caballero*
> *Norma Baraldi Briseño*

Bibliography

Bennett, Wendell C., and Robert M. Zingg. (1935) *The Tarahumara: An Indian Tribe of Northern Mexico.* Chicago: University of Chicago Press.

Nabakov, Peter. (1971) *Indian Running.* Santa Barbara, CA: Capra Press.

Pennington, Campbell W. (1963) *The Tarahumara of Mexico: Their Environment and Material Culture.* Salt Lake City: University of Utah Press.

MEYFARTH, ULRIKE

(1956–)

GERMAN HIGH JUMPER

When Ulrike Meyfarth competed in the high jump in the Munich Olympics at age sixteen, she was at the time the youngest woman to have competed in the Olympics. When she won, she be-

Ulrike Meyfarth of Germany during the high jump event at the 1984 Summer Olympics in Los Angeles. Meyfarth set an Olympic record with a jump of 2.02 meters. (AP Photos)

came the youngest athlete, male or female, to win a gold in track and field, a record that was still standing in 1999. She is the only woman to have won track and field gold medals in the same event in Olympics twelve years apart.

Meyfarth was born in Frankfurt on Main, West Germany, on 4 May 1956. She entered the international sporting stage at the 1972 Olympics in Munich with considerable flair. She drew much attention from the media, not only because of her young age, good looks, and school-girl persona, but also because of her dramatic victory in the high jump, in which she tied the world record held by her Austrian rival, Iona Gusenbauer. Meyfarth's victory was unexpected, as she was only the third-ranked high jumper on the German team; her winning jump was two and three-quarter inches higher than her previous best. The greatest drama came at the end of the competition, when Yordanka Blagoyeva of Bulgaria jumped higher than Meyfarth, but the jump was ruled a miss when the bar fell after she had already left the landing pit.

The victory made Meyfarth a European celebrity, but many experts believe that the stress of the dramatic competition and her unexpected success damaged her career. She performed poorly in international events until the early 1980s, when, more mature and physically developed, she won the World Cup high jump event in Rome in 1981 and the European title in Athens in 1982, setting a world record in the process. After finishing second in the world championships in 1983, she set another world record with a jump of 2.03 meters later in the year. In 1984 at the Olympics in Los Angeles, twelve years after her surprise victory at Munich, she won gold again, becoming the only woman to win medals in track and field in Olympics so many years apart.

After retiring from competition, Meyfarth married Dr. Roland Nasse in 1988. She became a fashion model and achieved considerable notoriety when she posed nude for the sculptor Arno Breker.

Gherardo Bonini

Bibliography

Matthews, Peter, Ian Buchanan, and Bill Mallon. (1993) *The Guinness International Who's Who of Sport*. Enfield: Guinness Publishing.

Quercetani, Roberto Luigi. (1991) *Storia dell'atletica moderna (1860–1990)*. Milano: Vallardi & Associati.

Umminger, Walter. (1992) *Die Chronik des Sports*. Harenberg: Chronik Verlag.

MILITARY SPORTS

Military sports for women began in World War II, the first war in which women served in physically active duty, if not combat. As it did for male soldiers, the military used sports to keep women recruits fit and to provide recreation.

HISTORY

In Western culture, the story of the woman warrior begins with the mythological Amazons, women who were said to remove a breast so that they could shoot a bow and arrow better. The Amazonian tradition notwithstanding, most cultures have denied women the opportunity to participate in defense. As a result, most women involved with the military have been either extraordinary, as was the case with Joan of Arc, or have been able to serve only if disguised as men.

This began to change in the twentieth century. In China, during the Long March of Mao Zedong's followers to refuge in Yenan in the 1930s, young women carried guns and helped defend the army as it retreated. Likewise, various guerrilla movements in Asia and Latin America began to use women members in combat roles. In the West, women first joined the service of the United States in 1917, when the U.S. Navy actively recruited telephone operators, who eventually worked alongside men on an equal basis during World War I, albeit not in combat.

Although military officials did show some concern for the physical fitness of these women, the overwhelming emphasis in Western armies during World War I was on improving the physical stamina and conditioning of the male soldiers and sailors. The U.S. Army focused on sports as a means of keeping the men fit to fight, and in so doing, followed the lead of the British. In the years between the two world wars, military planners met regularly to discuss the extent to which the military's sport program had successfully met its goals. They still gave little thought to women's sports, should women be admitted to military service in the future.

When World War II began in Europe, the British turned to young women as an important adjunct to their war effort. Women in uniform fired antiaircraft guns, operated communications equipment, and worked in other noncombat positions. In 1941, after the Japanese attacked Pearl Harbor and the Americans entered the war, the U.S. government was pressured to allow women to serve, and eventually all branches of the armed forces added women to their ranks. This marked the point when military officials began to consider how to keep those women fit and strong for the work they would be doing.

Because many of the women who joined the armed forces had had previous experience playing softball and other sports, a sport program quickly developed for women within the military. Teams of women from naval bases met teams from army posts to play softball, baseball, basketball, and to bowl. Similarly, individual units conducted competitions in other sports, including badminton and archery.

Despite their athletic skills, these women were subject to mockery and insult by the men with whom they served. Men questioned the value of assigning coaches to women. They asked whether military women could maintain their femininity while participating in sports. And they found ways to demonstrate their own supposed superiority in athletics. This was the case, for example, in some of the "mock" baseball games played between men's and women's military teams during the war. Men put on silly costumes and teased the women against whom they were competing.

Although the number of women in the armed forces declined rapidly after the war, the U.S. military continued to permit them to enlist. In 1948, during the Israeli war for independence, women also served in the armed forces there, although like the United States, Israel continued to keep women out of combat positions.

SPORT AND SERVICE ACADEMIES

With the second wave of feminism in America, women began to demand the right to attend the nation's all-male military academies. Once they were admitted, officials tried to devise appropriate opportunities for those women to play sports. Their task was complex; each military academy had a long tradition of requiring future officers to be skilled in multiple sports. At the Air Force Academy, for example, the male cadets had always been forced to learn to box, although they were taken off flight status if they suffered concussion. When the Air Force decided that the women's sport program should include fencing rather than boxing, many male cadets were bitter, believing that the difference in sport requirements was unfair to them. Each academy also struggled with the question of how far to push the physical fitness standards for women. Because women tend to have less upper body strength but more endurance than men, fitness and sport programs were first modified to reflect this. These modifications were also subject to criticism.

Although the struggle to define an appropriate level of physical fitness for military women continues, women within the American armed forces, as well as women at the military academies, continue to pursue their interests in sports. In so doing, they are applauded if they bring national championships to the academies, as has been the case at the Naval Academy. Likewise, women's athletic success is welcomed where it brings glory and recognition to their outfits. In this, sport programs for military women have come more and more to resemble sport programs

Women of the British Auxiliary Territorial Service camping in Kent do aerobic exercises. (Hulton-Deutsch Collection/Corbis)

for military men. The United States Military Academy at West Point, New York, has cadets participating in 25 intercollegiate sports. Female cadets compete in basketball, cross-country running, indoor track, outdoor track, rifle shooting, soccer, swimming, tennis, softball, and volleyball.

The past decade has brought a tremendous amount of change to the military, and women's sport programs have benefited from those changes. Military women have far more athletic opportunities today than they had in the past. Women in the armed forces compete in sports as varied as shooting and the luge. In doing so, they broaden the definition of what is physically appropriate competition for all women.

Wanda Ellen Wakefield

Bibliography

Holm, Maj. Gen. Jeanne. (1992) *Women in the Military: An Unfinished Revolution.* Rev. ed. Novato, CA: Presidio Press.

Stiehm, Judith Hicks. (1981) *Bring Me Men and Women: Mandated Change at the U.S. Air Force Academy.* Berkeley, CA: University of California Press.

Wakefield, Wanda Ellen. (1997) *Playing to Win: Sports and the American Military, 1898–1945.* Albany: State University of New York Press.

MILLER, CHERYL

(1964–)

U.S. BASKETBALL PLAYER

With her athletic prowess and her engaging and exuberant style of play, Cheryl Miller contributed to the growing popularity and visibility of women's basketball in the United States in the 1980s. In 1995 her achievements earned her a spot in the Naismith Memorial Basketball Hall of Fame.

Miller was born on 3 January 1964 in Riverside, California. She learned to play basketball on a backyard court with her father, Saul, a former college player, and her younger brother, Reggie, who would go on to be a star player in the National Basketball Association (NBA) and the Olympics. Six-foot-three-inch Miller propelled Riverside Polytechnic High School to a 132–4 record, including an 84-game winning streak. She averaged 33.8 points per game and once scored 105 points in a single game. In her senior year, she led her team to the California state title, scoring 41 points in the championship game. Miller was the first high school athlete, male or female, named as a Parade All-American four years in a row (1979–1982).

Of the nearly 250 offers she received, Miller chose a scholarship from the University of Southern California (USC). Her first year, USC won the NCAA national title and Miller was named most valuable player (MVP) of the tournament. That summer Miller led the United States to a gold medal at the 1983 Pan American Games, scoring 99 points in five games. That same summer, at the world championships, Miller was the leading scorer on the U.S. team, which lost the gold medal to the Soviets by two points.

In 1984, USC repeated as national champions and Miller again was named tournament MVP. That summer in Los Angeles, Miller sparked the United States to its first Olympic gold medal in women's basketball, leading the team in scoring, rebounds, steals, and assists.

In her junior and senior years at USC, Miller averaged over 26 points per game and saw post-

American Cheryl Miller dribbles the ball and looks toward teammate Lynette Woodard in a basketball game against the Cuban team in the 1983 Pan-American games. (Bettmann/Corbis)

season play each year, with her team finishing second in the NCAA tournament in 1986. She was a four-time All-American and three-time Naismith Player of the Year. She left USC with a 112–20 record, having set records at the school for most career points, rebounds, field goals, and free throws. Her jersey, bearing the number 31, was the first basketball jersey retired in USC history.

In the summer of 1986, Miller helped end the Soviet dynasty in women's basketball. As the U.S. team triumphed in the Goodwill Games and the world championships, both held in Moscow, Miller scored the most American points in both competitions.

A severe knee injury rerouted her passion for basketball in new directions. She coached at her alma mater for seven years, posting a 44–14 record during her two years as head coach (1993–1995).

Miller also worked as a sports commentator for several television networks and in November 1996 became the first woman to do play-by-play reporting for a nationally televised NBA game. When the Women's National Basketball Association (WNBA) started in 1997, Miller became the head coach and general manager of the Phoenix Mercury. She motivated her team to reach the playoffs during the league's first two seasons.

Kelly Nelson

Bibliography

California High School. (1997) *Cal-Hi Sports Record Book and Almanac.* Long Beach, CA: Student Sports Magazine.

Kirkpatrick, Curry. (1985) "Lights! Camera! Cheryl!" *Sports Illustrated* (November 20).

USA Basketball. (1999) <http://www.usabasketball.com>.

MILLIAT, ALICE

(1884–1957)

FRENCH ADVOCATE FOR WOMEN'S SPORTS

Born in Brittany and endowed with the independent spirit that is said to characterize that Celtic region of western France, Alice Million Milliat was a pioneer in the promotion of women's track-and-field sports in her own country and throughout the world. She began her career as a member of Fémina Sport, a Parisian club founded in 1911 to encourage sports among upper-class women. Her own favorite sport was rowing. In 1917, when Fémina Sport joined a number of other clubs to form the Fédération des Sociétés Féminines Sportives de France (FSFS), Milliat was named the federation's treasurer. Two years later, she became president. After the FSFS staged France's first track-and-field championships for women in 1917, Milliat worked hard to organize additional national championships in soccer, basketball, and a number of other sports. Early married, early widowed, and childless, Milliat had the time, the

energy, and the material resources to dedicate herself wholeheartedly to women's sports.

Although a number of historians have erroneously asserted that Milliat was the organizer of the Women's Olympics that were staged in Monte Carlo in the summer of 1921, that honor belongs to Camille Blanc, mayor of Beaulieu and president of the socially exclusive International Sporting Club of Monaco. On 31 October 1921, only five months after the games at Monte Carlo proved the viability of international competitions for women, Milliat founded the Fédération Sportive Féminine Internationale (FSFI) and began to plan for the first Jeux Internationaux Féminins (Women's International Games). These games, which were referred to as the Jeux Olympiques Féminins (Women's Olympic Games), were held in Paris on 10 August 1922. Over 20,000 spectators crowded Le Stade-Pershing to watch athletes from five nations compete in the eleven-event program, which included a 1000-meter race, a distance then considered to be an enormous challenge for a young woman.

Although the French press was enthusiastic about these women's games, the International Amateur Athletic Federation (IAAF) and the International Olympic Committee (IOC) were not. Despite this initial opposition, for the next fifteen years Milliat campaigned for the right of female athletes of all social classes to compete as freely as their male counterparts. (As a fully committed feminist, she also fought for the right of women to vote.) While Milliat acknowledged the appeals of traditional femininity, she argued that a woman's strength, endurance, and speed were as socially desirable as charm, poise, and grace. Unlike many advocates of women's sports, she seems to have had no qualms about muscular development for women.

Between 1922 and 1934, Milliat was the main force behind three highly successful Women's International Games at Gothenburg, Sweden (1926), Prague (1930), and London (1934). She also presided over no fewer than nine international conferences on women's sports (held in Paris, Gothenburg, Amsterdam, Prague, Vienna, London, and Berlin).

Milliat's bold initiatives compelled the IAAF and the IOC to reconsider their initial hostility to women's sports. Although Sigfrid Edström, the

Swedish IOC member who was also the founder and president of the IAAF, was unhappy about Milliat's challenge, he eventually opted for compromise and persuaded Milliat, in 1926, to renounce all use of the word Olympique and to accept IAAF rules and regulations (revised for women when necessary). The IAAF then persuaded the International Olympic Committee to include women's track and field in the program for the 1928 games in Amsterdam.

Milliat's victory was partial. The IOC limited women's track and field to a mere five events: the 100-meter and 800-meter races, the high jump, the discus, and the 4 × 100–meter relay. Even this partial victory was endangered by the IOC's hysterical reaction to the sight of women who were exhausted by the 800-meter race. The IOC voted in 1929 to drop women's track and field. Thanks in part to assistance from America's Avery Brundage, who was then a major figure in the IAAF, Milliat managed to persuade the IOC to change its collective mind and keep women's track and field on the program for the 1932 games in Los Angeles. (The vote was 17–1.)

During the Berlin Olympics of 1936, the IAAF agreed officially to sponsor women's events and to accept the FSFI's records, which were two of Milliat's goals, but she lost the fight to maintain the FSFI as a separate organization. The last of the FSFI's quadrennial sports festivals, held in Vienna in 1938, was officially sponsored by the IAAF, and it was downgraded to the level of a European championship. Milliat, now over fifty, retired from the international stage.

Allen Guttmann

Bibliography

Bernett, Hajo. (1988) "Die ersten 'olympischen' Wettbewerbe im international Frauensport." *Sozial- und Zeitgeschichte des Sports* 2, 2: 66–86.

Durry, Jean. (1996) *Almanach du sport: Des origines 1939*. Paris: Encyclopedia universalis.

Guttmann, Allen. (1991) *Women's Sports: A History*. New York: Columbia University Press.

Hubscher, Ronald, Jean Durry, and Bernard Jeu. (1992) *L'Histoire en mouvements: Le sport dans la société française*. Paris: Armand Colin.

Leigh, Mary H., and Thérése M. Bonin. (1977) "The Pioneering Role of Madame Alice Milliat and the FSFI in Establishing International Trade [*sic*] and Field Competition for Women." *Journal of Sport History* 4, 1: 72–83.

Serra, Luciano. (1969) *Storia dell'atletica europea, 1793–1968*. Rome: Edizioni di Atletica leggera.

MITTERMAIER, ROSI

(1950–)

GERMAN ALPINE SKIER

Rosi Mittermaier was the most successful of the three Mittermaier sisters (the others being Heidi and Evi) who skied for Germany in the Olympics and on the world tour in the 1960s and 1970s. Mittermaier actually had something of an inconsistent career, winning ten World Cup races from

Rosi Mittermaier competing in the World Cup at Copper Mountain, Colorado, in 1976. (AP Wide World Photos)

1969 to 1976, but never entering the ranks of the best Alpine skiers until 1976 when she took three Olympic medals and the World Cup.

Mittermaier was born in Reit-im-Winkel, West Germany, on 5 August 1950. As part of a skiing family, she won her first German title in 1967 and began competing in the just-organized World Cup, which pitted the best skiers in the world against one another on the toughest Alpine courses. Although technically talented, and expected to do well, she was inconsistent and never rose to the top of the sport. This changed, however, in 1975–1976, her last season of competitive skiing, when the opportunity for victory was opened up to all women skiers by the temporary retirement of Annemarie Moser-Proell (1953–), the Austrian who had won thirty-six World Cup races in the previous three seasons. Mittermaier took advantage of the opening and won the overall World Cup (for combined victories in the downhill, slalom, and giant slalom), becoming the first German to do so.

Her success on the World Cup tour made her one of the pre-Olympic favorites for the 1976 Alpine events, with the possibility that she might win all three downhill races, something never achieved by a woman. Only two men, Toni Salier of Austria in 1956 and Jean-Claude Killy of France in 1968, had ever won all three events. Mittermaier won the slalom, then the downhill (the first and only time she won the event in her career), and then missed winning three golds when she finished second in giant slalom by twelve-hundredths of a second behind the surprise winner, Kathy Kreiner (1958–) of Canada. Due to poor weather, the giant slalom was run in only one (rather than two) heats, a unique decision in the history of winter Olympics, and it is likely that Kreiner benefited from the smooth course she encountered as the first skier down the hill.

Following the Olympics, Mittermaier retired, enjoying celebrity status in Germany and the Alpine skiing community. She married former German Alpine skier Christian Neureuther and became a one-woman publicist for skiing, appearing on numerous television and radio talk shows, writing magazine articles and books about skiing, and starring in videos about skiing.

Gherardo Bonini

Bibliography

Oddo, Guido. (1976) *Il libro dello sci.* Milan: Arnoldo Mondadori Editore.

Umminger, Walter, ed. (1992) *Die Chronik des Sports.* Harenberg: Chronik Verlag.

MOSER-PROELL, ANNEMARIE

(1953–)

AUSTRIAN ALPINE SKIER

Annemarie Proell—Moser-Proell after her marriage in 1973—is generally considered to be the best female Alpine skier of all time. Although she won only one Olympic gold medal and thus won little international acclaim outside her sport, she won six World Cup overall championships, four more than any other woman skier.

Annemarie Proell was born in Kleinarl, Austria, on 27 March 1953. Her parents were farmers and outdoorspersons, and she and her seven brothers and sisters were encouraged to ski and engage in other outdoor winter sports. She taught herself to ski and at the close of the 1968–1969 season took second place in one of the last downhill races of the season.

Her real success began in 1970 when she took the bronze medal in the downhill at the world championships. In the following year, her dominance of Alpine skiing began when she won the first of five consecutive (1971–1975) World Cup overall titles, an achievement never duplicated by any other female or male skier. The major disappointment in this five-year run was her failure to take a gold at the 1972 Olympics in Sapporo, Japan, as she finished second to Switzerland's Marie Therese Nadig in both the downhill and the giant slalom. Nonetheless, it was a combination of these five titles, victories in individual races on the tour, her aggressive style and competitiveness, and her superior speed that led experts to label her the best woman skier of all time.

Annemarie Proell relaxes after winning her fourth straight World Cup downhill race in 1973. (Bettmann/Corbis)

At the end of the 1975 World Cup season, Proell stunned the skiing world by announcing her retirement, at the age of only twenty-two and with the prospect of several more successful years ahead. She had married Herbert Moser, an Austrian soccer (association football) player, in 1973, and after retirement had a child, opened a café, and sat out the 1976 Olympics in Innsbruck, Austria. By the end of 1976, however, she resumed training and then competed on the World Cup tour. In 1979, she took her sixth World Cup overall title and in 1980 at the Olympics in Lake Placid she took her sole gold Olympic medal, in the downhill, this time defeating Nadig. She then retired for the second time, with a total of sixty-two victories in World Cup events, a record for women and second only to Swedish skier Inge-

mar Stenmark. She was elected to the International Women's Sport Hall of Fame in 1982.

Gherardo Bonini

Bibliography

Matthews, Peter, Ian Buchanan, and Bill Mallon. (1993) *The Guinness International Who's Who of Sport.* London: Guinness Publishing.

Oddo, Guido. (1976) *Il Libro Dello Sci.* Milan: Arnoldo Mondadori Editore.

Umminger, Walter, ed. (1992) *Die Chronik des Sports.* Munich: Chronik Verlag.

MOTA, ROSA

(1958–)

PORTUGUESE MARATHONER

Rosa Mota, one of Portugal's most successful international athletes, was one of the leading women marathoners of the 1980s. Mota was born on 29 June 1958 in Porto, Portugal, and started to run as a child because, by her own account, she was afraid of the darkness and wolfmen. In 1972, when she was fourteen years old, she entered her first school track and field meet and in the following year began her career in running.

Mota specialized in the distance events and in 1981 drew international attention when she won the prestigious Saint Silvester Race, in Sao Paulo, Brazil. (In the years following, she won the Saint Silvester Race seven consecutive times.) She won her first marathon at the European championship in Athens in 1982, and in April 1983 she won the Rotterdam Marathon. In the 1984 Olympics (the first Olympic Games in which women ran a separate marathon), Mota won the bronze medal. The following year she won the marathon in the Stuttgart European championship. In August 1987 she won the gold medal in the Rome world championship, and she also won the Boston Marathon. When she repeated her victory in the Boston Marathon the following year, she became the first woman to win two consecutive Boston Marathons. Later in the year, she won the gold medal at the Olympics in Seoul. This series of victories in major marathons placed her, with Grete Waitz and Ingrid Kristiansen of Norway, among the leading female marathoners in the world in the 1980s.

Her success also made her a celebrity at home, and she did much to promote sports in Portugal. In January 1989 she had to drop out of the Osaka marathon, but she finished second in the Los Angeles Marathon and first—for the third time in each—in the Boston Marathon and the European championship. At the London World Cup in 1991, she won her last major race with a time of 2 hours 26 minutes 14 seconds. Later that year, she had to drop out of the Tokyo Marathon. Recovering from surgery, she also failed to finish the 1992 London and 1994 Tokyo Marathons. From then on, she raced for pleasure and to support social causes rather than to win major races.

During her career Mota won more major city marathons (London, Tokyo, Chicago, Boston, Rotterdam, and Osaka) than any other woman. In addition to the marathon, from 1977 to 1985 she competed internationally in races from 1000 meters to 20,000 kilometers, and during that time she held nineteen Portuguese records.

Manuela Hasse

Wilma Rudolph (right), winner of three gold medals in track and field in the Rome Olympics in 1960, training her 14-year-old daughter in 1973. (Bettmann/Corbis)

MOTHERHOOD

Motherhood affects a woman's participation in physical activity and sports in several ways. The first is through a loss of the free time needed to play a sport or engage in some recreational fitness activity, such as running. The second is through diminished energy, as taking care of children and home is a physically demanding task, one that may leave women without much interest in further activity. On the other hand, motherhood can have a positive impact on girls' and women's involvement in sports, as it affords women the opportunity to involve their daughters in sports and to share that experience with them.

CULTURAL PERSPECTIVE

In the Western world, women's lives have been, and are still, determined by the gender-specific segregation of work that has given them the primary responsibility for domestic work and child care. The combination of paid employment and unpaid housework is the basis and precondition of the functioning of modern industrial societies. However, the reality for many women, today and in the past (particularly working-class women), has been a dual role that combines paid and unpaid work in the public and private spheres. The combination of paid employment and unpaid housework is the basic division of labor of modern societies.

Many studies confirm that housework and domestic labor remain women's work. Motherhood, however, places an even greater demand on women's lives. A considerable body of literature and research suggests that "mothering" is in effect defined by each society, with the prevailing beliefs identifying what it means to be a good mother. This places powerful emotional, social, and physical responsibilities on women that can have a tremendous effect on the rest of their lives. Women react differently to situations that combine paid work and mothering; they experience different contradictions, negotiate different compromises, and derive different pleasures. Indeed, the same woman may react differently to these combined responsibilities at different stages of her life. Part of the question, for many women, is how they combine these things with leisure activities.

LEISURE AND MOTHERHOOD

Little research has focused specifically on leisure and motherhood. The studies that have been done tend to emphasize the constraints on women's leisure. One key issue in understanding women's experiences of leisure is the significance of time: women's time is frequently fragmented among various responsibilities, and this fragmentation affects their opportunities to take part in leisure activities. The very notion of a separate sphere defined as leisure has little meaning for many women with children. For many mothers, leisure is not an activity or something that they do, but rather a moment snatched for quiet thought between meals, a meeting with other mothers on the playground, or fifteen minutes to read.

The responsibilities of caring for children do not eliminate free time, but they do mean that advance planning of leisure activities is difficult, at times impossible. For many women, much of their time is devoted to the leisure of their children or partners. Women make possible the leisure activities of others, often at the expense of either having or using leisure of their own. Many women's leisure is also affected by lack of mobility and lack of money, particularly women with small children.

Child care is clearly a crucial problem for mothers who want to pursue leisure activities. Often, women find it takes so much time and money to organize child care that it is easier to forgo the leisure activities.

Mothers' leisure lives are not, however, totally determined by the restrictions imposed by time, finance, partners, and other outside factors. The question is, how do women use their leisure time and how do they negotiate time and space in spite of the many restrictions imposed on them? New studies of women's lives see leisure activities not only as problematic but also as having the potential for resistance—meaning that women can find ways to use their leisure to resist expectations about their duties and their roles. For instance, if women meet with other women and talk about their problems, then they can see that it is not their own fault that they do not manage to be a "perfect" mother, homemaker, or employed worker. They can learn how to manage or deal with this expectation. Perhaps by refusing a task or by asking the husband to take over responsibilities, women can use their leisure to get stronger, physically and psychologically. Women create their own positive experiences and gain relative freedom in their leisure lives, a perspective that is also linked to the notion of leisure as empowerment. Furthermore, just as the term *women* cannot be used to describe the lives and experiences of all women, neither can the term *mother* be used without recognizing that each mother is different.

CHILDREN WELCOME ON THE LPGA TOUR

The Ladies Professional Golf Association is one of the most child-friendly professional sports associations. It created the first day-care program for professional women athletes when it initiated a child care program to accompany the tour with support from the Smuckers Corporation. In 1999 women golfers on the tour had a total of 77 children in the program. The LPGA also allows children under the age of 15 to attend its tournaments for free when accompanied by an adult.

Women run with baby carriages in the Royal Victoria 8-km race outside the parliamentary buildings in Victoria, British Columbia, Canada. (Kevin R. Morris)

PHYSICAL ACTIVITIES OF MOTHERS

Being a mother, it would seem, could have a powerful influence on women's opportunities to take part in sport. Documenting this contention is difficult; little research, either quantitative or qualitative, has examined how motherhood affects the physical activities of women or of active athletes who combine motherhood with a physically active lifestyle. Some studies conducted in Germany and in Norway indicate that mothers are less active in sport than childless women of the same age and that mothers who do keep participating in sport do so less intensely and for less time.

Another study yields further information about the meaning and function of sport in the lives of mothers. Some 200 women were interviewed in England, Norway, and Germany. The group included forty mothers with small children; all subjects were active in tennis, soccer, or aerobics/gymnastics. One of the central questions concerned the way in which women organize their daily lives and how they find the time and opportunity to participate in sport. Regardless of the country, women with children mentioned very similar problems and used very similar strategies to cope with them.

The interviews with mothers showed clearly how important sport was in their lives, although this group might not be typical because they were the ones who remained active in sport despite the responsibilities and burdens of family life. Balancing that, however, was the finding that mothers report the same motives for their involvement in sports that are mentioned in broader participation surveys: fun, enjoyment, relaxation, social life, slimness, fitness, and health. Women with small children would often have some specific reasons for taking part in a sport. For example, they particularly emphasized relaxation and compensation for the isolation and weight of their family responsibilities. They also used sport to channel aggression, to break out of the daily routine, and to meet other people.

NEGOTIATING THE CONSTRAINTS

Women can achieve these positive effects, however, only by negotiating the many responsibilities that constrain them. One of the key problems mothers mentioned in the interviews is lack of time. This, in turn, is often connected with a feeling of guilt because mothers perceive that they do not have enough time for all their responsibilities. Some of them doubt if they have the right to take time for themselves to play and enjoy sport. Pressured by insufficient time, women are forced to set priorities and organize their work very efficiently. The mothers interviewed, however, found ways and means to deal with their time restrictions. Some changed to a different sport or participated less.

Child care is another major issue for mothers who want to be active in sport. Many of the women interviewed were convinced that they were responsible for arranging child care during their physical activities. Others imposed this same expectation on them, an expectation that some identified as a major pressure. Around one-third of the women interviewed in the three countries had arranged regular care for their children during their sport time. Although relieved once this care had been arranged, arranging it nevertheless involved considerable organization. Others interviewed had no fixed routine and so had to find new arrangements each time they wanted to play or take part in sport. For mothers with small children, it is extremely difficult to meet on short notice to go for a jog or play tennis.

The women most frequently used family members as baby sitters, which had advantages and disadvantages. Partners played the most important role in looking after the children, and most of the women appreciated the support they received from their partners. At times, however, conflicts arose when the partner had priorities other than his family or when both partners wanted to take part in some activity. To resolve this, many of the women who were involved in tennis or soccer took their children to the sport venue with them, especially if the children were school age.

Few of the women had access to or made use of institutional childcare. Nurseries or day-care centers tended not to be open when the women wanted to participate in their sport, and the women had often fixed training hours, frequently in the early evenings. Therefore few women, not surprisingly, mentioned institutional child care as a solution. Some fitness studios offered child care as a special service. Some of the mothers welcomed this service in principle but pointed out, also, that it did not solve all their problems. Often child care is expensive, offered only at certain hours, or not of high quality.

Perhaps most important was the mention that many mothers made of how much time and energy are required to transport a baby either to the studio or to grandparents. A baby has to be satisfied, fed, and dressed in new diapers; fresh diapers, food, fresh clothes and toys, a cart or a carrying bag must all be carried along. Understandably, then, some mothers prefer to stay at home even if child care is offered.

A key issue is the responsibility and sense of duty that many women feel toward their children. Many women feel that they should be their children's sole caregiver. Many face the classic triple bind: the conflicting demands of paid work, child care, and sports or leisure. Many of these women feel that because they are already leaving their children for their employment, they should not take time for themselves that again takes them away from their children.

"K2 IS NOT FOR MOTHERS"

If the question remains whether mothers have the right to leave their children to take part in sports or other activities, then mothers taking risks and participating in dangerous sports enter a still more contested terrain. High-risk sports have been and are often still viewed as a demonstration of masculinity. What have women and even mothers to seek in sports like car racing or mountaineering? The deaths of the famous "mountaineering mum" Alison Hargreaves while climbing K2 in 1995 and of the Austrian downhill ski racer Ulrike Maier led to a heated debate about whether women with children have the right to take risks with their lives in their sports. Alison Hargreaves herself felt pulled in two, as she confessed in her diary, wanting her children and wanting K2. Whereas the media described the death of Hargreaves as tragic and emphasized her status as a mother, the fatal accidents of male climbers are often depicted as heroic deeds, even if they leave a pregnant wife or children behind.

Though mothers engaged in dangerous sport activities are still confronted with a great deal of criticism, mothers in top-level sport are increasingly accepted. In the 1940s the "flying housewife," Fanny Blankers-Koen, was famous not only because of her gold medals at the Olympic Games in London in 1948, but also because she had two children. Today there is no doubt that motherhood has no negative effect on sport performances, and among the top-level athletes are several mothers. Some of them, such as the Norwegian long-distance runner Ingrid Kristiansen, can even improve their performance after having a baby. Another good example is the German long jumper Heike Drechsler, who won her gold medal at the Games in Barcelona in 1992, when her child was three years old.

CONCLUSION

Sport can play—indeed it does play—an important role in the lives of women even after they have children. Physical activities have similar meanings for mothers as for women in general and can contribute to the well-being of all. Physical recreation appears to be especially important as a way of relieving the strain of mothers' daily work. However, mothers have to arrange child care if they are to participate in sport, and results of research showed that this remains the woman's responsibility and is a complex and time-consuming task.

Providing high-quality child care, then, remains a priority if mothers are to remain involved in sports. Another solution to the dilemma of child care could be to arrange sport activities for families, as is done in Germany and Norway. Family sport can also be played independent of clubs and organizations by going to swimming pools, skating rinks, parks, lakes, and other facilities. In a German survey, around 40 percent of the married women who were active in sports reported that they participated with someone from their family. Many mothers are playing sports with their children and see this as a positive aspect of family life. Family activities, however, have disadvantages as well; they do not meet the needs of many mothers who seek time for themselves, away from responsibilities of the home and children.

Gertrud Pfister

Bibliography

Deem, Rosemary. (1986) *All Work and No Play: The Sociology of Women and Leisure.* Milton Keynes, U.K., and Philadelphia: Open University Press.

Fasting, Kari, Gertrud Pfister, Sheila Scraton, and Ana Bunuel. (1997) "Transnational Research on Women and Sport: Some Theoretical, Methodological and Practical Challenges." *Women in Sport and Physical Activity Journal* 6, 1: 85–109.

Green, Eileen, Sandra Hebron, et al. (1990) *Women's Leisure, What Leisure.* London: Macmillan.

Henderson, Karla, and Deborah Bialeschki. (1994) "Women and the Meanings of Physical Recreation." *Women in Sport and Physical Activity Journal* 3, 2: 21–37.

Pfister, Gertrud. (1998) *Sport im Lebenszusammenhang von Frauen: Ausgewählte Themen.* Schorndorf, Germany: Hofmann.

Schön, Bärbel, ed. (1989) *Emanzipation und Mutterschaft: Erfahrungen und Untersuchungen über Lebensentwürfe und mütterliche Praxis.* Weinheim and Munich: Iuventa.

Shaw, Susan M. (1994) "Gender, Leisure, and Constraint: Towards a Framework for the Analysis of Women's Leisure." *Journal of Leisure Research* 26, 1: 8–21.

Wimbush, Erica, and Margaret Talbot, eds. (1988) *Relative Freedoms.* Milton Keynes, U.K., and Philadelphia: Open University Press.

MOTIVATION

What motivated Wilma Rudolph to overcome her battle with polio and racism, prevailing as the first female African-American Olympic hero? Why are Muslim women motivated to participate in sports despite the oppressive disapproval of their country? What motivates a mother to play an instrumental role in her children's athletic success by providing a virtual taxi service between their lessons and competitions?

Motivation is a fascinating, complex entity that has become the focus of psychological research, primarily in the past twenty-five years. Though significant progress has been made in examining the components of this multidimensional construct, the study of motivation is in its infancy, particularly with respect to gender differences in motivation. Consistent with the majority of sport research, considerable overlap seems to exist in achievement behavior of males and females. The differences that have been uncovered may be related to societal influences on sex roles, as opposed to biological factors.

The term *motivation* is used in divergent contexts. Within the scope of this article, motivation will be defined by two major components: drive and direction. *Drive* refers to the energy or effort allocated to a particular behavior. Drive is manifested in behaviors such as persistence, intensity, and willingness to attend to performance of an action. *Direction* refers to the form and venue that action takes and indicates goals for the behavior. In explaining why someone participates in sports, the question involving choice of sport relates to the motivational direction, while the effort allocated to perfection of the sport refers to the motivational drive.

At the foundation of motivated behavior is personality. Influences on the development of personal reality define the direction in which one proceeds and the energy assigned to the efforts. Examples of major elements in personality development include; society, genetics, significant others (e.g., parents, peers, teachers), culture, spirituality (morals, values, and truths about the world), and environment (action consequences, success and failure experiences). With so many components involved, the massive complexities associated with personal motivation and motivated behaviors begin to emerge.

THEORIES OF MOTIVATION

Motivational theories have developed from the early 1900s, when prevailing sentiments regarded "mechanistic" views as appropriate models for explanation. These views held that people were motivated by internal drives for maximal pleasure (hedonism) and maintenance of equilibrium (stability of the system). These innate "mechanisms" were thought to determine the direction and intensity of behavior, and the individual was considered passive in terms of effect on motiva-

tion. In the 1940s the emergence of behaviorism in psychology influenced theorists to view motivated behavior in terms of input and output. Consequences were viewed as the main determinants in shaping motivated behavior. In the 1980s, the expansion of psychological theories to include cognition dramatically influenced motivational theories. The idea that a person has the capacity to think, reason, and create, independent from environmental conditions, provided impetus for modification in hypothesized composition of the motivational process. Later developments included a movement to address social influences on behavior. Contemporary social-cognitive theories have examined influences of the social environment on perception, emotion, and motivation.

Several social-cognitive approaches have provided useful insight, identifying components and uncovering operations involved in the motivational process. The major areas of sport motivation research have focused on elements of self-perception and their effects on motivation. Four theories that have been applied readily to the sport environment include: need achievement, attribution, self-efficacy, and goal perspective.

NEED ACHIEVEMENT THEORY

According to need achievement theory, personality factors drive an individual to strive for achievement or avoid failure. Motivation related to striving for success is predicted to elicit feelings of pride and to foster a selection of tasks that are challenging but not impossible to accomplish. This choice provides opportunity for accomplishment through effort. For example, a proficient volleyball player may choose to try out for her high school team, recognizing she could easily join a recreation league, but desiring the challenge of playing with more accomplished players.

Motivation by drive to avoid failure is predicted to foster feelings of shame and a selection of very easy or very difficult tasks. The easy task has a low risk of failure, and the difficult task carries with it no expectation for success, thus no shame for failure. An example might be the skillful golfer who avoids challenging competition due to her fear of losing, electing instead to play with unskilled golfing friends.

Research has supported the possibility of predicting the behaviors of individuals driven by the motive to achieve success, but predictions for those driven to avoid failure are sometimes inaccurate.

ACHIEVEMENT ATTRIBUTION THEORY

Achievement attributions involve beliefs about one's self and environment within an evaluative situation. Three dimensions are projected to influence motivation: locus of control, causality, and stability. Locus of control involves that which we can influence, as opposed to that which we cannot. An athlete can control the content of her own gymnastic routine but cannot control her opponent's. Causality refers to internal versus external factors. The effort one puts into her performance is an internal factor and the condition of the arena is an external factor. Stability refers to permanence. A relatively unchanging factor is one's own talent and an unstable factor is luck. The attributions that one makes about her situation influences expectations, emotions, and motivation.

A self-serving bias exists where failure is attributed to external factors and success is attributed to internal factors. This mechanism serves to protect and enhance one's self esteem. In general, winners make more internal attributions than losers. Some research indicates that women have lower perceptions of competence and less expectations for success than males. This may encourage females to attribute successes to external, unstable factors while attributing failure to internal, stable causes. This tendency is particularly evident for females in stereotypically masculine sports. Societal expectations for women in such sports seem to foster self-defeating attributions of performance outcomes, resulting in decreases in motivation.

Attribution to controllable factors provides empowerment through opportunity to influence outcome, increasing motivation to act. Attribution to uncontrollable elements fosters helplessness and decreases motivation to act. Athletes' assignment of performance attributions affects their emotional reactions, influences their expectations, and subsequently affects their motivation.

SELF-EFFICACY THEORY

Self-efficacy is a term used to indicate self-confidence and expectations for success in a given situation. It is influenced by information from past performance, vicarious learning (modeling), persuasion from others, and emotional arousal. For example, if an athlete has experienced success in the past, has watched coaches demonstrating a skill, is encouraged by others, and interprets arousal as "readiness to perform," then levels of self-efficacy would be very high. Levels of self-efficacy are associated with performance. If an athlete expects to perform well, it is likely that she will be successful, and vice versa. Low levels of expectation have characteristically been associated with women's athletics. Messages from society have historically discouraged females from participating in athletics. In addition, role models for athletics have been, and continue to be, predominately male. The self-efficacy model explains how these influences can detrimentally affect performance.

GOAL PERSPECTIVE THEORY

The goal perspective theory maintains that personal goals are a direct result of one's perception of reality. Multidimensional influences on goal composition include social, personal, and

---

HOW TO STAY FIT DURING THE WINTER

Many people (women and men) find it hard to keep up their motivation to remain physically active and exercise during the cold winter months. The Melpomene Institute, which promotes physical activity for improved health for girls and women, suggests that motivation can be maintained by keeping an exercise log, trying new activities, exercising in different locations, exercising with a partner, and rewarding one's self for small accomplishments.

developmental elements. Demonstrating competence by accomplishing goals affects achievement motivation. Individual perception of ability is determined by assigning success or failure labels to achievement behavior. The function and meaning of goal behavior must be addressed in understanding achievement motivation. Success is defined uniquely by individual athletes.

There are two prominent goal perspectives in achievement settings: mastery and ability. The mastery focus involves task accomplishment and learning. An athlete who develops a mastery perspective will be interested in executing her sport skill to the best of her ability. She uses herself as a reference point when setting goals and determining success. The mastery focus fosters belief that success is related to internal factors such as hard work and effort. In opposition, athletes who develop an ability perspective emphasize comparison with others. There is a focus on ego and competition as well as the belief that success is related to external factors like talent or ability. An athlete with an ability perspective will be most interested in beating others and winning.

Research has indicated that differential behavioral patterns develop from goals that are derived from these two perspectives. In the mastery focus, athletes tend to develop persistence, strong work ethics and optimal performance. With an ability perspective, athletes are inclined to develop maladaptive behavior patterns, such as decreased effort, quitting, making excuses, and less than optimal performance. The ability perspective fosters development of low perceived competence, increased anxiety, and other negative emotions including disappointment and embarrassment. A task perspective cultivates practicing, learning new strategies, and positive emotions such as enjoyment and pleasure. There is evidence that the ability perspective encourages tolerance for deceptive and illegal tactics for the purpose of gaining an advantage in competitive situations. Female athletes tend to be more mastery oriented.

ADDITIONAL ELEMENTS OF MOTIVATION

Although there has been little cross-cultural research, there is some indication that different social norms will influence personal definitions of success and failure, as well as other motivational constructs. For example, the self-serving bias of the attribution theory is not evident in the Hong Kong Chinese. The explanation offered for this difference involves the Asian tradition of modesty. This may be particularly valid with respect to Asian women. In the African-American population, it appears that females are driven by social comparison while males are more mastery focused. It is probable that as more research is conducted, cultural differences in motivational dispositions will continue to emerge.

Female biological and physiological constituents suggest a unique framework for athletic performance. Evidence of restraints imposed by anatomical factors is limited, particularly with respect to motivation. In addition, it appears that predominately female athletic problems (e.g., eating disorders) may better be explained by social factors.

SIGNIFICANCE OF MOTIVATION IN WOMEN'S SPORTS

As women's participation in athletics continues to increase, it will be beneficial for research on motivation to focus on components specific to the female athlete. With contemporary support for health and fitness benefits of athletics, it becomes important to develop a motivational climate conducive to female participation. In addition, the notion that performance is influenced by motivation begs the question of whether the majority of female athletes have reached their potential. Society as a whole has yet to provide a motivational foundation of encouragement for female athletes. With this in mind, it is possible that we have only begun to witness the evolution of female athletic prowess.

Valerie J. Willman

Bibliography

Fox, Kenneth R., ed. (1997) *The Physical Self: From Motivation to Well-Being.* Champaign, IL: Human Kinetics.

Gill, Diane L., ed. (1986) *Psychological Dynamics of Sport.* Champaign, IL: Human Kinetics.

Horne, Thelma S., ed. (1992) *Advances in Sport Psychology.* Champaign, IL: Human Kinetics.

Roberts, Glyn C., ed. (1992) *Motivation in Sport and Exercise.* Champaign, IL: Human Kinetics.

Singer, Robert N., Milledge Murphy, and Keith L. Tennant, eds. (1993) *The Handbook of Research on Sport Psychology.* New York: Macmillan.

Weinberg, Robert S., and Daniel Gould, eds. (1995) *Foundations of Sport and Exercise Psychology.* Champaign, IL: Human Kinetics.

MOTORCYCLE RACING

Members of the Manchester Ace Motor Club engage in a new sport at Holmes Chapel. Two women ride on small "surfboards" which are pulled along behind the motorcycles. (Hulton-Deutsch Collection/Corbis)

Perhaps there is no vehicle or sport that is so closely associated with male sexuality as is the motorcycle and motorcycle racing. Since the sport emerged in Europe near the close of the nineteenth century, it has been closely linked with danger and later with a fierce sense of independence, individuality, and an alternative lifestyle. Not surprisingly, women have not played a major role in motorcycle racing as innovators or competitors, although the sport has involved a few women since its earliest days. In the 1990s, several women enjoyed some success at the top level of international racing, but the sport remained male-dominated, with women most often portrayed as "biker babes" who support the male riders.

HISTORY

Motorcycle racing began with the invention of the motorcycle—the marriage of an engine and a bicycle. Perhaps the first to combine the two successfully was Sylvester Roper, an American from Roxbury, Massachusetts. In the second half of the 1860s, he amazed the public by challenging horse riders to races with his own prototype, the engine being a steam engine he built himself.

The allure of riding may have first developed in Paris when Ernst Michaux invented the pedals and the chain drive. The bicycle became immediately popular and several bicycle clubs were born, created mostly by rich bourgeois and nobles looking for new adventures and entertainment. Women were among these enthusiasts. The opportunity to ride not only provided adventure but also imbued them with a sense of modernity and glamor as they rode along the streets of the French capital.

It was a short and relatively easy step from the bicycle to the bicycle with an engine. In 1885 the German engineer Gottlieb Daimler built and experimented with a wooden motorcycle with the first small four-stroke engine, and in the same year another German technician, Carl Benz, built a three-wheeled vehicle with a four-stroke engine and electric ignition. On one occasion Benz's wife Berta took the tricycle, without her husband's knowledge, and left at dawn from Mannheim with two of her children to travel to Pforzheim, about 100 kilometers away.

Berta Benz's vehicle was a tricycle. The first motorcycles and motorcycle races involved tricycles, which were considered safer than bicycles because of the third wheel and a more stable frame. The first "female championship" was held on 15 August 1896 on race tricycles in Paris. The competition was organized by the French daily *Echo de Paris* and took place in the Bois de Boulogne, a park at the edge of the city. Six women participated and Léa Lemoine won, completing the two laps in 11 minutes and 6 seconds, while De Grandval and Bossu arrived second and third. Another French woman, Laumaillé, is considered the first woman who raced against men; she competed on a tricycle in the Marseille-Nice race in 1898.

In 1896 the Werner brothers, two Russian journalists living in Paris, patented the name "motorcycle" and started producing the two-wheeled, motorized vehicles that were the forerunners of modern motorcycles. The new cycles were safe, reliable, and faster than the tricycles and quickly replaced them in races. In order to promote the new cycles, championships with specific rules were organized.

The new cycles and the circuit of races made motorcycling a sport. While men took the lead, several women were involved in developing the new sport. In 1902, when she was only twenty years old, Muriel Hind of England bought her first motorcycle, a Singer 2HP, without her family's approval. Her next motorcycle was a Rex, whose frame had been modified by the firm that built it, based on Hind's design (to accommodate her large skirt). In 1905 Hind got her racing license, and in 1906 she won her first gold medal in Edinburgh. Until 1912 she participated in several competitions with good results. Her activity was so unusual that at the beginning Hind could not find an insurance company willing to give her a policy. Around 1910 Hind was employed by *Motorcycling* magazine and she wrote an essay, "The Lady Motorcyclist," which helped attract other women to the sport.

In 1904 in St. Paul, Minnesota, George Wagner developed the Wagner, a motorcycle with a four-horsepower engine. In 1910 his eighteen-year-old daughter, Clara, participated in a race from Chicago to Indianapolis on a motorcycle built by her father. She completed the race, but since her participation was unofficial, she was not listed in the results. The other racers contributed money to buy a medal for her.

In Italy several women also became involved in motorcycle racing in these early years of the sport. One, Vittoria Sambri of Ferrara, riding a Borgo 500 motorcycle, used to bet with men, challenging them in short races on tracks during local festivities. Also in Italy, in 1911 Teresa Boni opened a motorcycle workshop for her three sons and asked that they use a small golden lion on an azure background as their trademark.

World War I ended the races but accelerated the development of all forms of motor vehicles, including the motorcycle, which proved to be versatile, agile, and fast. After the war, motorcycle manufacturers began viewing the motorcycle not only as a machine for the wealthy but also as a product to offer to a larger group of potential customers. The appeal of the motorcycle was further heightened by interest in nations such as Spain, Germany, and Italy, which saw racing victories as a means to win acclaim for their national political and economic agendas. These races evolved into the European championships. Women were little involved in this stage of the evolution of the sport, although some women did race: Hanni Koehler from Berlin, known as the best German motorbike rider in the 1920s; Gina Soriani of Italy, who amazed everyone by participating in the Lario circuit for the "Italian Tourist Trophy," and also at Monza; and Marjorie Cottle and Edyth Foley of England, who were part of the all-women team that won for Great Britain in the 1927 International Six Day Trial in England.

WOMEN IN THE ROAD RACE WORLD CHAMPIONSHIP

The growth of motorcycling as a sport was interrupted by World War II but resumed in 1947 with the reopening of the international competitions. Interest now was greater than ever, as the motorcycle had come into much wider use as a means of everyday transportation. Among the popular vehicles, the Vespa, a scooter produced in Italy by Piaggio, was a particular success. The Vespa became a symbol of a society that was quickly changing and becoming part of the international community. Christa Solbach took the lead in founding the Italian Vespa Club, then a European one, and then a world club, which organized meetings, races, and contests of many kinds.

The modern era of motorcycling world championship races in different classes began in 1949. Women were not involved in world championship events at first, although women did race. The early 1960s saw the first efforts of women to compete in world championship races. In 1962 Beryl Swain signed on for the Tourist Trophy. The most famous motorcycle race in the world, the Tourist Trophy featured "touring" motorcycles and was run over the mountains on the Isle of Man in Great Britain. No women had entered the race before and none has raced since because at the end of the race the Tourist Trophy Pilot Association forbade women to race in the competition.

In 1972 a female team of Gabrielle Toigo and Anne Marie Lagauche was on the starting line for the 24-hour race at the Bol d'Or, the oldest of the time trial races, run on the hard track at Le Mans, France, with large motorcycles of the Grand Prix class. Also visible at this time on the race circuit was the team of Rudi Kurt of Switzerland and his wife, Dane Rowe of England, who raced as passenger in the sidecar; they became famous on the sidecar race circuit.

The beginning of the 1970s were ripe for the larger participation of women at motorcycles races. The road was opened by an Italian, Maria Teresa Ravaioli, who competed in the national speed championship in the 125 class, with good results. In the United States, Diane Cox, a nineteen-year-old from Salem, Oregon, earned a certain notoriety as the only woman with a professional license from the American Motorcycle Association (AMA); in 1976 she became famous in the national championship riding a fast, powerful Harley Davidson. Women's participation in speed races was more frequent but without striking results in the 1970s.

In 1982 Jerrie Van Rooyen of the Netherlands became the first woman to win the 24-hour endurance trial at the Italian Bol d'Or, on the Imola track, valid for the endurance world championship. The same year, Gina Bovaird of the United States raced her Superbike in the AMA championship, and she also placed eighteenth at Imola in the international 200-mile race. In 1989 the first motorcycling speed championship for women only was initiated by Maria Chiara Andreoli of Italy. Against men at the world championship level, Taru Rinne of Finland performed credibly in 1989. In August she finished second in practice behind the world champion, Jorge Martinez, and later finished seventh in the German Grand Prix and eighth at the Holland Grand Prix.

One of the most noted racers of the late 1990s was Katia Poesgen, of Hockenheim, Germany, home of a famous German motorcycle track. The daughter of a Suzuki dealer who encouraged her interest in the sport, she first raced in 1993 in the 125 and then moved up to the 600 Super Sport, in which she competed at the 1997 national championship. After recovering from a serious injury in 1997, Poesgen led for the international Supermono championship in 1998, an event previously monopolized by men. Also important in the 1990s was the Japanese 125-class rider Tomoko Igata, who fin-

ished seventh in the Czechoslovakian Grand Prix and eighth in the Malaysian Grand Prix.

Gianna Rivola

Bibliography

Bourdache, Jean. (1989) *La Moto en France, 1894–1914*. Poitiers, France: Edifree.

Foster, Gerald. (1978) *Ride It!* Somerset, U.K.: Haynes.

Gottmann, Günther. (1993) *Motorräder aus Berlin*. Munich: BMW A.G.

Harris, Nick. (1990) *TT 1907–1989*. Richmond, U.K.: Hazleton.

Italia Motociclistica 1901–1950. (1951) Milan: Edisport.

Luraschi, Abramo Giovanni. (1960) *Storia della Motocicletta*. Milan: Bruno Bacchetti Editore.

Patrignani, Roberto, and Michele Verrini. (1973) *Motogare 72–73*. Rome: L'Editrice dell'Automobile.

Rauck, Max J. B. (1986) *Kultur & Technik*. Munich: Zeitschrift des Deutschen Museums.

Rivola, Luigi. (1975) *La Rumagna de' Mutor*. Faenza, Italy: Astorre Editrice.

Rivola, Luigi, and Gianna Rivola. (1991) *Storia del motociclismo mondiale dalle origini ad oggi (Su strada)*. Milan: Vallardi & Associates.

Scott, Michael, et al. (1995) *Motocourse 1995–1996*. Richmond, U.K.: Hazleton.

Sheldon, James. (1971) *Veteran and Vintage Motor Cycles*. Brentford, U.K.: Transport Bookman.

Smith Hempstone, Oliver. (1957) *Automobiles and Motorcycles in the U.S. National Museum*. Washington, D.C.: Smithsonian Institution.

MOUNTAIN BIKING

Mountain biking is a form of recreational and competitive bicycling that requires the use of a bike with wide tires and other features that enable use in rough terrain. It got its start in the mid-1980s, when affordable mountain bikes began to be produced. Women were among the early mountain bikers, and surveys show that they are taking up the sport in increasing numbers.

Mountain biking differs from road biking in that mountain bikes are built with heavy-duty frames, fat tires, and cantilever brakes. These features, among others, allow a mountain bike to go

Jinny Weatherly mountain bikes through the woods of Sun Valley, Idaho, in 1996. (Karl Weatherly)

where a road bike cannot, and its upright position is more conducive to scenery viewing. For mountain biking enthusiasts, the attraction lies in pedaling up a steep mountain grade and later flying down that same mountain at superhuman speeds.

HISTORY

The history of mountain biking is often debated, but Joe Breeze, an engineer, is generally credited for creating the first off-road bike in the early 1980s. Before the development of the mountain bike, road bikers who sought closer views of the mountains transferred motorcycle parts to single-speed bicycles to make them sturdier. Soon after the early mountain bikes were created, affordable "production" bikes were developed, and mountain biking became extremely popular.

Mountain biking has experienced unprecedented growth during the past decade due to such factors as advances in equipment and tech-

nology, media coverage of events, increased access to trails, and the popularity of the sport's best riders. Mountain biking is so popular today that bikes with fat tires account for 80 percent of total bicycle sales.

Competitive mountain biking—racing—was formalized by the National Off-Road Bicycling Association (NORBA). The purpose of NORBA is to guide, service, and promote mountain biking as a competitive sport and outdoor activity. NORBA was established in 1983 to meet the need of a growing sport and to work toward the development and preservation of mountain bike trails. U.S.A. Cycling, the governing body for cycling competition in the United States, bought NORBA in 1989 with the aim of unifying the sport. Since 1989, NORBA has grown by 100 percent and has close to 33,000 members. The organization issues more than 1,000 permits per year for off-road events in the United States.

WOMEN'S INTERESTS

Shortly after NORBA was founded, Jacquie Phelan of Marin County, California, organized the WOMBATS (Women's Mountain Biking and Tea Society), the premier mountain biking organization for women. Phelan was already considered one of the best racers in the field. The WOMBATS provide a forum for women to find riding partners, stay current with riding trends, and enhance awareness of bicycles as modes of transportation. Women who join the WOMBATS also receive a newsletter and may take part in riding clinics, organized trips, potluck dinners, and general female camaraderie. There are three international chapters (British Columbia, Sweden, and Norway), four regional chapters in the United States (California, Colorado, New Mexico, and Massachusetts), and twenty-one local chapters.

During 1997, 31.5 percent of women surveyed by the National Sporting Goods Association reported participating in off-road bicycling, indicating growth of 8.8 percent from the previous year. In 1996 mountain biking was added as an Olympic sport. The women's races (downhill, cross-country, dual slalom, and observed trials) featured thirty entrants from twelve countries. Mountain biking attracts younger, more affluent men and women, with 42 percent of mountain bikers between the ages of twenty-five and thirty-four, 32 percent with household incomes of more than $50,000, and 51 percent with college degrees.

RULES AND PLAY

Equipment and technology advances have helped popularize mountain biking by making it safer and more comfortable to navigate bumps and rocks. One key aspect of technology that has revolutionized the sport is the development of suspension or shock absorption components. A suspension bike, with shock absorbers in front, back, or both, was developed with the idea that it would enhance cycling velocity and braking capacity due to better contact between the tire and the ground. Proponents also claim that they expend less energy and experience less physical stress with these bikes because they are not subjected to the full impact of bumps and vibrations.

The International Mountain Biking Association (IMBA) has suggested six rules that safe and courteous mountain bikers should observe. First, ride on open trails only. This means that riders should respect trail and road closures and avoid riding on private property. Second, leave no trace. Riders should not pedal in conditions where they will leave evidence of passing, nor should they leave trash on the trails. Third, always stay in control—which means maintaining a reasonable speed. Fourth, always yield on the trail. Riders should let others know (via bell, horn, or voice) that they are approaching, and they should assume that others may be around blind corners. Fifth, never spook animals. Sixth, plan ahead. No rider should try a trail without knowing her equipment, how it matches her abilities, the terrain, and weather in which she will be riding. Further, helmets are mandatory, and supplies such as sunscreen and extra food are highly recommended.

Competitive mountain biking offers various options. Types of races include cross-country, point-to-point, hill climb, downhill, dual slalom, stage, and ultraendurance. The cross-country race is a mass start event of 3.2 kilometers or longer that takes place on dirt roads and trails. The point-to-point race is a mass start event, similar to a cross-country race, that starts at one point and ends at another. Some races require riders to ride loops; the difficulty in the point-to-point race, however, is that riders do not become familiar with the course, as they would if they were riding a loop. The hill climb is a timed event designed to see who can reach the top of a summit in the least amount of time. The downhill event is a timed event in the opposite direction. Downhill events are the most dangerous mountain bike races. The dual slalom requires riders to compete next to each other (side by side) in a format similar to dual slalom ski racing (that is, with penalties for false starts, crashing, or missing a gate). Each rider must go through the gate from her course, and riders switch courses for the second run. The best combined time from the two runs wins the event.

A stage race typically combines several types of races, such as cross-country, uphill, and downhill. Winners of each event are awarded points such that the rider with the highest point total (or lowest combined time) wins. Ultraendurance events, which are typically longer than 121 kilometers, are mountain biking's answer to the marathon. Other types of events include stunt

TRAIL ETIQUETTE

As outdoor recreation has become increasingly popular, mountain bikers, hikers, runners, and equestrians often find themselves using the same trails. To prevent accidents and conflicts, rules have been established by outdoor recreation and conservation clubs to help manage trail behavior. The basic rules are that equestrians have the right of way and mountain bikers yield to hikers and runners. Experts also advise that as trail users approach each other, each should slow down and greet the other. All users should leave the trail in a condition that makes it useable by everyone.

competitions in which competitors jump over logs, curbs, or even park benches; and mountain bike polo, in which riders mount bicycles instead of horses, matches consist of two ten-minute halves, and each team has four players. At the Winter X Games (a principal competitive forum for extreme sports), riders stud their tires with quarter-inch wood screws and edge them into the slopes like a set of skis for competition in snow mountain bike racing.

FAMOUS WOMEN IN MOUNTAIN BIKING

Jacquie Phelan is considered one of the premier mountain bikers. She won every race she entered between 1980 and 1986, including NORBA world championships in 1984 and 1985. Cindy White-head won the 1987 women's division of the Raleigh Technicum World Mountain Bike Championships (downhill), and the 1986 NORBA national championship. Other notable contemporary names include Ruthie Matthes, the 1992 World Cup champion; Silvia Furst, the 1992 cross-country world champion; Missy Giove, the 1994 downhill world champion; Juli Furtado, the 1995 world cup champion; and Alison Sydor, the reigning cross-country world champion in 1999.

MOUNTAIN BIKING AND THE ENVIRONMENT

Naturalists, hikers, and horseback riders who share trails with bikers are increasingly critical of mountain biking and in some cases seek to have bikers banned from wilderness areas and trails because the sport, they say, causes erosion and other damage to ecosystems and interferes with the esthetic beauty of wilderness areas. Some bikers, for example, fail to ride along designated trails. In the desert, this means damage to fragile cryptoganic soil, which in turn disrupts plant life and diminishes the already sparse food available to desert wildlife. Other bikers lock their rear brakes on descents, creating gullies that can lead to increased erosion. Mountain bikers of both sexes face the challenge of convincing these critics that bikers can be responsible trail users as the sport, and women's participation in it, continues to grow.

Lynda B. Ransdell

See also Cycling

Bibliography

Clark, Jim. (1996) *Mountain Biking in the National Parks: Off-Road Cycling Adventures in America's National Parks.* San Francisco, CA: Bicycle Books.

Davis, Don, and Dave Carter. (1994) *Mountain Biking.* Champaign, IL: Human Kinetics.

Editors of Mountain Bike and Bicycling Magazine. (1996) *Mountain Biking Skills.* Emmaus, PA: Rodale Press.

Mariolle, Elaine, and Michael Shermer. (1988) *The Woman Cyclist.* Chicago: Contemporary Books.

National Sporting Goods Association. (1997) *Survey of Sports Participation, 1997.* <http://www.nsga.org/research>.

MOUNTAINEERING

Mountaineering as a sport consists of ascending and descending mountains under the climber's own power. At one end are the relatively gentle climbs for which climbers need little if any equipment; at the other are ascents of the world's highest and most daunting peaks, involving months of preparation. Though it began as an exclusively male pursuit, mountaineering slowly became an acceptable activity for women, and it now has many female adherents, including some of the top climbers.

Mountaineering and its companion sport, rock climbing, are simultaneously recreational and competitive. They are recreational in the sense that most climbers climb for love of the sport, but competitive when climbers seek to climb first, highest, or by a new route. In recent years, both men and women have adapted mountaineering and rock-climbing techniques to indoor sport climbing on vertical surfaces.

HISTORY

The sport of mountaineering is generally considered to have started in August 1786, when two Frenchmen made the first ascent of Mont Blanc (4,807 meters) in France. It was the British, however, who turned it into a sport, regularly traveling to the Continent for the climbing season. Clergymen, professionals, and men of leisure, often titled, hired local men to guide them in the Alps. In

1857 a few climbers founded the London-based Alpine Club, for men only. It set a male, upper-class tone to mountaineering that did not begin to change significantly until after World War II.

The first climb by a woman was in 1808, when Maria Paradis of Chamonix climbed Mont Blanc, the first woman to do so. Although details about her are sketchy, it is certain that she was poor and only undertook the climb because the guides who frequented the little stall where she sold refreshments and other sundries urged her to go. They said it would improve her business. Finally persuaded, Paradis set out for the two-day climb. At one point, she was so spent she urged the guides to simply push her into a crevasse and go on. They did not, and finally, she stood on top of the magnificent mountain. Indeed, as a result of her climb, business did improve. Curiosity-seekers came by the droves to make purchases from "Maria of Mont Blanc."

Her ascent was not repeated by a woman for several decades. Mountaineering at the time was an activity made difficult for women for multiple reasons. Societal views were perhaps the strongest; it simply was not an appropriate thing for women to do. If they climbed only with guides but no chaperone, they risked sullying their reputations. Even if suitably accompanied, they violated prevailing standards for healthful physical activity for women. If they persisted, their attire hampered them further, unless they rejected feminine dress.

Nevertheless, they persisted, although slowly and not in large numbers. Thirty years after Paradis made her climb, a French aristocrat, Henriette d'Angeville (1794–1871) decided to climb Mont Blanc. One speculation is that Angeville thought climbing the mountain would bring her enough fame for the coming social season to outshine her rival, the writer and feminist who used the pen name George Sand. Virtually all her friends and family opposed her plan to climb the mountain. Undaunted, Angeville continued making arrangements, hiring six guides and six porters to carry provisions for the men in the party. She would dine on lemonade, chicken broth, plums, and blancmange.

Prior to setting out, she consulted a doctor, made a will, and wrote letters to her closest friends. At 6 A.M. on the appointed day, wearing pantaloons underneath a below-the-knee skirt (according to an 1838 line drawing published in *La Montagne*), she bade farewell to the crowds that lined the galleries of her hotel. At first she "flew" up the mountain so fast the guides had to caution her to slow down. Refusing their help, she leapt across crevasses with impressive agility. By the second day of the ascent, she was experiencing the effects of the high altitude. Nonetheless she persisted, reaching the summit at 1:30 P.M. Angeville then released a carrier pigeon to the Comte de Paris, telling of her ascent. (As it turned out, somebody shot the bird over Les Contamines.) The party descended, spending a second night out. Finally, the climber arrived in Chamonix, triumphant, to waiting crowds and a correspondent of the Paris newspaper, the *Journal des Debats*.

"The Bride of Mont Blanc" became famous. After her highly publicized ascent, Angeville took up mountain climbing, garnering twenty-one ascents of various mountains (one in winter) during the next twenty-five years. At the age of sixty-nine she stood on top of her last mountain, the Oldenhorn.

Lucy Walker (1835–1916), an Englishwoman whose mountaineering career began in 1858, was the first woman to climb regularly in the Alps. She always went with the Swiss guide Melchior Anderegg and her father, brother, or both. Although Walker had climbed ninety-eight major peaks and made the first ascent of the Balmhorn (in 1864), she is best known for being the first woman to stand on top of the Matterhorn (4,477 meters) in 1871, six years after its first ascent. The English magazine *Punch,* in its issue of 26 August 1871, published a poem about Walker titled "A Climbing Girl." The final stanza is:

> No glacier can baffle, no precipice balk her
> No peak rise above her however sublime
> Give three times three cheers for intrepid Miss Walker
> I say, my boys, doesn't she know how to climb!

The honor of being the first woman to climb the Matterhorn might well have gone to a young Italian woman, Felicitas Carrel, in 1867, had she worn trousers. However, she was forced to abandon the climb 300 feet below the summit because a strong gale was blowing her skirt and crinoline above her head, making it dangerous to continue.

The "Col Felicité" pass is recorded as her high point.

Meta Brevoort (1825–1876) was the first American woman to climb extensively in the Alps. After she introduced her nephew, W. A. B. Coolidge, to the sport, it became his obsession. Brevoort was the first woman to climb the Bietschhorn. Although her account of the climb appeared in the 1873 *Alpine Journal*, published by the Alpine Club, authorship was attributed to Coolidge; women were not permitted to contribute under their own names.

Between the 1870s and the early 1900s, many women made impressive climbs in the Alps, including some winter ascents. They include: Mary Isabella Straton-Charlet; Kathleen (Kate) Richardson; Mary Paillon; Mary Petherick (Mrs. A. F.) Mummery, Mrs. Edward Patten Jackson; the sisters Anna and Ellen Pigeon; and Gertrude Bell. Lily Bristow made major ascents both with and without guides. In 1893 she led four famous male climbers as far as the foot of the Petit Dru, one of the earliest recorded examples of a female leading a roped party of males. However, no woman had as much influence on female mountain climbing as Elizabeth (Mrs. Aubrey) Le Blond (1861–1934).

"Lizzie," as she was called, outlived her first two husbands, Fred Burnaby and John Frederick Main, but was survived by the third, Aubrey Le Blond. She wrote eight books about climbing and illustrated them with her very proficient photographs. During her twenty-year climbing career, she summited all the main peaks of the Alps in summer, beginning with Mont Blanc and the Grandes Jorasses (4,208 meters).

Although her own family tried to dissuade her from climbing, considering it scandalous, Le Blond persisted. She was one of the earliest mountaineers to attempt winter ascents and was the only woman of her era to have led a guideless party in both winter and spring. Perhaps most remarkable of all, in 1900 she and Lady Evelyn McDonnel made an ascent of Piz Palü (3,905 meters), almost certainly becoming the first *cordée feminine* (feminine rope). Elegant and steeped in Victorian traditions, Le Blond always began her climb wearing a skirt (over trousers), which she ditched after she had passed the last inhabitants.

In 1907 Le Blond was a founder and first president of the Ladies' Alpine Club, which attracted qualified members from all over the world. Through meetings and the club journal, they met one another and published accounts of their experiences. Probably the club inspired the women of Scotland and Switzerland to found similar organizations. (After the Alpine Club voted to admit women in 1974, the Ladies' Alpine Club and Alpine Club merged.)

In 1898 the formidable Fanny Bullock-Workman (1859–1925), an American, and her husband took the first of eight trips to the Karakorum Range, part of the Himalayas. As was the custom of the day, they paid European guides to accompany them. Fanny vied with other climbers for the record of highest altitude attained. One of her rivals for this record was Annie Smith Peck (1850–1935), who, with Bullock-Workman and two other women, helped found the American Alpine Club in 1902. After Smith Peck climbed Mexico's highest mountain, Orizaba (5,609 meters) in 1897, she held the record for the highest mountain climbed by a woman. However, in 1906, Bullock-Workman's ascent of Pinnacle Peak (6,952 meters) gave her the record. Then, in 1908, Smith Peck announced that she had been to 23,000 feet (7,010 meters) when she climbed the North Peak of Peru's highest mountain, Huascuran, that year. Not so, countered Bullock-Workman, who then proceeded to spend thousands of dollars proving it. Indeed, the resulting survey showed that Smith Peck had only reached 21,812 feet (6,648 meters), giving the woman's high-altitude record to Bullock-Workman.

The Australian Freda du Faur (d. 1935), became the preeminent female climber of the Southern Alps in New Zealand. In 1907 she climbed Mount Sealy with the well-known guide Peter Graham. In 1910 du Faur, Graham, and his brother climbed Mount Cook (3,764 meters). Her finest climb occurred in 1913 when she, Graham, and Dave Thomas made the first traverse of the three peaks of Mount Cook, which Unsworth calls "possibly the hardest route done by a woman anywhere at that time." Mount du Faur, in New Zealand's Southern Alps, is named for her.

POST WORLD WAR I: GUIDELESS AND MANLESS

Following World War I, more and more women, many of modest means, began climbing not only without guides but without any male companions. Mountaineering historian Francis Keenlyside attributes this, in part, to the fact that the French Groupe de Haute Montagne, founded in 1919, initially admitted men and women from around the world on an equal basis, provided they passed the organization's demanding criteria. However, not all of the era's remarkable female climbers were French. Dorothy Pilley Richards and Nea Barnard Morin were English; Miriam O'Brien Underhill and Georgia Engelhard Cromwell were American; and Loulou Boulaz was Swiss.

Dorothy Pilley Richards was a founding member of the influential Pinnacle Club, the first rock-climbing club created by women for women in 1921. Concentrating on climbs in Wales and the Lake District of England, the British mountaineering club was the first to own a hut. Richards was considered the preeminent female climber of the early 1920s, climbing in the Alps as well as in Great Britain.

Georgia Engelhard Cromwell (1906–1986) climbed most of the Cascade volcanoes in the United States and made thirty-two first ascents in Canada. She could carry as much as any man in her party and was often faster than her guides.

Miriam O'Brien Underhill (1899–1976) in 1927 made the first woman's ascent of a route on the Torre Grande in the Dolomites of Italy that her guide named the "Via Miriam." In 1929 Underhill set off with the French climber Alice Damesme. Word spread that they were going to attempt the first women-only traverse of the Grépon, a formidable pointed peak that includes the famous Mummery Crack. As Underhill later observed, no leader had ever fallen out near the top of the crack and lived. But Damesme and Underhill managed the climb well, and an enthralled audience watched. Their successful ascent dismayed a number of men, including Etienne Bruhl. That evening, he sadly said, "The Grépon has disappeared . . . now that it has been done by two women alone, no self-respecting man can undertake it. A pity, too, because it used to be a very good climb." In 1932 Underhill and Damesme made the first all-women ascent of the Matterhorn.

Loulou Boulaz was the first woman to attempt to climb the infamous North Face (Nordwand) of the Eiger (3,970 meters); she attempted the climb in both 1937 and 1962. Some called Boulaz's two attempts on the Eiger's Nordwand in bad weather more noteworthy than the first successful climb by a woman in good weather. That honor fell to Daisy Voog, a Dutch woman working as a secretary in Munich, in 1964.

In 1933 Nea Barnard Morin, with her two French companions, sister-in-law Micheline and Alice Damesme, made the first all-woman traverse of the difficult Meije (3,983 meters) in the Alps. The year after that, the same trio set out to make an all-women ascent of all three summits of the Aiguille de Blaitière. (*Aiguille* means "needle.") It took some convincing to persuade Damesme's husband and Morin's husband not to accompany them, but finally the men agreed to the arrangement. There were a few problems. Shortly after leaving the hut, Alice discovered that she had taken one of her crampons (devices for walking on steep snow and ice) and one of her husband's; fortunately, she was able to make adjustments so it fit her boot. Then, several hours later, she accidentally dropped her ice axe. The climbers remained undeterred and completed their outstanding, successful climb. After her husband's death during World War II, Nea and her daughter, Denise Morin (Evans), became a strong team.

That same year, 1933, a woman's first of a different sort occurred. Wren Corry (Robinson) from England rescued her guide, Mark Lysons, after he broke a leg as they descended Mount Goldsmith in New Zealand. Using a split ski, Corry improvised a splint, binding it to Lysons's leg with puttees and a leather belt. Then she assisted him as he slowly made his way across glaciers, using a pair of ice axes as crutches. After a long night's bivouac, they finally reached the Almer Hut twenty hours after the accident. In 1961 the New Zealand Alpine Club named a tributary of Spencer Glacier below Mount Goldsmith "Corry Glacier."

For thirty-five years, the Canadian Phyllis James Munday (1894–1990) and her husband explored the inaccessible Coast Range of Canada to an extent no one has since equaled. In 1924 Munday became the first woman to climb Mount Robson (3,954 meters). The Mundays made sixteen attempts on what they called "Mystery Mountain," later renamed Mount Waddington (4,016 meters), considered North America's most difficult climb until the 1950s. On one attempt, the husband-and-wife team turned back only fifty feet from the top. In 1936 Bill House and Fritz Wiessner climbed Waddington using pitons and rope for safety, devices the Mundays had carried but rarely used. Phyllis Munday climbed 100 peaks, achieving both first ascents by a woman and first ascents by a man or woman.

In 1938 Una Cameron of Britain became the first woman to climb both peaks of Mount Kenya (Nelion and Batian) in Kenya, while Geraldine Sladen and her brother, from South Africa, made the first guideless ascent of Mount Kenya. (The Englishwoman Gertrude Benyam probably made the first ascent by a woman of Mount Kilimanjaro [5,895 meters], a very easy mountain, technically, compared to Kenya.) In 1940 two Americans, Betsy Cowles (Partridge) and Elizabeth Knowlton, and two men made first ascents in the Santa Marta Range, Colombia, South America. Then World War II severely curtailed mountain climbing as a sport.

POST–WORLD WAR II: SLOW BUT STEADY PROGRESS

Following the war, with safer techniques and equipment available, more and more excellent climbers turned to rock climbing. They found worthy goals in the form of boulders, sea stacks, ocean cliffs, desert spires, canyon walls, and some magnificent rock walls that required many days to climb. (Rock climbing is described below.) Women began pushing various standards, although most climbers of both sexes continued to believe the myths about females—that they had weak arms and lacked the physical and psychological strength to do long, hard climbs and certainly to lead them. Gradually, the myths were dispelled.

In June 1950, two Frenchmen, Maurice Herzog and Louis Lachenal, broke an important symbolic barrier when they ascended Annapurna (8,091 meters) in Nepal. It was the first peak to be climbed of the world's fourteen peaks that are over 8,000 meters. Men—and a few women—began flocking to Nepal after it was finally open to Westerners. In October of 1950, Betsy Cowles (Partridge) joined a party of four men, the first Westerners to visit the Khumbu region and reconnoiter Mount Everest from its Nepalese side. Three years later, Edmund Hillary and his Sherpa companion, Tenzing Norgay, made the first ascent of the world's highest peak, Mount Everest (8,848 meters).

In 1955 four members of the Ladies Scottish Climbing Club set out to explore the Jugal Range, in Nepal, a week's trek northeast of Kathmandu. The members of the first all-women expedition to the Himalayas, after sleeping out at their highest camp, concluded that women adapted to cold better than men and that it was likely that small women who were wiry and spirited would do well in the Himalayas. As expedition member Elizabeth Stark wrote: "The higher we went, the less fearful we became. At 20,000 feet there was a serenity about us and we got on even better with one another than usual." The next year, Joyce Dunsheath of Great Britain organized an all-women expedition of members of the Ladies' Alpine Club to the Himalayas. That same year, she became the first Englishwoman to climb Mount Elbrus (5,633 meters) in the Caucasus. The decade ended with the most ambitious women's expedition of all–an attempt to make a first ascent of Cho Oyu (8,201 meters) in Nepal. The renowned woman climber Claude Kogan was the leader.

In 1951 Claude Kogan and Nicole Leiniger had become the first women to climb Quitaraju (6,180 meters) in the Cordillera Blanca range of the Andes. The following year, Kogan returned to Peru with partner Bernard Pierre and an American team to make a first ascent of Salcantay (6,096 meters). Over the next few years, she made first ascents on Nun Kun (7,135 meters) and Ganesh Peak (7,406 meters). In 1955 Kogan, an honorary member of the Ladies' Alpine Club, became the first female to give a speech in the male bastion of the Alpine Club. But her 1959 trip to Cho Oyu ended tragically; she, Ang Nurbu Sherpa, and Claudine Van der Stratten from Belgium disappeared in an avalanche that swept the highest camp on Cho Oyu. Criticism followed the ill-fated expedition. Still, women persisted in treading where only men had gone before.

BREAKTHROUGHS

All-female teams made successful ascents of such peaks as Mrigthuni (6,855 meters) in 1964 by Indians; Denali (6,194 meters) in 1970 by Americans; Annapurna III (7,577 meters) in 1970 by Japanese; Gasherbrum II (8,035 meters) and Gasherbrum III

PASANG LHAMU, HEROINE OF THE SHERPAS

Controversy surrounds the 1993 death of Pasang Lhamu. According to Sherpa sources, Pasang wanted to lead a team of Nepalese women up Mount Everest. However, the Nepalese government declared that Pasang would have to join a party of Indian women who were planning an expedition to Everest in the late spring of 1993. Because Pasang was told she could not be co-leader, she organized her own expedition. The Nepalese government then demanded 500,000 rupees for a peak permit. Normally Nepalese can travel free within their country.

Pasang's husband accompanied her part way up Everest, then turned back. After she made the summit on 22 April, a storm moved in, trapping her and a companion. Both died. The international climbing community severely criticized Nepal for its part in the tragedy. In response, the government offered Pasang's husband a rebate on the climbing permit, which he refused.

An account published in the 1994 *American Alpine Journal* states that Pasang was not an expert mountain climber, although she had made three previous attempts on the mountain prior to her final one. She was a thirty-year old housewife and mother of three children who helped her husband run a trekking agency in Kathmandu. Nonetheless, she was utterly determined to climb Mount Everest on behalf of Nepalese women, regardless of any personal danger.

Following the climb, one of the disaffected members of Pasang's team said Pasang had not even known the basic technique of downclimbing (climbing down) while wearing crampons (steel spikes fastened onto the soles of boots to climb hard/steep snow and ice), thus forcing Pasang to descend very slowly. Moreover, Pasang ascended the mountain more slowly than the average Everest climber.

After Pasang's death, the king and the prime minister of Nepal sent their condolences to her family. The government named a Kathmandu street for her, issued a postage stamp bearing her picture, and established a fund to pay for her children's education. A memorial to Pasang was erected in the Sherpa community of Namche Bazar and the Pasang Lhamu Mountaineering Institute was established. As a final tribute, a 7,350-meter peak, Mount Pasang Lhamu Chuli, was named for her.

(7,952 meters) in 1975 by Polish; Annapurna (8,091 meters) in 1978 by Americans (and two Sherpa men); Bhrigupath (6,797 meters) in 1980 by Americans and Indians; and Ama Dablam (6,856 meters) in 1982 by Americans. Gwen Moffat became the first female certified professional guide in Great Britain (1953). Thirty years later, after six years of training and field exams, Martine Rollard became the first woman in France to become a certified mountain guide.

During the 1980s, Louise Shepherd, one of many Australian female climbers, pioneered several dozen difficult rock routes in her native Australia. Although Shepherd had partnered with American Jean Ruwitch Goresline in 1980 to make the first free all-female ascent of the Diamond of Long Peaks (4,345 meters) in Colorado, she considered herself a rock climber rather than a mountaineer. It is a distinction that many modern climbers make. Shepherd has written that the part of rock climbing that appeals to her most is "the unique amalgamation of physical, mental, and psychological stresses" (Robertson 1990, p. 158).

In 1989 women in Latin and South America, long isolated and in a minority when on a climb with men, formed the Union of Latin American Women Climbers (ULAMM). Writer/climber Rachel da Silva says that many of the women in ULAMM feel that "geographical barriers and self-limiting attitudes, rather than social pressures, contribute to the low numbers of women in Latin American mountaineering." Still, South American women are climbing ever more challenging mountains both within their continent and outside it. Climbers such as Julia Meza Ramirez of Chile, Luisa Gallardo of Ecuador, Rosa Pabon and La China Arana of Venezuela, and Tatiana Cartwright of Colombia are leading the way.

MOUNT EVEREST: A WOMAN'S PLACE

Although the outstanding Swiss climber, Yvette Vaucher, was the first woman to attempt Mount Everest in 1971, a Japanese woman, Tabei (1939–), became the first woman to actually reach the summit in 1975. In 1969 Tabei had founded the Japanese Ladies Climbing Club, which became a major factor in the large number of excellent female climbers who began to emerge in Japan. Still, it was not easy. After Everest, she later commented that climbing Everest was easier than

THE CALL OF THE MOUNTAINS (1986)

Excerpt from Mountaineer Julie Tullis' Autobiography
Clouds from Both Sides (1986)

But I cannot allow the mountains to become a dominating passion. Even though Terry is the most understanding husband I could have, every time I go away we have problems with our relationship. After twenty-five years of living very closely together my travels have caused us to live very different lives for at least three months at a time. It is harder perhaps for my husband as I walk back into his everyday routine, feeling a little resentful that I am immediately plunged back into the routine of a housewife. The initial difficulty is that I do need time alone to come back from one world to another, which appears very anti-social when I have been away for so long. And of course any activity which takes one away for a long period and attracts a lot of publicity is bound to place a severe strain on a marriage. However, friendship has always been a strong part of our relationship and I am sure that will survive.

We both know that a sacrificial end to my mountaineering and filming is not the answer. Life must go forward. After all, if it had been Terry's vocation that took him away from home there would be less of a problem. It has always been socially acceptable for husbands to go off on business trips—or to climb mountains—while the wife sits patiently waiting at home. It is genuinely far more difficult for a woman, however modern-thinking and sympathetic the husband may be.

Unfortunately my situation is far from unique. It seems that many men in their late forties and fifties have reached a time in their lives when they want to sit back and relax; the career struggle is over and a quiet settled home life is important. Women of the same age, on the other hand, have just become free from the responsibility and ties of caring for children and are ready to take up the challenge of life again, to spread their wings. Sadly life and relationships are never properly balanced.

Mountaineering provides that challenge for me, but the challenge is to myself not the mountain. Sport is about finding out whether you can run faster, jump higher, work in better harmony as a team to score more goals. Most sports use competition as the challenge to push up personal standards and at the ultimate level to break records. There is not this incentive of competition in either climbing or marital arts: no goals are scored or points won. You have to learn to push yourself through a desire to want to know more.

And this is what draws me back to the mountains time after time. Even though I know that the odds of injury and survival must be shortening, I have to go back. One in twelve Himalayan mountaineers die for their ruling passion. But life is short and there has to be a reason to live beyond purely surviving, an extension of that force of nature of which my body and spirit are a part, just as a river has to flow and broaden or it will stagnate.

Julie Tullis died on K2 in 1986.

JULIE TULLIS
(1986) Clouds from Both Sides. *London: Grafton Books.*

counteracting the prejudice against her in Japan because she had forsaken the traditional role of a wife and mother.

Eleven days after Tabei's ascent, a Tibetan woman, Phatog, followed, as part of a Chinese team. Wanda Rutkiewicz of Poland was the first European woman to ascend Everest in 1978, followed by Hannelore Schmatz of West Germany in 1979 (who died on the descent), and Bachendri Pal of India in 1984. In 1986 Canadian Sharon Wood was the first woman to climb Everest by a new route. In 1988 Stacy Allison, an American, summited, followed by fellow team member Peggy Luce. In 1996 Cathy O'Dowd became the first South African and the first from the continent of Africa to climb Everest. Tabei became the first woman to climb the highest points of the seven continents, known as the Seven Summits, in 1992.

TRAGEDIES

As women—and men—climbed ever more difficult routes on ever higher mountains, tragedies followed. None is more poignant than the one that occurred in 1974 in the Pamir Mountains in the former Soviet Union. Eight Soviet women set out to make a traverse of Peak Lenin (7,132 meters). They wore old-style leather boots, cooked on unreliable stoves, and slept in cotton tents with button-loop closures and wooden poles. After a severe storm moved in on their camp, high on Peak Lenin, they were trapped. Slowly, one by one, still in radio contact with base camp, the entire party perished. Consequently, Russian men, who dominate mountaineering in their country, have permitted few women to join them on expeditions, and all-women parties are not allowed.

Some very fine female climbers died in the last decades of the twentieth century. A partial list follows. In 1986 Julie Tullis, English (b. 1939), died on K2 (8,611 meters) after a successful ascent. Catherine Freer, American (b. 1949), disappeared while bivouacking on the Hummingbird Ridge of Mount Logan (6,050 meters) in 1987. Wanda Rutkiewicz (b. 1943), from Poland, disappeared on Kanchnjunga (8,586 meters) in 1991. She had already climbed eight 8,000-meter peaks, a women's record and one that very few men have equaled. Alison Hargreaves, British (b. 1962), died in 1995 while descending K2, the world's second-

Teenage girls from Liverpool, England, rock climb during an outward bound course in 1955. (Hulton-Deutsch Collection/Corbis)

highest mountain. In 1993 she had made solo climbs of six classical climbs in the Alps, including the Matterhorn and the Eiger, via the north faces, while her husband, J. B. (Jim) Ballard, looked after their two young children. Hargreaves was the first woman to climb Everest solo.

ROCK CLIMBING

From its beginning as a sport, mountaineering consisted of treading on snow, ice, rock, or combinations thereof. However, in the late 1800s, rock climbing became a sport in its own right, spurred on by a British barrister, Walter Parry Haskett Smith (1859–1946). He was the first person to record rock climbs in the Lake District, which led to his publishing *Climbing in the British Isles* in 1894. Because he believed in climbing rocks for their own sakes—not merely as a means to the summit—Haskett Smith is credited with being the founder of British rock climbing. Frequently climbing solo, he eschewed using ropes or other equipment, an attitude that many British climbers held for decades.

After Haskett Smith came the Abraham brothers, Ashley P. (1876–1951) and George D. (1872–1965). Professional photographers, they popularized the sport with their pictures and wrote influential guidebooks on climbing in the British Isles and the Alps. In 1906 they helped found the Fell and Rock Climbing Club of the Brit-

Climber Marsha Collins climbs in the remote area of Canon Tajo, Mexico. (Greg Epperson)

ish Lake District, which admitted women. The brothers' wives were competent enough climbers to be admitted to the club and, in fact, George and his wife went rock climbing on their honeymoon in 1902. However, in his book, *On Alpine Heights and British Crags*, George Abraham said, "I would strongly urge that no serious climbing should be undertaken with a lady tied second on the rope. This has led to several parties being lost."

Unlike Haskett Smith, the Abraham brothers did not regard it as "cheating" to attempt to make rock climbing as safe as possible. In fact, they are credited with inventing the "belay," a device and technique to protect a rock-climbing party roped together from the effects of a member's fall. However, the reality was that the only available ropes, commonly made of hemp, but sometimes made of linen, silk, or cotton, usually broke if a leader fell from only eight or ten feet above a belay point. Moreover, if the rope was *not* tied around a belay point, only the second person's great strength and balance and enormous good

luck could prevent the leader from pulling off the entire party.

Ironically, the prime mover behind the Pinnacle Club for women, Emily ("Pat") Kelly, died less than a year after she had helped found it in 1921. A "loose stone . . . moved and brought disaster" on Tryfan (917 meters) in Wales (Pilley, p. 87). She had been climbing solo, without protection, in the accepted British style.

In the early 1900s, metal spikes called pitons began coming into use, though they were scorned in Britain until after World War II. Essentially, pitons were portable belay points. In the event that the leader fell, a securely placed piton permitted the second person on the rope to use a technique known as a "dynamic belay," which put considerably less strain on the rope than the "static belay." In *Give Me the Hills*, Miriam Underhill mentions that at first there was such a stigma attached to pitons that when her guide, Alfred Couttet of Chamonix, began using them in 1926, he wanted it kept a secret.

The use of pitons found favor first in the Alps, spreading east to west, and then in the United States. Climbers trained in European techniques brought the use of ropes and pitons to the United States. For example, after Robert Ellingwood (1888–1934) returned to Colorado Springs in 1914, having learned climbing techniques while studying in England, he taught fellow Colorado College teacher Eleanor Davis (Ehrman, 1885–1991) how to rock climb. She was so agile and unafraid of heights, endowed with a natural "kinesthetic sense," that he trusted her to be second on the rope. Because Ellingwood seldom used pitons, it is doubtful that Davis could have caught him had he fallen. However, Ellingwood never fell; until 1924 he led Davis and others on impressive first ascents in Colorado.

European-trained climbers spread the word about climbing techniques in the United States, beginning on the East Coast, eventually spreading to the West Coast. Although American women did climb rocks prior to World War II, their companions were almost exclusively men. Even Miriam Underhill gave up the *cordée feminine* after 1932, preferring to climb with her husband, Robert.

After World War II, nylon climbing rope became available. It was many times stronger than natural fiber rope. Gradually the great walls of California's Yosemite National Park in the United States replaced Britain as the international rock climbing hub. Francis Keenlyside observed that new methods of climbing had to be developed to climb in Yosemite because of the area's intense summer heat, lack of water, and the high level of difficult routes on the 3,000-foot granite walls.

In the 1950s, 1960s, and 1970s, primarily in the United States, it became generally acceptable to climb difficult routes using "direct aid," that is, physically relying on devices other than the rock itself. Pitons became obsolete as ever more sophisticated belaying devices were developed. It became routine for the leader to fall as he or she attempted difficult moves on the rock. So "aid climbs" by women, such as the first all-female ascent of the 3D Route on El Capitan in Yosemite in 1973 by Sibylle Hechtel and Beverly Johnson, were applauded. So was the first all-female ascent of the 2,000-foot wall known as the Diamond on Longs Peak in Colorado in 1974 by Molly Higgins, Stephanie Atwood, and Laurie Manson. However, as equipment improved and as the standards for free climbing escalated, aid climbing came into disfavor, fueling controversies.

Increasingly, women in all parts of the world began climbing as teams. In 1981 Coral Bowman established what is probably the world's first rock climbing school for women, Great Her-izons, in Eldorado Springs, Colorado. As rock climbing gained in popularity, it inspired sport climbing and climbing competitions.

SPORT CLIMBING AND COMPETITION

In the 1980s, sport climbing, defined as "climbing with protection bolts already in place," made its appearance. Although the Soviets had held speed-climbing competitions in the 1970s, it was not until a decade later that Europeans and Americans became interested in sport climbing competitions. First held outdoors in southern Europe, climbing competitions became popular after they were brought indoors. In perfect comfort, audiences of several thousand watched climbers ascend walls on artificial handholds and footholds. Quite a few women, often of slight stature, with small fingers, and a high strength/weight ratio, began excelling at what some mountaineers scornfully call "acrobatic climbing." Two outstanding ones, Catherine Destivelle and Lynn Hill, alternated between sport climbing and traditional or alpine climbing. Destivelle, French (born in Algieria in 1960), had been a full-time professional since 1986, a status easier to achieve in Europe than elsewhere, earning money from magazine advertisements, movies, and climbing competitions. At home on rock and ice, she made the first female solo climb of the North Face of the Eiger in winter (1993) as well as the extremely difficult, rarely climbed Bonatti route on the North Face of the Matterhorn, solo, and in winter. Hill, American (b. 1961), made the first free climb of the Nose (using only holds provided by the rock), a 3,000-foot rock wall on El Capitan in Yosemite in 1993. A year later she blazed the same route in fewer than twenty-four hours. Her feats had not been duplicated as of January 1999.

GUIDED CLIMBING

For two centuries, men and women have hired guides to take them up mountains. However, the number of commercially guided expeditions on the world's highest mountains has proliferated ever since Dick Bass made the summit of Everest in 1985. A Texan with more money than climbing experience, he paid mountaineers to guide him to the high point of each of the seven continents, the last being Everest. His well-publicized success launched dozens of commercial guide services that offered trips up the Seven Summits.

On 10 May 1996, the hazards of such ascents were brought home when five people died on Everest after having made successful ascents. All were members of commercially guided expeditions, one headed by New Zealander Rob Hall, the other by American Scott Fischer. (That spring there were at least ten commercial expeditions out of a total of 30 on the mountain.) Among the dead was Yasuko Nama of Japan, who at age forty-seven was the oldest woman to have climbed Everest. Two American women, Sandy Hill Pittman and Charlotte Fox, members of Fischer's team, escaped death only because of the actions of others.

Clients had paid as much as $65,000 each to join a guided team. Thus, before the expeditions ever began to set foot on the mountain, there was enormous pressure on Fischer and Hall, who were rivals, to "deliver" the summit to their clients. Almost certainly Fischer and Hall made decisions based not on their soundest mountain sense and extensive experience, but rather on their driving desire to have their clients reach the summit.

Although the initial outcry following the 1996 Everest tragedies was loud and prolonged (a total of twelve people died before the season was over), several Everest climbers have predicted the outrage will fade away and the muddy ethics of guiding paid clients up Himalayan mountains will remain unresolved.

Janet Robertson

Bibliography

Abraham, George D. (1916) *On Alpine Heights and British Crags*. Boston and New York: Houghton Mifflin.

Allison, Stacy, with Peter Carlin. (1993) *Beyond the Limits: A Woman's Triumph on Everest*. Boston, New York, Toronto, and London: Little, Brown.

Birkett, Bill, and Bill Peascod. (1989) *Women Climbing: 200 Years of Achievement*. London: A & C Black.

Blum, Arlene. (1980) *Annapurna: A Woman's Place*. San Francisco: Sierra Club.

Coburn, Broughton. (1997) *Everest: Mountain without Mercy*. Washington, DC: National Geographic Society.

Darmi, Peter. (1992) *The Sport Climbing Competition Handbook*. Evergreen, CO: Chockstone Press.

da Silva, Rachel. (1992) *Leading Out: Women Climbers Reaching for the Top*. Seattle, WA: Seal Press.

Engel, Claire Eliane. (1952) *They Came to the Hills*. Great Britain: Hunt, Barnard.

Hargreaves, Alison. (1994) *A Hard Day's Summer: Six Classic North Faces Solo*. London: Hodder and Stoughton.

Hill, Lynn, producer and director. (1997) *Free Climbing the Nose*. (video).

Himalayan Journal. (1929–).

Keenlyside, Francis. (1975) *Peaks and Pioneers: The Story of Mountaineering*. London: Paul Elek.

Krakauer, Jon. (1997) *Into Thin Air*. New York: Villiard.

Ladies' Alpine Club Yearbook/Journal. (1927–1975).

Main, Mrs. (1892). *My Home in the Alps*. London: Sampson Low, Marston.

Mazel, David, ed. (1994) *Mountaineering Women: Stories by Early Climbers*. College Station: Texas A & M University Press.

Olds, Elizabeth Fagg. (1985) *Women of the Four Winds: The Adventures of Four of America's First Women Explorers*. Boston: Houghton Mifflin.

Pilley, Dorothy. (1935) *Climbing Days*. New York: Harcourt, Brace.

Robertson, Janet. (1990) *Magnificent Mountain Women: Adventures in the Colorado Rockies*. Lincoln: University of Nebraska Press.

———. (1998) *Betsy Cowles Partridge: Mountaineer*. Niwot, CO: University Press of Colorado.

Satayev, Vladimir. (1987) *Degrees of Difficulty*. Seattle, WA: The Mountaineers. (Originally published 1977 in the Soviet Union.)

Smith, Cyndi. (1989) *Off the Beaten Track: Women Adventurers and Mountaineers in Western Canada*. Jasper, Canada: Coyote.

Stephens, Rebecca. (1994) *On Top of The World*. London: Macmillan.

Tullis, Julie. (1987) *Clouds from Both Sides: An Autobiography*. San Francisco: Sierra Club.

Underhill, Miriam. (1956) *Give Me the Hills*. London: Methuen.

Unsworth, Walt. (1992) *Encyclopaedia of Mountaineering*. London and Sydney: Hodder & Stoughton.

Vause, Mikel, ed. (1990) *Rock and Roses*. La Crescenta, CA: Mountain'n' Air.

Williams, Cicely. (1973) *Women on the Rope: The Feminine Share in Mountain Adventure.* London: George Allen & Unwin.

MOVIES

Despite the use of athletes in early cinematic experiments (as a means of demonstrating motion within the medium), depictions of athletics within movies have not been widespread enough for sport films to have developed as a separate film genre. Only about 300 films have been made that feature athletics as key plot devices (out of more than 21,000 films), and less than twenty of these films have been about women in athletics.

Cinematic depictions of sports have fallen into a range of cinematic genres, including biographical sketches, comedies, documentaries, dramas, musicals, mysteries, and science fiction. Films about sports do not exist as a separate category of cinema; instead, films within these genres sometimes have sports as plot devices or athletes as lead characters.

In 1878 the cinematic pioneer Eadweard Muybridge offered photographic sequences of athletes to demonstrate the fluidity of the developing medium. Early silent strips often featured real athletes (usually male, in keeping with Victorian principles) to provide a human element in depictions of movement that commonly represented technologies, such as locomotives and factory production lines. Despite the early value of using athletes within the medium, sport did not become a cinematic staple following the advent of scripted movies, presumably because the thrill of sport lies with the uncertainty of the live moment rather than in its recreation. Through the twentieth century, most films depicting athletes or athletics have been American and have been either biographical sketches or comedies. Films about women athletes have also fallen into this pattern. However, for sport films about women, a third subcategory exists—that of post–Title IX films (mostly made for television) representing the struggles of the first women on teams as either coaches or athletes.

FILMS MADE PRIOR TO THE SECOND FEMINIST WAVE

The earliest full-length feature film on sports was *The Champ* of 1931, an Academy Award–winning film about the relationship between an aging boxer and his child. The only feature film with women as lead characters to appear before the feminist-influenced wave of film produced in the 1970s was *Hard, Fast and Beautiful* (1951), a film about women's tennis directed by Ida Lupino, one of the only female Hollywood directors of the period.

Perhaps the most significant (and definitely the most controversial) film about sports involving women was *Olympia* (sometimes featured as *Olympiad*), directed by Leni Riefenstahl in 1936. Ostensibly a documentary of the 1936 Berlin Olympics, *Olympia* is notable for its extensive and equal representation of women athletes. For Riefenstahl, the true subject of the film was the athletic ideal, as witnessed through the achievements and struggles of the human body, regardless of the race or gender of those bodies. Because this Olympic contest was used by Hitler as a means of promoting the Nazi party worldwide, and due to other affiliations Riefenstahl had with Hitler, *Olympia*'s achievements as a film about sport is overshadowed. If left to stand on its own, *Olympia* is arguably the best film ever made about athletics, as new cinematic techniques were developed to represent the movement and pace of athletics, and because the supremacy of the camera's focus lay with a multitude of athletes regardless of the sport pursued, medals won, or the participants' gender, race, or nationality.

THE INFLUENCE OF TITLE IX

With the advent of the second wave of feminism in the 1970s and the impact of the passage of Title IX of the Education Amendments Act, a number of films about pioneering women athletes were produced in the late 1970s and early 1980s. These films fall into a subgenre of films about women that represent the incorporation of women into fields previously perceived to be male-dominated. Most of these films were quickly produced for television.

These films reflect a range of genres, primarily biographies, comedies, and dramas, and were similar to those made about athletes overcoming racial barriers (although more films were made in that subgenre). It is notable that, with the exception

FILMS ABOUT WOMEN IN SPORTS

The Feminist Second Wave, which began in the 1970s, and the associated growth of women's sports following the enactment of Title IX led to an increase in films and more inclusive topics in films about women's sports and women athletes. Especially prominent have been movies that depict women in athletic roles previously reserved for men. These include films which feature women as hockey players, baseball players, wrestlers, body-builders, race car drivers, multi-sport athletes, and as coaches.

of two documentaries—*Olympia* and *Pumping Iron II*—all of the films about women athletes have been representations of white women, while all films about black athletes have been about black men, thus effectively erasing women of color from any cinematic testament of athletics.

A chronological listing of these films begins with the "sex-ploitation" film *Kansas City Bomber* (1972), starring Racquel Welch as a roller derby champ; followed by *Babe* (1975), a biographical treatment of superlative athlete Babe Didrikson Zaharias, starring Susan Clark; *The Coach* (1978), starring Cathy Lee Crosby as an Olympic medalist hired to coach a boy's basketball team when it is mistakenly assumed she is a man; *All the Marbles* (1981), a Robert Aldrich film about women's wrestling; *Hockey Night* (1984), a Canadian film about a female who makes an all-male team; and *Wildcats* (1986), starring Goldie Hawn as a high school football coach.

Also made during this period was *Dallas Cowboy Cheerleaders* (1979), one of the most successful made-for-television movies of the 1970s. With a focus on breasts and sexual innuendo that dispelled cultural fears about women (notably fear of women athletes), it was so successful that it spawned a self-named sequel the following year. Indeed, the most pervasive roles that women have had in films about sports have been as sexual prizes for successful male athletes or as understanding and supportive wives. Even in the 1990s, despite the real advances women have made, the athletic field (like the battlefield) remains a culturally iconographic place in which masculinity is achieved.

Probably the most successful film of the sports subgenre was *Bad News Bears* (1976), a comedy starring Tatum O'Neal as a female Little League pitcher who takes her team to the championship despite their initial resistance to her involvement. This film spawned two sequels and a television series and was responsible for drawing media attention to girl athletes.

The sole documentary of this era, *Pumping Iron II: The Women (1985)*, was a landmark film not only because it introduced a wide audience to a little known sport, but also for the impact the film had on the sport itself. The follow-up to *Pumping Iron*, a successful 1977 film about men's bodybuilding, this film solidly depicts the trials of forming a new sport (women's bodybuilding was in its fifth year when the documentary was made, and was newly-removed from its beauty show beginnings).

In *Pumping Iron II*, the emotional debate between originators, sponsors, and athletes over esthetics versus strength forms the narrative focus of the film. The documentary effectively captures the battle, one so integral to women's athletics as to transcend this particular sport. While a range of athletes are featured, the focus of the contest is largely between Texas beauty queen Rachel McLish (who was favored to win) and Australian power lifter Bev Francis, who entered the contest expressly to challenge the beauty standards held in the contest.

MAJOR CINEMATIC RELEASES

Rarely is sport considered to be the experience of women, despite the thematic value of sport as a simplistic metaphor for struggle. Only three major Hollywood studio releases have involved women athletes as key figures: *Personal Best, Heart Like a Wheel,* and *A League of Their Own*.

Personal Best (1982) is the only film about women and athletics that represented lesbian athletes. It must be noted that this depiction is not fully positive, as lesbianism is constructed more as the temporary result of women being surrounded by women, rather than as a true sexual orientation. It traces the track and field careers and romantic relationship of two athletes, Chris Cahil (Mariel Hemingway) and Tory Skinner (Patrice Donnelly), beginning with the 1976 Olympic trial and ending with the 1980 U.S. Olympic track and field trials. The strongest aspects of *Personal Best* as a film about athletics are its concentration on the sport of running, its portrayal of women athletes as tough, competitive winners, and its depiction of the beauty of strong, athletic females (although this focus becomes so concentrated as to be overtly sexual).

Heart Like a Wheel (1983) did not get the distribution or have the box-office success of *Personal Best*. A biography of three-time world top fuel racing champion Shirley Muldowney (played by Bonnie Bedelia), this film depicts the obstacles women had to overcome to even be allowed to compete with men. Muldowney was the first woman to compete in professional automobile racing, beginning by running informal circuit races in 1956 and progressing to the professional circuit in 1966 when she not only qualified on her first attempt but broke the existing track record. *Heart Like A Wheel* is outstanding for its depiction of the barriers placed in front of women athletes; not only does it offer an accurate account of Muldowney's life, but it contextualizes her efforts within the larger sphere of 1970s women's liberation and other athletic events, such as the landmark "battle of the sexes" tennis tournament between Billie Jean King and Bobby Riggs.

A League of Their Own (1992) is a fictionalized account of the All-American Girls Professional Baseball League, which was founded during World War II. The film depicts the rise and dissolution of the league by focusing on one of the league's many teams, the Rockford Peaches. Unfortunately, the film loses a great deal of the exciting and important history of the league (which existed from 1943 to 1954) through attempts at easy laughs and a focus on sibling and female rivalry. The narrative conflict of the film is provided by the struggle between two sisters, Kit Keller (Lori Petty) and Dottie Hinson (Geena Davis). Keller, the younger sister, has the greater desire to be on

Women athletes are a rare sight on the silver screen, which is true to an even greater degree for African American women athletes. Tennis star Althea Gibson (far left) played a non-athletic-role in the 1959 movie *The Horse Soldiers*. (Corbis/Bettmann)

the team but lacks the talent of her older sister. This box office success' greatest contributions to women's athletics are its representation of a little known athletic league and its focus on the dual roles women have been expected to play as athletes and beauty objects.

Molly Merryman

See also All-American Girls Professional Baseball League; Muldowney, Shirley

MULDOWNEY, SHIRLEY

(1940–)

U.S. RACE CAR DRIVER

In 1999, more than twenty years after her victory, Shirley Muldowney was still the only woman who had won a world championship in auto racing.

Shirley Muldowney drag-racing in Pomona, California, 1974. (AP Photos)

Though alone in this distinction, throughout her career she was joined by more and more women drivers who were able to enter the sport because of her achievements.

Born Shirley Roque on 19 June 1940, she grew up in Schenectady, New York. Her boyfriend John Muldowney introduced her to motor sports. "I had my [driver's] permit about a week and Jack put me behind the wheel. I was going 120" (*Current Biography*, p. 397). She quit high school at sixteen to marry Muldowney. Their son John was born a year later. The couple became regulars on the semiprofessional drag racing circuit, with Shirley driving and Jack acting as crew chief. She acquired the nickname "Cha Cha," which she disliked, when someone wrote it on her car.

Professional drag racing licenses, which sanction drivers to compete in major national events, were traditionally denied to women, who were viewed by the male racing establishment as too fragile mentally and physically to handle a dragster. There was also concern about negative publicity should a woman be injured in a crash. In 1965, when women were first allowed to apply for licenses, Muldowney became the first woman licensed by the National Hot Rod Association (NHRA) to drive a Top Gas dragster. In 1971 she began a business and personal partnership with racer Conrad "Connie" Kalitta. When the Top Gas class was eliminated that year, she moved to one

of his "Funny Cars." Competing as "The Bounty Huntress," she won the first regular Funny Car race she entered. A divorce in 1972 and a serious crash in 1973 derailed her drive to the top. After recovering from the accident, Muldowney became the first woman to race a Top Fuel dragster, a 2500-horsepower car, shaped like an arrow, that reaches speeds of nearly 300 mph (482.7 kph) in less than six seconds. Kalitta became her crew chief, and they later married.

By 1975 Muldowney was a top driver whose hot pink dragster appeared often in the finals. Her 1976 Top Fuel victory at the NHRA Springnationals was the first by a woman in a national professional drag race, and she was, moreover, the only driver to be clocked under six seconds. In 1977 she became the first driver to win three NHRA Top Fuel events in a row and captured the championship. She was named 1977 Top Fuel driver of the year by *Drag News* and Person of the Year by *Car Craft*.

Male drivers usually have corporations clamoring to sponsor them after their first win, but even after her world championship Muldowney had trouble getting major sponsors. At the same time, her stormy relationship with Kalitta ended in divorce. For the next two years her career went into a decline that many critics attributed to the loss of Kalitta. Muldowny was unable to vie for the points title again until 1980, when she became the first driver to win the NHRA Top Fuel championship twice. She improved her own record when she won it a third time in 1982.

In 1983, *Heart Like a Wheel*, a feature film starring Bonnie Bedelia and based on Muldowney's life, was released. The film acquainted the general public with a tough, talented woman and gained her many fans. On 29 June 1984 she suffered a life-threatening crash in Montreal and sustained multiple severe injuries. Incredibly, she returned to racing less than two years later and clocked the fastest quarter mile of her career at the 1986 Pomona Winternationals (5.470 seconds). She won the last of eighteen International Hot Rod Association (IHRA) national titles at the 1989 Fall-nationals in Phoenix, Arizona.

Through the 1990s, Muldowney continued to compete on the IHRA circuit, where she won several times and twice finished second in the points standings (1996 and 1997). By the end of the decade, she was driving her pink dragster more for pleasure than for competition. While a few women had competed in drag racing before Muldowney, she opened the door for those who came after. The derision of the early years, from fans who did not want to see a woman on the track, turned to cheers for her grit and her outstanding and lengthy career. She is the only women driver in the Motorsports Hall of Fame. Says Muldowney, "I'm a bit of a toughie, and I had to be in the early days or I would not have survived. I like to think that I made it easier for other ladies" (Vader 1989, p. 25).

Suzanne Wise

Bibliography

Densmore, Dave. (1983) *Popular Hot Rodding: 1983 Drag Racing Yearbook.* Los Angeles, CA: Argus Publishers.

Duden, Jane. (1988) *Shirley Muldowney.* Mankato, MN: Crestwood House.

Vader, J. E. (1989) "Two Foes Bury the Hatchet, But Not the Competition." *Sports Illustrated* (4 September): 22–26.

Woolum, Janet. (1992) *Outstanding Women Athletes.* Phoenix, AZ: Oryx Press.

MULHALL, LUCILLE

(1885–1940)

U.S. RODEO COMPETITOR AND WILD WEST ENTERTAINER

One of several popular Wild West female entertainers, Lucille Mulhall was the first woman to compete against rodeo cowboys, and she was often called the first American cowgirl. Mulhall was born to Zack and Agnes Mulhall on 21 October 1885. Zack Mulhall had settled a homestead near Alfred, in the Oklahoma Territory, during the land rush of 1889. When the town was asked to change its name by railroad officials, citizens called the town "Mulhall," after Zack, who was then the mayor of the town.

Zack and Agnes developed their settlement into a 160-acre working cattle ranch, where the Mulhall children learned to ride horses and rope cattle, skills that made them effective ranch hands even before their teens. At roundup time, cowhands from area ranches would stage friendly competitions to see who could be the best "cowboy"—who could throw the lariat most accurately, and who could rope and brand the most cattle the fastest. With Wild West shows becoming a popular form of entertainment throughout the United States, Zack Mulhall seized the opportunity to go into show business.

He gathered the best cowboys he could find and in 1899 formed the Congress of Rough Riders and Ropers. Zack Mulhall and his talented children were the star attractions of the show, as were a number of undiscovered western performers who were just getting their starts in show business. Will Rogers and Tom Mix credited Mulhall with giving them the opportunity to perform in their early days.

Although there were many female Wild West show entertainers like Annie Oakley and May Lillie who performed shooting or rope tricks, Lucille Mulhall was the first woman to compete in riding and roping events with cowboys. At the age of thirteen, she competed in relay horse races and steer roping contests, demonstrated the art of the lasso, and performed tricks with her trained horse, Governor. Because she competed alongside cowboys, Mulhall was called the first cowgirl.

Mulhall was strong and tough. In 1910, she drew the fury of the Society for the Prevention of Cruelty to Animals (SPCA) when she accidentally killed a steer during a roping event. The SPCA took the Mulhall show to court, but the judge refused to believe that Mulhall could have killed a steer. However, he fined her father and several other male members of the company for breaking a rarely enforced law against roping cattle.

Throughout her life, Mulhall remained captivated by show business and more loyal to her father than to any other man. Her two marriages ended in divorce, and she rarely saw her son, born in 1909, because she was always on tour. Though she was a top draw at Wild West shows and had run her own company, Lucille Mulhall's Round-up, many people considered her an ineffective wife and mother because she had never learned to do "women's work" such as house-cleaning and cooking.

Although Wild West shows became less popular and less financially viable starting in the mid-1910s, Mulhall and her brother Charley continued to perform in them through the 1930s. Attendance at Wild West shows waned in the shadow of the polio epidemic, the entry of the United States into World War I, and the Great Depression; however, Lucille seemed unable to pull herself away from the limelight. She made her last known public appearance in September 1940.

Lucille Mulhall died less than a mile from the Mulhall Ranch in an automobile accident on 21 December 1940. She was only fifty-five years old. In December 1975, Mulhall was inducted into the Rodeo Hall of Fame, a unit of the National Cowboy Hall of Fame. She was also made an Honoree of the National Cowgirl Hall of Fame.

Wendy Painter

Bibliography

Stansbury, Kathryn B. (1992) *Lucille Mulhall: Her Family, Her Life, Her Times*. Mulhall, OK: Homestead Heirlooms.

MUSLIM GAMES *see* Islamic Countries' Women's Sports Solidarity Council and Games

MUTOLA, MARIA

(1972–)

MOZAMBICAN MIDDLE DISTANCE RUNNER

Maria Mutola is one of the most successful women runners from Africa, and her career is often cited as a example of the success of the International Olympic Committee (IOC) in developing women's sports in less developed nations.

Maria Mutola in the women's 800-meter race at the 1996 Olympic Games in Atlanta. (Ales Fevzer/Corbis)

Mutola was born in Maputo, Mozambique, on 27 October 1972, as the sixth and youngest child of Joáo and Catarina Mutola. Her father was a railroad clerk and her mother raised vegetables to sell in the city market. Mutola began playing soccer with boys in the streets when she was five and was so good that she was allowed to play on a boys' team. In 1988, when she was fifteen, she was spotted by José Craveirinha, the well-known Mozambican poet, who recognized her athletic ability and brought her to the attention of his son, Stleo, a track and field coach. They encouraged her to compete in middle-distance track events and supplied her with equipment and a training facility; later that year she competed in the 800-meter run at the Seoul Olympics, finishing seventh in her heat. She continued to compete in Africa and internationally and finished first in the 800- and 1500-meter events in the African championships in 1990 and first in the 800-meter run at the African Games in 1991.

In 1991 she was selected for an Olympic solidarity scholarship provided by the International Olympic Committee to athletes from less developed nations. The scholarship enabled her to move to Springfield, Oregon, to train with Margo Jennings and Jeff Fund, while she lived with Doug and Judy Abramson and their two children and attended the local high school. At the age of nineteen, she was older and more physically and emotionally mature than her classmates. The relocation adjustment was not without its problems, including a ruling that she was not eligible to compete on the high school track team but was eligible to compete in cross-country.

With the benefit of a more stable life (life in Mozambique had been disrupted by a civil war that ended in 1992) and regular training, her international career took off. At the Olympics in Barcelona in 1992, she finished fifth in the 800-meter run and then won forty consecutive races, including the world championship in 1992. In 1994 she again won the world championship and the Goodwill Games and was the dominant 800-meter runner in 1995. In 1996 she was the pre-Olympic favorite in the 800-meter and a threat in the 1500-meter run, but she took only the bronze in the 800-meter event. After seven years in the United States, Mutola has assimilated to American society and continues to live in Oregon, now with her teen-age niece whom she brought over in 1995.

David Levinson

Bibliography

Layden, Tim. (1996) "Long Run." *Sports Illustrated Olympic Daily.* July 27. <http://channel.cnnsi.com/events/1996/olympics /daily/july 27/muto.html>.

MYTHOLOGY

Mythology refers to the study of the traditional narratives of peoples around the world, as well as to the myths themselves. Myths include traditional folk tales, fairy tales, fables, and legends. The boundaries between these different forms of narrative are simply convention. Classical mythology refers to the mythology of Greeks and Romans in antiquity. Although myths exist in every culture, and physical competition and sporting events figure in many myths, there has not been a systematic study of women's sport in world mythology.

This entry focuses, therefore, on classical mythology, where various mythical competitions are associated with goddesses and heroines. In Olympia, for instance, Hippodameia is said to have introduced the running contests (Greek: *agones*) of girls; Palaistra is held to be the founder of wrestling; and the women's festival, with its rhapsodic contests (i.e., declamation of Homeric poems), dancing, running, and weaving, which took place at Brauron at regular intervals, is believed to go back to Artemis.

MYTH OR REALITY

Although myths are not a mirror of past societies, they nevertheless transport real elements and images that contribute to an understanding of earlier times. Mores and folkways show themselves in myth, as do attitudes toward many issues of everyday life, from birth and death to marriage and relationships. Myths show that games and sports have been made part of systems of religious worship and social ritual, and that they also have long provided relaxation as leisure and communal activities. In classical mythology, sport is predominantly understood as a male domain.

Despite all the elements of fantasy inherent in myth, myths reflect historical reality. The poet, for example, in the twenty-third book of the *Iliad* (eighth century BCE) tells about the funeral games of Patroclus, a friend of Achilles, which included chariot racing, boxing, wrestling, running, hoplomachia (fighting with heavy arms), discus, archery, and javelin. Historians disagree about whether Achilles, Patroclus, and Odysseus were real people, but they do not dispute the existence of the competitions and other details contained in the narrative.

The same holds true for Pausanias' (second century CE) story about the foot races for virgins of different ages at the Heraia at Olympia. According to Bachofen, who believed that matriarchy existed among the pre-Hellenic Eleans (northwest Peloponnese), these women's races were later replaced by the patriarchal Olympic games. Regardless of whether this interpretation is correct, Pausanias's narration is based upon the idea that women's and girls' races have taken place in historical time.

Competitions such as beauty contests are very similar in this regard. A historical example would be the *kallisteia* of Lesbos (recorded by Alcaeus, late seventh century BCE). The best known example is the Judgment of Paris, in which Hera, Aphrodite, and Athena competed for being the most beautiful goddess, but myths also tell of other beauty contests between Hera and Side, Hera and the daughters of Proitos, and also between the Nereids and Cassiopeia, Athena, and Medusa. Contests for beauty (which also exist for men—*euandrias agon*) are not the only kind of contests that can be found in myth. Contests in the art of weaving (between Athena and Arachne), in singing (between the Muses and Thamyris; the Muses and the Sirens), in poetry (between Corinna and Pindarus), in foot race (Atalanta and Chloris), in wrestling (Thetis and Peleus), and in discus throwing (Artemis and Orion) can also be found.

Such legendary mythical contests are also known outside Greek mythology. Brunhilde in the Nibelungenlied is a case in point. In Japanese mythology, as gathered in the *Nihon Shoki* (712 CE) and the *Kojiki* (720 CE), the sun-goddess Amaterasu, who binds her hair in male fashion and ties her skirt into the form of trousers, challenges her brother, Susanowo, with her bow and her sword. He meekly surrenders, and she bites his sword to bits and tosses it to the winds.

In these myths (Greek or otherwise), competitive spirit is truly congruent with feminine mentality. Nike, the goddess of victory, a sister of Zelos (rivalry), Kratos (strength), and Bia (force), as described by Hesiod around 700 BCE in *Theogony*, rules over all athletic, equestrian, and musical contests and represents the competitive spirit. The goddesses Nemesis and Hecate are also sometimes connected with athletics.

The mythical contests show that girls and women are also granted the ambition to outdo others in a certain discipline or with regard to a certain trait (*aristeia, philotimia*: excellence, prowess; love of honor, ambition). The well-known pedagogical maxim of the *Iliad*, "always to be the best and excel over others," seems to apply to the female sex as well.

FEMALE CONTESTS IN CLASSICAL MYTHOLOGY

Ancient Greece is famous for its festivals and events of athletic competition, which formed an important part of Greek culture and society. This image of Greece exists in part because sport events of all kinds can amply be found in texts as well as in pictorial representations—and not only in texts that are directly concerned with sport. Similes and metaphors taken from sport are often used in contexts unrelated to sport (such as political speeches, love poetry, and even in the Bible).

Hence athletic activities often appear as important elements in myth. The spectrum ranges from the mere reference to the carrying-out of games on different occasions to the detailed descriptions of specific contests (wrestling, boxing, or others). Gods actively participate or help the hero; prizes for participants and victors are listed and elaborately described; injury, death, and fraud occur; spectators' reactions are considered noteworthy; and finally, athletic achievements are a constant element of the life course of Homeric heroes.

WOMEN'S PLACE

A different picture emerges as soon as sport historians focus on the role of women. Given how much mythological material exists and the frequency of women's prominent participation in myth, as well as the frequency of sport events mentioned, the scarcity of female contests in myth is astonishing. One explanation for this may be that female contests were of minor public significance in Greek city-states; another may be that women were not given due recognition in the male-dominated literary production. But this absence is also associated with the fact that literary genres had certain taboos of content, that is, they always omit certain areas when portraying social reality. One will search in vain for pederast scenes in epics, for example, even though other sources (vase paintings, graffiti) and other literary genres (lyrics, for example) document this form of interpersonal behavior extensively. Concerning the extent of female contests in Athens, Claude Bérard was able to supplement the meager literary documents by interpreting vase paintings.

In the oldest examples of European literature, the epics *Iliad* and *Odyssey,* attributed to the poet Homer (eighth century BCE), sport plays a major role in the lives of heroes. Athletic activities, for example, are extensively described on the occasion of the funeral games for the slain Patroclus, or on the occasion of the contests during Odysseus's stay with the Phaeacians. They were also a pastime during the siege of Troy, descriptions of which portray various sports. But women play only a marginal role in these sport events: they are mentioned as spectators in the Homeric *Hymn to Apollon* (146); Thetis organizes the funeral games for her son, Achilles (*Odyssey* 24.85); and women can be given as prizes of victory to male contestants (*Iliad* 22.162).

BALL GAMES

In addition to descriptions of this passive type of participation in sport, there is mention of a ball game played by Nausicaa, the daughter of the Phaeacian king Alcinous, and her friends at the seashore (*Odyssey* 6.99). This game is accompanied by *molpé* (dance or rhythmic movement with song) that, like *paizein* (defined as "play like a child," or "sport" or "dance"), points to a possible connection with round dances, where Nausicaa probably acted as leader of the choir. A somewhat fiercer competitive spirit is depicted in another scene (*Odyssey* 6.115), in which Nausicaa's throw misses the target. Some sport historians compare this game with the ball game known as *ourania* (sky-ball). Brief references to ball games played by young women can also be found in the work of Apollonius Rhodius (Greek author, third century BCE), who compares the Argo, the ship of the Argonauts, with a ball that the Nereids pass around to one another. Although a source (a late one, however) mentions Nausicaa as the inventor of the ball game (the Kerkyraeic scholar Agallis, quoted by Athenaeus, *Deipnosophistae* 1.14d), ball games are not limited to women, as the connection between ball games and dance is verified for young men in the *Odyssey.*

These scenes of sport clearly are images taken from the everyday life of the poet, no matter how they are interpreted. Various interpretations may portray them as mere pastimes, as competitive games of a combative nature, or as playful preparations for a dancing performance of a cult. Non-mythical evidence shows that these scenes—even if the figure of Nausicaa is not historical—do not consist of fictional elements.

RUNNING

Investigation of women's running contests yields a more diversified picture. Pausanias (Greek author, second century CE) transmits the origin myth concerning the running contests, known from historic time, on the occasion of the Heraia (festival in honor of Hera) at Olympia, where girls of various age classes participated. "They trace the girls' games to antiquity as well as the men's: they say Hippodameia (daughter of Oinomaos, mythical king of Elis, and his wife, Sterope) first gathered the sixteen women to give thanks to Hera for her marriage to Pelops, and first celebrated Hera's games with them, and they also record that the winner was Chloris, the only surviving daughter of Amphion" (Pausanias, *Description of Greece* 5.16.4). These and similar running contests are often interpreted as survivals of initiation rites. A completely different situation is encountered in the myth of Atalanta, the daughter of Schoeneus, to whom various references exist. She refuses to marry, but because of her beauty many suitors court her nevertheless. Atalanta demands of them that they defeat her in a running contest, wherein the suitors are permitted a head start and Atalanta runs wearing heavy arms. When she catches up with them she kills the suitors. Only Milanion (or, according to a different source, Hippomenes) beats her with a trick. He successively drops three apples made of pure gold given to him by Aphrodite. Atalanta loses the race because she pauses to pick up the apples. This depiction is a reversal of more common ones: in a traditional bridal race several men engage in a race to win a girl, usually a daughter of a king, as a wife—and subsequently the kingdom as well. The motif of erotic chases is also found, which calls to mind several basic elements—among them that girls are wild and have to be tamed by marriage, that girls are violently torn away from their families and are subjugated to an unknown man, and similar notions. The narration of Atalanta can be seen as a counterpart to these. Here the bride-to-be challenges the suitors herself and her intention is that no marriage take place; even when finally defeated in the race and married, she is not tamed but hunts together with her husband—an activity that in real life was restricted to men. This myth does not simply represent evidence for athletic performance of young women. It is, rather, the depiction of a reversed world and is meant to draw attention to socially important forms of behavior.

WRESTLING AND OTHER SPORTS

Atalanta is not only known for this running contest, she also figures as a wrestler. In this context she is an exception, too: she is the only heroine participating in this event during funeral games (for Pelias); in it she defeats Peleus, who is famous for his wrestling skills. No further details of this fight survive. Other sources do not mention Atalanta; only male victors for the wrestling competition at these games were recorded. The fight, however, became a popular subject for vase painters. Thus the character of the pictures changed over time. At the beginning of the pictorial tradition (since the sixth century BCE), one finds the representation of the wrestling contest; these were later replaced by vase paintings that show Atalanta apart from the actual fight.

The above-mentioned Peleus had to get through another wrestling contest with a woman: the woman he desired, Thetis. The daughter of the sea god Nereus, she could change her shape and appear as fire, as water, or as a beast before him. Following the advice of the wise centaur Cheiron he was finally able to capture her while she was changing shapes. He did not let her go until she had regained her original form. One mythical version about the god Dionysus and the daughter of Sithos, Pallene, reported by Nonnus (Greek author, fifth century CE) in his epic *Dionysiaca*, shows the erotic manner in which this sport could be pursued. Other early sources illustrate how a love scene is described in the language of a wrestling contest.

Besides these more or less extensively documented wrestling competitions, the goddess Athena is mentioned as Theseus's mentor in wrestling, and Palaistra as the inventor of the wrestling contest. She is the daughter of Hermes, who is himself sometimes considered the inventor of the school of wrestling (*palaistra*).

AMAZONS: THE LAST NATION OF WOMEN

The Amazons, a mythical nation of women warriors frequently referred to in Greek mythology, are often mentioned in discussions of women's sports. The Amazons actually have nothing to do with women's sports, but rather with the image of women as aggressive, warlike, strong, fierce, and a threat to men.

The myth of a nation of women warriors spread from Greece to other parts of Europe and then to the New World. Spanish explorers claimed to have encountered Amazons in South America, and, according to some accounts, so named the Amazon River. Much information about the Amazons is subject to debate, including the meaning of the word "Amazon." In one version, it is claimed to mean "without breast" as the Amazons were reported to have removed their right breasts to aid shooting with bow and arrow. In another version, it is thought to mean "without grain" because Amazons hunted for their food.

The Amazon nation of ancient Greek mythology was located on the edge of the Greek world and they were described in some detail by the historian Herodotus in the 5th century BCE. However, no one ever observed an Amazon or discovered the Amazon nation, and modern classicists and historians have viewed the notion of Amazons and an Amazon nation as a myth. This view has been challenged recently as archaeological finds in southern Russia suggest that some peoples living in the region during the time of ancient Greece allowed women to serve as warriors including graves in which some women are buried with weapons. These were certainly not the Amazon nations described in myth, but the presence of women warriors suggests that the myth may have been based on some reality.

All further references to women in sports are purely marginal. Hippodameia, the founder of the race at the Heraia, is portrayed on vase paintings standing on the chariot next to her spouse Pelops, a version to which Pausanias refers. According to a short note by Hesiod in *Theogony*, the goddess Hecate is responsible for horse races but apparently has no further connection with sport.

On a vase painting Atalanta is portrayed riding as a huntress with her favorite weapon, the bow and arrow, with which she killed Rhoikos (Rhoecus) and Hylaios (Hylaeus), two drunken centaurs who tried to rape her. This weapon was also used by the goddess Artemis who is said to have killed the giant Orion, known for his passion for hunting, when Orion challenged her in discus throwing. And famous for their skills in archery were the Amazons, the legendary female warrior tribe.

CONCLUSION

Myths can be heard all over the world. They are told for different purposes: to explain natural phenomena as well as to legitimize a new dynasty, to tell the beginnings of the world as well as to explain strange cults or traditions. Though a great deal of information can be found in myths, one has to be careful when using them as a source for the past; it is not always possible to decide whether a single piece of information can be used as proof for a widespread trend or if it is just an exception to that trend, noted, in fact, for its uniqueness rather than its generality.

The mythology of Greece and Rome offers a wide range of information on social behavior, including, of course, sport. Women, however, are seldom mentioned in this context: we hear of etiological myths, where women are the namegiving heroines for a sport (e.g., Palaistra as the one who invents wrestling) or where they introduce a specific contest (e.g., Hippodameia in Olympia). The most detailed descriptions are from myths where a woman is not willing to marry, and the suitor has to fight with her—but these scenes do not reflect widespread practice. They have to be read the other way around: young women were expected to marry willingly and to have children, thus meeting the needs of society. Some myths, however, seem to reflect historical reality (at least of the time when the myths where written down),

and we hear of ball games, dancing, and running contests of young girls and women.

Peter Mauritsch
Ingomar Weiler

See also Art; Greece, Ancient; Literature; Marathon and Distance Running; Rome, Ancient

Bibliography

Angeli Bernardini, Paola. (1988) "Le donne e la pratica della corsa nella grecia antica." In *Lo sport in Grecia*, edited by Paola Angeli Bernardini. Rome-Bari: Editore Laterza, 153–184.

Arrigoni, Giampiera. (1985) "Donne e sport nel mondo greco: Religione e società." In *Le donne in Grecia*, edited by Giampiera Arrigoni. Rome-Bari: Editore Laterza, 55–201.

Bachofen, Johann Jakob. (1861) *Das Mutterrecht*. Stuttgart: Krais und Hoffmann.

Bérard, Claude. (1989) "The Order of Women." In *A City of Images: Iconography and Society in Ancient Greece,* by Claude Bérard et al. Princeton: University Press, 89–105. Originally published in French, 1984.

Bremmer, Jan N. (1996) *Götter, Mythen und Heiligtümer im antiken Griechenland*. Darmstadt: Wissenschaftliche Buchgesellschaft. Originally published in English, 1987.

Calame, Claude. (1997) *Choruses of Young Women in Ancient Greece: Their Morphology, Religious Role, and Social Function*. Lanham, MD: Rowman & Littlefield. Originally published in French, 1977.

Eisen, George. (1976) "Sports and Women in Antiquity." Ph.D. diss., University of Massachusetts.

Golden, Mark. (1998) *Sport and Society in Ancient Greece*. Cambridge: Cambridge University Press.

Graf, Fritz. (1996) *Greek Mythology: An Introduction*. Baltimore: Johns Hopkins University Press. Originally published in German, 1985.

Hampl, Franz. (1975) " 'Mythos'—'Sage'— 'Märchen.' " In *Geschichte als kritische Wissenschaft,* edited by I. Weiler. Darmstadt: Wissenschaftliche Buchgesellschaft, 2: 1–50.

Harris, H. A. (1972) *Sports in Greece and Rome*. London: Thames and Hudson.

Huizinga, Johan. (1991) *Homo Ludens: Vom Ursprung der Kultur im Spiel*. Reinbek bei Hamburg: Rowohlt Taschenbuch Verlag. Originally published in the Netherlands, 1938.

Kirk, Geoffrey S. (1980) *The Nature of Greek Myths*. Harmondsworth: Penguin Books.

Laser, Siegfried. (1987) *Sport und Spiel*. Göttingen: Vandenhoeck & Ruprecht (*Archaeologia Homerica,* Kapitel T).

Lefkowitz, Mary R. (1986) *Women in Greek Myth.* London: Gerald Duckworth.

Lévi-Strauss, Claude. (1955) "The Structural Study of Myth." In *Myth: A Symposium,* edited by T. Sebeok. Bloomington: Indiana University Press, 81–106.

Lexicon Iconographicum Mythologiae Classicae (LIMC). (1981–1997) Zurich-Munich: Artemis.

Ley, Anne. (1990) "Atalante—Von der Athletin zur Liebhaberin." In *Nikephoros* 3: 77–90.

Poliakoff, Michael Baron. (1986) *Studies in the Terminology of the Greek Combat Sports.* Frankfurt/Main: Hain.

Scanlon, Thomas F. (1984) "The Footrace of the Heraia at Olympia." *Ancient World* 8: 77–90.

Sourvinou-Inwood, Christiana. (1991) *"Reading" Greek Culture: Texts and Images, Rituals and Myths.* Oxford: Clarendon Press.

Specht, Edith. (1989) *Schön zu sein und gut zu sein.* Vienna: Wiener Frauenverlag (Frauenforschung, Vol. 9).

Weiler, Ingomar. (1974) *Der Agon im Mythos: Zur Einstellung der Griechen zum Wettkampf.* Darmstadt: Wissenschaftliche Buchgesellschaft (Impulse der Forschung, Vol. 16).

———. (1989) *Der Sport bei den Völkern der Alten Welt.* Darmstadt: Wissenschaftliche Buchgesellschaft.

Weiler, Ingomar, G. Doblhofer, M. Lavrencic, P. Mauritsch, W. Petermandl, U. Schachinger, eds. (1991–1998) *Quellendokumentation zur Gymnastik und Agonistik im Altertum.* Vienna-Cologne-Weimar: Böhlau-Verlag.

N

NAGINATA

Naginata is a Japanese martial art that has for centuries been associated with women. It is practiced by women, and some men, in virtually all schools and colleges in modern Japan. Although it began as a system of warfare, naginata is not a modern means of self-defense. It is instead practiced as a physical discipline and method of personal d-evelopment. Around the world, some 80,000 people study naginata, almost all practicing *atarashi naginata*, the modern sport form of naginata. There are naginata federations in Japan, the United States, France, Brazil, New Zealand, Belgium, the Netherlands, and Sweden. Outside Japan, men and women practice in about equal numbers.

HISTORY

During the ninth century, Japanese warfare underwent radical change with the proliferation of the curved cavalry sword known as the *tachi*. This corresponded to the rise of the aristocratic mounted *bushi* (warrior class). Lower-ranking warriors began fighting with a curved blade mounted on a stout oak shaft, similar to a European halberd or glaive. These weapons were known as *naginata*, meaning "long blade" or "reaping blade."

These single-edged, slightly curved blades were fashioned with the same laminations of hard and soft steel used for sword blades. Despite variations in the proportion of shaft to blade, the length of the entire weapon has almost always been the same, somewhere between 2.1 and 2.4 meters in length (7–8 feet).

These first naginata were heavy, and were used to cut the legs of horses and to slash through an enemy's defenses. They were also used in thrusting attacks, with either the blade or the metal-capped butt end. The naginata began to be supplanted in the fourteenth century with the reintroduction of spear fighting. Spears could more easily be used in close formation and required far less training time to be effective. The naginata became a rather uncommon weapon of war by the mid-sixteenth century.

NAGINATA AND WOMEN

Naginata has long been associated with women. It was considered most appropriate to women's physique, and to the circumstances in which they would fight, generally speaking, defending their homes. A strong, lithe woman, armed with a naginata, could keep all but the best warriors at a distance, where the advantages of physical strength counted for little.

The imposition of the Tokugawa government in the early seventeenth century led to strict social controls on all strata of society, controls that fell heavily upon women. The bushi woman was expected to center her life in unquestioning service to her family, much as the samurai was in service to his lord. The naginata became an emblem of a glorious past, a means of training women to stoic acceptance of a life of subservience. The use of the naginata became more formalized and stylized in specific *ryu-ha* (martial traditions), which then became associated with women. Movements became precise and quick, and the weapons themselves had small, slender blades and light shafts.

In the mid-1800s, Japan began to consolidate as a modern nation-state. The newly created grammar school system played a significant role. Martial arts training was made a regular part of the school curriculum. As the old martial arts, with their emphasis on forms, were not amenable to teaching school children en masse, they were restructured into martial sports such as *judo* and *kendo*.

These innovations brought the practice of naginata to a crossroads. Judo, kendo, and later *karate* were developed to be practiced in standardized forms. This had not yet happened with naginata, which was still split among many dif-

THE BUSHIDO IDEAL (1899)

Fencing and similar exercises, if rarely of practical use, were a wholesome counterbalance to the otherwise sedentary habits of women. But these exercises were not followed only for hygienic purposes. They could be turned into use in times of need. Girls, when they reached womanhood, were presented with dirks (kai-ken, pocket poniard), which might be directed to the bosom of their assailants, or, if advisable, to their own. The latter was very often the case; and yet I will not judge them severely. Even the Christian conscience with its horror of self-immolation, will not be harsh with them, seeing Pelagia and Dominina, two suicides, were canonized for their purity and piety. When a Japanese Virgin saw her chastity menaced, she did not wait for her father's dagger. Her own weapon lay always in her bosom. It was a disgrace to her not to know the proper way in which she had to perpetrate self-destruction. For example, little as she was taught in anatomy, she must know the exact spot to cut in her throat; she must know how to tie her lower limbs together with a belt so that, whatever the agonies of her death might be, her corpse be found in utmost modesty with the limbs properly composed.

INAZO NITOBE
(1899) Bushido: The Soul of Japan.

ferent groups, all with different curricula. Therefore, competitive practice became more and more popular, both as a means of training among different groups and to hold the interest of modern young women.

Light wooden practice weapons, covered with leather, were first used; later, for safety, bamboo strips were attached to the end of a wooden shaft. This modern replica is light and whippy, allowing movements impossible with a real naginata. As rules developed, and point targets were agreed upon, the techniques useful for victory in competition began to differ from those used by the old martial traditions, each of which had been developed for different terrain and different combat situations. Thus, naginata was transformed into a sport and became known as *atarashii naginata* or "new naginata."

During World War II, some naginata teachers, notably Sakakida Yaeko, created a set of standardized forms consisting of prearranged choreographies of one naginata form against another. In 1953, after a hiatus caused by a ban on martial arts by the occupying forces after the war, Sakakida and several of the leading naginata instructors created the All Japan Naginata Federation.

RULES AND PLAY

Atarashii naginata is composed of two parts: form practice and freestyle competition. The forms, or *kata*, are a set of simple movements requiring straight posture and sliding footwork. They are used in contests, where two pairs of contestants perform at the same time and are judged on the correctness of their movements. A solid wood naginata is used for kata practice. Live blade naginata are rarely used today.

The freestyle competitions are very similar to the kendo competitions. The contestants are armored and there are ten designated targets. Strikes are to the ribs (at the side of the chest), the top and sides of the head, the throat, the shins, and the wrists. The hip protector is not a target. Winning points are decided by referees; the target area must be struck with accuracy and authority. The contestants hold their bodies upright on the balls of their feet, so as to be able to slide and jump quickly toward or away from their opponent.

Atarashii naginata has spread around the globe since World War II and there have been international tournaments since the early 1990s. Women are involved throughout the world in

Women practicing naginata martial arts. (Michael S. Yamashita/Corbis)

the practice and development of the sport. The United States Naginata Federation, the first branch federation outside Japan, was established by Helen Michiyo Nakano and Yasuko Yamaguchi in 1974. Nakano is the president of the Southern California Naginata Federation, as a member of the Technical Committee for the International Naginata Federation, and was the first director of the Pan-American Zone for the International Naginata Federation, which was formed in Japan in 1990. There are naginata practitioners in California, Florida, Minnesota, and Nebraska. Because naginata is one of the least known martial arts, many students (who are commonly practitioners of other martial arts, especially kendo and aikido) are geographically isolated and often practice alone and must travel to gatherings for practice and competition. Women make up about 50 percent of U.S. naginata students.

Atarashii naginata is neither an archaic system of warfare nor a modern system of self-defense. Instead, it is a method of personal development. Participants believe that through confrontation with one's own weaknesses, which are revealed by dedicated practice, repeated failure and success, and the modeling of one's instructor (an individual further down the same road of personal development) each practitioner can achieve the ideal of calm and self-mastery.

Ellis Amdur

See also Kendo

Bibliography

Amdur, Ellis. (1995) "The Development and History of the Naginata." *Journal of Asian Martial Arts* 4, 1: 32–49.

———. (1996) "The Role of Arms-Bearing Women in Japanese History." *Journal of Asian Martial Arts* 5, 2: 10–35.

International Naginata Federation (1999) <http://www.naginata.org>.

Southern California Naginata Federation (1999) <http://members.aol.com/naginata/index.html>.

Additional information provided by Sue Kent (Southern California Naginata Federation).

NAMIBIA

Namibia is located in southwest Africa and has a population of about 1.7 million. The region came under German control in 1890 and was then under South African rule from 1915 until it became an independent nation in 1990. Prior to the arrival of European settlers and missionaries, the traditional African education system included specific sporting activities for both males and females.

During the colonial period (1890–1990), education was structured along racial lines, with separate schools for blacks and whites and far more resources devoted to the education of whites. This pattern of segregation and discrimination also applied to physical education and sports with white schools having more and better facilities and equipment and white boys and girls encouraged to participate in European sports. During this period, white women in Namibia participated in swimming, equestrian events, netball, track and field, volleyball, tennis, and gymnastics while black women were restricted mainly to netball, volleyball, and track and field.

Participation in international sports was through South Africa and was open only to whites. The end of South African rule in 1990 and the end of apartheid in Namibia opened sport participation to women and for the first time girls and women of all races had unlimited access to all sporting facilities. In the 1990s, Namibian women participated in the two Summer Olympic Games, the Commonwealth Games, the All-Africa Games, world championships in several sports, and regional games.

In the newly independent Namibia there was a disparity between urban areas and the rural regions as almost all sporting facilities were located in cities. Consequently, girls growing up in rural areas were often not able to participate in sporting activities such as lawn bowls, tennis, swimming, gymnastics, basketball, and other sports that required indoor facilities.

Sport in Namibia in the 1990s was organized along institutional lines, by schools, colleges, and other institutions, with a broad range of sports for men and women. There were several teacher training institutions and a university that trained teachers of physical education, who frequently served as coaches in the schools. Government policy requires that physical education teachers be placed in schools in all regions. The most popular sports in Namibia are cycling, rugby, soccer (association football), horse riding, lawn bowls, track and field, gymnastics, swimming, tennis, volleyball, and netball. Field hockey and basketball are also developing rapidly. Save for rugby and soccer, women participate in virtually all other sports.

To underline the seriousness that the government attaches to women's sport, Namibia hosted the second World Conference on Women's Sport in May 1998 at Windhoek. At the end of that meeting, two Namibians were elected to the key posts of president and secretary-general of the International Working Group on Women in Sport.

Moni Wekesa

See also International Working Group on Women and Sport; South Africa

Bibliography

Amukugo, Elizabeth Magano. (1998) *Education and Politics in Namibia.* Windhoek: Gamsberg Macmillan.

Katjavivi, Peter. (1978) *A History of Resistance in Namibia*. London: UNESCO.

Toetemeyer, Gerhardt. (1978) *Namibia Old and New*. London: Hurst & Co.

NATIONAL ASSOCIATION FOR GIRLS AND WOMEN IN SPORT

The National Association for Girls and Women in Sport (NAGWS) is a not-for-profit U.S. organization whose roots come from a committee created in 1899 to write rules for women's collegiate basketball. NAGWS is the sole professional educational organization devoted to providing opportunities for girls and women athletes. Its membership is composed of professional educators in the field of physical education and sport. Members are teachers, coaches, and administrators for grades K–12 and the college/university level. NAGWS has championed the cause of girls and women in sport since 1899. NAGWS fosters quality and equality in sport for girls and women. NAGWS is one of six national associations of the American Alliance for Health, Physical Education, Recreation, and Dance (AAHPERD).

At a conference held in 1899 by the American Physical Education Association (APEA, later to become the AAHPERD), Alice Foster of Oberlin College read a paper on women's basketball. At that time, women's basketball was being played under several different rule formats. Foster's paper identified this problem and suggested a meeting to consolidate the rules. During the conference, Foster chaired the committee that included Senda Berenson, Smith College; Ethel Perrin, Boston Normal School of Gymnastics; and Elizabeth Wright, Radcliffe College. The committee investigated the various rules being used for women's basketball and produced the first official women's basketball rules book in 1901. However, the committee represented only the American Association for the Advancement of Physical Education (AAAPE), one of six sport organizations in the United States at that time.

The American Physical Education Association (APEA) authorized a standing committee on women's athletics in 1916. A year later, this committee sponsored the first meeting of a women's group at the APEA convention. Subsequently, a women's basketball committee of APEA was formed and divided into subcommittees including the women's rules and editorial subcommittees. By 1922, the editorial subcommittee had published guides and rule books in hockey, soccer, (association football), swimming, and track and field, as well as in basketball.

The Depression years marked important gains for the women in sports within the APEA. A section on women's athletics was formed for representation on the council of APEA. In 1928, the rating of officials began. The reorganization of APEA in 1932 led to the formation of the National Section on Women's Athletics (NSWA).

The Women's Division of the National Amateur Athletic Federation (NAAF) merged with NSWA in 1940. The joint efforts of the two groups proved successful. The name was changed to the National Section on Girls and Women's Sports (NSGWS) in 1953 to emphasize that NSGWS served secondary schools as well as college and adult women. NSGWS made an important decision in 1958 when it gave up independent status to become part of AAHPERD. The NSGWS became the Division for Girls and Women's Sports (DGWS) within AAHPERD.

In 1974, when AAHPERD restructured, DGWS became the National Association for Girls and Women in Sport (NAGWS), one of six national associations within AAHPERD. The mission of NAGWS continues with the common thread it has maintained since 1899, to promote opportunities for girls and women in sport through conferences and clinics that focus on teaching, coaching, and current issues concerning girls and women in sports.

Diana Everett

NATIVE AMERICAN GAMES AND SPORTS

Native American women have become regular and serious participants in both traditional Native games and mainstream sports, and some have also gone on to succeed in these games and sports outside their Native communities. Native elite athletes are role models for a large group of Native girls and women who embrace sport as an important part of their life.

HISTORY

Indigenous peoples have lived on the North American continent for at least 12,000 years. The ancestors of today's Native peoples, which include the Inuit (Eskimo), Indian, and Metis, viewed physical activities as part of their lives and cultures. European travelers began documenting these practices in the sixteenth century. From these accounts, we learn that girls and women participated in sports and games for both ceremonial purposes and recreation.

After the United States and Canada were in control of North America, they began to legislate what they viewed as appropriate physical activities for Native peoples. In the 1880s, government officials outlawed some traditional ceremonies, and teachers and government agents directed Native peoples away from traditional activities toward non-Native sports and games. Until the 1970s and 1980s, when all women gained greater access to sports, Native women, like other women, had fewer opportunities for participation in mainstream sport than did the men. The same sequence occurred in indigenous sports, with women slowly participating more fully in traditionally male domains. As Native women's opportunities have expanded in community life, they have also broadened in both mainstream and indigenous sports.

TRADITIONAL PARTICIPATION

Native women traditionally participated in a variety of indigenous sports and games. Ball games were especially popular, such as double ball, handball, and football, which were primarily played by women. Men and women also competed together in certain ball games. The women of the Choctaw tribe, formerly of the southern United States and then relocated to Oklahoma, played a handball game along with men. Men and women of the Dakota, a plains tribe, played lacrosse together, with women allowed a five-to-one ratio over men.

Women competed in athletic activities that were essentially extensions of other aspects of their lives. Horse racing, rodeos, and sled dog racing were all popular in certain regions of the country. Running games were likewise common. Accounts exist of Native women in foot races at the end of the nineteenth century. Running was also part of the puberty rituals of Navajo and Apache women. The running symbolically shaped her body and soul into strong, upright, and beautiful forms, while also making her brave, energetic, and industrious.

In some situations, both women and men participated, but in different parts of the event. Pow-wows were gatherings where both men and women took part in competitive dancing, but females traditionally had a supporting role, and their dancing style was very modest. Male domination, both in organization and in the vigor of their dancing, reflected the tradition of male leadership among Northern Plains tribes.

Women were completely banned from competing in some sporting and ceremonial activities, or even from touching the equipment to be used. Hand-guessing games, archery, snowsnake, hoop and pole, and Inuit games of skill and self-testing were all off-limits for women. Some experts argue that women were not involved in Alaskan Tlingit hand-guessing games because items owned by men were used for wagering. Women were viewed as impure during menstruation, and so their contact would bring bad luck. These games thus allowed men to symbolically express their honor and prestige apart from women, and so reinforce their dominant role in the culture.

CONTEMPORARY PARTICIPATION

Indigenous sports have changed over the years to include more women. The Northern Games are a competition of traditional Inuit and Dene (Dene means "people" in some Native American lan-

BECENTI, RYNELDI (1971–): A ROLE MODEL FOR HER PEOPLE

Ryneldi Becenti was an All-State high school basketball player and the first from her Navajo reservation to play university basketball. When she was drafted into the American Basketball League in 1998, she faced a promising future as a professional basketball player and a role model for Native American youth.

Becenti grew up on the Navajo Reservation in Arizona and began playing basketball at age five. Both her parents participated regularly in reservation basketball. They helped her develop the mental and physical strength to be a great basketball player. Aware that Native basketball players did not have any Native role models, Becenti resolved to succeed and become a role model herself.

Growing up, Becenti's life centered on basketball. Not only her parents but also her four brothers, teachers, and the community gave her support. Her family did not have much money, so she knew she would have to get a scholarship if she wanted a university education. She became a high school All-State player, and won a full scholarship to the University of Arizona in 1988.

She was the first on her reservation to play university basketball, and many people would travel over five hours to join with Native supporters from Phoenix to watch her play. Becenti completed her university basketball career in 1994, and went on to play professional basketball in Europe. She returned to school and finished her sociology degree in 1997.

As she began her professional career, she planned to work with Native youth, encouraging them to aspire toward a university education and develop the self-esteem and confidence necessary to achieve that goal. She did not forget her childhood resolve to be a role model for Native children. While she saw the value of sport, she clearly believed that education was more important. She thus encouraged others—especially those who faced financial difficulties—to pursue sport if it would help to pay for their education.

Becenti also learned about the ways in which Native peoples were mistreated historically, and this awareness also motivated her to succeed. As she began her professional career, she continued to take great pride in her Native heritage and maintain her cultural practices.

guages and is also the name some nations use for themselves) games that have been held annually across the Northwest Territories in Canada since 1970. The World Eskimo Indian Olympics, involving only participants of Native heritage, has been held annually in Fairbanks, Alaska, since 1961, and also includes Eskimo and Indian traditional games. Both competitions include women competing in traditionally male Inuit games such as knuckle hop, one foot high kick, and ear pull. World champions such as Meika McDonald from Canada, and Carol Pickett and Nicole Johnston from Alaska, have become role models for aspiring competitors in Inuit sports. In powwows, women are now involved in all aspects of the competition and are performing more vigorous "fancy dances," such as the jingle dress and shawl dances.

Junior women occasionally compete in traditional Iroquoian snowsnake competitions held in Ontario and Quebec. This activity involves par-

ticipants throwing a javelin-shaped stick down a preset snow track, with the greatest distance being the goal. Hand-game competitions in the Yukon have women, men, and junior participants. Even an Iroquois national women's lacrosse team has been formed, complementing the Iroquois national men's team, and both compete in world championships. These developments are part of women's broadening roles in Native communities.

All-Native Games

All-Native sports competitions, open only to those of Native descent, also offer athletic opportunities for women. The North American Indigenous Games, begun in 1990, have a number of mainstream sport events for women athletes. The National Indian Athletic Association has also provided Native women with single-sport competitions, such as basketball, golf, baseball, and softball. Female athletes are thus involved in a variety of competitive settings—both Native and non-Native—when they play mainstream sports.

Mainstream Sports

Native women have also become involved in a wide variety of mainstream sporting activities. Family and community support has been substantial for these athletes, with sports involvement complementing their feminine identity. Among the Choctaw, for example, females have expressed positive attitudes toward sport. Parents encourage young girls to develop physical coordination and abilities, and the girls choose female athletes as role models. They are comfortable competing with and beating males without fear of rejection, and athletic accomplishment is seen as an attractive feature of women. Both men and women in the Choctaw culture value womens' sports, and women believe that it is important that they be strong and healthy. Brief sketches of some successful female athletes provide a sense of their range and accomplishments.

Sharon and Shirley Firth (Gwich'in) became involved in cross-country skiing as teenagers in the Northwest Territories and went on to compete for Canada in four Olympic Games and several world cups during their twelve-year career (1972–1984). Both were awarded the Order of Canada medal in 1987.

Princess Redbird, Emma Blackfox, and Good Elk were all Native women who competed in mainstream rodeo at the start of the twentieth century. At that time, most Native women were only allowed to race in so-called Squaw events, but this designation was dropped, and women have continued to compete successfully both in the All-Indian Rodeo circuit, started in the 1970s, and in mainstream competitions. Shelly Bird-Matthews, for example, was the 1990 barrel racing champion at the Indian National Rodeo Finals, as well as a rookie qualifier for that event at the National Finals Rodeo in 1991.

Alaskan Native women have participated in the sport of sled dog racing. For three years in a row—1952 to 1954—Effie Kokrine (Athabaskan) of Alaska won the Women's North American competition. Twenty years later, Roxy Wright-Champain (Athabaskan) won the Women's Fur Rendezvous World Championship sprint race in Anchorage on her way to competing in the Idita-rod sled dog race and winning numerous times against men in the Open North American competition and the Open Fur Rendezvous World Championship sprint race during the 1980s and the 1990s.

Ryneldi Becenti (Navajo) and Crystal Robinson (Cherokee) have had successful careers as professional basketball players, both in Europe and in North America. Robinson had an outstanding career with the Colorado Explosion in the American Basketball League, while Becenti played on teams in Sweden and Greece since competing with the United States women's basketball team at the World University Games in 1993.

Angela Chalmers (Sioux) has had an outstanding career in track. She represented Canada and won a bronze medal in the 3,000-meter race at the 1992 Olympics. She also won four gold medals while competing at the Commonwealth Games in 1990 and 1994. She was awarded a National Aboriginal Achievement Award in Canada in 1995.

Controversies

Although women athletes are highly regarded in many Native communities, the same bias that favors male athletes in non-Native societies is apparent in aspects of Native sport. The athletic awards provided to Native athletes, for example, have largely gone to men. In Canada, the Tom Longboat Award has been given since 1951 to those demonstrating character, leadership, and sportsmanship. Only one female—Phyllis Bomberry (Iroquois) in 1969—won this award during the first twenty-three years of its existence. She was a fastball catcher who played on the Canadian women's championship team. The American Indian Hall of Fame, begun in 1972 to honor those who have brought distinction through sports to themselves and the Native community, had inducted only one female—Angelita Rosal (Sioux) in 1973—among the fifty-seven people inducted by 1985. Rosal made the United States table tennis team when she was only seventeen years old. These awards thus tended to promote male rather than female role models in sport.

Some Native communities have not valued women's sports to the same degree as men's sports. For example, Inuit girls from Holman

Island in the Northwest Territories may now freely participate in sports, and have greater opportunities to do so. Like boys, they have been influenced by cultures to the south to value mainstream sporting activities. Girl athletes, however, do not gain the same prestige as boys who play sports, and seem to move from sports to adult responsibilities at an earlier age than do the boys in their community. These cases suggest that females still face inequality in some Native sport settings.

Inequities notwithstanding, the North American Indigenous Games, begun in 1990, have gender-equitable rules that require equal numbers of men and women on the coaching, management, and chaperone staffs. These contrasting examples make clear the variety of approaches taken toward women's sport in Native cultures, and the need to look at particular Native cultural situations to get a clear picture of the status of Native women in sport.

Another source of controversy has been the use, by Native organizers, of the restrictive, government-defined term for "Status Indian" when determining participants in all-Native sports competitions. The Indian Act in Canada, until 1985, created a systematic bias—women who were legally classified as Indian lost their Indian status (as did their children) when they married men who lacked that status, while Indian men did not. The use of government-generated definitions of "Indian" for all-Native sport competitions thus worked against women and their offspring who had so lost their status. New legislation (Bill C-31) was passed after a long struggle, allowing both women and children to have their status reinstated.

SIGNIFICANCE OF THE DEVELOPMENT OF WOMEN'S SPORTS

Native women within mainstream sport have continued to push the boundaries of achievement. Roxy Wright-Champain, for example, is considered among the best dog mushers in the world—male or female, Native or non-Native. Female athletes such as Wright-Champain serve as role models for other Native girls and women in sport (and boys as well). Basketball player Ryneldi Becenti shows, for example, that Native girls can get university athletic scholarships, compete successfully, and get an education at the same time, while staying in touch with their cultural practices.

Meika McDonald, a world champion in traditional Inuit games, demonstrates to young girls that competing in indigenous sports is as rewarding as being active in non-Native sports. Young girls need to know more about the achievements of these women.

CONCLUSION

Native women have continued to ensure that their needs, as well as those of men, are met in sport. Native athletes have laid the groundwork to inspire Native youth to become involved in sports. Native women have shown that participation in sports is personally rewarding and important for the well being of their communities.

Victoria Paraschak

Bibliography

Blanchard, Kendall. (1981) *The Mississippi Choctaws at Play: The Serious Side of Leisure*. Chicago: University of Illinois Press.

Condon, Richard, and Pamela Stern. (1993) "Gender-Role Preference, Gender Identity, and Gender Socialization Among Contemporary Inuit Youth." *Ethos* 21, 4: 384–416.

Heine, Michael. (1991) "The Symbolic Capital of Honor: Gambling Games and the Social Construction of Gender in Tlingit Indian Culture." *Play and Culture* 4: 346–358.

LeCompte, MaryLou. (1993) *Cowgirls of the Rodeo: Pioneer Professional Athletes*. Chicago: University of Illinois Press.

Nabokov, Peter. (1981) *Indian Running: Native American History & Traditions*. New Mexico: Ancient City Press.

Oxendine, Joseph. (1995) *American Indian Sports Heritage*, 2d ed. Lincoln: University of Nebraska Press.

Paraschak, Victoria. (1990) "Organized Sport for Native Females on the Six Nations Reserve, Ontario from 1968 to 1980: A Comparison of Dominant and Emergent Sport Systems." *Canadian Journal of History of Sport* 21, 2: 70–80.

———. (1996) "An Examination of Sport for Aboriginal Females on the Six Nations Reserve, Ontario, from 1968 to 1980." In *Women of the First Nations: Power, Wisdom, and Strength*, edited by Christine Miller and Patricia Chuchryk. Winnipeg: University of Manitoba Press.

Silman, Janet, ed. (1987) *Enough Is Enough: Aboriginal Women Speak Out*. Toronto: The Women's Press.

Vennum, Thomas, Jr. (1994) *American Indian Lacrosse: Little Brother of War*. Washington, DC: Smithsonian Institution Press.

NAVRATILOVA, MARTINA

(1956–)

CZECH, AND LATER U.S., TENNIS PLAYER

Martina Navratilova is one of the most successful, outspoken, and controversial women athletes of all time. She was the dominant women's tennis player for the much of the 1980s, and her on-court rivalry with Chris Evert made the sport popular with an entire generation of spectators. Off the court, she has worked in many ways to promote women's full participation in sports.

Martina Šubertova was born in Prague, Czechoslovakia, on 18 October 1956. Her father, Miroslav Šubert, was a restaurant manager in Prague. Her mother, Jana, was responsible for the house, the family, and a full-time railroad job. Jana enjoyed many sports but was passionate about skiing. By the age of two, Martina was learning to ski. Her parents divorced in 1958 and Martina and Jana moved to Revnice, Czechoslovakia. Jana joined a tennis club and took Martina along regularly. It was there that Jana met Miroslav (Mirek) Navratil; they married and Martina Šubertova became Martina Navratilova. In 1963, her mother and stepfather presented her with a baby sister, Jana.

With her mother as a role model, Navratilova soon discovered that a woman could be an athlete, a worker, and a mother. In her stepfather, Mirek, she found a loving disciplinarian who provided stability and nurturing. She received unconditional love and support from her father's mother who invested time in Navratilova, accepting her as unique and encouraging her to enjoy life. Her maternal grandmother was also quite a tennis player and was a member of the Czech national tennis team before World War II.

An administrator at the tennis club, Mirek Navratil took a serious interest in the development of Navratilova's tennis career. When she was only eight years old, he coached her in her first tournament and she reached the semifinals. Soon after, she met George Parma, whose job was to develop promising tennis talent. As a youngster, playing tennis seemed to make Navratilova more independent and more self-confident. By the age of ten, she traveled alone to practice one or two days a week in Prague. By the time she got home, she had barely time to do her homework before she went to bed, exhausted.

By the age of fourteen, Navratilova won her first national tournament, and by the time she was sixteen she was the best female tennis player in Czechoslovakia. She reigned as national champion from 1972 to 1975 and also won the Wimbledon Junior Girls Championship in 1973. By that time, Navratilova was traveling to tournaments around the world, including the United States, where she discovered that she thoroughly enjoyed junk food. She quickly gained twenty pounds and her movement around the court suffered as she became somewhat sluggish. She then confronted Chris Evert, at the time an up-and-coming tennis star. After suffering her first loss to Evert, Navratilova shed the excess weight and began beating most of the world's best players.

The communist government of Czechoslovakia included tennis in its grand plan to gain international prestige via sports achievements, and the Czech Tennis Federation was told to begin producing champions. Navratilova had other ideas. Frustrated by the federation's restrictions, she decided, in 1975, to defect to the United States. Unable to say goodbye to her mother, stepfather, sister, and *babicka*, Navratilova left Czechoslovakia, knowing that she could probably never return so long as the country remained under communist rule.

The next several years were exceptional ones. By 1977, she was ranked as one of the top three players in the world, but for some reason, she was still unable to win the Grand Slam events—Wimbledon, the Australian, French, and U.S. Opens. Perhaps her defection and the adjustment to the United States distracted her from tennis. By 1978, Navratilova was able to focus on her game. She won her first Wimbledon singles title, defeating Chris Evert in the finals. In 1979, she won both the singles and doubles tournaments at Wimbledon, and by 1980 she was the leading money earner on the women's tour.

After becoming an American citizen in 1981, she dominated the professional women's tennis scene for much of the remainder the decade. From 1982 to 1987 she was the ranked the number one tennis player in the world. She won the Wimbledon singles title in 1982, 1983, 1984, 1985, 1986, and 1987; the Australian Open in 1981, 1983, 1985; the French Open in 1982 and 1984; and the U. S. Open in 1983, 1984, 1986, and 1987. Equally impressive during the decade was her string of doubles championships with partner Pam Shriver.

Determining that her weight, nutrition, sleep, and training techniques were all important components of her game and required attention to take her tennis to another level, Navratilova enlisted former basketball player Nancy Lieberman to serve as her personal trainer. Weight training was beneficial for her play, but her exceptionally toned physique led to innuendos in the press about her sexual orientation. In her independent style, Navratilova confirmed that she was, in fact, a lesbian and that her sexual orientation had nothing to do with her ability to play tennis. For a period, Navratilova was seen as an inappropriate person to endorse products, but public indifference to her lesbianism brought back the sponsors.

In 1986, for the first time since her defection, Navratilova returned to Czechoslovakia as a member of the United States Federation Cup team. Her return was beyond her wildest dreams. The Czech people embraced her as one of their own and threw bouquets of flowers on center court before, during, and after play.

Navratilova's singles career ended in 1994. Knee injuries decreased her mobility to the point where retirement was the only option as she could no longer play her aggressive service-and-volley game. As a tennis superstar, she had won fifty-four Grand Slam titles (singles, doubles, mixed doubles), second only to Margaret Court Smith (sixty-two). For ten years, she and Chris Evert provided the world with phenomenal tennis. In the finals of the Grand Slam, Navratilova won ten of their fourteen encounters. In all, she won 166 tournaments, including 1,400 singles matches (and nearly $20 million in prize money). She was named the Female Athlete of the Decade by National Sports Review, United Press Inter-

Martina Navratilova competing at Wimbledon in 1987. Her on-court success and off-court activism have made her a leader in the women's sports movement. (Mike King)

national, and the Associated Press. She also served as President of the Women's Tennis Association Tour Players Association in 1994. In that role as well as in unofficial capacities she was a strong voice for women's tennis.

Darlene A. Kluka

Bibliography

Blue, Adrianne. (1995) *Martina: The Life and Times of Martina Navratilova.* New York: Carol Publishing Group.

Harrington, Denis. J. (1995) *Top 10 Women Tennis Players.* Springfield, NJ: Enslow Publishers.

Navratilova, Martina. (1985) *Martina.* New York: Ballantine Books.

NETBALL

Netball is a game that resembles basketball but uses a smaller ball and has somewhat different rules. It was invented by women physical educators in England in the late nineteenth century. Though netball's early expansion was rapid, it has remained almost exclusively confined to former areas of the British Empire, including Australia and New Zealand, Africa, and the Caribbean. In many places netball has been variously referred to as basketball, basket ball, and women's basketball, although netball has become the common international name for the sport. Netball has remained almost exclusively a women's game, which may account for its survival despite the spread of the far more popular sport of basketball.

HISTORY

James Naismith's invented game of basketball was imported to England from the United States in 1895 by an American physical educator named Dr. Toll. By the late 1890s, English female physical educators thought that a modified form of the game would suit their female pupils. In 1901 women physical educators of the Ling Association in England devised the first set of netball rules. Netball, as with other sports played by women in the late nineteenth and early twentieth centuries, initially developed in schools, usually in single-sex private schools. It spread rapidly within Britain and then to other parts of the British Empire, and by 1906 the game had reached Australia and New Zealand.

In the first decade after its invention, netball rapidly gained a large following among women and, unlike many other sports taken up by women, received mostly positive press reporting. Netball's success has been attributed largely to the fact that men did not play the game in its early years and that women were always a majority among officials running the sport. Indeed, many netball associations put in their constitutions that only women could serve as executives. When the Otago Association in New Zealand held their first tournament in 1915, the local press stated:

> On Saturday afternoon over 100 interested spectators gathered at Woodhaugh Gardens to witness the first tournament under the auspices of the Otago Basket Ball Union. . . . Seven teams entered; and as every team played every other team in 10-minute matches, the two grounds were in a state of constant excitement until very late in the afternoon. During all this time the keenness of the players and the enthusiasm and excitement of the spectators never flagged, which is evidence of the hold which basket ball has taken in Dunedin.

The first national tournament was held in New Zealand in 1926 as part of the Empire Exhibition in Dunedin. Press coverage was minimal, but the *Otago Daily Times* covered the event and argued that netball was "a game eminently suitable for every girl, especially the business or industrial girl, who gets practically no exercise during the week"; the article also reported that netball was played in every primary school and most secondary schools in the country. By 1929, the *Christchurch Sun* hailed netball as "A New National Game." National associations appeared in New Zealand in 1924, England in 1926, Australia in 1927, and South Africa in 1933.

As with New Zealand, netball in Australia and South Africa, for white women at least, was rapidly organized as provincial and national unions emerged and competitions developed. The first international netball tour took place when Australia and New Zealand played each other in 1938. Due to the differing team sizes, though, international competition between the two countries was difficult. Other international competitions were also hard to sustain as resources were few and support for tours minimal. In England, netball remained entrenched as a schoolgirls' game. In 1957, a meeting of representatives from Australia, New Zealand, South Africa, the United States, and Great Britain took place to discuss the framing of international rules. As a result of differences between countries, the International Federation of Netball Associations (IFNA) was not formed until 1960, in Ceylon. In the 1960s, international competition became more formalized with world championships (from 1963) and more regular tours between the main netball-playing countries. Australia has dominated the world championships held every four years, winning seven of the nine tournaments held between 1963 and 1997 and every tournament from 1983 onward, with New Zealand being close behind. Trinidad and Jamaica have also fared well, as did South Africa in the 1960s and 1990s.

In the 1970s and 1980s, South Africa was excluded from world championships and official international tours due to its apartheid policies. Though netball became increasingly popular in the "Coloured" (mixed race) communities of the Cape Province and among black women in Johannesburg townships, the sport's organizational structures remained firmly segregated in South Africa until the 1990s.

Although netball began in England, it has failed to develop there as a mass sport for women in the way it has in Australia and New Zealand and to a lesser degree in South Africa. In Australia and New Zealand, various estimates show that between 10 and 15 percent of all women play netball at some level. In New Zealand, netball is one of four sports that receives free television coverage and a major news reporting along with the male-dominated sports of rugby union, rugby league, and cricket. Netball is regarded as the national sport of the Cook Islands, perhaps the only country where the national sport is one played primarily by women.

Netball appeared as a demonstration sport in the 1990 Commonwealth Games and was a regular part of the Commonwealth program in 1998. In Australia and New Zealand, the game appears to be very healthy both at elite and mass levels although the limited number of nations that participate at the international level does not bode well for the future of the game as a global sport. Australia remains dominant, sweeping a three-match test series with New Zealand in 1998. The 1999 Fisher and Paykel Cup, however, was dominated by New Zealand with a 60–48 win. While South Africa and Jamaica and Trinidad are competitive, the West Indian sides were decimated in the 1990s by the great popularity of basketball.

RULES AND PLAY

Netball, in terms of the ways the body is used, the restrictions on player movement within the court of play, and penalties for contact, resembles the six-a-side basketball that many women once played in North America. Netball differs from basketball in several distinct ways in that the ball is smaller, players are not allowed to dribble the ball, movement with the ball is restricted, and players stop to shoot at goal from a largely stationary position. The Code of Rules of Netball states that the number of players per side is seven. While most countries adopted the seven-a-side version of the game, in New Zealand, schools, clubs, and provincial associations played with nine-a-side before the 1960s. Women involved in New Zealand netball argued that their version allowed more girls and women to play—a good

Girls from Stepney's Central Foundation School go through warm-up exercises before a netball game. Netball spread from Britain to many of its colonies, with Australia, New Zealand, and Caribbean nations producing the best teams in the 1990s. (Hulton-Deutsch Collection/Corbis)

thing because facilities were limited. Except for pre-1960s New Zealand, however, the seven-a-side version dominated with players confined to certain areas of the court. The goal shooter (GS) and goal keeper (GK) on each team are allowed in their respective attacking and defensive thirds of the court; the goal attack and goal defense are also allowed in their respective shooting circles along with the GS and GK but can use two-thirds of the court. Mid-court players are the wing attack and wing defense and the center; none of these players is allowed in the goal circles or to shoot at goal.

PUBLIC PERCEPTION

Media coverage of netball initially denigrated the sport but then rapidly moved to promote netball as an ideal healthy activity for young women (when coverage appeared at all). Shifts in media and public pronouncements about netball occurred during the 1960s, in the context of a general improvement of the status of women in Western societies. Women were entering the work force in greater numbers in nations such as Australia and

Netball was invented in England, but its true home is Australia and New Zealand, where the best players and best teams play. In the ten world championships contested since the first in 1963, teams from one of these two nations have taken first place each time, with Australia winning eight times and New Zealand twice. Second place is much the same with New Zealand finishing second six times and Australia twice. Only England, South Africa, and Trinidad and Tobago (in a tie with Australia) have also finished second. In the 1999 championships, Australia won its eighth title, defeating New Zealand in the final match.

New Zealand where netball was widely regarded as the national sport for women.

It was at this time that the media began to focus on the sexual characteristics of players, and reports concentrated on those deemed to be the most attractive to men, rather than on their netball skill. In the 1980s and early 1990s, netball received unprecedented media coverage as women began to play many other sports, including those previously defined as male. The focus on the sexual characteristics of some players attracted wider attention to netball, not in terms of drawing male support for netball as a sport, but rather drawing the male gaze to women playing the game. Cartoons, like the one published in New Zealand's *Evening Post* during the first world championships in 1963, evidence the shift. The cartoon depicted a man leering at two passing national netball players while his wife lamented to a friend about her husband's new support for the sport.

New Zealand's top player of the 1960s, Joan Harnett, was portrayed more for her sexual appeal than her playing prowess, with such descriptions as "a long-legged beauty," "the male's ideal sportswoman," and "the essence of femininity." The power of the sexualization process was such that Harnett internalized the attention. She stated that she was initially embarrassed, but got used to it as it gave netball publicity. A 1982 book entitled *New Zealand's Champion Sportswomen* written by a former women's national cricket representative continued the framing of Harnett in terms of sex, discussing her beauty and even listing her measurements. That the author of the book was a woman illustrates the dominant power of images of female beauty in the presentation of women sporting participants to the wider public.

Margaret Carlisle Duncan argues in *Sociology of Sport Journal*, in an article on portrayals of women athletes, that photographs, like other mass media images, are politically motivated. Photography works to make the interests of the dominant group legitimate. As a result, often unbeknownst to the subject or the observer, photos still shape opinion and validate existing social arrangements.

Beyond portrayals in photographs there is also much written material that frames netball players as feminine, sexually attractive, and conforming largely to dominant male norms. Netball has benefited in some ways from such coverage in that many see the sport as one that is still ideally suited to young women, although it is now one of many sport options for young women in the countries where it is played. The need for greater media coverage and demands of sponsors have forced many women's sports such as netball, basketball, softball, and hockey in Australia to adopt what are viewed as sexier Lycra bodysuit uniforms even though many players do not like them. Nevertheless, they are part of the search for more funds and greater media coverage.

SUMMARY

Netball at the highest level of competition is played only in a few nations that were former British colonies such as Australia, New Zealand, Jamaica, and Kenya. And in some of these nations such as those in the Caribbean and Africa, it is losing ground as a major sport for women to more recently introduced sports such as basketball, soccer (association football), and running. These newer sports are popular because of ties to the United States and Western European sports cultures, and also because they provide the opportunity for well-paid, international professional careers.

Nonetheless, netball is gaining ground and thriving in some new places. For example, in neighborhoods in the Bronx and especially Brooklyn in New York City, thirty-six teams competed in a tournament sponsored by the Caribbean Netball Association in the summer of 1998. There are now forty-six teams and over a thousand players across the United States in New York, New Jersey, California, Texas, and Florida.

In nations where netball has become a popular national sport for women, netball has generally been dominated by men, and especially executives in the television and advertising industries who provide the major financial support for the sport. Women-dominated netball associations have lost power. Thus, as with some other women's sports such as basketball that are popular spectator sports, male control has no doubt helped netball grow but some critics question at what cost to women's sport in general and the public perception and role of women athletes.

John Nauright

See also Australia; Basketball; New Zealand; Unionism

Bibliography

Beran, Janice. (1993) *From Six on Six to Full Court Press: A Century of Women's Basketball in Iowa.* Iowa State University Press.

Duncan, Margaret Carlisle. (1990) "Sports Photographs and Sexual Difference: Images of Women and Men in the 1984 and 1988 Olympic Games." *Sociology of Sport Journal* 7, 1: 22–43.

Nauright, John. (1995) "From Private to Public: Historical and Social Factors in the Development of Women's Sport in Australia and New Zealand." *European Physical Education Review* 1, 2: 137–147.

———. (1995) "Netball, Media Representation of Women and Crisis of Male Hegemony in New Zealand." In *Sport, Cultures and Identities in New Zealand: Historical and Contemporary Perspectives,* edited by John Nauright. Sydney: Australian Society for Sports History.

———, and J. Broomhall. (1994) "A Woman's Game: The Development of Netball and a Female Sporting Culture in New Zealand, 1906–70." *International Journal of the History of Sport* 11, 3: 387–407.

NETHERLANDS, THE

The Netherlands is a small, densely populated European nation with a population of about 15.7 million people. Nearly half of all women are employed outside the home, compared to 70 percent of all men, and two-thirds of Dutch men and women take part in organized sport. Men and women, however, do not participate to the same extent in all sports. Some sports are mainly for boys or men and some are mainly for girls or women, while others, such as tennis, volleyball, and hockey, are played by people of both sexes. Additionally, sport participation varies by ethnic background, as many people of non-Dutch ethnicity (mainly people from former Dutch colonies in Southeast Asia and the Caribbean and South America), and especially the women in these minority groups, participate less in organized sports than do the ethnic Dutch.

RECREATIONAL SPORTS

The Netherlands has many rivers, lakes, and canals that have for centuries been used for ice-skating. In fact, ice-skating scenes—including female skaters—were among the most popular motifs for sixteenth- and seventeenth-century artists like Henrik Averkamp. Another winter sport, *kolf*, is believed by some to have evolved into modern golf, although other experts believe that golf began in the British Isles. *Korfball*, which is similar to basketball, is the only national team sport in which men and women play together. Developed as a coed school sport, in the 1990s it was the fourth most popular team sport, following soccer (association football), volleyball, and hockey.

Soccer is the major national sport, with more than one million players participating in organized leagues. The women's soccer program was

Dutch speed skater Sandra Zwolle slows down after competing in the women's 1000-meter event during the 1998 Winter Olympic Games. (Wally McNamee)

recognized by the national soccer federation in 1971. Since then the number of organized female participants has grown rapidly and in 1998 was more than 60,000 girls and women. Since 1996, girls and boys have been allowed to play together on mixed-gender teams until they reach eighteen years of age. Tennis in the 1990s has emerged as the second most popular sport with some 800,000 tennis players, including 286,000 women, making it the most popular sport among adult women. The third most popular sport is gymnastics with 250,000 participants, including 131,000 girls and women, making it the most popular sport for girls. Among those identified as gymnasts or tennis players, 84 percent and 48 percent, respectively, are girls or women. Several sports are incorporated in the physical education programs in the primary and secondary schools, with most offered on a coed basis until students reach the ages of sixteen to eighteen. Most people in the Netherlands participate in sports through membership in sport clubs, which have some four to five million members. More than 50 percent of Dutch youth are members of sports clubs.

Since the 1980s, women have been involved in increasing numbers in such noncompetitive fitness activities as aerobics, which take place in sport halls, neighborhood centers, and private fitness clubs. Government initiatives to encourage more participation by women are mainly aimed at older women and ethnic minority women.

Although women participate in all sports as athletes and as coaches, managers, and policy makers, they are largely underrepresented in leadership positions. In 1995, 11 percent of all certified coaches were women. The percentages of certified women coaches ranged from 50 percent in swimming to less than 1 percent in soccer. Nearly 50 percent of women coaches coached youth teams. Women held only 10.3 percent of the board positions of sport clubs, compared to 20.4 percent of board positions at voluntary organizations in general. To rectify this disparity, both the government and the Dutch Sport Association are initiating programs to increase the number of women in leadership positions.

ELITE SPORTS

In 1920, a female swimmer was the first, and only, woman member of the Dutch Olympic team; in 1996, 44 percent of the members of the Netherlands Olympic team in Atlanta were women. However, only 7 percent of the coaches, 11 percent of the team managers, and 13 percent of the other attendants were women. Since that first female team member, swimmers have won a sizable share of Dutch Olympic medals. In 1920, two Dutch women's water polo teams brought attention to Dutch swimming. In Berlin in 1936, Hendrika Mastenbroeck swam for three gold medals and a silver. In track and field, the "flying housewife," Fanny Blankers-Koen, became one of the most famous Dutch athletes of the century, competing in three Olympic Games (1936, 1948, 1952) and winning four gold medals at the 1948 games in London. The success of double-gold-medalist Marianne Timmer at the 1998 Winter Olympics is evidence of the continuing Dutch strength in speed-skating.

SPORT IN DUTCH CULTURE

The Dutch have a generally low-key attitude toward sport, other than men's soccer and men's and women's speed skating. At the symbolic and cultural level, sports, especially men's soccer, remain one of the most male-centered activities in the Netherlands. Soccer is seen as a manly endeavor where the male body and heterosexuality are the norm. The print and television sport media focus on men's soccer, with more than 50 percent of media sport coverage devoted to soc-

FANNY BLANKERS-KOEN—DUTCH HOUSEWIFE

The Netherlands was the home of Francina "Fanny" Blankers-Koen, the track athlete whom some experts consider the first truly "global" female sports figure. Later experts might award that honor to Norwegian figure skater, Sonje Henie, or American multi-sport athlete, Mildred "Babe" Didrikson Zaharias. However, in the 1940s, Blankers-Koen dominated European short-distance sprint and hurdle events and won multiple medals in the Olympics. Part of her appeal was her humility, her combining her track career with her roles as wife and mother, and her comment that "I am, after all, a Dutch housewife," which led to her nickname, "the Flying Housewife."

cer during the season. On the other hand, women's soccer is hardly ever shown on television or reported in the press, and coverage of women's sports accounts for only about 5 percent of the media coverage during the soccer season. Men's soccer at the top levels is also accompanied by spectator violence, in the form of public brawling called "hooliganism." On the whole, male Dutch trainers, coaches, and soccer players continue to view soccer as a sport that is not suitable for women, and they assume that women cannot play it very well. Women's soccer tends to be undervalued in the Netherlands, except by the participants themselves. To what extent this undervaluation is due to the large and visible lesbian presence in women's soccer is not known.

GENDER EQUITY

Dutch sport in general is seen as a place where equal opportunity exists. Some sport federations refuse to register the gender of participants and leaders because they assume sport is gender-neutral. Equal opportunity, the results of new programs designed to encourage female participation, and research are all thus difficult to monitor. Since sport participation is seen as a voluntary activity, it is assumed that anyone who wants to participate or coach can do so. The underrepresentation of women and people of color as trainers, coaches, managers, and board members is often attributed to a lack of interest, motivation, or ability. Research indicates that this explanation is not accurate, but translating theory

into practice has proven to be a daunting task for women's sport advocates.

Agnes Elling
Annelies Knoppers

See also Korfball

Bibliography

Guttmann, Allen. (1991) *Women's Sports*. New York: Columbia University Press.

NEW ZEALAND

New Zealand lies in the southwest Pacific Ocean, some 1,600 kilometers southeast of Australia. Composed of two large islands separated by the tumultuous waters of the Cook Strait, and several smaller islands, New Zealand was initially settled between the tenth and twelfth centuries by the Maori, who arrived in canoes from other Polynesian islands. The Maori called this land Aotearoa, or Land of the Long White Cloud. European settlers arrived in there in the early nineteenth century. New Zealand has a population of 3.6 million.

Sport has played a major role in shaping the cultural and national identity of New Zealand. In the twentieth century, the country distinguished itself as a nation in two ways: on the battlefields of international military conflicts and on the rugby playing fields throughout the British Commonwealth. Rugby is an icon of this small island nation and the sport has also had a significant impact on the role of women in sports and in society at large.

EARLY HISTORY

The 1840 Treaty of Waitangi granted possession of the lands, forest, and fisheries to the Maori and sovereignty to the Queen of England. In an effort to colonize the islands, the New Zealand Company, based in Great Britain, offered assisted passages to Englishmen and women willing to make the difficult, dangerous, three-month voyage. Many accepted, willing to take the risk in exchange for a fresh start away from England's often harsh living conditions.

Initially, twice as many men as women settled in New Zealand. It was not until the second half of the twentieth century that women reached demographic parity with men. This domination, in pure numbers, significantly affected the construction of the country's cultural and sporting values.

Rugby was among the diversions that the settlers brought with them. The game adapted well to the frontier spirit and personality, and New Zealand teams established a good reputation in Britain. Rugby was, however, in keeping with the British tradition, solely a men's game and considered too rough for women. As in other British colonies, rigorous physical exertion for girls and women was strongly opposed by the government. Men—and many women—considered such activities unladylike and likely to damage the woman's reproductive capacity, despite the obvious contradiction that pioneer women's hard labor had helped build the new colony. Furthermore, crews of Maori women competed in whale boat races in Port Chalmers (Dunedin), and women played in holiday sports. In some rural areas, women played hockey alongside men when numbers were short, without reported ill effect.

Riding a bicycle was a political action for some nineteenth-century New Zealand women. Symbolizing political as well as physical independence, women were seeking full citizenship through voting rights. As "Theta," who compiled the ladies' page of the *New Zealand Wheelman* put it in 1893, "The dainty wheel gives [cycling girls] a larger world to live and move in." Some women cyclists were also involved with the clothing reform movement—wearing "rational dress" of loosely fitting clothing, split skirts, or bloomers, which enabled them to move more freely than traditional corsets and bustles would allow. Many women cyclists suffered abuse, including being knocked off their bikes, by "larrikins," or what we would call hooligans today, as well as by more respectable "well-dressed persons."

In 1893, New Zealand became the first nation to grant women the vote. Ironically, the national assembly was motivated less by the desire to grant greater freedom to women or to acknowledge them as full citizens than by trying to bring more of the "right kind" of male influence into the ballot box. Some politicians who supported the women's franchise hoped that women would vote the same way as their husbands, thus increasing the influence of the "settled family man," and reducing the corrupting voice of the "loafing single man." Though electoral independence reinforced male domination in New Zealand society, it did increase opportunities for women in sports.

TWENTIETH CENTURY

In the early twentieth century, drill, dance, calisthenics, Greek friezes (where a group of girls would assume the static pose of ancient statues), and other physical activities that focused on posture and deportment dominated the physical education of girls. These activities, as an 1898 school prospectus explained, were designed to counter the possible debilitating effects of study by teaching girls to "carry themselves well and gracefully" without unduly stressing the body and particularly the reproductive organs. Educators also believed that keeping young girls busy with this sort of gentle physical activity would contribute to keeping them on a high moral path.

As the century progressed, athletics for girls became more acceptable. Schools slowly introduced games into the curriculum: often tennis and swimming in the summer, and hockey and basketball in the winter. School principals saw these sports as fundamental to establishing "house spirit" within the schools, and this spirit was "the foundation of an understanding of good citizenship." Netball, a modified and less strenuous form of basketball that was invented in Britain, became popular both in the schools and with working "girls," and quickly became the national women's sport. The sport became popular largely because it maintained the nineteenth-century ideal of femininity. According to a 1929 news report, published in the *Christchurch Sun*, netball "provides splendid exercise for those engaged in it, but it has the added charm of not being too rough." Unlike basketball, netball does not include dribbling, and each player has a limited zone in which to play. The rules prohibit all body contact, and when an opponent attempts to score a basket, the defense must remain at least one meter from the shooter. Even today, netball players from New Zealand wear the pleated skirts and colored panties of their great-grandmothers seventy years earlier. Similarly, the rules of the game remain rooted in Victorian notions of restricted and protected femininity, despite the increasing athleticism of the players.

In specific instances, New Zealand society has demonstrated a tolerance for women's sport that deviates from ideal images of femininity. Women who bestowed pride on the nation through success in international sporting events have been revered. The first swimmer to participate in the Olympic Games was a woman—the young Violet Waldrond, who swam at Antwerp in 1920 and finished fifth in the 100-meter freestyle. An affectionate public smiled on Waldrond, referring to her as "that splendid girl swimmer." Although women have won only two Olympic gold medals—Yvette Williams in the long jump (1952), and Barbara Kendall in the sailboard (1992)—they have led the world in non-Olympic sports, such as squash (Susan Devoy), marathon running before it became an Olympic sport for women in 1984 (Lorraine Moller, Anne Audain, and Allison Roe), and in those sports that rely on the ability to navigate rugged land, air, and water. Aviator Jean Batten established numerous world records in the 1930s. Erin Baker led the world in the ironman triathlon in the late 1980s and early 1990s.

Women have made inroads into some areas of predominantly male sports. Although women played rugby in New Zealand as early as 1891, their participation was more of a sideshow than a serious sport. In a country where rugby symbolizes and measures the health of the nation, it took nearly 100 years for women to gain official recognition. Women have enjoyed real success in the game, perhaps because of their lifetime exposure. New Zealand finished second in the first World Cup for rugby in 1991 and won the event in 1998. Unlike countries in the northern hemisphere, where women's unions administer the sport independently from the men, the New Zealand Rugby Football Union (NZRFU) governs both men's and women's rugby, with mixed results. Many representative female rugby players acknowledge the advantages of having the NZRFU as a governing body. Although the financial commitment to women's rugby by the

VOTING AND NETBALL

In 1893, New Zealand became the first nation to grant women the right to vote. This decision was followed in the early twentieth century by increased opportunities for women to participate in physical activities, including sports. Within a few decades the British sport of netball was adopted in the schools as the sport for women, primarily because it provided physical activity but was not too rough. Netball has remained popular in New Zealand ever since.

NZRFU represents only 3 percent of the total amateur budget, the amount is still more than a fledgling women's association could dream of acquiring in its first ten years of existence. The NZRFU, however, is male-dominated and unashamedly sexist. In 1994, NZRFU did not allow the women's team to participate in the women's World Cup because the cup was not recognized at that time by the male-dominated International Rugby Football Union.

Some women see the game of rugby as a symbol of the male domination of society and oppose supporting it, as spectators or participants, because they believe it maintains the unequal balance of power between men and women. In 1981, serious political upheaval resulted over the NZRFU's decision to allow a South African rugby team to tour New Zealand, contrary to an international ban on sporting relations with the apartheid country. Women, and Maori women in particular, led protests, which also served as a catalyst for the expression of deep concerns about the effect of the game and of the rugby culture, on women's subordinate position in New Zealand.

Maori women are heavily involved in rugby and netball and participate with distinction in other European sports. In 1952, Ruia Morrison reached the quarter-finals at Wimbledon—"an excellent advertisement for New Zealand race and gender relations," wrote one journalist at the time. Her success underscores Maori women's participation in European sport but also indicates that most indigenous sporting activities have disappeared. For example, although the *poi*, small round balls on strings that are swung and twirled by girls and women with a highly skilled wrist action, remains a feature in the physical activities of some Maori and European women, it is more closely associated with cultural, rather than sporting, endeavors. Young girls might learn *poi* in Polynesian culture groups at school and give demonstrations at cultural festivals. There has been a recent upsurge in canoeing, outrigging, and dragon boating among Maori women—activities that bear some resemblance to pre-European sports.

THE FUTURE OF WOMEN'S SPORT

In 1997, Beatrice Famouina won the world championship in the women's discus throw, rep-

resenting New Zealand. An impressive and articulate woman of Samoan descent, Famouina was voted New Zealand Sportsperson of the Year in 1997. She won the award over male athletes, notably Jeff Wilson, rugby's "golden boy." Her success in establishing herself, not only as an athlete but also as a leading national figure, points to a positive future for women's sport in New Zealand. Although women continue to play netball in pleated skirts, and women's rugby is controlled by a male-dominated governing body, Famouina has shown that a large, strong woman from a non-European culture can become a role model.

Nevertheless, women's success in sport is still not accepted by all. The same year that Famouina triumphed as Sportsperson of the Year, male athletics officials disqualified the women's national pole vault record-holder, Melina Hamilton, from participating in the men's pole vault at the national club championships. It is an illustration of what many people believe is the inferior position New Zealand women continue to hold in a society that has been dominated by men.

Annemarie Jutel

See also Commonwealth Games; Netball; Unionism

Bibliography

Fry, Ruth. (1985) *It's Different for Daughters: A History of the Curriculum for Girls in New Zealand Schools, 1900–1975*. Wellington: New Zealand Council for Educational Research.

Graham, Jeanine. (1981) "Settler Society." In *The Oxford History of New Zealand*, edited by W. H. Oliver. Oxford: Oxford University Press.

Macdonald, Charlotte. (1993) *Organisations in Sport, Recreation and Leisure*. Wellington: Daphne Brasell Associates Press.

Nauright, John. (1995) "Netball, Media Representation of Women and Crises of Male Hegemony in New Zealand." In *Sport, Power and Society in New Zealand: Historical and Contemporary Perspectives*, edited by John Nauright. Sydney: Australian Society for Sports History.

Palenski, Ron, and Terry Maddaford. (1983) *The Games: The Pride and Drama of New Zealanders at Olympic and Commonwealth Games*. Auckland: Moa Publications.

Phillips, Jock. (1987) *Te Whenua, Te Iwi: The Land and the People*. Wellington: Allen and Unwin.

———. (1996) *A Man's Country*. Auckland: Penguin.

Simpson, Clare. (1995) "The Development of Women's Cycling in Late Nineteenth Century New Zealand." In *Sport, Power and Society in New Zealand: Historical and Contemporary Perspectives*, edited by John Nauright. Sydney: Australian Society for Sports History.

Simpson, Helen M. (1962) *The Women of New Zealand*. Auckland and Hamilton: Paul's Book Arcade.

Sinclair, Keith. (1980) *A History of New Zealand*. London: Allen Lane.

———. (1986) *A Destiny Apart—New Zealand's Search for National Identity*. Wellington: Allen and Unwin.

NIGERIA

Nigeria is a West African nation with a population of about 110 million. Most Nigerians live in rural farming communities, although many Nigerians are moving to the cities. More than half the country's labor force is still involved in agriculture. Increasingly, girls and women are taking part in both recreational and competitive sports. Although cultural, religious, and social barriers remain, they are not as difficult to surmount as in the past.

HISTORY

The traditional place of Nigerian women has been the home, where women have served as housekeepers, cooks, childbearers, and child rearers. Historically, when men were involved in such traditional games and physical activities as wrestling, boxing, acrobatics, swimming, spear throwing, and arrow shooting, women would watch and applaud. These activities were featured prominently in cultural events and ceremonies such as initiations into manhood, funerals, and the new yam harvest festival. During these ceremonies, women and girls would perform traditional dances.

During the British colonial period from 1900 to 1960, missionary-sponsored schools introduced compulsory physical education programs for boys and girls. The annual Empire Day celebrations to honor Queen Victoria became a showcase for modern physical education and competitive sports in Nigeria, and established a continuing legacy for women's participation in sports. In the 1990s, physical education was compulsory in primary and junior secondary schools for both boys and girls, and girls were active participants in competitions between schools and universities.

In 1949, netball, a popular girls' game similar to basketball, was introduced to Nigeria, and became the first game to be organized and controlled by women. It has since been replaced by basketball as the premier team sport for girls and young women. Lady Abayomi, founder of the Girl Guides of Nigeria, introduced athletic competition for girls in what was then the capital city of Lagos, and in 1950 the "ladies sports club" was founded to promote women's participation in sports.

ELITE SPORTS FOR WOMEN

In 1956, Nigerian sportswomen were invited to participate in an international competition in the Gold Coast, the nation now known as Ghana. In 1958, Nigerian women entered the Commonwealth Games. At the first All-Africa Games held in Brazzaville, Congo, in 1965, several Nigerian women were victorious. Helen Okwara won the gold medal in javelin; Amelia Okoli won the gold in the high jump; and women runners won gold medals in the 100-meter sprint and the 4 × 100-meter relay. At a competition in New Zealand, Modupe Oshikoya won a gold medal in the 100-meter event, a silver medal in high jump, and a bronze in the 4 × 100-meter relay. Since then, Nigerian women have achieved success in many national and international competitions. The women's volleyball team won the first-ever international tournament in 1979. Nigerian women handball players won medals in the All-Africa Club championships in 1979, 1983, 1986, 1988, and 1991.

In Tokyo in 1964, Nigerian women participated in the Olympics for the first time with Amelia Okoli in the high jump and Clarice Ahanotu in the short sprints. Among the participants in the 1968 games were Ronke Akindele, Mairo Jinadu, Regina Okafor, and Ashanti Obi. Amelia Edet and Nnena Njoku joined the 1972 team in Munich; and Kehinde Vaugham and Gloria Ayanlaja took part in the Moscow games of 1980. Nigerian

Nigerian relay runners celebrate a good run at the 1992 Barcelona Olympics. (Jean-Yves Ruszniewski; TempSport/Corbis)

women have continued to participate in the Olympics with twenty-three in 1992 and fifteen in 1996, a greater number than from any other African nation other than South Africa.

Chioma Ajunwa became the first Nigerian woman to win an Olympic gold medal, when she won the long jump competition in 1996 in Atlanta. Her teammates included Mary Onyali-Omagbemi, who took the bronze in the 200-meter dash; Mary Tombri and Fatima Yusuf, in the 100- and 200-meter events; Falilat Ogunkoya, who took the bronze in the 400-meter run; and Charity Okpara, also in the 400-meter event.

RECENT DEVELOPMENTS

Women have made great strides in sports, and girls and women participate in growing numbers in recreational and competitive athletics as sports are no longer the exclusive domain of Nigerian men. Women are also becoming active in sports that have traditionally been male, including football, boxing, wrestling, and weightlifting. In 1995, Kofo Nwokedi was elected the first female chairperson of the Weight Lifting Association of Nigeria.

Women do remain very much underrepresented at the policy- and decision-making levels of sport. They have, however, begun to play active roles as coaches, referees, and organizing secretaries in several sports. Several women have assumed government management positions. For example, Margaret Nzombato served as the director of sports for the State of Adamawa, and Amelia Okpalaoka served as a senior officer of the Ministry of Youth and Sports.

Cultural, religious, and social barriers continue to bar Nigerian women from full participation in sport. Traditional interpretations of gender roles in the Islamic community in northern Nigeria often limit the opportunities for girls and women to take part in sport. Throughout the nation, poverty, illiteracy, and a lack of political power combine to create continuing obstacles. In most cases, women's sports are administered by men, and women's sports are promoted and supported less than are men's sports.

The Nigerian government initiated the National Sports Festival in 1973 in Lagos to create opportunities for both male and female athletes. Nevertheless, critics believe that men's competition receives more attention than do women's events. Talented female athletes often stop competing in sports out of a sense of frustration, insecurity, or occasionally because of sexual harassment. Some Nigerians, prompted by their traditional concerns for propriety, frown on the participation of women in sport events. Some public disapproval continues of women's track and field uniforms, which are thought to be too revealing.

In 1990, at the initiative of F. B. Adeyanju of the Department of Physical and Health Education, Ahmadu Bello University, in Zaria, the Nigerian Association of Women in Sports (NAWIS) was established. NAWIS is working to create national awareness of the need for active participation by girls and women in sports in Nigeria. The association holds conferences and seminars, publishes papers, and advocates for gender equity, equal access to sports programs, and for facilities and equipment for women's sports.

F. B. Adeyanju
Mickey Friedman

NORDIC SKIING *see* Skiing,
Cross-Country; Ski Jumping

NORTHERN IRELAND *see* Ireland, United Kingdom

NORWAY

Norway is a Nordic nation with a population of about 4.4 million. Sport has a long history in Norway and many Norwegians have always been involved in exercise and sport in their leisure time. In 1996, the Norwegian Olympic Committee and Confederation of Sport had more than 1.7 million members from a network of 13,549 voluntary sports clubs, organized into 56 sports federations, and 20 district associations. "Sports for All" has been the organization's long-term objective, and it has worked to ensure that the people of Norway have been able to engage in sports according to their wishes and needs. It has also been responsible for the administration and preparation necessary for Norway's participation in the Olympic Games.

Norway has a long tradition in winter sports, as demonstrated by this young woman who, wearing a long embroidered dress, skates across the frozen lake at Lillehammer. (Adam Woolfitt)

HISTORY

At the end of the nineteenth century, women participated in many kinds of informal sporting activities such as ice-skating, skiing, hiking, and swimming. In later years, when it came to competition, there were a few sports in which women were allowed to compete to almost the same degree as men: tennis, swimming, figure-skating, and equestrian events. In 1924, sport in Norway was organized into two umbrella organizations. Of the two, Arbeidernes Idrettsforbund (AIF, workers sports federation) was more positive toward the introduction and the development of women's sport than was Landsforbundet for Idrett (national federation for sport). By the end of the 1930s, Norwegian women participated in badminton, fencing, track and field, handball, orienteering, equestrian events, rowing, skiing, skating, swimming, tennis, and gymnastics. Gymnastics, which generally did not involve competition, was by far the most popular sport among women. Before 1940, there was considerable resistence to women competing in sports. The resistance was related to the popular beliefs about femininity, which focused on motherhood and judged all activities according to their alleged effect on the health and beauty of mothers and children.

After World War II, the two former umbrella organizations united to form the Norwegian Confederation of Sport (NCS), which in 1996 merged with the Norwegian Olympic Committee to form the Norwegian Olympic Committee and Confederation of Sport. At the beginning of 1946, NCS had twenty-three sport federations, with programs for women in about half. In 1951, women made up 23 percent of the membership. By 1961, women's membership had increased to 25 percent and then to 31 percent in 1971, 36 percent in 1981, and 38 percent in 1997.

Women's sport in Norway has never been organized into gender-based organizations and

THE GRETE WAITZ INSPIRATION—40,000 WOMEN RUNNING FOR FUN

In Oslo, Norway, the Grete Waitz Run (GWR) has been held annually since 1984. It is named after its founder, the internationally famous female long distance runner, Grete Waitz, who has remained actively involved in the run for its entire history. Only women can participate in the GWR. Starting with 3,300 women runners, by the late 1990s more than 40,000 participated each year. Waitz stated that the aim of the run was "to inspire women of all ages to experience pleasurable exercise." Most of the runners are average Norwegian women, though the race is organized so that elite runners can compete in their own class. Disabled women are integrated among the other runners, and there is a little girls' GWR of approximately 200 meters. A survey among the participants in 1995 showed that the youngest was eleven years old and the oldest was ninety-six, with an average age of forty-two. About 75 percent were married or lived with somebody, 75 percent were mothers and 85 percent were gainfully employed. "The Run" is a motivating factor for exercising. About 22 percent in the mentioned survey answered that they exercised especially for the GWR. Most women, about half of them, alternated between walking and jogging during the run. Many runners were from various kinds of women's groups and voluntary organizations, and they tended to run the race together. Other groups of women sing while they run or dress in different kinds of fancy costumes, sometimes symbolizing their work. They might appear as fish, trolls, witches, police, waitresses, etc.

What is the motivation for participating in the Run? Interviews done in 1993 and 1996 showed that two themes, though expressed in different ways, were mentioned by almost everyone: the run itself was fun and the social aspects of the run were also enjoyed. The participants in the survey were also asked what they thought were the main reasons for the Run's great popularity. The five most often mentioned reasons were: inclusiveness, women's fellowship and atmosphere, informality, fun, and the fact that the race was for women only.

The GWR can be interpreted as an alternative or counter-culture sports model: as an expression of a female sports culture, it challenges the traditional male model of sport by transforming it. It also fits into the concept of feminist culture, which has elements of freedom, liberation, and change. As one of the participants declared:

It's so nice that we women have something for ourselves. Men would never have managed to develop anything like this. They are sitting in the living-room at home, but we do something about it—you would never have seen so many lively men, if it had been a men's run. Never. It would have been so strict if the men should have participated. They are so grave and too serious.

clubs to the same degree as in other countries. Men have, however, always been more numerous in most sport federations although women have formed the majority of members in a few sports, including gymnastics, team handball, equestrianism, volleyball, and dance.

After 1945, many sport federations within the Confederation of Sport appointed "women's committees" with the responsibility of developing women's sports. These committees were often chaired by men. Most of these committees disbanded around 1960, probably because most people believed that gender equity in sport had been achieved and that it was therefore no longer necessary to have special committees for women.

With the election of a new NCS president in 1984, women's committees were revived and the work to promote women's sports seemed to speed up. A new women's committee recommended that all units within Norwegian sport organizations (clubs, districts, and federations) should have women's committees. The long-term goal was to ensure that women and men would have the same opportunities to enjoy sport, to hold leadership positions, and to enter sport careers as trainers and officials. In the early 1990s, these committees again declined in importance, and in the 1990s women's sport was more often promoted through special projects, particularly when it came to educating and electing more female coaches, administrators, and officials. An example of such a project was the Norwegian Women's Project, which began in January 1995 and was scheduled to last until the year 2000. The main aims of the project were to develop women's sports to the point where female athletes win ten to fifteen medals in the Nagano and Sydney Olympic Games and to promote women's involvement so that women constitute at least 20 percent of the leaders, coaches, and team support personnel. The latter goal was reached in the Winter Olympic Games in Nagano in 1998.

PHYSICAL EDUCATION

Physical education is mandatory in elementary and secondary schools (students six to eighteen years of age). The number of classes varies from one to three per week and it is also possible for secondary school students to choose physical education as an elective (from two to five sessions per week). Gender-mixed physical education is required in all schools at all levels. Competitive sport is not a component of the school to the extent that it is in the United States and some other nations. There are a few intramural sports but they are not that popular. To compete in a sport as an individual, one must become a member of a sport club and practice outside of school hours.

WOMEN'S PARTICIPATION

Women in the Norwegian Olympic Committee and Confederation of Sports accounted for 38 percent of the memberships in 1997. Among girls under seventeen years of age, membership was even greater, at 43 percent. The most popular women's sport, based on number of member-

ships, was soccer (association football), followed by team handball, gymnastics, and Nordic skiing. Women's soccer was officially accepted into the Norwegian Soccer Federation in 1976. It has been very successful with about 67,000 girls and women playing soccer in 1997.

National polls taken since 1992 indicate that as many women as men exercise regularly, at least once a week, and about 60 percent of the female population are regular exercisers. The most popular activities among women are hiking/walking, bicycling, cross-country skiing, jogging/running, swimming, and gymnastics.

ELITE SPORTS

Norway has had a long tradition of developing female athletes who are successful in international competitions in several sports. As a result, the fifty-four female athletes on the 1996 Summer Olympics team formed over 50 percent of the team.

The ice-skater Sonja Henie was among the first Norwegian women to gain international recognition. She participated in four Olympic games and won gold medals in 1928, 1932, and 1936. By contrast, the first international medal for women in cross-country skiing came comparatively late. It was not until 1966 that the breakthrough came for the female elite skiers who won the silver medal in the world championship cross-country relay. Since then many Norwegian women have medaled in cross-country races. Norwegian women have been especially successful in long-distance running. Ingrid Kristiansen and Grete Waitz were among the world's best track athletes in the 1980s. Kristiansen set world records in the 5,000- and 10,000-meter runs and the marathon, and won four world championships. Grete Waitz won the world marathon championship in 1983, a silver medal at the 1984 Olympic Games, and the New York City marathon nine times. She also founded the Grete Waitz Run in 1984, the most popular women's run in the world. By the 1990s, this 5-kilometer run drew some 40,000 participants each year and took place each spring in Oslo.

In the 1990s, Norwegian female athletes added handball, soccer, and some field events to cross-country skiing and distance running as sports in which they excelled at the highest level of international competition. At the 1997 track and field world championship, Hanne Haugland won the high jump, and Trine Hattestad, the javelin. At the Olympic Games in Barcelona in 1992, the women's handball team won a silver medal, and in 1995 the Norwegian women's soccer team won the world championship in Stockholm.

Kari Fasting

See also Henie, Sonja

Bibliography

Årsrapport 1997. (1998) Oslo: Norwegian Olympic Committee and Confederation of Sports.

Aschehoug & Gyldendals Store Norske Leksikon. (1979) Oslo: Kunnskapsforlaget.

Bryhn, Rolf, and Knut Are Tvedt, eds. (1990) *Idretts-leksikon*. Oslo: Kunnskapsforlaget.

Fasting, Kari. (1996) *Hvor går Kvinneidretten?* Bærum: Norwegian Confederation of Sports.

Lippe, Gerd Von der. (1993/1994) "Women's Sports in Norway in the 1930's: Conflict Between Two Different Body Cultures." *Stadion* 19/20: 178–187.

Norwegian Confederation of Sports—Women's Committee. (1990) *Program 1985–90: Women in Sport*. Bærum: Norwegian Confederation of Sports.

The Norwegian Women Project. An Introduction to the Norwegian "Olympiatoppen"'s Campaign to Increase the Number of Top Level Female Athletes and Female Leaders. (1998) Bærum: Norwegian Olympic Committee and Confederation of Sports.

Olstad, Finn, and Stein Tønneson, eds. (1987) *Norsk Idretts Historie: Forsvar, Sport, Klassekamp 1961–1939*, part 2. Oslo: Aschehoug.

NUTRITION

The general increase in women's participation in sport has prompted substantial interest in how diet affects athletic performance. Among researchers, this interest has translated into a growing number of studies on the nutritional needs of female athletes.

NUTRITION, RESEARCH, AND DIET

As a field of scientific and applied study, nutrition is more than 200 years old. Sport nutrition is a relatively new subdiscipline that applies the principles of nutrition to the enhancement of athletic performance. Sport history is rich with anecdotes about unusual, even bizarre, dietary practices of athletes. For example, Milo of Croton, a Greek wrestler of the sixth century BCE who participated in seven Olympiads and won six wrestling victories, was said to have trained on a daily diet of twenty pounds of meat, twenty pounds of bread, and eight quarts of wine. Only since the early 1900s has the relationship between nutrients and physical performance been studied scientifically.

Basic dietary principles apply to both women and men, but some nutritional matters are extremely important to active women. Iron and calcium are two such concerns. A national survey found that 56 percent of women in the United States fail to get 70 percent of their Recommended Dietary Allowance (RDA) for iron while 49 percent get less than 70 percent of the RDA for calcium. Their diets may be inadequate for various reasons—the nutrient-rich food may not be readily available, they may simply choose to eat an unhealthy diet, or they may not eat enough even if they do have healthy diets. The less food a person eats, the fewer nutrients she takes in.

ENERGY NEEDS

People assume that athletes need to eat more than do nonathletes. This is not always true. Many athletes, especially those who must maintain a low body weight, may eat even less than their peers who do not take part in a sport. At the same time, training for some sports requires less energy—and hence less food—than for others. Gymnasts, for example, spend a significant amount of time sitting or standing and listening to the coach, watching teammates, or rehearsing routines in their minds. This means that an hour of training for a gymnast with Olympic aspirations may entail only thirty or forty-five minutes of actual physical activity, resulting in an energy expenditure during that hour of 420–630 kjoules (100–150 calories) for a girl who weighs 45 kilograms (99 pounds). In contrast, another 45 kilogram female who runs to enhance her health would expend about 1,785 kjoules (425 calories) on a one-hour run at a 11.9 kilometer-per-hour pace (5.5 mph).

Dietary surveys of female athletes have found that some do not eat as much as nutritional estimates suggest they need. Why this is so is a matter of debate; the athletes may report eating less than they actually do; they may have adapted to lower energy intake, or both—or the estimates themselves may be incorrect. Arguably, if an athlete is maintaining her ideal competitive weight and shows no signs of malnutrition or reduced performance, she is consuming enough energy regardless of her expected requirement.

Energy is provided by fat, carbohydrate, protein, and alcohol. For some athletes, alcohol is a normal part of the diet, and this must be considered in the mix of energy distribution. For others, alcohol consumption is not a factor.

Protein

For more than a century, researchers and athletes both have debated the importance of protein for athletes. In 1842, the German chemist Justin Von Liebeg reported that protein was the major fuel for muscular contraction. Although studies conducted in the late 1890s failed to confirm this finding, the idea lingered that athletes needed extra protein to build muscle, and consuming this extra protein became common practice, particularly for athletes in sports such as weightlifting.

Because protein is not the major fuel for muscle contraction does not mean that it is not important. It is. Research has shown that it can provide up to 15 percent of the energy needed to run a marathon. Numerous studies have found that athletes do have greater protein requirements than do nonathletes. Athletes' protein requirements increase as they grow, and when they are training. Persons on a low-calorie or vegetarian diet may not get adequate protein.

Experts note that this relationship—fewer calories, more protein needed—is important to remember when determining a person's ideal protein intake, as is the type of protein they consume. In the United States, nutritionists derive recommendations for dietary protein from studies of people who are consuming adequate calories. Not everyone in the world does, in fact, get enough to eat. Another important factor is that about 65 to 75 percent of the protein in those studies was from foods of animal origin (meat, fish, poultry, dairy products, and eggs). These are forms of dietary protein that have high biological value. The higher the biological value of dietary protein, the less of it a person needs to eat to meet the requirement. An adult male or female who consumes adequate calories and gets two-thirds or more of the protein from animal sources has an RDA of 0.8 grams of protein per kilogram of body weight.

Some nutritionists believe that the U.S. recommendation for protein is adequate for all adults, including athletes, who consume a typical American diet. However, research and experience show that athletes do need more protein, and for them, the appropriate recommendation would be 1.5 to 2.0 grams per kilogram of body weight daily. This would come out to 99 to 130 grams of protein a day for a 66 kilogram (142 pound) athlete.

Female athletes may not be meeting their protein needs if they restrict calories or exclude milk, cheese, yogurt, beef, pork, fish, eggs, or poultry from their diets. This does not mean that a vegetarian diet is inevitably deficient in protein. Well-planned vegetarian diets can meet and even exceed protein requirements. However, if no animal products are consumed, protein requirements may be higher (as much as 2.5 grams of protein per kilogram of body weight) because of the lower-quality protein and digestibility of plant foods.

Carbohydrates

Early in the twentieth century, two Scandinavian scientists studied how changes in the diet affected a person's ability to perform prolonged, hard work. They found that as the intensity of exercise increased, so did the contribution of carbohydrate as a source of fuel to the muscles. In the late 1960s and early 1970s, further studies demonstrated that body carbohydrate stores (glycogen) play an important role in endurance exercise. Thus evolved the dietary recommendation that athletes consume a high-carbohydrate diet. What investigators (and athletes) did not consider was that most of the research on carbohydrate and performance was conducted in laboratories with men running on treadmills or riding stationary bicycles. They assumed that the findings from those studies applied to athletes in other sports. Since data on athletes participating in other sports did not exist, the sport world readily accepted the recommendations of high carbohydrate for all.

Later studies proved this wrong. A 1993 study showed that not all athletes require high carbohydrate intakes to train or compete. Cyclists and runners consuming moderate-carbohydrate (five grams of carbohydrate per kilogram body weight per day) did have 30 to 36 percent less glycogen in their muscles on days five and seven of the seven days of training. This did not hinder their training or have a negative effect on their performance. These and other studies have made it possible for nutritionists to make more specific recommendations on how much carbohydrate an athlete needs to support training and performance, based on body size and the intensity and duration of training. Female athletes participating in sports requiring short bursts of energy such as basketball, soccer, and tennis need about five grams of carbohydrate per kilogram of body weight daily to maintain muscle glycogen stores. This is equivalent to 330 grams of carbohydrate for an athlete weighing 66 kilograms (145.2 pounds). Those who train aerobically for ninety or more minutes daily may need eight to ten grams of carbohydrate per kilogram of body weight. For the same 66-kilogram athlete, this would be 527 to 659 grams. Interestingly, research shows that physical work and athletic performance can also be maintained on a high-fat diet.

Fat

The body is adaptable. It can burn fat, carbohydrate, alcohol, and even protein to get the energy it needs. Which one it uses at any given time depends on body stores, diet, and type of activity. For example, when sitting and reading a book or watching a play, the body uses mostly fat for energy. When exercising, it uses varying combinations of fat and carbohydrate and, in some cases, protein.

Nutrition scientists interested in high-fat diets studied Alaskan Eskimos in the early 1970s. Although the diet of the Eskimos studied varied slightly based on the availability of whales, seals, walrus, caribou, and polar bears, of the 2,300–4,500 daily calorie intake, approximately 50 percent were from fat and 30–35 percent were from protein. Carbohydrate accounted for only 15–20 percent of the calories. The average blood cholesterol levels of these physically active hunters were not significantly different from the general U. S. population, but their serum triglycerides levels were markedly lower than that of the white population in the United States.

Another study of fat consumption comes from the Committee on Military Nutrition Research (CMNR), which reviews scientific research and makes recommendations to the U.S. Department of Defense about the nutritional needs of the military. In considering what military personnel need in cold and in high-altitude environments, restriction of fat calories to 30 percent in these environments is not appropriate.

The studies on Eskimos and the findings of the CMNR have, in part, prompted researchers to evaluate the effect of high-fat diets on athletic performance. Their findings were mixed. Scientists have found that severe restriction of dietary fat can be detrimental to performance, that the working muscle adapts to a high-fat diet, and that some athletes perform better on a high-fat diet.

That humans can perform and even excel on high-fat diets has been overshadowed by the emphasis on fat as a possible factor in certain diseases in some people. This makes health professionals reluctant to recommend a high-fat diet. The public attention given to fat, and the fact that many countries are encouraging their population to reduce fat intake, has in some cases resulted in lower fat intakes.

Many athletes reduce their fat intake, not only out of concern for their health but also in an attempt to improve their appearance. Unfortunately, in the United States, health messages about the dangers of eating too much fat coupled with the emphasis on thinness have resulted in a distorted view of dietary fat. Weight-conscious athletes often go to extremes to avoid fat in the diet. While excessive dietary fat may not be desirable, trying to avoid fat completely leads to monotonous, nutritionally inadequate diets. For example, in an effort to reduce dietary fat, athletes often exclude foods rich in nutrients, such as meat, milk, eggs, and cheese and choose fat-free items such as rice cakes, pretzels, salads, and bread.

At the invitation of the Food and Agriculture Organization (FAO) and the World Health Organization (WHO), an international group of nutrition experts met in Rome in 1993. The resulting report titled *Fats and Oils in Human Nutrition* provided, among other information, recommendations on minimum desirable and upper limits of fat intakes. The experts concluded that most adults should make fat no less than 15 percent of their energy intake. For women of reproductive age, this figure rises to 20 percent. The upper limit of fat intake recommended is 30 percent of energy for sedentary individuals and 35 percent for active people.

While many people in the United States are obsessed with fat, low-fat eating is not uniquely American. A survey conducted in the United States, the United Kingdom, France, and what was formerly West Germany in 1992 showed that Europeans are as interested as Americans in controlling their fat intake. According to the survey, 77 percent of Britons consume low-fat products, as do 53 percent of Germans and 39 percent of the French. This is in comparison to 68 percent in the United States. Some of the most popular low-fat products include margarine, cheese, yogurt, dressings, sauces, mayonnaise, and sugar-free beverages.

VITAMINS AND MINERALS

Protein, carbohydrate, and fat supply the energy the body needs. Vitamins and minerals are necessary for the body to metabolize these energy-producing nutrients. Vitamins help to regulate how the body metabolizes nutrients. Minerals are essential for many reactions, such as regulation of body fluids, muscular contraction, heartbeat, and conduction of nerve impulses. Athletes with high energy needs usually eat more food to get the calories needed and in doing so they also increase their vitamin and mineral intake. If an athlete is consuming a diet low in calories, the risk increases that she is not getting enough vitamins and minerals. Several reasons may explain why some female athletes have low energy intakes. They may simply be small in stature and thus not need to eat very much. However, girls and women who avoid particular food groups or have monotonous diets are also at risk of inadequate vitamin and mineral intake.

Iron and calcium are two minerals of particular concern for female athletes, regardless of age and nationality. Studies of female athletes' diets show that they often have low levels of these two nutrients. As with all essential nutrients, athletes need iron and calcium to perform and to be healthy. They need iron to carry oxygen to the cells and to produce hemoglobin and myoglobin. Iron deficiency affects numerous metabolic functions related to energy production and thus, female athletes who do not consume enough dietary iron risk iron depletion and impaired physical performance.

Iron

Iron is found in small amounts in a number of foods, and the amount the body absorbs depends on several factors. For example, if a person is deficient in iron, her body will absorb more. The type of iron consumed also affects how much the body can absorb. Approximately 40 percent of the iron in meat, fish, and poultry is heme iron, of which the body absorbs about 23 percent. Nonheme iron is the remaining 60 percent of iron in meat and the type of iron found in plant foods, ready-to-eat cereals, and dietary supplements. Nonheme iron is absorbed at about 3–8 percent depending on other factors in the diet, such as the amount of vitamin C, meat, and fiber, among others. Low-energy intakes and diets that supply little or no meat are often low in iron. A woman can increase her iron intake by including more iron-rich foods in her diet, such as ready-to-eat cereal, dried fruits, cooked beans, dark leafy green vegetables, whole grains, and foods containing vitamin C (for example, citrus fruits). The use of iron cookware can also increase iron intake.

Iron deficiency affects more than 2 billion people—more than one-third of the world's population. Although it occurs in all population groups, iron deficiency is most common among infants, young children, and women of childbearing age. Iron deficiency has serious effects. It impairs growth, and cognitive development and functioning. It causes fatigue and reduced productivity. Iron deficiency is the most common nutritional deficiency in humans and the most common cause of anemia. It occurs most frequently in developing countries; however, in the United States, an estimated 58 percent of healthy women may have some degree of iron deficiency. The World Health Organization, in 1990, estimated the prevalence of anemia in women between the ages of fifteen and forty-nine at 44 percent in Africa, 58 percent in Southern Asia, and 8 percent in North America. Thus, treatment with diet and/or supplements is prudent. Consuming too much iron should be avoided because some people can be harmed by supplementation. People at risk for hemochromatosis, sickle cell, or thalassemia can develop iron overload or otherwise be harmed by iron supplementation.

Calcium

Calcium, in addition to being a major component of bones and teeth, helps control muscular contraction and regulate numerous metabolic reactions. During childhood and adolescence, optimal calcium intake is important to attain peak bone mass and to prevent osteoporosis. Although all women need to consume enough calcium, it is particularly important for women with amenorrhea (whose menstrual periods are at least ninety days apart). These women are at increased risk for low bone density due to low estrogen levels.

The recommended intakes for calcium vary among countries, depending on the native diet, public health concerns, and physiological adaptations. The WHO recommendation for calcium is 400–500 milligrams for adults. Calcium recommendations for the United States are higher: 1,300 milligrams daily for adolescent girls nine to thirteen years old and 1,000 milligrams daily for women ages nineteen to fifty.

In countries where they are consumed throughout adulthood, milk and milk products are the primary sources of calcium. In the United States they provide more than half the calcium in a typical diet. Other calcium-rich foods include dark green leafy vegetables, canned fish with soft bones, and foods fortified with calcium. Calcium-set tofu (tofu processed with a calcium salt) and calcium-fortified soymilk are important sources in diets of many vegetarians. Hard water can also contribute calcium to the diet.

Young female athletes need to be aware that diet and other life-style factors affect bone health. Research shows that although most women in the United States know that calcium is necessary for bone health, most still do not have enough calcium in their diet, even though when asked, they say they believe they do.

DIETARY SUPPLEMENTS

Not so long ago, iron-deficiency anemia was still referred to as "tired blood," and before the word osteoporosis was coined, the condition was called "brittle bones." One treatment for tired blood was to stick iron nails in an apple. The type of iron in the nails was basically not absorbable by the human body, but the apple could absorb it. The vitamin C in the apple then converted the iron to a form more readily absorbed by the human body. The person with tired blood would then eat the apple, making it one of the first dietary supplements. Ground egg shells and fish bones were early calcium supplements.

Augmenting the diet today is much easier, given the wide variety of vitamins, minerals, manufactured high-protein foods, and other substances available in food stores, nutrition shops, and by mail order. The issue is no longer obtaining supplements, but establishing guidelines for their use.

FLUIDS

The human body is approximately 55 to 60 percent water, and a muscular athlete's body can be 70 percent water. Since all body cells work best when they are hydrated (have adequate water), water is essential for both mental and physical performance. Water is second only to oxygen as being essential to life. While a person could live without food for thirty days, depending upon various conditions, one could survive only four to ten days without water.

Under normal conditions, people need between 1.5 and 4.0 liters of water a day. They get this water from food, fruit and vegetable juices, soft drinks, milk, tea and coffee, as well as plain water. While thirst is the major regulator of fluid intake and the kidneys regulate fluid excretion, aging, illness, use of medications, and exercising in the heat are among conditions that can interrupt the balance.

Working muscles produce heat, which increases the temperature of the body. Sweating is one of many methods the body uses to help maintain normal temperature, and thus, the harder one exercises the more one sweats. To keep cells hydrated, it is essential to replace the water lost in sweat. An athlete who does not replace this water then suffers dehydration, which not only can impair performance but can be life-threatening. Research has shown that athletes exposed to high temperatures, high humidity, and sunlight can experience sizable fluid losses—two to three liters of sweat per hour. When an athlete becomes dehydrated, she may not perform as well, and in cases of severe dehydration, heat-stroke can occur.

CONCLUSION

Nutrition is a growing concern in sports. While both female and male athletes need to be concerned with proper nutrition, women have some unique concerns relating to issues such as calcium intake and the need to maintain proper diet so as to prevent eating disorders, a problem in a small but significant percentage of women athletes, as well as bone loss and amenorrhea. Nutrition has become a big business, both inside and outside of sport, and many nutritional supplements are now widely available. While such supplements have their benefits, they have further clouded the basic issue of developing nutritional standards and recommendations for male and female athletes in different sports.

Ann C. Grandjean
Jaime S. Ruud

See also Amenorrhea; Anemia; Eating Disorders; Osteoporosis

Bibliography

Bean, Anita, and Peggy Wellington. (1995) *Sports Nutrition for Women*. London: A & C Black Ltd.

Greenleaf, J. E., and M. H. Harrison. (1986) "Water and Electrolytes." In *Nutrition and Aerobic Exercise*, edited by D. K. Layman. Washington, DC: American Chemical Society, 107–124.

Ruud, Jaime S. (1996) *Nutrition and the Female Athlete*. Boca Raton, FL: CRC Press.

Wells, Christine L. (1991) *Women, Sport & Performance: A Physiological Perspective*. Champaign, IL: Human Kinetics.

Wolinsky, Ira. (1997) *Nutrition in Exercise and Sport*. 3rd ed. Boca Raton, FL: CRC Press.

OAKLEY, ANNIE

(1860–1926)

U.S. SHOOTER AND ENTERTAINER

In 1926 Will Rogers, the American entertainer and columnist, described Annie Oakley as "the greatest woman rifle shot the world has ever produced. . . . She is a greater character than she was a rifle shot . . . [and] her lovable traits, her thoughtful consideration of others will live as a mark for any woman to shoot for" (*American Rifleman* 1998).

Annie Oakley was born on 13 August 1860 in Patterson Township, Ohio. The fifth of eight children, Phoebe Anne Oakley Moses had a grim and tortured childhood. Her father died when she was four, and her mother had to work long hours as a nurse. The young girl was sent to an orphanage at age nine. The following year she was adopted by a family that made her toil from dawn to dusk on their Ohio farm. At age twelve she ran away and rejoined her mother.

To help support the family, Annie took up hunting. With her father's rifles, she hunted small game, such as rabbits and quail, and sold them in Cincinnati. At the age of sixteen, she met Frank Butler, ten years her senior, a touring vaudeville show performer whose specialty was target and trick shooting. She defeated Butler in a shooting contest, and a year later she became his wife. The Butlers embarked on a career as touring shooting professionals and competed at various shows across the Midwest.

At the height of their popularity, the Butlers were celebrity figures, enjoying the sort of following normally associated with the stars of stage, theater, and music hall. In fact, Oakley was more entertainer and show business luminary than sportswoman, although her skills most certainly mark her as an athlete of the highest order

and she was honored for those skills by induction into the American Trapshooting Hall of Fame. In 1885 Oakley joined Buffalo Bill's world-famous Wild West Show and quickly became the top-drawing star for the circus-style rodeo spectacular. Because the show was sensationally popular in Great Britain and Western Europe as well as the United States, Annie Oakley became an international celebrity

The diminutive Oakley, who was just 5 feet tall and less than 100 pounds—and, interestingly, a Quaker—became the first female athlete to achieve worldwide superstar status. Crowd favorites performed by Oakley included splitting a playing card at a distance of 30 yards, shooting a cigarette from Frank Butler's lips, and hitting a dime tossed into the air. She also had a routine in which she shot standing, in a prone position, and on horseback.

Oakley's trapshooting skills were extraordinary. She regularly broke 100 targets in a row. In 1922, when she was sixty-two, she was still able to perform this feat which was described in the *New York Times* of 17 April 1922 as "a new world's record among women gunners." Her marksmanship was so widely known that entertainment complimentary tickets were once called "Annie Oakleys" because their pattern of punched holes looked like the result of a shotgun blast. During World War I Oakley entertained soldiers at military camps with feats of marksmanship. Her fifty-year marriage to Frank Butler ended with his death in 1922. Oakley herself died four years later.

Oakley's life has been subject to several stage and film treatments, albeit part fact, part fiction. Barbara Stanwyck starred in *Annie Oakley* (1935). Closer to reality was *Annie Oakley* (1985), part of the *Tall Tales and Legends* series produced by Shelley Duvall. With Jamie Lee Curtis as Oakley, the film included footage of Annie Oakley taken by Thomas Edison in 1923. The best-known movie is *Annie Get Your Gun* (1950) with Betty Hutton as a glamorous Oakley in the Hollywood version of

Annie Oakley teaching women to shoot in 1918. (Bettmann/Corbis)

Irving Berlin's Wild West Show musical. The musical was produced again in a slightly revised version on Broadway in 1999.

Scott Crawford

Bibliography

Flynn, Jean. (1998) *Annie Oakley: Legendary Sharpshooter*. Springfield, NJ: Enslow.

Kasper, Shirl. (1992) *Annie Oakley*. Norman: University of Oklahoma Press.

OFFICIATING

The official, an essential partner in the sports arena, ensures that the rules and procedures of the game are followed, resulting in an impartial situation for all competitors. An official—often known as a referee or umpire—fills several functions related to competition. Officials start and stop play, judge the quality of the skills performed, supervise the adherence of the performance to specifically set criteria, and enforce rules of play. Officials in a team sport also monitor the interaction between the opposing athletes.

Sports are recognized by the International Olympic Committee (IOC) and are controlled by the governing bodies of individual sports. These bodies formulate rules, conduct international competitions, and certify officials. Nations, through the power of their national sports organizations, have the right to modify specific rules or procedures for athletic events conducted within their own borders. During international competitions, however, they must abide by international rules. International officials learn only one set of rules, gaining experience with the international rules every time they work.

The United States often deviates from international rules by formulating variations of the rules of games for play at the youth or scholastic levels; rules may also vary between men's and women's sports. Therefore, officials in the United States are required to learn a set of rules for each level of play and modifications for each gender.

Women's professional leagues, although they exist around the world, have been slow to develop in some sports (basketball, softball, volleyball) in the United States. In other sports, however, such as tennis, golf, and figure skating, women have experienced great success as professional athletes. Building on their experience with women's collegiate or national sports, women work as officials with great success in these professional sports. Women have faced increasingly difficult competition and obstacles, however, as they have attempted to obtain higher certification levels. In actuality, the number of women officials has decreased with the increased popularity of women's sports because more men have wanted to officiate women's games.

TRAINING, CERTIFICATION, AND ASSIGNMENTS

Officials work their way up to the elite levels of the performance pyramid with each higher certification. Women and men are eligible to work at all levels of competition for either gender if they can demonstrate competence and obtain the required certification.

Women need not be elite athletes to become officials in a particular sport, but they must be willing to understand the technique, strategy, and rules of the sport, as well as the techniques of officiating. Officials are required to attend rules clin-

ics, practical evaluation or rating sessions, and critique sessions with clinicians. Officials generally begin working in entry-level positions (such as lane judges, turn or stroke judges, and linespersons or umpires). As women learn the rules of the game and the officiating methods to interact with coaches and other officials, they are rated by their supervisors and they try to earn assignments for higher-level competitions. Once a woman obtains certification at the national level, she must be nominated by the national governing body to attend an international officials' clinic. Nominations for international certification from each country must be approved by each sport's international federation. Candidates for international rating must meet age guidelines in addition to passing the written and practical exams. Finally, candidates, while trying for certification, work under the scrutiny of a jury. Once certified, female officials must negotiate the obstacles of gender and cultural or political discrimination. Future assignments depend on the evaluations of work in this biased environment, and they are limited by the finite number of international competitions and the difficulties involved with the required traveling. A retirement age or fitness qualification to maintain certification may also be imposed.

On average it takes six to ten years for an individual who chooses to concentrate on an officiating career to earn the necessary credentials to qualify for nomination as an international official. In some sports the time required to move through the rating levels may be closer to fifteen years. Depending on the total number of officials in the pool of each country and the need for international officials, it might take even longer.

Officials must learn to deal with the pressure that comes with performing under stress and with constant criticism as they work in front of spectators whose emotions often run high. Women must remain unflappable under the added pressure of an environment dominated by men. The male-dominated system creates a political environment in which women often work with male coaches, officiating partners, administrators, and media personnel.

An international competition requires only a small number of working officials. Countries that send athletes to the competition may send a ref-

Women referees often start their careers officiating interscholastic games. (Richard Cummins/Corbis)

eree for each team. As an option, the host country may provide several officials, and then the sport federation invites neutral officials to complete the officiating crew. Neutral officials ensure that national bias does not interfere with the fairness of the competition. Officials from an athlete's country are not allowed to officiate any match that could have an impact on the status of that athlete's position in the competition results. In sporting events for which a panel of judges determines the final placement, officials are selected from a balanced mix of countries that reflects the demographics of the athletes or the competing countries. The old-fashioned concept that men are assigned men's events and women are assigned women's events is disappearing, although it may occasionally influence the assignments.

GENDER ISSUES

Women's advances in athletic participation have not been matched in the area of officiating. Women officials face many difficulties as they work their way up through the ranks of certification. At all levels of competition, the number of male officials, coaches, and assigners far surpasses the number of females in the same positions. The reasons are complex and varied and include the following. As there are more male coaches in women's athletics than female coaches and men feel more comfortable with male officials, fewer women are chosen as officials. Because female officials are less willing to tolerate the increasing level of unacceptable behavior demonstrated by players, coaches, and spectators, they are more prone than male officials to leave the profession. It is also possible that, because some female officials have family and career responsibilities that conflict with afternoon schedules or prevent them from traveling distances, they have less opportunity to officiate than do male officials. And, last, because officials join male-controlled local and national official associations in order to receive training and assignments, women are discriminated against and receive fewer assignments than their male counterparts do.

Although women have achieved officiating success at the highest levels of athletic competition, the number of women at this level remains quite low. Women officials are becoming more visible internationally as they break the barriers and achieve assignment to sporting events like the Olympics and world championships. And women have finally been hired to officiate in several professional sports leagues, including professional basketball, in the United States. Women role models, with their excellent standard of performance at the highly visible and competitive levels of competition, have opened doors for other women. But women are still in a position that requires them to work harder and under closer scrutiny than their male colleagues in order to achieve the same level of success.

PERSONALITY TRAITS OF OFFICIALS

Research has been conducted to identify the characteristics of a good official, to indicate whether personality traits differ across officials in various sports, and to determine if male and female officials behave in the same ways. Effective officials show concern for the welfare of each athlete, exhibit high standards of honesty and integrity, demonstrate knowledge of the rules, maintain objectivity and alertness, react quickly to situations, and are consistent in their interpretation and enforcement of the rules. Many officials and coaches believe that experience is the key factor to success. Studies have shown that many officials have dominant and self-confident personality characteristics. Female basketball officials must be tough-minded, realistic, self-reliant, self-sufficient, responsible, and decisive. Officials must also be able to demonstrate emotional stability in the face of pressure and stress.

Using the eighteen-trait California Personality Index (CPI), one study found that national volleyball officials were socially oriented, with men more so than females, and that female officials

---

OATH OF THE OFFICIALS OF THE GAY GAMES

The officials who govern and officiate in the Gay Games take an oath. The following is the oath, usually recited by an official during the Opening Ceremonies.

I, [Name],
On behalf of all officials in this stadium
Pledge to fairly officiate in the Gay Games

To honor the spirit of their origins by celebrating the true meaning of sportsmanship
By judging impartially and without prejudice
I pledge to respect the talents of all athletes who come to these Games
Where self-esteem is fostered through fairness
To all competitors who seek and find victory in a personal best.

were more sympathetic and sensitive than male volleyball officials. It also reported that both males and females were more dominant, assertive, sociable, ambitious, and self-confident than the general population. Male officials were more self-accepting of themselves than were female officials or the general population. The best officials approached their responsibilities with a professional manner, made instantaneous decisions under pressure, and walked away "unremembered."

THE OFFICIAL AND UNSPORTING BEHAVIOR

The increased popularity of sports has provided opportunities for participants of all ages to learn many of life's valuable lessons. Athletes learn to practice and play the game giving their total effort, and learn that sometimes, even if they give everything they have, their opponents may still be better. Teammates learn to trust, care about, and rely on each other as they work together toward a common goal throughout the season. Each team member gains a sense of accomplishment and increased self-esteem as new skills are learned and improved on. But perhaps the most important lesson is that all aspects of life require elements of basic human dignity, which in sports is called good sporting behavior.

Officials take positive steps to minimize poor sporting behavior during competition by enforcing the rules fairly and consistently for both teams. Officials can never satisfy both teams with any particular decision; one team always walks away in defeat. Every official's goal is to call an impartial and consistent game without controversy. Officials work hard to ignore comments from spectators and sometimes even from players and their coaches. Officials who begin to listen to these comments risk missing a call or giving the benefit of the doubt to the complaining team, which unfairly influences the game. Officials must enforce the rules regardless of the team, the score, or the situation. And they must penalize any show of unsportsmanlike behavior from coaches or athletes during the competition. At the end of the game, officials immediately leave the playing area, often escorted by security personnel to limit the possibility of interaction with irate fans.

OFFICIATING AND LIABILITY

Legal liability is based on the principle that a person is responsible for the cost or damages to another individual if he or she does, or fails to do, something that a reasonable or prudent person would do in the same situation. A reasonable and prudent official, in terms of liability, is one who knows the rules that are designed to protect the players. He or she makes the call to stop any play that puts an athlete at risk for injury or puts one team at a disadvantage. A reasonable and prudent official enforces the rules with integrity in all situations. Decisions are based on the rules—regardless of the score, the time remaining, or the reaction of the players, coaches, or fans. And, most important, the official does not allow anyone or anything to prevent the completion of those duties.

The official is responsible for the athletic event from the time it begins until it is over. The official must see that the safety conditions specified by the rule book are satisfied before the contest starts. If the competition is allowed to continue under unsafe conditions and a participant is injured, the official becomes liable for the damages incurred. Despite all the preventive steps taken by the officials, injuries may still occur, and so many officials purchase liability insurance.

Athletes who experience a career-ending injury resulting in the loss of future income may include the official in a lawsuit. Negligent or not, an official with liability insurance will be covered for any financial damages assessed or costs associated with the lawsuit. Officials should also be aware that they should not discuss any aspect of the game, controversy, or injury with the media or with anyone except their attorneys. Statements made without the advice of a lawyer may involve the officials in a future lawsuit. Officials should not respond to baiting or harassment from spectators, as confrontations between officials and spectators can escalate into violence and result in assault charges.

OFFICIATING LANGUAGE

Officials communicate through sign language and, in many sports, a whistle. Players, coaches, and spectators want to know why the game was interrupted and what will happen next. The whistle starts and stops the action. Blowing the whistle is an art for the successful official, and its use distinguishes the experienced and self-confident official. The whistle should give a sharp, loud tone, capable of being heard in a crowded gymnasium or an open stadium filled with cheering spectators. Plays are started with short, crisp blasts and are stopped by a longer, sharp, single blast. Occasionally, a double whistle is used to interrupt the action during the play. Time-outs and substitutions have special sound patterns so that players do not begin to play without permission. Regardless of the whistle style or the sound pattern produced, there should be no doubt that the official is in charge.

When play ends, officials give additional information through the use of arm signals. Many signals have become universally accepted in everyday life. Using the hands to form a "T" means "Stop, I want a time-out." Holding both hands high in the air signifies that a goal has been scored. A sweeping outward motion with both hands indicates that everything is all right or safe. Each sport also has hand and arm signals that convey specific meanings.

Officials follow a specific pattern when stopping play during a game. They blow the whistle when the play is considered over, indicating with the appropriate signal the infraction of the rule. Officials then award the penalty or the points to the proper competitor before play continues.

WOMEN OFFICIALS

In some sports, women have been accepted internationally as officials for years, whereas in others, women have only recently begun to officiate at the professional or international level. Opportunities for women to officiate in high-profile sports increased dramatically in the 1980s and 1990s. Since the 1984 Los Angeles Olympic Games, women have received international certifications in many major sports. Despite this progress, in many sports female officials constitute only one-quarter to one-third of the total certified officials, and far fewer women than men achieve international certification. The United States has been a leader in the effort to certify women and nominate them to work major international competitions.

The woman who first obtained the International Basketball Federation (FIBA, Fédération Internationale de Basketball) certification was also the first assigned to officiate at the Olympic Games. Since the 1984 Olympics in Los Angeles, women have been assigned to officiate in every basketball game of the Olympic Games and world championships. In 1999 eleven American women were internationally certified by FIBA. The first three-woman crew for a men's National Collegiate Athletic Association (NCAA) Division I basketball game was in 1990. In 1991 the first woman was hired to work a professional basketball game for the United States Basketball League, and in 1997 the first women were hired by the National Basketball League (NBA) as referees. In 1983 the International Volleyball Federation (FIVB, Fédération Internationale de Volleyball) certified the first woman international referee. However, women were not assigned to work either the Olympic Games or the world championships until the 1996 Olympic Games in Atlanta, when women were certified as international beach volleyball referees; four women were assigned to work this first beach volleyball event. The FIVB established a second level of international certification required of officials assigned to major international indoor competitions. No woman has yet been nominated to this level.

WOMEN OFFICIALS IN MEN'S SPORTS

The first four American women to be employed as full-time officials in men's professional sports leagues were Dee Kanter and Violet Palmer in the National Basketball Association in 1998 and Nancy Lay and Sandra Hunt in the Major Soccer League also in 1998. Although some coaches and players objected at first to women officiating men's games, once the women proved that they would stand up to players and coaches in confrontations, they were accepted.

Women have officiated for many years at the highest level of softball competition. Since 1978 approximately forty women have been certified by the International Softball Federation (ISF) as officials for international competition. Eighteen of these women are from the United States. Softball was included as a medal event during the 1996 Olympic Games, and five of the twelve officials assigned to the Atlanta Olympic Games were women. Women officials have penetrated professional baseball; four women have umpired in the minor leagues.

Many women have achieved International Football Federation certification (FIFA, Fédération Internationale de Football Association) as international soccer (association football) referees. Soccer officials are classified as referees or assistant referees. There are sixty-six women referees and approximately the same number of certified assistant referees. In 1995 the first woman was assigned to referee at the women's World Cup in Sweden, and in 1996 the first woman was assigned to work as a referee assistant at the Olympic Games in Atlanta. Three women have been nominated to the FIFA for international certification as referees.

The U.S. Hockey Association, following the commitment of the International Hockey Federation (IHF) to promote women officials at its competitions, sent one female referee and two linespersons to the 1996 Olympic Games and to the 1997 world championships. In addition, two women work in men's professional minor league ice hockey. Only eight women are certified to officiate ice hockey at the international level.

Swimming requires many officials during a single event. There are turn and stroke judges, as well as the starter and the head referee. From the United States, three women are certified by the International Amateur Swimming Federation (FINA, Fédération Internationale de Natation Amateur) as starters and head referees. One of these was the first woman to be assigned internationally as a starter during the 1996 Atlanta Olympics.

Track and field competition officials follow a classification format similar to that of swimming officials, requiring a head official, starters, umpires, and field judges. The number of women assigned to officiate during International Amateur

Carolina Domenech was the first woman to referee a Premiere League soccer match. (AFP/Corbis)

Athletic Federation (IAAF) track and field meets is increasing in a continued attempt to obtain gender equity within the officiating pool. Several women have been assigned to major competitions since the 1984 Olympic Games.

Women are now competing at the national and international levels in the sport of wrestling. There are two types of wrestling officials: mat officials and pairing officials. Although traditionally men have been mat officials and women pairing officials, women have worked on the mat; and women have been sent to the Olympic Games and the world championships.

Other Olympic-level sports have a history of female officials working at major international competitions. Since the early years of organized tennis, women have served as chair umpires and linespersons for the International Tennis Federation (ITF). Several women from the United States have achieved assignments at U.S. open tournaments and have been invited to work at numerous international tennis tournaments. The sport of gymnastics unofficially requires that women judge female competitions. They must also have one female coach on the floor during competition. In golf, the tournament director for the Ladies Professional Golf Association (LPGA) has also served on the Professional Golf Association's rules committee in addition to serving as a rules committee official for many of its major tournaments.

Women have long served as officials during international figure skating competitions. Judges evaluate the competition, present the marks for each performance, then rank the winner chosen by the majority of judges. Referees control the competition environment and monitor that the judges' scores fall within acceptable ranges of variation. The International Skating Union (ISU) had restricted the number of international judges (12) and referees (6) allowed certification from each member country, but this restriction has been lifted. The number of women eligible to obtain their international ratings will increase according to the ability of each country to train and nominate new international officials.

Many of these female pioneers and groundbreakers currently work as officials, but they are also involved in numerous administrative functions nationally and internationally. These women continue to help future female officials improve their skills and reach their dreams of becoming the internationally certified officials of tomorrow.

There are two organizations in the United States with open membership for officials from all sports: the National Association of Sports Officials (NASO) and the National Federation Interscholastic Officials Association (NFIOA). In the United States, high school and college athletic directors work with local officials' associations to arrange for the training and development of officials for interscholastic sports, where both women and men generally begin their officiating careers. In addition, the national governing bodies for most sports in the United States and around the world have officiating directors who provide information and local contacts for those interested in becoming sports officials.

Terry Lawton

Bibliography

Barber, Perry. (1998) "In the Fraternity." *Referee* [Journal of the National Association of Sports Officials] 23, 3 (March): 31–36.

Fratzke, Mel R. (1975) "Personality and Biographical Traits of Superior and Average College Basketball Officials." *Research Quarterly* 46: 484–488.

Furlong, William. (1975) "Dominant, Hostile, Objective." *Los Angeles Times* (20 December): Pt 3; 1, 6.

Goldmeyer, Alan. (1984) *Sports Officiating: A Legal Guide*. New York. Leisure Press.

Johnson, Lee. (1999) "Where are the Female Officials?" *Officials Quarterly* [Journal of the National Federation Interscholastic Officials Association] (Spring): 6–7.

Kroll, Walter. (1977) "Psychological Scaling of AIAW Code of Ethics for Officials and Spectators." *Research Quarterly* 48: 475–479.

Lemaire, Sue. (1981) "Personality Traits of National Volleyball Officials." Master's thesis: California State University, Long Beach.

Megargee, Edwin. (1972) *The California Psychological Inventory Handbook*. San Francisco: Jossey-Bass.

Scheer, Janet K., and Charles J. Ansorge. (1979) "Influence Due to Expectations of Judges: A Function of Internal and External Locus of Control." *Journal of Sports Psychology* 1, 1: 53, 58

Schurr, Evelyn L., and Joan A. Phillip. (1971) "Women's Sports Officials." *Journal of Health, Physical Education and Recreation* 42: 71–72.

Thompson, William A., and Richard Clegg. (1974) *Modern Sports Officiating: A Practical Guide*. Dubuque, IA: Wm. C. Brown.

Information was also provided by Esse Baharmast (U.S. Soccer, Director of Officials), Tom Blue (U.S. Volleyball, Vice President Officials Division), Merrill Butler (U.S. Softball, Director of Officials), John Davis (U.S. Track & Field, Director of Officials), Claire Ferguson (U.S. Figure Skating, President), Shawn Ford (U.S. Basketball, Director of Officials), Don Hart (U.S. Swimming, Director of Officials), Richard Kaufman (U.S. Tennis, Director of Officials), Matt Leaf (U.S. Ice Hockey, Director of Official Education), Connie Maloney (U.S. Gymnastics, Junior Olympic Program), and Sue Siar (U.S. Wrestling Officials, National Pairing Director).

OLYMPICS

In 1894, when Pierre de Coubertin (1863–1937) invited "the youth of the world" to compete in the first Olympic Games of the modern era, the French baron extended his invitation to men only.

Two years later, when the first Games took place in Athens, only men competed. During his long tenure as president of the International Olympic Committee (IOC)—1896 to 1925—Coubertin never wavered in his conviction that women should participate as spectators but not as athletes. Their proper role was to encourage the men and to admire male athletic achievement.

EARLY HISTORY

Despite Coubertin's opposition, at least twelve women competed in the Games of 1900. Margaret Abbott, a member of the Chicago Golf Club, had come to Paris to study art, but she lay down her brushes, picked up her clubs, and became the first American woman to bring home an Olympic gold medal. Her mother, Mary Abbott, came in seventh in the same competition. In tennis, Great Britain's Charlotte Cooper, the Wimbledon champion of 1895, 1896, and 1898, defeated Hélène Prévost of France 6–1, 6–4. In mixed doubles, Cooper teamed with Reginald Dougherty to vanquish Prévost and her Irish partner, Harold Mahoney, by a score of 6–2, 6–4. Some historians believe that the very first female Olympian was American-born Helen de Pourtales, who may have accompanied her Swiss husband, Hermann, competing on the yacht *Lerina*.

A mere twelve nations sent athletes to the 1904 Olympics in St. Louis. Archery was the only sport for women—and all eight contestants were Americans. In 1908, in London, figure skating was added to archery, and tennis returned to the program, raising the number of female athletes to forty-three, or 2.1 percent of all Olympic athletes. Germany's Anna Hübler teamed with Dr. Heinrich Burger to outskate two brother-sister couples from Great Britain. In that less specialized age, England's Charlotte "Lottie" Dod was able to add a silver medal in archery to her five Wimbledon tennis trophies.

During these Olympics, members of the Fédération Internationale de Natation Amateur (International Amateur Swimming Federation) voted to admit female swimmers and divers to the 1912 Games, scheduled for Stockholm. When the New South Wales Ladies' Swimming Association selected Sarah "Fanny" Durack and Wilhelmina "Mina" Wylie to represent Australia at these Olympics, the organization's president resigned in protest because she thought it indecent for male spectators to watch female athletes. Durack, Wylie, and thirty-nine European women competed in 100-meter freestyle and 400-meter relay races, and in platform diving. The Australians finished first and second in 100 meters. Du-

PIERRE DE COUBERTIN
ON FEMALE ATHLETES (1910)

Can one permit women . . . to appear as female jockeys? Could one look calmly on from the stands while they broke their skulls? Should female teams be allowed to compete in polo and soccer matches? By no means!

Respect for individual liberty requires that one should not interfere in private acts. If a woman wishes to pilot an airplane, no policeman has a right to stop her. . . . But, when it comes to public sports competitions, women's participation should be absolutely prohibited. It is indecent that the spectators should be exposed to the risk of seeing the body of a woman smashed before their eyes. Besides, no matter how toughened a sportswoman may be, her organism is not formed to sustain certain shocks. Her nerves dominate her muscles, this is nature's will. Finally, the . . . discipline that is brought to bear on male competitors in order to establish the good order and decorum of a contest is jeopardized by female participation.

PIERRE DE COUBERTIN
(1910) "Chronique du mois: Défense aux femmes," Revue Olympique, *109–110.*

Young Greek girls in Olympia, dressed in appropriate Greek costumes, light the Olympic torch. (Bettmann/Corbis)

rack's time of 1:22.2 was a world record. British women won the relay. Twelve of the thirteen divers were Swedes, and so it was no surprise when Greta Johansson and Lisa Regnell, both from Sweden, took first and second place. Perhaps because archery was dropped, the total number of women at Stockholm increased to only fifty-five.

BETWEEN WARS

There were no female American swimmers or divers at the 1912 Games because James Sullivan, head of the Amateur Athletic Union (AAU), was adamantly opposed to women's sports. His death in 1914 removed the main impediment to women's participation, and American women dominated the swimming and diving in Antwerp in 1920. Ethelda Bleibtrey set world records for the 100- and 300-meter events and helped to set a third in the 4 × 100-meter relay. France's flamboyant Suzanne Lenglen, perhaps the greatest tennis player of the era, easily defeated Britain's Dorothy Holman 6–3, 6–0, and went on to take a second gold in mixed doubles.

At the 1924 Games, celebrated in Paris as a favor to Coubertin, Denmark's Ellen Osiier won the first-ever fencing competition. There were also three new events for the swimmers: 100-meter backstroke, 200-meter breaststroke, and 400-meter freestyle. The total number of female athletes nearly doubled, from 76 to 136. In addition, 120 Frenchwomen performed a gymnastics display, which doubtless influenced the IOC's decision to accept gymnastics as a team sport in 1928.

There was also strong pressure to introduce women's track and field at the 1928 Amsterdam Olympics. In 1922 Alice Milliat, who had founded the Fédération Sportive Féminine Internationale (FSFI) the previous year, staged an international sports festival in Paris, the first of five quadrennial "Women's Olympics." In response to this challenge, Sweden's Sigfrid Edström, founder and president of the International Amateur Athletic Federation (IAAF), concluded in 1926 that a compromise was in order; if the FSFI dropped the word "Olympics," he would recommend that the IOC experiment with five track and field events at the 1928 Amsterdam Olympics.

Together with the swimmers, divers, fencers, and newly invited gymnasts, the 101 track and field athletes (from nineteen countries) raised the total number of women at the 1928 Olympics to 290 (9.6%). In the absence of British women, who boycotted because they felt that the five-event program was too limited, Canadians were the leaders, with gold medals for the high jump and the 4 × 100-meter relay and silver and bronze for the 100-meter race. In winning the high jump, Ethel Catherwood cleared 1.59 meters (5.24 feet). Unfortunately, a storm of controversy followed the 800-meter race, which Germany's Lina Radke won in world-record time (2:16.8). After the race, the runners sprawled on the ground, and the *New York Times* reported hysterically that they had been exhausted by their strenuous efforts. In a panic, the IOC's executive board voted in July 1929 to eliminate women's track and field from the program for 1932.

At this point in the prolonged struggle over women's participation, Gustavus T. Kirby, an influential American member of the IAAF, threatened a boycott of men's track and field at the Los Angeles Olympics if the IOC did not reverse its discriminatory decision. At the Olympic Congress

A *NEW YORK TIMES* EDITORIAL ON THE EFFECTS OF ATHLETICS ON WOMEN

After the athletic contests between school and college girls in Paris on Sunday certain spectators concluded from the severe exhaustion shown by some of the participants after their victories, and especially after their defeats, that such "games" were not proper for women, or, at any rate, not for girls—that they might be seriously and even permanently affected by the strains to which in the excitement of competition they subjected their hearts and other muscles.

That there is some truth in this criticism hardly can be questioned, but it can be applied as fairly to young men as to young women, and too much could easily be made of the fact that in several instances the girls fell into fits of hysterical crying. Anybody who has been near the finish of college boat races has seen young men do the same thing, not often, of course, but frequently enough to show that this reaction to physical exertion carried to the very limit of endurance is about the same in both sexes. By no means all the girls taking part in the Olympic games cried when they were beaten; the majority of them showed only a weariness that was little if any more than wholesome, and not at all likely to have lasting effects.

That the American team made only 31 points while the Britons made 50 is not surprising, but it probably should give rise to no more thought than the fact that the competitions were more vigorous than those in which the majority of girls now would think of taking part—more vigorous than any girls, a few years ago, would have dreamed of engaging in.

New York Times. *(1922) "Effects of Athletics on Women" 23 August.*

held in Berlin in 1930, the exhibition of prowess by German female athletes was so impressive that another influential American, Avery Brundage, joined Kirby in advocating a reversal of the IOC's decision. The delegates endorsed women's track and field by a vote of 17–1.

At Los Angeles, Poland's Stanislawa Walasiewicz (later known, as an American, as Stella Walsh) won the 100-meter run in world-record time (11.9), and Helene Madison (United States) won three golds in swimming. But the most publicized female athletes at the 1932 games were a pair of polar opposites. Mildred "Babe" Didrikson excelled in baseball, basketball, volleyball, golf, and tennis as well as in track and field. At the 1932 national track and field championships, she won six gold medals and set four world records. At Los Angeles, limited by Olympic rules to only three events, she set a world's record in the 80-meter hurdles (11.7) and far surpassed her German rivals in the javelin. In the high jump, she tied for first with Jean Shiley with a world's record of 1.657 meters (5.51 feet) but was awarded the silver medal on the grounds that she dove over the bar using the then-prohibited western roll. While the journalist Paul Gallico ungallantly described Didrikson as "the muscle moll to end all muscle molls," photographers jostled one another to snap pictures of Eleanor Holm, whose Olympic record in the 100-meter backstroke (1:18.3) interested the press corps less than the fact that she was "the most beautiful girl athlete" at the Games.

En route to the 1936 Games in Berlin, Holm was also the most gregarious "girl athlete." She made her clandestine way to the ship's first-class deck, flirted, danced, drank, missed a curfew, and was expelled from the American team. Newspapers published photographs of the "water nymph," and pilloried "spoil-sport" Avery Brundage, then head of the American Olympic Committee. The press might better have criticized him for his adamant insistence that the United States participate in the "Nazi Olympics" despite

Germany's violation of the Olympic Charter. At these Games, German Jews were excluded from the German team.

Among the excluded was high-jumper Gretel Bergmann, whose leap of 1.6 meters (5.28 feet) had set a national record. Despite her absence, German women performed impressively. Gisela Mauermayer, who had triumphed in the first-ever women's pentathlon at the FSFI's 1934 London games, won the discus with an Olympic record of 47.63 meters (157.1 feet). Tilly Fleischer hurled the javelin 45.18 meters (149 feet) for a second gold while their German teammates won two silver medals and two bronzes. Although the 4 × 100-meter relay squad set a world's record in the opening round, a dropped baton spoiled their chance to win the race.

Ironically, in light of the Nazis' refusal to allow Bergmann to compete, the "Aryans" were defeated by Ibolya Csak, a Hungarian Jew, whose best jump was two centimeters better than Bergmann's German record. There was a second irony. Although her father was a Jew, flaxen-haired fencer Helene Mayer, who had won a gold medal in 1928, was allowed to represent Germany in the foils. Standing on the victors' podium to receive her silver medal, she raised her arm in deluded tribute to the man who was soon to send women like her to the gas chambers.

THE POSTWAR YEARS

The outbreak of war in 1939 forced the cancellation of the 1940 and 1944 Games. At the first postwar Olympics, held in London in 1948, Micheline Ostermeyer of France won the shot put and the discus and was third in the high jump. The winning jumper, Alice Coachman, was the first African-American woman to earn Olympic gold. Her leap of 1.68 meters (5.5 feet) was an Olympic record. The year's most spectacular female athlete, however, was undoubtedly the Dutch runner Francina (Fannie) Blankers-Koen. As a fifteen year old, she had competed in 1936. Then, she was completely overshadowed by her teammate Hendrika Mastenbroek, who swam for three gold medals and one silver. Now, twelve years, one husband, and two children later, Blankers-Koen earned gold medals in the 100- and 200-meter sprints, the 80-meter hurdles, and the 4 × 100-meter relay. Avery Brundage, often criticized for

his alleged hostility to women's sports, raved about her as "a new type of woman," goddess-like, "lithe, supple, physically disciplined, strong, slender and efficient." Brundage's enthusiasm did not signal a revolution in men's attitudes toward women's sports. The Daily Graphic (London) reported in a headline: "Fastest Woman in the World Is an Expert Cook."

It is doubtful that culinary skills were widely present among the female athletes of the Soviet Union's first Olympic teams. They were professional athletes trained from childhood to compete, to win, and to prove to the world that communism was the wave of the future. Win they did. At Helsinki, Finland, in 1952, Soviet women participated in their first Olympics and garnered seven of the nine medals awarded for the shot put, the discus, and the javelin. They also dominated gymnastics, which now consisted of individual as well as team competition. Led by Maria Gorokhovskaya, they took four gold and five silver medals. It was the first of the Soviet Union's eight consecutive Olympic championships. The Hungarian gymnasts (two golds, one silver, four bronzes) and swimmers (four golds) were also impressive. Another representative of the communist world, Dana Zatopek (Czechoslovakia), won the javelin with a throw of 50.47 meters (166.5 feet).

Eastern European women were, however, not yet a match for the Australian runners, then near the peak of their remarkable careers. Marjorie Jackson equaled the world's record for 100 meters (11.5) and won the 200 meters as well, while Shirley Strickland did the 80-meter hurdles in world-record time. Australia was the favorite in the 4 × 100-meter relay, and the team set a world record (46.1) in the first heat, but a poorly executed baton pass between Winsome Cripps and Marjorie Jackson allowed the United States to win its lone track and field gold. In diving, however, the American women made up for disappointments elsewhere. Led by Patricia McCormick, they took five out of six medals.

For the first time, women competed along with men in dressage. Denmark's Liz Hartel won a silver medal on Jubilee even though she was partially crippled by polio.

Four years later, in 1956, the Games were in Melbourne, and the Australian women had a home court advantage. Although they were only

16 percent of their nation's contingent, they won more than half their team's medals and led the way to Australia's third-place finish in the unofficial medal count (behind the United States and the Soviet Union). Betty Cuthbert won the 100- and 200-meter races, and Strickland repeated her 1952 victory in the 80-meter hurdles. Both ran on the 4 × 100-meter relay team that obtained the gold medal that had eluded them in 1952. In the pool, Lorraine Crapp won the 400-meter freestyle, and Dawn Fraser, who was second in that race, won gold in the 100-meter freestyle in world-record time (62 seconds). The two of them joined Faith Leech and Sandra Morgan to take still another gold—and set another world record—in the 4 × 100-meter freestyle relay.

In gymnastics it was another story. Despite strong competition from the thirty-five-year-old Ágnes Keleti, who won gold for the uneven parallel bars and the balance beam and tied for first place in the floor exercise, the Soviet Union's Larissa Latynina became the all-around champion. By the time Latynina concluded her career, in 1964, her medal collection included an amazing nine golds, five silvers, and four bronzes.

In 1960, in Rome, Dawn Fraser continued to be unbeatable in the 100-meter freestyle, but she had to settle for two silver medals in the relays. The most memorable athletic performance was probably Wilma Rudolph's. As the youngest member of the 1956 American team, she had been eliminated in her 200-meter heat. By 1960, she had matured—and had completely overcome the effects of polio, which had crippled her as a child. Tall, graceful, and fast, she sped to victory in the 100 meters, ahead of Britain's Dorothy Hyman, and in the 200 meters, ahead of Germany's Juta Heine. She also anchored the 4 x 100-meter relay team, which finished ahead of the German and Polish teams. The 800-meter race was contested for the first time since 1928 (after a close IOC vote of 26–22). It was won by the Soviet Union's Ludmilla Shevtsova, who equaled the world's record of 2:04.3.

Among the millions who watched Rudolph at the 1960 Games, which were the first to be televised throughout Europe, was Irene Kirszenstein, a fourteen-year-old Polish Jew who had been born in a camp for displaced persons. Four years later, in Tokyo, she was on the Polish team that

Speed skating became an Olympic sport in the 1960 Squaw Valley Games through the campaigning of the Soviet Union, which dominated the competition in its infancy. Pictured is Russian skater Anna Savelyeva, competing in the 1998 Nagano Olympics. (Wally McNamee)

won the 4 × 100-meter relay in world-record time. She was second in both the 200-meter race and the long jump. At Mexico City in 1968, she would win the 200-meter event in the world-record time of 22.58 seconds. Betty Cuthbert won the first-ever 400-meter race, adding a fourth gold to the three she acquired in 1956. In the field events, Tamara Press (Soviet Union) was victorious in shot put and discus, and her sister, Irina Press won the first-ever pentathlon. In gymnastics, Czechoslovakia's Vera Caslavska won gold on the balance beam and in the vault and wrested the combined title from Larissa Latynina. Although Japan had produced few truly great female athletes since Hitomi Kinue starred at the International Women's Games of 1926 and 1930, the Japanese volleyball players upset a much taller, much more experienced Soviet squad. Trained for years by an extremely severe coach, they were adulated as symbols of national *seishin* (spirit).

Despite Mexico City's high altitude, which thinned the air and made distance races especially arduous, the women's 1968 performances were stellar. Wyomia Tyus (United States), who had won the 100-meter race in Tokyo, sped to a second victory in that event while Madeline Manning, another black runner, came within a second of breaking the two-minute barrier for the 800-meter. France's Colette Besson was the surprise winner of the 400-meter event, while West Germany's favored Ingrid Becker won the pentathlon. Among the swimmers, Debbie Meyer (United States) led with gold for the 200-, 400-, and 800-meter freestyle. That the swimmers set a record number of Olympic records was nearly inevitable; six of the fourteen races were new (200- and 800-meter freestyle, 100-meter breaststroke, 200-meter backstroke, 200-meter butterfly, and 200-meter individual medley). In gymnastics, Vera Caslavka had her greatest moment. Against the political background of the Soviet invasion of her homeland, the Czech won three events—vault, uneven bars, floor exercises—and defeated the favored Russian Natalia Kuchinskaya for the all-round title.

In the summer of 1972, the Games returned to Germany. As expected, Munich was the scene of intense drama as the representatives of the Federal Republic of Germany were challenged by those from the German Democratic Republic, competing for the first time under their own flag. The East German women, led by sprinter Renate Stecher, were thought to be unbeatable. They did, indeed, win six of the fourteen track and field events, but their rivals took four of them, including the high jump, won by sixteen-year-old Ulrike Meyfarth, who would do it again in 1984. Australia's Shane Gould swam for three world records (and was overshadowed by Mark Spitz, who set or helped to set seven). Although the Soviet Union's Ludmilla Tourischeva was the best gymnast at the Games, Roone Arledge of ABC-TV anticipated the transformation of the sport from women's gymnastics to children's acrobatics; he ordered the cameras to focus on Tourischeva's diminutive pixie teammate, Olga Korbut. The Games were overshadowed by a tragic drama that summer: Palestinian terrorists invaded the Olympic Village and murdered eleven Israeli athletes. This heralded a period in which politics would play an increasingly prominent role in the Games.

THE ERA OF THE BOYCOTTS

At the Games held in Montreal in 1976, the total number of athletes was reduced by the departure of most of the African teams, angered by the IOC's refusal to bar New Zealand, which had played rugby against white-ruled South Africa.

Thanks in part to the absence of all-male African teams, women were a record 20.6 percent of the athletes. Another reason for the increase was that the IOC had given its belated approval to women's basketball and team handball as well as to six new rowing races. In all, there were forty-nine events for female athletes; women from the Soviet bloc won forty-five of them. They also garnered fifteen of eighteen possible medals in women's rowing. Their dominance in track and field and in rowing was no surprise, but their triumph in swimming was startling. Shirley Babashoff was expected to lead a parade of Americans to the victors' stand, but East Germany's Kornelia Ender won three individual gold medals and her teammates collected seven more. They also won the 4 × 100-meter relay. In all, they equaled or bettered nine world records. Babashoff refused to congratulate Ender and gave vent to a bitter innuendo about anabolic steroids. Revelations in the 1990s, after the unification of East and West Germany opened secret files, proved her right. Happier memories cluster around Romania's Nadia Comaneci, who received the first perfect score given in Olympic gymnastics. Her charm was so great that she was forgiven for her defeat of Olga Korbut, once the idol of the West.

Although most Western European teams defied their governments and competed in Moscow despite an American-sponsored boycott of the 1980 Games (a response to the Soviet Union's invasion of Afghanistan), female athletes from Western Europe were once again overwhelmed by those from the Soviet bloc. Italy's Sara Simeoni was memorable simply because her unexpected win in the high jump was one of the few occasions when three Eastern Europeans did not embrace on the victors' stand. Of sixty track and field medals, the Soviet women won fifty. Eight of the ten medals won by other Europeans went to the British for two third-place finishes in the relay races. In swimming, twelve of thirteen golds went either to East Germany or the Soviet Union. French women dominated fencing, but all the medals in gymnastics, rowing, and kayaking went to representatives of the Soviet bloc. It was the same story in basketball, handball, and volleyball.

Four years later, it was tit for tat. The Soviet Union refused to send a team to Los Angeles. Fortunately for the fans of women's gymnastics, Romania defied the Soviet Union, and Ecaterina Szabo's challenge to America's Mary Lou Retton provided a moment of high drama. Otherwise, the parade of American victors was almost an embarrassment. African Americans like Evelyn Ashford (100 meters) and Valerie Briscoe-Hooks (200 and 400 meters) dominated the shorter distances. Although the mass media had touted the new 3000-meter race as a contest between America's Mary Decker Slaney and South Africa's Zola Budd (running for the British team), the former accidentally spiked the latter, tripped, and fell. Romania's Maricaca Puica won the race. In the first-ever women's marathon, Joan Benoit (United States) endured the blazing California sun better than her Norwegian rivals, Greta Waitz and Ingrid Kristiansen.

The 3000-meter race and the marathon were not the only firsts. In addition to a 79.2-kilometer (49.1 miles) road race for cyclists, won by Connie Carpenter Phinney (United States), there were added events in kayaking and shooting and new events exclusively for women: solo and duet synchronized swimming, both won by the United States, and rhythmic gymnastics, won by Canada's Lori Fung. If the IOC was more open to women's sports than it had been, one reason was that the IOC now had female members. At the Baden-Baden Olympic Congress (1981), Flor Isava (Venezuela) and Pirjo Haeggman (Finland) ended the eighty-six-year male monopoly.

Although there were threats of still another boycott, the 1988 Games, celebrated at Seoul (South Korea), went smoothly. In addition to a new sport—table tennis—the IOC added a number of events, including a 10,000-meter race, won by Olga Bondarenko (Soviet Union). The proliferation of events for women tended, however, to diffuse the impact of the individual athletes. Some patterns were familiar. Russians and Romanians divided the gold medals in gymnastics (three each). East Germans took five of the six golds in rowing. Eastern European athletes also dominated track and field, but they failed to achieve the fame (and subsequent endorsements) of Florence Griffith-Joyner, the flamboyant African American winner of the 100-meter and 200-meter races and anchor of the winning 4 × 100-meter relay team. German fencers, led by Anja Fichtel, won gold, silver, and bronze and defeated the Italians for the team title. Although American television watchers might have thought Janet Evans—winner of the 400- and 800-meter freestyle races and the 400-meter individual medley—was the only swimmer in Seoul, Germany's Kristin Otto won the 50- and 100-meter freestyle races, the 100-meter backstroke, and the 100-meter butterfly. Otto added two more golds in the 4 × 100-meter relay and the 4 × 100-meter team medley. To no one's surprise, Germany's Steffi Graf triumphed in singles tennis—the sport returned after an absence of sixty-four years. Other patterns were brand-new. Portugal's Rosa Mota won the marathon, and divers from the People's Republic of China were spectacular in platform (Xu Yanmei) and springboard (Gao Min) diving.

AFTER THE COLD WAR

At the 1992 Games in Barcelona, women of African descent continued to excel in the sprints; Gail Devers and Gwen Torrence won the 100- and 200-meter races, and the latter joined Evelyn Ashford, Esther Jones, and Carlette Guidry to win a second gold in the 4 × 100-meter relay. Jackie Joyner-Kersee (United States) repeated her 1988 victory in the heptathlon and another African American runner, France's Marie-José Pérec, won the 400-meter race. The field events, the 400-meter hurdles, and most of the longer races were won by white women. Algeria's Hassiba Boulmerka, the first Islamic woman to become a world-class runner, won the 1500-meter race.

Canadian women won three of the six golds awarded in rowing, while Germans took three of the four in kayaking. The Italians outfenced the Germans, and the Eastern European gymnasts continued to dominate the gymnastics events. Surprisingly, Korean women took only two of the eight weight classes in the demonstration sport of *taekwondo*. This was, however, a better showing than that of the Japanese *judokas* who, in the seven weight classes of this newly introduced sport, managed to win three silver medals and two bronzes but not a single gold. The strongest swimmer was Hungary's Krisztina Egerszegi (100- and 200-meter backstroke, 400-meter individual medley). Shannon Miller (United States) was the only Westerner to dent the communists' control of gymnastics; she was second on the balance beam, third on the uneven bars and the floor exercises, and second as all-round. Chinese women won both golds and both silvers in table tennis while Koreans took all four bronze medals. The honors for team sports were distributed among the Koreans (handball), the Spanish (field hockey), the Cubans (volleyball), and the members of the Unified Team—the former Soviet Union (basketball).

At the Centennial Olympics in Atlanta, the women's program expanded to include soccer (association football), softball, and beach volleyball as well as new events in previously contested sports. Swimming and track and field, which began in 1912 and 1928 with two and five events each, now had nineteen and twenty. The record number of female athletes—3,779, or 36.4 percent of the 10,361 Olympians—stood in extreme contrast to the handful of women who participated in 1900.

Although the American women's total of seventeen victories was nearly twice the count of their Chinese rivals, who had nine, female athletes from twenty-seven other nations collected one or more gold medals. Great athletes like sprinter Marie-José Pérec (200- and 400-meter) and swimmer Krisztina Egerszegi (200-meter backstroke) repeated earlier Olympic successes, and there were new stars, like Ireland's Michelle Smith, who swam to three golds and a bronze, but the 1996 games were remarkable for victories won by small countries that had rarely if ever seen their athletes—male or female—mount the victory stand. Chioma Ajunwa (Nigeria) was first in the long jump, Ghada Shouaa (Syria) in the heptathlon, Claudia Poll (Costa Rica) in the 200-meter freestyle, and Lai-Shun Lee (Hong Kong) and Kristine Roug (Denmark) in sailing. In addition, the Danes won the handball tournament, and a Brazilian pair finished first in beach volleyball. Oddly, the most memorable woman at the Games was none of these. In an Olympic career that stretched from 1980 to 1996, sprinter Merlene Ottey (Jamaica) competed in ten finals and won two silver and five bronze medals. She never achieved her lifetime goal of Olympic gold.

WINTER GAMES

Despite Coubertin's opposition to winter sports (because they were not practiced worldwide), the IOC voted in 1921 to schedule them. The first of the series took place at Chamonix, France, in 1924. Until alpine skiing was introduced in 1936, the only event

for women was figure skating, won at the first Winter Games by Hungary's Herma Planck-Szabo. Unnoticed, in last place, was eleven-year-old Sonja Henie. The charismatic Norwegian was destined to star at the next three Winter Olympics—at St. Moritz (Switzerland), Lake Placid (New York), and Garmisch-Partenkirchen (Germany)—and then in Hollywood. Her films popularized the sport.

After World War II, the Winter Games resumed in 1948. At St. Moritz, Canadian figure skater Barbara Ann Scott won the most coveted honor of the Games (and was praised in *Time* for her "peaches-and-cream complexion"). The downhill slalom, introduced that year, was won by Gretchen Fraser (United States). Four years later, at Oslo, Andrea Lawrence (United States) won both the slalom and the giant slalom. All three medals in the newly introduced 10-kilometer cross-country race were taken home by the Finns. Britain's Jeannette Altwegg was first in women's figure skating while Ria and Paul Falk (Germany) won the pairs competition. Second to Altwegg was Tenley Albright (United States), who would win the gold in 1956. Second to her in that year was Carole Heiss (United States), who would win in 1960. The pattern repeated when Sjoukje Dijkstra (Netherlands) won silver in 1960 and gold in 1964.

At the 1956 Games, held in the Italian town of Cortina d'Ampezzo, a 3 × 5-kilometer cross-country relay race was introduced (won by the Finns), but the Soviets' request for women's speed skating was rejected. The program for Squaw Valley in 1960 was greatly expanded as the Soviet Union finally got its wish for women's speed skating. Their star was Lydia Skoblikova, who won both the 1500- and 3000-meter races.

Four years later, at Innsbruck, Austria, Skoblikova repeated these victories and swept the competition by adding two more over 500 and 1,000 meters. Luge was introduced in 1960 and won by East Germany's Ortrun Enderlein.

In 1964, the French sisters Christine and Marielle Goitschel emerged as the world's best alpine skiers. They finished first and second in the slalom and second and first, respectively, in the giant slalom. At the 1968 winter games, held in Grenoble, Marielle completed the women's slalom 0.29 seconds ahead of Canada's Nancy Greene; another French skier, Annie Famose, finished second, behind Greene, in the giant slalom. In figure skating, Peggy Fleming (United States) was far and away the best individual skater, and Oleg Protopopov and Ludmilla Belousova (Soviet Union) were as unbeatable a pair as they had been four years earlier in Innsbruck.

At Sapporo, Japan, in 1972, Switzerland's Marie-Theres Nadig defeated her favored countrywoman, Annemarie Proell, in the alpine events. In Nordic skiing, the Soviet Union's Galina Kulakova collected three gold medals. Women's figure skating, a perennially popular attraction, was won by Austria's Beatrix Schuba. Aleksei Ulanov and Irina Rodnina, who had beaten Protopopov and Belousova in the 1969 European championships, won the pairs competition. With a new partner—Aleksandr Zaitsev—Rodnina would triumph again in 1976 and 1980.

The 1976 Winter Games returned to Innsbruck (after Denver's voters rejected the Games). German alpine skier Rosi Mittermaier (two golds and a silver) shared the limelight with Dorothy Hamill (United States), winner of the individual figure skating contest.

Although the women at the Lake Placid Games in 1980 were overshadowed by the American hockey players' upset win over the Soviet Union, Liechtenstein's Hanni Wenzel made headlines by winning the slalom and the giant slalom. East Germany's Annett Pötzsch took the figure skaters' title but never became remotely as popular as her charismatic rival, Katarina Witt.

Witt starred at the 1984 Games in Sarajevo, Yugoslavia, winning gold with a routine of American show tunes. Witt's dance to the music of Bizet's *Carmen* in 1988 at Calgary, Canada, would give her a second victory. She would also make an exciting comeback at Lillehammer, Norway, in 1994, when she paid tribute to war-torn Sarajevo by skating to "Where Have All the Flowers Gone?"

If anyone outshone Witt in 1984, it was the British ice dancers Jayne Torvill and Christopher Dean. Their victory that year interfered with what, at century's end, had otherwise looked like a monopoly of the sport by the Soviet Union/Russia. At the Calgary Games, the gold for pairs competition went to Ekaterina Gordeeva and Sergei Grinkov of the Soviet Union; they repeated their triumph in 1994. At these 1988 Olympics, speed skater Bonnie Blair (United States) began her spectacular career with a world-record 39.10 seconds over the 500-meter course.

Blair won two more golds (500- and 1000-meter races) at the 1992 Games in Albertville, France. She and champion figure skater Kristi Yamaguchi (United States) were that year's most popular winners, but forty-year-old Raisa Smetanina (Unified Team), appearing in her fifth consecutive Olympics, was surely the most remarkable. She added a gold medal in cross-country skiing to the three golds, five silvers, and one bronze she had already accumulated.

There were also indications that the Winter Games were no longer a monopoly of Europeans and North Americans. Speed skaters Qiaobo Ye and Li Yan won China's first-ever winter medals. The former, returning to competition after a suspension for steroid use, won the 500- and 1000-meter races while the latter was second in the 500-meter short-track contest. With a second-place finish in the slalom, New Zealand's Annelise Coberger became the first winter medalist from Oceania.

MEDIA COVERAGE OF WOMEN'S SPORTS

The Olympics are especially important to women's sports and to women athletes because it is one of the few events in which women's sports are given broad media coverage. Television coverage of the 1996 Olympics by NBC Sports was criticized, however, for its failure to fully cover the popular softball games and soccer competitions in which the United States teams won the gold medals. NBC said coverage would be different in Sydney in 2000, and Sports Chairman Dick Ebersol was quoted in *Real Sports* (Winter 1999, p. 50) as promising that "Every second, every minute of every U.S. women's basketball, softball, and soccer game will be shown in its entirety."

TRAMPOLINE

The newest Olympic sport, contested for the first time at the 2000 Olympics, is trampolining. The sport is a gymnastic discipline which consists of four events: individual trampoline, synchronized trampoline, double mini trampoline, and tumbling. In structure and scoring it is similar to gymnastics and also resembles diving as competitors perform compulsory and voluntary skills and routines which are scored by a panel of judges. The basic move is the somersault with twists, tucks, and rotations added to make the moves more difficult. Depending on the event, competitors work on a full-size or mini trampoline or a sprung floor. Trampolining is popular in Australia, Russia, Ukraine, Germany, Great Britain, Sweden, and France. It is less popular in the United States, as trampolining largely disappeared from the public schools in the 1970s due to concerns about safety and liability raised by insurance providers.

The 1994 Lillehammer Games were the first to be celebrated between the Summer Games rather than in the same year. Bonnie Blair sped to victory once again in the 500- and 1000-meter races, bringing her Olympic total to five golds and a bronze, but the most decorated athlete at the Games was Italy's cross-country skier, Manuela DiCenta, who was first in the 15- and 30-kilometer races, second in the 5-kilometer and the pursuit, and third in the 4 × 5-kilometer relay. No athlete, male or female, received more adulation than Nancy Kerrigan (United States), the bronze medalist from 1992. Already immensely popular, Kerrigan won the world's sympathy after she was the victim of a physical assault by a friend of rival skater Tonya Harding (whom the media had already cast as the "tough girl" of the sport). That Kerrigan was finally (and perhaps unfairly) judged second to Oksana Baiul (Ukraine) seemed only to enhance her popularity (and her endorsement income). The demise of the amateur rule enabled Ekaterina Gordeeva and Sergei Grinkov of the Soviet Union, who had become openly professional after they won the gold in 1988, to return to Olympic competition and win the pairs competition.

The dramatic contrast in Nagano, Japan, in 1998, was not between good and evil, which is how the media tended to portray the Kerrigan-Harding rivalry. It was between the womanly grace of Michelle Kwan—all of seventeen years old—and the childlike energy of Tara Lipinski—fifteen. Kwan, the favorite, arrived after the Games had begun and stayed in her hotel room in order to concentrate on the task before her. Tiny Lipinski lived in the Olympic Village, posed with the massive sumo wrestler Akebono, and quickly became the most widely recognized spectator at the Games. Though Kwan skated beautifully, Lipinski, twirling and jumping like a symbolic embodiment of youthful energy, won. In the pairs competition, Artur Dmitriev, who had won gold and silver medals with Natalya Mishkutenok (1992, 1994), partnered Oksana Kazakova for a second gold. It was the tenth consecutive pairs victory for the Soviet Union/Russia.

In the alpine events, Germany's Katja Seizinger triumphed in the combined and in the downhill and was third in the giant slalom. America's Picabo Street failed to win a medal in the downhill, her specialty, and then surprised the experts with a win in the super-giant slalom. Russian skiers took all five gold medals in the Nordic events. Playing as roughly as the men, the American women defeated their Canadian rivals at ice hockey. Canadians took comfort in the tamer excitements of a win in curling, which had its Olympic debut in Nagano. Canadian spectators also rejoiced in the victories of speed skaters Catriona LeMay Doan (500-meter) and Annie Perrault (500-meter short track). Dutch fans screamed their enthusiasm for Marianne Timmer, who won the 1,000-meter and 1,500-meter races. Thanks to the *klap* skates introduced a few years earlier by Dutch speed skaters and soon adopted by nearly everyone else, world records were broken and broken again at almost every distance. The Japanese women skaters and skiers came away with a single bronze medal but, had there been a world's record for Olympic hospitality, the Nagano organizers might well have won it.

Allen Guttmann

Bibliography

Findling, John E., and Kimberley D. Pelle, eds. (1996) *Historical Dictionary of the Modern Olympic Movement.* Westport, CT: Greenwood.

Guttmann, Allen. (1991) *Women's Sports.* New York: Columbia University Press.

———. (1992) *The Olympics: A History of the Modern Games.* Urbana: University of Illinois Press.

Simri, Uriel. (1977) *A Historical Analysis of the Role of Women in the Modern Olympic Games.* Netanya, Israel: Wingate Institute.

ORIENTEERING

Orienteering competitors read a map at the Nantahala Outdoor Center before beginning a race in North Carolina in 1989. (Dave G. Houser)

The sport of orienteering is also known as the "thinking sport" or "cunning running." In orienteering, the athlete must navigate as quickly as possible on unfamiliar terrain using a map and compass to find predetermined locations. Men and women compete on relatively equal terms in orienteering, although often on separate courses, but proportionately fewer women participate.

Orienteering is a sport that appeals to outdoor enthusiasts who want to get off the beaten track and experience both a physical and mental challenge. The sport caters to the serious elite competitor as well as the casual map walker—often at the same event. Events will usually have suitable categories for a variety of lengths and difficulty levels. For these same reasons many people consider orienteering to be an ideal family sport.

A successful elite orienteer needs speed, agility, physical stamina, and the ability to read and interpret maps while moving quickly. Recreational orienteers may choose to walk or jog slowly.

HISTORY

The sport of orienteering officially celebrated its 100th anniversary in 1997. Orienteering evolved in Scandinavia from military exercises at the end of the nineteenth century. The Boy Scout movement adopted the sport during the first part of the twentieth century and organized the first nonmilitary competitions. Ernst Kilaander (1881–1958), a Swedish Scout leader, was instrumental in popularizing the sport and has become known as the father of orienteering. The first international event was held in 1932 between Sweden and Norway. The sport's popularity spread to other parts of Europe starting in the 1930s. Today, orienteering is practiced on all the continents. Scandinavians continue to dominate the orienteering elite.

The sport is governed by the International Orienteering Federation (IOF), which was formed in 1961. Approximately fifty countries worldwide have national orienteering associations that are affiliated with the IOF, along with thousands of regional and local orienteering associations. Orienteering is recognized by the International Olympic Committee (IOC) but has not been on the program of the Olympic Games. Those involved in the sport are lobbying the IOC for inclusion in the Games.

Outside of the Scandinavian countries, the sport tends to have a low to average media profile. This is partly because, by nature, orienteering is not much of a spectator sport. The IOF and other orienteering associations are working to change that by using new technologies that inform spectators of the whereabouts of the competitors and their times since they started at any point during the course.

RULES AND PLAY

Orienteering events offer course lengths and levels of difficulty for all ages and levels. Novice courses are generally all set on trails to ensure relatively easy navigation. The more difficult courses take the participant off the trails and require greater route choice. Higher-level competitors navigate not only by trails but also by valleys, ridges, hills, streams, lakes, and other geographic features, all of which are detailed on the orienteering maps. The goal is to find the various spots on the map in a predetermined order. In the actual terrain these spots will be marked by a small three-sided flag (also called a "control"). When participants reach a control, they mark a card (either manually or electronically) with a unique marker. Participants hand this card in at the finish, and event officials use it to determine whether the participants actually reached all the spots indicated on the map.

Starts are staggered so that competitors do not follow each other. Participants also receive a clue sheet to help them locate the control once they are in the vicinity and to verify that they are at the correct control. Both the flags and the clue sheets will be marked with letters or numbers so that the

orienteers can confirm that they are at the correct location. These clue sheets use international symbols that enable participants to compete in events all over the world without knowing the local language.

Orienteering requires a specialized and extremely detailed map. In most cases, the map is adapted and enhanced from an aerial photo. The maps are usually scaled at 1:15,000 or 1:10,000. Orienteering is done on different types of terrain in both rural and urban areas: forested areas, city parks, deserts, plains, treeless areas, and other areas. Participants use compasses for navigation. Specialized clothing is also available: shoes, trousers, gaiters, and the like designed for orienteering—lightweight and fast-drying. Special attire is not required, however, and many participants wear clothes and footwear suitable for any outdoor activity.

The IOF recognizes four types of orienteering: foot orienteering, ski orienteering, mountain bike orienteering, and trail orienteering. Foot orienteering—the basic kind described earlier—is the most popular of the four disciplines. Ski orienteering is done during the winter on cross-country skis, and the concepts of the sport are essentially the same. Mountain bike orienteering is done in a wilderness area with many trails and, to limit environmental damage, participants are required to stay on the trails. Trail orienteering is designed for participants with limited mobility. The controls are placed close to an accessible path, and the participants must choose which control in a cluster corresponds to the information that is included on the control description sheet and the map. Time is not a factor in trail orienteering. Many disabled athletes enjoy the mental challenge of trail orienteering. Winners are determined using a point system.

ELITE COMPETITION

The major orienteering events in the world attract many participants. The largest of these, the Swedish O-Ringen, attracts upward of 25,000 participants annually, making it one of the largest sporting events in the world.

Women and men participate in orienteering on a relatively equal basis. Events include courses for both genders. They compete within the same time frame and use the same maps. Men and women often compete on the same course, albeit in different categories. Despite the equal nature of orienteering competitions, overall, fewer women than men participate in the sport. The number of women in the sport has been growing since 1965. Estimates are that 30 to 40 percent of participants are women.

Orienteering is a very labor-intensive and time-consuming process for those who plan and set up courses for the variety of levels at an event. It is also a participatory sport; that is, the officials and event organizers tend to be people who are also active orienteers. The time commitment required to organize the sport is in some cases a barrier to greater participation by women. Volunteer burnout can be an issue in this sport as in many others.

Several research studies undertaken to discover what types of people enjoy orienteering found that participants in this sport tend to be well educated, have healthy lifestyles, often participate with family members, and are interested in outdoor activities.

That orienteering is viewed as a good family sport is a factor in the number of women who participate. Research has shown that a woman's family members often participate in the sport along with her. Women with husbands and children may find it much easier to participate in the sport because they are able to incorporate it into their family life without undue conflict between their domestic and athletic roles. This may be why more women in their thirties take part in orienteering, proportionately, than in other sports.

The same studies have also found that women who participate in the sport enjoy the accomplishment of successfully completing a course. Also, research into how people tend to get involved in the sport indicated that hearing about orienteering from a friend or family member was the primary method of attracting new participants. Barriers to greater participation include significant travel and time required to reach various events. Balancing this, perhaps are the minimal costs of equipment.

The sport of orienteering appeals to the outdoor enthusiast who enjoys both a physical and mental challenge. The sport-for-all aspect of the activity is one of its most appealing features, as people of all ages and levels of fitness can participate at the same time.

Charlotte MacNaughton

See also Wilderness Adventure

Bibliography

Andresen, Steve. (1977) *The Orienteering Book*. Mountainview, CA: World Publications.

Boga, Steven. (1997) *Orienteering: The Sport of Navigating with Map and Compass*. Mechanicsburg, PA: Stackpole Books.

Disley, John. (1978) *Orienteering*. London: Faber and Faber.

Hogg, David. (1996) "The Social and Lifestyle Characteristics of Australian Orienteers." *Scientific Journal of Orienteering* 12: 9–18.

Ottoson, Torgny. (1995) "Swedish Orienteers: A Survey Study." *Scientific Journal of Orienteering* 11: 31–37.

Renfrew, Tom. (1997) *Orienteering*. Champaign, IL: Human Kinetics.

Thompson, Shona. (1985) "Women in Sport: Some Participation Patterns in New Zealand." *Leisure Studies* 4: 321–331.

OSTEOPOROSIS

Osteoporosis is a condition characterized by progressive loss of bone mass. Bone loss, a natural phenomenon associated with aging, accelerates rapidly in women during the years immediately after menopause, leading to osteoporosis and, as a result of weaker bones, to fractures. Because the condition results in significant injury, illness, and death—directly or indirectly caused by the fractures—public health officials recognize it as a major concern. Medical expenditures attributable to such fractures in 1995 were estimated at $13.8 billion, with the highest incidence of fractures occurring in white women over seventy.

Regular physical activity and exercise are very important in maintaining bone health, or, in medical terms, skeletal integrity. The skeletal system essentially is the framework that holds the body up, just as the frame of a house supports the house, although the skeleton also helps the body to withstand the forces of gravity and allows it to move. The skeletal system is continuously transformed throughout life. During the first two decades of life, bones grow to their maximum length and bone mass reaches its peak. As a result, exercise during this time may help to minimize bone loss later in life and to prevent osteoporosis.

Genetic background is the primary factor that affects bone mass, and that is an unchangeable, predetermined part of a person's makeup. But other factors—including nutrition, hormonal levels, physical activity, and exercise— alter the state of bone. Osteoporosis is one element in the related health problems known as the "female athlete triad." The other elements are amenorrhea (cessation of menstrual cycles) and eating disorders.

MECHANICAL LOADING

Weight-bearing activity (for example, running) and muscle contraction, which result from the mechanical stress of exercise, play a major role in bone health and a strong, intact skeleton. Subjecting the bones to weight—mechanical loading—in the form of exercise appears to help develop and maintain strong bones (bone mass). Muscle contraction and the force of gravity are the two primary forces that are applied to bone. Muscle contraction, by itself, also stimulates bone growth. Bone tissue responds immediately to mechanical loading, which increases the pull of gravity, and the response is very specific to the bone site exposed to the load. Lifting a weight with the right arm, for example, affects the bones in that arm but not those in the other arm. Research suggests that the bone cells have within them some sensory mechanism that detects a force applied to the bone—a bone strain—and helps to set in motion a series of cellular events that promote the depositing of new bone.

Bone tissue responds to the mechanical loading of exercise by actions of the force of gravity. Muscular contraction, for its part, sets in motion a cascade of events that increase the rate of bone formation above the rate at which bone is lost (the resorption rate), resulting in greater bone mass. The increased mechanical loads (exercise) stimulate bone-building activity, resulting in a higher rate of bone formation. In contrast, during periods of immobility, prolonged bed rest, and the weightlessness of space flight, bone is subject to a much lower degree of mechanical stress, or weight. This triggers the process of reshaping bone, but this time the amount of bone loss (resorption) is greater than the degree of bone formation. What this means is a net loss of bone mass. Other factors, including hormones and nutrition, also affect how bone tissue responds to weight-bearing activity, or mechanical loading.

PEAK BONE MASS

Peak bone mass is the term for the highest density (value) of bone achieved during an individual's lifetime. Over the entire life span, bone may be most responsive to the bone-building stimulus of exercise during the primary years of growth. More important, the largest gains in bone mineral density may occur during the year before puberty and during the first few years following puberty. This growth depends greatly on the sex hormones, particularly estrogen. In females, bones stop growing longer in the second decade of life, which means that women reach their peak height between the ages of eighteen and twenty-one. Studies show, however, that bones continue to add strength-giving minerals as two types of bone mass. These are (1) *cortical bone*, the compact bone found in the shafts of long bones, which makes up 80 percent of the skeletal mass, and (2) *trabecular bone*, the spongy bone found in the ends of the long bones and the vertebrae. Bone mass, then, increases in the twenties and peaks at around age twenty-eight. Traditionally, doctors believed that peak bone mass was reached during the third decade of life. Recent research, however, points to a more complex situation, in which trabecular bone may actually begin to decrease as early as the third decade, whereas cortical bone mass does not begin to decline until the fifth decade of life. In fact, 90 percent of peak bone mass is attained by age twenty.

Researchers have suggested that attaining a high peak bone mass during adolescence and young adulthood may significantly affect the prevention of osteoporosis later in life. Individuals who attain a higher peak bone mass during early adolescence and young adulthood can lower their risk of later fractures and osteoporosis. For exam-

CONSEQUENCES AND PREVENTION

Bone loss is part of the aging process and a major health concern for post-menopausal women. The primary consequence of bone loss is weakened bones and fractures, especially in the hip and long leg and arm bones. Although medical researchers continue to search for the best prevention model for women, current thinking stresses the use of regular exercise, a calcium-rich diet, and hormone replacement therapy to limit bone loss and prevent fractures.

ple, among two groups with a high and low bone mineral density, the group with the lower peak bone mass at maturity had a higher incidence of fractures later in life than the group with a higher peak bone mass at maturity. According to these findings, attainment of a high peak bone mass during the first two decades of life is important to minimize fracture risk later in life.

ADOLESCENT ATHLETES

Regular exercise and sport increase the mineral density in the bones of young women aged twenty-two to thirty. Only limited information is available on how exercise affects bone mass in girls before puberty and in adolescence, ages eleven to twenty. Data indicate that girls who take part in such weight-bearing exercise as gymnastics, dancing, and running during puberty gain significant amounts of bone mineral density. In girls between the ages of nine and ten, ten months of weight-bearing exercise resulted in significant increases in bone mineral density compared to girls who did not exercise. Similarly, before puberty, active gymnasts also have higher bone mineral densities than nongymnasts. In fact, even among former gymnasts, the bone mineral density is similar to or greater than normal controls. Together, these data support the notion that exercise during this critical time of development is a powerful stimulus for the accumulation of bone mass.

Hormones and nutrition may affect the benefits of exercise (mechanical loading) on bone mineral density in young adolescent females. For example, some adolescent female dancers with abnormally low levels of estrogen have been found to have a lower bone mineral density. These data suggest that exercise is not enough to maintain bone mass in adolescents who participate in a vigorous level of activity but have chronically low levels of estradiol, a form of estrogen.

YOUNG ADULT ATHLETES

Several studies have evaluated the effect of exercise on bone mineral density in young adult female athletes. Among female tennis players, studies have shown that exercise leads to a higher bone mineral density in their dominant arm. This same effect has also been seen in the dominant arm of squash players and in baseball players. The key point here is that higher density (hypertrophy) occurs in the place where the exercise is most strenuous—where mechanical load is applied. Several other reports have confirmed that other female athletes, such as runners, figure skaters, gymnasts, and volleyball players, have an increased bone mineral density at the specific site most involved in their form of exercise, for example, spine and hip. These sites are especially important for the prevention of osteoporotic fractures.

How much of an effect exercise training has on bone mineral density seems to vary depending on whether the form of exercise is weight bearing. Non-weight-bearing activities, such as swimming, seem to be less beneficial for spine and hip bone mineral density than weight-bearing sports, such as running, volleyball, and gymnastics.

Several investigators have noted that resistance training—weightlifting, for example—may provide extra benefits on bone mass that are equal to or perhaps greater than the benefits of typical weight-bearing exercise. High-resistance muscle contractions, such as those that occur during weightlifting, provide a greater mechanical load to the bone than regular weight-bearing exercise and so act as a more powerful stimulus to bone formation. Bodybuilders and female athletes participating in activities with a high component of resistance training have a higher spinal bone mineral density than do sedentary women. It appears, too, that women who practice resistance training have a slightly higher bone mass than female athletes who take part in other sport activities without a significant resistance-training component.

These findings suggest that exercise training, especially weight-bearing and resistance activities, increase bone mineral density. The observations, however, are of female athletes with apparently normal menstrual cycles. In female athletes who do not have normal menstrual cycles and stop menstruating, bone mass is actually lower. An equally vital point, then, is understanding the importance of menstrual history and menstrual cycles on bone mass in athletes.

THE RESPONSE OF BONE

Studies have identified the following five principles that describe how exercise affects bone mass.

1. Specificity: bone mass will be gained at the specific site to which the mechanical load is applied.

2. Overload: that exercise will lead to a gain in bone mass only if the mechanical load is greater than normal.

3. Reversibility: unless exercise is continued, its positive effects will be quickly lost.

4. Initial status: those who begin with the lowest bone mass have the greatest capacity for improvement whereas those who begin exercising with average or above-average bone mass will gain the least.

5. Diminishing returns: each person has a limit, or biological ceiling, that determines how much of an effect exercise training has on bone mass. As this ceiling is approached, gains in bone mass will eventually slow and level off.

MENSTRUAL DISTURBANCES IN YOUNG ADULT ATHLETES

Several investigators have observed that athletes who menstruate only every ninety days or so—a condition called *amenorrhea*—have a lower bone mineral density than do athletes who menstruate regularly. Amenorrhea is a medical condition characterized by the loss of menstrual periods in a female who was previously menstruating or who fails to experience menstrual cycles by the age of sixteen. Also characteristic of amenorrhea are very low levels of estradiol, a hormone produced by the ovary that is critical for bone health.

Trabecular bone seems to be most affected in women with exercise amenorrhea; cortical bone is not as significantly altered. Particularly alarming is the finding that among women with exercise amenorrhea, bone mineral density at these trabecular sites compare to the much-decreased bone mass in postmenopausal women.

The beneficial effects of exercise training on bone mineral density, then, diminish when the menstrual cycle is altered. Medical intervention is critical when a young female or a female of reproductive age stops menstruating. Typically, the medical strategy for combating the bone mass loss associated with amenorrhea is to rule out all other potential causes of the altered menstrual cycle, including pregnancy, and to place the patient on hormone therapy or oral contraceptives, check her calcium intake, and see if she is consuming an adequate diet.

Interestingly, less severe forms of exercise amenorrhea do not negatively affect bone mass simply because the estrogen status in these athletes remains within normal limits despite low progesterone levels, the classic hormonal characteristic of these menstrual disorders.

MENOPAUSAL WOMEN

Bone loss is a part of the normal aging process. Approximately 0.75–1.0 percent of bone mass is lost per year in the average woman from as early as age thirty to the onset of menopause. Later, during the postmenopausal years, a decrease in bone mass of approximately 2.0–3.0 percent annually is observed, which may result in the development of osteoporosis and associated fractures. Estrogen deficiency is clearly associated with bone loss in both premenopausal and postmenopausal women, and this accelerated bone loss is attributable primarily to the low levels of estrogen associated with menopause. Thus, bone loss is a product of both the aging process and the hormonal alterations associated with menopause.

The first observation of the association between osteoporosis and menopause was made in 1940 by Fuller Albright. Half a century later, Riggs and Melton hypothesized that osteoporosis can be divided into two types: type I, or postmenopausal, osteoporosis, and type II , or age-related osteoporosis. Type I osteoporosis affects women within their first fifteen years after their menopause. The decrease in the ovarian production of estrogen is probably the single most significant factor related to the decreased bone mass in women during the immediate postmenopausal years. It is during the first three years after menopause that bone loss occurs at an accelerated rate. Although bone loss during periods of estrogen deprivation and menopause is evident at all skeletal sites, trabecular bone is lost three to four times faster than cortical bone. Osteoporosis in postmenopausal women is most frequently characterized by decreased bone mineral density in the spine (lumbar vertebrae) and the hip (proximal head of the femur).

TREATMENTS

One of the major treatments available to postmenopausal women—and to athletes—is hormone replacement therapy (HRT). It is an established means of preventing bone loss during this critical period of accelerated bone turnover in postmenopausal women, though exercise itself, as well as adequate diet, continue to be effective methods of maintaining bone density. Many investigators have documented the positive effects of estrogen therapy at several different skeletal sites, including the hip, spine, and wrist. If estrogen therapy is initiated within the first three years of menopause, modest increases in bone mineral density can be observed within a two-year period. If estrogen therapy is delayed several years beyond the menopause (greater than five to ten), the degree of bone protection possible appears to be minimized. Nonetheless, estrogen therapy appears to be effective not only at the onset of menopause but also in women with established osteoporosis.

Hormone replacement therapy is usually based on dosages of estrogen, often combined with progesterone (to minimize the risk of endometrial cancer that is apparent with the use of estrogen alone). Another HRT is androgen therapy, which uses a male hormone, in this case a form of testosterone called synthetic methyl-testosterone. Estrogen replacement therapy is associated with a decrease in bone resorption whereas androgen therapy may actually stimulate bone formation density. Unfortunately, methyl-testosterone can reduce HDL-cholesterol levels and it has been associated with masculinizing effects such as virilization, hirsutism (excessive hair growth), and deepening of the voice. As with estrogen and progesterone, micronized forms of testosterone are available and are being evaluated for efficacy in preventing bone loss while minimizing adverse changes in cholesterol, or lipid, levels and masculinizing effects.

Calcium plays an important role in the maintenance of the skeleton and, when intake is inadequate, circulating levels are maintained via mobilization from bone. Thus, calcium supplementation should also be initiated if dietary intake of calcium is below recommended dosages. The current recommendation for postmenopausal women is 1000–1500 mg, depending on their hormone status. Calcium has a beneficial effect on bone mineral density in older women and fracture risk is significantly lower in women receiving adequate calcium. Vitamin D is important for the promotion of active absorption of calcium across the intestinal wall and may play a role in skeletal mineralization. Evidence, however, has not supported a role for vitamin D in maintaining bone mineral density in women without a vitamin D deficiency. Some evidence has supported a role for vitamin D in vitamin D–deficient women when taken in conjunction with calcium supplements. Supplementation should not, however, be considered an adequate intervention to maintain bone mineral density and prevent osteoporosis-related fractures in high-risk women who are estrogen-deficient.

Alternative HRT includes phytoestrogens, which represent a natural approach to the management of menopause. Many women prefer this strategy, especially because it does not present the woman with concerns regarding breast cancer. Phytoestrogens are substances derived from plants, act on the estrogen receptor, have a chemical structure remarkably similar to the estrogen produced by the human granulosa cells, but have much weaker estrogenic activity. Phytoestrogens appear to represent a viable and safe alternative to traditional HRT though there is little published data to support a specific role for phytoestrogens in the prevention of osteoporosis. Nonetheless, the available data have demonstrated that dietary soybean, a source of phytoestrogen, prevents significant bone loss in ovariectomized rats and that, in postmenopausal women, bone mineral density was maintained and even increased.

SUMMARY

Bone is a dynamic tissue that changes continuously throughout life. During the first three decades of life, bones lengthen and reach their peak mass. Although exercise, along with other factors, including hormones and nutrition, affects peak bone mass and its maintenance, the genetic component is the major predetermined factor affecting bone mass.

Bone loss occurs as a natural phenomenon with aging. Unfortunately, bone loss can lead to osteoporosis and osteoporotic-associated fractures. Achieving a high peak bone mass may minimize later bone loss, and some forms of exercise may be means of increasing bone mass.

Several studies have shown that bone mineral density is higher in women who exercise than in women who do not. The effects of exercise as a bone-building (osteogenic) stimulus depend largely on the ability of the mechanical load to stimulate bone formation at a level greater than bone mass loss. Some studies have shown a positive effect of vigorous weight-bearing exercise on bone mineral density; more recent research has suggested that resistance training has a greater site-specific bone-building stimulus than weight-bearing activities.

Among athletic women with normal menstrual cycles, physical activity seems to have a positive effect on bone mass during the early adult years. Women whose menstrual cycles have been altered by exercise have decreased spinal bone mineral density, which has been linked principally to their lower levels of estrogen. Exercise training, especially resistance training, seems to reduce the loss of spinal bone mineral density. The exercise regimen must be maintained, however, or the benefits gained will be quickly lost. The ultimate test of the effectiveness of any regimen to improve bone mass—whether mechanical

loading, improved diet, or HRT—is a reduction in fracture risk. Future studies will need to focus on the relationship between changes in bone mass and the structural quality of bone.

Mary Jane De Souza
Brian E. Miller

See also Aging; Amenorrhea; Anemia; Biomechanics; Eating Disorders; Menstrual Cycle; Nutrition

Bibliography

Albright, F., E. Bloomberg, and P. H. Smith. (1940) "Postmenopausal Osteoporosis." *Transactions of the Association of American Physicians* 55: 298–305.

Arjmandi, B. H., L. Alekel, and B. W. Hollis. (1996) "Dietary Soybean Protein Prevents Bone Loss in an Ovariectomized Rat Model of Osteoporosis." *Journal of Nutrition* 126: 161–167.

Bass, S., G. Pearce, M. Bradney, et al. (1998) "Exercise Before Puberty May Confer Residual Benefits in Bone Density in Adulthood: Studies in Active Prepubertal and Retired Gymnasts." *Journal of Bone & Mineral Research* 13: 500–507.

Breslau, N. A. (1994) "Calcium, Estrogen and Progestin in the Treatment of Osteoporosis." *Rheumatic Disease Clinics of North America: Osteoporosis* 20, 3: 691–716.

Chapuy, M. C., M. E. Arlot, P. D. Delmas, and P. J. Meunier. (1994) "Effect of Calcium and Cholecalciferol Treatment for Three Years on Hip Fractures in Elderly Women." *British Medical Journal* 308: 1081–1082.

Davis, S. R., and H. G. Burger. (1996) "Androgens and the Postmenopausal Woman." *Journal of Clinical Endocrinology and Metabolism* 81: 2759–2763.

De Souza, M. J., B. E. Miller, A. A. Luciano, et al. (1997) "Bone Health is Not Affected by Luteal Phase Abnormalities and Decreased Ovarian Progesterone Production in Female Runners." *Journal of Clinical Endocrinology and Metabolism* 82, 9: 2867–2876.

Drinkwater, B. L., B. Bruemner, and C. H. Chestnut. (1990) "Menstrual History as a Determinant of Current Bone Mineral Density in Young Athletes." *Journal of the American Medical Association* 263: 545–548.

Drinkwater B. L., S. K. Grimston, D. M. Raab-Cullen, et al. (1995) "ACSM Position Stand on Osteoporosis and Exercise." *Medicine and Science in Sports and Exercise* 4: 27, i–vii.

Eddy, D. M., C. C. Johnston, S. R. Cummings, et al. (1998) "Osteoporosis: Review of the Evidence for

Prevention, Diagnosis, and Treatment and Cost-Effective Analysis." *Osteoporosis International* 4: S7–S80.

Erdman, J. W., R. J. Stillman, and K. F. Lee. (1996) "Short-Term Effects of Soybean Isoflavones on Bone in Postmenopausal Women." Proceedings of the Second International Symposium in the Role of Soy in Preventing and Treating Chronic Disease. Brussels, Belgium, 15–18 September.

Fehling, P. C., L. Alekel, J. Clasey, et al. (1995) "A Comparison of Bone Mineral Densities Among Female Athletes in Impact Loading and Active Loading Sports." *Bone* 17: 205–210.

Haapasalo, H., P. Kannus, H. Sievanen, et al. (1994) "Long-Term Unilateral Loading and Bone Mineral Density and Content in Female Squash Players." *Calcified Tissue International* 54: 249–255.

Heinrich, C. H., S. B. Going, R. W. Pamenter, et al. (1990) "Bone Mineral Content of Resistance and Endurance Athletes." *Medicine and Science in Sports and Exercise,* 22 (5): 558–563.

Komulainen, M., H. Kroger, M. T. Tuppurainen, et al. (1999) "Prevention of Femoral and Lumbar Bone Loss with Hormone Replacement Therapy and Vitamin D in Early Postmenopausal Women: A Population Based 5 Year Randomized Trial." *Journal of Clinical Endocrinology and Metabolism* 84: 546–552.

Luciano, A. A., M. J. De Souza, M. P. Roy, M. J. Schoenfeld, J. C. Nulsen, and C. V. Halvorson. (1993) "Evaluation of Low-Dose Estrogen and Progestin Therapy in Postmenopausal Women." *Journal of Reproductive Medicine* 38: 207–214.

Luciano, A. A., B. E. Miller, C. A. Benadiva et al. (1998) "Effects of the Sublingual Administration of Micronized Estradiol, Progesterone, and Testosterone on Bone Metabolism in Postmenopausal Women." *Bone* 23: S364.

———. (1998) "The Pharmacokinetics of the Sublingual Administration of Micronized Estradiol, Progesterone and Testosterone in Postmenopausal Women." *Fertility and Sterility* 70 (Suppl. 1): S280.

Marcus, R. (1996) "Physical Activity and Regulation of Bone Mass." In *Primer on the Metabolic Bone Diseases and Disorders of Mineral Metabolism,* 3d ed., edited by M. J. Favus. Philadelphia, PA: Lippincott-Raven.

Morris, F. I., G. A. Naughton, J. L. Gibbs, et al. (1997) "Prospective Ten-Month Exercise Intervention in Premenarcheal Girls: Positive Effects on Bone and Lean Mass." *Journal of Bone & Mineral Research* 12: 1453–1462.

Raisz, L. G., B. Wiita, A. Artis, A. Bowen, et al. (1996) "Comparison of Estrogen Alone and Estrogen Plus Androgen on Biochemical Markers of Bone Formation and Resorption in Postmenopausal Women." *Journal of Clinical Endocrinology and Metabolism* 81: 37–44.

Ray, N. F., J. K. Chan, M. Thamer, et al. (1997) "Medical Expenditures for the Treatment of Osteoporotic Fractures in the United States in 1995. Report from the National Osteoporosis Foundation." *Journal of Bone & Mineral Research* 12, 1: 24–35.

Reid, I. R., R. W. Ames, M. C. Evans, G. D. Gamble, and S. J. Sharpe. (1995) "Long Term Effects of Calcium Supplementation on Bone Loss and Fractures in Postmenopausal Women: A Randomized Controlled Trial." *American Journal of Medicine* 98: 331–335.

Slemenda, C. W., T. K. Reister, S. L. Hui, et al. (1994) "Influences of Skeletal Mineralization in Children and Adolescents: Evidence for Varying Effects of Sexual Maturation and Physical Activity." *Journal of Pediatrics* 125: 201–207.

Welten, D. C., H. C. G. Kemper, G. B. Post, et al. (1994) "Weight-Bearing Activity During Youth is a More Important Factor for Peak Bone Mass Than Calcium Intake." *Journal of Bone & Mineral Research* 9: 1089–1096.

OSTERMEYER, MICHELINE

(1922–)

FRENCH FIELD ATHLETE

Although she won two gold medals and one bronze medal at the 1948 London Olympics, little has been written about Micheline Ostermeyer. She is the only French female athlete to have won Olympic gold in field events. Micheline Ostermeyer was born in Rang de Fliers on 23 December 1922. Little is known about her early years or about who or what encouraged her to participate in athletics.

After finishing third at the 1948 French discus championship, she was entered in the Olympic discus competition as an afterthought. She had been selected for the high jump and the shot put, but it was not anticipated that she would perform as well as she did. She took the gold medals in the discus and the inaugural women's shot put—two

Discus thrower and concert pianist Micheline Ostermeyer throwing the discus in her gold medal performance at the 1948 Olympics in London. (Bettmann/Corbis)

of the ten gold medals that France received at the 1948 Games. Her bronze medal came in the high jump. Ostermeyer celebrated her victories by playing recitals of Beethoven's piano music at the headquarters of the French Olympic team.

Although Ostermeyer participated in the 1952 Helsinki Olympics, her best shot put of 45 feet 1¼ inches was eclipsed by over 5 feet by the Soviet Union's Galina Zybina. Ostermeyer's medals in the throwing competitions were the last before women representing the Soviet Union and other East European nations dominated those events. These women were larger, heavier, better trained, and more exclusively dedicated to sports than Ostermeyer was. By 1956 these athletes had improved on Ostermeyer's winning discus throw of 1948 by 30 feet.

Ostermeyer had another interest far from the world of sport. Just before going to London to take part in the 1948 Games, Ostermeyer had finished her music education at the Paris Conservatory of Music and had graduated with high honors as a concert pianist. It must have been extraordinarily difficult for somebody in a field of study as all-encompassing as music to find the time to practice for her sporting events, but Ostermeyer did and succeeded at both. Unfortunately, winning three Olympic medals had a negative impact on her music career as she found it difficult to gain acceptance in the music world after competing in sport at the elite level. She did manage to have a successful concert career, although for years she refused to play the music of Franz Liszt because his physically demanding compositions were so "sportif," so athletic, that they evoked her other life.

J. P. Anderson

Bibliography

Greenberg, Stan (1991). *The Guinness Olympics Fact Book.* Middlesex: Guinness Publishing.

Killanin, Michael, and John Rodda, eds. (1979) *The Olympic Games.* London: Macdonald and Jane's Ltd.

Wallechinsky, David. (1996) *The Complete Book of the Olympics.* London: Aurum Press.

OTTEY, MERLENE

(1960–)

JAMAICAN TRACK ATHLETE

Merlene Ottey won more medals in major international sprint competitions, competed in more Olympics in the same event (the 200-meter sprint), and competed at the top of the sport longer than any other male or female track and field athlete in history. In the late 1990s, she continued to compete and often finish among the top three finishers in major international races.

Merlene Joyce Ottey was born in Jamaica on 10 May 1960. She trained at and competed for the University of Nebraska (it was, and still is, a common practice for Caribbean athletes to attend American universities) in the early 1980s and first competed for Jamaica at the 1980 Olympics in Moscow, where she took a bronze in the 200-meter sprint. This was to be the first of a record five Olympic appearances for Ottey, who competed in the 100- and 200-meter sprints and the 4 × 100-meter relay. No other track athlete has competed in the same event in five consecutive Olympics. At the 1996 Olympics, Ottey finished second in both the 100- and 200-meter sprints and third as part of the Jamaican 4 × 100-relay team. In all, she won three silvers and five bronzes over the course of her Olympic career. Although she won three medals at the 1996 Olympics, Ottey found the Games that year to be a personal disappointment; at the age of thirty-six and competing against women in their twenties, it was probably her last chance to win an Olympic gold. In the 100-meter sprint she lost in a photofinish to Gail Devers of the United States, with the same times recorded for both women and, in the 200-meter sprint, she was overtaken in the last 20 meters by Marie-José Pérec of France.

By 1998, Ottey had won thirty-five medals in major international competitions, including the world championships, Olympics, and Goodwill Games; from 1983 through 1998, she was ranked among the top ten female sprinters in the world. Only three of her medals have been gold, however, and her failure to win more major races has probably prevented her from being rated the greatest sprinter of all time. Nonetheless, she is considered to be one of the greatest athletes, and the most consistent, of the last two decades. It is possible that some early second- and third-place finishes in the 1980s to sprinters from Eastern Europe may have been the result of drug use by her competitors.

Her longevity, many successes, and near wins, along with her desire to compete against younger women, have made her a legend ("the Queen of Track") and a major marketing draw on the European track and field tour. At the age of thirty-seven, she entered the 1998 European tour by commenting, "Beating Marion Jones [the then top woman sprinter in the world] is my target for the year." On 18 August 1999, the track and field world was stunned by the announcement that Ottey had tested positive on 5 July for the use of the banned steroid nondrolone. Ottey claimed that she had not used the substance and this was the only positive result in some 100 tests during her career. She denied using the substance and in

Merlene Ottey competes in the 200-meter event at the 1996 Olympic Games, where she won the silver medal. (Mike King)

2000 was cleared in Jamaica to compete on the Jamaican 2000 Olympic team.

David Levinson
Karen Christensen

Bibliography

The Jamzone! Sports Page Track & Field. (1999) <http://www.geocities.com/The/Tropics/Cabana/4929/trackfield.htm>.

OTTO, KRISTIN

(1966–)

EAST GERMAN SWIMMER

Kristin Otto of East Germany was one of the most successful and versatile swimmers of the 1980s. In

Kristin Otto racing at the 1988 Olympics where she won six gold medals. (Dimitri Lundt)

the 1990s the validity of her achievements was questioned amid charges that she and other East German female swimmers had used performance-enhancing drugs as part of East Germany's effort to build an international sports program.

Kristin Otto was born in Leipzig, in the former East Germany, on 5 August 1966. Identified by German sports authorities as a potential athlete, she was involved in athletic and swimming training at a young age and, in 1981, when she was fifteen, began competing at the international level. During her eight-year career, she proved to be the most successful and most versatile female swimmer in the world, as well as the leader of the East German women's swim team, which dominated international competitions until 1989 (the year of the collapse of the communist governments of Eastern Europe). Competing mainly in the backstroke but also in the individual medley and freestyle events, she won seven world titles and nine European championships, but her best and most visible achievements came in the Olympics.

When the Games were hosted in 1984 by Los Angeles, Otto, then at the height of her career, missed the opportunity to compete when East Germany and other communist nations boycotted the Games in response to the boycott of the 1980 Games in Moscow led by the United States. In

place of the Olympics, the Soviets in Moscow organized the Friendship Games, a mini-Olympics for athletes from nations that boycotted the Los Angeles Olympics. Otto won both the 100-meter and 200-meter backstroke races, with times that bettered those of the gold medalists in Los Angeles. Four years later, in the Olympics of Seoul, when politics no longer interfered with competition, Otto won six gold medals: in the 200-meter backstroke, as a member of the 400-meter medley and freestyle relay teams, and in the 100-meter backstroke, butterfly, and freestyle races. The six gold medals in this diverse mix of events was a unique feat in international swimming competition, men's as well as women's. And no other woman had ever won six gold medals in a single Olympics. The Olympic medals made Otto a celebrity in East Germany although, in international swimming circles, charges and rumors circulated that she and other East German swimmers used performance-enhancing drugs. The charges were routinely denied by German sports leaders, who attributed the success of East German athletes to their better training techniques. Otto retired after the European championship in Bonn in 1989.

In the 1990s, following the reunification of the two German nations, researchers and investigators began looking into charges concerning the use of performance-enhancing drugs. Documentation pointed to a government-sponsored program that supported widespread use of drugs to enhance the strength of women athletes, with the drug use often beginning when the athletes were girls in government training programs. Otto, as a premier athlete, was listed as an offender, a charge that was supported by the discovery of documents suggesting that, in trials for the 1989 European championship, Otto and three other female swimmers had unusually high quantities of testosterone detected in urine drug tests although they had not been disqualified. Otto, who became a journalist after her athletic career ended, consistently denied the charges. However, some former East German officials have indicated that the government did frequently use performance-enhancing drugs in its sports program.

Gherardo Bonini

Bibliography

Matthews, Peter, Ian Buchanan, and Bill Mallon. (1993) *Guinness International Who's Who of Sport.* London: Guinness Publishing.

Umminger, Walter, ed. (1992) *Die Chronik des Sports.* Munich: Chronik Verlag.

OWNERSHIP

Women who occupy ownership positions in professional sports are the exception rather than the rule. This is so because the team and league structures were developed to support men's sports. It is the structure established for men's sports, specifically baseball, that dictates the ownership patterns in today's professional women's team sports.

Women's ownership of sports is intertwined with business, economics, and the development of the dominant model for professional sports. Professional sports have become a big business that follows a private ownership model and strives for profit maximization. The most lucrative professional sports have developed in urban industrial societies. These societies have efficient transportation and communication systems and a standard of living that allows people the time to watch sports and develop into fans by purchasing tickets to games and following their favorite teams and athletes through newspapers, television, and radio. Though some global change is evident, a private ownership model for team sports is a North American phenomenon.

NORTH AMERICAN OWNERSHIP MODEL

Virtually all professional sports teams in North America are privately owned by very wealthy individuals or by corporations. It takes a sizable financial investment to become involved in contemporary sports at the ownership level. For example, the owners of the Jacksonville Jaguars had to pay a franchise fee of $140 million just to join the National Football League (NFL). In 1996 the three most valuable professional sport team franchises were the Dallas Cowboys of the NFL (worth $272 million), the Miami Dolphins of the NFL (worth $214 million), and the New York Yankees (worth $209 million). Beyond the initial costs of ownership, it takes a lot of money to make money by owning a professional sport team.

History

Professional sport teams are not always money-makers for owners. In the early years of professional sport leagues, it was more likely that teams would fold rather than turn a profit. According to Ted Vincent, 850 men's professional sport clubs were founded between 1869 and 1900. Of these clubs, 650 went out of business in two years or less and only 50 lasted longer than six years. During this time, anyone seeking to affirm his "leading citizen" status, enhance his political power in the community, or increase patronage in his shop, restaurant, or saloon would give sport ownership a try. But many teams, for financial reasons, could not complete their schedules. Then, too, many players would roam from club to club, in what was called "revolving" and would play for whichever team owner offered them the most money. During this time, club owners placed more emphasis on making money for themselves (called *utility maximization*) and ignored the welfare of the league as a whole (called *profit maximization*). Thus, clubs competed against each other both on the field and in the accounting ledger. The result was a very large number of teams and players selling their talents to the highest bidder. In business terms, the supply of sport exceeded the demand for sport, and labor costs were driven up by the players' practice of revolving. Many communities could not provide enough gate receipts to offset costs. Thus, in this "twilight" period of league formation, as David Voigt aptly calls it, many teams folded. Simply put, this was a financial environment for ownership failure rather than success.

The professional sport team landscape was radically altered on 2 February 1876, when a small group of baseball owners met at the New York Grand Central Hotel. The meeting was called by William A. Hulbert, owner of a Chicago baseball club, and was passed off to the media as being a rules committee meeting. But Hulbert had a different agenda. He wanted to establish a new league for baseball that would include his own club, which would be named the Chicago National League Ball Club (later renamed the Cubs). Hulbert proposed that the owners in the new league, to be called the Major League, would act together to ensure the financial success of each team. Although plagued by many difficulties during its formative years, the Major League survived and set a precedent for business practices in all North American team sports. Most team owners of that period were forced to make a decision either to join the Major League or to try to survive alone. Since then, no successful sports leagues have ever followed a path radically different from that begun by Hulbert.

The Contemporary North American Ownership Model

Ownership positions in sport have been held almost exclusively by men. This has been the case regardless of whether the leagues were made up of male or female athletes. Profitability is the goal of the private ownership model. Since men control most of the wealth in North American societies, they have tended to invest in and promote sports that serve their interests. These have been traditional men's sports or women's sports that show potential to make a profit.

Although there is a tendency to think of North American team sports as the epitome of competition, it is the owners' willingness to cooperate with each other that ensures league success. And, in the long run, Hulbert's model for league structure ensures that the ownership of professional sport franchises is turned over to affluent men. Though he could not have foreseen it, Hulbert's grand experiment contained three elements that would be taken for granted as features of the North American sports industry: cartelization, monopoly, and monopsony.

Cartelization is a term that applies to owners of business firms (including sports teams) acting together to make decisions about the production and distribution of their product (in this case, sports). Professional sport owners, acting as a cartel, have a remarkably complex set of rules designed to restrict business competition for athletic labor and divide geographical markets for individual franchises. Even though each team is a separate entity, the owners have worked out rules for

conducting business in ways that represent their collective interests. For example, all leagues have rules for revenue sharing among teams. And owners, acting as a cartel, vote on the placement, ownership, and number of franchises in the league. Owners also set the franchise fees for expansion teams.

Monopoly practices manipulate the sale of league sports to fans. For example, television and radio broadcasts, admission to games, and sale of team-related merchandise are all subject to league regulations. *Monopsony* practices manipulate the costs of acquiring players by restricting interteam bidding. For example, league rules specify the procedures for drafting new players and binding them to contracts, thereby assuring that bidding wars will not break out for athletic talent. Though the sports cartel has been challenged from time to time by rogue owners, taken together these business practices have established Major League Baseball, the National Football League, the National Hockey League, and the National Basketball Association as some of the most powerful businesses in the history of North American capitalism. This ownership/league model is so dominant that no one will sponsor a women's professional team sport until it shows the potential to be organized by these principles and offers the prospect for quick return on investment.

The Private Ownership Model and Women's Professional Sport Teams

The dominant private ownership and league model has supported men's sports since 1875 but was not used to promote women's sports successfully until the mid-1990s. A possible exception to this rule was the women's All American Girls Professional Baseball League, which flourished from 1943 to 1945. But this was a special case; this league was founded by owners of Major League baseball not as a vehicle for promoting women as baseball players as such but rather as a way to sustain and develop interest in men's baseball during World War II.

Over time the private ownership model for professional sports has passed through a series of stages. Not until the most recent stage of corporate-backed sport team ownership have women's professional sport teams been promoted at a broad level. Still, almost all team owners are men, as are the sponsorship groups of these new women's leagues. The changing pattern of sport ownership has paralleled the development and success of the league model for North American sports. Because this model ensures the profitability of franchises in the prestige leagues, rival leagues are either financial disasters or are merged into existing leagues. The increasing power of the existing leagues has established professional sports as a business venture in which only the wealthiest individuals or corporations can engage.

In the early stages of men's professional sports, team owners were individuals whose whole business was sports. They made their money by promoting their sports and thus helped provide stability for young leagues. The second stage of owners consisted of individuals whose financial fortunes were linked to other businesses and who used sport teams to advertise their other products. The most recent stage of ownership is marked by increasing corporate involvement in professional sports. The value of men's sport franchises has been pushed higher and higher as a result of the leagues' marketing strategies and their success in manipulating the business environment for professional sports. Corporations or partnerships of wealthy individuals are buying a growing number of franchises, and they operate the teams solely as profit-seeking business ventures. It is at this stage that private investors have shown increased interest in sponsoring women's professional sports teams. Given this context, it is fair to say that the motivation for forming professional leagues for women is directed toward making money and, if these new leagues are not financially profitable, they will probably fold.

Professional women's basketball appears to have the best potential to thrive under this model in the United States. Prior to the 1990s, there were four attempts to establish professional women's basketball; each ended in financial failure. Many people blame the leagues' failures on the lack of spectator interest in women's sports. Others cite the owners of these leagues for using marketing strategies that did not appeal to people who already supported girls' basketball all over the United States. Whatever the explanation, in the end owners of these teams did not believe that

enough profit potential existed for their financial investments. In the mid-1990s, however, two more professional women's basketball leagues were formed, though only one showed evidence of financial success.

The two women's basketball leagues founded in the 1990s were the American Basketball League (ABL) and the Women's National Basketball Association (WNBA). Many people watched closely to see if these two rival leagues could survive. The history of men's professional sport leagues suggested that they could not. The ABL, which tipped off its first game in October 1995, folded in December 1998. Though some of the teams in the ABL attracted loyal and dedicated fans, organizers of the league reported that it did not have the financial resources to continue. The ABL simply could not compete against the better funded WNBA for sponsorship and media coverage. The ABL and the WNBA differed greatly from one another in ownership structure. In fact, the ownership structure of the ABL differed from all other professional sports in the United States. Three investment groups backed the league, and each player owned stock in the league. Approximately 10 percent of ABL stock was owned by the players, which in effect made every athlete in the league a part owner. By contrast, the WNBA, which began in 1997, is owned by the same individuals and corporations that own the men's National Basketball Association (NBA) and is supported by the NBA.

In addition to women's basketball, a number of other professional team sports hoped to launch their inaugural seasons in the 1990s. All these leagues are supported by private investment groups or corporate ownership structures. They include a Women's Professional Ice Hockey League (WPHL), the Women's Professional Volleyball Association (WPVA), and the Women's Professional Fastpitch (WPF) softball league.

Women Owners of North American Men's Team Sports

Though the exception, women have been, and continue to be, owners of men's sports teams. Three women have owned professional baseball clubs, and two have owned professional football franchises. In each case, these women have played active roles as owners and have made decisions

---

FOR THE LOVE OF THE GAME

Helen Britton, the First Female Owner of a Professional Sports Franchise, Communicates Her Passion for Baseball

I can honestly say that I have always loved baseball. My father and uncles talked about baseball ever since I can remember. My father insisted that I keep score. . . . I grew up . . . in an atmosphere of baseball. I even played it when a girl and am glad to know that the game is played in a somewhat modified form in hundreds of girl camps and elsewhere by young ladies all over the United States. Played in that way, I believe it is a healthful and interesting diversion though I realize that anything which resembles a professional type is distinctly a man's game. . . .

I realize that my position as the only woman owner in the major leagues is a peculiar one. And I don't pretend to know the game as intimately from a playing stand-point as a man might do in my place. I appreciate the fact that baseball is a man's game, but I also appreciate the fact that women are taking an increasing interest in the sport."

HELENE BRITTON
Owner of the St. Louis Cardinals, 1911–1917
Baseball Magazine, *February 1917.*

---

that affect the day-to-day operations of their teams.

The first woman to hold a majority ownership position of a major professional team was Helene Robinson Britton. From 1911 to 1917, Britton owned 75 percent of Major League Baseball's St. Louis Cardinals. When Stanley Robinson died on 24 March 1911, his thirty-two-year-old niece Helene Robinson Britton inherited the team. The other major league owners were unhappy with Robinson's choice of successor, maintaining that baseball ownership and management were the proper domain of men only. Britton was an active baseball owner and an active suffragette, which brought even more resentment from her male contemporaries. She participated in all the league's annual meetings and even made it a point to sit in the front row for all the annual league pictures. In 1916 Britton assumed the presidency of the team. She sold the Cardinals in 1917 for $375,000.

The second woman to assume the role of a professional sport franchise owner was also involved in baseball. From 1935 to 1948, Effa Manley was co-owner of the Newark Eagles, a Negro League team. Effa Manley shared an active own-

ership role with her husband, Abe. She assumed responsibility for daily operations of the team while her husband concentrated on player recruitment. Effa Manley's responsibilities included making all the team's travel arrangements, managing the payroll, purchasing equipment, and handling publicity. In addition, she was active in civic affairs and a crusader for African American rights, often using the Newark Eagles' games to promote social causes. During the time she was co-owner of the Eagles, Manley was also the treasurer of the National Association for the Advancement of Colored People (NAACP), a supporter of black military units in World War II, and an activist for black women's equality. In 1935 she cofounded the Citizens League for Fair Play and picketed stores in Harlem that refused to hire black women. She led a group of marchers down 125th Street in New York City, with the slogan "Don't shop where you can't work." In addition to her duties with the Eagles and her social activism, Manley handled all the finances of the Negro National League, although her husband was the official treasurer.

After Manley's tenure with the Newark Eagles, four decades passed before a woman would hold ownership in professional baseball. In 1981 Marge Schott became a limited partner of Major League Baseball's Cincinnati Reds. Schott became the majority owner of the Reds on 21 December 1984 and team president and chief executive officer on 8 July 1985. Though often controversial, Schott managed to retain control of the Reds during the stage of corporate-owned sport franchises while keeping ticket prices among the lowest in professional sport. Schott became a businesswoman by necessity when her husband, Charles Schott, died in 1968, leaving her in charge of a financial empire that included such divergent holdings as an auto agency; cement, truck, and brick companies; and real estate. She is the first woman ever to be awarded a major metropolitan General Motors auto dealership and the first woman to be named to the board of trustees of the Cincinnati Chamber of Commerce. Like Britton and Manley before her, Schott assumed an active role in the day-to-day operations of her baseball team. Schott is currently the only woman involved in the primary ownership of a Major League Baseball franchise.

Women have held majority ownership positions for two different football teams in the NFL. Clearly, the most powerful ever to have been a part of professional football is Georgia Frontiere, chairwoman and chief executive officer of the St. Louis Rams. Frontiere assumed ownership of the Rams in 1979 after the death of her husband Carl Rosenbloom. She served as sole owner of the franchise from 1979 to 1995. In 1995 she relocated the Rams to St. Louis from Los Angeles and took on a limited partner. During her tenure as head of the Rams organization, the team competed in a Super Bowl, reached the NFL playoffs eight times, and advanced to the National Football Conference championship game three times. In addition to her activities with the football team, Frontiere became involved with educational programs and arts and youth groups in the St. Louis community.

In 1997 Denise DeBartolo York was named owner of the San Francisco 49ers and became the second woman to own controlling interest in a National Football League team. York had been active as an executive in the Edward J. DeBartolo Corporation for over twenty years when her brother, Eddie DeBartolo Jr., resigned as head of the 49ers. The family has vast holdings in real estate and sports, but its public profile was based on the ownership of the 49ers and the Pittsburgh Penguins hockey team, which York managed, making her one of the few women executives in the National Hockey League. In 1997 *Forbes* magazine listed York as number 245 on the list of the richest Americans, with a net worth of $745 million.

Kimberly S. Schimmel

See also Baseball; Basketball; Management; Marketing; Schott, Marge

Bibliography

Berlage, Gai Ingham. (1994) *Women in Baseball: The Forgotten History.* Westport, CT: Praeger.

Coakely, Jay J. (1998) *Sport in Society.* Boston, MA: Irwin McGraw-Hill.

Leonard, Wilbert Marcellus, II. (1993) *A Sociological Perspective of Sport.* New York: Macmillan.

Noll, Roger. (1974) *Government and the Sports Business.* Washington, DC: The Brookings Institution.

Schimmel, Kimberly S., Alan G. Ingham, and Jeremy W. Howell. (1993) "Professional Team Sports and the American City: Urban Politics and Franchise Relocations." In *Sport and Social Development,* edited by Alan G. Ingham and John W. Loy. Champaign, IL: Human Kinetics Publishers, 211–244.

"Sports: The High Stakes Game of Team Ownership." (1996) *Financial World Magazine* 165, 8 (20 May): 52–70.

Vincent, Ted. (1981) *Mudville's Revenge: The Rise and Fall of American Sport.* New York: Seaview.

Voigt, David. (1966) *American Baseball: From Gentleman's Sport to the Commissioner System.* Norman: University of Oklahoma Press.

P

PAIN

Pain can be simply defined as a distressing sensation in a particular part of the body, mental or emotional suffering, or torment. This definition expands greatly when applied to medical conditions. In those circumstances, pain may vary in intensity from mild discomfort to intolerable agony. In most cases, pain stimuli are harmful to the body and tend to bring about reactions that cause the body to protect itself. Studies have shown that women tend to be more sensitive to pain but at the same time are better able to cope with it than are men.

Pain may be either a warning signal or a sign of injury. It is one of the primary symptoms of inflammation, which is a by-product of all injuries, however mild or severe. Pain varies greatly from person to person, and individual thresholds of pain vary greatly. Pain can be specific to a particular body part or may be in a general anatomical location. It may manifest itself in different symptoms and thus may be classified as various kinds of pain.

TYPES OF PAIN

Aching pain generally refers to pain associated with infectious disease, such as flu or fever. Burning pain may be due to superficial skin wounds, burns, and nerve-related injury. Cramplike pain is related to muscle spasm or gastrointestinal distress. Dull pain is generally continuous with mild throbbing. Acute pain is sharp and associated with specific inflammation; that inflammation, in turn, is linked to an increase in symptoms of a chronic condition or a new injury or illness. Growing pains are usually related to nonspecific aching of joints and surrounding muscles in adolescents going through a growth spurt. Referred pain is pain arising in an area other than at its origin, such as leg pain resulting from a back injury.

If pain has no detectable physical basis, it is called subjective pain. Many other definitions of pain are specific to types, body location, and particular diseases and injuries.

CAUSE OF PAIN

Pain is a universal symptom that occurs with most illness and injury. Each person perceives pain in a slightly different way, and that perception is influenced by a variety of physical, chemical, social, and psychological factors. Pain associated with injury is caused by mechanical or chemical insult to the nerves.

Pain impulses are transmitted by nerves of small diameter and slow transmission, as opposed to large-diameter, fast-transmission nerves, which carry such sensations as touch, temperature, and sensations originating within the body. Both types of fibers communicate with the spinal cord. Impulses from afferent fibers (those that run from distant body parts to the central nervous system) are transmitted through the spinal cord to the brain.

In response to stressors—in this context, things that generate pain of any kind—the body produces pain-killing chemicals similar to morphine called beta-endorphins. These chemicals work by blocking the specific places in the brain that transmit pain. The brain produces endorphins in several different sites. Stress produced by physical exercise, mental stress, and injury and illness trigger the release of endorphins into the cerebrospinal fluid. Researchers believe that endorphin release creates a feeling of euphoria that often occurs among long-distance runners and other physically active people who participate in prolonged exercise bouts.

The central nervous system provides a set of psychological and emotional filters that affect how people perceive pain and how they then express their feelings of pain. Social and cultural factors can also be powerful influences on the level of pain people can tolerate. In American society, for example, it is much more acceptable for females to express feelings of pain than for males.

A track official attempts to comfort an injured Mary Decker after Decker's fall in the women's 3000-meter run at the 1984 Summer Olympics. (Bettmann/Corbis)

Personality and mental states can also significantly affect pain.

RESPONSE TO PAIN

The body's response to injury is a well-documented, predictable process. The first phase is the acute inflammatory phase, which lasts for approximately four days following injury. During this phase, subcellular agents are rushed to the site to remove the damaged tissue. During a period of six weeks following the injury, repair and regeneration take place. The remodeling phase is the final phase and can last up to a year or more as tissues strengthen and become reoriented.

Pain is an important factor in assessing and evaluating any injury related to an activity. The pain that a person perceives can indicate what structures may be injured and how badly they are injured. There are two categories of pain: somatic and visceral.

Somatic pain arises from the skin, ligaments, muscles, bones, or joints and is the most common type of pain encountered in sports injuries. Somatic pain is then divided into two major types: deep and superficial. Deep somatic pain is described as diffuse, deep, or nagging, as if intense pressure is being applied to the structures. This type of pain lasts longer and usually indicates significant tissue damage either to bone, internal joint structures, or muscles. Superficial somatic pain resulting from injury to the top several layers of skin is usually a sharp, prickly type of pain that tends to be brief.

Visceral pain results from disease or injury to an organ in the chest or abdominal cavity. As with deep somatic pain, people perceive it as deeply located, nagging, and pressing. It is often accompanied by nausea and vomiting. Referred pain is a type of visceral pain that travels along the same nerve pathways as somatic pain. The brain perceives it as somatic; the injury is in one area but the brain considers it in another. A common example of referred pain occurs when an individual has a heart attack. The person may feel pain in the chest, the left arm, and sometimes the neck. Pain can also travel the length of any nerve and be referred to another region. Low back pain may produce pain in the gluteal region, radiating down the back of the leg. If a nerve is injured, a person may feel pain or change in sensation (such as numbness or burning) along the length of the nerve.

When evaluating injury or illness, questions about the location and severity of pain are key indicators. Pain is central to evaluating the condition: where it hurts, how much it hurts, and how extensive it is. Various characteristics of pain can help identify the problem. A person who awakens in the morning with pain and stiffness may have a chronic inflammation caused by swelling or arthritis. An athlete, for example, who feels a sharp, stabbing pain during activity may have an acute injury, such as a ligament sprain or muscle strain. A dull, aching pain aggravated with activity may indicate a chronic muscle strain. If rest relieves pain, that means soft tissues are involved. Pain not affected by rest or activity may indicate an injury to a bone. In addition, muscular pain is characterized by a dull, aching, feeling that is difficult to pin down precisely. Bone pain is characterized by a very deep, localized pain. Nerve pain is characterized by a sharp, burning, or numbing sensation that may radiate the length of the nerve.

PAIN MANAGEMENT

Health care providers use the term *pain management*. Eliminating pain generally involves eliminating the underlying condition, and that may take time—or it may be impossible. But pain can generally be lessened. Pain is managed in a variety of ways. In many cases, a health care professional will recommend medication, either prescription or over-the-counter, to control pain. Local anesthetics eliminate short-term pain in a particular body part or region by blocking afferent (sensory) nerve transmissions along peripheral nerve pathways. These drugs are identified by their -caine suffix (for example, lidocaine, procaine, and marcaine). They may be applied to the skin as creams or salves for minor irritations. Such anesthetics may also be introduced into tissue under the skin tissue via phonophoresis or iontophoresis (using electric current to apply a substance under the skin); these drugs are commonly used in the treatment of bursitis and tendonitis). In other cases, the physician may inject a medication into soft tissue areas or near peripheral nerves to create a nerve block, which serves to interrupt nerve transmission.

Analgesics (painkillers) and nonsteroidal anti-inflammatory drugs (NSAIDs) are commonly used to widen blood vessels and slow the production of prostoglandins, substances that increase local blood flow and edema (swelling) that is associated with inflammation. These drugs decrease inflammation and relieve mild to moderate pain. The NSAIDS are best administered in the early stages of healing, when prostoglandins cause the most pain and edema. Using these drugs for more than two weeks, however, may actually slow the healing process. Examples of analgesics and common NSAIDs include aspirin, acetaminophen (with brand names such as Tylenol), and ibuprofen (under brand names such as Advil, Nuprin, Motrin, and Aleve).

Aspirin is the most commonly used drug to relieve pain and inflammation. Because it slows or reduces blood clotting (necessary to stop bleeding) it is not used during the acute phase of injury. Aspirin has various adverse side effects, including stomach irritation. Ibuprofen and other NSAIDs are administered primarily for pain relief and anti-inflammatory effects. These may cause gastrointestinal problems, though to a lesser degree than aspirin. Corticosteroids can be used to decrease edema and inflammation. Physicians may apply these drugs to the skin, give them by mouth, or inject them into a specific area such as a tendon or joint. Skeletal muscle relaxants may be used to relieve a muscle spasm that causes pain. Muscle spasms can result from certain injuries to the muscles, tendons, or other parts of the musculoskeletal system or from inflammation. Muscle relaxants break the pain spasm cycle; in doing so, they decrease pain and improve a person's ability to move the affected area.

Ice is one of the simplest but most effective ways to reduce pain. Ice constricts blood vessels in the area where applied, slowing circulation and inhibiting swelling. It also produces an extremely effective anesthetic affect. When ice is applied to an injured area, it should be separated from the skin with a moist cloth to protect the skin from frostbite.

SEX DIFFERENCES

Recent studies have focused on women's sensitivity and reaction to pain as compared to men's. Although women may be more sensitive to pain than men, women are better able to cope with pain, recover more quickly from pain, and do not let its presence control their lives. In research results presented by the National Institutes of Health, women demonstrated a superior ability to men in dealing with pain. A study of men and women suffering from arthritis found that women tended to have a keener sense of pain than men but that men were more likely to let the discomfort affect their mood. Women tended to regard pain as a call to action and took measures to overcome the discomfort, often relieving it through emotional coping mechanisms. This coping included distracting activities, venting emotions, and seeking support of others.

Researchers have long known that individuals' perception and response to pain is learned in childhood. Children tend to evaluate their own injuries by how their parents react; they look to their parents to learn the response to injury. Thus, a parent who sees an injury and responds by saying, "Well, that looks painful, but I'm sure we can make it feel better," is likely to be shaping that child's future response; so is the parent who looks at a minor injury and rushes a child to the emergency room.

Psychological and sociological influences greatly affect how people perceive and respond to pain. Researchers have long speculated about how the hormones estrogen and testosterone affect people's perception and tolerance of pain. As yet, they have reached no well-documented conclusions, and they need to do much more research on the question.

People tend to think of pain as a bad thing—as, indeed, it in many ways is. What they may overlook is that pain is a vital signal, one that reveals that something is wrong. An athlete who injures herself and feels no pain may keep going and so worsen the injury drastically. Pain is a warning signal that needs to be addressed and managed to ensure injury-free sport participation.

Marjorie J. Albohm

Bibliography

Anderson, Marcia K., and Susan J. Hall. (1995) *Sports Injury Management*. Philadelphia: Williams & Wilkins.

Tabor's Medical Dictionary. (1971) Philadelphia: Davis.

PAN AMERICAN GAMES

The Pan American Games are the only sport festival to bring together all the countries in the Western Hemisphere, involving the nations of North America, Central America, South America, and the Caribbean. The Games were first held in Buenos Aires, Argentina, in 1951. Twenty-one countries and approximately 2,500 athletes participated in nineteen events, including five for women.

HISTORY

While the Games are a postwar development, there was actually an earlier attempt to hold such an event. During World War II, Avery Brundage (at the time a representative of the International Olympic Committee) tried but failed to organize Pan American Games as a substitute for the interrupted Olympic cycle. After the first Games in 1951, this international sport festival has been held every four years, and the numbers of participating countries and of athletes have increased dramatically. The athletic program has also expanded, especially in terms of the number of sports for women.

At the first Games, the women's program consisted of track and field, fencing, swimming, diving, and tennis. In the five track and five field events, female athletes from the United States, Argentina, Brazil, and Chile figured most prominently, although a Peruvian woman won the 100-meter race. Women from the United States won the 4 × 100 meter relay, a feat they would repeat in eight future Pan American Games. Pat McCormick of the United States won gold and silver medals in diving.

The 1955 Games in Mexico City, Mexico, added women's basketball and synchronized swimming and volleyball for both sexes. The women's team from the United States won the gold in basketball that year, and the team repeated the achievement in 1959, 1963, 1975, 1983, and 1987. In volleyball, women from Mexico placed first and the United States placed second.

In 1959 in Chicago, Illinois, synchronized swimming was left out, and women began competing in gymnastics and equestrian events. Lucinda Williams and Wilma Rudolph, both of the United States, finished first and second, respectively, in the 100-meter event, and Williams repeated her victory in the 200-meter race. Both were on the 4 × 100–relay team that won the gold medal. Althea Gibson of the United States won the gold medal in tennis singles and the silver in doubles. Brazil triumphed in volleyball, beginning a history of strong performances in this sport. The Brazilian team won again in 1963 and placed in the medals in two other future Games. Peru won the bronze in volleyball in 1959 and earned medals—five of them silver—in seven future Games.

In 1963, for the São Paulo, Brazil, Games, the women's program added sailing and restored synchronized swimming to the program. This was also the first time that women ran the 800-meter event, marking the first inclusion of a women's track event longer than 200 meters in the Pan American Games. (The Olympic Games of 1960 were the first to offer women's races longer than 200 meters; this was also done at the

1928 Olympics.) The Brazilian María Bueno won tennis singles (later becoming a well-known professional), and Darlene Hard of the United States won third in singles and first in doubles.

At the Winnipeg, Canada, Games in 1967 women's sailing and again synchronized swimming were dropped, and canoeing was added. Women from the United States won volleyball for the first and only time.

For the Cali, Colombia, Games in 1971, women's canoeing and tennis were dropped and synchronized swimming was again restored. The women's track and field program expanded to include a 400-meter event, the 4 × 400–meter relay, and 100-meter hurdles (in earlier Games the hurdle distance was 80 meters). The Cuban team won volleyball, beginning a string of gold medals that lasted throughout all later Games.

Tennis returned to the women's program in 1975 in Mexico City. Continuing the trend of increasing running distances for women, a 1500-meter event was added to the track program. Women from the United States continued to dominate gymnastics.

New women's events in San Juan, Puerto Rico, in 1979 were archery, softball, and roller-skating. Evelyn Ashford of the United States continued that country's tradition of dominance in the sprints when she won gold medals in 100- and 200-meter events. Mary Decker (also of the United States) won the 1500-meter race, setting a new Pan American record. A new event, the 3000-meter run, was added. Ana Fidelia Quirot from Cuba appeared for the first time among medalists as a member of the second-place 4 × 400–meter relay team. Cuba's María Colón won in the javelin event. Quirot later became an Olympic medalist, and Colón became the first Latin American woman to win an Olympic gold medal (in 1980). The U.S. women won in softball (repeating in 1987, 1991, and 1995, and finishing second to Canada in 1983). Tracy Caulkins of the United States won four individual swimming medals and two relays. She would repeat her two gold medals in the 200-meter and 400-meter medleys in 1983.

Beginning with the 1983 Games in Caracas, Venezuela, the women's program was increased notably. New events that year were 400-meter hurdles, shooting, judo, rowing, Sambo wrestling (a specialty of Venezuela), and table tennis. Sailing was restored to the program. Roller-skating was dropped that year. Ana Quirot won the silver medal in the 400-meter event, behind Canadian Charmaine Crooks's Pan American record-setting run. Joan Benoit of the United States achieved the gold medal in the 3,000-meter event, nearly 15 seconds ahead of the second-place runner.

KELLER MAKES CENTRAL AMERICAN GAMES A DREAM COME TRUE

In the early 1970s, sport leaders in Guatemala received IOC approval for a new series of games which would include only the geographic region of Central America. They wanted to provide more opportunities for competition for the athletes of the countries of the region, without the dominating influence of sport powers such as Cuba, Mexico, and the United States. The central figure in negotiations with Avery Brundage and other IOC officials was the executive secretary of the Guatemalan National Olympic Committee, former athlete Ingrid Keller. Keller began her crusade for Central American sport at the meetings of the Central American and Caribbean sport organization in Panama in 1970.

There she was elected to membership in the organization and had an opportunity to speak with General José Clark Flores of Mexico, the vice president of the IOC. General Clark died before she could cultivate his support, but she continued to travel extensively, mostly at her own expense, to seek the support of Latin American sport leaders and IOC officials. She eventually received approval for the Central American Games from Avery Brundage, just as he was leaving the IOC presidency, and then from Lord Killanin, who became president in Munich, in 1972. When the first games were held, in 1973, Keller was Executive Secretary of the Organizing Committee.

American Amanda Borden competes on the balance beam at the 1995 Pan American Games in Argentina. (AP Photos)

In 1987 in Indianapolis, Sambo wrestling was dropped, roller-skating and canoeing were restored, and team handball and field hockey were initiated. Ana Fidelia Quirot won gold medals in the 400-meter (setting a new Pan American record) and 800-meter events (repeating in 1991). Jackie Joyner-Kersee won the long jump. The marathon, 10,000-meter run, 10-kilometer walk, and heptathlon were added for women. Sylvia Poll of Costa Rica won eight medals (three gold) in swimming. The next year she won an Olympic silver in Seoul, South Korea, and then another Pan American gold medal in 1991.

For 1991 in Havana, Cuba, women's bowling and rhythmic gymnastics were added. Professionals were allowed to participate in tennis, and Pam Shriver of the United States won the gold medal for singles.

The Games returned to Argentina (at the seashore resort of Mar del Plata) in 1995. New sports for women included badminton (also new for men), karate, racquetball, squash, triathlon, and water skiing, and women's competitions were added in cycling and Tae kwon do. Women's basketball was canceled due to the small number of entries. The U.S. women won their fourth gold medal in softball and Cuban women won their seventh gold medal in volleyball.

The first Winter Pan American Games, held in 1990 in Las Leñas, Argentina, included Alpine skiing for women. The 1999 Pan American games were held in Winnipeg. Around 5,000 athletes competed in some forty-two sports, including all thirty-five Summer Olympic sports. The United States finished first with 295 medals (106 gold), Canada second with 196 (64 gold), and Cuba third with 157 (70 gold).

Richard V. McGehee

Bibliography

Ferreiro Toledano, Abraham. (1986) *Centroamérica y el Caribe a través de sus juegos.* Mexico City: Artes Gráficas Rivera.

Ferreiro Toledano, Abraham. (1992) *Historia de los once juegos deportivos panamericanos, 1951–1991.* Mexico City: Artes Gráficas Rivera.

McGehee, Richard V. (1994) "Los Juegos de las Américas: Four Inter-American Multisport Competitions." In *Sport in the Global Village,* edited by Ralph C. Wilcox. Morgantown, WV: Fitness Information Technology.

Ministerio de Educación de Guatemala. (1974) *Memoria de los Primeros Juegos Deportivos Centroamericanos 1973.* Guatemala City: Editorial José de Pineda Ibarra Ibarra.

Memoria III Juegos Deportivos Centroamericanos. (1986) Guatemala City: Litorama.

Memoria Oficial de los XVI Juegos Deportivos Centroamericanos y del Caribe. (1992) Tlalnepantla, Mexico: Impresora de Ediciones.

PARACHUTING

Parachuting is a form of recreation in which participants, wearing a strapped-on, tightly folded silk canopy, jump out of airplanes from varying heights and in various configurations. Parachuting is also used for military and civilian safety purposes, as when firefighters are parachuted into wilderness fires. Many women parachute, and some hold impressive records.

HISTORY

Leonardo da Vinci (1452–1519) had foreseen the use of a cloth umbrella to slow the fall of a body. Sketches survive that show a pyramid-shaped wooden frame covered with fabric, with a flyer precariously dangling from a central pole. For more than two centuries, however, no one followed up on the idea. After the advent of hot air balloons, the device was resurrected in 1785 as an air show attraction and was dubbed a *parachute*—something that protects (*parer*, in French) from a fall (*chute*, also used as abbreviation for *parachute*). Its use became known as *parachuting*, although the term *skydiving* is sometimes preferred to indicate purely sporting applications. Women entered the sport in 1798 and have participated ever since.

Leonardo's design was revived as an attraction by the French balloonist Jean-Pierre Blanchard, who made the first jump in 1785. The first woman parachutist was Jeanne Labrosse, wife of the French aeronaut André-Jacques Garnerin. On 10 November 1798 she flew a balloon solo from the Tivoli Gardens in Paris and then jumped using the open parachute that was suspended below the balloon. She later joined her husband in giving parachute exhibitions, achieving great fame throughout Europe for a decade. In 1815 a third Garnerin, their niece Elise, took up the tradition and made some forty successful jumps before retiring in 1836. Another French balloonist-parachutist was Marie Poitevin, who made several jumps in England in 1852 and across Europe, including Rome (in 1868), then still under papal rule.

By 1887, the Baldwin brothers in the United States developed the first stowable parachute; this was an important development, even though the parachute's cumbersome container was still fixed to the balloon basket. In Germany, Kathe Paulus discovered parachuting when she met Paul Lattermann, who was looking for someone to pilot the balloon from which he jumped. The couple was soon married and "Kätchen" ("Little Kate")

Georgia "Tiny" Broadwick of San Francisco before making a parachute leap from a plane 3,000 feet up in 1920. (Bettmann/Corbis)

made her first jump at Nuremberg in 1893, on her third flight. A few days later, despite poor weather, she made the first "double jump," opening a second chute after a brief descent and then abandoning the first one. This technique, called a cutaway, is still in use in a modified version.

In 1908, fifteen-year-old Georgia "Tiny" Broadwick became the first U.S. woman to jump from a balloon, marking the start of a 1,000-jump career as a performing parachutist with a traveling carnival. But the days of the parachute as crowd-puller were numbered, its lure largely stolen by airplanes. On 21 June 1913, Broadwick would become the first woman to intentionally parachute from an airplane, near Griffith Field in Los Angeles. She demonstrated the new "parachute coat" devised by her adoptive father Charles—in essence a canopy stowed in a pack worn on one's back, although still deployed by a "static line," a cable fixed to the aircraft.

Meanwhile Paulus, who in 1910 had earned a pilot's license, saw the potential of the traditional parachute as a safety device and exploited the experience of her 197 jumps to become a supplier of parachutes to the German army during World War I, eventually employing forty workers. The classic canopy-shaped parachute was finally perfected by Leslie Irvin in 1919, who dispensed with the static line in favor of a handle that the jumper could pull at will to release a small chute that, in turn, deployed the main canopy.

Despite this great improvement, the parachute as safety device was slow to gain acceptance. In 1926 Bessie Coleman, the first black woman to earn a pilot's license, died during an air show when she fell out of her rolling airplane without her parachute. Not much later, Fay Gillis Wells jumped from a falling airplane and thus became the first woman member of The Caterpillar Club, which gathers people who survived air crashes by using their parachutes. (A similar group, The Tie Club, was set up after World War II for those saved by Martin-Baker Ltd. ejection seats, but details of women's membership are not available).

After this early period of activity, only limited sport parachuting seems to have taken place between the wars. In 1921 the U.S. pilot Phoebe Omlie (1903–1975) set a women's world record by jumping from an altitude of more than 4600 meters (15,180 ft.). Smaranda Braescu, the first woman parachutist in Romania, earned her parachuting license in Berlin in 1928. In 1931 she set a world record, jumping from 6000 meters (19,800 ft.), following up on 19 May 1932 with a 7233-meter (28,869-ft.) absolute record. In 1931 Helmi Pakkala became the first woman parachutist to perform in an air show in Finland.

During World War II, all the major powers trained soldiers to use parachutes so that these troops could be dropped behind enemy lines. After the war, this training led to the development of parachuting as a sport, in competition and for recreation. Like gliding, parachuting served as a useful and affordable introduction to aviation in terms of experience, discipline, and meeting others interested in flying. In the Soviet Union, Svetlana Savitskaya started her career at sixteen by parachuting, then worked her way to piloting,

flight testing, and space, becoming the second woman astronaut in the world on mission Soyuz T-7, launched on 19 August 1982. Skydiving inherited the standard silk canopy chute from the parachute's military design, and this form continued to be used until the introduction of the flat Dacron parasail in the 1970s. This design allowed for greater precision and controllability, and it also led to derivative sports such as "paragliding," in which the parasail is used as a glider—inefficient, but very inexpensive, requiring minimum ground assistance.

RULES AND PLAY

Like other air sports, skydiving is regulated by the Fédération Aéronautique International (FAI) through national air clubs, with a range of competitions from the local level to biennial world championships. Individual and team events are held in specialties called "freestyle," precision landing, combined (which includes freestyle and precision landing), and four- and eight-person free-fall formation. When the Italian team took the four-person freestyle bronze in the 1991 world championships, Marina Ugolini became the first woman to place in an absolute (not all-women) event.

Techniques have improved, and the sport has otherwise progressed, but skydiving contains an inescapable element of danger: the FAI considers an annual fatality rate of 1 per 1,800 divers acceptable.

WOMEN'S RECORDS

In the course of a 1991 international air rescue exercise, Takako Takano of Japan became the first woman to jump over the North Pole. The record for free fall—the most extreme form of skydiving, whose object is the longest possible drop before opening the parachute—was set in 1977, when E. Fomitcheva of the Soviet Union did a free fall of 14,800 meters (48,840 ft.). The record without the use of oxygen stands at 10,150 meters (33,495 ft.) and was set on 11 December 1993 at Brescia (Italy) by Barbara Brighetti (1966–). She jumped at an altitude of 10,900 meters (35,970 ft.) with an air temperature of $-65\ °C$ and winds of 180 kilometers per hour (111.6 mph) without breathing until, 40 seconds later, she reached 6,000 meters (19,800 ft.), eventually landing about a minute later. Because of the costly equipment and long training required to survive such descents, these record attempts attract some sponsorship and are, apart from instructing, the only professional segment of parachuting.

Although it is unlikely that parachuting will ever become a mass sport in terms of participation or spectators, its role as an introduction to air sports, the element of character-building through risk, and its military and safety applications will probably ensure its continuing popularity for the foreseeable future.

Gregory Alegi

Bibliography

De Bernardi, Fiorenza, ed. (1984) *Pink Line. A Gallery of European Women Pilots.* Rome: Aeritalia.

Devlin, Gerard M. (1979) *Paratrooper!* New York: St. Martin's Press.

Franchi, Bruno, ed. (1991) *Annuario Aero Club d'Italia,* Rome: Aero Club d'Italia.

Mason, Francis K. and Martin Windrow, eds. (1970) *Air Facts and Feats. A Record of Aerospace Achievement.* New York: Doubleday.

Rado, Gheorghe. (1993) *Prioritati si recorduri mondiale de aviatie.* Bucharest: Tehnoprod.

Taylor, Michael, and David Monday, eds. (1984) *Aircraft Facts and Feats.* London: Guinness.

PARALYMPICS

The Paralympic Games is the international sport competition for disabled athletes that is the counterpart of the Olympic Games, having the official sanction of the International Olympic Committee. The Games were founded by six international organizations for sports for the disabled: the Comité International Sports des Sourds (CISS), the Cerebral Palsy Sport and Recreation Association (CP-ISRA), the International Blind Sports Association (IBSA), the International Association Sport for Persons with Mental Handicap (INAS-FMH), the International Stoke Mandeville Wheelchair Sports Federation (ISMWSF), and the International Sports Organization for the Disabled (ISOD). The "Olympic style games" for athletes with disabilities were first held in 1960 under the name of the International Games for the Disabled. In 1964 the event became known as the Paralympics.

HISTORY

Organized sports for athletes with disabilities have existed since World War II. Sports for these athletes originally were established as a means of rehabilitating the many injured servicemen and servicewomen after the war. Ludwig Guttman was instrumental in the treatment and rehabilitation of such people at the Stoke Mandeville Hospital in Great Britain. His rehabilitative method quickly evolved into competitive sport, primarily for wheelchair athletes, and the first Stoke Mandeville Games were held in 1948 in London. Three women were among the competitors in these games.

An earlier example of competitive sports for disabled people are the World Games for the Deaf (WGD), which was founded in 1924. Deaf athletes have competed in separate games, because they have no "physical" disability that requires special classification in competitions, as do athletes who are blind, those who are paraplegics or amputees, or athletes who have cerebral palsy.

In 1960, the first International Games for the Disabled (now Paralympics) were held in Rome for physically disabled athletes, particularly those with a spinal-cord injury. Disabled female athletes were included in the Paralympics from the onset. But little research has been done on the history of sports for disabled athletes, and even less specifically on disabled female athletes. Wheelchair basketball for disabled women athletes was introduced in the 1968 Paralympic Summer Games in Tel Aviv, Israel. Amputee and blind athletes joined these games in 1976, and athletes with cerebral palsy were included in 1980. The international organizations for these four groups of disabled athletes founded the International Coordinating Committee of the World Sports Organizations for the Disabled (ICC) in 1984. The four founding organizations were IBSA, ISMWSF, ISOD, and CP-ISRA.

The ICC helped to win the support of the International Olympic Committee (IOC), but the IOC stipulated that the ICC and disability sport organizations refrain from using the word "Olympics." The alternative terminology selected was

Paralympian Di Coates. (Richard Bailey/Corbis)

Paralympics, *para* meaning "attached to," as in "attached to" the Olympics, not as in "paraplegic." The Paralympics were officially recognized by the IOC in 1985. The ICC continued to govern the Paralympic Games until the International Paralympic Committee (IPC) was established in Düsseldorf, Germany, in 1989. The Paralympics were founded by six international organizations for sport for the disabled: CISS, CP-ISRA, IBSA, INAS-FMH, ISMWSF, and ISOD.

The IPC has multiple objectives. The first is to organize paralympic and multidisability world games and world championships (the IPC is the only world organization with the right to do so). The second is to act as a liaison with the IOC and all other relevant international sport bodies. The third is to seek the integration of sports for the disabled into the international sport movement for the able-bodied, although always safeguarding its own identity. The fourth is to supervise and coordinate the conduct of the Paralympics and other multidisability world and regional games and to coordinate the calendar of international and regional competitions, while guaranteeing to respect the athletic technical needs of the individual disability groups. The fifth objective is to assist and encourage educational programs, research, and promotional objectives of sports for disabled people. The sixth is to promote the practice of sports for disabled people, without discrimination for political, religious, economic, sexual or racial reasons. The seventh objective is to seek expansion of the opportunities for disabled people to participate in sports and of their access to training programs designed to improve their proficiency.

PARALYMPIC COMPETITIONS

The Paralympic Games (summer and winter) are held alternately every two years in the same country as the Olympics. The Summer Games have grown tremendously since the first Paralympics in Rome in 1969, which involved 400 athletes from twenty-three countries in wheelchair events. Recent games draw around 4,000 athletes from 100 countries in fifteen sports (archery, athletics, basketball, boccie, cycling, equestrian events, fencing, goalball, judo, powerlifting, shooting, soccer, table tennis, tennis, and volleyball) and three demonstration sports (wheelchair racquetball, wheelchair rugby, and sailing) with various disabilities (amputees, blind, cerebral palsy, mentally handicapped, and paraplegics). The Winter Games also continue to grow since the first competition in Oshevik, Sweden, in 1976.

Athletes in the Paralympic Games are classified according to their functional ability. For example, there are nine classifications for athletes with spinal injuries, nine for amputees, eight for athletes with cerebral palsy, and three for visually impaired athletes. The classifications are intended to promote equal opportunity for all athletes.

Like most sporting events, the Paralympics are dominated by men. This includes coaching and leadership positions at various levels within the Games. Disabled female athletes, like their able-bodied counterparts in other international competitions, make up about one-third of the total population. For example, in the 1996 Paralympics in Atlanta, Georgia, 2,522 male athletes competed, compared to 788 female athletes.

The IPC reported that 49 of the 104 nations that participated in the 1996 Paralympics did not bring any female athletes. Currently, 13 percent of sport chairpersons in the IPC are women; 14 percent of the sport council executive members are female, and only 9 percent (two of twenty-three) women serve on the IPC executive committee.

Historically, women in general have been discouraged from developing their physical skills and participating in sports. Women with disabilities face even greater obstacles in breaking through the barrier of the male-dominated sport environment. Disabled men were applauded for their strength and courage in developing their physical strength through sports. In contrast, disabled women were often discouraged from participation in sports. Female athletes with disabilities still face multiple challenges. These include the small number of role models; lack of organized sport programs at local and regional levels; lack of informal early experiences in sport; lack of accessible sport facilities; lack of access to coaches and training programs; and economic, psychological, and sociological factors.

As evidenced by their outstanding performances in the Paralympics and other international competitions, disabled female athletes are breaking down these barriers. Tanni Grey of Great Britain won four gold medals at the 1992 Barcelona games in wheelchair racing events (100-, 200-, 400-, and 800-meter races) and also holds British records in 1500-meter and 5000-meter races, half marathons, and full marathons, establishing world records for the number of medals won. LeAnn Shannon of the United States—at thirteen years old the youngest athlete to compete in the Paralympics—broke two world records in the 1996 Games in Atlanta in the 100-meter and 400-meter wheelchair races. She also took the gold medal in the 200-meter race and the silver in the 800-meter race.

The women's 1500-meter wheelchair race in the 1996 Paralympics was one of the most exciting competitions at the Games: six women broke the world record. Australia's Louise Sauvage took the gold in 3 minutes 30.45 seconds, Canada's Chantal Petitclerc grabbed the silver in 3 minutes 30.63 seconds, followed by U.S. competitor Jean Driscoll for the bronze in 3 minutes 30.83 seconds. Three other athletes finished under the old world record of 3 minutes 36.66 seconds. Linda Mastandrea of the United States broke the world rec-

ord in the 200-meter wheelchair event in 1996 at 35.30 seconds and picked up the gold medal. Marla Runyan, a blind athlete from the United States, broke the pentathlon record at the 1996 Games after competing in four of the five events.

Outstanding swimmers include Priya Cooper of Australia, who established world records in the freestyle, backstroke, and medley races; and Sarah Bailey of Great Britain and Gemma Dashwood of Australia, who shared almost all of the world records in the classifications between themselves. Tricia Zorn, a blind athlete from the United States, won ten gold and two silver medals at the 1992 Paralympics, and Beth Scott, a blind swimmer also from the United States, won seven medals. The women's Alpine ski team from the United States produced multiple medal winners at the 1998 Nagano Winter Paralympics, with Sarah Will capturing three gold medals and one silver, Sarah Billmeier and Mary Riddell winning four medals each, and Muffy Davis and Maggie Buhle each taking a bronze medal.

CONCLUSION

Women and girls with disabilities have far greater opportunities than their predecessors to participate in sports at all levels of competition. Indeed, sport competition for disabled women is still in its youth. The Paralympics have yet to experience the explosion of talent and success from disabled women in sport. Improvements in coaching, training methods, medical advances, education, and opportunities to compete at younger ages will enhance athletic performances and open unlimited opportunities for female athletes in the Paralympics. The IPC, in conjunction with the IOC, is committed to addressing the underrepresentation of women in the Olympic movement and has established the Working Group on Women and Sport Committee to recommend how to increase women's participation in sports and how to include more women in the decision-making process.

Rebecca A. Clark

See also Deaf Olympics; Disability Sport

Bibliography

Depauw, Karen P. (1998) "Disabled Women and Sport." In *Encyclopedia of Women and Sport in America,* edited by Carole A. Oglesby, Doreen L. Greenberg, Ruth Louise Hall, Karen L. Hill,

Francis Johnston, and Ridley, Sheila Easterby. Phoenix, AZ: Oryx Press, 70–74.

Depauw, Karen P., and Susan J. Gavron. (1995) *Disability and Sport.* Champaign, IL: Human Kinetics.

Dunne, Cara. (1998) "Cycling and Women with Disabilities: Faster, Higher, Stronger." In *Encyclopedia of Women and Sport in America,* edited by Carole A. Oglesby, Doreen L. Greenberg, Ruth Louise Hall, Karen L. Hill, Francis Johnston, and Ridley, Sheila Easterby. Phoenix, AZ: Oryx Press, 61–63.

International Paralympic Committee Home Page. (1998) <http://www.lboro.ac.uk./ipc-info>.

PARENTING *see* Motherhood

PEDESTRIANISM

Women have participated in running and walking events for centuries, but their accomplishments have often been ignored. Some sources have claimed that such women were brazen entertainers violating Victorian morality, who made only a small contribution or even a negative contribution to women's sport. Recent findings reveal accounts of women in professional walking and running to refute this thesis. Current research presents nineteenth-century pedestrianism as a vital thread in the history of women's sport.

HISTORY

Accounts of women walking and running long distances for prizes date back to the eighteenth century, if not considerably earlier. In the nineteenth century, hundreds of women, diminutively known as *pedestriennes,* performed professional feats of endurance. Women endurance runners and walkers performed in England and the United States, and to a lesser extent in Canada, Australia, Mexico, and Germany. Pedestrian events garnered significant enough attention to appear in popular sporting newspapers and metropolitan newspapers. In England, girls and women walking long distances for money were reported in *Annals of Sporting* beginning in 1823. Large U.S. metropolitan newspapers, such as the

New York Times, published the achievements of pedestriennes as early as the 1850s. At least two accounts of women walkers illustrate some legitimacy in their walks. In 1857 the *New York Times* reported the exhibition of Mrs. Bentley, a single mother who walked sixty consecutive hours in a New York City church, the Broadway Tabernacle. In 1876 the *London Times* reported the performance of Bella St. Clair, who walked 1,000 miles in 950 hours at North Woolrich Gardens.

Women's achievements in the 1870s and 1880s included walking day and night for twenty-eight days, and walking and running more than 400 miles in six days. Most of the events were held on small sawdust ovals, within smoke-filled theatres and saloons. Occasionally, women defeated men in pedestrian contests, but most events were solo exhibitions and women-only competitions. Though pedestrian events were depicted as scenes for gambling and drunkenness, they were increasingly popular by the late 1870s. Pedestrian achievements were chronicled in sporting and theatrical newspapers such as the *New York Clipper, Chicago Field,* and *National Police Gazette,* and high circulation metropolitan newspapers such as the *Boston Post, New York Sun, Philadelphia Inquirer, Washington Post, Cincinnati Inquirer, Chicago Tribune,* and *San Francisco Chronicle.*

LEGITIMATION OF PEDESTRIAN SPORT

German-American immigrant Bertha Von Hillern and Englishwoman Ada Anderson were two notable pedestrian performers. Von Hillern partially legitimized pedestrianism when she was advertised as an example of women's physical culture, and her walks were supported by medical doctors. Rising popularity increased women's participation, as events were held in New York City, Chicago, San Francisco, New Orleans, Washington, D.C., and dozens of other cities and towns. From 1876 to 1878, Von Hillern was supported by middle-class women who saw her as a symbol of female strength and endurance. Editorials favoring her efforts appeared in the premier women's suffrage newspaper, *Woman's Journal.* From 1877 to 1880, Anderson was also promoted as a symbol of women's abilities. Her day and night walk of twenty-eight days—2,700 consecutive quarter miles in 2,700 consecutive quarter hours—further symbolized the potential strength and endurance of women. Ada Anderson's achievement in Brooklyn, New York, received national and international attention through metropolitan and sporting newspapers. Her story and illustrations of her performance received front-page recognition in *Frank Leslie's Illustrated News* and the *New York Illustrated Times*. Anderson's speeches, and their subsequent publication in newspapers, promoted walking for improving women's health. Anderson's solo exhibition was also favorably compared to the shorter public walks of Princess Louise, one of Queen Victoria's daughters. Madame Anderson's exhibition also gained significant attention for its reported gate receipts ($32,000) and athlete's wages ($8,000).

Women's pedestrianism became a commodity in the burgeoning sports entertainment industry, attracting hundreds of women participants, selling hundreds of thousands of tickets and concessions, and becoming the interest of in-depth newspaper stories throughout the United States. The zenith of women's pedestrianism occurred in 1879, when competitive six-day races with ten or more participants were held in New York's Madison Square Garden and San Francisco's Mechan-

ics Hall. Newspaper reports, sometimes on the front page, fueled interest in the contests. Many pedestrians were working-class women and immigrants with limited opportunities for social mobility. Some were untrained for pedestrian efforts but walked because of economic desperation. These performers frequently saw sporting entertainment as an avenue for material progress. Some of the more notable performers were Mary Marshall and French-Canadian Exilda La Chapelle. Women billed as English, German, Spanish, and Russian also participated. Pedestrian women of color included Native American Tek Sek and African-American Madame de Cristoral.

EXPLOITATION, SUPPRESSION, AND HISTORICAL MARGINALIZATION

Pedestrianism violated Victorian moral standards, and acts of worker exploitation and brutality against women performers did occur. Ada Anderson's walks in 1879 were protested by religious groups in Brooklyn, Pittsburgh, and Chicago because they were held on Sundays amid gambling and alcohol use. Newspaper coverage in the *New York Tribune* and *Chicago Tribune* reported on the

MADAME ANDERSON: PIONEERING WOMAN OF ENDURANCE (1877–1880)

Madame Anderson gained brief international recognition as a pioneer in women's endurance efforts of the late 1870s. Her most famous walk was a successful effort of twenty-eight days and nights—2,700 consecutive quarter miles in 2,700 consecutive quarter hours—in Brooklyn, New York, from 17 December 1878 to 13 January 1879. Anderson began the first of her twenty multi-day walks in Newport, South Wales, in 1877. She continued her walks in England at Plymouth, Boston, Leeds, Skegness, King's Lynn, and Peterborough. Her performances in the United States occurred in Brooklyn, Pittsburgh, Chicago, Cincinnati, Louisville, Detroit, Buffalo, New York City, and Baltimore. The intrepid pedestrian's accomplishments transcended sport because they symbolized women's capacity for strength and endurance in an era that considered ladies too frail

for public lives. Madame Anderson spoke freely about injustices against women and the benefits of exercise for women's health. She performed many exhibitions under extreme hardships that included walking outdoors in torrential rain, enduring cigarette and cigar smoke, suffering from sleep deprivation, and having decayed teeth extracted between laps. Anderson's efforts prompted a pedestrian craze that fueled a growing sport industry, but her efforts were condemned by some religious groups, including Brooklyn's Women's Christian Temperance Union, for being performed on Sundays amid gambling and alcohol consumption. Anderson's efforts were uncovered in some magazine articles in the 1960s and 1970s. With few exceptions, however, Madame Anderson's pioneering efforts were largely forgotten in women's sports history until the late 1990s.

evils and excesses of pedestrianism, and the Philadelphia Medical Society called for a suspension of women's pedestrianism to safeguard women. By 1880, New York City government authorities placed restrictions on women's pedestrianism to safeguard women's health and morality. Women's pedestrianism continued to be popular and competitive in San Francisco, where Amy Howard and Sarah Tobias broke the 400-mile barrier in a six-day race.

Pedestrianism was on the wane by the early 1880s. The most promising pedestrian, Amy Howard, competed for a few years, went into vaudeville with her husband, then died in childbirth in 1885. Madame Armaindo, May Stanley, and others moved into bicycle racing and other sporting entertainment. The last known multiday races occurred in Baltimore and Washington, D.C., in 1889. The participants included Sarah Tobias, Bella Kilbury, and Millie Roze, all of whom had pedestrian careers spanning ten years or more. In the last known event of its kind, Tobias and Kilbury came to blows during the race, and Tobias was arrested. Both participants, however, finished the race, and received a portion of the reported $4,000 in winner's wages. During the winter of 1890–1891, Spanish-American Zoe Gayton walked from San Francisco to New York. Gayton continued to walk for wages in 1896, the same year that a Greek woman, Stamata Revithi, ran the inaugural Olympic marathon course. In the early twentieth century, a few accounts of women long-distance walkers appeared in the *New York Times*. The most notable long-distance woman walker of the early twentieth century was Eleanora Sears, who was better known for her tennis achievements.

CONCLUSION

The long but fragmented history of women in endurance sports shows that some women pedestrians of the nineteenth century consciously strove for and briefly experienced public recognition and acceptance. Thousands of newspaper stories of women walkers and runners fueled an immensely popular pedestrian craze. The pedestrian craze, however, led to excesses and abuses that provided reasons for public interference and suppression. Pedestrian performances should have defeated the myth that women were too frail for endurance sports, but the evidence was triv-

ialized and then forgotten. By the early twentieth century, historical recognition of nineteenth-century *pedestriennes* was limited. Popular and favorable accounts of the *pedestriennes* surfaced in the 1960s and 1970s, and *pedestriennes* began to receive some scholarly attention in the 1990s. The story of the *pedestriennes* has contemporary significance because it demonstrates how groups with special interests can influence a sport—whether to support it or to suppress it—by using the media and government policy. Powerful groups sometimes define a sport as worthy and profitable, or attack it as revolutionary and immoral, thus determining how history is written.

Dahn Shaulis

See also Walking, Fitness

Bibliography

Brailsford, Dennis. (1969) *Sport and Society: Elizabeth to Anne*. Toronto, Ontario: University of Toronto Press.

Cumming, John. (1981) *Runners and Walkers*. Chicago: Regnery Gateway.

Drinkwater, Barbara. (1986) *Female Endurance Athletes*. Champaign, IL: Human Kinetics.

Guttmann, Allen. (1991) *Women's Sports: A History*. New York: Columbia University Press.

Howell, Reet. *Her Story in Sport*. West Point, NY: Leisure Press.

Osler, Tom, and Ed Dodd. (1979) *Ultra-Marathoning: The Next Challenge*. Mountain View, CA: World Publications.

Tricard, Louise Mead. (1996) *American Women's Track and Field*. London: McFarland and Company.

Vertinsky, Patricia. (1990) *The Eternally Wounded Woman*. Manchester, England: Manchester University Press.

PENTATHLON, MODERN

The pentathlon in its original form dates to the ancient Olympics, while the modern pentathlon is a child of the modern Olympics. It is a sport of mili-

Heide Rosendahl (in front) in hurdles action during the pentathlon competition at the 1972 Munich Olympics. (Bettmann/Corbis)

tary skills—horseback riding, fencing, pistol shooting, swimming, and running. Women have competed since 1981.

HISTORY

The pentathlon has a long history. The first time it was staged as an Olympic event was 708 BCE. Originally, the pentathlon consisted of what would today be called athletics or track and field. Events included running the length of the stadium, jumping, throwing a spear and a discus, and wrestling. Baron Pierre de Coubertin, the person responsible for the revival of the Olympic Games in the late nineteenth century, greatly admired the idea of a pentathlon competition. Beginning in 1909, he attempted to have the modern pentathlon reintroduced to the Olympics. Like the ancient competition, this modern pentathlon did not include women. Baron de Coubertin did not believe that women should have any place in

sport except as spectators, so it is not surprising that the modern pentathlon was a sport so steeped in masculinity. It was first held at the Olympics in Stockholm in 1912. The first world championships were held in 1949. Women did not compete in the world championships until 1981.

The idea behind the sport is to have the athlete perform the exploits of a Napoleonic cavalry officer. As a messenger, this officer had to take an important document across the country. To do this, he first had to ride a horse through enemy territory, then he had to fight his enemies with a sword and pistol. He then had to swim a river and run cross-country, where his mission was completed.

RULES AND PLAY

To replicate the feats of the cavalry officer, pentathletes compete in cross-country riding, fencing, pistol shooting, swimming, and cross-country running. One of the principal challenges to the modern pentathlete is that she or he must ride a horse selected by lot and provided by the organizers. Competitors have 20 minutes and five practice fences to get to know their horses before they ride over a course 350–450 meters (381–490 yd.) long and negotiate twenty obstacles. They fence using the épée-type sword, and when a competitor is hit or touched with the tip of the sword, the bout is won. Each bout may last no longer than one minute, and if that time passes and neither competitor registers a win, then both register a defeat. The competitors must go through twenty bouts, so if there are fewer than twenty people, then they fight each other twice. In the pistol shooting event, the competitors shoot at a snap target with a .22 caliber pistol. Each competitor has twenty shots at a range of 10 meters (11 yd.). The competitor has a time limit of 40 seconds to fire each shot. The shooting is done in four sets of five scoring shots, for a total of twenty shots. The participants then swim 300 meters (327 yards) freestyle. The cross-country course is 4000 meters (4360 yards) long and is rugged. This running event must always be completed last. The winner is the athlete who collects the most points during the competition.

Men and women compete at the same events with only a few minor variations. Women swim a shorter distance of 200 meters (218 yards) and run a cross-country course half as long, at 2000 meters (2180 yards).

Scoring for the modern pentathlon is complicated. The pistol shooting is scored out of a possible 200, with each of the twenty shots worth a possible 10 points. A score of 172 is worth 1,000 pentathlon points. Any score above or below that either has 12 points added or subtracted. The competitor who earns 1,000 points, with a total score of 70 percent, wins in the fencing. A competitor earns 1,000 pentathlon points in the swimming if her time is the benchmark figure: 2 minutes, 54 seconds. Any score above that benchmark is rewarded 4 points for every half second, and those below it are penalized by the same margin. The running event is also set on a specific time; for women it is 7 minutes, 40 seconds, and any second above or below this will lose or gain 5 points. The riding section is scored on the performance and timing of the rider in negotiating the course.

Competitors start with 1,100 points and lose points if they make mistakes. The rider loses 40 points for a refusal, 30 points for a knockdown, and 60 points if the competitor falls off the horse; 3 points are deducted for each second beyond the allotted time for the completion of the course.

Given its emphasis on military skills, the modern pentathlon usually attracted participants who had served as soldiers in countries with a background in cavalry and classic sports such as fencing and shooting. As a result, those countries with an emphasis on such military sports—mostly European countries—were much more successful in the modern pentathlon than those countries that did not, such as the United States.

The modern pentathlon competition used to be held over four or five days. While this was less grueling for the competitors, it was not particularly exciting for the spectators. With the numbers of watching public diminishing at major championships and events, it was decided at the 1996 Atlanta Olympics that all events that make up the modern pentathlon would be held on the same day. The women's events, although not yet in the Olympics, followed the same pattern in non-Olympic championships.

Illicit drug use also figured in the change to a single day. Competitors were accused of taking beta blockers, which slow the heartbeat. This helped the penthaletes in shooting events because even the beat of the heart would jar the competitor enough to affect the accuracy of the shot. Beta blockers do have an adverse affect on a competitor in a running event, but when the pentathlon was spread over a period of days, the competitors would have time to recover between the shooting and running events. When all events are held in one day, competitors are not be able to use the calming drugs necessary for shooting or the stimulant drugs for running because the effects would be counterproductive. By compressing the time span of the modern pentathlon, the authorities were able to discourage drug use.

WOMEN'S PARTICIPATION

In the modern pentathlon world championships, the rules are the same for men and women, with the modifications described above. There are three different levels of competition for women in the modern pentathlon: the women's event, the junior women, and youth, which is for girls seventeen to eighteen years old. The youth event is usually held over two, or sometimes three days, and the participants do not take part in the riding component. There are three elements to the world championship competition: two parts that make up the individual event and a third part, the team relay competition. In the individual event, the athletes qualify for the final in two or three groups of semifinalists. The top ten and the two highest eleventh places qualify for the final.

Individual and team medals are awarded. The team medal is decided by adding three individual team member's scores together. The team relay is a separate competition altogether and consists of twelve teams with three members competing in a continuous relay in one day. Each team member fires ten shots, swims 100 meters (109 yd.), takes part in one bout of fencing, runs 1000 meters (1090 yd.), and rides a horse over eight show jumps.

As with the men's competition, the women's modern pentathlon is generally dominated by European countries. Since 1987, the Polish have not been out of the top three in the team event. Other individuals such as Eva Fjellerup from Denmark have won the world championships four times.

The World Cup is the second elite event. This competition was first held for men and women in 1990. The athlete has her three best results posted on a league table. The top sixteen athletes are chosen from the World Cup qualifying competitions, and they challenge for the World Cup. There is prize money, but given the modest number of participants, the modern pentathlon obviously does not have the resources that are available in other sports. The 1997 women's World Cup final, won by Swede Jeanette Malm, included a $5,000 award. Second and third prize were $3,000 and $2,000, respectively. The 2000 Olympics in Sydney represent the first Olympics in which women compete in the pentathlon.

J. P. Anderson

Bibliography

Glenesk, Neil. (1984) "Modern Pentathlon." *Journal of Physical Education, Recreation and Dance* 55, 4 (April).

Greenberg, Stan. (1991) *Olympics Fact Book*. Middlesex, England: Guinness Publishing.

Additional information was provided by Union Internationale de Pentathlon Moderne et Biathlon.

PERFORMANCE

Women compete in a broad range of sporting events. Each competitor strives to perform to the best of her ability, but her actual performance results from the complex interaction of multiple factors. These factors include physiological and psychological components as well as technique and skill in performing specific motor tasks. Additionally, each woman enters her sport event with a set of predetermined genetic traits, which have been developed to varying degrees by sport training. The contribution of each of these components to a successful performance may vary among sport events, among individual competitors, and even among repeat performances by the same individual athlete.

PHYSIOLOGICAL FACTORS

Each sport or event has a set of underlying physiological requirements. The body's physiological systems provide energy, cardiorespiratory endurance, and muscle strength and power for the athlete to be fast, jump high, score a goal, or perform other feats. Virtually all systems of the body are involved, but the capacities of the metabolic, cardiovascular, and neuromuscular systems are most important. The importance of each of these systems depends on the performance requirements for a specific event. In general, the shorter the event, the greater the need for strength and power; more sustained events require more cardiorespiratory fitness, heat-regulating capacity, and a substantial ability to supply energy for long periods of time.

Actually, most sports are more complex in their physiological requirements because they do not involve a single sustained kind of activity. A general look at what happens during a soccer game illustrates this point. Players are continuously active for two 45-minute halves. During each game, they cover distances ranging from 7 to 12 kilometers (4.3

AN INVITATION TO PERFORM DURING THE REIGN OF QUEEN ANNE

Near London these wakes, like Hampstead or Deptford wakes, were well kept up; and there was my Lady Butterfield in Epping Forest, of whose entertainment and calf-roasting we have already had a description through Ward's instrumentality. Here is one of her advertisements: 'My Lady Butterfield gives a Challenge to all England, to Ride a Horse, Leap a Horse, Run on Foot or Hallow with any Woman in England Ten years younger, but not a Day older, because she would not under value herself. Gentlemen and Ladies, whilst in the Spring 'tis worth your while to come to hear the Nightingal Sing in Wanstead within a Mile of the Green Man, in Essex, at my Lady Butterfields at Nightingal Hall. This is to give notice to all Gentlemen and Ladies, and all the best of my Friends, that on the last Wednes-day of April is my feast, where is very good Entertainment for that Day, and for all the Year after from my Lady Butterfield.'

Or another: –

TO ALL GENTLEMEN AND LADIES.
If Rare Good young Beans and Pease can
    Tempt Ye,
Pray pass not by my Hall with Bellies Empty;
For Kind Good Usage every one can tell,
My Lady Butterfield does all excell;
At Wanstead Town, a Mile of the Green Man,
Come if you dare and stay away if you can.

JOHN ASHTON
(1882) Social Life in the Reign of Queene Anne Taken from Original Sources. *London: Chatto and Windus.*

to 7.4 mi.). More than 10 percent of the total distance a player covers during a soccer game has been estimated to occur at sprint speed, with accelerations from standing to maximal effort occurring between forty and sixty-two times per game. It has also been estimated that players change pace or direction approximately every 5 seconds. Thus, the physiologic component of performance in a particular sport is governed, in part, by the movement patterns of that event (that is, fast or slow, high or low intensity, short or prolonged).

The physiological demands of most sporting events are similar for men and women athletes. Likewise, training methods seem to be similar, and existing evidence suggests that men and women respond to the same training in qualitatively similar ways. Several gender-related physiological differences may limit the effects of training on a woman's performance. For example, women typically have smaller hearts, smaller blood volume, and lower hemoglobin concentrations, thus limiting oxygen transport. These factors, combined with a woman's higher percentage of body fat,

may limit maximal oxygen uptake and therefore limit performance in endurance events. In addition, while men and women will respond to resistance training with similar patterns of strength gain and changes in muscle cross-sectional area, the male athlete is typically stronger (mainly because of the hormonal effect of testosterone on muscle mass) than the female athlete. This will give him a performance advantage in sport events requiring strength and power. The magnitude of gender-related performance differences is remarkably similar across events, other than those in which power to move body weight against gravity is the main determinant of success.

Athletes also need adequate energy and nutrient intake for optimal performance. To supply movement energy, the athlete's body uses a combination of fat and carbohydrate. Since fat stores are virtually unlimited, athletes seeking energy balance should focus on the consumption of adequate calories and enough carbohydrate to keep glycogen stores full. It is generally accepted that 8 to 10 grams of carbohydrate daily per kilogram of body weight (600–650 grams of carbohydrate for the average person) are necessary to maintain maximally full glycogen stores. With a normal calorie diet, this translates to a carbohydrate intake of 60 to 70 percent of the diet. In addition to maintaining a daily energy and carbohydrate balance, many endurance athletes also follow carbohydrate-loading regimens before important competitions. During typical carbohydrate loading, the athlete increases her dietary carbohydrate to 75 percent of energy intake for four days before competition. But recent research has cast doubt on the usefulness of this practice for female athletes. Further investigation of this apparent gender difference is needed before carbohydrate loading can be recommended for women athletes.

Another major physiological consideration is the maintenance of fluid and electrolyte balance. For athletes to maintain body temperature within tolerable limits, their bodies must generate a high rate of heat loss to balance the high rate of heat production that occurs with prolonged exercise. This requires a high sweat rate and the resultant loss of fluids and electrolytes. Distance running and sports that last longer than one hour, particularly when done in a hot environment, place large thermoregulatory demands on male and female athletes. Athletes can apparently train themselves to tolerate fluid consumption during endurance exercise and this ability should be incorporated into their training.

SKILL OR TECHNIQUE

Each sport event requires the athlete to be proficient in a set of very specific skill techniques for optimal performance. The components of these motor skills are multifaceted and complex. They may include sensory motor (for example, reaction time), psychomotor (for example, hand-eye coordination), sensory perceptual (such as pain/discomfort threshold), and cognitive (information-processing) components. Investigators agree, in general, that motor skills are important determinants of sport performance, but they do not agree about training methods that contribute to improvement of these parameters.

Research has demonstrated that athletes acquire motor skills through practice with appropriate feedback, that is, getting feedback that tells the athlete what works and what does not. For example, a certain way of swinging a tennis racquet may result in the ball landing in the court, while a different way of swinging results in hitting it out. The appropriate feedback is the athlete's distinction between the two. Most athletes train by repetitions of the specific movement patterns of the competitive event. It is not possible to predict either the amount of time an athlete will need to develop these skills or the final level of skill that she will reach.

PSYCHOLOGICAL FACTORS

An athlete may possess all the physiological and technical attributes necessary for a good performance, but unless she also possesses the necessary psychological skills, she may be unable to perform at her potential. Successful athletes control their psychological responses and are able to find the delicate balance of being optimally aroused without becoming overanxious. Investigators frequently describe the relationship between arousal and performance as an inverted *U*, with a moderate level of arousal necessary for optimal performance. Too much or too little will result in less than optimal performance.

REQUIREMENTS FOR SUCCESS

How well a woman performs in a sport is determined by a complex mix of factors. Among these are the physiological requirements (energy use, endurance, strength, speed, agility, power) of the sport, skill and technique, psychological factors such as arousal and anxiety, genetic predisposition and training. Successfully maximizing the positive factors often leads to high performance.

An athlete who is insufficiently aroused may give an apathetic performance (athletes sometimes refer to this a "being flat"). At the other extreme, overarousal may make the athlete overanxious and tense, with a tendency to make many errors. Optimal levels of arousal may differ among sports and among individual competitors. For example, golfers may require lower levels of arousal than track sprinters. Factors such as anxiety, emotion, attention, stress, and motivation all contribute to the athlete's level of arousal.

The athlete's ability to concentrate on the task at hand actually has the greatest impact on whether she can maintain an appropriate level of arousal. Concentration is a learned skill that includes cultivating the ability of not being distracted by irrelevant stimuli. The stimuli can be either internal (self-doubts) or external (behavior of an opponent). Successful athletes use goal setting, stress management, visual imagery, and mental rehearsal to control their state of arousal and to therefore perform at their best.

GENETIC ENDOWMENT

Genetic endowment clearly contributes to athletic performance. In fact, researchers agree that a strong genetic potential is absolutely essential for success in elite-level competition. But an athlete must be careful to evaluate her performance not only in terms of external outcomes (winning), but also in terms of realistic expectations based on her unique combination of genetic potential and state of training. That is, is she performing to the best of her ability? The degree of the genetic influence on performance may vary according to the specific requirements of a particular event. For example, twin studies have documented a strong genetic influence (estimated to be between 45 percent and 75 percent of performance ability) in sprint running performance. Conversely, in distance running, the genetic contribution has been estimated to be less than 30 percent. Even less is known about the genetic influence on the ability to learn motor skills or to be psychologically capable of consistent optimal performances.

TRAINING

No matter how strong the genetic influence, an athlete will not be a champion without appropriate training. The type, intensity, and duration of training should mirror requirements of the particular event. The athlete's performance will then depend on how much she improves in the capacity for energy transformation (aerobic and anaerobic), aspects of neurophysiologic function (coordination, skill, and reaction time), and the capacity for strength and power generation. Training to improve performance can be described as a stimulus–response model, in which the stimulus is a training overload and the response is the physiologic adaptations that allow the athlete to go faster, jump higher, or be stronger. Much is known about the physiologic adaptations that occur during the initial stages of exercise training. Much less is known about the adaptations that occur in athletes to improve performance by very small amounts (often the difference between winning an event and finishing out of contention). Athletes may need large amounts of training, while avoiding the pitfalls of overtraining, to produce very small improvements in performance.

Overtraining, an unexplained decline in performance with or without specific physiological and psychological signs or symptoms, can be a serious problem for the competitive athlete. It is, in fact, difficult to determine the amount of training an athlete needs to optimize performance. An amount of training that may be optimal for one athlete may undertrain or overtrain others. To complicate the issue further, undertraining and overtraining may result in performance plateaus. The usual response to a performance plateau is to increase the amount and intensity of training. If the athlete has hit the plateau because of undertraining, additional training may be of benefit. If, on the other hand, overtraining is the problem, further training will make it worse and will in all likelihood lead to further decrements in performance.

CONCLUSION

Successful performances are the result of optimal physiological conditioning, high levels of sport-specific skill, and the ability to control such psychological factors as arousal and concentration. Winning performances result when athletes optimize these factors through appropriate training if they also have a high genetic potential for athletic success.

Mary L. O'Toole

See also Biomechanics; Burnout; Endurance; Environment; Injury; Mental Conditioning; Motivation; Nutrition; Stress and Stress Management

Bibliography

Fleck, Steven J., and William J. Kramer. (1987) *Designing Resistance Training Programs.* Champaign, IL: Human Kinetics.

Noakes, Timothy D. (1991) *Lore of Running.* Cape Town, South Africa: Oxford University Press.

Wells, Christine L. (1991) *Women, Sport, and Performance: A Physiological Perspective.* 2d ed. Champaign, IL: Human Kinetics.

Wilmore, Jack H., and David L. Costill. (1994) *Physiology of Sport and Exercise.* Champaign, IL: Human Kinetics.

PERSONALITY TRAITS

There are many measurable personality traits and personal dispositions by which people vary and which make each individual unique. The terms *trait* and *disposition* are interchangeable. Some examples of traits and dispositions are: extraversion–introversion, stability–instability, conscientiousness, endurance, dominance and submission, sociability, intelligence, gender and sexual styles, and achievement motivation. Traits are usually studied by administering a personality test, questionnaire, or inventory. These instruments are scored and interpreted according to a strict set of norms and statistical regulations yielding a personality profile for each individual. A profile purports to capture the unique character and modes of expression of the individual. Such profile comparisons have been used in the study of women in sport.

The sources, descriptions, and measurements of traits selected for study make the field of personality interesting, since all do not agree on the traits to be studied. Students of personality have sought to understand the relationships of traits to many psychological behaviors and outcomes. These include social adjustment, health status, aging and life passages, gender development, and, most important, sport participation and sport achievement.

If traits are the dimensions of personality upon which people vary, then why do they vary? Personality evolves from many influences that may be divided into three broad categories: physical, personal, and sociocultural. Physical influences are due to inherited and other biological characteristics. Personal influences are due to the unique events experienced by a particular individual. Sociocultural influences are internalizations from the social environment, for example, via parents, education, and the media.

HISTORY

The psychological sciences have existed for approximately 120 years (the first laboratory was founded by Wilhelm Wundt in Leipzig, Germany, in 1879). Four schools of thought have competed as the major models for explaining human behavior, including personality: psychoanalytic, behavioral, cognitive, and neurological. Each of these models has been used in attempts to understand personality traits and their influence on women in sport, although many will argue that the psychoanalytic and the behavioral have lost momentum when compared to the cognitive and neurological. To these four major schools a fifth emphasis may be added in the study of personality in sport. This is the prosocial emphasis, which may also be called the moral or ethical model in sport. This model addresses questions of how sport is best integrated into the individual's development and personality as a constructive force. As the competence experiences of sport generalize to other aspects of life, sport and exercise can lead to increased adjustment and to long and fulfilling lives for the individual. Sport can also be a negative experience leading to stress, increased anxiety, and sometimes injury and drop-out. The moral dimension to sport, when studied in relationship to women's competence development in cultures throughout the world, may yield important results in the future.

IS THERE AN ATHLETIC TYPE?

This is a complex question due to the methodological issues underlying it. One may give a general response in the affirmative: There is a general

---

THE INDIVIDUALISTIC OUTLOOK (1969)

A Sociological Explanation
for Women's Gravitation to Individual Sports

Team play does not have much of an appeal to most women. The contests women enter are usually those in which they function alongside one another. Women are evidently more individualistic in temper, more self-contained than men. They live in their own bodies while men spend their time and energy on projects, some of which demand team work. . . .

There are, of course, exceptions. Women make good partners in tennis, and good members of teams in field hockey, basketball, and lacrosse. These exceptions do not belie a general tendency of women to perform as individuals. That tendency is support by the fact that team sport invite undesirable injuries, and the fact that a woman's acceptance of her body, gradually intensified as she develops, encourages an individualistic outlook. This persists even when she makes a strong effort to abstract from her natural body condition and tries to identify herself with her body in the way male athletes identify with theirs. . . .

PAUL WEISS
(1969) "Women Athletes." Sport: A Philosophical Inquiry. Southern Illinois University Press.

athletic type for most sports. Women who do well in sport tend to score highly on measures of competence, achievement motivation, activity level, endurance, risk taking, and ability to withstand stress. (Competence here means an individual's expectation that she will interact effectively with the environment in the future, an expectation based on her cumulative past experiences in similar situations.)

The study of personality is a study of complex interaction effects, not linear relationships. That is, different personality traits vary interactively with other variables for every question asked. Consider the following: (1) Women most attracted to or suited to a sport may not be those encouraged to stay in it by the sport culture, officials, or demands of participation; (2) personality changes may occur over time as women adapt to and adjust to intense sport subcultures and other demands of performance; (3) gender and sex role adjustment of women and men in sport are in continual evolution and are in some cases extreme, which must be taken into account by the researcher; (4) persons who participate in individual sports tend to yield different personality profiles than persons who participate in group sports, and this produces error variance in many sport studies; (5) positions played on teams and levels of achievement reached similarly produces error variance when one seeks general conclusions. Given these complexities, it is a tribute to the field that students of personality have persevered to the current level of understanding of the competent, high-activity-level, robust type of woman who succeeds in many sports.

The woman who chooses to invest in sport and persevere within it will tend toward higher scores on dominance, extraversion, confidence, resilience, activity level, endurance, aggression, and competence. She may also, as she perseveres, manifest an ethical or moral investment in sport as it is fairer and more regulated than some other avenues of life. Although competitiveness, if improperly managed, can yield a tough, uncaring, and low-insight profile, this destructive side of sport must not be permitted to negate the positive psychological and health benefits reflected in the feelings of well being that characterize those who are physically fit and who exercise or engage in sport regularly. High achievers in sport are often in a constant struggle to balance constructive and destructive elements, and a positive outcome fre-

RECOMMENDED SPORTS MODIFICATIONS FOR NATURALLY WEAKER FAIR SEX (1912)

Some of the specific mental and physical qualities which are developed by athletics are increased powers of attention, will, concentration, accuracy, alertness, quickness of perception, perseverance, reason, judgment, forbearance, patience, obedience, self-control, loyalty to leaders, self-denial, submergence of self, grace, poise, suppleness, courage, strength and endurance. These qualities are as valuable to women as to men. While there is some danger that women who try to excel in men's sports may take on more marked masculine characteristics . . . this danger is greatly lessened if the sports are modified so as to meet their peculiar qualifications as to strength, height, weight, etc.

Inasmuch as the average woman is inferior to the average man in nearly all physical qualifications, all the apparatus used and the weights lifted, as well as the height and distance to be attained in running, jumping, etc., should be modified to meet her limitations. Considering also the peculiar constitution of her nervous system and the great emotional disturbances to which she is subjected, changes should be made in many of the rules and regulations governing the sports and games for men, to adapt them to the requirements of women.

DUDLEY A. SARGENT, M.D.
(1912) "Are Athletics Making Girls Masculine?"
The Ladies' Home Journal. *March.*

---

quently yields the character growth and competence observed in mature athletes.

MEASURES OF PERSONALITY

Published measures of personality have appeared in the scientific literature since the 1920s. Through the years (1938 to 1995) Oscar Buros's *Mental Measurements Yearbooks* have been the standard reference works summarizing and evaluating the measures and alerting users to their ethical, statistical, and construction merit or demerit. Note that with Buros's death, the most recent volume is edited by J. C. Conoley and J. C. Impara. Some examples of specific tests are the *Revised NEO Personality Inventory and NEO Five-Factor Inventory* (NEO-FFI), *Minnesota Multiphasic Personality Inventory* (MMPI), *California Psychological Inventory* (CPI), *Personality Research Form* (PRIF), *Locus of Control Scales,* and *Sixteen-Personality Factor Questionnaire* (16 PF test). These tests all measure personality traits or styles and have been much used in sport studies. A second group of tests, called sport-specific measures, have appeared over the past twenty years, and 314 of these can be found, described in detail, in another reference work compiled by Andrew Ostrow titled *The Directory of*

Psychological Tests in the Sport and Exercise Sciences (1996). These more recent measures yield scores on personal dispositions, motivations, and styles that are manifested in sport behaviors. Examples of these measures are the *Athletic Motivation Inventory, Sport Motivation Scales, Sport Competition Anxiety Test, Test of Attentional and Interpersonal Styles, Sport Aggression Questionnaire,* and *Sport Locus Of Control Scale.* The Buros and Ostrow reference works are the best sources for students and researchers to find an overview of the measures available.

FIVE BASIC TRAITS OF PERSONALITY

P. T. Costa and R. R. McRae (1992) have sought to integrate work in personality by proposing five basic dimensions. Using cross-cultural data, hundreds of separate studies and the technique of factor analysis, they have named and studied five "universal" factors of personality. These are: (1) extraversion, (2) agreeableness, (3) conscientiousness, (4) neuroticism, and (5) openness to experience.

These factors are measured by the *Revised NEO Personality Inventory (NEO-PI-R).* The writers have advanced studies of the five and have sought to assign the above labels for consensus and unity in the diverse field of personality. The typical profile for the woman doing well in sport would be a high score on all of the factors except neuroticism. As in all personality studies, there are many exceptions to this typical profile.

A DISPOSITIONAL MODEL: MOTIVATIONAL STYLES IN SPORT

A sport-specific example of personal dispositions in sport and their measurement is to be found in the motivational theory and measurement of Dorcas S. Butt (1987). The model (see Figure 1) supposes that individual motivation evolves between two major sources: biological motivation on level one and the reinforcements conferred through social sanctions and structures on level four. Psychological motivation on level two is represented in the three basic energy models of aggression, conflict, and competence, while social motivation on level three may be either competitive or cooperative. The solid and dotted arrows indicate the greater and lesser degree of association thereafter. Aggressive motivation and conflict are most likely to lead to competitive social motivation and, to a lesser extent, to cooperation. Competence motivation is most likely to lead to cooperative social motivation and to a lesser extent to competitive motivation. The competitively and cooperatively motivated will be affected by the reinforcements of sport. However, external rewards will be most important to the competitor and internal rewards to the cooperator.

The basic personality traits described within the theory are aggression, conflict, competence, competition, and cooperation. These constructs have been measured and studied locally, nationally, and internationally. It is becoming increasingly apparent that competence and cooperation are the crucial concepts for understanding personal and social constructiveness, health, and longevity in sport, particularly for women.

THE FUTURE

There are two areas of study that will advance knowledge about women in sport and personality. The first is the relatively new perspective offered from the study of evolutionary and biological processes underlying personality and sport behavior. Sport represents a contest in which sta-

tus in groups is determined and in which the physical fitness and robustness, so necessary in our evolutionary past, finds expression. Testosterone level rises with competitive success and also after sexual intercourse, apparently for both sexes. If social status and dominance are increased with competitive success in groups, then it may be that women, through sport, may realize more leadership roles and influence in society at large.

Constructive leadership and sport behavior must be mediated by the knowledge and practice of ethical and value considerations. Thus the second major theme that will see rapid development is the combined study of sports, ethics, and personality. Sport is played within a set of rules, supported and nurtured with constructive participation. It is clear that problem athletes may short-cut the rules at any opportunity to gain unfair advantage. However, it is also clear that the good leader in sport and in society does not benefit or advantage only a few but looks to the good of all. Thus the study of constructive versus destructive sport behaviors and of personal integrity in sport are crucial to women's continuing sport participation.

Dorcas Susan Butt

Bibliography

Butt, Dorcas S. (1987) *Psychology of Sport: The Behavior, Motivation, Personality and Performance of Athletes.* New York: Van Nostrand.

Conoley, J. C., and J. C. Impara. (1995) *The Twelfth Mental Measurements Yearbook.* Lincoln: University of Nebraska, Buros Institute of Mental Measurements.

Cooper, Colin. (1998) *Individual Differences.* New York: St. Martin's Press.

Costa, P. T., Jr., and R. R. McCrae. (1992) *Revised NEO Personality Inventory (NEO-PI-R) and NEO Five-Factor Inventory (NEO-FFI) Professional Manual.* Odessa, FL: Psychological Assessment Resources.

Dabbs, J. M., Jr., and S. Mohammed. (1992) "Male and Female Salivary Concentrations before and after Sexual Activity." *Physiology and Behavior* 52:195–197.

Mazur, A., A. Booth, and J. M. Dabbs, Jr. (1992) "Testosterone and Chess Competition." *Social Psychology Quarterly* 55:70–77.

Leith, L. M. (1994) *Foundations of Exercise and Mental Health.* Morgantown, WV: Fitness Information Technology.

Ostrow, Andrew C. (1996) *Directory of Psychological Tests in the Sport and Exercise Sciences.* Morgantown, WV: Fitness Information Technology.

Robbins, R. W., S. D. Gosling, and K. H. Craik. (1998) "Psychological Science at the Crossroads." *American Scientist* 86: 310–313.

Shields, D. L. L., and B. J. L. Bredemeir. (1995) *Character Development and Physical Activity.* Champaign, IL: Human Kinetics.

PHYSICAL EDUCATION

Young women perform an exercise to improve the flexibility of the spine during training at the Bergman Osterberg Physical Training College in England. (Hulton-Deutsch Collection/Corbis)

Scholars seldom discuss the fact that physical education and sports represent two very different approaches to what some academics now refer to as "kinesiology," the study of movement. The two approaches differ in such fundamental ways that one can see them almost as opposites. Sports and physical education are often discussed together in British and American books, while French and German publications refer to "éducation physique et sport" and to "Leibesübungen" (physical exercises) or "Körperkultur" (body culture), categories that include all kind of issues such as posture, deportment, and even grooming.

With the exception of ancient Sparta, where girls as well as boys were trained for eugenic purposes so that they might bear healthy sons to fight in their city's incessant wars, physical education is a modern phenomenon. It began in Germany at approximately the same time that modern sports were born in England. While the focus of physical education was on health, the emphasis of sports was on physical prowess and athletic skills, especially those demonstrated in competition.

These differences created extreme tensions in some countries. In the Netherlands, situated between Germany and England, there was a long cultural conflict that Dutch sociologists refer to as "strijd over sport" (strife over sports). Nineteenth-century and early-twentieth-century Dutch schoolteachers looked to Germany and made noncompetitive German gymnastics the core of Dutch physical education. Their pupils, however, looked to England. As soon as they were released from their gymnastics classes, schoolboys rushed to play soccer (association football) and other modern sports. The conflict between gymnastics and sports occurred everywhere, first in Europe, North America, Australia, and New Zealand, then in South America, Asia, and Africa. Everywhere, the conflict was eventually resolved in favor of sports. This triumph of sports over physical education occurred sooner for boys and young men than for girls and young women, but there is no doubt that schools everywhere are now much more likely to emphasize sports rather than calisthenics and drills. This is true even in Islamic countries, where girls' physical education classes are safely shielded from male eyes.

Modern physical education can be traced back to a group of German pedagogues known as the

PHYSICAL EDUCATION IN THE 18TH CENTURY

Two French women contributed to the development of physical education for girls as early as the eighteenth century. Stéphanie-Félicité du Crest, la Comtesse de Genlis (1746-1831), was governess to the children of the powerful Duc d' Orléans and instructed Louis-Philippe, the future King. Her most famous work was *Adéle et Théodore*, published in 1782. The book contains numerous recommendations concerning the health of children and is loosely based upon ideas of Rousseau, Locke, and other contemporary as well as classical sources. It enjoyed a great success for many years in several countries. The wide variety of exercises which the Comtesse provided for her large retinue of children is best described in the *Leçons d'une gouvernante à ses élèves* (1791).

She did not intend, however, that physical education should be only for the rich and well-born. In her *Discours sur l'éducation du peuple* (1791) Mme. de Genlis insisted that all children will benefit from physical education and that gymnastics must be restored to the curriculum in the public schools. She also insisted that physical education must be made an important part of the education of the girls and recommended for them many of the exercises which she suggested for boys.

Another teacher, Jeanne-Louise-Henriette Genêt Campan (1752-1822), received a good education thanks to a father who was convinced that his large family should have such opportunities. She served as teacher to the three daughters of Louis XV and became a close friend of Marie Antoinette. During the Revolution Mme. Campan retired to the country and, finding herself burdened with debts incurred by her husband, founded a boarding school. This establishment at Saint German soon attracted the daughters of important French and foreign families. The curriculum included games and physical exercises, music, and dancing. Mme. Campan's reputation as a teacher became so substantial that Napoleon named her the directress of the school at Ecouen which he established in 1808 for daughters of members of the Legion of Honor.

Philanthropen (lovers of humankind). In the late eighteenth century, these men—the best known of them was Johann Christian Friedrich Guts-Muths—founded a number of schools where they paid serious and systematic attention to the bodies as well as the minds of the sons of the upper and middle classes. In addition to Greek and Latin, and geometry and algebra, the boys were taught to swim, climb ropes, vault over brooks, run, jump, lift, throw, swing, and clamber. Their progress was carefully measured, and the measurements were carefully recorded. The system practiced at Schnepfenthal and other schools was described in a number of books by Guts-Muths and his colleagues.

A generation later, another schoolmaster, Friedrich Ludwig Jahn, took his pupils (all male) to the suburbs of Berlin and constructed a Turnplatz, that is, a place to do gymnastic exercises. Jahn's exercises, which were accompanied by a good deal of nationalistic rhetoric, became widely popular in gymnastic clubs that sprang up all over Germany. Led principally but not exclusively by Adolf Spiess, German educators transformed Jahn's boisterous open-air activities into an indoor routine closely akin to military drill. Spiess published a widely used instructional manual in which he described and categorized all the imaginable ways to march, hang from a bar, move one's arms, bend from the waist, and otherwise exercise the body. Three pages of his two-volume work were devoted to games for children. The purpose of this curriculum was clearly to promote the pupils' health and not to indulge them in the joys of physical play.

As early as 1826, one year after Karl Beck had introduced Turnen to the boys at the Round Hill School in Northampton, Massachusetts, there were efforts to extend the healthful benefits of gymnastic exercises to girls and women. W. B. Fowle, a Boston teacher, tried to adapt German gymnastics for females. He failed to attract enough women and girls to make a go of it, but

German reformers were more successful. In 1829, the Swiss Phokian Clias published *Kalisthenie*, the source of our modern term "calisthenics" (from the Greek for beauty and strength). Although Clias favored moderate exercise to improve a girl's health, he rejected ballgames because they were allegedly too great a strain on a girl's shoulder and breast muscles. Five years later, in *Gymnastik für die weibliche Jugend* (Gymnastics for Young Females), Johann Adolf Ludwig Werner suggested that schoolgirls be allowed to swim, throw light objects, jump, balance on wooden beams, and clamber up poles. His concern was for health and hygiene and he warned against overexertion, which was thought to be a dangerous consequence of female athletic competition.

Within a generation, the German conception of physical education was exported to the rest of Europe. The Czechs were especially enthusiastic and their club-based gymnastics movement, known as *Sokol* (Falcon), was a mainstay of Czech nationalist resistance to Austrian rule. Gymnastics, without the nationalistic rhetoric, became a part of the educational curriculum for girls as well as boys. At a much slower pace, gymnastic systems on the Czech or German model spread through the primary and secondary schools of Poland, Hungary, and—somewhat later—the other nations of Eastern Europe. In the schools, as opposed to the clubs, the rationale for gymnastics and calisthenics was always the same: health and hygiene for boys and girls (with an eye, of course, to their future roles as soldiers and mothers).

After the failed Revolution of 1848, hundreds of thousands of middle-class Germans emigrated to the New World. Among them were numerous *Turner* who introduced German gymnastics from Cincinnati and Chicago to Buenos Aires and Santiago de Chile. Their influence on physical education in both North and South America was incalculable.

Meanwhile, in Sweden, Per Henrik Ling, another man influenced by GutsMuths, created a rival system of gymnastic exercises, which was generally assumed to be especially appropriate for females. From the Central Institute that Ling established in Stockholm in 1814, teachers like Martina Bergman-Österberg set forth to convert the world to Lingian or Swedish (as it was frequently called) gymnastics. Scandinavia was fertile ground for the propagation of Ling's system, which was soon dominant in the schools of Denmark and Norway as well as Sweden. In 1881, Bergman-Österberg became superintendent of physical education in London's public schools. At the Physical Training College that she established in Hampstead four years later, she trained an entire generation of women whose influence on British physical education—for women—was immense.

As early as 1861, when he opened the Boston Normal Institute for Physical Education, Dioclesian Lewis preached the doctrine of physical education for girls and women. When Vassar College

MARY HEMENWAY

Mary Hemenway was an early and important supporter of physical education for girls in the United States. Usually labeled a philanthropist, she was also an educational reformer who pushed for education for women; physical education; courses in American history, home economics, and industrial education; and interdisciplinary teaching. Some experts believe that several of her ideas continue to inform educational reform in Massachusetts. Hemenway was born in 20 December 1820 in New York City, the daughter and youngest child of Thomas Tileston, an innovative and wealthy ship-builder. In 1840 she moved to Boston and married Augustus Hemenway, who like her father, was a wealthy business man with an interest in new business ventures and opportunities. The couple had four children and following her husband's death in 1876, Hemenway devoted the remaining 22 years of her life to philanthropic activities that promoted education for young men and women. She continued, nonetheless, to see women's role as primarily in the home and neither worked for nor against suffrage.

in New York State opened in 1865, Delia Woods introduced his system to the students in the college's Calisthenium. Similar programs of physical education were established at the American women's colleges of the Northeast and at state universities everywhere.

In 1889, Amy Morris Homans and Mary Hemenway founded the Boston Normal School for Gymnastics and hired Nils Posse to drill young women in the Swedish manner. This institute, which offered a two-year course in physical education, trained the women who eventually controlled women's physical education throughout the United States. In 1913 the school became a part of Wellesley College, but it continued to be extremely influential.

A year after the founding of the Boston Normal School for Gymnastics, the Boston School Board voted to adopt the Swedish system. In the long run, however, Lingian gymnastics had less success in the United States than in England because German immigrants to the Americas were avid, persuasive, and numerous proponents of *Schulturnen* ("school gymnastics").

Late in the Meiji period (1868–1911), Ling's influence was felt even in distant Japan, where his "scientific" gymnastics were thought to be especially suitable for schoolgirls. (The boys were allowed the pleasures of baseball.)

In France, a Frenchman of Spanish origins, Francisco Amoros, propagated still another gymnastics system. Throughout the century, in Europe, in the Americas, and even in Japan, there were fierce controversies among the followers of Jahn, Ling, Amoros, and others, but they all agreed—more or less—that systematic noncompetitive exercises, commonly performed by groups under the strict control of a single instructor, were the right answer to the physical dysfunctions of modernity. And they all agreed—more or less—that sports were definitely not the answer. For the true believer in physical education, sports for boys were almost as objectionable as sports for girls.

One problem with sports was that they could be positively unhealthy. It was all too easy to construct a catalog of sports-related injuries. Physical educators like Amherst's Edward Hitchcock, Harvard's Dudley Allen Sargeant, and Vassar's Alida Avery were all medical doctors. Their European colleagues—Germany's Alice Profé, for instance—were also likely to be trained physicians whose focus was on physiological principles applied to health.

Despite the fitness-and-health focus of physical education professionals, the passion for modern sports eventually overwhelmed the highminded commitment to German or Swedish gymnastics. This occurred even in Germany, the bastion of scientific physical education. In other words, the boys and girls won the battle with their teachers.

In England, it was hardly a contest. Early in the nineteenth century, British schoolmasters like Thomas Arnold of Rugby recognized that modern sports were a way to organize and discipline what had been the unruly and barbaric pastimes of English schoolboys. By the end of the century, it was an article of faith that the Battle of Waterloo had been won on the playing fields of Eton. The popularity of cricket was thought to be proof positive

STEREOTYPES ABOUT PHYSICAL EDUCATION TEACHERS

Both scholarly research and portrayals in mass media indicate that women physical educators in the United States are stereotyped as being masculine, physically fit and active, interested in sports, lesbian, aggressive, unattractive, and less intelligent that other educators. A survey of physical educators conducted by Mary B. Harris and Joy Griffin of the University of New Mexico in 1995 indicates that women physical educators agree with some and disagree with others of these stereotypes. They believe, like the general public, that women physical educators are more active and interested in sports, are more aggressive than other women, and are less intelligent than other educators. But they do not agree with the stereotypes that they are masculine, unattractive, or lesbian.

that the English were the most civilized people on earth, devoted to fair play, good sportsmanship, and the burdens of empire. Unlike their continental counterparts, English physical educators were convinced that there was no logical contradiction between competition and cooperation, no conflict between individualism and teamwork. By and large, physical educators working in the rest of the English-speaking world agreed.

Despite the craze for sports that swept through nineteenth-century Rugby, Eton, Harrow, Winchester, and the other schools for privileged British boys, there was considerable hesitation among female physical educators. Were the manly virtues inculcated by team sports appropriate for young women? Among the "foremothers" of English higher education for women was Dorothea Beale, principal of Cheltenham Ladies College from 1858 to 1906. Beale required calisthenics and introduced Swedish gymnastics in 1890, but she was typical of her generation in that she steadfastly opposed ballgames because she disliked competition in any form. It is doubtful that she understood what sports are all about. When she observed a game of field hockey, she was upset. "The children will hurt themselves," she said, "if they all run about after one ball. Get some more balls at once." Pressure from the students and from the younger teachers eventually caused Beale to compromise. At the time of her death, Cheltenham had twenty-six tennis courts and facilities for fencing, riding, and swimming. Beale was never wholly reconciled to this. "I am most anxious," she wrote, "that girls should not overexert themselves, or become absorbed in athletic rivalries, and therefore we do not play against other schools."

The first women's colleges at Cambridge were founded in 1869 and Oxford followed in 1879. There was no effort to impose a system of physical education upon the students. They were free to establish sports clubs, which they did almost from the day of their matriculation. In the United States, it was a different story. Vassar College's first annual catalog announced to prospective students that a "suitable portion of each day is set aside for physical exercise and every young lady is required to observe it as one of her college duties."

Since the catalog mentioned not only calisthenics but also riding, boating, swimming, skating, and gardening, it seems that someone at the school realized that hanging from a bar or swinging an Indian club is not as much fun as Guts-Muths and Ling thought it was. While Woods stressed disciplined exercises in her classes in the Calisthenium, the students organized a pair of baseball teams. When Smith College opened its doors, a decade after Vassar, there was the same progression from calisthenics to sports. The earliest catalogs noted that regular gymnastic exercises were prescribed under the direction of an educated lady instructor.

Like Vassar, Smith initially relied on teachers trained by Dioclesian Lewis. An alumna, Edith Naomi Hill, looked back on the dreary regimen. The students, she wrote, "in their twilled flannel with long drawers, their ankle-length skirts and high collars," exercised "to slow music with dumbbells and Indian clubs, wands and chest weights." Like their sisters at Vassar, the Smithies were eager to finish their exercises and get on with the ballgame. In the spring of 1878, Minnie Stephens and her friends began to play baseball on the lawn in front of Hubbard House. The college promptly banned baseball, but the sport was revived fourteen years later. At approximately the same time, Senda Berenson made the newly invented game of basketball the center of her physical education program.

At Wellesley College, the transition from calisthenics to sports was very slow. The catalog for 1876–1877 boasted of a large gymnasium "where the students are instructed in Calisthenics." The faculty disapproved of intramural sports and adamantly opposed intercollegiate athletics. The students, however, expressed a strong preference for the challenges of competition. The faculty relented and introduced basketball in 1898. Not until 1906, however, did Wellesley require sports within its physical education program. (Smith waited until 1925.)

In her *History of Physical Education in Colleges for Women* (1930), Dorothy S. Ainsworth asserted flatly that the students preferred calisthenics to sports. There is little doubt that Ainsworth preferred exercise programs to sports contests, but she was wrong about the students. They agitated for sports. In the 1920s and 1930s, Mabel Lee and other prominent female physical educators gradually surrendered ground and substituted intramural sports contests for the dreary repetitions of the calisthenics class.

At the very time that Lee and others shifted their emphasis from calisthenics to sports, between the two world wars, Italian, German, and Japanese physical educators devised programs that stressed fitness and health. In the schools (and in the out-of-school programs) of these fascist regimes, male bodies were hardened in preparation for the rigors of war while female bodies were strengthened in preparation for the ordeal of (repeated) childbirth. Sports were a part of the physical education curriculum, just as they were a part of Italy's *Opera Nazionale Dopolavoro* (National After-Work Organization) and the *Bund Deutscher Mädel* (Association of German Girls), but sports were never an end in themselves. They were always, as German physical educators stressed, part of *"politische Leibeserziehung"* (political physical education).

In the postwar reconstruction of these societies, programs of physical education became increasingly similar to those in the United States. In a linguistic shift that would have horrified Adolf Spiess, German schools now have *Sportunterricht* (instruction in sports) rather than *Turnenstunden* (gymnastics classes). The Italians, too, are increasingly likely to refer to *Sport* rather than *educazione fisica*. Even the Japanese have begun to speak of *spôtsu* instead of *taiiku* (physical education). Fitness and health are still listed as justifications for the expenditure of time and money in scholastic and collegiate physical education programs, but students and teachers know that fun is now the name of the game. Ironically, calisthenics—in the form of aerobics and other exercise programs—has moved out of the classrooms that were once its natural habitat. The drills that Ling and Spiess and their followers once imposed on the world's reluctant schoolchildren are now the self-induced routines of men and women working out in fitness studios or before the TV set.

Allen Guttmann

See also Ling Gymnastics; Sokol Movement

Bibliography

Ainsworth, Dorothy S. (1930) *The History of Physical Education in Colleges for Women.* New York: A. S. Barnes.

Bernett, Hajo, ed. (1966) *Nationalsozialistische Leibeserziehung.* Schorndorf, Germany: Karl Hofmann.

Blecking, Diethelm, ed. (1991) *Die Siawische Sokolbewegung.* Dortmund, Germany: Forschungsstelle Ostmitteleuropa.

Bulger, Margaret A. (1981) "American Sportswomen in the Nineteenth Century." *Journal of Popular Culture* 16, 2: 1–16.

Fletcher, Sheila. (1984) *Women First: The Female Tradition in English Physical Education, 1880–1980.* Bristol, U.K.: Athlone Press.

Frasca, Rosella Isidori. (1983) *E il Duce le volla Sportive.* Bologna: Patron Editore.

Gerber, Ellen W. (1971) *Innovators and Institutions in Physical Education.* Philadelphia: Lea & Febiger.

Gori, Giliola. (1996) *L'Atleta e Ia Nazione.* Rimini: Panozzo Editore.

Guttmann, Allen. (1991) *Women's Sports.* New York: Columbia University Press.

Irie, Katsumi. (1986) *Nihon Fashizumu to no Taiiku Shisô.* [History of Japanese Fascism and Physical Education] Tokyo: Fumaidô.

Kamm, Josephine. (1958) *How Different from Us.* London: Bodley Head.

Kleindienst-Cachay, Christa. (1980) *Die Verschulung des Turnens.* Schorndorf, Germany: Karl Hofmann.

Krüger, Michael. (1993) *Einführung in die Geschichte der Leibeserziehung und des Sports,* Parts 2 and 3. Schorndorf, Germany: Karl Hofmann.

McCrone, Kathleen E. (1988) *Playing the Game.* Lexington: University Press of Kentucky.

Marks, Jeannette A. (1898) "Outdoor Life at Wellesley College." *Outing* 32 (May): 117–124.

Peiffer, Lorenz. (1987) *Turnunterricht im Dritten Reich.* Cologne, Germany: Pahl-Rugenstein.

Pfister, Gertrud. (1983) *Geschlechtsspezifische Sozialisation und Koedukation im Sport.* Berlin: Bartels & Wernitz.

Roden, David. (1980). *Schooldays in Imperial Japan.* Berkeley: University of California Press.

Stell, Marion K. (1991) *Half the Race: A History of Australian Women in Sport.* Sydney: Angus & Robertson.

Stokvis, Ruud. (1979) *Strijd over Sport.* Deventer, Netherlands: Van Loghum Slaterus.

Thibault, Jacques. (1977) *Les Aventures des Corps dans la Pédagogie Française.* Paris: Vrin.

———. (1979) *Sports et Éducation Physique 1870–1970,* 2d ed. Paris: Vrin.

Van Dalen, Deobolf, and Bruce L. Bennett. (1971) *A World History of Physical Education,* 2d ed. Englewood Cliffs, NJ: Prentice-Hall.

Verbrugge, Martha H. (1988) *Able-Bodied Womanhood.* New York: Oxford University Press.

PING PONG *see* Table Tennis

POLAND

The Republic of Poland is in north central Europe and has a population of 38 million. The history of the modern Polish state and the development of modern sports in Poland virtually begin with the founding of the second Polish Republic in 1919. Until that year the Polish nation was split among the then-powerful states of Germany, Austria-Hungary, and Russia. Each section participated in the process of social and political modernization in its own way and established physical education and sports on different terms. Women's participation in sport was limited during this era, although in some large cities women took part in sport clubs. Women's participation increased later in the twentieth century.

Cultural autonomy was the most advanced in Galicia, which was part of the Austrian section of Poland. Here, as early as 1867, a district school council was established under Polish administration. In the same year the first Polish gymnastics club was also formed in eastern Galicia, in the town of Lvóv (Lemberg). Under the name Sokol (falcon), new sport clubs were also founded after 1884 in the Prussian section, which was economically and socially the most advanced part of Poland. In the Russian section, the Russian administration suppressed efforts to create cultural autonomy by the Poles.

The nationalistic Sokol gymnastic clubs offered almost no room for female involvement. This was not exclusively due to the clubs' repressive legislation that, for example, long prohibited women from being members of Prussian political clubs. Another important reason was that Polish Catholic agrarian society, with its own concept of women's roles and behavior, could not accept the image of women performing gymnastics. Nevertheless, in Warsaw, Kraków, Poznan, and Lódz—the larger cities of divided Poland, where women were more active outside the home—sport clubs were established in the nineteenth century; the Warsaw rowing club was one example.

The situation changed drastically in the second republic, between the world wars; women became heavily involved in most of the newly established sport clubs as Polish sports became organized. A National Olympic Committee (NOC) was formed and sport associations were established across the country. On 28 February 1925 an organizational committee of all the Polish women's sport associations (Komitet Organizacyjny Polskiego Zwizku Sportowego Kobiet) was founded. The committee's main purpose was to act on behalf of the women and their national and international activities. For practical reasons the committee soon merged with the Polish track and field athletics association and formed their own women's board. On the one hand, this merger shows the importance of track and field for Polish women's sport. On the other hand, the action illustrated the difficulty of establishing independent representation for women.

At the end of the 1920s, there was one last attempt (which was unsuccessful) to provide representation for women by creating a general information and communication committee of women (Międzyzwiązkowe Komitet Porozumiewawczy Paň). But the track and field athletics clubs did not agree with that concept. Nevertheless, women's departments existed on the level of sport administration and in several sport associations.

Under government auspices, two congresses took place to discuss the problems of women's sports, one in 1928 and the other in 1934. The sport magazine *Start* was dedicated to the issue of women's sports between 1927 and 1936. At that time Polish women began to compete in international championships. In Budapest in 1934 the Polish team won third place at the world gymnastics championships and was also successful at the world championship in Prague four years later.

Track and field athletes were even more successful. The first Polish women's championships had taken place as early as 1922, and emphasis on the sport produced women athletes who could compete on the international level (for example, Halina Konopacka and Stanisława Walasiewicz). Konopacka won the first Olympic gold medal for Poland with the discus at the 1928 Olympic Games in Amsterdam. The 100-meter sprinter Walasiewicz (who later lived in the United States but competed for Poland under the name Stella Walsh) did even better. In 1932 and in 1936 she won the gold and silver medal, first in Los Angeles and then in Berlin, and over the course of her career she set ten world records and eight European records. Between the wars, Polish women also met international success in rowing, archery, ice skating, figure skating, and skiing.

Germany's occupation of Poland from 1939 to 1945 was a catastrophe not only for the Polish state but also for its society and culture. Over 5 million Poles were killed, and the survivors faced massive destruction of the country's infrastructure, including 50 percent of its sport facilities. But as early as November 1945 the first delegates' meeting of the Polish athletics association took place. Sports continued to be valued and were revived with the Polish "Dream Team," which won seventeen Olympic medals from 1956 to 1966. The team consisted of males and females, and it was an indication of the importance placed on women's sports in Poland.

At the Olympic Games in Melbourne in 1956, Elzbieta Krzesińska won the first postwar Olympic medal—a gold medal in broad jump—and she broke her own world record in the process. In 1960 she took a silver in the event. In Tokyo in 1964, Irena Szewińska (Kirszenstein) emerged as Poland's best athlete, one who was to influence the future of sports in Poland. She won the gold medal in the 4 × 400–meter relay and silver in the 200-meter sprint and the broad jump. In Mexico City four years later she won a gold medal in the 200-meter sprint and also a bronze medal in the 100-meter sprint. At the Olympic Games in Munich in 1972, Szewińska won only the bronze medal for the 200-meter sprint, but in Montreal four years later she triumphed again and won the gold medal in the 400-meter run. With seven Olympic medals, ten European championship medals, and ten world records, Irena Szewińska had become the most successful Polish athlete in history.

At the end of the 1970s, economic and political crises disrupted life in Poland and had a negative impact on sport participation at the international level. The era of success for Polish women in track and field ended, although some women still competed with excellent results. Wanda Panfil-Gonzales won the 1991 world championship marathon, and women continued to excel in archery and the modern pentathlon. In the 1990s, the future of women's sport in Poland again rested with Szewińska, who had become the president of the Polish Women's Sport Association (Stowarzyszenia Sportu Kobiet), the Polish Athletics Association, and the vice president of the National Olym-

pic Committee. In 1998 she was elected to the International Olympic Committee, where she is expected to not only represent Poland's interests but to help promote women's sports.

Diethelm Blecking

See also Sokol Gymnastics; Szewinska, Irena Kirszenstein; Walsh, Stella

Bibliography

Chmielewski, Zbigniew. (1998) "Rozmowa z Ireną Szewińska." (Talking with Ireną Szewinska).

Rotkiewicz, Maria. (1979) "Rozwój sportu kobiet w Polsce okresu międzywojennego." (The development of women's sports in Poland between the wars). In *Sport Wyczynowy* 3–4, 7: 3–21.

Woltmann, Bernard, ed. (1994) *Lekkoatletyka w Polsce, 1919–1994.* (Track and field in Poland). Warsaw: Polskie Towarzystwo Naukowe Kultury Fizycznej.

Woltmann, Bernard, and Jerzy Gaj. (1997) *Sport w Polsce, 1919–1939.* (Sport in Poland). Gorzów Wlkp: Polskie Towarzystwo Naukowe Kultury Fizycznej.

POLITICS

The link between sports, politics, and gender is strong, long-standing, and complex. Sports and sport training, throughout much of human history, have been the training ground for the men who held political control. These same men have used sports as a force to unify societies—witness the intense national loyalty that is the essence of the Olympic Games.

At the same time, most societies excluded women from sports and from participation in the political process. In the twentieth century, women's struggle for political power has run parallel to their growing involvement—also frequently a struggle—in physical activity and sports. Now more empowered in both arenas, women nevertheless face many questions about how to proceed and what the future might bring.

Throughout human existence, the ways that men and women have participated in the athletic cultures of their societies have been correlated with definitions of enfranchisement and citizenship.

There has been a correlation between this participation and the relative power of men and women in the political institutions of their societies. In general, historical, anthropological, and archeological evidence all yield the conclusion that where one sex dominates in sports, it will also dominate in politics and the exercise of brute force. Sports are physical rituals that rehearse and celebrate the actual skills and actions of domination in societies where exercising force and waging war are central values. Whether we speak of the religious court ball games of pre-Columbian Mesoamerica, of the Olympics of ancient Greece, or of the global football networks of the late twentieth century, sports codify and transmit the fundamental values, roles, and relationships of their cultures.

FROM ANTIQUITY TO THE EIGHTEENTH CENTURY

For 99 percent of the time in which *Homo sapiens* has existed, humans lived in stateless societies. They dwelt in small, self-regulating groups with complementary social divisions of labor based on age and gender. Within these groups were smaller groups that made decisions, but these people lacked the material structures—treasuries, armies, police, courts, ministries, and estates—that characterize a mature state. About 10,000 years ago, the development of horticulture and agriculture created the possibility of producing a relative abundance of food. This in turn brought about major change in the specialization of labor and technology, and eventually it led to new social structure and organization. Ancient city-states, supported by surrounding farms, grouped artisans, merchants, and laborers in urban settlements that were ruled by powerful land-owning families, a priesthood, and a public administration.

Some cultures may have reached this stage of development without more or less constant warfare. But the ones that eventually gave rise to the modern world came largely from warlike civilizations that relied on their armed forces and coercive capacities to reach the height of their political formation. These were the patriarchal civilizations of ancient Mesopotamia, Greece, Rome, India, and China. These societies were internally stratified along the lines of class, caste, and gender. They valued the arts and spirit of the warrior, and their sports expressed this value.

Foot races, javelin throws, wrestling, sword fighting, horsemanship, and chariot racing—classical Greek and Roman events—all directly enacted the arts of war and conferred status on those men who were skilled in these arts. The martial cultures of groups such as the Japanese samurai—with their focus on archery and swordplay—developed in response to similar conditions.

Men's specialization in matters of force and coercion led directly to their monopoly of political power. Evidence from every continent shows that many individual women have been warriors, commanders, and regents, and even that women banded together as warriors in Asia Minor and Africa. Among the ancient Greeks, whose athletic culture was, on the whole, fiercely sex-segregated (with women in subordinate positions), in one city-state (Sparta) young women participated in a variety of sports and were politically influential. This evidence shows clearly that women can be aggressive and violent when their societies value these forms of behavior or when invasion or attack force them into these roles. There is also evidence of individual women or groups of privileged women participating in sports, but nowhere, until modern times, did women's sport participation approach that of men. The example of ancient Sparta, where young women did participate in a variety of sports, suggests that there may not have been the correlation between political and athletic participation that seems to be the case in modern times as well as in most ancient societies.

The feudal epoch in Europe—the time from which most contemporary sports evolved—witnessed many variations on the "monarch–landed liege lord" state. In medieval times, the state was barely more than a tribal council for the allocation of land and power, but by the sixteenth century a few monarchical states developed large armies and centralized administrative structures.

In medieval and early modern times, sports were games and contests, differentiated by class and gender. The male aristocracy engaged in jousting and hunting—activities related to combat and land ownership. Other activities, such as the precursors to modern tennis and golf, evolved as pleasurable physical activities requiring considerable leisure and a good deal of space. The emergent middle classes of European cities turned to archery and eventually to marksmanship with firearms. These classes organized themselves into guilds from which women were usually, but not invariably, excluded. The men and women of the popular classes played communal games, especially folk football, which were rowdy and often violent (women also participated actively in the stickball games of the North American Indians).

The aristocracy and landed gentry sometimes attended popular events, making these occasions moments of political bonding. Some scholars suggest that while women's games were not recorded and not celebrated in public ways, women of all classes took up on their own the games played by their men. This may be true, but because so few records exist of such women's activities, the true nature and extent of their involvement in their own or mixed athletics is not known. Queens such as Elizabeth I of England were known sportswomen, and aristocratic women rode and took an enthusiastic part in court where permitted. Yet organized games, which formed the basis of spectacle and celebration, were ordinarily reserved for males and transformed into ritual the actions and ideal qualities of the masculine role for each class.

WOMEN, SPORTS, AND POLITICS 1800–1980

The growth of mercantilism and small-scale manufacturing during the sixteenth, seventeenth, and eighteenth centuries eventually transformed a layer of feudal artisans and merchants into the haute bourgeoisie. They became the great venture capitalists and manufacturers of the nineteenth century whose economic initiatives fueled the Industrial Revolution, financed the growth of the nation state, and supported the colonial policies of the European powers. When a series of bourgeois political revolutions from the late eighteenth to the mid-nineteenth centuries in Europe and North America brought liberal-democratic governments into existence, certain freedoms—of religion, expression, association, and suffrage—were decreed to be the inalienable rights of man. What they were, in fact, were the rights necessary to form political parties and other influential organizations, which were needed by the industrially based middle classes to debate and decide issues of state formation and public policy. On the eve of the twentieth century, however, full political rights had still not been accorded to women.

Industrialization produced liberal democracy and what historians have called a "separate spheres" gender order. In this order, men were expected to be public actors while women were expected to provide personal and social services within the private, domestic realm. Nineteenth-century European and American ideals of womanly virtues (female chastity), family arrangements (the family wage system), economic enterprise (laissez-faire capitalism), and state formation (the limited state) all expressed this ideology. Although women's sports became common in the upper and middle classes, sports continued to be seen mainly as an agent to enhance virility, something that would equip men to be political and military actors.

The separate-spheres ideology proclaimed that the "essential" differences between men and women limited women's physical activity and their involvement in sports, just as they established women's unsuitability for politics. Medical science promoted the notion that women needed to reserve all their energy for menstruation, pregnancy, and lactation. Mental, physical, and sexual activities were thought, in this context, to weaken women's maternal capacities, sacrifice their femininity, and hence, in the rhetoric of late-nineteenth-century eugenics, to lead to "race suicide"—in which the white middle classes were overwhelmed by lower-class foreigners or by those with darker skins.

But views about the innate weakness and inferiority of women's bodies and minds clashed with women's subjective experiences and with their own aspirations to liberty, equality, and fraternity—ideals that were articulated in the liberal-democratic and social-democratic rhetoric of the times. Accordingly, women began the first stage of an extended struggle to end their exclusion from political institutions and public authority. As part of the first wave of feminism (roughly 1850–1925), upper- and middle-class women demanded suffrage as an elementary right of political enfranchisement. Women organized and fought for entry into institutions from which they had been excluded: schools and universities, the legal and medical professions, and public administration.

At the same time, feminist leaders adamantly rejected the views of male authorities on women's ability to participate in physical activities and sports. Arguing that vigorous physical activity produced strong, healthy women as well as men, these reformers advanced views about women's physicality that were radical by the standards of their day. Concurrently, some women's athletic leaders raised questions about the apparently antisocial values of men's sports and cautioned against women adopting such values. From the late 1880s through the 1920s, a significant wave of athletic as well as political emancipation washed over society as women increasingly took part in physical leisure activities and sports in North America and Europe. Numerous women's sporting associations were created, most of them led by women and independent of men's organizations. Sport-based physical education was established as part of upper-class girls' education, and middle- and working-class women played baseball and basketball. Thanks to Japanese modernizers and to YMCA and YWCA workers in China and the Philippines, there were efforts to involve Asian girls and young women in calisthenics and sports.

Although women's participation in all sports by the start of the twentieth century effectively eliminated the evidence supporting the ideology of women's weakness, this ideology remained remarkably tenacious within men's sport organizations and the mass media. This tenacity attested to a resistance on the part of many men to sharing with women the associations, experiences, spectacles, mythology, and status of sports. As Jennifer Hargreaves has noted, in the Victorian period the physical body was a fundamental symbol of power relations for men and women. The sports that developed in the male-exclusive schools, regiments, and private clubs transformed folk football into soccer, rugby, American football, and Australian rules football; sports also rehabilitated pugilism, revived Greek athletics, and helped to make legitimate and to celebrate men's powerful, aggressive, athletic bodies. Modern sports were supported through public facility subsidies at city, regional, and national levels and were integrated into public educational and recreational systems. Although some men were enthusiastic proponents of women's physical education and sports, the growth of men's sport may be said to constitute an unnamed men's movement that regrouped men along gender lines and acted as a repository for antifeminist beliefs and sentiment.

The granting of the vote to women in the 1920s in the United States and England followed seventy years of organizing by women, of changing roles and ideas of gender, and of transforming ideas of the role of government and the state. The twentieth century has witnessed the rise and fall of many different forms of government—provisional revolutionary states, totalitarian dictatorships, bureaucratic command economies, and parliamentary democracies. All the types of governments have attempted to mobilize sports to promote their particular projects and interests. Indeed, one dramatic feature of twentieth-century culture has been the growing identification among class, racial, municipal, and national groupings with team sports and Olympic athletes. The Olympic stage was thoroughly politicized, ranging from the socialist and workers' Olympics in the 1920s and 1930s, to the 1936 Nazi Olympics in Berlin, to the cold war Olympics (mostly be-

WARTIME FITNESS

Physical fitness campaigns—for both men and women—are often initiated in nations during times of war. The underlying idea is that physically fit men will make better soldiers and physically fit women will be able to better support the war effort at home. In response to the threat of fascism in Italy and Nazism in Germany, Great Brit-

ain began a National Fitness Campaign in 1937. In a report, the Chief Medical Officer of Health wrote that "'Keep Fit' classes are multiplying, and girls and women are showing themselves to be as enthusiastic as their brothers and husbands for open-air games and pastimes, where the opportunity is given to them to take part."

Skiers carry their nation's flags as they ski downhill during the opening ceremony for the 1992 World Cup Freestyle Event in Colorado. (Bob Winsett/Corbis)

tween the United States and the Soviet Union) from the late 1940s to the late 1980s. The football (soccer) mania of such countries as Brazil, Zambia, and the United Kingdom has long been highly politicized and has often spilled over into real violence. In the 1950s and 1960s, athletes such as Jackie Robinson and Mohammed Ali used their athletic success to support the civil rights movement in the United States.

In addition, the sites of professional men's sports have been used for political and military projects. In 1973, when General Augusto Pinochet overthrew the democratically elected regime of Salvador Allende in Chile, thousands of political prisoners were held and tortured in the football stadium in Santiago. In 1991, U.S. President George Bush used the NFL Super Bowl to mount support for war in the Persian Gulf.

From the 1950s to the 1980s, during a long wave of economic expansion and prosperity in North America, Europe, and the capitalist economies of East Asia, an ideal of a government that

represents all members of society shaped the development of the industrialized nation states. This form of government and state formation concerned itself with public welfare and not simply the collection of taxes, the building of an infrastructure for business, and the exercise of force. This idea of the state as an enlightened and egalitarian public authority was linked to the political activation of working people in liberal, social democratic, and Communist parties. It was also linked to the integration of large numbers of women into the paid work force in the service sectors (teaching, nursing, clerical work), into civic and national politics, and into the apparatus of the state; and to the sustained political activity of disadvantaged minority groups.

Accompanying this ideal of state formation came a larger rhetoric of equal opportunity and a recognition that the system contained barriers to particular disadvantaged groups. In addition, there was a new wave of feminism that targeted the activation of girls and women in sports as an important goal to be supported by political and state initiatives.

WOMEN, SPORTS, AND NEOLIBERAL POLITICS SINCE 1980

With the end of postwar expansion, and the start of a long period of recession, the industrialized world entered a new political period in the 1980s—a period of transnational corporate globalization. Throughout the industrialized world, conservative political parties undertook to implement particular domestic and international fiscal policies that would reshape the structures of the nation-state in accordance with the precepts of neoliberal economics. This reshaping included divesting and privatizing public resources, enterprises, and services; expanding the coercive apparatus of the state (prisons, police, military); and restricting representative forums (through private corporate concentration of the mass media). The third piece of the reshaping was the state's divesting of key regulatory functions and service apparatus that are directly and indirectly involved with restrictions on the flow of private capital (including labor standards and employment, environmental protection, health service provision, and public education).

These policies have had two major effects on an international scale, noted alike by scholars and international organizations such as the United Nations. First, they have brought about a transfer of wealth from the less affluent to the more affluent, thus increasing economic disparities and concentrating global wealth into ever fewer hands. Second, they have eroded those powers of the nation-state that allow it to regulate private capital. Hence these policies have undermined the ability of the nation-state to act on behalf of the majority of its citizens, undermined its democratic features, and reversed the dominant trend in postwar state formation.

In the political discourse of neoliberalism, the market is seen as the effective arbiter of economic prosperity to which restrictive governments and states must give way. Being competitive in this market has been presented as the most important precondition for an individual, group, or society's economic viability. Elite and professional men's sports—the dominant sports today—play an unparalleled role in modeling and celebrating such competitiveness in contemporary culture. They are crucial sites for the ritual confirmation and spectacular celebration of the ideology of winners and losers. (As one chief executive officer of Xerox said at the time of the 1996 Atlanta Summer Olympics, "The ideals associated with the Olympics—world class competitiveness and the tireless pursuit of excellence—are parallel to the ideals we have established at Xerox.") Indeed, Olympic sport has joined with other professional sports in making young athletes comply in sustaining a system in which only a fraction of them can win. At the same time, sports sponsors and marketers make use of audience identification with the heroics of sports to promote consumerism as a way of life that must be pursued, defended, and extended. Hence, neoliberal movements enthusiastically support professional sports—linked to corporate sponsorship and supported by a public educational and recreational infrastructure—as a practice that will promote active consumerism and compliance with the corporate reshaping of society.

WOMEN'S INVOLVEMENT

Since the 1970s and the rise of second-wave feminism, women in significant numbers have taken on and succeeded in sports and leisure activities that were previously the exclusive domain of men. Women have made great strides in claiming rights to physical activity, and winning increased resources and attention for women's sport. In the late 1990s, women have multiplied their athletic numbers by significant measure—constituting about one-half of recreational exercisers and about one-third of competitive athletes in North America. Under the protection of Title IX (1972) in the United States (which made it illegal to discriminate against girls and women in school sports) and similar forms of equity legislation in other countries, far-reaching changes have been made. These changes have affected many levels of public education and recreation systems, as well as the sport-scholarship system. Several professional team sports leagues for women have been established. Only time will tell whether a permanent television audience will develop to observe the athletics of girls and women, but it is certainly possible. The principle of women's equal right to participation in sports has largely been established in sport rhetoric in most societies, and there has been a steady progression to-

American softball fans show their patriotism and loyalty to the U.S. softball team at the 1996 Olympics in Atlanta. (Wally McNamee/ Corbis)

ward more complete integration of women. We may count all these developments major, if not consistent or secure, steps toward gender equality.

In contrast, we have seen nothing like the mass incursion by men into sports such as figure skating or competitive gymnastics (sports that can provide a more expressive gestural repertoire) or into nonsport physical disciplines such as dance. Also, the athletic participation of large numbers of U.S. women has had the unforeseen effect of reducing the percentage of women's sports teams coached by women, even as the absolute number of female coaches has risen. In nearly every instance, the combining of programs of men's and women's sports has meant that a man became the chief administrator and a woman became—at best—his assistant. Throughout the Olympic organization and the international and national sports federations, men continue to occupy a large majority of the positions of power. Thus women's inclusion in the world of sports has changed the ratio of men to women in what was once a male preserve, particularly at the school, club, and university levels, and it has certainly created new beliefs about women's athletic abilities among large numbers of people. But it has not changed the core culture of the dominant men's professional sports or the effect of their culture on larger social ideals and values. While liberal feminists welcome women's participation in the present system of modern sports, Marxist feminists are sharply critical of the values implicit within the present system.

How do aggressively competitive and thoroughly commercialized sports affect political attitudes and actions with respect to economics, government, and state formation? A culture that worships only masculine qualities in its physical culture—and that links these qualities to elite competition—may easily come to accept these values as universally valid. The megaprojects of professional sports (for example, publicly financed stadium construction), routinely supported by neoliberal and neoconservative municipal politicians, continue to receive subsidies worth hundreds of millions of dollars each year, while the social infrastructure withers.

CONCLUSION

Women who are active and athletic are dedicated believers in the virtues of sports for girls and women, emphasizing its physical, emotional, and psychological benefits. Yet in sports, as in the paid labor force, government departments, and the military, the substantial increase in participation by women has not translated into equal power to shape and direct the evolution of sport institutions or equal representation within sport culture. Women remain subordinated in sport's heroic mythology and in its athletic and economic elites. In the many moments when sport and political identifications unite (be they civic, national, racial, or ethnic), women almost always occupy the role of spectator rather than that of hero. They may enjoy men's sports and the forms of sociability that take place around them; they may even play these sports with other women or men. But women athletes have not yet become political symbols for city, nation, or empire the way that men have. As yet, we have no female equivalent of Muhammad Ali, Pelé, or Akebono.

If women decide to seek such status by competing at the upper echelons of professional sport, what will be the consequences? At the individual level, women athletes must grapple with the trade-offs between the pressures they encounter when they enter the sport system and the rewards that success in that system may bring. On a case-by-case basis, these trade-offs may well be positive for many. But at the broader political level the issues are more contradictory. Women athletes are living proof of women's physical strength and accomplishments in the realm of symbolic warriorhood. Nevertheless, these very qualities may be co-opted to increase the legitimacy of a social practice and a value system that discourage the political policies and democratic processes so important to the empowerment and well-being of women, their families, and communities. Women's embrace of sports as they exist may inadvertently support the idealization of a "macho" state; a highly unequal economic, gender, and racial order; and a system of communications (cultural industries) in which ownership and profitability are the dominant determinants of political expression and of the power to shape athletic culture.

The inclusion in mainstream physical culture—sports in this case—is an essential part of women's struggle to achieve sociopolitical equality with men. The principle linking political equality with participation in physical culture holds true in the contemporary world as much as it did in ancient societies. It holds true in Norway, where women are exceptionally active in sports and leisure activities (with men and in their own organizations) and have achieved a greater degree of inclusion in government and state institutions than anywhere else. And it also holds true in Afghanistan, where revived traditions of women's physical confinement correlate to complete political disenfranchisement. Nevertheless, simple integration into the existing dominant sport culture may ultimately work against women's broader objectives for gender and social equality and the right to a life that includes physical activity. Hence, the historic task before women may be to work toward transforming sports and political institutions in similar, prosocial directions. Women have a political interest in broadening participation in dance, Eastern disciplines, noncompetitive games and pastimes, and developing new forms of athletics, not only for their own physical well-being and personal development but also for the development of political consciousness.

Varda Burstyn

Bibliography

Birell, Susan, and Cheryl Cole, eds. (1994) *Women, Sport, and Culture.* Champaign, IL: Human Kinetics.

Burstyn, Varda, and Dorothy Smith, eds. (1999) *The Rights of Men: Manhood, Politics, and the Culture of Sport.* Toronto, Ontario: University of Toronto Press.

Cahn, Susan K. (1994) *Coming on Strong: Gender and Sexuality in Twentieth-Century Women's Sport.* New York: Free Press.

Gilroy, Sarah. (1997) *Working on the Body: Links Between Physical Activity and Social Power. Researching Women and Sport.* London: Macmillan.

Guttmann, Allen. (1991) *Women's Sports: A History.* New York: Columbia University Press.

———. (1994) *Games and Empires: Modern Sports and Cultural Imperialism.* New York: Columbia University Press.

Hargreaves, Jennifer. (1994) *Sporting Females: Critical Issues in the History and Sociology of Women's Sports.* London: Routledge.

Jansen, Sue Curry, and Donald F. Sabo. (1994) "The Sport/War Metaphor: Hegemonic Masculinity, the Persian Gulf War, and the New World Order." *Sociology of Sport Journal* 11, 1 (March): 1–17.

Kimmel, Michael. (1990) "Baseball and the Reconstitution of American Masculinity, 1880–1920." In *Sport, Men, and the Gender Order: Critical Feminist Perspectives*, edited by M. A. Messner and D. F. Sabo. Champaign, IL: Human Kinetics.

McKay, Jim. (1997) *Managing Gender: Affirmative Action and Organizational Power in Australian, Canadian, and New Zealand Sport.* Albany: SUNY Press.

Messner, Michael A., and Donald F. Sabo, eds. (1994). *Sex, Violence, and Power in Sports: Rethinking Masculinity.* Freedom, CA: The Cossing Press.

Taylor, Ian. (1982). "Class, Violence, and Sport: The Case of Soccer Hooliganism in Britain." In *Sport, Culture, and the Modern State*, edited by H. Cantelon and R. Gruneau. Toronto, Ontario: University of Toronto Press.

Vertinsky, Patricia. (1989) "Feminist Charlotte Perkins Gilman's 'Pursuit of Health and Physical Fitness' as a Strategy for Emancipation." *Journal of Sport History* 16, 1 (Spring): 5–26.

POLL, SYLVIA

(1970–)

COSTA RICAN SWIMMER

Sylvia Poll won Costa Rica's first-ever Olympic medal in 1988 with her second place finish in the 200-meter freestyle event. Poll was born on 24 September 1970 in Managua, Nicaragua, where her father managed a cotton processing plant. Her parents, both from Germany, moved the family to Costa Rica in the late 1970s to avoid the political unrest in Nicaragua. Soon afterward, nine-year-old Poll began swimming at Costa Rica's only 10-lane pool under the guidance of coach Francisco Rivas.

Poll splashed onto the international swimming scene at the 1987 Pan-American Games in Indianapolis, where she won an unprecedented eight medals, including three golds (100-meter and 200-meter freestyle, and 100-meter backstroke). She was named Best Athlete of the Games and received offers of scholarships from several American universities. Instead, she opted to continue training in Costa Rica. Poll had become a naturalized Costa Rican citizen only one year earlier, but her adopted country gave her a hero's welcome. At 6 foot 2 inches, with white-blonde hair, Poll was an easily recognizable celebrity. Her accomplishments grabbed just as many headlines as the Nobel Peace Prize won by the country's president. One Costa Rican newspaper named her Woman of the Year. The following year she traveled to Seoul to compete in the Olympics. Poll did not disappoint: She captured a silver medal. In a tiny country with virtually no world-class athletes, Poll was easily named Costa Rican Athlete of the Decade (1980s).

At her peak in the late 1980s, Poll's name regularly appeared in the world rankings, including three top ten rankings in 1987. She continued to be a contender, winning a gold at the Pan-American Games (100-meter backstroke) and a silver at the world championships (50-meter backstroke) in 1991. She competed in the 1992 Olympics in Barcelona, finishing fifth in the 200-meter backstroke.

She retired from swimming in 1994. Two years later her younger sister was in the spotlight. Claudia Poll (21 December 1972 –) won the gold medal in the 200-meter freestyle at the 1996 Olympics in Atlanta.

Kelly Nelson

Bibliography

"Bañada en Plata: Sylvia Poll, la Primera Medallista Olímpica de la Historia." (1996) *La Nacion.* <http://www.nacion.co.cr/deportes/pagina08.html>.

Kinzer, Stephen. (1988) "Olympic Profile: Sylvia Poll." *New York Times* (28 August): 8, 4.

Muckenfuss, Mark. (1987) "Poll Getting Ready for Seoul." *Swimming World* (October): 100.

Robb, Sharon. (1988) "Silver Not Small Change in Costa Rica." *Sun-Sentinel* (18 December): 15C.

POLO

Polo is a team sport played on a grass field between two teams of four players each, mounted on horses and using mallets to hit a ball between goal posts. The aim is to drive the ball between the goal posts. Polo is reputed to be the oldest mounted game, and it is largely a sport of the elite. Women have played polo since ancient times but never in numbers equal to men.

HISTORY

Polo apparently originated in the central plains of Asia and spread to ancient Persia, China, and India. British Army officers picked up the game in the 1850s while serving in India, and it was promptly adopted by many regiments in England and in British colonies, mainly Australia and New Zealand. James Gordon Bennett, publisher of the *New York Herald,* is generally credited with the introduction of the game into the United States in 1876. In that same year, the first documented match took place in Argentina, played between English and Scottish settlers.

It is documented that in Persia, as well as in China, women played polo. The Persian poet Nizami (1126–1200) relates how the beautiful Shirin, wife of Kushrau Parviz who ruled in the sixth century, together with her ladies-in-waiting, played a game of polo against the king and his men.

When Kusrau reached the polo ground,
The fair-faced ones curvetted on their steed with joy.
They started play, when every Moon
Appeared a Sun, and every partridge a hawk.
At times the Sun bore off the ball, at times the Moon.
Now Shirhin won and now the Shah.

In China, polo has had a long history and has been a favorite subject of many artists. There are numerous depictions of women as polo players, including a mortuary figure of a horsewoman engaged in a polo match and a ceramic sculpture dating from the eighth-century T'ang dynasty. As in Persia, polo in China was strictly a royal and aristocratic game.

RULES AND PLAY

A polo team is composed of four players, numbered one through four; number four is also called the "back." Number one plays forward and is usually the top goal scorer. Number two is a roamer and more adept in attack, although she also acts as a marker for the opposing number three. The best player on the team usually plays number three and is the pivot between offense and defense. The defense is covered by number four, who should be able to hit the ball a good distance. Players have an official handicap based on quality of play (not number of goals scored) ranging from minus two goals for beginners to ten goals for top players. The goal difference is given to the weaker team at the start of the match. Any breed or size of horse can be used, although they must be in good health with no handicaps, and they must show no behavioral problems.

The object of the game is to hit the ball between the goal posts to score points. The team with the most points at the end of the game wins. The players line up in their teams facing the umpire, who throws the ball in midfield to begin the game. The ball is hit with a mallet. The ball can be hit on either side of the pony, and players are permitted to bump each other (though not at dangerous angles). The hooking of an opponent's mallet is also permitted but only when striking the ball. The basic rule is that of "right of way," which extends ahead of a player in the direction she is riding and permits the ball to be hit on the offside (right side) of the pony. This rule focuses on the safety of both the players and the mounts.

The playing field is 274 × 146 m (300 × 160 yards) if the sides are boarded. If the sides are not boarded, the width can be extended to 183 meters (200 yards). The goal posts must be at least 3 meters (10 feet) in height and are placed 2.4 meters (8 feet) apart in the center of each back line. They are made light enough to break upon collision, thus reducing the risk of injury.

Matches consist of between four to eight periods, depending on the importance of the tournament. Each period, known in England as a

Women participate in a polo match. (Paul A. Souders/Corbis)

chukka (*chukker* in Argentina), lasts 7 minutes; there is an interval of 4 minutes between periods, during which players may change ponies. If there is a tie at the end of regulation time, then play extends until either a goal is scored or the ball goes out of play.

There are ten different penalties that can be called in a game, although most penalties are called for the crossing infringement. Two mounted umpires make the calls, and there is also one referee who sits on the sidelines to resolve cases in which the two umpires do not agree.

THE TWENTIETH CENTURY

The first documented women's polo game in Argentina took place in 1927 at Las Pingüinas Club between players representing the home side and another foursome called Estancia Josefina. Actually, all the players were close friends and relatives. Women also served as umpire and timekeeper. After four chukkers (playing periods), Las Pingüinas emerged victorious, 4–1.

The Braun Menéndez family may be considered the pioneers of women's polo in Argentina; in England the distinction belongs to the Pearsons from Cowdray Park in Surrey. Harold Pearson, second Viscount Cowdray, founded the Cowdray Park club in 1910, and his son John contributed to the revival of polo in England after World War II. John's three sisters, Yoskyl, Angela (his twin), and Daphne, played polo, although they were not allowed to compete with men in official tournaments. However, after the war they played in many competitions. Daphne was married to John Lakin, one of the top English international players.

In the United States, Mrs. Thomas Hitchcock, Sr., wife and mother of top polo players, was a prominent player and coach. At Aiken, South Carolina, and at Meadowbrook, Long Island, she coached the youthful Meadow Larks team, whose members went on to achieve international status as top players.

The first woman to have a handicap in Argentina was Alicia Pamela Greenshields, later Mrs. Storey, in 1937. However, Marjorie Lancaster, a player from the club Sayago in Uruguay, was the first one to participate in official tournaments in Argentina. Sue Sally Hale from California, a tireless worker of behalf of women's polo, was the first U.S. woman to be officially rated by the U.S. Polo Association (USPA), which was founded in 1890.

The most important women's tournament is the U.S. Handicap, first played in 1979 and won by Carmel Valley of California with a team formed by Sue Sally Hale, her daughters Sunset and Stormie, and Susan Welker of Texas. The competition has been played without interruption at different venues since its inception.

An all-women's club, the Naperville Women's Polo Club, was founded in Naperville, Illinois, in 1981. It was formally affiliated with the USPA, and it listed its colors as tan and blue. It became inactive in 1991.

The Women's Intercollegiate Championship was inaugurated in 1976 for a trophy presented by Katydid Farms. Ann Hewitt, Molly Baldridge, and Jacqueline Chazey, all representing Yale University, were the first winners. The Interscholastic Championship started in 1991. The cup was donated by Dan and Julie Calhoun and won by Charlotte Dishman, Elizabeth Roeser, Jessica Bailey, Katherine Roeser, and Michelle Lopez, all of Santa Ynez, California.

LEADING PLAYERS

Polo is very much a sport in which attention is focused on the skills of the individual players. Claire Lucas Tomlinson, the daughter of Arthur Lucas who was one of the first to revive polo in England after World War II, played on the Oxford University Polo team. After graduation she worked in Argentina as part of a research firm studying fertilizers, but she managed to find time to improve her polo skills. Married to Captain Simon Tomlinson, a four-goal army officer, they have their own team, Los Locos, in England. Los Locos has been extremely successful in medium and high polo, although not without a struggle. Lavinia Roberts Black shares the credit with Tomlinson for leading the movement to allow women to compete in high-goal polo in England. In 1979 the Hurlingham Polo Association would not

WOMEN AND POLO TOURNAMENTS

Polo began and remains primarily a men's sport. However, in the twentieth century, some women have reached the highest levels of the sport. In the United States, there are now three major tournaments for women: the Women's Intercollegiate Championship, which began in 1976; the U.S. Handicap, which began in 1979; and the Interscholastic Championship, which began in 1991. Leading women polo players are also ranked by the U.S. Polo Association and have played on international teams representing Great Britain and France.

All-women polo team. (Bettmann/Corbis)

allow the team to take the field. Tomlinson and Black threatened to take the association before the Equal Opportunities Commission, and the threat alone was sufficient for the association's stewards to change their policy. (In that year, 1979, Tomlinson's husband was one of the association's stewards. It is not known whether he took part in the deliberations or the vote.) Claire Tomlinson later became a member of the powerful Handicap Committee.

In 1979 Los Locos won the very first high-goal tournament of the season—the Queen's Cup at Royal Windsor—and was the runner-up in the Warwickshire Cup. Since then, they have played in all the major tournaments in England, including the British Open for the gold cup at Cowdray Park. In 1998 Tomlinson's daughter Emma represented England in the successful elimination games for the World Polo Championships, and her son Luke was on the British team that took the Eu-

ropean Eight-Goal Championship. After reaching a five-goal handicap, Claire Tomlinson became the highest-rated woman in the history of the game. Black, who maintained a two-goal handicap for twenty years, is the daughter of Alan Roberts, one of the founders of the Henley Polo Club and patron of the Maidensgrove team. Journeys to Argentina helped Black hone her polo skills acquired with the Pony Club; she was, for a time, the best woman player in the United Kingdom.

In the United States, Sue Sally Hale was among the first women to be officially rated by the USPA, together with Jorie Butler Richardson, Elizabeth Dailey, and Virginia Merchant, a member of the National Capitol Park in Washington, D.C. Sue Sally Hale runs the Moorpark Polo Club in California. Her daughter Stormy was the first U.S. woman to reach a 4-goal rating.

Vicky Armour was the first woman to play in high-goal polo in the United States; she breeds and trains ponies in Florida. Susan Stovall, one of the best players in the United States, also manages the Eldorado Club in California, which has more than 1,000 ponies, more than 150 players, and up to 40 teams competing in any one tournament.

Related to and forming an integral part of the game, Martha "Marty" LeGrand was editor of *Polo* magazine for several years, maintaining that publication as the best periodical devoted to the sport.

Hollywood stars Pamela Sue Martin and Stephanie Powers have contributed to the increasing visibility of the game by adding glamour and crowd interest in may benefit games that have heavy participation by celebrities. Frenchwoman Caroline Anier, now rated at four goals, plays in both her native country and in the United States. She started playing at age fourteen, and within a few years she was the manager of the Polo Club de Bouloy. After that came invitations to play in Jamaica and in the United States. By the end of the 1990s she was one of the top-ranked women in the world. She and Kathy Batchelor are the co-owners of the Tri Valley Polo Club in La Quinta, California. Other players of note are Leigh Eckstrom, from Giant Valley in Connecticut; Californians Susan and Mary Alizon Walton; and Lesley Ann Masterton-Fong Ye, a three-goaler from Kingston, Jamaica, who has wide international experience. In 1992 Julie Roenisch became the first woman to play in the U.S. Open, while Deborah Couples was the first to sponsor a team competing in the Open. She was a member of the squad as well.

POLO IN ART

The French painter Adrienne Jouclard (1881–1971) made polo her particular subject. Her best known polo painting is *Le Polo a Bagatelle*. A late-twentieth-century U.S. artist, Peggy Kauffman, has gained visibility with her realistic bronzes; the seven castings of "Archie," Paul Withers' famous polo pony, are the most sought after of her works. Another U.S. painter, Marilyn Newmark (1928–), a disciple of the talented Paul Brown, also sculpted some beautiful bronzes on the subject of polo. Englishwoman Amy Oxenbould (1921–) produced four bronzes showing a player executing the four basic strokes. Author and painter Diana Thorne, born in Canada in 1895, wrote and illustrated the adult book *Polo* and the children's books, *Tails Up, Pepito the Polo Pony,* and *Roughy;* she also painted several watercolors depicting such famous players as Tommy Hitchcock from Long Island, New York, and colorful scenes of international matches. Two contemporary Argentine artists, Adriana Zaefferer and Inés Menéndez Behety, have also made their mark on the polo artistic scene.

Polo remains an elite sport that is likely to retain a small but intensely loyal following among women as well as men. It was an Olympic sport, featured at the Games in 1900, 1908, 1920, 1924, and 1936, although no women ever competed.

Horacio A. Laffaye

Bibliography

Laffaye, Horacio A. (1989) *El Polo Internacional Argentino.* Buenos Aires: privately published.

————. (1995) *Diccionario de Polo.* 2d ed. Weston, MA: Polo Research.

Laufer, Berthold. (1975) "Early History of Polo." In *Horse and Horseman,* edited by Peter Vischer. New York: Arco.

Russell-Stoneham, Derek, and Roger Chatterton-Newman (1992). *Polo at Cowdray.* London: Polo Information Bureau.

Spencer, Herbert, ed. (1986) *Chakkar: Polo around the World.* Zurich: City-Druck.

POLO, WATER

Water polo has always been a rough-and-tumble sport associated with men and with masculinity. Though modern rules have made water polo more a game of speed and finesse than it used to be, the introduction of women into the game has been slow and difficult, and has not really changed the image of water polo as a macho sport.

HISTORY AND RULES OF WATER POLO

The first rules of water polo were defined by the Metropolitan Swimming Association in London in 1870. In this "football in the water," the ball had to be brought to and put on a floating goal on which a goalkeeper was standing and looking at the adversaries. Indeed, the text mainly referred to rugby-football. Players reproduced in the water the fights and the strategies used on the ground. In 1877, in Glasgow, another set of rules were invented to emphasize the spectacular aspects of the game and to make the annual swimming club galas more attractive. After some adaptations, a synthesis of the various proposals was carried out in 1888 with new rules, which considered the spirit of soccer (association football) as a model for water polo.

In this version, the goals were vertical, not horizontal. The hand had to be located above the wrist to handle the ball, thus making a rugby-style carry under the arm more difficult. Time was reduced to two seven-minute periods to limit the tiredness of players and to reinforce the quality of the spectacle. The principle of free-throw was also taken from soccer. In order to limit team regroupings and to develop a faster and more mobile play, the ball could be either carried or thrown through the goal. A specific rule of offside was adopted within a limit of two yards from the goals. Last, a player could not keep the ball when he was pushed under water by a defender.

These main rules became more universal with the creation of the Fédération Internationale de Natation Amateur (FINA) in 1908. Until the middle of the century, they did not change very much. However, two distinct styles developed in Europe, where the game was most popular. The first one, adopted by the Hungarians and, later, by the Italians, favored speed, sense of anticipation, and technical skills; the other, used by the Belgians, English, Germans, and French, was based on force, individual duel, slyness, and even trickery, the latter being favored by the difficulty of refereeing players in an aquatic and opaque environment.

During the interwar period, water polo remained a sport of collective violence that was criticized by most observers. The game had also been developing in South America, and after 1948, an approving attitude grew toward the more moderate South American code, which had itself been influenced by basketball rules. New rules included use of substitutes, the exclusion of any player who made four faults, and especially the possibility for a attacker to move before the signal (whistle) of the referee authorizing a free-throw.

This last rule led water polo toward a game of speed, without totally abandoning its original physical violence.

The new rules did not facilitate the work of the referees, and the matches degenerated regularly into pugilism. At the Melbourne Olympics in 1956, Hungary beat the Soviet Union in a semifinal match of unbelievable intensity—within a minute of playing, the water reddened with the blood of the adversaries.

Several attempts to modify the rules were tried in the 1960s and 1970s in order to make the game still less tough, but they generally resulted in making it more complex both for players and for spectators and more broken up during the matches. The introduction of double refereeing in 1976 helped to reduce the violence of the game. Later, FINA proposed various modifications to give more continuity to the game and to make it more attractive for the media and the spectators.

BEGINNINGS OF WOMEN'S PARTICIPATION

At the end of the nineteenth century, the aggressive and violent forms of water polo did not favor the integration of women. The sport quite simply was considered as too tough for women. However, within the swimming associations recently created for their own use, some English women dared to face the contempt of men and to risk scandal by including demonstrations of water polo in their activities. The Swansea Ladies Water Sports Club officially sponsored a water polo group from 1899. Some of the matches against other clubs were held over the objections of the male members of those clubs.

By 1900, women's water polo was exclusively British and generated little interest. Nonetheless, as more women became interested in swimming and more strong swimmers began to appear, the popularity of water polo for women began to increase. First, the London Water Polo League proposed the creation of a water polo championship for women. In 1923, a regional association was created, the Southern Counties Ladies' Water Polo Association, which met some Belgian teams after 1930.

Women's water polo gradually followed the development of men's water polo. The first non-British women's teams appeared in Belgium,

LADIES GO SLOWLY (1915)
An Early Twentieth-Century Female Water Polo Player Comments on the Development of the Sport

Water polo as regards ladies has received no support from official sources. The governing bodies in the swimming world have let it go its own way, and the clubs promote and control the game quite alone. It is true that some male players take a very practical interest in polo for ladies, and individually they help and encourage our play, but collectively they do not recognise us yet. Naturally, polo for ladies is in its infancy, and we must expect to go slowly.

Swimming Magazine, *1915*.

France, and the Netherlands. A demonstration between two Dutch teams of seven women was presented at the Olympic Games in Antwerp in 1920. In 1922, three Parisian clubs competed for the French national championship.

The diffusion of women's water polo remained very limited and usually took the form of demonstrations, frequently with little or no publicity. If swimming was still considered the ideal feminine sport, water polo had a totally different status; women were not welcomed in an activity that placed strength and brutality as its most prized attributes.

Attempts to extend water polo to women generally went through proposals for softened plays, in conformity with women's supposed brittleness: friendly demonstrations or matches rather than real championships; use of the South American rules, which limited the more brutal static play; and use of the "push-ball," a ball so large (diameter 60 centimeters, about 24 inches) that it could not be carried.

WATER POLO FOR WOMEN COMES OF AGE

After 1950, because of the decline of static play—characterized by strength and brutality—particularly after the modification of the rules in 1976, water polo began to attract more women. The development of international meets for women was marked by the supremacy of the Dutch during the 1950s, the Australians during the 1960s, and the Americans in the 1970s. In 1979, a FINA Water Polo Cup was dedicated to women. In 1983, a Eu-

ropean women's tournament was held in Belgium. In 1985, the first women's European championship was organized in Oslo. In 1986, during the first world championships for women, the Australians, with a more physical style, dominated the Dutch, who played a more dynamic and collective game. In 1990, the Dutch won the world tournament. In 1994, Hungary, and in 1998, Italy, two countries with a water polo tradition, won the world championship. In Sydney in 2000, women's water polo finally became an official Olympic sport.

THE MODERN GAME: CHARACTERISTICS AND CHALLENGES

The women's style of playing water polo is generally different from the men's. Offensive responsibilities, for example, are better distributed throughout the team. Conversely, the central forward is less of key figure than in men's water polo. Less aggressive defenses also alter the strategies used, particularly in the dueling between the goalkeeper and multiple attackers.

Neither women's nor men's water polo are widely popular sports. Moreover, the women's game continues to fall victim to the machismo associated with water polo generally, and has difficulty attracting players and coaches.

Thierry Terret

Bibliography

Beulque, Paul, and A. Descarpentries. (1923) *Méthode de Natation. Le Water-Polo.* Tourcoing, France: Ed. Frère.

Charroin, Pascal, and Thierry Terret. (1998) *L'Eau et la Balle. Une Histoire du Water-Polo.* Paris: L'Harmattan.

Hale, Ralph W., ed. (1986) *The Complete Book of Water Polo.* New York: Simon & Schuster.

Hines, Charles. (1967) *How to Play and Teach Water Polo.* New York: Associated Press.

Keil, Ian, and Don Wix. (1996) *In the Swim: The Amateur Swimming Association from 1869 to 1994.* Loughborough: Swimming Time.

Lemhenyi, Dezso, and Jacques Meslier. (1969) *Waterpolo: Technique-Jeu-Entraînement.* Paris: Amphora.

Rajki, Belá. (1958) *Water Polo.* London: Museum Press.

Rinehart, Robert E. (1996) "Fists Flew and Blood Flowed: Symbolic Resistance and International Response in Hungarian Water Polo at the Melbourne Olympics, 1956." *Journal of Sport History* 23, 2 (summer): 120–139.

Terret, Thierry, and Pascal Charroin. (1998) "From England to France . . . via Belgium: The Diffusion of Water-polo in West-Europe in Late Nineteenth Century." In *From West to East and from East to West*, edited by Liu Yueye and Gertrud Pfister. Berlin: Academia Verlag.

POOL *see* Billiards

PORTUGAL

Portugal is a nation on the Iberian Peninsula in southwestern Europe with a population of about 10.5 million. Women there have long participated in casual recreational sport along with their families. With the rise of competitive sports in the nineteenth century, women who sought to participate faced opposition from some elements of society that thought it improper. By the mid-twentieth century, physical education was being taught in the schools, and Portuguese women were taking part in sport at many levels.

HISTORY

As various sports were established in Portugal, women joined their families in sailing, rowing, tennis, riding, shooting, gymnastics, walking, moun-

tain climbing, and skating. They participated with the general support of men, as a social experience that was fun and healthful and, in some cases, fashionable. In Lisbon, by the summer of 1889, a group of society women formed a club to promote fencing and shooting. Some years later, in 1918, women established a female football (soccer) club in Póvoa do Varzim, a fishing region in the north.

About that time, sport became less casual and more competitive. By the 1920s, competitive sports such as cycling, track and field, and football were becoming more popular, and new clubs and associations were being formed. When women tried to join this new kind of sport experience and compete among themselves, they met clear and discouraging criticism from some sectors of Portuguese society. Critics viewed the idea of women competing in public, sweating and striving to win, unsuitable and ludicrous.

PHYSICAL EDUCATION

The first legal consideration of physical education in schools came in 1911, but to no practical effect. By 1920, new regulations were adopted in schools which emphasized the need for physical education teachers and the physical development of Portuguese children. The Belgian Gymnastics perspective influenced these new regulations, although it was considered too military to be adopted in boys' and girls' public schools.

From 1938, Mocidade Portuguesa Feminina was the official organization responsible for promoting sport to girls, and the group offered schoolgirls the opportunity to take part in many sport activities. Girls could do this in government programs, where instructors could make sure they maintained good habits and proper behavior as well as emphasizing the healthful benefits of sports. Many schools had extensive equipment and facilities. Scouting and camping were also important. They provided physical exercise and sports, and at the same time gave girls, in a controlled environment, the opportunity to enjoy outdoor living and improve social skills and self-discipline. In addition, it was a way to use leisure time productively in a healthful and active fashion.

Until the mid-1970s, school programs favored gymnastics, traditional dances, and introductory-level sports. Schools promoted school and inter-scholastic competition in most sports, including

Portuguese runner Fernanda Ribeiro wins the gold medal for the 10,000-meter run with an Olympic record time of 31:01.63 at the 1996 Atlanta Olympics. (Wally McNamee/Corbis)

badminton, handball, football, gymnastics, basketball, volleyball, and track and field. School gymnastics have since declined, but general interest in sports has increased, and classes include boys and girls in the same groups.

ELITE COMPETITION

Portuguese women first participated in the 1952 Olympics in Helsinki. Three gymnasts, Laura Amorim, Dália Cunha, and Natália Cunha, took part in those games. Portugal did not send a team to the Olympics in 1956, but in Rome, in 1960, three gymnasts, Dália Cunha Sammer, Maria Helena, and Esbela da Fonseca, and a swimmer Maria Regina Louro were on the team. Only one woman, gymnast Esbela da Fonseca, took part in the Tokyo Games in 1964, and two female gymnasts went to Mexico City in 1968. In 1972 and 1976, Portugal again sent no national team. In Moscow in 1980,

one woman gymnast was there, Avelina Alvarez. Portugal sent a relatively substantial contingent of women to the Los Angeles Games in 1984: the country's five best runners, Albertina Machado, Aurora Cunha, Conceição Ferreira, Rita Borralho, and Rosa Mota; two gymnasts, Margarida do Carmo and Maria João Falcão (rhythmic gymnastics); a swimmer, Joana Figueiredo (diving); and a shooter, Maria Isabel Chitas.

Los Angeles was a significant occasion for the Portuguese women because it was there that Rosa Mota won her first Olympic medal in the marathon, taking the bronze with a time of 29:06.58. Four years later she won the gold medal at the Seoul Olympics. In 1996 in Atlanta, Fernanda Ribeiro won the gold medal in the 10,000-meter race with a time of 23 minutes 06.69 seconds.

These events changed the Portuguese perception of sports. People wanted to know not only who would represent Portugal at the Games and in other international competition, but also how the athletes had trained and what kind of support they had received. While the Olympics remain the major athletic event, there is increasing support for athletes who do not as yet compete in the Olympics.

Distance running remained Portuguese women's strength. Aurora Cunha, a long distance runner, won multiple gold medals in international elite competitions. Albertina Dias, another runner, also won various world championships. Many other outstanding runners have competed as well, earning the respect of the Portuguese people and serving as valuable role models for girls and young women. Women have also competed in racewalking, cycling, weightlifting, surfing, and judo.

Some women athletes have gone on to become coaches, as did Esbela da Fonseca in gymnastics, Jenny Candeias in rhythmic gymnastics, and Maria do Sameiro Araújo in track and field. Portuguese sports associations and federations remain controlled by men, but in the future that may change as Portuguese women continue to gain attention in regional and international sport competitions.

Manuela Hasse

Bibliography

Crespo, Jorge. (1990) *A História do Corpo.* Lisbon, Portugal: Difel.

Esteves, José. (1967) *O Desporto e as Estruturas Sociais.* Lisbon, Portugal: Editora Prelo.

Hasse, Manuela. (1987) "A Mulher e o Desporto em Portugal." *Cadernos da Condição Feminina* 21.

———. (1993) "A Situação dos Estudos sobre a Mulher e o Desporto em Portugal." *Cadernos da Condição Feminina* 38.

Additional information was provided by Federação Portuguesa de Judo (Lisboa, Portugal), and by the Federação Portuguesa de Vela (Lisboa, Portugal).

POWERLIFTING

Powerlifting is a competition to determine who possesses the greatest brute strength. A powerlifting competition consists of three lifts—the squat, the bench press, and the deadlift. The winner is chosen based on the total weight, computed by adding together the heaviest successful attempt in each category. Unlike weightlifting, which requires a high level of flexibility and explosiveness, powerlifting is a sport that women can begin at any age.

HISTORY

The birth of women's powerlifting is generally dated to the mid-1970s. Before that time, various women did participate in these displays of raw strength. The professional strongwoman Jane de Vesley reportedly deadlifted 176.6 kg (392.5 pounds) in 1926; and Ivy Russell of Great Britain claimed to have made 184.7 kg (410.5 pounds) in the same lift at a bodyweight of approximately 56.2 kg (125 pounds) in the early 1930s. Jean Ansorge of Grand Rapids, Michigan, hosted a meet on 17 October 1943, in which women competed in the overhead press, the squat, and the deadlift.

In the United States, following the passage of Title IX in 1972 (which made discrimination against girls and women in school sports illegal), a few individual women began appearing in local men's competitions. At the Chattanooga Open in May 1975 three women entered the men's contest, marking the first time more than one woman was officially entered in a men's meet. At that meet, Jan Todd of Georgia deadlifted 394.5 pounds (177.5 kg) while Cindy Wyatt Reinhoudt of New York lifted in the 165-pound (74.2-kg) men's class and Rebecca Joubert of Tennessee lifted in the 148-pound (67.1-kg) class. But there were sometimes problems. As Todd wrote in 1982, "Within six months we began to hear from other places around the country that more women were entering men's contests. . . . Reports began surfacing of young women who entered contests and were told that since no women referees were present, they would have to weigh in the nude before male judges. But the girls persevered, continued to show up at the meets, and slowly the men accepted us. We became less 'freaky,' more fellow athletes."

In 1976, at the World Powerlifting Championships for Men, Todd and Reinhoudt met with Joe Zarella, the newly elected president of the United States Powerlifting Federation (USPF), and together they laid plans to hold the first USPF-sanctioned contest for women. Zarella agreed to host the meet in Nashua, New Hampshire, and in May 1977, twenty-five women participated in the All-American Women's Open. Six of those competitors were Todd's high-school students from Nova Scotia, Canada, where she had moved in 1976. This marked the first time that women powerlifters competed internationally. In 1978, Zarella received a sanction from the USPF to host the first official Women's National Powerlifting Championships. Seventy-four women attended this competition, including several lifters from Canada and Australia.

After the lifting at these championships, Todd and Reinhoudt organized a meeting for the women competitors to talk about the formation of some sort of women's organization. After considerable discussion, the women voted to stay within the USPF, and Reinhoudt was named as the first chairwoman of the USPF Women's Committee. At the International Powerlifting Federation (IPF) World Congress in November 1978, Zarella was asked to head up a similar committee for the IPF, and over the next year this committee—consisting of Zarella, Todd, Reinhoudt, Roz Basile of Australia, Mabel Rader of Nebraska, and Natalie Kahn of California—drafted rules for uniforms,

weight classes, and other items that affected women's participation.

The first IPF World Championships were held in 1980. Zarella again played host in Nashua, New Hampshire. Eight nations participated in the contest: the United States, Canada, Australia, Japan, Norway, Brazil, Finland, and the Netherlands Antilles. By 1982, women's powerlifting had spread to many of the IPF member nations. Except for the United States, Australia, and Canada, the other nations participating in the early days of women's powerlifting did not hold national championships for women until the early 1980s. England held its first meet in 1981 and then went on to bring home one gold, two silver, and two bronze medals at the 1981 world championships in Hawaii. Japan, also a participant in the first IPF World Championships, held its first national championships in 1981 and had six women certified as referees by 1982. Brazil also hosted its first national championships for women in 1981, as did Belgium. Norway and Finland held their first nationals in 1982, as did Germany, which hosted a national meet in the spring of 1982 and a German cup for women in November. Sweden did not have a sanctioned meet just for women

WOMEN'S POWERLIFTING RECORDS, INTERNATIONAL POWERLIFTING FEDERATION, JANUARY 2000

Women's Junior (90+ kilo category)

Squat	280.0	Lee Chia-Sui	Taiwan
Benchpress	152.5	Lee Chia-Sui	Taiwan
Deadlift	247.5	Lee Chia-Sui	Taiwan
Total	672.5	Lee Chia-Sui	Taiwan

Women's Open (90+ kilo category)

Squat	280.0	Lee Chia-Sui	Taiwan
Benchpress	178.5	Chao Chen-Yeh	Taiwan
Deadlift	263.5	Katrina Robertson	Australia
Total	677.5	Lee Chia-Sui	Taiwan

Women's Master (82.5 kilo category)

Squat	202.5	Vicki Steenrod	United States
Benchpress	132.5	Vicki Steenrod	United States
Deadlift	212.5	Vicki Steenrod	United States
Total	500.0	Vicki Steenrod	United States

until 1983, although they did hold Nordic Championships in 1982 that attracted lifters from Finland, Sweden, and Norway.

DRUG TESTING AND POWERLIFTING

Women powerlifters led the fight for drug testing within their sport. In the early 1980s, legislation was introduced in both organizations to begin a drug-testing program at world and national meets. The IPF agreed and started a drug-testing program for women in 1982, but the USPF refused to begin a similar program. This decision splintered the U.S. organization. A large number of lifters, particularly women lifters, abandoned the USPF to join the newly formed American Drug Free Powerlifting Association (later renamed USA Powerlifting). Several years later, when the IPF told the USPF that they would have to adopt a testing program or else lose IPF membership, another group of lifters split away to form the American Powerlifting Federation (APF), which advertised that their contests would never include drug testing. Over the next decade a number of other associations were also formed. This makes discussions of records and best performances nearly impossible because rules are not consistent among the organizations.

Four women have been inducted in the International Powerlifting Hall of Fame: Jan Todd for her work as an administrator, and Beverly Francis of Australia, Ruthie Schafer of the United States, and Cathy Millen of New Zealand as lifters.

RULES AND PLAY

Before a competition begins, all lifters must be weighed, their lifting costumes must be inspected, and all equipment (plates, bars, platforms, benches, and the like) must be certified by the referee in charge. Lifters are then divided into age and body-weight divisions and the order of competition is set. Most contests operate under what is known as the rounds system, in which the competitors are divided into "flights" of approximately fifteen lifters. This group of lifters will then do all three attempts at a particular lift (for example, the squat) before the next flight begins the same lift. Flights can be determined by weight and age divisions or by the weights chosen by the lifters for their first attempts.

In competition, each lifter gets three squat attempts, three bench press attempts, and three deadlift attempts, in that order. If a competitor begins with a weight that is too heavy and misses all three attempts, she cannot continue in the competition. The winner of each weight class and age group is determined by the total, computed by adding together a lifter's best attempt in each lift. In most competitions, best lifter awards are also given to the athletes who lift the most weight pound-for-pound in the various divisions of the contest (open, masters, juniors, etc.). World, national, and state records can be made in each of the individual lifts as well as in the total.

The Squat

The squat is a test of leg, hip, and back strength. To begin the lift, the competitor removes the bar from a squat rack by placing the bar across her upper back and shoulders. She then steps away from the rack and assumes an erect position with the knees locked. At the referee's command of "squat" the lifter lowers her body until the top surface of the thighs at the hip joint is slightly lower than the top of the knee. This means that the angle at the knee is slightly below ninety degrees. From this deep position, the lifter rises, and stands erect with locked knees. As soon as the head referee is satisfied that the lifter has the bar under control, the verbal command to "rack" the bar is given to signal the end of the lift. The lifter then places the bar back in the squat rack. Squatters are most commonly disqualified because they do not squat low enough. Another common error occurs when the lifter does not wait for the referee's signals to begin and end the lift.

The Bench Press

This test of arm, chest, and shoulder strength begins when the lifter lies on her back on a bench and takes the barbell at arms' length. In IPF competition, the head referee then gives a verbal command to begin the lift, the competitor lowers the bar to the center of her chest, pauses briefly, and then pushes the bar upward until the elbows are locked and the head referee says "rack." During the performance of the lift, the head, shoulders, and hips must remain in contact with the bench, and the lifter may not move her feet. Lifters are most commonly disqualified during this lift for raising the hips off the bench while performing the lift and for not waiting for the judges' signals.

Before 1999, the IPF used different rules for the bench press. In those earlier contests, no signal was given until the bar was motionless on the lifter's chest. Once motionless, the referee said "press" and the lifter raised the bar to arms' length. As soon as the elbows were locked and the referees could see that the bar was under control, a "rack" signal was given to end the official attempt. This method of benching is still used by the second largest international powerlifting federation, the World Drug Free Powerlifting Association (WDFPA).

The Deadlift

The deadlift is a test of back, hip, forearm, and thigh strength. In this event, the lifter stands close to the bar, bends down, grips the bar, and then pulls it upward until the body is erect. Once the bar is "locked out," the referee says "down," and the lifter returns the bar to the platform. During the upward movement of the bar, the lifter may not shift her feet, "hitch" the bar by rebending the knees, or allow the bar to move downward, even if only fleetingly. The most common cause of disqualification in the deadlift is that the lifter is unable to get the shoulders into proper alignment without hitching.

ORGANIZATIONS FOR POWERLIFTING

Partly because powerlifting is not an Olympic sport, there have been many—some very short-lived—international organizations vying for control of the sport. The IPF is by far the oldest, largest, and best organized of these rival associations. In 1998 the IPF recognized seventy-five member nations and held world championships for men and women in junior, open, and masters divisions. Until drug testing became a hotly contested issue within the sport of powerlifting, the IPF was the only governing body for international powerlifting, and it was the IPF that sanctioned (in 1980) the first world championships for women.

In each of its seventy-five member nations, the IPF recognizes one national governing body. Since 1998, the governing body for the United States is USA Powerlifting. Although USA Powerlifting and several other member nations still have women's committees that make decisions affecting women lifters, the IPF dissolved its women's advisory committee in 1998.

Given the increasing popularity of weightlifting among women, powerlifting as a recreational and competitive activity would seem to have a promising future. Whether it will ever attain Olympic status remains an open question.

Jan Todd

Bibliography

Kelso, Paul. (1996) *Powerlifting Basics, Texas-Style*. Nevada City, CA: Ironmind Enterprises.

Todd, Jan. (1998) *Physical Culture and the Body Beautiful: Purposive Exercise in the Lives of American Women 1800–1870*. Macon, GA: Mercer University Press.

PREGNANCY *see Reproduction*

PROFÉ, ALICE

(1867–1946)

GERMAN SPORTS PHYSICIAN AND WOMEN'S RIGHTS ADVOCATE

The first practicing female doctor in Berlin, Alice Profé was also Germany's first female sport physician and a lifelong advocate for the rights of women to participate in sports. Profé grew up in a large, well-to-do family, the eleventh of fourteen children. After graduating from a girls' high school, she decided to become a teacher, one of the very few professions then open to women.

For some years she taught in Germany and in England. With broader horizons came the ambition to become a medical doctor. Since women were not admitted to Prussian universities until 1908, she went to Switzerland to realize her dream. After her examinations, she established herself in 1905 in Berlin. As a general practitioner and specialist for pediatrics and sport medicine, she worked in Berlin until her death in 1946.

ALICE PROFÉ ON MUSCLE AND GENDER

There is no such thing as a muscle with feminine form or function. No muscle is made to respond in any special way to the demands of physical education. There's no special female blood or respiration that allows a woman to move gracefully. None of this kind of assertion about female difference is scientifically proven. Women don't eat differently from men in order to function nor do they need to be provided with a different kind of physical education.

From Gertrud Pfister, ed., Frau und Sport. *Frankfurt: Fischer, 1980. Translated by Allen Guttmann.*

She dedicated her life to the improvement of the situation of girls and women. Before World War I, she was active in the radical wing of the women's movement, which was then engaged in a battle for the right to an education and for access to the ballot box. The focus of her work was on girls' and women's physical education. Her first article on this topic appeared in the journal *Körper und Geist* (Body and Mind) in 1906. She spoke frequently on women's issues, criticizing traditional stereotypes about female debility and demanding support for girls' and women's physical education. Her essays and her speeches reduced female anxieties about strenuous activity and encouraged girls and women to participate in sports.

Because of her engagement, she was asked in 1912 to become a member of the influential *Zentralausschuss für Volks- und Jugendspiele* (Central Committee for the People's and Youth's Games). Eventually, she chaired the women's committee of that organization.

After World War I, she was mainly active as a writer and speaker who advocated revolutionary ideas about the place of women in modern society. In this role, she appeared in 1925 as keynote speaker at a large, groundbreaking congress sponsored by Germany's largest and most influential sports organization, the *Deutsche Turnerschaft* (German Gymnastics Federation). In another keynote address, in Berlin in 1929, she refuted widespread myths about femininity.

In these years, Profé became prominent as a member of several professional organizations in physical education as well as medicine. Her scientific credentials as a medical expert were especially valuable, because the stiffest opposition to women's sports came from the medical profession, which warned repeatedly that physical exertion of any kind endangered a woman's reproductive organs. She offered empirical evidence that strenuous competition in such sports as long-distance running and rowing was not detrimental to a woman's health.

In addition to her more public role as advocate of women's rights, Profé worked for a long time as a doctor and teacher at a girls' high school. She swam, hiked, and skated with her pupils. She was a member of a women's gymnastics club, she rowed, and she loved mountaineering.

Her last article, published in 1936, proves that she refused to adapt her ideas to conform to National Socialist (Nazi) ideology and terminology. Her obituary paid tribute to her steadfastness: "You have never changed your ideas about life in order to reap material rewards or to advance professionally. You stayed yourself."

Gertrud Pfister

Bibliography

Pfister, Gertrud. (1998) "'Macht die Schleppe kürzer und Ihr macht die Schwingen länger': Alice Profé (1867-1946)." In *Für eine andere Bewegungskultur,* edited by Ulrike Henkel and Gertrud Pfister. Pfaffenweiler, Germany: Centaurus.

PROFESSIONALISM

Professionalism is covered here in two articles. The first article, by Allen Guttmann, discusses the meanings and history of amateurism and professionalism in sports and the controversies that have arisen because of the distinctions made between amateur and professional athletes. The second article, by Debra Ballinger, covers the professionalization of women's sports.

AMATEURISM AND PROFESSIONALISM

The concept of amateurism was a nineteenth-century invention of the British upper and middle classes. Its original purpose was, quite simply, to allow leisured men and women to compete among themselves without the unwelcome intrusion of the "lower orders." The amateur rule was an intensification of cricket's eighteenth-century distinction between the "gentlemen," who were members of the upper or middle classes, and the "players," who were members of the working class. (Both, however, were allowed to play on the same cricket team.)

Amateurism took its most extreme form in the exclusionary regulations of the 1879 Henley Regatta: "No person shall be considered as an amateur oarsman or sculler . . . who is or has been by trade or employment for wages, a mechanic, artisan, or labourer." The extreme form of the amateur rule was at least logical. A less severe version of amateurism—one that still survives in the anachronistic rules of the National Collegiate Athletic Association (NCAA)—excluded only those men and women who were paid to play a game or who received some kind of material compensation for their performance. This less severe version was completely illogical because it ignored the difference between occasional participation in an activity and a lifetime commitment to it. For instance, the guardians of amateurism decreed that a wealthy woman who played golf nearly every day of the year but never won a prize was an amateur while her maid, who once won $5 in a footrace at a picnic, had to be defined as a professional athlete.

The original rationale for total exclusion of working-class men (and women) was their alleged inability to understand the ethos of fair play and good sportsmanship, which the ideologues of amateurism traced back to medieval chivalry. This conviction was bluntly expressed by an adamant early-twentieth-century spokesman for the amateur rule: "It is argued, with much show of truth, that the average workman has no idea of sport for its own sake." Still another aspect of amateurism was the Renaissance humanist's scorn for the specialist. In other words, amateurs played an occasional game of tennis for the intrinsic pleasures of tennis while professionals practiced endlessly and played daily because they were motivated by extrinsic rewards. For the latter, tennis was a vocation rather than the avocation it was for the former.

In order to convince themselves that this amateur–professional distinction was more than simply a class-based exclusionary technique, E. Norman Gardiner and other defenders of "sport for its own sake" argued that victors at the ancient Olympics shunned monetary and material rewards and were content to be crowned with a wreath of olive leaves. David Young and other modern scholars have shown conclusively that this view of the ancients was a modern myth. Antiquity's Olympic victors received rewards comparable to those of modern professionals.

Whether motivated by reverence for an imagined antiquity or simply by a revulsion against the "lower orders," the ideologues of amateurism fought fiercely to prevent direct payments to athletes, to ban reimbursements for time lost at work, to limit expenses incurred by travel, to restrict the time allowed for practice, and to segregate amateur sports from professional sports. The history of modern sports is rife with bitter conflicts over different interpretations of the concept. Typical among them was the long controversy that finally split rugby football between the Rugby Football Union (amateur) and Rugby League (professional).

There were also controversies over individual athletes. The famed Finnish distance runner Paavo Nurmi, for instance, was barred from the 1932 Olympics because it was alleged that he had earned money from his sport. Austria's leading skier, Karl Schranz, was banned from the 1972

RICH AND POOR NEED TO ENJOY SPORTS—SEPARATELY (1895)

A Nineteenth-Century Opinion on Alleviating Class Strife

Why there should be such constant strife to bring together in sport the two divergent elements of society that never by any chance meet elsewhere on even terms is quite incomprehensible, and it is altogether the sole cause of all our athletic woe. . . . The laboring class are all right in their way; let them go their way in peace, and have their athletics in whatsoever manner best suits their inclinations. . . . Let us have our own sport among the more refined elements, and allow no discordant spirits to enter into it.

CASPAR W. WHITNEY
(1895) A Sporting Pilgrimage. *New York: Harper & Bros.*

winter games for the same reason. France's Suzanne Lenglen, the flamboyant tennis player who dominated the women's game in the 1920s, was condemned by all the major tennis federations when it was revealed that she had signed a contract with promoter C. C. "Cash and Carry" Pyle. Mildred "Babe" Didrickson, the track and field star of the 1932 Olympics, was suspended by the Amateur Athletic Union (AAU) of the United States because she endorsed Dodge automobiles and was allowed to purchase one on the installment plan.

Lenglen and Didrikson were exceptions. Male athletes were far more likely than female athletes to be disbarred for "professionalism" because very few female athletes were offered the opportunity to earn money at their sport. Those who did support themselves by their athletic prowess tended to be women from the working class—like the Irish weightlifter Kate Roberts and the American wrestler Mildred Burke—for whom amateurism was never an option because their sports were totally unacceptable (for women) at the amateur level. Neither of these women was likely to enter a golf or tennis tournament.

In the 1980s and 1990s, as a significant number of female athletes began to earn large sums of money in sports that had been dominated by men, and just as professional leagues for female athletes became economically viable, the ideology of amateurism became moribund. The International Olympic Committee (IOC), which had long been the bastion of amateurism, abandoned the struggle and relegated the question of Olympic eligibility to the international sport federations. The Olympics are now, in most sports, an "open" competition among the world's best athletes, most of whom are indeed professionals in the sense that they specialize in and are rewarded materially for sport performances.

The NCAA continues to decry the thought of direct monetary payment to the "student-athletes" whose specialized performances bring millions of dollars (and invaluable publicity) to their universities. Today, most of the student-athletes who accept under-the-table payments or sign secret contracts with sport agents are male. It is likely that this particular form of gender inequality will diminish if the continued commercial success of women's professional sports sends boosters and agents to the campus in search of fresh talent. It is less likely that the NCAA will abandon its anachronistic eligibility rules.

Allen Guttmann

Bibliography

Gardiner, E. Norman. (1930) *Athletics of the Ancient World*. Oxford: Clarendon Press.

Gerber, Ellen W. (1974) *The American Woman in Sport*. Reading, MA: Addison-Wesley.

Glader, Eugene A. (1978) *Amateurism and Athletics*. West Point, NY: Leisure Press.

Guttmann, Allen. (1985) "The Belated Birth and Threatened Death of Fair Play." *Yale Review* 74 (summer): 525–537.

Savage, Howard J. (1927) *Games and Sports in British Schools and Universities*. New York: Carnegie Foundation.

Young, David C. (1984) *The Olympic Myth of Greek Amateur Athletics*. Chicago: Ares.

THE PROFESSIONALIZATION OF WOMEN'S SPORT

The transition from amateur to professional sport for women is an exciting outgrowth of the twentieth century and another milestone in the drive for equity begun with women's suffrage in the early part of the 1900s. A cursory look at the opportunities for a career in sport for young women would seem to lead to a bright future and to positive change in defining the sporting arena. But is professional sport for women truly a positive development, when viewed from the perspective of self-development and progress toward a woman's identity? To determine the true value of professional sport for women, one is cautioned to consider the meaning of sport, in general, and more specifically the benefits of sport participation for girls and women.

DEFINING PROFESSIONAL SPORT

The earliest professional sporting opportunities came from three driving forces: (1) the demand for teachers and coaches; (2) a need for individuals to market and demonstrate equipment for manufacturers of clothing and sporting goods; and (3) the desire of society to be entertained.

As amateur sport participation grew, more individuals sought out instructors to assist them in their skill development. The earliest teachers were usually parents or family friends who also played sport. Private clubs eventually hired professionals to fulfill the role of teacher for the members, and eventually, such professionals were banned from competition in the sport with amateurs. A division in competitive sports such as tennis and golf between amateur and professional players arose out of the sense of fairness in competition being tantamount to the definition and essence of the sporting environment. Even school teachers who made a living in the physical education field were sometimes considered professionals and therefore banned from amateur competitions, including the Olympics. With team sport development, early coaches were usually player-coaches and emerged in a leadership role as the member of a team. But once coaches were hired and compensated for their duties, they also fell under the umbrella of professional, and their player-coach role changed, as did their status as amateur athletes.

Early sporting goods manufacturers such as Wilson quickly saw the need for professional athletes to sell their wares. In the early 1900s, such competitors as Helen Hicks and Mildred "Babe" Didrickson were hired by American sporting goods companies to travel to cities and private clubs to give clinics and to market equipment and clothing. In golf, this led to the development of the first professional tournaments, and the delineation between amateur and open championship competitions.

The entertainment value of sport has been documented for centuries, with the best-known annals being the Roman coliseum events, where man's prowess was pitted against warriors or animals before crowds of thousands of spectators. The fight to the finish and the crowd's control over the ultimate survival or demise of the participants set the stage for the word "fanaticism" in sport viewing. There has long been an almost separate sport ethic that separates professional and amateur sport, when considering sport as entertainment compared to sport for the joy of participation. This distinction must be more carefully examined before women can judge whether professional sport is a positive or negative development for the future of womanhood, or even humanity, in general.

AMATEUR SPORT PARTICIPATION

Sport psychologists and sociologists report that there are many reasons why individuals choose to participate in sport. Children play sports primarily to have fun and to learn new skills. Older players have superior skills and consider winning to be a primary motive. Other differences between child and adult participation relate to the preferred coaching style. Research shows that child competitors prefer a relationship-oriented coaching style. College-age athletes have low relationship needs and prefer more task-oriented coaching. Professionals expect the coach not only to be task-oriented but also to use insight, intelligence, and communication of knowledge in coaching. Child athletes of various ages will almost surely quit a team or sport without warm coach-athlete interaction, while the professional athletes whose careers and salaries are dependent on performance are very task-oriented.

In general, the reasons for participation across gender have been the same, but some subtle differences emerge when reviewing the reasons. In surveys in which boys are asked why they participate, the following reasons and ranking emerges: be a part of a team, improve skills, demonstrate competence, have fun, and compete. When girls are given the same choices in surveys, they select and rank as follows: have fun, make and enjoy friends, improve appearance, control weight, and be a part of a team or group. Even with adults, there appear to be some gender differences, which may be critical to the success of women in professional sports. Adult males have been found to be motivated more by such extrinsic rewards as money, trophies, and fame—and their ego-involvement is enhanced by the world of professional sport. Women have been shown to seek out sport for intrinsically rewarding reasons such as the playing of sport as an end in itself—for fun, enjoyment, and affiliation. As the athlete shifts from amateur to professional and to playing for money, the motivation to compete shifts from a personally gratifying orientation to one that is being controlled externally.

More research needs to be conducted to determine if the female motives to compete shift substantially with this transition from amateur to professional, and what effect that has on the individual. As the level of play increases, gender differences may disappear. More research needs to be done to examine similarities and differences in team cohesion and reasons for participating for both male and female professional athletes. Trends indicate that professional athletes often lose intrinsic motivation for playing sports, and are governed by monetary rewards, fame, and celebrity status.

EFFECTS OF PROFESSIONALISM ON WOMEN'S SPORTS

Research has not yet determined the fundamental differences in reasons for sports participation between professional men and professional women athletes. Nor are the changes that occur as athletes enter professional status fully understood. Still, the casual bystander can offer some opinions about fundamental differences in the performance of amateur and professional athletes. Professional sport is designed to make money for the owners of teams, to provide a career for the professional athlete, and to entertain the spectator. To do so, players are forced to meet spectator and owner demands to change appearance, attend fundraising events, move to new cities, and spend many nights in hotels in unfamiliar cities. Participation for the joy of movement, for self-expression, for affiliation, and to stay in shape are no longer overriding goals. One must question how much joy can be derived from playing through pain and injury, from being on the road the better part of the year, or from masking personal emotions and giving up personal identity to take on the role of "heroine" and role model for the unknown entities and faces in the crowd.

Anecdotal reports from professional female athletes also cite conflict between roles and desires for bearing children and raising a family as concerns about professional lifestyles. While some professional athletes such as golfer Nancy Lopez have successfully overcome this barrier, others have not been able to achieve the same balance and resolution of the conflict. These concerns need to be tracked over time to determine what the actual sacrifices on family will be for professional female athletes, as well as the best means to satisfactorily resolve the personal conflict associated with motherhood and professional sports careers.

Even the medical profession is responding to the rise of professionalism in sport by changing how it treats athletic injuries in young athletes. Now, when deciding upon the most effective forms of treatment, the emphasis is to make early return to competition a priority. The incidences of overuse and training injuries in knee, shoulder, and back joints has dramatically increased for young girls, as they are being driven to keep up with the boys and train at higher intensity levels. One of the first questions asked by orthopedic doctors is whether a return to sport participation is critical to the well-being of the athlete, and aggressive forms of therapy are often the first choice in physical therapy clinics. The fear of athletes, and pressures by parents, that a few weeks or season lay-off will critically affect the career and scholarship opportunities for girls has contributed to changes in paradigms for care.

Young athletes are better served when they are reminded that amateur sport participation provides many joys and benefits, including the development of positive self-esteem, leadership opportunities, strength of character, and physical strength. The affiliation derived from participating in team sport is a gift to be cherished, and the bonds of friendship among teammates and between teams can lead to lifelong support systems for athletes, male and female alike.

These positive effects of sport participation fundamentally change when sport becomes career. Much of what many feminists have fought to gain may actually be given back as women cater to the demands of the sport as entertainment model. Fans will clamor to be entertained, and while expert play is beautiful to the trained eye, the larger crowd still clamors for the coliseum effect—kill or be killed. Fans demand a different type and style of performance, and a different type of heroine. The individual is sacrificed for the image, and the athlete is on display—to be criticized or admired for any number of characteristics. Looking at the male professional sport model, one finds aggression, violence, substance abuse, and angry outbursts abounding, a standard of conduct that is not so admirable in traditional society. Professional athletes sacrifice their personal lives to meet the demands of the fans—and the question arises as to whether the monetary rewards and fame merit the sacrifices of losing one's joy of sport and the self-control of one's destiny.

Debra A. Ballinger

Bibliography

Anshel, M. (1997) *Sport Psychology: From Theory to Practice.* Scottsdale, AZ: Gorsuch, Scarisbrick.

Chelladurai, P. (1984) "Discrepancy Between Preferences and Perceptions of Leadership Behavior and Satisfaction of Athletes in Varying Sports." *Journal of Sport Psychology* 6: 27–41.

———. (1990) "Leadership in Sports: A Review." *International Journal of Sport Psychology* 21: 328–354.

———., and A. V. Carron. (1983) "Athletic Maturity and Preferred Leadership." *Journal of Sport Psychology* 5: 371–380.

Deci, E. L. (1975) *Intrinsic Motivation.* New York: Plenum.

———., and R. M. Ryan. (1985) *Intrinsic Motivation and Self-determination in Human Behavior.* New York: Plenum.

Gould, D. (1984) "Psychosocial Development and Children's Sport." In *Motor Development during Childhood and Adolescence,* edited by J. R. Thomas. Minneapolis, MN: Burgess.

Roberts, G. C. (1993) "Motivation in Sport: Understanding and Enhancing the Motivation and Achievement of Children." In *Handbook of Research in Sport Psychology,* edited by R. N. Singer, M. Murphy, and L. K. Tennant. New York: Macmillan.

PUBERTY

During puberty and in the following period of adolescence, bodily and psychosocial changes and conflicts are closely connected. Puberty initiates developments and demands that are embedded in social contexts and transformed by social influences. These changes also have immediate impact on the sporting engagement of both sexes, but especially on the physical activities of girls.

THEORETICAL CONSIDERATIONS

Development from childhood to adulthood can be described using different theoretical approaches as a backdrop. These theories shed light on different aspects of this developmental process. Theories of socialization with a socioecological perspective, especially theories on gender-specific socialization, can show how girls and boys themselves appropriate not only norms, values, and behavior patterns, but also femininity and masculinity in a given society. The typical expectations and the processes of dealing with these demands in adolescence are main topics of developmental theories.

The theoretical approaches of youth sociology emphasize, among other things, the tasks that must be fulfilled in adolescence. These are the development of ego-identity; the development of gender identity, including the appropriation of gender roles; dealing with social expectations; a wide range of physical issues, including changes

TO HANDLE A GIRL IN ATHLETICS (1912)

A Ladies' Home Journal *Article Warns of the Dangers
of Girls' Participation in Vigorous Athletics*

By slow and careful preparation a girl who is organically sound may be trained to participate safely in almost any form of athletics. But inasmuch as the heart, lungs and other important organs do not attain their full power and development until a girl is about eighteen to twenty years of age no girl should be pushed to her limit in physical or mental effort before that time, if ever.

It is during the youthful period of from ten to fifteen years of age that girls are most susceptible of improvement if judiciously looked after; it is during the same period that they are most likely to be injured if they are not wisely cared for. For this reason every girls' school where athletics are encouraged should have a special teacher to look after the physical condition of the girls, who should not be left to become victims of their own zeal and the unbridled enthusiasm of a partisan school community.

Parents should insist upon the supervision of the physical as well as the mental training of their girls, especially if the girls are encouraged, through school politics, to engage in athletic contests. Most of the colleges for women have directors of physical training and instructors in athletics and gymnastics whose duty it is to look after the physical condition of the girls and to supervise their athletic sports and games as well as their gymnastic exercises.

It is largely on account of the intelligent supervision of the physical work in the women's colleges that athletics are less likely to be overdone than in many of the schools for girls where there is little or no supervision, though it is much more necessary than in the colleges.

DUDLEY A. SARGENT, M.D.
(1912) "Are Athletics Making Girls Masculine?"
The Ladies' Home Journal. *March.*

of the body, appropriation and use of the body, sexuality, and acceptance of appearance; gaining independence from the parent family; and building close relations to peers of the same and of the other sex. The metaphor of "life course" makes clear that, on the one hand, lives are directed by society, but that individuals, on the other hand, use these given "normal" life courses in an individual way, constructing their own specific lives.

Girls and boys deal differently with these tasks and expectations. It is, for example, easier for boys than for girls to gain autonomy by identifying themselves as different from their mothers. Conversely, while girls find it easier to learn social and communicative skills because of their identification with the mother, it is harder for them to develop an autonomous individuality.

CHANGES OF THE BODY

Prepuberty starts with girls at the age of around ten years, puberty at around thirteen. In this pe-riod of hormonal changes, the sexual functions and the secondary characteristics of the female sex develop. These changes affect the size and proportions of the body and influence movements, motor competence, and sport performances. Cognitive developments and new social expectations are closely intertwined with the changes of the body. It is not easy for girls to deal with all these changes and solve the connected difficulties in order to develop a positive self-concept and a stable identity.

It is difficult for many girls during puberty to accept these changes, which they cannot influence. Research in Europe and in the United States in the 1990s showed clearly that weight is of central importance for a majority of girls at this age. In a representative survey about the health of young people in Germany, more than half of the young women (59%) but only one third of young men (35%) reported to be dissatisfied with their body and with its weight. In other studies, the

NO MORE CLIMBING TREES

A Fictionalized Account of Puberty's Effect on a Girl

In her tree climbing days the ascent would have taken only a few minutes. But she had given up climbing when she started to grow her hair and stopped wearing shorts every day during the summer holidays. Since she was thirteen when her periods began, she felt she was pregnant with herself, bearing the slowly ripening embryo of Melanie-grown-up inside herself for a gestation time the length of which she was not precisely aware. And, during this time, to climb a tree might provoke a miscarriage and she would remain forever stranded in childhood, a crop-haired tomboy.

ANGELA CARTER
(1986) The Magic Toyshop. *London: Virago.*

percentage of girls who thought they were not slim enough was two-thirds. Of girls with less than the normal weight, a full 23 percent thought they were too heavy.

Further indicators of a widespread culture of slimness are the propagation of diets and the increasing number of eating disorders. According to a representative study in Germany, the number of girls having experience with dieting was more than double the number of boys. Of the persons with anorexia or bulimia, 90 to 95 percent are girls and women. Virtually all studies available, in spite of different methods and samples, demonstrate that girls evaluate their appearance in a more negative manner than do boys. Two-thirds of girls asked in a German study feared that their appearance was not good enough.

Consistent with these results was an indication that girls tended to trust their bodies less than boys and that girls, far more than boys, thought that they could not perform well in sports or that their athletic abilities were not relevant. These tendencies could be found even before puberty (in a period of life in which there are no decisive gender-specific differences in physical ability and performance). These empirical results are consistent with the everyday experience of teachers, coaches, and parents. The question that demands attention is: Why are so many girls not happy with their bodies?

When one compares the above-mentioned theoretical considerations with the research re-

sults, one finds many connections between ruling social ideals, images, norms, and values, on the one hand, and the reactions of the girls, on the other. Girls must deal with contradictory and unrealistic expectations concerning femininity. To a high degree, femininity is defined by body and appearance, and women depend much more than men on their physical appearance; they experience a great deal of pressure to live up to the myth of femininity. One problem is that the ideals transmitted by the mass media and advertisements are always unreachable. In addition, these ideals change frequently. The ideal of being slim, compact, and without any fault contradicts the female body and its physiological changes (puberty, pregnancy, old age).

MENSTRUATION

A central event during puberty is the first menstruation. Scientific interest in how menarche and menstruation influence the body and the self-concept of girls and women is relatively new. In sport science, menstruation as social construct has not been a topic. In 1994 Karin Flaake gathered information about the experiences of girls and women with menstruation. Girls and women themselves, when interviewed by Flaak about how they interpret and evaluate menstruation, were either ambivalent or negative toward this experience.

Searching for the causes of the conflicts connected with menstruation, one is confronted with contradictions. On the one hand, menstruation

A CHANGING BODY

An Account of Childhood Perceptions of Physical Development

Slight and slender were my grown up ambitions. Too often for comfort my mother, statuesque and on the heavy side, had teased (in front of my father) that I was going to inherit her ample bosom. No I won't, I'd mutter, in awe of what I'd seen when we'd shared a bath. Even worse was the fear that I might not develop at all, that I'd be wearing undershirts for the rest of my life.

SUSAN BROWNMILLER
(1984) Femininity. *New York: Lindon Press.*

symbolizes womanhood and adulthood; on the other hand, menstruation must be hidden because it is surrounded with numerous taboos. On an individual level, menstruation is a sign of good health, but socially, it has associations with weakness, illness, and impurity. These contradictions make it difficult to use menstruation as a chance to develop a positive relation to the body. The ambivalent attitude toward menstruation has negative effects on sport activities. It is frequently regarded as abnormal to be active when menstruating. Even though modern physicians may advise physical activity as a remedy for problems with menstruation, many girls do not feel at ease when they participate in sport or competition during menstruation.

SELF-CONCEPT AND FEMALE IDENTITY

Many studies reveal that girls, more often than boys, experience adolescence as a phase of destabilization and decreased self-esteem. Especially for an active girl (whom society sometimes calls a "tomboy") puberty brings change in many areas. Not only does the body change, but the environment increases the pressure on girls to adapt to the norms and the ideals of femininity. Studies from North America describe how girls who revolted as children against barriers and restrictions lost their autonomy during puberty. For independent girls, after puberty the appropriation of the culturally defined concept of femininity is connected with conflict. They cannot act and behave like boys, nor are they accepted as women.

Often, girls replace their lost self-confidence with a boyfriend and thus develop a new self-concept. Having a boyfriend, as well as having the "right" clothes and the "right" behavior, brings status and acceptance within the peer group. Thus, self-confidence becomes based more on attractiveness and success with boys than on the person herself and her abilities. In the United States, dating and popularity are specific concepts connected with rules and rituals of central importance for young people. In this context, sport is much less important for girls than for boys.

PHYSICAL ACTIVITIES AND SPORT ENGAGEMENT

During adolescence, male and female youths develop in different directions. Membership statistics of sport clubs, as well as surveys of the population, reveal the same trend in many countries: the interest of girls in physical activities and sport decreases continuously after puberty—at least until the age of thirty. Coaches and physical education teachers frequently complain that it is very difficult to motivate girls for gym class or training. Because peer acceptance becomes more important and because sport activities contribute relatively little to their popularity, girls often turn to different leisure activities, such as shopping, and telephoning. Often girls adapt their interests to the wishes of their boyfriends. So, for example, they watch their boyfriends playing sports instead of being active themselves.

The problems of sport activities in the context of adolescence depend on the type of sport. On the one hand, sports can increase adolescent conflicts, especially if the sport does not fit ideals of femininity. On the other hand, sport activities can help to resolve expectations that confront girls and can provide a measure of self-confidence. Sport activities and success can, for example, strengthen girls when they have conflicts within their families or when they feel lonely.

While conflicts with sport activities, femininity, and self-concept can develop, especially in a male-dominated sport, ballet and rhythmical gymnastics present a different set of problems. The pressure to demonstrate a certain type of femininity and to present a type of "child-woman" can lead to discrepancies between the real and the ideal body and self. Gymnasts, for example, often suffer from both the real and imagined evaluation of others. The necessary presentation of the body during practice and competition can be connected with the fear of not reaching this ideal. It seems paradoxical that some "feminine" types of sport, such as gymnastics, cannot be easily combined with becoming a grown-up female.

Whether sport is a central part of the lifestyle of young people depends on many factors. Social level, ethnic origin, environment, economic status, and sport culture are all important. While some girls give up their sport interest and engagement during or after puberty, many others enjoy the possibilities offered by sports, solving the problems connected with sport activities in this phase of life. It is a challenge for physical education teachers and coaches to strengthen the commitment to sports for all girls in order to motivate them for lifelong sports engagement.

Gertrud Pfister

See also Amenorrhea; Eating Disorders; Menstrual Cycle; Reproduction; School Achievement; Socialization

Bibliography

Delaney, Janice, Mary Jane Lupton, and Emily Toth. (1988) *The Curse: A Cultural History of Menstruation.* Illinois: University of Illinois Press.

Flaake, Karin. (1994) *Ein eigenes Begehren? Weibliche Adoleszenz und das Verhältnis zu Körperlichkeit und Sexualität.* Berlin: ZE Frauenforschung.

Gilligan, Carol, and Lyn Mikel Brown. (1992) *Meeting at the Crossroads: Women's Psychology and Girls' Development.* Cambridge, MA: Harvard University Press.

Hancock, Emily. (1989) *The Girl Within.* New York: Dutton.

Horstkemper, Marianne. (1987) *Schule, Geschlecht und Selbstvertrauen.* Weinheim and Munich: Juventa.

Lee, Janet, and Jennifer Sasser-Coen. (1996) *Blood Stories: Menarche and the Politics of the Female Body in Contemporary U.S. Society.* New York: Routledge.

Nathanson, Constance A. (1991) *Dangerous Passage: The Social Control of Sexuality in Women's Adolescence (Health, Society, and Policy Series).* Philadelphia, PA: Temple University Press.

Palzkill, Birgit. (1990) *Zwischen Turnschuh und Stöckelschuh: Die Entwicklung lesbischer Identität im Sport.* Bielefeld, Germany: AJZ.

Pfister, Gertrud. (1997) "Der Widerspenstigen Zähmung. Körper und Bewegungskultur von Mädchen in der Adoleszenz" In *Jugendsport,* edited by Jürgen Baur. Aachen: Meyer and Meyer, 255–281.

Pipher, Mary. (1995) *Reviving Ophelia: Saving the Selves of Adolescent Girls.* New York: Ballantine Books.

Ussher, Jane M. (1989) *The Psychology of the Female Body.* New York: Routledge.

Vertinsky, Patricia. (1990) *The Eternally Wounded Woman.* Urbana: University of Illinois Press.

R

RACE AND ETHNICITY

Racism in sports may take various forms. The first is exclusion, which may mean exclusion from facilities, participation, or leadership positions. Members of one race or ethnicity may hold low-paying jobs more frequently than those of other groups. Because they do not have much money, sport participation becomes difficult, at times impossible. Joining sport or fitness clubs with high-quality facilities is expensive; swimming teams for youth may have practice fees; gymnastics requires long and costly training. Exclusion may not be the intent in these cases, but it is the result.

Women in some cultures face difficulties when they try to gain access to proprietary sports and fitness facilities. In some cultures, family money is controlled completely by the dominant male, who may refuse a woman financial support for activities related to sports, thus creating financial exclusion. If the woman is a member of a race or ethnic group that is generally limited to lower-paying jobs, she stands little chance of getting access to proprietary sports or fitness facilities. Without money, she may use only free facilities that are almost certainly less desirable or in poorer condition than those enjoyed by the people of the dominant race or ethnic group.

Basketball, track, and cross-country are among the sports that, unlike golf, tennis, or swimming, typically do not require fees or highly specialized facilities. Thus, the targets of society's racism are often disproportionately represented as participants in sports that do not charge fees to participate.

Racism may also limit access to leadership positions. This is particularly true for women of color. Research in the United States has shown that in intercollegiate athletics, only 6.5 percent of all athletics directors are members of a minority group: African American, Hispanic, Asian, or Native American. Of the 6.5 percent, less than 1 percent are women. Additionally, the National Collegiate Athletic Association (NCAA) reported that in 1997 the percentage of black coaches of women's teams was decreasing, as was the number of black women administrators of women's intercollegiate sports programs.

In the United States, people of color are more likely to find it hard to gain access to participation and leadership positions. This is the same group of people who suffer disproportionately from high blood pressure and heart disease, health concerns that may be related to exercise level. It is also this same group of people who are typically underrepresented as role models by way of leadership positions in sport. In women's athletics, the presence of females in leadership positions increases the likelihood of greater representation of women as coaches. The same is likely to be true when race is the focus. Thus, the absence of African-American women in leadership positions responsible for hiring works against their representation in other leadership positions.

Stacking is a second manifestation of racism in sports. Also referred to as centrality of position, stacking occurs when players from a particular racial or ethnic group are either over- or underrepresented at certain playing positions in team sports—for instance, when players of color are assigned to play positions that the assigner classifies as nonthinking. Similarly, positive stereotypes about racially enhanced levels of speed or strength often cause stacking to occur in positions where those qualities are critical. For example, according to Jay Coakley, in women's intercollegiate sports, black players seem to be overrepresented in the spiking position in volleyball, while white players are most visible in the setter and bumper positions.

Segregation is another form of racism in which people from one racial or ethnic group are

---

WALKING OUT LIKE A LADY (1958)

Althea Gibson Reflects on Combatting Racial Stereotypes

Those days, I probably would have been more at home training in Stillman's Gym than at the Cosmopolitan Club. I really wasn't the tennis type. But the polite manners of the game, that seemed so silly to me at first, gradually began to appeal to me. So did the pretty white clothes. I had trouble as a competitor because I kept wanting to fight the other player every time I started to lose a match. . . . After a while I began to understand that you could walk out on the court like a lady, all dressed up in immaculate white, be polite to everybody, and still play like a tiger and beat the liver and lights out of the ball. I remember thinking to myself that it was kind of like a matador going into the bull ring, beautifully dressed, bowing in all directions, following the fancy rules to the letter, and all the time having nothing in mind except sticking that sword into the bull's guts and killing him as dead as hell.

The Cosmopolitan members were the highest class of Harlem people and they had rigid ideas about what was socially acceptable behavior. They were undoubtedly more strict than white people of similar positions, for the obvious reason that they felt they had to be doubly careful in order to overcome the prejudiced attitude that all Negroes lived eight to a room in dirty houses and drank gin all day and settled all their arguments with knives.

ALTHEA GIBSON
(1958) I Always Wanted to Be Somebody. *New York: Harper & Row Publishers.*

---

denied access to athletic facilities, such as private country clubs that have been maintained as the exclusive domain of another racial or ethnic group. Segregation, however, is not always the product of the dominant group in a society. For example, African-American athletes, long the victims of segregated country clubs, have sometimes created racially exclusive teams and/or leagues that exclude white athletes. A historic example of this may be found in the Negro Baseball Leagues of the 1940s, in which black athletes who had been excluded from the white leagues, in turn, barred white athletes from play.

In sports, segregation appears to be more common among males than females. One possible explanation is that large numbers of women could not participate in organized sports during the decades of rampant segregation. Most sport sociologists, though, believe that women generally function on a more inclusive level than men.

Marginalization is the fourth way in which racism affects sports participation. Some people are concerned only with appearances. Being able to point to a black or Jewish member of a country club, for instance, allows those so inclined to feel better about the racism they and their clubs practice. Such tokenism is also referred to as marginalization. The presence of a token is designed to erroneously convince outsiders that the club or team has a policy of accepting all members who meet the membership criteria, regardless of race or ethnicity.

In sport, racism is almost always applied or manifested toward darker-skinned people of either gender. Indeed, racism seems to be generally free of gender discrimination although the research direction concerning the topic may be a bit gender-biased. Research is increasing on males who participate in sports. That there is very little research documenting the presence of racism among female athletes may, in itself, be a function of the lower level of concern about female participation in sport in general.

RACISM AND THE ATHLETE

In 1989 the Women's Sport Foundation published the result of a national survey involving 14,000 high school sophomores in the United States in 1,015 public schools from 1980 to 1986. The results showed that sport-participation patterns, as well as the patterns of how sport benefited students,

ASHE TAKES TENNIS TO INNER CITY

The National Junior Tennis League was founded in 1969 by tennis players Arthur Ashe and Charles Pasarell and businessman Sheridan Snyder in order to provide tennis lessons for children in inner cities. The NJTL is administered by the United States Tennis Association and supported by the Association and corporate and individual donations. The best-known player involved in the program is Venus Williams who participated in Compton, California, before achieving top-5 status on the women's professional tour. The purpose of the program is to make tennis more widely available, especially to minority children who would not otherwise have the chance to play or take lessons.

varied among racial and ethnic groups. Although the study focused solely on African Americans, Hispanics, and whites, its extent provides interesting insight into broader issues.

The results of the study suggest the following general conclusions. Minority athletes are more socially involved than members of minority groups who are not athletic. These minority athletes, too, tend to score higher on standardized tests and to get better grades in school. Among some minority groups, sport participation can increase the likelihood of staying in school. In some categories, minority athletes were more likely to attend college; these categories included African-American males from cities and both rural and urban Hispanic females. Sport participation benefited male and female minority athletes equally.

In some areas the WSF study found that race had a negative effect on whether minority students benefited from sport participation. For example, Hispanic girls were the most likely to reap positive benefits from sport-participation, and African-American girls were the least positively affected by sport-involvement. In fact, sport may have hurt them socially in school and may have had hindered their upward mobility.

Minority athletes are sometimes encouraged to use their athletic talents to obtain professional sports contracts. This motivation deceives the young male athlete because his potential for success and glory in professional sports is ephemeral. Only one out of 25,000 collegiate scholarship male athletes of any racial group ever obtains any type of professional sport contract. Therefore, minority male athletes might be better served by being offered more accurate and realistic motivations.

Ownership and other leadership roles in professional sports teams are generally the domain of wealthy white males; they need not be athletic. Very few minorities, male or female, serve as owners, managers, and coaches in professional sports.

Why are minorities missing from professional sport management? Some would argue that society has sent both subtle and overt, yet erroneous, messages to would-be owners and managers of professional teams: "Because of your minority status, you do not have the talent or capability to succeed as coaches and managers." If racism is keeping talented minority males out of leadership positions, its effect on female minorities is even more powerful.

CONCLUSION

Sports has often been characterized as a universal venue, where all people, regardless of race, are welcome and accepted. Reality has shown that sports may instead be perpetuating society's racism through means both subtle and blatant. Racism is a quiet killer of spirit and should be rejected in both society and its microcosm, sport. Participation in sports activities and the benefits to be derived from them should be available to all people, regardless of race and gender.

R. Vivian Acosta

Bibliography

Acosta, R. Vivian, and Linda Jean Carpenter. (1994) "Status of Minority Women." In *Women's Intercollegiate Athletics—1994*. Unpublished study.

Birrell, Susan, and Cheryl L. Cole. (1994) *Women, Sport, and Culture*. Champaign, IL, Human Kinetics.

Brooks, D. D. and R. C. Althouse. (1993) *Racism in College Athletics: The African-American Athlete's Experience*. Morgantown, WV: Fitness Information Technology, Inc., 101–142.

Bryant, J. E. and M. McElroy. (1997) *Sociological Dynamics of Sport and Exercise*. Englewood, CO: Morton Publishing Company.

Coakley, Jay J. (1997) *Sport in Society, Issues and Controversies*. Boston: Irwin, McGraw-Hill.

Corbett, Doris, and W. Johnson. (1993) "The African-American Female in Collegiate Sports: Sexism and Racism." In *Racism in College Athletics: The African-American Athlete's Experience*. Edited by D. D. Brooks and R. C. Althouse. Morgantown. WV: Fitness Information Technology, Inc., 179–204.

Edwards, Harry. (1980) "The Myth of the Racially Superior Athlete." In *Sport and American Society: Selected Readings*, edited by G. H. Sage. Reading. PA: Addison-Wesley Publishing, 317–322.

Eitzen, Stanley D. (1993) *Sport in Contemporary Society: An Anthology*. New York: St. Martin's Press.

Eitzen, Stanley D. (1997) *Sociology of North American Sport*. Dubuque, IA: Brown and Benchmark.

Green, Tina-Sloan. (1993). "The Future of African-American Female Athletes." In *Racism in College Athletics: The African-American Athletes's Experience*. Edited by D. D. Brooks and R. C. Althouse. Morgantown WV: Fitness Information Technology, 205–223.

Lapchick, Richard E., and K. L. Matthews. (1992) *1997 Racial Report Card*. Northeastern University's Center for the Study of Sport in Society.

Smith, Yvonne R. (1992) "Women of Color in Society." *Quest*, 44: 228–250.

Women's Sports Foundation. (1989) *The Women's Sports Foundation Report: Minorities in Sports*. New York: Women's Sports Foundation.

RACEWALKING

Racewalking is a relatively obscure sport that developed in Europe. Classified as an event within track and field, it has been an Olympic sport for men since 1932 and for women only since 1992. Men compete in 20- and 50-kilometer races and women in 10- and 20-kilometer races. The sport is classified within track and field, and competitors are judged on speed and technique. Thus, racewalkers consider it a sport and an aesthetic form, as well as an activity that provides major physical fitness benefits for participants at all levels of the sport.

HISTORY

Racewalking developed from the sport of pedestrianism, "the art of rapidly covering great distances on foot," which originated in England in the eighteenth century. In 1835 organized footracing was introduced to the United States, where it soon became headline material. Women participated regularly in pedestrian events in Europe and North America. Pedestrians had competed indoors in large halls and arenas, where they circled for days in quest of such prizes as the Sir John Astley belt, which pitted the Americans against the British in a fiercely competitive battle. The atmosphere was much like horse racing, with spectators gambling on the athletes. By the twentieth century, as the event shifted from entertainment to sport, racewalking had replaced the alternate run-walk gait of the pedestrian, and track and road courses had replaced the halls and arenas.

Racewalking's first appearance in the Olympics was in 1932, for men only. For some years, the only event was the 50-kilometer race; then, in 1956 a 20-kilometer race was added. Not until 1992 did racewalking become an Olympic sport for women, with a 10-kilometer race. Women also compete in 20-kilometer races outside the Olympics. Often featuring a dramatic finish, racewalking draws considerable media and spectator attention at the Olympics. After completing most of the race out of sight on roads, the leading racers enter the stadium for the final lap in a state of near exhaustion, pushing themselves to the limit while trying to maintain their strange gait. The spectators rise to cheer them home, and the winner can be assured of much, though brief, attention from the media.

In the 1990s racewalking experienced considerable growth and became a worldwide sport. At the top level of the women's sport, China and Italy dominate, followed by Russia.

RULES AND PLAY

Racewalking is "the progression of steps taken so that unbroken contact with the ground is maintained" while the "knee of the supporting leg is straightened as it passes under the centre of the body," according to the handbook of the International Amateur Athletic Federation (IAAF), which governs track and field internationally. The definition emphasizes that racewalking is a skill, as well as a strength and endurance sport. It is correct style and its enforcement that justify the existence of racewalking. Judges enforce the rules at intervals along the racecourse and may caution or disqualify a racewalker for lifting (failing to maintain contact with the ground with at least one part of one foot) or creeping (failing to straighten the supporting leg). An athlete must receive a disqualification (red card) from each of three judges to be removed from the race. Unfortunately, as in any judged sport, controversies have hurt the sport during its history as judging leaves athletes exposed to political considerations.

Racewalking, unlike the other events in track and field, is an art and, as such, is exposed to a certain amount of subjective judgment. Although aesthetics are not at issue, and the judges are supposed to judge only correct technique, the walker who looks the smoothest and most relaxed will usually manage to avoid the attention of the judges. Racewalkers today attain speeds at which it is almost impossible for the human eye to tell whether the athlete is maintaining contact with the ground. Judges try different techniques, such as judging from a supine position, but most look for cues, such as bouncing shoulders, a bent-over waist, and other indicators of fatigue that often lead to a breakdown in technique. Whatever method judges use, athletes would nevertheless benefit from greater objectivity because they and their sport suffer from the occasionally blatant politics of judging. Racewalkers compete on tracks and roads, but only results achieved on tracks are considered as world records.

Women have participated in the racewalk at an international level since the early 1900s, although the first world cup of racewalking for women was not awarded until 1979 at Eschborn, Germany. The event was a 5-kilometer race won by Marion Fawkes of Great Britain in 22 minutes 51 seconds, followed by Carol Tyson, also of Great Britain, and Thorill Gyler of Norway. Some sources indicate that the first world cup for women actually took place in 1968, although that event was probably not sanctioned by the IAAF as the 1979 event was. The men's world cup (the Lugano) started in 1961. World cups are held every other year, with a 10-kilometer race, which

M. Mullens wins the 880-yard race at the Fourteenth Annual Sports Gala of Siemens Sports Club held at Charlton in 1936. (Hulton-Deutsch Collection/Corbis)

became the official women's distance in 1985. The first Pan American Games event for women was in Indianapolis in 1987 (for men in 1951). Maria Colin of Mexico won the 10-kilometer event in a time of 47 minutes and 17.15 seconds. She was followed by Ann Peel of Canada and Maryanne Torrellas of the United States. At the first Olympic 10-kilometer event for women at the 1992 Olympic Games in Barcelona, Spain, Yueling Chen of China won with a time of 44 minutes and 32 seconds, followed by Yelena Nikolayeva of Russia, and Chunxiu Li, also of China. The race was very dramatic and highly controversial, with Alina Ivanonva of Ukraine taking the lead over the last 150 yards. Her technique was so unacceptable, however, that she received two red cards in the final lap and was then disqualified after finishing first, giving the victory to Chen. The fourth finisher, Ileana Salvador of Italy was also disqualified, allowing Li to move from fifth to third place.

The world record progression statistics show steady and rapid improvement in women's times over the years. In 1943 the best time for the 10-kilometer race was 52 minutes and 6.6 seconds. By 1990 it had dropped to 41 minutes and 56.23 seconds, which remained the track world record as of 1998. It was set in Seattle by Nadezhda Ryashkina of the Soviet Union. The women's world record in 1998 for the 10-kilometer road race was 41 minutes 4 seconds, set by Yelena Nikolayeva of Russia in 1996. Linca Alfridi of Italy holds the world record in the 20-kilometer race at 1 hour, 28 minutes, 13 seconds.

SUMMARY

The continuing interest shown in racewalking and its increasing worldwide popularity in the 1990s is certainly due in part to the interest in fitness in North America. Racewalking is an excellent form of exercise. When the correct technique is used, every muscle group comes into play. Even with less than perfect technique, rapid walking provides cardiovascular benefits.

The Editors

See also Pedestrianism

Bibliography

Jacobson, Howard. (1980) *Racewalk to Fitness.* New York: Simon & Schuster.

Schiller, Curt. Racing Walking World. (1999) <www.monmouth.com>.

Strangman, Denis. (1990) *An Annotated Bibliography of Race Walking and Related Topics.* Belconnen, Australia: National Sport Information Centre.

Ward, Elaine. (1990) *Walking Wisdom for Women.* Pasadena, CA: North American Racewalking Foundation.

Additional information was provided by Wayne Wilson (Amateur Athletic Foundation, Los Angeles).

RACQUETBALL

Racquetball is a court game played indoors with a small racquet and a hard ball. The fashionable game of the late 1970s and early 1980s at health and recreation centers, it declined in popularity in the late 1980s but has experienced a revival as part of the fitness movement in the 1990s. Racquetball now has a larger following, including more women, than ever before. Racquetball's appeal has much to do with its value in promoting fitness. Participation even at the recreational level burns calories, tones muscles, enhances flexibility, promotes cardiovascular fitness, and helps improve balance and coordination. Although the sport has been international since the early 1980s, it continues to be dominated at the elite level by American and Canadian women athletes.

HISTORY

Racquetball was invented by Joe Sobek in 1949 on a Connecticut handball court. Seeking a game with fast pace that was easy to learn, Sobek designed the first short strung paddle, devised rules combining the basics of handball and squash, and named his modification "paddle rackets." His experiment was an overnight success; the sport caught on quickly and evolved into racquetball as we know it today.

By the early 1970s, court clubs could be found in every state, and the sport enjoyed a rapid and steady rise in popularity. As Americans sought new and challenging athletic activities, the timing was perfect for racquetball—courts were accessible nationwide, and the sport was fun and easy to learn. In the late 1970s and early 1980s, racquetball became one of the fastest-growing sports in America. To meet the demand for playing time, thousands of new racquetball courts were built at health and fitness clubs around the country.

Interest in the new sport peaked in the mid-1980s and then declined, with some racquetball-only clubs going out of business and fitness clubs using racquetball courts for other purposes. By 1987 the sport had found its base market, and, from an original core group of loyal enthusiasts, participation had grown to some 6.8 million players. Over the next few years, the sport continued to grow at a slow but steady pace and enjoyed a resurgence in the early 1990s. For the first time in more than a decade, racquetball showed a significant increase in participation—more than half a million more people played racquetball in 1996 than the previous year (from 6.3 million to 6.8). Of these, 2.2 million were women, with 17 percent between the ages of eighteen and thirty-four.

The sport also spread internationally, with world championships held every other year since 1981, the addition of five events approved by the International Olympic Committee (IOC), and its debut as a Pan American Games sport in 1995. At the close of the century, racquetball was being played in some ninety nations.

The international governing body for the sport of racquetball is the International Racquetball Federation (IRF). A current member of the International Olympic Committee, the IRF governs ninety-one countries' racquetball federations. The IRF, originally the International Amateur Racquetball Federation (IARF), was founded in 1979 with thirteen countries as members.

RULES AND PLAY

Racquetball may be played by two or four players. When played by two, it is called singles and when played by four, doubles. Racquetball, as the name implies, is a competitive game in which each player uses a racquet to send and return the ball. The objective is to win each rally by serving or returning the ball so that the opponent is unable to keep the ball in play. A rally is over when a side makes an error or is unable to return the ball before it touches the floor twice, or when a hinder (obstruction) is called. Points are scored only when the serving side serves an ace or wins a rally. When the serving side loses a rally, it loses the serve. Losing the serve is called an out in singles. In doubles, when the first server loses the serve, it is called a hand-out, and when the second server loses the serve, it is called a side-out. The first side to win two games wins the match, with each game being played to 15 points. In the event that each participant or team wins one game, the match is decided by an 11-point tiebreaker.

WOMEN AND RACQUETBALL

Racquetball has maintained a women's professional tour since the early 1970s, now known as the Women's International Racquetball Tour (WIRT). One of very few professional sporting organizations devoted solely to promoting women athletes, the WIRT ended its 1997–1998 season with seven-time professional national champion Michelle Gould (1970, Boise, Idaho) capturing the season crown by 245 points over 1992 champion Jackie Paraiso (1966, El Cajon, California). As of 1998,

After peaking in popularity in the mid-1980s, racquetball experienced a revival as part of the 1990s fitness craze. (Dennis O'Clair/Corbis)

Gould had won eight of the previous nine amateur national singles championships—more than any other player, male or female. While retaining her amateur status, the Idaho resident has captured seven of the previous eight pro tour titles, including six in a row. Before the emergence of the 5-foot 11-inch Gould, the women's professional tour was firmly in the grasp of Canadian Heather McKay (1941) and American Lynn Adams (1957). McKay had dominated the international squash circuit for almost two decades before deciding to try racquetball. Her switch resulted in four pro tour titles (1980, 1981, 1983, 1984).

The only player on the tour to challenge McKay was former collegiate track star Lynn Adams of Oregon Coast College. Courageously fighting through multiple sclerosis, Adams managed to win six tour crowns (1982, 1985–1988, 1990). Both Adams and McKay were 1997 inductees into the Racquetball Hall of Fame. Athletes such as Adams, McKay, and Gould might never have had the chance to earn a living from the sport if it not been for Peggy Steding (1947). This vibrant Texan seemed to revolutionize a sport that had been controlled by men since its inception. Steding dominated women's racquetball from 1973 to 1976. She was ranked number one for three years on the professional tour and for three years as the top U.S. amateur.

The United States Racquetball Association (USRA) is doing its part to seek more participation by women. In November of 1996 the USRA's inaugural Promus Hotel Corporation U.S. Open racquetball championships took place and attracted more sponsorship and prize money than any racquetball event in the history of the sport. Held at the prestigious Racquet Club of Memphis Tennessee, the 1998 U.S. Open budget increased the women's prize money and provided more female players with such amenities as cars, cellular phones, and personal services than in the past.

All professional matches, from the men's and women's quarterfinals on, are played on the made-for-television portable glass court. Because it is played on such a television-friendly court, the event has been picked up by the sports network ESPN. With its title sponsor, Promus Hotel Corporation, signed through 2001, the U.S. Open will continue to feature the sport that many call the fastest in the world.

All ages compete at national and world levels in racquetball. Athletes as young as six compete at the annual junior world and national championships, whereas players through the age of eighty-five compete for their respective national crowns at the national singles and doubles championships. The senior players can also compete at the International Racquetball Federation World Seniors Championships in Albuquerque, New Mexico. With divisions running from ages thirty-five and over to eighty-five and older, the IRF event has become one of the most internationally popular racquetball events.

For the elite international racquetball athlete, the biannual IRF world championships have been a long-standing goal. Since the first world championship in 1981 and then again in 1984, the event has been held in Orlando, Florida (1986); Hamburg, Germany (1988); Caracas, Venezuela (1990); Montreal, Canada (1992); San Luis Potosí, Mexico (1994); Phoenix, Arizona (1996); and Cochabamba, Bolivia (1998).

Here, as was the case with the professional and U.S. amateur circuits, Michelle Gould has dominated. She captured gold at the 1992, 1994, and 1996 tournaments and finished second to Canada's Heather Stupp at the 1990 world championships. At fourteen years of age, Gould took the silver medal in doubles at the 1986 world championships. Gould's current rival on the women's professional tour, Jackie Paraiso, has enjoyed her share of success on the international level, winning three world doubles titles (1990, 1994, 1996). The 1996 title was won with her identical twin Joy MacKenzie.

SUMMARY

The close of the twentieth century marked an exciting time for the sport of racquetball for both female and male participants. With increasing exposure to a growing market of recreational and competitive players—combined with the sport's proven record of steady annual growth and the promise of achieving the Olympic dream—racquetball was well positioned for the future, both in terms of leisure participation and national and international competition.

Kevin Vicroy

Bibliography

Adams, Lynn, and E. Goldbloom. (1991) *Racquetball Today.* St. Paul, MN. West Publishing.

Mojer, Linda, ed. (1990–present), *Racquetball.* Colorado Springs, CO: Luke St. Onge/United States Racquetball Association.

Stafford, Randy (1990) *Racquetball: The Sport for Everyone.* 3d ed. Memphis, TN: Stafford.

RECRUITMENT

The recruiting of talented athletes by representatives of teams and sports programs has probably been going on for as long as there have been competitive sporting events, but skilled female athletes were not widely recruited until the 1990s. Today, women are recruited in ever-increasing numbers by colleges and professional teams in sports such as basketball and volleyball.

THE PROCESS OF RECRUITING

Recruiting takes place at just about every level of female sports, and competition is keen for the most skilled and talented athletes. Sport recruiting usually refers to college-level athletics.

Clearly, that is where the most intense recruiting takes place because, at the majority of American institutions, sports are an integral part of the collegiate scene and there is fierce competition to field the best teams. Strong sport programs bring recognition and esteem to colleges and are in themselves a tool for recruiting students.

Recruiting also takes place in other situations, though on a smaller, less formal scale. Increasingly, adolescent girls are invited to join clubs or select traveling teams by coaches eager to field competitive programs. Olympic hopefuls and other elite athletes, after being recruited, sometimes move away from their hometowns to train with well-known coaches. Some high school coaches dazzle talented female athletes with the unique benefits offered by their schools in hopes of securing their attendance, though this practice is not allowed by many school districts.

Another area in which recruiting takes place is in professional sports. The best female athletes in the United States and around the world are highly sought after, and some are able to earn their living by playing sports and by endorsing products. Many of them, like male professional athletes, are represented by sports agents.

Recruiting for college athletes is usually carried out by coaches, who try to secure the best players for their teams. A major incentive that many colleges offer talented sportswomen who join their athletic programs is the sport scholarship. Unlike loans or other kinds of financial aid, scholarships do not have to be repaid. The sport scholarship not only carries a monetary incentive but also validates the value of the athlete to the college. Colleges that offer athletic scholarships are usually able to attract the best athletes.

The availability of athletic scholarships for females has steadily increased, along with the growth of women's participation in sports at U.S. colleges and universities. Much of the credit for this goes to Title IX, the federal law that mandates equal opportunity for women and girls in education, including sports. Although Title IX was passed in 1972, it took strong measures, such as lawsuits, to put teeth into the law and to force colleges to bring their athletic programs into, or close to, compliance.

To comply with the law, colleges added sports for women and raised many intramural sports to the intercollegiate level. Because recruiting the female athlete was a relatively new phenomenon, many high school girls and their parents—even many coaches and high school counselors—did not understand the recruiting process: what it was, how it happened, and what girls could do to enhance their chances of being recruited.

WHY MORE YOUNG WOMEN DO NOT SEEK SCHOLARSHIPS

There are four myths that keep many females from even looking into the possibility of pursuing a sport scholarship. For girls to be successful in the recruiting game, each myth has to be dispelled.

The first myth that should be debunked is that only superstars win a sport scholarship. In fact, only 1 percent of high school athletes are considered superstars, or "blue-chip athletes." They are only a handful of the thousands of skilled female athletes who play sports—from badminton to basketball, soccer to squash, tennis to track and field—and who make an important contribution to college sports teams every year. Coaches need skilled, hardworking athletes to fill their rosters and make up their teams.

The second myth is that college coaches automatically know about any high school athlete who is good enough to warrant their attention. In fact, college coaches will probably never find out about most of these talented athletes unless they are brought to the coaches' attention. Thousands of young athletes across the country who excel at sports in their hometowns are never seen by coaches outside their region. The word does not spread automatically; time and limited recruiting budgets prohibit coaches from scouring the countryside looking for talent.

The third myth is that an athlete has to be capable of Division I competition (the highest level of collegiate athletic competition) to get a sports scholarship. Many student athletes think only about Division I schools because these are the colleges that often appear on television or the sport pages. In fact, several thousand other colleges (four-year and some two-year schools) offer competitive sport programs and award athletic scholarships.

The last myth is that there are very few sport scholarships for women athletes. In fact, scholarships are increasingly available for female athletes.

In 1972, when Title IX passed, there were no athletic scholarships for female athletes. By 1998, 33 percent of the more than $600 million per year awarded in sport scholarships went to women.

STRATEGIES TO ATTRACT ATHLETIC RECRUITERS

Recruiters believe that female athletes need to market themselves. Though young women frequently underestimate their prospects, recruiting experts advise that they must assume a proactive attitude and take specific steps to draw the attention of college coaches. Student athletes are advised to plan their approach years in advance, as early as the sophomore year of high school. The first step is to research colleges. Libraries offer a wide selection of college guides for two- and four-year institutions, and athletic directories that describe college programs. Additionally, most universities have their own Web sites that give detailed and up-to-date information. Matching up athletic programs with a list of colleges that interest the student gives her a preliminary slate of colleges to contact.

Once a student athlete has decided which schools interest her, she must initiate the recruiting process by contacting college coaches. This is especially important advice for females, because, despite the improvements since Title IX, there are still fewer scholarship opportunities for women than there are for men, and the limited money allotted for recruiting tends to go for male athletes. This increases the chances that girls, many of whom could make a significant contribution to a college sports program, will simply not be noticed. The student athlete should send a brief letter to the coach, indicating interest and requesting information about the college and the athletic program. Coaches usually respond promptly with a packet of information and request that the athlete fill out a player profile sheet.

To increase her prospects, experts advise that the student athlete prepare a range of materials that will display her potential to the coaches of prospective schools. She should prepare a résumé—a summary of academic, athletic, and personal accomplishments—to elaborate on the limited information the coach has received. Along with the résumé; a cover letter, several letters of recommendation, an upcoming game or event schedule, copies of newspaper clippings and awards, and a photo all help a coach to learn about the prospective athlete, and perhaps to go to see her compete (or send a representative to do so). The student athlete sends this packet to all the appropriate coaches at all the colleges in which she has an interest. Follow-up calls and notes at intervals indicate continued interest in the program and establish rapport with the coach. Additionally, girls should have their athletic performances filmed in case a videotape is requested.

Coaches are interested in the potential recruit's academic as well as her athletic achievements. Colleges and athletic associations, of which the National College Athletic Association (NCAA) is the largest, set minimum academic requirements athletes must meet to participate in collegiate sports. When coaches are considering two athletes of similar skills, the one with the best

HOW TO GET A COLLEGE ATHLETIC SCHOLARSHIP

Athletic scholarships are an important source of higher education financial aid for young female athletes in the United States. Recruitment is a two-way street. Coaches seek out well-known high school players and visit well-known teams and schools. But athletes must also market themselves to coaches because there is much competition for athletic scholarships and coaches cannot visit every school. Experts suggest that athletes market themselves by writing letters to coaches at schools they would like to attend, visit the schools, send videotapes of themselves in action, and follow up with phone calls. Gaining the support of local alumni of the college or university can also help.

grades and highest assessment test scores usually has the edge because she is viewed as having the greater potential for success at the college level. Thus, a student athlete can enhance her prospects by having good grades and other academic achievements.

When a student athlete reaches her senior year, she may be recruited by several coaches, all trying to encourage her to play her sport at their college. To help her make a decision, experts advise that she should always visit the schools, get to know the coaches, and talk to other athletes about their experiences with each school and its programs. When a coach makes a scholarship offer, it is important to weigh it carefully before deciding. If there is more than one offer, each should be considered and compared. Some scholarships are for all expenses, including tuition, room and board, books, and supplies. Others are partial scholarships, paying a portion of overall expenses. These can sometimes be combined with other scholarships or financial aid. The student athlete and her parents will want to consider the size of the scholarship with other criteria they have developed in selecting a college. Signing a letter of intent is the final stage in the recruiting process, signaling the commitment of the college and student to her education and sports involvement.

Today, athletic talent can pave the way to college and pay expenses, too. Increasingly, professional opportunities are opening up to female athletes around the world. Whatever the level, it is vital that female athletes who do not want to be left on the sidelines take an assertive role in the recruiting process. There is growing demand for top female players, a situation that influences girls' and young women's participation in sports throughout much of the world.

Penny Hastings

See also Intercollegiate Sports; Title IX

Bibliography

Hastings, Penny. (1999) *Sports for Her: A Reference Guide for Teenage Girls.* Westport, CT: Greenwood.

Hastings, Penny, and Todd D. Caven. (1999) *How to Win a Sports Scholarship,* 2d ed. Los Angeles, CA: First Base Sports.

Sporting Goods Manufacturers Association. (1998) *Gaining Ground: A Progress Report on Women in Sports.* North Palm Beach, FL: Sporting Goods Manufacturers Association.

Walker, Ron, ed. (1998) *Peterson's Sports Scholarships & College Athletic Programs.* Princeton, NJ: Peterson's Guides.

Women's Sports Foundation. (1997–1998) *College Athletic Scholarship Guide.* East Meadow, NY: Women's Sports Foundation.

REFEREEING *see* Officiating

RELIGION

Religion may determine what opportunities and barriers women encounter in physical education and sport. Women have particular roles in each religion, and those roles influence whether and how women may be physically active. At the same time, religion also has a powerful influence on society's notions of femininity and masculinity, as well as on how women themselves think of these concepts.

RELIGION, SPORT, AND PHYSICAL EDUCATION

Many religious doctrines outline beliefs, attitudes, and practices about the body, as well as the relationship between body and soul. Part of this may involve the religion's stance on sports and physical recreations. At the same time, physical activities have played and continue to play distinct roles in various religions. Whether and how women participated depended on each religion's ideas about physical activities linked with ritual and its views on women, their role in society, and the relative status of men and women. In many preindustrial societies, physical activities were part of cults and rituals, some of which involved women. In ancient Greece, for example, the Heraia—the women's equivalent of the Olympic Games—was a form of worship of the goddess Hera. Similarly, South American stick ball games and log races, like many of the dances in African cultures, related women's physical activity to religion.

Catholic nuns at a fantasy baseball camp in Port Charlotte, Florida, in 1992. (Tony Arruza/Corbis)

In both industrialized and secular societies, the connection loosened between cult and physical activities; for example, none of the three concepts of physical activities developed from the turn of the nineteenth century—Swedish gymnastics, German gymnastics (*Turnen*), and modern sports—has any official outspoken connection with religion. At the same time, religions existed and still exist whose doctrines about the body essentially kept women—and sometimes men—from participating in sports. Numerous studies have also shown that some religious beliefs are connected to certain attitudes, ideals, and physical techniques, for example, Buddhism and yoga.

Since the mid-nineteenth century, the dominant concept of modern sports shows the strong connection between sports and philosophy of life. Drawing on the insights of Max Weber, sports historians and sociologists have shown that the countries with the highest participation rates and greatest success in the Olympic Games have been those in which what Weber termed the Protestant ethic (work brings success) was combined with a relatively high level of secularization and industrialization. In contrast, countries in which the dominant religions advocated contemplative or fatalistic ways of thinking showed much less interest in modern sports. Empirical studies of participation in the Olympic Games also show that religion influences the involvement of women much more than that of men. In some Islamic countries, religious beliefs and ethos about both the body and the role of women limit or wholly preclude these nations from sending female athletes to the Olympics.

CATHOLICISM AND WOMEN'S SPORT

For centuries the attitudes of the Catholic church toward sports in general and women's sports in particular determined whether Catholic women participated in sports and, if they did, when and how. In the Middle Ages, for instance, a strong strain of asceticism physically immobilized many women in convent cells, but the church had no objection to other women participating in Whitsuntide ball games or in aristocratic pastimes like falconry. In early modern times, the church tended to adopt conservative attitudes toward social change. From the middle of the nineteenth century to the latter half of the twentieth century, the Catholic church demonstrated mistrust in sports; it viewed the body with suspicion and perceived sports as sensual if not positively sinful. Church doctrine, too, prized the soul above the body; consequently, the church had little interest in physical education for boys, and even less for girls.

The turn of the century brought growing numbers of positive evaluations of sports, including some from influential clerics. But within the church a consensus still held that sports should not be played for their own sake nor should participants overvalue sports and make them into a fetish. An emphasis on physical achievements in the form of quantified records was strictly condemned.

The church's attitude toward women's sports was influenced not only by its general views on sports but also by women's roles in Catholicism. The point of departure and the fundamental belief of the church were that the genders are polar opposites. Women and men are said to differ decisively and basically, not only in their physical characteristics but also in their "natures," their characteristics and competencies, and especially their destinies in the world. Gender differences are mirrored in the structure of the church, which excludes women from the priesthood, and in society. The submissiveness of women guarantees the continuity and the order of the family, which is the nucleus of the religious community. Political and social emancipation of women was judged as wrong and was decisively rejected. Sexual liberation was anathema.

Gender polarity and beliefs about the specific destiny of the "weaker sex" were the central arguments in the evolving discourse of the Catholic church about women and sports. In the first half of the twentieth century, discussions dealt mainly with two problems: the moral dangers of women's participation in sports and the effects of physical activities on gender hierarchy. Because the church claimed that gender arrangements based on polarity and hierarchy were natural and the will of God, it rejected the participation of women in "male" sports. As more girls and women became involved in physical education and sports, especially in state-run and Protestant-affiliated schools, the Catholic church focused on the fundamental differences between physical activities appropriate for men and women and demanded that physical education for girls in Catholic schools take into consideration their physical and mental condition and destiny. Activities planned for girls and young women should aim at enhancing their health and preparing them for motherhood.

The church was also concerned about protecting boys and men from the sexually stimulating sight of girls and women participating in sport. This led to a strict segregation of the sexes during physical activities and modest sports clothes for girls and women. Women's public appearances in gymnastics exhibitions and sports competitions were condemned.

The church also tried to control women's participation in sport by offering acceptable physical activities in church-sponsored sports organizations. Today, the influence of the Catholic church in the world of sports has greatly diminished. Recent popes have softened traditional views of human sexuality, and the sensuality evident in sports is now widely accepted—within limits.

PROTESTANTS AND SPORTS

The Protestant churches were, on the whole, quicker to accept sports, including women's sports, as a legitimate activity. Seventeenth-century Puritans admitted that men and women needed "lawful recreations"—as long as the Sab-

Crowds gather on Whit Monday to watch a game of cricket played by women and men in the churchyard of St. Martin-in-the-Fields, in London, 1935. (Hulton-Deutsch Collection/Corbis)

bath was not disturbed. In the eighteenth century, Anglican ministers looked kindly on female cricketers (but disapproved of lower-class female boxers and wrestlers). Although the "muscular Christianity" of the nineteenth century was meant primarily for men, the YWCA and the church-related women's colleges of Great Britain and the United States advocated field hockey, basketball, and other appropriate sports for young women. Fundamentalist churches in the American South had views very similar to those of the Catholic church, but their restrictive views were gradually abandoned in the course of the twentieth century.

JUDAISM AND WOMEN'S SPORT

Jewish women's participation in sports has changed over time and still differs between the Orthodox and Reform sectors of the religion. Orthodox Jewish attitudes are still sticking to the same rules that prevailed a hundred years ago—it is forbidden on the Sabbath even to turn on the lights. Orthodox Jewish religion has a fixed gender order in which women and men depend on each other but are responsible for different tasks. Women's main tasks involve caring for the family, which plays a central role in the Jewish community. Women belong in the home, and they

THE CHURCH'S DECREE ON LAWFUL RECREATION IN STUART ENGLAND

The sports enumerated are 'Dauncing, either men or women, Archery for men, Leaping, Vaulting, or any other such harmless Recreation.' From these the people are not to be debarred, 'nor from having May-games, Whitson Ales, & Morris Dances & the setting up of Maypoles, and other Sports therewith used, so as the same be had in due & convenient time without impediment or neglect of Divine Service: And that women shall have leave to carry rushes to the Church for the decoring of it, according to their old custome. But withall We doe here account it still as prohibited all unlawfull games to be used on Sundaies onely, as Beare and Bull baitings, Interludes, and at all times in the meaner sort of people by law prohibited, Bowling.' Why Bowling? we ask in some perplexity.

'And likewise We barre from this benefite and liberty all such known Recusants either Men or Women, as will abstain from coming to Church or Divine Service, being therefore unworthy of any lawful Recreation after the said Service that will not first come to the Church & serve God.

'And Our pleasure is, That this Our Declaration shall bee published by Order from the Bishop of the Diocese through all the Parish Churches, and that both Our Judges of Our Circuit, and our Justices of the Peace bee informed thereof.'

JESSIE BEDFORD
(1904) Social Life Under the Stuarts. By Elizabeth Godfrey. London: Grant Richards.

are responsible for the material side of the religious rules and rituals, including the preparation of kosher food. Religious scholarship, schools, and synagogues are the domains of men. Although mothers are much revered, men dominate traditional Jewish community life, and women are officially subordinated. Their lower status is produced by, and mirrored in, various laws and rules that range from the laws on divorce to the position of women in the Jewish community to their exclusion from many religious practices.

Orthodox Jews define women to a high degree according to their bodies, against whose sexual attractiveness and potential impurity men have to be protected. Several practices aid in this protection, especially the rule that men should avoid women as much as possible. The key reason for a purification ceremony before spouses resume sexual relations after menstruation is the men's anxiety about being overwhelmed by, or in, a woman's body. It is also the reason this purification has taken the specific form of a woman's immersion in a *mikvah,* a ritual bath.

The role of women and the meaning of physical education and sport in Orthodox Jewish communities can best be demonstrated using some examples from history. One has to bear in mind that Orthodox Jews still believe in, and follow, the rules of the Talmud. In many phases of Jewish history, for example in the Eastern European stetls (Jewish villages) of the nineteenth century, it was not only accepted but expected that women work outside the home. Women were supposed to be strong and healthy. Masculinity was not connected with military fitness and aggressiveness; on the contrary, the ideal man was the pale and ascetic scholar. Thus, Judaism permitted men to express emotion and women to be strong and capable.

Adler describes the gender roles in Jewish communities as follows: "Jewish men denigrated physical prowess as cultural ideal. Instead, they cultivated intellectual and spiritual pursuits. . . . This absence of the 'macho mystique' freed Jewish men and women from the sharpest differentiation of gender characteristics: the strong, emotionally controlled, yet potentially violent male vs. the weak, emotional, and tender female. Jewish culture 'permitted' men to be gentle and emotionally expressive and women to be strong, capable and shrewd." These gender ideals led to identity conflicts for Jews who had emigrated to Germany or the United States because they were not compatible with the ruling myth of masculinity and femininity.

Although wrestling and hunting appear as valued activities in Hebrew Scriptures, in the Jewish culture of the Diaspora, bodily strength and physical education were marginal. Even small boys were obliged to rate Talmudic knowledge and piety over physical abilities. Orthodox Judaism has never valued physical education and sports as highly as Talmudic study. When a reformed branch of Judaism gained popularity in the eighteenth century, members of the Jewish communities of Europe (but not those of the Middle East) began to participate in sports at least as much as the non-Jewish population. In the twentieth century, Reform and secular Jewish women became involved in sports competitions, often under the aegis of the Young Women's Hebrew Association. The Makkabi sports movement offered sports opportunities to Zionist women. In the 1920s the percentage of Jewish women in European Makkabi organizations was actually higher than the percentage organized in German sports clubs.

ISLAM AND WOMEN'S SPORTS

Islam has no general interdiction of sports, even for females, and the Prophet Muhammad apparently favored physical activity for girls and women. Over time, however, this early openness has been transformed to a far more restrictive situation.

According to traditional interpretations of the Quran; women are subordinate to men. Many Islamic norms and values, rules, and laws restrict women, especially in terms of marriage, divorce, and inheritance. Women's sexuality is defined as dangerous and must be strictly controlled by segregating the sexes and covering the body.

There are often differences, however, between the interpretations and practices of traditional Islamic scholars and the behavior of ordinary Muslims.

Health is valued in Islam as in other religions and should be supported and improved by hygiene, physical training, and exercise. According to Islamic authors, the Prophet Muhammad advocated a harmonious balance between the spiritual and physical dimensions of the being. Muhammad encouraged people to engage in such sports as riding, swimming, and archery. These had particular use for military preparedness. He is said to have proposed that children of both sexes be taught swimming and archery.

Thus, initially, Islam had a positive attitude toward women and sport. L. Sfeir notes: "Islamic religion in no way tries to depreciate, much less deny, sport for women. On the contrary, it attributes great significance and function to physical strength and sport activities. Islam is a constant concern with one's body, cleanliness, purification and force, without segregation of sexes. But certain religious elements, such as Islamic fatalism . . . have been dominant factors in controlling general access to sport."

Hence, according to Sfeir, Muhammad's promise about the status of women did not last but disintegrated over time. Traditional Islamic societies did set up barriers to protect their customs, such as veiling, seclusion, and segregation of the sexes. In 2000, Muslim women are still influenced by these customs. And the problem in some countries, therefore, is that sport for women may be considered contrary to traditional values, which instruct women to be obedient, to be economically dependent on men, and to confine their activities to housework and procreation.

Shahizah Daiman has put together many of the ideas found in Islam and statements of important people in Islam relative to the topic of women and sports. She concludes that sporting activities should be obligatory for women particularly for reasons of health. Those who exercise, however, must follow the rules of Islam, particularly those on covering the body and segregating the sexes. Thus, according to Islam, women's entire bodies, excepting the face, hands, and feet, must be covered. Clothes should be loose, not tight. (Men, too, must observe rules of attire, with the body covered from the navel to the knee.)

Although Islam's concept of the body is not oriented toward abstract performance and competition, modern sports spread in Islamic countries, together with the globalization of economy and culture. Islamic countries, such as Egypt, now accept women's sports, especially if female athletes follow the rule requiring the covering of the body. Other countries, such as Iran, permit women to participate in sport only when the segregation of the sexes is guaranteed. Some Islamic countries do not send women athletes to international competitions and the Olympic Games. Instead, they organize women's games that exclude men. To guarantee women access to the Olympic competitions, an initiative from Western countries called Atlanta Plus demanded that the International Olympic Committee (IOC) exclude all countries of the Olympic family that prohibit their women athletes from participating in the Games. The IOC did not accept this proposal, and the discussions and initiatives for the inclusion of Islamic women in the world of sports are certain to continue.

Gertrud Pfister

Bibliography

Adler, Rahle. (1983) "The Jew Who Wasn't There: Halakha and the Jewish Woman." In *On Being a Jewish Feminist*, edited by S. Heschel. New York: Shocken Books. 12–18.

Cantor, Aviva. (1995) *Jewish Women/Jewish Men*. San Francisco: Fresh Meadows.

Daiman, Shahizah. (1983) "Women in Sport in Islam." *ICHPER-SD Journal* 32, 1: 18–21.

Geldbach, Erich. (1975) *Sport und Protestantismus*. Wuppertal, Germany: Brockhaus Verlag.

Guttmann, Allen. (1978) *From Ritual to Record*. New York: Columbia University Press.

Hoffman, Shirl J., ed. (1992) *Sport and Religion*. Champaign, IL: Human Kinetics.

Mernissi, Fatema. (1987) *Geschlecht, Ideologie, Islam*. Munich: Frauenbuch Verlag.

Pfister, Gertrud. (1996) "Der Einfluss der katholischen Kirche auf die Anfänge der Körper- und Bewegungserziehung von Mädchen in Deutschland und Spanien." In *Erziehung und Menschen-Geschlechter. Studien zur Religion, Sozialisation und Bildung in Europa seit der Aufklärung*, edited by M. Kraul and C. Lüth. Weinheim, Germany: Deutscher Studienverlag, 159–185.

Schneider, Gerhard. (1968) *Puritanismus und Leibesübungen*. Schorndorf, Germany: Karl Hofmann.

Sfeir, L. (1995) "The Status of Muslim Women in Sport: Conflict Between Cultural Tradition and Modernization." *International Review for the Sociology of Sport* 20: 283–306.

REPRODUCTION

If and how physical activity affects women's reproductive health has been an area of controversy for decades. For much of that time, the medical profession, with the backing of society in general, cautioned women against taking part in sports or other activities because it might compromise their destiny as future mothers. One such controversy was the issue of jumping. The medical profession, basing its opinion on myths and theories, suggested that jumping would displace the uterus and cause reproductive abnormalities. It was 1992 before women were able to compete in the triple jump at the Olympics.

As modern medicine advanced and scientific evidence accumulated, that issue has been resolved to some extent. Exercise in moderation can be beneficial, and more women are enjoying active, healthy life-styles, with little or no problems with reproductive health.

ACTIVITY, CONCEPTION, AND PREGNANCY

For women with normal menstrual cycles, moderate physical activity should play no role in preventing conception. Once conception has occurred, recreational activity in moderation has not been linked to early pregnancy loss or miscarriage. Traditionally, physicians have advised pregnant women to rest during pregnancy. That outdated medical advice does not address the increasing participation of pregnant women in sports and recreational activities. In addition, a growing number of women work throughout pregnancy in strenuous and nontraditional occupations (such as police work, fire fighting, and military service). Pregnancy is a unique process in which almost all the control systems of the body are modified to try to maintain the maternal and fetal environment. Under these circumstances, adding exercise to a woman's normal activities may represent a significant challenge to the well-being of the mother and fetus. This is especially true at higher intensities of physical work. The scientific literature suggests, however, that low- to moderate-intensity exercise in a healthy pregnancy benefits mother and baby. Some of these benefits include improved physical fitness and muscular endurance, improved stamina for labor and delivery, promotion of appropriate maternal weight gain throughout pregnancy, improved mood and decreases in anxiety and depression following pregnancy.

According to recent medical advice, if a woman has been active before pregnancy, she can maintain that level of activity during pregnancy. If, in contrast, she has not been active, she should not start an exercise program during pregnancy. Although this advice is more modern than the traditional directive of bed rest, it does not give pregnant women concrete guidelines for exercise. Unfortunately, many physicians are still adhering to this old advice because it seems to be based on common sense.

Common sense, however, has long been the closest thing to guidelines that physicians could offer. No formal guidelines for exercise during pregnancy existed until, in 1985, the American College of Obstetricians and Gynecologists (ACOG) published a bulletin that suggested such guidelines. The most controversial of these was that a pregnant woman should not let her heart rate rise above 140 beats per minute. These guidelines generated considerable discussion among physicians and health-care professionals, but even so, ACOG was the first organization to put in writing any guidelines for exercise during pregnancy and to publish and distribute them to other organizations. In 1994 ACOG released another bulletin on exercise during pregnancy. The organization apparently ignored the controversial issue of exercise heart rate in this bulletin; there are now no guidelines for this. Pregnant women and their physicians in the United States are still unhappy with the present guidelines because this information is lacking.

In Canada, exercise and pregnancy guidelines are found in the PARmed-X for Pregnancy document that was published by the Canadian Society for Exercise Physiology (CSEP) in 1996 and endorsed by Health Canada, the federal health agency in Canada. This document was developed by Dr. Larry Wolfe of Queen's University and Dr. Michelle Mottola of the University of Western Ontario. The PARmed-X for Pregnancy document includes a medical prescreening questionnaire to

Expectant mothers exercising in Amsterdam, Netherlands in 1991. (Owen Franklin/Corbis)

identify contraindications to exercise during pregnancy, a list of safety considerations, and aerobic and muscle conditioning guidelines. In addition, the Canadian Association of Sports Medicine (sports medicine physicians) has recently published a position statement on exercise during pregnancy that includes the PARmed-X for Pregnancy document.

Before taking part in an exercise program, pregnant women should confirm a healthy pregnancy with a physician or midwife. The PARmed-X document contains a list for the physician (or midwife) to check for contraindications to exercise. Medical professionals advise prescreening because studies have identified several potential risks. Each of these appears to have a dose–response relationship—that is, the more intense the exercise, the greater the potential risk.

In a healthy pregnancy, low- to moderate-intensity exercise seems to pose no threat to mother or fetus. Nevertheless, since researchers have not identified a threshold for intensity or duration of exercise—the point above which problems might occur—it is important that medical screening take place to ensure a healthy pregnancy before a woman begins to exercise. Guidelines promoting exercise intensities of 60 to 70 percent of maximum oxygen consumption (moderate aerobic exercise) are within accepted levels for healthy pregnancies. The PARmed-X for Pregnancy document provides guidelines for these levels of intensity. Aerobic ac-

VIGOR AND HEALTH FOR FUTURE MOTHERS (1883)

A Nineteenth-Century Woman's View on the Necessity of Exercise for Girls

Women are burdened with heavy clothing, and every vital organ restricted by bands and bones. It is not unusual to count from sixteen to eighteen thicknesses of cloth worn so tightly about the pliable structure of the waist that actual deformity is produced.

The pelvis and chest are naturally well guarded from intrusion by the ribs and pelvic bones. But just at the point where belts are adjusted there is no protecting wall. Thus these parts are easily deformed, consequently digestion become imperfect, the circulation obstructed, the respiration restricted, and what is worse than all, the viscera crowd down upon the womb, the citadel of life.

Thus, by abuse, the maternal organism fails of fulfilling the divine charge committed to it by the Creator. The wonder is that intelligent, educated woman has ordinarily no thought of her relation to posterity, and her responsibility to offspring.

Exercises adapted to develop the muscles of the trunk and abdomen, giving breathing power and room for all the viscera, will be found very satisfactory in their results, to women who will arrange their clothing suitably.

The restraint placed upon young girls, according to the usages of society, at the time when they most need exercise and muscular development, is not only mistaken wisdom, but a cruel physical wrong. They *must be ladylike!* So, perforce, they must not jump nor skip; they must not run upstairs two steps at a time, *like a boy. No romping allowed!* The physical freedom which is everywhere accorded to a boy, and by which he all unconsciously fits himself for manhood, is forbidden the girl. So she grows up without strength of nerve or muscle, and readily becomes a victim to all the ills that woman is heir to.

ALICE B. STOCKHAM
(1883) Tokology: A Book for Every Woman. *Chicago: Sanitary Publishing Co.*

tivity is defined as exercise in which large muscle groups are being moved, such as walking, stationary cycling, swimming, aquatic exercise, or low-impact aerobics.

Pregnant women should carefully monitor intensity of exercise. The PARmed-X for Pregnancy form provides three ways to check that the aerobic activity is not too high. The first way is by using a chart of exercise heart rate (pulse rate) guidelines based on the age of the pregnant woman. Women who are younger than twenty should exercise between a target heart rate of 140 and 155 beats per minute, women twenty to twenty-nine years old should exercise between the ranges of 135 and 150 beats per minute, women between the ages of thirty and thirty-nine should exercise from 130 to 145 beats per minute target heart rate, and women

forty and older should stay within the range of 125 to 140 beats per minute. Asking a pregnant woman who is exercising how hard she thinks she is working is the second way to ensure the appropriate intensity for exercise. On a 20-point scale (rating of perceived exertion scale, Borg 1962), she should be within twelve and fourteen, which is considered "somewhat hard." The final check for intensity is called the "Talk Test"; a pregnant woman is exercising too intensely if she cannot carry on a conversation while she is exercising. If she is out of breath and breathing heavily and cannot talk, she must reduce the intensity to lower her heart rate. A healthy pregnant woman who has not exercised before should begin at the lower end of the target heart rate zone for her age and monitor her intensity closely.

A pregnant woman should exercise three times per week, even if she is just beginning an exercise program, increasing up to a maximum of four to five times per week. Perhaps the best way to begin an exercise program is to have a day of rest in between the exercise days to avoid undue fatigue. Each exercise session should include approximately 15 minutes at the target heart rate intensity, increasing by 2 minutes every week until a maximum of 30 minutes per session is reached. Women should not increase either the intensity or the time of each exercise session after the twenty-eighth week of gestation because of fatigue. Many women in the third trimester exercise less intensely and for less time because they tire more easily. Each exercise session should start with 5 to 15 minutes of warm-up and end with 5 to 15 minutes of cooldown at a lower intensity. All pregnant women should know the safety signs and consult a physician if they experience any contraindications to exercise.

Women who have been exercising before pregnancy have been advised by the medical profession to continue exercise during pregnancy. Before they do so, however, they should consult a physician to determine the frequency, intensity, duration, and type of exercise. They should also have a medical prescreening to rule out problems that would contraindicate exercise. The aerobic guidelines presented for women who have not exercised before pregnancy (see above) are also suggested for the recreational athlete. The recreational athlete may be able to exercise at the higher end of the target heart rate zone based on age, for the maximum of 30 minutes four to five times per week. If a woman has been jogging before pregnancy, she may continue within the aerobic exercise guidelines unless she develops joint problems or is uncomfortable with this type of exercise. Switching to a stair climber (with no jarring movements) or to a kind of exercise that supports the body weight, swimming or biking, would be recommended.

Muscular strength or conditioning exercise is activity that includes stretching, abdominal exercise, and resistance or weightlifting exercise. The PARmed-X for Pregnancy document also includes suggestions for these activities. The major precaution for muscular conditioning exercise is that women must perform no activity lying on the back past four months of pregnancy. This guide-line has also been suggested by the ACOG because of possible blocking of the major blood vessels in the abdomen (inferior vena cava and/or abdominal aorta) by the weight of the pregnant uterus pushing on them during exercise on the back. The inferior vena cava is the major vein that returns blood to the heart, and the abdominal aorta is a major artery that supplies the lower body with blood, including the pregnant uterus. Instead of lying on her back, a woman past four months of pregnancy can do sit-up exercises for the abdominal muscles in a side-lying, sitting, or standing position.

Physicians used to advise women who had not exercised not to start an exercise program during pregnancy. Recent scientific literature and guidelines, however, suggest that, if no contraindications to exercise exist and if the pregnancy is healthy, women may start an exercise program in the second trimester. Women should not start to exercise in the first trimester because of potential risks. Many women do not feel well in the first trimester and may be discouraged from exercise if the exercise is started at that time. The best time to start an exercise program is at about sixteen weeks.

Pregnancy is not the time to engage in athletic competition or strenuous activity that would place the mother at risk of bodily injury. Women who have been exercising strenuously before pregnancy should reduce the intensity, frequency, and duration of exercise and follow the exercise guidelines recommended above. Strenuous high-intensity exercise by the mother provides no known benefits to the fetus, and the risks to the fetus far outweigh any maternal benefits. Of the few studies available describing the effects of strenuous exercise on mother and fetus, most are case studies that record the efforts of one individual or are reports of past activity and are not scientifically controlled experiments. Thus, no guidelines exist for pregnant women who engage in strenuous exercise although researchers are investigating this population group of pregnant athletes.

Activity that pregnant women perform as part of their occupation also needs to be taken into consideration, whether the woman is a homemaker or a nurse working 12-hour shifts and lifting patients. This day-to-day activity level is important and must be considered when prescribing an exercise program. If the pregnant woman is engaging in high-intensity physical activities in her occupation, a recreational exercise program should complement the activities performed in everyday life. This will prevent unnecessary fatigue, as well as injuries from overuse, and will decrease the potential risk to the fetus.

Recent studies suggest that physical activity on the job may play an important role in the outcome of pregnancy. Military women on active duty who gained fewer than 25 pounds (11.25 kilograms) during pregnancy developed an earlier labor more often than pregnant women in general. The risk of early labor (before forty weeks) was also increased in women who worked regularly in the evening or at night, whose occupations required long hours of standing, and who continued to work through late gestation.

In a national survey of nurses in the United States, factors significantly associated with earlier birth included number of hours worked per week, per shift, and while standing. Other factors were noise level, physical exertion, and occupational fatigue. In addition, another study found a link between moderate to high-intensity physical activity in the workplace and a twofold increase in the risk of severe high blood pressure compared to mild activity on the job. In general, research suggests that occupations including prolonged standing and/or walking continued into late gestation, as well as work that involves several strenuous factors in combination, appear to increase the risk of earlier delivery. It was also recommended that working pregnant women avoid extremely heavy physical exertion (close to maximum) in early pregnancy and late gestation. Heavy lifting on the job and the impact on spontaneous abortion is inconclusive and requires further study.

ACTIVITY AFTER DELIVERY

Many pregnant women are concerned about when they can safely return to exercise after the baby is born. This depends on the number of complications during labor and delivery. If these processes are uncomplicated, a woman can usually return to aerobic exercise once vaginal bleeding from delivery has stopped or her postpartum checkup with her physician is normal. Women should begin an exercise program at the lower-intensity heart rate range based on age and follow the same guidelines that would apply if she were pregnant. Avoiding unnecessary fatigue is an important consideration for any new mother, and walking while pushing a baby carriage is an excellent way to start to regain activity. If the woman has had a cesarean section or complications during labor and delivery, she should wait at least ten weeks or until labor and delivery complications have healed or returned to normal.

Muscular conditioning exercises are also recommended for women after they give birth. They should return to these exercises after the first postpartum checkup with the physician or after vaginal bleeding from delivery has stopped. Abdominal exercises can be started as well and may be performed while lying on the back.

Women who breast-feed and choose to exercise usually have no problems. Exercise of mild or moderate intensity has little adverse effect on milk quality or quantity or on infant weight gain. Infants detect sweet and sour tastes, and studies suggest that infants may refuse to nurse or may fuss during a feeding that follows the mother's exercise because the increase in the lactic acid content of the breast milk may produce a sour taste. Maximal exercise has been shown to have this effect; aerobic

EXERCISE AND PREGNANCY

Before 1985 there were no medical guidelines for exercise during pregnancy, and the traditional medical view was to advise pregnant women not to exercise at all. Since then much research on the relationship between pregnancy and childbirth has led to the current view that exercise during pregnancy often benefits the mother and possibly the fetus as well. However, an exercise program should not be initiated without the advice of a qualified medical professional.

exercise of mild to moderate intensity performed four or five times per week beginning six to eight weeks postpartum had no adverse effect on breast-feeding. It would seem that mild to moderate exercise is well tolerated postpartum, but women should avoid strenuous (near maximum) aerobic activity until they stop breast-feeding.

CONCLUSION

Engaging in mild to moderate-intensity exercise should not be a problem for the reproductive health of active women. Pregnancy is a time when women improve their health habits to provide a good environment for the unborn. These changes include improving eating habits, abstaining from smoking and alcohol consumption, and starting or continuing an exercise program. All these changes can be carried forward into the postpartum period. Many health professionals believe that pregnancy is a good time to incorporate permanent healthy life-style habits, integrating activity into a healthy, active life-style that leads to healthy mothers and healthy babies.

Michelle F. Mottola

See also Amenorrhea; Menstrual Cycle

Bibliography

Ahlborg, G. (1995) "Physical Work Load and Pregnancy Outcome." *Journal of Ocupational and Environmental Medicine* 37, 8: 941–944.

American College of Obstetricians and Gynecologists (ACOG). (1985) "Pregnancy and the Postnatal Period." *ACOG Home Exercise Programs*. Washington, DC: ACOG.

American College of Obstetricians and Gynecologists. (1994) "Exercise During Pregnancy and the Postpartum Period." *ACOG Technical Bulletin*. 189 (February): 2–7.

Borg, G. (1962) "A Category Scale with Ratio Properties for Intermodal and Interindividual Comparison." In *Psychophysical Judgement and the Process of Perception*, edited by H. G. Geissler and P. Petzold. Berlin: VEB Deutscher Verlag der Wissenschaften.

Canadian Society for Exercise Physiology. (1996) *PARmed-X for Pregnancy*. Ottawa, Canada: Canadian Society for Exercise Physiology, 1–4.

Carley, G. B., T. J. Quinn, and S. E. Goodwin. (1997) "Breast Milk Composition After Exercise of Different Intensities." *Journal of Human Lactation* 13, 2: 115–120.

Clapp, J. F. (1996) "Pregnancy Outcome: Physical Activities Inside Versus Outside the Workplace." *Seminars in Perinatology* 20, 1: 70–76.

———. (1996A) "Exercise During Pregnancy." In *Exercise and The Female—A Lifespan Approach. Perspectives in Exercise Science and Sports Medicine*. Vol. 9, edited by O. Bar-Or, D. Lamb, and P. M. Clarkson. Cooper: U.S.A., 413–451.

Dewey, K. G., C. A. Lovelady, L. A. Nommsen-Rivers, M. A. McCrory, and B. Lonnerdal. (1994) "A Randomized Study of the Effects of Aerobic Exercise by Lactating Women on Breast-milk Volume and Composition." *New England Journal of Medicine* 330: 449–453.

Fortier, I., S. Marcoux, and J. Brisson. (1995) "Maternal Work During Pregnancy and the Risks of Delivering a Small-for-gestational-age or Preterm Infant." *Scandinavian Journal of Work Environment & Health* 21, 6: 412–418.

Kardel, K. R., and T. Kase. (1998) "Training in Pregnant Women: Effects on Fetal Development and Birth." *American Journal of Obstetrics & Gynecology* 178, 2: 280–286.

Koltyn, K. F., and S. S. Schultes. (1997) "Psychological Effects of an Aerobic Exercise Session and a Rest Session Following Pregnancy." *Journal of Sports Medicine & Physical Fitness* 37, 4: 287–291.

Lenskyj, H. (1986) *Out of Bounds—Women, Sport and Sexuality*. Toronto, Ontario: Women's Press.

Luke, B., N. Mamelle, L. Keith, F. Munoz, J. Minogue, E. Papiernik, and T. Johnson. (1995) "The Association Between Occupational Factors and Preterm Birth—A United States Nurses Study." *American Journal of Obstetrics & Gynecology* 173: 849–862.

Magann E. F., M. I. Winchester, D. P. Carter, J. N. Martin, T. E. Nolan, and J. C. Morrison. (1996) "Military Pregnancies and Adverse Perinatal Outcome." *International Journal of Gynecology & Obstetrics* 52, 1: 19–24.

Mottola, M. F., and L. A. Wolfe. (1994) "Active Living and Pregnancy." In *Toward Active Living. Proceedings of the International Conference on Physical Activity, Fitness & Health*, edited by H. A. Quinney, L. Gauvin, and A. E. Wall. Champaign, IL: Human Kinetics, 131–140.

Spinillo, A., E. Capuzzo, L. Colonna, G. Piazzi, S. Nicola, and F. Baltaro. (1995) "The Effect of Work Activity in Pregnancy on the Risk of Severe Preeclampsia." *Australian & New Zealand Journal of Obstetrics & Gynecology* 35, 4: 380–385.

Wallace, J. P., G. Inbar, and K. Ernsthausen. (1992) "Infant Acceptance of Postexercise Breast Milk." *Pediatrics* 89: 1245–1247.

Wolfe, L. A., P. J. Ohtake, M. F. Mottola, and M. J. McGrath. (1989) "Physiological Interactions Between Pregnancy and Aerobic Exercise." *Exercise and Sport Sciences Reviews* 17: 295–351.

Wolfe, L. A., and M. F. Mottola. (1993) "Aerobic Exercise in Pregnancy: An Update." *Canadian Journal of Applied Physiology* 18: 119–147.

Wolfe, L. A., I. K. M. Brenner, and M. F. Mottola. (1994) "Maternal Exercise, Fetal Well-being and Pregnancy Outcome." *Exercise Sports Sciences Reviews* 22: 145–194.

RETTON, MARY LOU

(1968–)

U.S. GYMNAST

Mary Lou Retton leaped into the limelight at the 1984 Los Angeles, California, Olympics, where she vaulted to the all-round title (and to the most lucrative product-endorsement contracts ever for a gymnastic champion). Her achievement and her cheery charisma sent thousands of little girls in search of a gymnastics coach.

Mary Lou Retton on the balance beam. (Neal Preston/Corbis)

Mary Lou Retton was born in Fairmont, West Virginia, in 1968. She began gymnastics training at age seven in her hometown and, under the tutelage of Gary Rafaloski, qualified for elite status seven years later at age fourteen. In 1982 at a U.S. Gymnastics Federation meet, Retton met her Olympic coaches, Romanian-born Bela and Marta Karolyi, who had coached Nadia Comaneci a decade earlier. She spent the next year trying to convince her family to send her to Houston to train with the Karolyis.

She arrived in Houston in 1983. Coach Karolyi recalled in his book that she "wasn't a fantastic talent" when he first saw her perform, but he recognized her potential when she came to his gym. Under the Karolyis' guidance, Retton entered the Chunichi Cup (Japan) in 1983. Competing against some of the world's best gymnasts, she won the all-around title, a first for an American. Her teammate Diane Durham won the bronze. In June 1984, only weeks before the Olympics, she suffered a knee injury that threatened to keep her out of the competition. Much credit is due Dr. Richard Caspari, who quickly repaired her knee and enabled her to participate. The Karolyis remained Mary Lou's coaches until the American Cup in 1985, at which time she completed her string of three consecutive all-around titles. She retired in 1986.

Following the Olympics, Retton was proclaimed Sportswoman of the Year by *Sports Illustrated* and was the Associated Press Athlete of the Year. Her photograph, with arms stretched in victory, was the first of a female athlete to appear on a Wheaties cereal box. Although the "Golden Vault" was a special moment in American Olympic history, Retton also won the individual silver medal for that event, bronze medals for the uneven bars and the floor exercise, and a silver team medal for the team's performance.

Since retiring, Retton has appeared as a motivational speaker. She was a commentator for NBC sports and wrote a column for *USA Today* during the 1988 Olympics. She married Shannon Kelley in 1990 and has two children.

A. B. Frederick

Bibliography

Götzt, Andreas, and Eckhard Herholz. (1992) *Das Turnjahrhundert der Deutschen*. Berlin: Edition OST.

Gutman, Dan. (1996) *Gymnastics*. New York: Viking.

Lessa, Christina. (1997) *Gymnastics Balancing Acts.* New York: Universe Publishing.

Marshall, Nancy Thies, and Pam Vredevelt. (1988) *Women Who Compete*. Old Tappan, NJ: F. H. Revell Co.

Moran, Lyn. (1978) *The Young Gymnasts*. New York: K. S. Giniger.

Retton, Mary Lou, Bela Karolyi, and John Powers. (1986) *Mary Lou*. New York: Dell.

Ryan, Joan. (1995) *Little Girls in Pretty Boxes*. New York: Doubleday.

Silverstein, Herma. (1985) *Mary Lou Retton and the New Gymnasts*. New York: Franklin Watts.

Simons, Minot, II. (1995) *Women's Gymnastics: A History*. Carmel, CA: Welwyn Publishing Co.

Straus, Hal. (1978) *Gymnastics Guide*. Mountain View, CA: World Publications.

RINGETTE

Developed for women in Canada in 1963, ringette is unique in that it is a composite of many aspects of older sports, including basketball, ice hockey, soccer, and team handball. It requires complex motor skills within an environment of explosive speed and finesse. Ringette combines ice skating, controlling a ring, reading and reacting to an ever-changing environment, delivering and receiving passes, and stopping and starting at full speed, all while in full equipment (helmet with face mask; neck protector; elbow pads; girdle with genital, hip, and tailbone protection; shin pads; and gloves), and carrying a stick. It is one of the fastest sports in the world and is played in various countries.

HISTORY

Ringette was invented in 1963 by a Canadian, Sam Jacks, who created the game as an alternative winter team sport on ice to provide girls with a safe activity that did not involve body contact and one that they could play to develop their skills, court sense, and fair play. The first set of rules, which dates from 1965, has been revised over the past thirty years in response to the women who play it. Ringette players today are stronger, faster, and more strategic than their predecessors.

Following its inaugural season, 1963–1964, ringette and its administrative structure gained momentum well beyond any early expectations. The sport grew from slightly more than 4,000 registered members in 1979 to more than 21,000 in 1985. During the 1997–1998 and 1998–1999 seasons, there were 32,000 registered players across Canada. During the mid-1980s, Ringette Canada used the slogan "The winter sport for females." Today, with other opportunities available, it is no longer an accurate statement. During the early and mid-1980s, ringette was one of the most popular team sports in Canada.

The rules of the game have developed to meet the needs of the players and so have the events. The first national championships in Canada were held in 1979 in Winnipeg, Manitoba. This competition has grown to become the annual elite ringette showcase. Players involved at lesser competitive levels may also take part in tournaments and events. In all countries most ringette clubs offer or attend some type of organized tournament each season.

The International Ringette Federation (IRF) was founded in 1986 by six countries under the direction of Betty Shields, president of Ringette Canada. This group now sanctions the World Ringette Championships, which have been held every other year since 1990. World tournaments were held in Ontario; Helsinki, Finland; Minneapolis, Minnesota; and Stockholm, Sweden. In 1998 the event was canceled because of a lack of international representatives—notably, the United States, Russia, and France were not able to commit. As an alternative, Finland and Canada organized a Summit Series, which combined a European tour to promote the sport at an elite level with an opportunity to battle for the 1998 series title. The two national teams traveled and played their way through Turku and Helsinki in Finland; Stockholm, Sweden; Osnabrück, Germany; and Colmar, France.

Along with Canada, Finland has long been in the running as the international leader of the sport. In 1978 ringette made its way to Finland, making it the first European country to be introduced to the sport. A hockey coach, Juhani Wahlsten, developed the game there and assisted in forming the first ringette club, Turku Ringette. Since then, the sport and its infrastructure have steadily evolved. In 1983 the Ringette Association of Finland was formed, and in 1985 the Finnish Central Sports Federation accepted the association as a member, making ringette an official sport in Finland. The Finnish team won the world champion title in 1994 and the 1998 Summit Series. The 3,000 registered members support the year-round (renamed) Finnish Ringette Association (FRA) office. The FRA has had a national team program (since 1990), a junior national team program (since 1996), and a strong grassroots youth leadership program through *Nuori Suomi* (Young Finland). At the twelve and under age group, called "E Juniors," the players all wear armbands that determine age and skill levels. This armband system ensures that all players have equal ice time and playing opportunities. It is a positive approach to teaching fair play and team skills.

Ringette has been played in the United States since at least 1986, and Minneapolis hosted the 1994 world championships. The sport is also an expanding activity in Sweden, France, Germany, and Russia, which all compete at the international level.

RULES AND PLAY

The sport has gained fame mostly for its scoring object and the method of controlling that object. Ringette is played not with balls or pucks but with a ring approximately six inches in diameter and one inch thick made of blue rubber for ice or hard plastic for gym and asphalt. The ring is maneuvered by a straight stick, with a shaft that tapers slightly at the tip for better control. Many of the sticks are wooden with tips of steel, aluminum, or hard plastic.

The game is played in teams of five, plus a goaltender. Much as in basketball, ice hockey, and indoor soccer, the five skaters, or out players, are broken down into two defense, two forwards, and one center. Players wear loose-fitting jerseys and long pants. Most players wear smaller equipment to balance safety with agility. For example, hockey players may prefer wide shin pads to help block shots, whereas ringette players may lean toward narrower shin pads to allow better mobility and speed. Regardless of the position, players must

wear helmets, full face masks, padding, and gloves. The five skaters' objective is to move the ring toward the opposition's net with control, with the ultimate intention of shooting and scoring. The goaltender's job is to prevent the opposition from scoring and to assist in her own defensive unit's breakout.

Ringette's equivalent of a jump ball or face-off is called the free pass. The free pass allows a player from one team 5 seconds of protection to make a pass from a predetermined spot on the ice. Many teams use this possession to key on set plays or skating patterns that enable the other four skaters on the ice to get open. One of the founding ideas behind ringette is that it should emphasize team play. When Sam Jacks put together the first working set of rules, he had the players pass over the blue lines that trisect the court into attacking, neutral, and defending zones. In basketball or soccer a player can control the ball and make her way down the court or field without having to pass to any teammates. In ringette, players may not carry the ring from end to end. Players must pass the ring over each blue line, as they are not allowed to carry the ring across these lines. The ring must touch another player (from either team) before the player can again touch the ring on the other side of the blue line. Today, that emphasis lives on; the ring must be passed, shot, deflected, batted, or legally kicked to another player across each blue line.

Although there are no competitive events for co-ed teams of any age, there are some recreational tournaments in various centers that allow co-ed teams. Internationally, very few attempts have been made to include male players, nor have any national or international events allowed male participation.

CONCLUSION

Some proponents of ringette cite the lack of male participation as a possible explanation for why the sport is not more popular. Others disagree, pointing out the positive: The game has evolved from a slow and controlled game to a fast-breaking, dynamic contest of ring skills and skating and has gained many female participants. For either argument the game of ringette is based on finesse and speed, not gender.

Tamara McKernan

Information was provided by Lorie Horne, 1999 Team Alberta, Canada Winter Games; Lyndsay Wheelans, 1996 World Champion Coach, Canada; and Ringette Canada.

ROBERTS, KATE

(1883–?)

BRITISH PROFESSIONAL STRONGWOMAN

Well known for strength and beauty, Kate Roberts was a music hall entertainer who specialized in feats of strength. The professional strongwoman "Vulcana" began life in 1883 as Kate Roberts, daughter of a Protestant minister in Wales. Roberts, who reportedly had unusual strength even as a child, made her professional debut at the age of fifteen when her brother asked her to perform at a gala he was organizing in the nearby town of Pontypool. Apparently the audience's response to her feats of strength convinced Roberts that she should become a professional.

It is not clear whether Roberts had done much traditional weight training before she began her career as a strongwoman. Once she began, however, she did not shy away from tackling the heavier weights. Encouraged by her brother, who had already been performing as a strongman under the name of Atlas, Kate adopted the stage name Vulcana. For at least a decade, Atlas and Vulcana performed their act with dumbbell and barbell throughout Great Britain, Europe, and Australia. By 1902, when she was featured in *Sandow's Magazine* and *Royal Magazine,* Vulcana claimed to hold all the world records in women's weightlifting and to have earned 120 medals in various strength competitions.

In her stage act, Vulcana lifted two 56-pound block weights overhead simultaneously, supported a 120-pound barbell overhead with a man hanging from it, and reportedly finished with a 224-pound overhead lift. In *Health & Strength* magazine, the bible for weight trainers at the time, her best was given as 141 pounds.

Roberts stood 5 feet 4 inches and weighed 150 pounds. Her biceps measured 14 inches, her calf 15 inches, and her thigh 27 inches. Compared to other professional strongwomen, such as Minerva and Athleta, Roberts seemed almost petite. Her beauty is mentioned in nearly every newspaper and magazine account from this era, and more than one journalist was quick to note that Vulcana proved that exercise need not "render woman mannish—or 'unbeautiful' viewed from the standard of what woman should be." This notion, that women could exercise and still be feminine and physically attractive, is Kate Robert's greatest legacy.

Jan Todd

Bibliography

Chapman, David. (1984) "Gallery of Ironmen: Kate 'Vulcana' Roberts." *Ironman.*

Desbonnet, Edmond. (1911) *Les Rois de la Force.* Paris: Librairie Berger-Levrault.

Holmes, H. J. (1902) "The Strongest Woman on Earth." *Royal Magazine* 8 (October): 580–582.

Reader, E. K., and L. M. Reader. (1902) "Types of Women Athletes." *Sandow's Magazine* 8: 251–256.

"Vulcana." (1902) *Health & Strength* (February).

RODEO

Professional rodeo is a multimillion-dollar sport. Although rodeo draws audiences by stressing its links to the mythical West and its status as a uniquely American creation, it actually grew out of the far older Mexican *charreada,* a mixture of bullfighting and cattle wrangling that dates back to the conquistadors. Barrel racing, the premier women's event, is the only standard rodeo contest that had no counterpart in the *charreada.* It was also the newest event, begun in 1948 by the Girls Rodeo Association (GRA), later the Women's Professional Rodeo Association (WPRA). In barrel racing the competitors attempt to ride a cloverleaf pattern around three barrels in the fastest time possible without toppling them. Every year, there are usually several barrel racers among rodeo's top twenty money winners. However, cowgirls

Cowgirl practicing calf roping. (Neil Rabinowitz/Corbis)

made up less than 10 percent of the athletes in big-time rodeo, and women's representation and status within the sport are precarious.

American rodeo evolved after the Texas Revolution and the subsequent U.S.–Mexican War, as Anglo-American cowboys adopted the skills, attire, vocabulary, and sports of their *vaquero* (Mexican cowboy) predecessors. Ranch-versus-ranch contests gradually sprang up, and bronc riding, bull riding, and roping contests appeared at racetracks and fairgrounds. In 1882 in North Platte, Nebraska, William F. (Buffalo Bill) Cody created the first major rodeo and the first Wild West show. This successful venture led Cody to organize his touring Wild West show while other entrepreneurs gradually created what became professional rodeo. Rodeos and Wild West shows enjoyed a parallel existence and employed many of the same stars, capitalizing on public fascination with the mythic West. Women joined the Wild

West and contest rodeo circuits in the 1890s, and their participation grew as the sport spread geographically. Rodeos and cowgirls enjoyed enormous popularity in New York, Chicago, Boston, and Philadelphia, as well as in London and Paris, in the 1920s and 1930s.

Despite numerous forays abroad before World War II, by the 1990s rodeo was significant only in North America. While it does exist in Australia and New Zealand, top athletes from those countries come to America to seek their fortunes. Some Latin American countries have contests called rodeos, but they include none of the events found in the North American version.

RULES AND ADMINISTRATION

Numerous organizations governed rodeo in the 1990s, each with slightly different rules, different roles for women, and different events. By far the most important was the Professional Rodeo Cowboys Association (PRCA), sponsor of over 700 rodeos annually. The PRCA crowns the world champions at the National Finals Rodeo (NFR), held since 1984 at Las Vegas, Nevada. With purses in excess of $3 million, the NFR is the world's richest rodeo, yet it is open only to the top fifteen money winners in seven events. The athletes with the most money, including NFR earnings, in each event become the world champions.

Contests are classified as either timed events, in which athletes try to be the swiftest, or roughstock events, in which athletes attempt to stay atop a bucking animal for a designated time. The PRCA timed events are calf roping, steer roping, team roping, and steer wrestling. Although steer roping is not included at the NFR, the WPRA barrel racing final is.

Bull riding, saddle bronc riding, and bareback bronc riding are the standard roughstock events. In PRCA rodeos, riders have to stay on the animals for 8 seconds. In Professional Women's Rodeo Association (PWRA) all-women rodeos, the time limit is 6 seconds. Other organizations have various time limits for different events. There are also additional timed contests for women sanctioned by some organizations. These include breakaway calf roping, flag racing, ribbon roping, and goat tying.

Other important rodeo governing bodies holding women's contests include the International Professional Rodeo Association (IPRA), Canadian Professional Rodeo Association (CPRA), American Junior Rodeo Association (AJRA) for contestants under twenty years of age, National Little Britches Rodeo Association (NLBRA) for ages eight to eighteen, Senior Pro Rodeo (SPR) for athletes forty years old or over, National High School Rodeo Association (NHSRA), and National Intercollegiate Rodeo Association (NIRA). All offer the standard rodeo events for men, as well as four or more timed events for women. Most were formed in the late 1940s and early 1950s, and each has its own regulations and its own particular means of naming champions. All organizations hold some kind of final rodeo. All require athletes to have membership cards or permits in order to compete. Ath-

letes are required to participate only in rodeos sanctioned by their own governing body or by a governing body having a mutual agreement with their own.

Local rodeo committees pay sanctioning fees to these governing bodies and, from their approved lists, employ the needed local stock contractors, judges, announcers, clowns, and barrel men. Female athletes actually outnumber males at the youngest ages, whereas in high school and college rodeo they are nearly equal. Women's participation has been most restricted in PRCA contests, where their only opportunity other than barrel racing has been as one of a pair of team ropers. The only organization offering women's competition in roughstock events is the PWRA, a subsidiary of the WPRA that has sanctioned fifteen to

TILLIE BALDWIN: RODEO'S ORIGINAL BLOOMER GIRL

Tillie Baldwin (1888–1958), born Anna Matilda Winger, was one of the most versatile and influential stars of pre-World War I rodeo. In only five competitive seasons Baldwin won ten major titles and became the first woman on record to bulldog a steer. In this most dangerous feat, contestants jump from the backs of their speeding horses onto a bull, grab the animal's horns, and wrestle it to the ground. At that time cowgirls wore ankle length divided skirts, sometimes of leather. Baldwin broke a major taboo by competing in a gym suit consisting of bloomers, middy blouse, and black stockings. Thus free, she performed headstands and riding tricks her competitors could never accomplish. She also captured titles in relay and Roman racing and bronc riding. If not for her competitive success at the most prestigious rodeos, Baldwin's costume would have been inconsequential. While the great Lucille Mulhall (1885–1940) called Baldwin's outfit disgusting, the advantage was obvious, and other women quickly began shortening their divided skirts and elasticizing the hems. Soon bloomers, then jodhpurs, and by 1924 trousers were the norm.

Baldwin participated in many sports as a child in her native Norway, and in 1908 emigrated to New York to study cosmetology. She also began riding lessons and within a year had joined the Wild West. She was in Will Rogers' 1910 vaudeville troupe and, subsequently, headlined the 101 Ranch Wild West. Her competitive career began in 1912 with multiple victories at Los Angeles and Pendleton. A 1913 picture postcard showed Tillie performing with the caption, "Tillie Baldwin: Only Woman Bulldogger in the World." Eleven years later Eloise "Fox" Hastings (1898–1948) erroneously claimed the title of first cowgirl bulldogger. At the 1913 Winnipeg Stampede, Baldwin defeated an otherwise all-male field to capture the Roman Racing crown, six years before Florence Hughes Randolph (1899–1971) launched her competitive career by accomplishing a similar feat at Calgary.

Athletic, attractive, and charismatic, Baldwin continued to grab big titles through the 1916 New York Stampede. She drew headlines, photographs, and interviews until World War I interrupted big-time rodeo, ending her competitive career. During the 1920s and 1930s, future hall-of-famers Hastings, Randolph, and Tad Lucas (1902–1990), won her titles and got credit for most of her achievements. Had she remained active, Baldwin would surely have been a star in the Golden Age of Sport, and taken her rightful place in the rodeo halls of fame.

twenty all-women rodeos annually and has held its own national finals. Only on the PRCA circuit, including WPRA barrel races, can athletes earn a living through rodeo winnings.

Such bureaucracy and regulation are relatively new; rodeo had neither central control, standard rules, nor eligibility requirements until the mid-1930s. During the formative years, men and women of diverse ethnicities and nationalities competed in over a hundred different contests. Each rodeo selected its own events, devised its own rules, and allowed entries according to its own traditions. In that wide-open era, women enjoyed their greatest success and fame. As rodeos were modernized and standardized, participation by cowgirls diminished, as did participation by Hispanics, African Americans, and Native Americans.

Before World War II the most popular events included trick and fancy roping, trick and fancy riding, and races. The first cowgirl superstars earned fame in these events. Trick and fancy roping contestants had to make figures and shapes with their lassos before unleashing them to capture one or several persons or animals. In trick and fancy riding, athletes performed gymnastic feats on horseback while circling the arena at top speed. Judging of both events resembled that of gymnastics or figure skating. The premier women's races included relays, in which riders changed horses after each lap of the arena, and Roman standing races, in which riders stood with one foot on the back of each of a pair of horses.

HISTORY OF WOMEN'S PARTICIPATION

Rodeo cowgirls before World War II usually had, at best, an eighth-grade education. They joined the circuit as teens, and more than 90 percent soon married rodeo cowboys. It was a difficult life, and two thirds quit after one or two years. Those who succeeded were versatile and tough. In addition to trick and fancy events and races, they rode broncs and bulls, and roped and wrestled steers. Many competed against men and won. Only the best cowboys and cowgirls, who also starred in vaudeville and Wild West shows, earned enough to live well.

Early cowgirl athleticism was seriously hampered by costumes that consisted of long, divided skirts. The first woman to break this tradition was

Tillie Baldwin (1888–1958). Her bloomer costume caused a sensation in 1912 and 1913, and her major victories motivated other women to alter their attire. By the mid-1920s trousers had become the standard cowgirl costume.

Four rodeos before World War I significantly influenced the history of rodeo and cowgirls. The Cheyenne Frontier Days, which began in 1897, remains the most significant community celebration. Women first competed in cow pony races at Cheyenne in 1899, and in bronc riding and relay racing in 1906.

Big-time producers ultimately controlled women's destinies. The organizer of the remaining major events was Guy Weadick (1885–1954), founder of the Calgary Stampede in 1912 and producer of the 1913 Winnipeg Stampede and the Sheepshead Bay, New York, Stampede of 1916, all offering women rich prizes in numerous events.

Lucille Mulhall (1885–1940), a vaudeville and Wild West trick roper who gained fame defeating men at steer roping was the top cowgirl of the era and star of Weadick's rodeos. Mulhall also formed her own rodeo company and produced several notable contests. Unfortunately many rodeos, including Mulhall's, were unable to survive World War I. How the sport and women's role in it might have developed with the charismatic Mulhall in a leadership position will never be known but, without her, rodeo remained a patriarchy.

After World War I three men and two organizations ruled the sport. Tex Austin (1887–1941) created the Madison Square Garden Rodeo, which quickly became rodeo's premier event, its winners long recognized as the unofficial world champions. Austin also produced the 1924 London Rodeo, the most successful international contest in rodeo history. Women starred in all Austin's productions. Competing in bronc riding, trick riding, and sometimes races, they often garnered most of the publicity. After Austin lost control of the New York venue, his influence diminished. Col. William T. Johnson (1875–1943) obtained the Garden contest and took it to new levels of professionalism while adding a string of other lucrative eastern venues to his domain. He was revered by cowgirls, whom he promoted and supported. Simultaneously, western rodeo producers in 1929 formed the Rodeo Association of

---

CHAMPION WOMAN BRONCO BUSTER OF THE WORLD (1909)

A 1909 Newspaper Account of Goldie St. Clair's Rodeo Beginnings

Her parents were riders, her mother being a noted relay rider, and the children were given the run of the range. Mrs. Goldie St. Clair and one of her brothers herded cattle while riding horses bareback as soon as the children were able to toddle. As they grew older the children rode horses to and from school and were such daring little experts that they nearly wore them out. At last the father restricted the children to some mules. They were small mules but could match with Steamboat or Rocking Chair [well-known bucking horses] when it came to bucking . . . As time went by they began to have bucking contests every Sunday afternoon. The exhibition ground was a wheat field, and the spectators were neighbors . . . It was in this wheat field that Mrs. St. Clair got the training which was afterward to make her the champion of the world.

Cheyenne State Leader, *21 August 1909.*

America (RAA) in an attempt to bring order to the chaotic sport. That same year, popular cowgirl Bonnie McCarroll (1899–1929) died in a bronc riding accident at Pendleton, Oregon. After her death the RAA refused to sanction women's events, which were dropped from many western contests. Led by Johnson, most eastern producers ignored the RAA, and cowgirls continued earning big headlines and big dollars at their rodeos.

The premier cowgirl of the 1920s and 1930s was Tad Lucas (1902–1990). She won virtually every major title available, including the prestigious MGM Trophy for the top cowgirl at Madison Square Garden, and six consecutive trick riding titles at Cheyenne. She also enjoyed unprecedented respect and popularity among her peers.

In 1936 cowboys, who did not share cowgirls' enthusiasm for Johnson, went on strike against his Boston Garden rodeo, demanding a fairer prize structure. Victorious, they formed the Cowboys Turtle Association (CTA), now the powerful PRCA, while Johnson sold his company and retired. Like the RAA, the CTA allowed women neither voice nor vote and, without Johnson, women had no advocate. Meanwhile, Hollywood star Gene Autry (1907–1998) had thrilled audiences with his singing at the Madison Square Garden rodeo, leading producers everywhere to hire western entertainers to attract crowds. Rodeo has paid dearly for this, as singers and not athletes have constituted the featured attraction ever since. Soon, Autry purchased most of the major companies and dominated big-time rodeo. He restructured the events to reflect the patriotic themes of the World War II era and eliminated all women's contests. Thereafter, cowgirls' roles were limited to beauty queen and entertainer.

Soon after the war, the CTA and RAA merged to become the PRCA and to assume total control of the sport. Never again would individual promoters wield the power of Johnson and Autry. By the mid-1950s the Madison Square Garden rodeo had declined, and the PRCA established the NFR. Women changed as well. A new generation of cowgirls, many college-educated, took independent action to attain a meaningful role in the sport. In 1947 two of them, Nancy Binford (1921–) and Thena Mae Farr (1927–1985) staged an All-Girl Rodeo at the Tri-State Fair in Amarillo, Texas. Their resounding success led participants the following year to form the WPRA. The organization hoped to provide women with the opportunity to compete in roping and roughstock events at all-girl rodeos and in legitimate, sanctioned contests at PRCA rodeos. All women rodeos enjoyed a heyday in the fifties as Binford and Farr formed a successful company to produce the contests across the country. Following their retirement, the contests dwindled to become a minor part of the sport, in which winnings were insufficient to meet expenses. The loss of Binford and Farr certainly contributed to the demise of the all-women rodeos.

Still, the WPRA succeeded in restoring cowgirl contests to PRCA rodeos. Barrel racing was the WPRA contest of choice, and it spread rapidly across the country. In 1955 WPRA president Jackie Worthington (1924–1987) and PRCA president Bill Linderman (1920–1965) signed a historic agreement, still in effect in 1999, urging the inclusion of WPRA barrel racing at PRCA rodeos and requiring that women's events at PRCA rodeos conform to WPRA rules and regulations. When the NFR began four years later, the WPRA launched a campaign to have its barrel racing championship included. It succeeded in 1967, with the help of the Oklahoma City NFR sponsors, who believed that the popular event would increase attendance.

Although barrel racing was in the NFR, cowgirl prize money was far below that of cowboys. In the wake of Title IX and the gender equity movement, the WPRA in 1980 sent an ultimatum to 650 rodeo committees nationwide stating that if prizes were not equal by 1985, the WPRA would not participate. Compliance was almost universal, and winnings more than doubled by the end of the decade. The only rodeo refusing to pay equally was the NFR, which insisted that the women were guests of the PRCA. Not wishing to be shut out of the premier rodeo, the WPRA obtained corporate underwriters to bring their NFR purse into compliance. Equally significant was a successful 1990 case against a cowboy who sued to participate in WPRA barrel races. The U.S. Court of Appeals ruled that the WPRA could remain an all-women's organization. Much of the credit for these achievements goes to Jimmie Gibbs Munroe (1952–), WPRA president from 1978 to 1993.

The biggest beneficiary of the WPRA's progress was Charmayne James (1970–), the most successful woman in rodeo history and the premier cowgirl of the late twentieth century. Winner of ten consecutive barrel racing championships, she was rodeo's leading money winner in 1987 and the first woman to wear the prestigious number 1 in the NFR. In 1988 her official prize money surpassed even the All Around Cowboy, who competed in two events. James, who from 1988 to 1995 competed as Charmayne Rodman, was the WPRA's first million-dollar cowgirl and was widely regarded as the most popular athlete in the sport from the late 1980s through the mid-1990s.

Although James's successors were also high on the money lists, none captured the public imagination in quite the same way that she did. As the millennium approached, the WPRA had reached a plateau, and the PRCA held the keys to any future progress. Adding more women's events to PRCA rodeos was almost impossible—rodeos were too long already. Additional women's contests could come only at the expense of men's. Whereas PRCA rules no longer prohibited female competitors, the complex qualifying system had precluded noticeable cowgirl participation. Perhaps recognizing the inextricable link to the PRCA, the WPRA moved its headquarters to the PRCA's longtime home, Colorado Springs. The benefits were soon evident. The cowgirls joined forces with the team ropers, who had been forced to split their NFR purses. Their threatened strike produced the desired result, and in 1998, for the first time, all NFR winners, male and female, received the same payoff. Despite the successful cooperation, the PRCA also has an uncertain future. Urbanization, changing public tastes, animal rights opposition, and inadequate television and press coverage threaten the entire sport. Both cowboys and cowgirls face formidable challenges in the twenty-first century.

Mary Lou LeCompte

Bibliography

LeCompte, Mary Lou. (1993) *Cowgirls of the Rodeo: Pioneer Professional Athletes*. Urbana: University of Illinois Press.

Roach, Joyce Gibson. (1990) *The Cowgirls*. Denton: University of North Texas Press.

McGinnis, Vera. (1974) *Rodeo Road: My Life as a Pioneer Cowgirl*. New York: Hastings House.

Wooden, Wayne S., and Gavin Ehringer (1996). *Rodeo in America: Wranglers, Roughstock & Paydirt*. Lawrence: University of Kansas Press.

ROME, ANCIENT

Italy had a long athletic tradition: the Etruscans (ninth–third centuries BCE) were enthusiastic wrestlers, boxers, and charioteers. They also participated in a sort of pentathlon of various races and field exercises such as throwing the disc—all frequently depicted in their tomb decorations. The Romans derived from Etruria an overall passion for athletics although the span of Roman civilization, in both time (eighth century BCE–fifth century CE) and area (Europe, North Africa, Near East, and present-day Turkey up to the Caspian Sea), produced very different concepts throughout the empire, and Roman women's participation in sports varied by social class and era.

In general, Romans did not consider sport an expression of a citizen's virtue and prowess but saw it merely as training to gain military effectiveness and a body capable of withstanding the strain of war. Athletics, therefore, comprised sprinting, running, boxing, javelin throwing, swimming, riding, fencing, and comparable activities. Competitions were regarded as shows and, since members of the upper class did not show off in public, athletes and performers belonged mainly to the lower classes, further contributing to the social marginalization of sports. People of higher rank practiced athletics in the baths or other buildings intended for physical fitness and entered the circus or amphitheater only to watch freedmen and others of the lower classes fight each other. Indeed *ludus,* the Latin word for game, is not associated with the idea of competition, which is instead present in the Greek *agón* ("contest"). Romans also objected strongly to appearing naked in public; the Greek habit of racing naked contributed to the Romans' view that sports corrupted youths.

In this framework in Rome, women's sports had no ritual or political meaning. Hence the paradox of the secondary role of women's sports in a society that granted women a certain freedom and allowed them to participate in several aspects of public life—the opposite of Greece, which attributed to women's sports symbolic meanings of much greater importance than women's role in society. In any case, first-century-CE conservative writers, such as Juvenal and Martial, accused some Roman women of spending too much time exercising in the gymnasium, which would seem to indicate that sports were widely practiced in private.

Sources, including the famous Piazza Armerina mosaics (Sicily, fourth century CE), attest to the participation of women in javelin and discus throwing, the long jump, and running. Here the women are shown wearing simple and practical clothing consisting of minimal shorts (*subligaculum*) and a narrow strip bra (*fascia pectoralis*). Ball games were also widespread, especially in baths and private gyms, as was swimming. There is no evidence of women chariot drivers, nor is there evidence of official sporting events for women. Such instances of women's sports in Roman times that can be documented have been traced to areas under Greek cultural influence, the continuity of the local athletic traditions underscoring their foreignness in the more properly Roman environments.

Among the Roman areas, there is no trace of women athletes during either the empire (eighth–sixth century BCE) or the republic (fifth–first century BCE), although the mythical character Clelia is said to have been praised by the Etruscan king Porsenna for swimming away from the place in which she was held hostage with other Roman maidens. According to the first-century-BCE historian Dionysius of Halicarnassus, Porsenna was so impressed that he presented her with a warhorse.

Athletics themselves are well documented in imperial Rome. In Greek-influenced traditional games, many women athletes' names have been preserved through inscriptions celebrating their achievements. In 23 CE the Isthmian Games in Corinth saw the introduction of a "maidens' contest," which can be interpreted as a race for unmarried women, the prevalent women's event of the Roman period. A maidens' race was also included in the Livian Games, established in Sparta by Tiberius or Claudius to honor Livia (mid-first century CE). An inscription from Delphi seems to indicate that, in the early first century CE, women could enjoy a "sporting career": the sisters Tryphosa, Hedea, and

BATHING IN ANCIENT ROME

A Description of Men's and Women's Shared Use of Roman Baths

In the days of Martial and Juvenal, under Domitian, and still under Trajan, there was no formal prohibition of mixed bathing. Women who objected to this promiscuity could avoid the *thermae* and bathe in *balneae* provided for their exclusive use. But many women were attracted by the sports which preceded the bath in the *thermae*, and rather than renounce this pleasure preferred to compromise their reputation and bathe at the same time as the men. As the *thermae* grew in popularity, this custom produced an outcropping of scandals which could not leave the authorities undisturbed. To put an end to them, sometime between the years 117 and 138 Hadrian passed the decree mentioned in the *Historia Augusta* which separated the sexes in the baths: "*lavacra pro sexibus separavit.*" But since the plan of the *thermae* included only one *frigidarium*, one *tepidarium*, and one *caldarium*, it is clear that this separation could not be achieved in space, but only in time, by assigning different hours for the men's and women's baths. This was the solution enforced, at a great distance from Rome, it is true, but also under the reign of Hadrian, by the regulations of the procurators of the imperial mines at Vipasca in Lusitania. The instructions issued to the *conductor* or lessee of the *balnea* in this mining district included the duty of heating the furnaces for the women's baths from the beginning of the first to the end of the seventh hour, and for the men's from the beginning of the eighth hour of day to the end of the second hour of night. The dimension of the Roman *thermae* made impossible the lighting which an exactly similar division of times would have required.

JÉRÔME CAROPINO
(1940) Daily Life in Ancient Rome; The People and the City at the Height of the Empire. *New Haven, CT: Yale University Press.*

Dyonisia, from Tralles, in Asia Minor, listed their victories between 40–50 CE in several events (running, chariots, music) in various Panhellenic games. In Chios, women were attested as winners in horse races in the first century CE. In his *Deipnosophistae*, the second-century-CE author Athenaeus reported wrestling matches open to both sexes. In Cyrene (Libya), women could watch male games but probably could not compete. In Antioch (Syria), under Commodus (180–192 CE), noblewomen competed in the local Olympics in running, wrestling, and music events. These games seem to have had an additional religious function because the winners, learned as well as athletic, then became priestesses. Later, in the fourth century CE, Nikegora of Patras won a race, which moved her brother to erect a suitably inscribed statue.

Further confirmation of the importance attached to sports in this cultural area can be inferred from the first-century-BCE funerary inscription of Damodika of Cuma (Southern Italy), which claimed that she had died "not without fame, as she left a son and a victory in the four-horse chariot [race]."

The Hellenizing tastes of the imperial age saw the introduction of games deliberately patterned on the Greek model. In 2 CE, Greek-style *Sebastà* games were established in Naples in honor of Augustus and included a race reserved for the daughters of magistrates. In 154 CE the race was won by Seia Spes. Seia's inscription, offered by her husband, makes her the only married woman known to have competed in public—something usually reserved for unmarried, childless maidens. The imperial biographer Suetonius reported that in 86 CE Emperor Domitian established Greek games, the *Capitolia* or *Certamen Capitolinum*, in Rome itself. This again included a women's race, which proved a real attraction.

The extent of women's participation in sports throughout the Greek area of imperial Rome is further confirmed by their presence among the *gymnasiarchoi* and the *agonothetes*, magistrates in charge of sponsoring athletic and cultural games and running gymnasia. Evidence is particularly abundant in Asia Minor between the third century BCE and the third century CE.

Typically Roman were gladiator fights, female participation in which drew great criticism from Juvenal and Tacitus. Ancient authors often mentioned professional women prizefighters, giving the impression there were many. But a further impression is that women's fights were included largely to add something extravagant and exotic to lavish productions. A bas relief from Halicarnassus (now in the British Museum) depicts two female gladiators whose noms de guerre, Amazone and Achillia, clearly served to dramatize their performances.

In the late third century CE, Septimius Severus banned professional women gladiators, declaring the sport too savage. The decision was adopted as part of a wider moralizing trend that strongly limited the public role of women. From then on, women's role in athletics and among the *gymnasiarchoi* declined steadily.

Francesca Garello
Angela Teja

See also Greece, Ancient

Bibliography

Harris, Harold A. (1972) *Sport in Greece and Rome.* London: Thames and Hudson.

Lee, Hugh M. (1984) "Athletics and the Bikini Girls from Piazza Armerina." *Stadion* 10: 45–76.

Mantas, Konstantinos. (1995) "Women and Athletics in the Roman East." *Nikephoros* 8: 125–144.

Moretti, Luigi. (1953) *Iscrizioni agonistiche greche.* Rome: Angelo Signorelli.

Teja, Angela. (1988) *L'esercizio fisico nell'antica Roma.* Rome: Studium.

Thuillier, Jean Paul. (1996) *Le sport dans la Rome antique.* Paris: Editions Errance.

ROPE JUMPING *see* Double Dutch

ROUNDERS AND STOOLBALL

Rounders and stoolball are bat and ball games that, like many of today's sports, originated in Britain in the late eighteenth century. Rounders has been said to be the precursor of American baseball, and the games do have similar elements: a bowled (pitched) ball struck with a wooden stick (bat), a home base, four posts (bases) around which players run, and nine players. First played by men and women, rounders and stoolball soon became primarily women's sports and are played predominantly by women or mixed teams on a recreational level or by students in physical education programs. Young women who can now play soccer (association football), basketball, or cricket associate rounders with old-fashioned school games. Rounders is played mostly in primary or elementary schools, whereas stoolball is a traditional English summer game for women.

HISTORY

Rounders and stoolball share a number of features in early history and styles of play but diverge in the way their growth was stimulated in modern urban society. Both emerged in rural England by the later eighteenth century as loosely structured spring and summer pastimes. There have been several attempts at antiquarian reconstruction, as part of an attempt to locate them in broader national folk roots, but the earlier evidence is sparse and its terminology unreliable. One assertion that continues to provoke angry disagreement is that both games contributed to the remarkably separate rise of cricket and baseball; it often seems to be the case that broadly similar activities are harnessed together to satisfy a hunger for origins. The use of wooden bats and wickets and thrown balls on grass fields may well be all these two games have in common with their supposed descendants. In England, rounders and stoolball often share the same grounds as cricket but are physically as well as symbolically marginalized because of their assumed feminine domination. When compared with cricket, they fall into an uneasy divide between sport and pastime.

Both sports owe their modern followings to late Victorian attempts to reconstruct an imagined country past and, particularly, to improve the health and leisure activities of young girls and married women. Both owe a subsequent rise in popularity to a growing emphasis on physical recreation as an essential part of education in English state schools after the World War I; their relative cheapness and team involvement made them particularly attractive, as did the fact that they could be played on asphalted urban yards if necessary. But they were never wholly gender-limited; at times there has been confusion, and even conflict, as to whom rounders and stoolball were designed for, and that is still far from resolved. The actual scale of participation, which is probably in the thousands, is very difficult to reconstruct because relatively small national organizations exist alongside a wide range of informal participation.

MODERN PLAY

Rounders is played on a five-sided pitch, or field, three of whose sides are 12 meters (39.5 feet) long whereas the other two are 8.5 meters (29 feet). The bat holder stands in an approximately 2-meter (6-foot) square at the junction of one of the longer sides with one of the shorter ones, opposite a bowler in a central 2.5-meter (8-foot) square. Each team has nine players, and the various roles—bowling, batting, and fielding—are rotated so that all share as a team; whatever the individual skills, play does not generate specialties. A game consists of two innings, during which each side bats twice. A hard leather ball up to 19 centimeters (7.5 inches) in circumference and weighing up to 80 grams (3 ounces) is thrown underarm to a round wooden bat or "stick" about 46 centimeters (18 inches) long. After the hit, the bat holder runs, counterclockwise, around four posts 1.2 meters (4 feet) tall, hoping not to be caught or "bowled out." To be bowled out means that a fielder hits one of the sticks with a retrieved ball before the runner reaches it. Each successful run scores a "rounder" and the next team member steps forward until all have completed or been caught out. The team with the most rounders wins. Two umpires watch for rule infringements. No special dress is required although most players wear some version of decorous sporting wear and teams may wear sweatshirts.

In stoolball, two teams, normally of eleven on a side, play with two wickets (30-centimeter [1-foot] square boards) mounted on poles 1.37 meters (4 feet 6 inches) tall and 5 meters (16 yards) apart. Soft balls, derived from tennis, are bowled underarm from one wicket to a bat holder standing at the other. The bat is normally wooden, shaped like a rather heavy table tennis bat—it is often claimed that the game's name derived from the fact that the first bats were three-legged milking stools. After striking the ball, the bat holder runs between the two wickets unless bowled or caught out. The winning team scores the highest number of runs, hence the claimed similarities with cricket. There are two umpires, who are normally male, whatever the gender of the players, who are predominantly female. The remaining members of the bowler's team are spread out as fielders.

FORMALIZATION, ECCENTRICITY, AND GENDER CONFUSION

Rounders had a relatively quiet history until the late nineteenth century, when it was adopted loosely as a useful game for younger boys and girls in some schools and as a team game for uniformed youth organizations. Some of the major new girls' private schools, such as Roedean in Sussex, adopted it, but often as a poor second to games such as hockey, which were regarded as more character-forming. Despite its reputation as a girls' game, it appeared in a number of contemporary texts as an option for "young sportsmen," a gentle preparation for more demanding and manly games. Rather grandiosely titled "governing bodies" appeared in 1889, when proper rules were drawn up. In that year in Scotland and the urban north of England, two more such bodies appeared, the Scottish Rounders Association and the National Rounders Association of Liverpool. In conjunction with the more rural Gloucester Association, they concocted the rules much as they still stand. It was 1943 before a proper National Rounders Association was formed, well away from London, to govern the sport throughout the country. It controls the rules and allows the formation of leagues, for which a minimum of three

THE GRASSHOPPERS' VICTORY

Literary references to rounders and stoolball are rare, but show that picturesque settings and social composition mattered more than skill in women's sports. The following is an account from Sussex, England, in 1878:

"A ten miles drive through shady lanes and by picturesquely grouped cottages and well-stocked farmyards brought us to our destination, a noble Elizabethan mansion, sheltered by the adjoining Downs [the local hills] and by its own extensive, rook-colonised woods, and as soon as the last carriage had arrived with its expected contingent of visitors, and an ample luncheon had been done justice to, the whole party adjourned to a spacious lawn in front of the house, and eagerly awaited the commencement, whether as actors or spectators, of the great event of the day . . . Two o'clock had struck before the fair athletes were ready for the fray—the sides were composed of the younger branches of the leading country families in the neighborhood . . . supplemented by a few village girls admitted to make up the indispensable twenty-two. The captain of one side was a bright-eyed damsel, wearing the badge of her local club representing a grasshopper . . . [The opposing side] had for its chief a lady becomingly attired in white and violet, but evidently inexperienced in the important matter of placing her field. . . . 'Point' [was] personified by a diminutive village girl of india-rubber elasticity. . . . At twenty minutes to six the last of our rustic auxiliaries, a small girl with a huge straw bonnet went in to bat."

The Grasshoppers won by 63 runs. The quaint had yet to become serious.

local clubs is required. The game also received a boost when it was recognized as a useful way of keeping soldiers fit in both world wars, being cheap, easily organized, and requiring little specialized equipment. As such, it featured with stoolball in a number of military handbooks as a means of useful and impromptu morale building between bouts of fighting. There, an essentially female game was harnessed to become a lesser recreation for men when more complex sports were difficult to organize. Although it has had some success at national and even international levels, particularly in Australia, where it proved popular in new private girls' schools for the socially ambitious around 1900, rounders remains essentially a localized game in which fun is paramount. The National Rounders Association continues to promote it as ideal for all ages and both sexes but especially as a family bonding activity. Its literature shows young men playing, but it is difficult to see it as other than a pastime for young women, away from its value in primary schools. It is essentially amateur.

Stoolball, by comparison, has a more checkered history. It was largely refounded in southeastern England in the 1840s by rural social matriarchs as a means of filling the little spare time of village girls with activities the women could supervise. The daughters of the wealthy were also encouraged to play in teams, which were occasionally drawn from mixed social classes, using country house lawns as part of rural fetes. Some village clubs grew on the edge of cricket fields, and men occasionally joined in, usually with one hand tied behind their backs. Small county organizations emerged, but most competitions took place between neighboring villages.

Stoolball would probably have remained very localized had it not attracted the attention of an eccentric lawyer, country landowner, and part-time soldier, William W. Grantham of Sussex, who saw in it a means both of reviving a local patriotism threatened by social and cultural changes and of helping wounded soldiers recuperate in preparation for returning to the trenches of the World War I. He organized hospital teams between patients and nurses and used his aristocratic connections ruthlessly to develop it as a fund-raiser for veterans' charities. For some years it was even played in the grounds of Buckingham Palace when the royal family was away. Grantham had it filmed and broadcasted on the BBC radio and took sets of playing gear on his travels around the world. Reduced versions were played on ocean

A stoolball match in London, 1938. (Hulton-Deutsch/Corbis)

liners, and scratch teams were formed wherever he turned up, in Switzerland, Iceland, and the United States among other places. In 1930s London, he developed strong links with Japanese diplomats, who formed their own teams, and he made the mistake of seeing stoolball as a means of generating international friendship to head off a Pacific war. Tireless as he was, Grantham made two serious mistakes in his attempts to revive stoolball as a national game. He used the game to promote a rather dotty revival of "Merrie England," in which he and other men played stoolball wearing idealized peasant costumes, opening the game to ridicule. Much worse, he alienated the social matriarchs, who regarded it as essentially a women's game and found him autocratic.

The real popularity of stoolball after 1920 lay with local women's organizations since it was offered as a game for virtually all ages and as a refuge from male interference. By the 1930s there were around 1,000 clubs scattered throughout England, but the battle for control was fought in southeastern England, the land of its roots. In 1923 Grantham formed a Stoolball Association of Great Britain, but it was male-dominated, and women in local federations fought it, even push-

ing Grantham out of his own county federation. They did not, however, bother to found a rival national organization, leaving Grantham to flounder on; when he died in 1942, his creation died with him.

England's postwar revival saw stoolball re-emerge rather more quietly. Most of the international dimension had gone, but the game was still played occasionally in schools throughout the country as part of a diet of physical recreation. The main focus was in local clubs and leagues in southeastern England, some village-based, others attached to employers, such as banks and food factories. In the late 1970s a new National Stoolball Association emerged, dealing largely with the southeast and some 200 clubs—though many more clubs remained without affiliation and do so to this day.

One major difficulty continues: the new association recognizes the major changes that have taken place in both sporting practice and alternative attractions for young women, and so it allows mixed teams. Some of the older members will not countenance this and insist on playing on all-female teams. The memory of Grantham lives on as disagreement about gender-specific play thrives. Nonetheless, it remains as a much-loved amateur game primarily for women, as important a symbol of the English summer locally as cricket is for men.

John Lowerson

Bibliography

Crawford, Ray. (1987) "Moral and Manly: Girls and Games in Early Twentieth–Century Melbourne." In *From Fair Sex to Feminism*, edited by J. A. Mangan and R. J. Park. London: Cass.

Lowerson, John. (1995) "Stoolball, Conflicting Values in the Revivals of a Traditional Sussex Game." *Sussex Archaeological Collections*, 133. Lewes, England: Sussex Archaeological Society.

———. (1996) "Stoolball and the Manufacture of Englishness." In *Spiele der Welt in Spannungsfeld von Tradition und Moderne*, edited by Gertrud Pfister et al. Sankt Augustin, Germany: Academia Verlag.

McCrone, K. E. (1988) *Sport and the Emancipation of English Women, 1870–1914*. London: Routledge.

National Rounders Association. (1994) *Know the Game, Rounders*. London: A. and C. Black.

ROWING

Competitive rowing is a form of racing in shells, that is, narrow boats made of wood or fiberglass that are powered by one, two, four, or eight rowers. Eight-oared shells also have a coxswain, who sits facing the crew, providing directional guidance and calling out the beat of the oars and, consequently, the speed of the boat.

The history of women's rowing is colored by a struggle to be accepted in a traditionally male sport. It is also something of a class struggle as women of all classes have tried to gain admission to what was predominantly an upper-class sport. During the first half of the twentieth century, women's rowing was viewed by most members of the male rowing establishment as, at best, a novelty and, at worst, an abomination.

Rowing as an organized sport for women is rooted primarily in Great Britain and the United States although there is evidence of parallel developments in Australia, Canada, and a number of European nations. Through the formation of their own organizations and competitions during the early part of this century and the promotion of rowing for women regionally, nationally, and internationally, women have been able to forge a place for themselves in this conservative sport.

Rowing has a strong tradition linked to both upper-class male chivalry and the military, and it also requires bodies that are very strong and powerful with a high tolerance for pain. These characteristics were (and, in many cases, still are) traditionally viewed as male and, therefore, women and their bodies were considered unsuited to such an effort. Women's participation was tolerated in some places, but more often than not, oarswomen were actively discouraged from entering the male preserve. Much has changed over the past fifty years with the inclusion of women in rowing clubs and competitions at all levels, but obstacles to true equality remain to be overcome. In the late 1990s, for instance, opportunities and financing for female rowers continued to lag substantially behind those available to men.

Women's double scull teams. (Joel W. Rogers/Corbis)

The physical training required for rowing can be very intense, so much so that sports scientists like to use oarspeople for research subjects when an extrapolated maximum is required; because researchers can usually encourage these athletes to "max out," no extrapolation is necessary. On average, a typical international-level rower will train ten to fifteen times a week for 20 to 30 hours. An elite national team training regime will usually include up to three sessions a day, two on water—on average, between 30 and 36 kilometers a day—and one on weights. Training also focuses on rowing techniques, which vary according to the type of boat. In most countries in the Northern Hemisphere, where much of the elite women's rowing in the world occurs, training is seasonal and dependent on weather conditions. In winter particularly, training changes in duration and frequency and becomes what is known as dry-land training. There is not a great deal of variety in training programs from country to country though, in some countries, the training programs have been changed with the introduction of formal national programs for coaches.

The world's most successful women's rowing coach—18 Olympic or world championship medals, including 10 gold, out of 24 entries since

1991—Al Morrow, the National Women's head coach of Canada, claims that there really are no significant technical distinctions between women's and men's rowing.

HISTORY

The modern version of the sport of rowing, with the sliding seats and outriggers that revolutionized the sport from a biomechanical perspective, is a relatively recent phenomenon, dating back less than 200 years. To recognize and understand the cultural and social conditions from which women's rowing has emerged, it is necessary to examine the deeper roots of the sport. Records of rowing races can be traced back through history to Roman times. The first written account of a rowing race is found in Book V of Virgil's *Aeneid*. As with other everyday modes of transportation, including running, horses, and chariots, people have been racing boats of all kinds for as long as they have used them for fishing, carrying goods, and ferrying passengers across rivers and lakes. During the Middle Ages, for example, watermen (that is, men who work on the water) in Britain were known to supplement their incomes by taking part in "wager" racing. This kind of wager racing influenced the attempts by the upper classes to keep the working class out of later competitions for both social and competitive reasons. Women were also involved in early recorded examples of boat racing; one such example is the women from the Italian town of Pellestrina racing against one another in Venice during the fifteenth century. As these two examples illustrate, racing that took place before rowing emerged as an organized sport consisted primarily of contests between people who used boats for their work and in their everyday lives. Thus, it is not difficult to imagine that both women and men, especially from the working classes, took part in boating contests that stemmed from the natural human desire to test strength and skill in competition against one's peers.

Rowing did not become a formalized sport in the modern sense until the early nineteenth century, at which time the first rowing and boating clubs were formed by individuals from the privileged classes in America and Britain. Amateur rowing clubs existed in England as early as 1817 and in the New York metropolitan area as early as

1828. The first race between Oxford and Cambridge Universities took place in 1829. Gentlemanly amateur rowing in Britain, North America, Europe, and Australia was clearly differentiated from professional rowing (for example, by fishermen and watermen) primarily to protect amateurs from "unfair" competition. The distinction between amateur and professional rowers played an important role in determining who controlled the development of the sport of rowing during the nineteenth century. This division based on social class resulted in the sport of rowing being governed by wealthy amateurs, who formalized the rules and formed national governing bodies, whereas professional oarsmen were responsible primarily for advances in rowing techniques and equipment over this period.

In the first half of the nineteenth century, rowing races in Britain were almost exclusively professional events that attracted large crowds and were used by towns and villages to boost tourism and fill local taverns. At the same time, the earliest rowing competitions between members of the social elite, who would later make up the ranks of the gentlemanly amateurs, were initiated within and between the universities and public schools (as private schools are called in Great Britain). For example, boys from Eton were rowing an eight with a coxswain as early as 1811. Boys from the public schools moved on to the universities of Oxford and Cambridge and began the tradition of rowing competition between these two institutions in 1829. Although amateur rowing in Britain had its start in the universities and public schools, it was in the first private rowing clubs, made up of the public school and university graduates, that the sport was formally organized later in the century. Although the amateur clubs began to exert a greater influence over rowing at this time, professional rowing continued to attract the majority of the public's attention.

The 1870s and 1880s represented the heyday of professional sculling in North America and included the likes of world champion (1880–1884) Ned Hanlan from Canada and Americans Charles Courtney, George Faulkner, and Michael Davis. By 1900 professional rowing had all but disappeared, but its legacy was evident in the improvements in amateur rowers' technique during the early twentieth century. The influence of professional rowers on amateur rowing was primarily the result of the use of professional oarsmen by college rowing teams; one such example was Matthew Taylor, who coached Oxford in 1857. As in North America, difficulties that faced professional rowing in Britain included the absence of rules to regulate races and gambling which, at times, resulted in disputes that could be settled only in the law courts. The decline of professional rowing in Britain and North America was for the most part due to the disappearance of the river watermen and the appearance of such new spectator pastimes as association football and baseball. Thus, with the departure of the professional rowers, the sport's future rested with the amateur oarsmen.

With the increase in the number of rowing clubs during the second half of the nineteenth century, there was increased formalization of rowing with respect to the organization of regattas and the rules of racing. This led to the formation of the National Association of Amateur Oarsmen in the United States in 1872, and the Amateur Rowing Association in Britain in 1882. At this time, definitions of what constituted an amateur were arrived at in the United States (1872) and Britain (1878) in order to release the amateur oarsman from the problems of gambling and cheating that were often associated with professional rowing. In England, amateurs were defined primarily by their class, and anyone who earned a living in a physical occupation was excluded, whereas in America the slightly more democratic definition excluded only athletes who earned prize money in rowing competitions. Similar definitions were formulated in other countries, such as Canada, Australia, and New Zealand. Thus, professional rowers were barred from the amateur ranks.

The shift from professional to amateur domination of the sport was not the only change during the nineteenth century; there were also significant changes in the technology of rowing boats that played an important role in the development of the sport. The boat used by Oxford in the first race against Cambridge University was more akin to a working boat (similar in shape to the lifeboats on a ocean liner) than a sleek modern rowing shell. The original Oxford boat had no sliding seats, no outriggers for the oars, and weighed over 600 pounds, well over twice the weight of a modern eight shell. The first major technological

Oxford University women's crew. (Hulton-Deutsch Collection/Corbis)

breakthrough was the invention of the iron outrigger by the Claspers, a family of professional rowers, which was first employed by Oxford and Cambridge for their 1846 race. In 1857 the universities used the first boats without keels, which represented a dramatic change in the design of rowing boats. Finally, in 1870 the sliding seat was invented by an American and first used in a Hudson River regatta. Technological advances in rowing equipment and in the use of improved rowing techniques during the nineteenth century are an integral part of rowing today.

During the nineteenth century, when rowing was being formed into a sporting institution by men, women's participation in rowing was limited strictly to pleasure or recreational boating. There are very few examples of women from the privileged classes engaging in competitive rowing, primarily because it was generally accepted that vigorous physical activity such as rowing was damaging to women's health. It was not until the late 1800s that women in the United States and Britain first organized rowing clubs at women's colleges, such as Mount Holyoke (1875) and Wellesley (1876), and Sommerville and Lady Margaret Hall at Oxford (1884). Rowing for women at these colleges was conducted under restrained conditions that focused on the healthful benefits of light rowing. Racing was avoided.

Women who were not affiliated with college rowing clubs, formed such clubs as the ZLAC club in San Diego, California (1892). These clubs, which were similar to the college crews, were socially and not competitively oriented. It was only in the early part of the twentieth century that women began to compete in organized rowing races which, for the most part, took place outside the established men's clubs and the organizing bodies for rowing.

Women's rowing competitions, on a broadly organized scale, were first initiated in Australia during the early decades of the twentieth century. These competitions took place in the states of Victoria and New South Wales prior to World War I. In 1907 the Ladies Sculling Championship of Australia was organized following the success of several women's regattas in previous years. In 1921 the Australian Women's Rowing Council was created.

In post–World War I England, women's rowing was received with greater acceptance, in part because women's involvement in industry and other essential services during the war had changed the public's perception of women and what was appropriate for women to do. "Victory Regattas," featuring ladies' races, assisted in promoting rowing races between women even as they emphasized the social role and status of the "lady" rower. In 1923 the Women's Amateur Rowing Association was formed.

Competitive women's rowing in the United States did not become accepted until well after it had become commonplace in Britain, Europe, and Australia. In 1938 Ernestine Bayer founded the Philadelphia Girls Rowing Club, but it was not until 1956 that her club competed against a team from Florida Southern University in one of the first eight-oared intraclub races for women held in the United States. In Europe, by comparison, French and Danish women's regattas had been organized prior to the men's European championships in 1951 and 1953; these regattas led to the first women's European championships, which were held on the Bobaan in Amsterdam in 1954. A decade later in 1964, the first national regatta in the United States, organized by the National Women's Rowing Association, drew fewer than 100 competitors. Two years after that, however, the regatta drew 650 participants, an indication of the rapid growth in women's interest in the sport. Although competitive women's rowing in the United States, and later in Canada, developed separately and later than rowing in Europe, Britain, and Australia, by the early 1970s representatives from these regions were able to demonstrate that women's rowing was ready to enter the realm of international sporting competition.

The 1970s was a turning point decade during which women's rowing entered the international stage. The first women's world championships were held in 1974, and two years earlier the International Olympic Committee had voted to include women's rowing in the 1976 Olympic pro-

CHRIS ERNST MAKES A DIFFERENCE

The documentary film, A Hero for Daisy, (1999) produced by Mary Mazzio, Theresa Mazzio, and Eric Hamilton, focuses on American rower Chris Ernst and her battle to win equal opportunity for female athletes. The film covers the protest in 1976 when Ernst and female teammates at Yale bared their Title IX marked breasts to win equal facilities for male and female rowers at Yale. It also covers her life before and following the Yale protest, documents women's efforts to gain equality in sports, and highlights the beauty of rowing as both a team and individual sport.

gram. The inclusion of women's rowing as an Olympic sport and funding from the federal government in Canada and from the United States Olympic Committee enabled North American rowers to catch up to their British and European counterparts, who had dominated the early European and world championships. This early dominance in rowing was evident at the 1954 world championships when the Soviet team won every event and was truly challenged only by the Romanian crew in the eights. Yet two decades later at the 1976 Olympics in Montreal, the U.S. eights were able to win a bronze medal even though the first United States championships had been held only a decade earlier. The 1970s, therefore, marked the arrival of women's rowing as a sport of international consequence, but with all that was achieved, clear inequalities with men's rowing persisted.

During the 1980s and 1990s, women's rowing continued to face obstacles to its acceptance in the rowing world. Examples of this continued resistance include restrictions on the women's competition in Britain's Henley Royal Regatta; the standards of race lengths and recognized boat classes for the world championships and the Olympic Games; and the slow movement of the sport beyond its North American, European, and Australasian foundation. The cost of a rowing shell was, and in many cases still is, prohibitively expensive for many women's programs.

In the late twentieth century, funding for oarswomen varied greatly from country to country, with many countries contributing very little financial support to women's rowing. The most strongly supported national teams were from the former Eastern Bloc countries, North America, Western Europe, and Australasia. For example, Canadian National team rowers had their travel and coaching paid for by the National Rowing Association (Rowing Canada). Sport Canada provided funding, with the amounts determined by a rower's place in the carding system (A card: top 4 in world; B card: top 8; C card: national team; D card: up and coming). Two female rowers in Canada made more than Can$100,000 annually in the late 1990s, but most oarswomen on the national team made little or no money. University oarswomen in Canada who were on the national team received free tuition. Other sources of funding included parents, part-time jobs, and private-sector sponsorship. The rowing clubs were supported by user or membership fees, fund-raising, grants from city governments to build facilities, private donations, and sponsorship from private businesses. Few club rowing events made any profit.

MODERN REGATTAS

In North America two of the largest club regattas are the Head of the Charles, which is held in the fall in Boston, and the Royal Canadian Henley, which is held in the summer in St. Catharine's, Ontario. These regattas represent the two distinct types of rowing races. The Head races are long-distance races held on rivers; the boats race in sequence, with the times calculated separately to determine the winner. Passing other boats on a narrow river in a Head race can be the most exciting part of the race, and it takes a great deal of skill to accomplish it without dangerous collisions. The blades of the oars often come into contact with the other boats or oarspeople and, for this reason the regulations state that the blades must be relatively thin to limit serious damage in case of collisions. The Royal Canadian Henley is the shorter, 2000-meter racing format—used in the world championships and the Olympics. These two major North American regattas are considered the unofficial national club championships of Canada. The Canada Cup is the interprovincial championship. National team trials in North America often take place in single shells or pairs to determine the candidate's rowing ability because the smaller boats require greater technical abilities. Most regattas in North America are hosted by clubs or universities.

There are major championship regattas for universities as well; the largest are held in San Diego, California; Philadelphia, Pennsylvania; St. Catharine's, Ontario; and Victoria, British Columbia. Most universities and high school teams rely on the presence of a strong rowing club nearby. For example, the city of Philadelphia has eight universities and seventeen high schools with rowing programs. To accommodate all the oarspeople, the very famous "Boathouse Row" was developed; it is the longest row of boathouses in the world. High school rowers row for their schools in the spring and for the clubs in the summer and fall. The largest North American high school rowing regatta takes place in the spring in St. Catharine's and is known as the School Boy Regatta, indicating clearly once again that rowing has been traditionally a male sport at all levels of competition. Another, more recent form of regatta that is becoming very popular in North America is the indoor rowing machine regatta, which reflects the extensive dry-land training that takes place.

LINGERING ISSUES OF INCLUSION IN MODERN ROWING

Although some of the obstacles for women have been overcome, rowing remains a male-dominated sport within which women must continue to struggle to maintain and improve their place. The Henley Royal Regatta (Great Britain) By-Laws, last revised in December of 1995, state that "Except in the Women's Single Sculls women may only compete as coxswains." This restriction on women's participation in this regatta reflects the persistence of the exclusionary position taken by many male rowing clubs toward women during the twentieth century. When women were first allowed to compete at Britain's Henley, they were not allowed to carry their rowing shells out of the boathouses down to the water—which men traditionally did in all regattas—because it was viewed as too masculine. It was not until the 1960s and 1970s that rowing clubs in Britain began to accept female members, and this change was in large part a financial decision to increase revenues at a time when rowing was becoming increasingly expensive.

Compared to other countries, Britain has traditionally been more restrictive toward women's participation in traditional men's events. At the Canadian Henley, for example, events for women were introduced into the program in 1972 and make up a significant part of the current regatta, unlike its British counterpart. It is also the case that the Canadian Henley does not have the rigid class barriers that still exist in Britain; in fact, this regatta is hosted by the mostly working class city of St. Catharine's, Ontario. Women seem to have made much greater progress in rowing where the social class distinction is not so prominent. Despite differences in the acceptance of women's rowing by specific groups in various countries, the progress made by women in international

rowing since the 1970s is readily apparent. Further examples of progress include the formation of an international junior championship for women in 1978, the introduction of lightweight classes, and the 1985 increase in race distances for international competition from 1000 to 2000 meters. Until the 1984 Olympic Games in Los Angeles, women rowed 1000 meters while men rowed 2000; after those Games all races for both women and men were 2000 meters, with the notable exception of races for master rowers (world championship held in Boston), where the races are 1000 meters. Women's and men's master rowing is grouped into age categories starting at age twenty-seven.

These later developments contributed to participation in women's rowing in a number of ways. The introduction of the international junior championships encouraged the development of a worldwide youth pool of athletes well experienced in international competitions. The introduction of weight classes for women had a great impact on the participation rates because, at the time, rowing was primarily a power sport (each event lasting only about 3 minutes) and was dominated by women who were very big and strong. Rowing favors bodies that are tall (for biomechanical leverage), typically ranging from 5 feet 9 inches to 6 feet 3 inches for women, and very strong and usually weighing in the range of 150 to 200 pounds. The results were twofold. First, the connection between masculine stereotypes (which were worsened by the abuse of male hormones in some countries) and rowing was reinforced. Second, a large number of women—and indeed many countries—were effectively excluded from elite-level competitive rowing on the basis of size alone. Thus, the introduction of weight classes has gone a long way to increase the level of women's participation in the sport throughout the world. Not all the effects of this decision were positive, however. There is a high incidence of anorexia nervosa and bulimia in lightweight women's rowing because many of the women competing in that weight category are not naturally healthy weighing under 130 pounds. Socially, women's lightweight rowing has received far less negative attention because it has been viewed as somehow less masculine than the heavyweight category. Finally, the movement to

Women row a dragon boat at the 1996 Water Splashing Festival in Xishuangbanna, Yunnan, China. (Keren Su/Corbis)

double the women's race distance from 1000 meters to 2000 (approximately 7 minutes' duration) has decreased the importance of the power factor somewhat and increased the endurance element, allowing for a slightly less powerful body type to succeed as well. Despite this progress, which has led to great increases in the participation rates in women's rowing, there are still more men's events than women's events. At the 1998 world championships in Cologne, Germany, there were fourteen classes for men and only ten for women. Although this is a much better ratio than Britain's Henley Royal Regatta program contains, there remains ample room for progress toward equality.

At the international level at the end of the 1990s, rowing competitions for women included the Olympic Games, the yearly world championship, and a World Cup circuit of three regattas leading up to the world championship. There are fewer rowing events at the Olympic Games than the world championships because there are fewer Olympic classes of boats for both men and women, given that only 550 rowers (both men and women) are allowed to compete. At both the world championship and the Olympics Games, there are more events for men than for women. This is justified by the Federation Internationale des Societes d'Aviron (FISA), the international rowing federation, on the basis that there are more male rowers worldwide than women rowers.

Although there are more women from a variety of countries rowing at the international level today than at any time in the past, there remain significant gaps in participation by women from certain regions—specifically Africa, South America, and Asia. International representation at the world championships and the Olympic Games provides some indication of the present-day distribution of women's rowing throughout the world. At the 1996 Olympics in Atlanta, there were thirty countries representing five continents. Although the medallists were primarily from North American and European countries, which also made up the majority of the entrants, representatives from South American, African, and Far Eastern nations were also present. For these regions, however, Argentina was the sole South American representative; Algeria and South Africa were the only African nations; and China, Korea, and Japan represented the Far East. Considering the difficulties faced by Muslim women in competing in most sporting events, it is not surprising that Middle Eastern nations were absent from the women's rowing competition.

Rowing for women today, as a worldwide phenomenon, is limited for several reasons. First, it is clear that many economically disadvantaged countries are not able to support rowing at the club level. For these countries, it is virtually impossible to send competitive national teams to international competitions. Second, women in some countries are not afforded the same freedom to take part in sports, especially traditionally male sports, because of prevailing social and religious conventions. As a result, rowing for women remains limited to relatively wealthy areas like Europe, North America, and Australasia.

CONCLUSION

Women's rowing has helped to break down gender stereotypes and to present as positive role models women who are both powerful and strong. In Canada, the international success of the women's rowing team has led to wider acceptance of female athletes. The success and consequent popularity of women's rowing has made elite oarswomen Elisabeta Lipa, and Veronica Cochela, both of Romania, and Marnie McBean into national celebrities and sports heroines. Canadian Silken Laumann reemerged dramatically as an oarswoman after a boat collision almost severed her leg, and she won a bronze medal at the 1992 Olympic Games in Barcelona. Such stories are also an integral part of the history of women's rowing.

Angela Schneider

See also Laumann, Silken Suzette

Bibliography

Adair, Daryl. (1994) "Rowing and Sculling." In *Sport in Australia: A Social History,* edited by Wray Vamplew and Brian Stoddart. Melbourne, Australia: Cambridge University.

Cleaver, Hylton. (1957) *A History of Rowing.* London: Herbert Jenkins.

Dodd, Christopher. (1989) "Rowing" In *Sport in Britain: A Social History,* edited by Tony Mason. Cambridge, England: Cambridge University Press.

Howell, Reet, and Maxwell L. Howell. (1986) "Women in the Medieval and Renaissance Period: Spectators Only." *Canadian Journal of History of Sport/Revue Canadienne de l'Histoire des Sports* 17, 1 (May): 11–37.

Huntington, Anna Seaton. (1998) "Women on the Water." In *Nike Is a Goddess,* edited by Lisa Smith. New York: Atlantic Monthly.

Kenny, Karen. (1982) "The Realm of Sports and the Athletic Woman 1850–1900." In *Her Story in Sport: A Historical Anthology of Women in Sport,* by Reet Howell. West Point, NY: Leisure Press.

King, Peter. (1980) *Art and a Century of Canadian Rowing.* Toronto: Amberley House.

Laumann, Silken, and Calvin Wharton. (1994) *Rowing.* Erin, Ontario: Boston Mills.

Lewis, Linda. (1992) *Water's Edge: Women Who Push the Limits in Rowing, Kayaking and Canoeing.* Vancouver: Rain Coast.

Mendenhall, Thomas. (1980) *A Short History of American Rowing.* Boston: Charles River Books.

Royal Candian Henley Regatta. (1999) <http://www.vaxxine.com/henley>.

Schuylkill Navy of Philadelphia. (1999) <http://www.boathouserow.org>.

Wigglesworth, Neil. (1992) *The Social History of English Rowing.* London: Frank Cass.

Woodhouse, Margaret K. (1980) "A History of Amateur Club Rowing in the New York Metropolitan Area 1830–1870." *Canadian Journal of History of Sport and Physical Education* 11, 2 (December): 73–92.

RUDOLPH, WILMA

(1940–1994)

U.S. RUNNER AND ACTIVIST

Wilma Glodean Rudolph's story reads like a fairy tale. Born into poverty, she was stricken with polio as a child and could not even walk, let alone run. She went on to become the first American woman to capture three gold medals in a single Olympics when she won the 100- and 200-meter runs and anchored the 400-meter relay to victory at the 1960 Olympic Games in Rome, Italy.

Rudolph, an African American, was born in St. Bethlehem, Tennessee, on 23 June 1940, and was raised in Clarksville, Tennessee. She was the twentieth of Ed and Blanche Rudolph's twenty-two children. She was born two months prematurely and weighed only 4.5 pounds at birth. During her early childhood she battled chicken pox, double pneumonia, whooping cough, measles, and the mumps. She had a tonsillectomy and an appendectomy. At four she was diagnosed with polio. For the next two years she and her mother would board a Greyhound bus each week to travel forty-five miles to Meharry Medical College in Nashville for treatment. The doctors prescribed a brace on her left leg and orthopedic shoes.

By age six she was hopping on one foot; at eight she was able to walk; and at nine she could walk without the aid of her brace for the first time in years. Later, she would write in her autobiography, *Wilma,* "I think I started acquiring a competitive spirit right then and there, a spirit that would make me successful in sports later on."

By the time she was a sophomore at Burt High School, Rudolph stood six feet tall. While starring for her high school basketball team in 1956, she caught the attention of Tennessee State College track and field coach Edward Temple. Under his guidance, she qualified for the 1956 U.S. Olympic track and field team that was to compete in Melbourne, Australia. She ran in the 200-meter and was a member of the 400-meter relay team that placed third.

Rudolph redefined the concept of femininity in athletics. Her swift, graceful running style on the track prompted the Italians to call her *La Gazella Nera* "the black gazelle". First, she won the 100-meter gold medal in a wind-aided 11.0 seconds after equaling the world record of 11.3 in the semifinals. Then, she won the 200-meter in 24.0 after setting an Olympic record of 23.2 in her opening heat. Finally, she combined with Tennessee State teammates Martha Hudson, Lucinda Williams, and Barbara Jones to win the 400-meter relay in 44.5, after setting a world record of 44.4 in the semifinal.

Wilma Rudolph crosses the finish line in a women's sprint event at the 1960 Olympics in Rome. (Bettmann/Corbis)

When she returned to Nashville after the Olympic Games in 1960, Rudolph refused to participate in a parade that was to be held in her honor unless African American and white citizens were permitted to participate together. She had her way, and it was the first integrated affair in the history of the city. But years later Rudolph found that the key to the city that she had been given would not open all doors. When she and 300 other black activists tried to integrate a local restaurant, the restaurant's owners locked the doors for two weeks.

Such instances of prejudice increased her determination to do what she could to make it a better world. She started the Wilma Rudolph Foundation to instill hope and courage in the young people of Indianapolis and to provide opportunities for them to excel. "I would be very disappointed," she said, "if I were only remembered as a runner, because I feel that my contribution to the youth of America has far exceeded the woman who was the Olympic champion."

Rudolph was diagnosed with brain cancer only four months before her death. She died on 12 November 1994 in her home in Nashville, Tennessee, at the age of fifty-four.

Urla Hill

Bibliography

Davis, Michael D. (1992) *Black American Women in Olympic Track and Field.* Jefferson, NC: McFarland.

Rudolph, Wilma. (1997) *Wilma.* New York: New American Library.

Tricard, Louise Mead. (1996) *American Women's Track and Field: A History, 1895 through 1980.* Jefferson, NC: McFarland.

RUGBY

Rugby, or rugby union football, has traditionally been a male sport, played by men and administered by men; and men's international teams compete for the World Cup that is the highest award for rugby. Despite the sport's history as a male game, women have begun to play rugby and have established rugby organizations run by women. In England, women's rugby is a fast-growing sport. The closing decade of the twentieth century saw significant inroads made by women playing rugby on all continents, a process furthered by the televised Women's Rugby World Cup in 1998.

HISTORY

The origins of rugby union football lie in folk football, variants of village and localized games, and the alleged shaping of rugby as a ball-carrying sport at Rugby School, England, in the 1820s. Running while carrying the ball distinguished rugby from soccer, and this remains a significant factor in the game's appeal for women seeking a physically vigorous open-air game. The printed rules of the game have been available since the 1840s and the (male) English Rugby Football Union appeared in 1871 as the first national governing body. This national organization was composed primarily of upper-class men with private school backgrounds. (Private schools are known in Britain as public schools.) England was to dominate international rugby administration for some 125 years, along with the other "home unions" of Scotland (formed in 1873), Ireland (1874), and Wales (1881), until the 1995 change to professional rugby.

The spread of rugby union illustrated the British Empire's colonization of some distant lands and its commercial and trade links with others. Male engineers, missionaries, teachers, settlers, military personnel, traders, diplomats, and colonial officials introduced, played, organized, taught, administered, and arbitrated rugby throughout the expanding nineteenth-century world. In Australia, for example, the Wallaroo Club had Richard and Montague Arnold, who had Rugby School connections, as 1870 foundation members, and the English wine merchants at Le Havre influenced the sport's origins in France. In New Zealand the influence of ex-public school masters in the education system was seen in their shaping of sport participation. Social structures and attitudes restricted women's involvement in such organized sports, and until the 1990s, women played rugby almost exclusively in backyard games, in siblings' informal matches and kick-arounds, and the occasional and unofficial gathering of women into two opposing rugby teams.

At the end of the 1990s, the seventy-eight member nations of the International Rugby Board had playing strengths ranging from two male rugby clubs in Andorra and three each in Luxembourg and the Bahamas to 1,200 in the United States, 1,757 in France, 2,049 in England, and 5,000 in Japan.

Despite that growth in men's rugby, women's rugby union experienced the faster growth of player numbers in the 1990s. Previously, the role of women in rugby had been peripheral—providing afternoon teas, caring for children, and washing rugby gear. Women were invariably excluded from aftermatch functions and, on occasion, were confined to waiting in parking lots for their male rugby-playing family members, even when their spouses were international players.

WOMEN AS PLAYERS

In the 1890s in New Zealand, a group of women organized themselves into a rugby team and proposed, under the leadership of Nita Webb, to make a national tour playing against other women's teams. The social standards of the time prevailed against such an initiative, and the male-controlled New Zealand Rugby Football Union prevented the women from carrying out their plans.

As early as 1908, and certainly in the 1920s, France saw women's rugby games played, but it was not until 1970 that the Association des Rugby Fémina (French Association for Women's Rugby) was created in the Haute Garonne area, with headquarters at Toulouse. This was the first national body administering women's rugby. (These headquarters are now located in Bourg-en-Bresse.) Each year a club championship is held, and France has about 3,000 women rugby players, who play on about ninety teams. In 1982 France played Holland in a women's rugby international but in 1986 France defeated Great Britain in the first official women's rugby test match.

The development of women's rugby has had variable success in the rugby home unions of Great Britain and Ireland. Wales has organized women's rugby, a group of clubs has been formed in Scotland, and there is an increasingly strong structure of clubs under the Rugby Football Union for Women (RFUW) in England. Many clubs have been started by students, sisters or friends of male participants, or women with common occupations, such as nurses. This participation in England exceeded 6,000 women players in 1994.

RULES AND PLAY

The biggest occasion for women's rugby before the end of the twentieth century was the first ever International Rugby Board–sanctioned World Cup, held in Amsterdam, the Netherlands, in May, 1998. New Zealand, which has traditionally been the foremost male rugby-playing nation in the twentieth century (along with South Africa), won this cup after being seeded fourth. England and the United States had won World Cups in 1991 and 1994, but it was the accredited 1998 event that placed women's rugby in the sports world spotlight.

The tournament rebutted criticism of women's rugby as lacking skill and revealed a sport in which women excelled with technical ability, fluid play by the champions, and an entertainment factor that owed nothing to male condescension. European countries (England, Scotland, Ireland, Wales, France, Spain, the Netherlands, Italy, Germany, and Sweden) were most prominent in the 1998 World Cup entries, but other participating nations included Russia, Kazakhstan, Canada, the United States, Australia, and New Zealand. The score for the World Cup final was New Zealand 44 and the United States 2. The name of the New Zealand women's rugby team—The Black Ferns—was reminiscent of the silver fern insignia of their male compatriots (the All Blacks), who had won the first men's rugby World Cup in 1987.

The world championship team included many Maori and Pacific Island women who had also achieved national success in sports such as netball and touch rugby. They are, essentially, an amateur team unlike their male counterparts. The Black Ferns also feature the performance of a *haka*, or traditional action dance challenge from New Zealand's indigenous people, the Maori.

The success of the official 1998 World Cup, recognized by the International Rugby Board, gave major impetus to women's rugby. Although still controlled primarily by men, the sport became the subject of an International Rugby Board Development Plan 1996–2001. This aims to "encourage participation of women in playing,

RUGBY TEAMS DEVELOP IN ENGLAND

Rugby was first played by women in England in the early twentieth century. It has since then become popular around the world and is in the twenty-first century a global sport. Still popular in England, rugby has more than 200 women's clubs which compete in league play. At the top of the league structure are the sixteen teams which play in the two National Premier divisions. Below them, the teams are aligned in six ranks of divisional and regional sections. Teams may compete for the Bread for Life National Cup or the North and South Junior Cups.

New Zealand rugby players compete. (Kevin Fleming/Corbis)

coaching, refereeing, and administration," and "to integrate women's rugby into all relevant aspects of the IRB's operation."

Internationally, the North American nations of Canada and the United States and the original home of rugby, England, have the greatest number of women rugby players. These countries face several challenges: to develop more top-level playing fixtures, to develop younger players, and to recruit talented players. Broadening the player base is also a real need, reflected in the imbalance of 200 college teams in North America and only seventy-two nonacademic teams.

CONCLUSION

Women's rugby is played in twenty-four countries that participate in world cups and tournaments, such as the international rugby club tournament at Leiden, the Netherlands. The sport still lacks the resources that men's rugby has and needs to shift its image of a sport associated with perceptions of masculine rugby's on-field brutality and alcohol consumption. At the grassroots club level, often seen as the lifeblood of rugby, the Consett Rugby Football Club, in Consett, County Durham, England, was the first club to establish men's rugby and women's rugby development officers to promote equitable participation in the sport. The club worked with schools and the local community to achieve this. The sport shows remarkable potential; the Sports Council in England, for example, noted women's rugby as that country's fastest-growing sport in the final decade in the twentieth century.

Robin McConnell

Bibliography

Bishop L. (1977) "Women and Rugby." *Arena Newsletter*, 1, $^3/_4$ (April/June):1–4.

International Rugby Football Union Website <http://www.irfb.com/women_rugby>.

Jordan, J. (1993) "Women and Rugby in the United States." *Rugby (New York)* 19, 11:40, 33.

———. (1993) "Women's Rugby: Challenges and Possible Solutions." Unpublished paper presented at the Asian Pacific Rugby Congress at Calgary, Canada, October 1993.

Kervin, A. (1998) "Women's Rugby. Rugby Union 99." *The Official RFU Annual Publication.* London: Absolute Sport Publications, 192–194.

McConnell, Robin C. (1997) "The New Zealand All Blacks—A World Champion Team in a Socio-Historical Context." Paper presented to North American Society of Sport Sociology Conference. Toronto, Canada, November 1997.

Potter, J. (1997) "World Cup 1998 Profiles." *Inside Rugby,* (September): 91.

Sedlock, D. A., F. I. Fitzgerald, and R. G. Knowlton. (1988) "Body Composition and Performance Characteristics of Collegiate Women's Rugby Players." *Research Quarterly for Exercise and Sport* 59, 1: 78–82.

Townsend, M. B., R. J. Sauers, and C. B. Weiss. (1992) "Physical Fitness Evaluation of Elite Women Rugby Athletes." *National Strength and Conditioning Association Journal* 14, 5: 42–45.

RUNNING *see* Cross-Country Running, Marathon and Distance Running, Track & Field—Hurdling and Running

RUSSIA AND BELARUS

The two nations, Russia (150 million people) and Belarus (15 million), were part of a single state for hundreds of years until their separation in late 1991 with the demise of the Soviet Union. The Soviet socialist experiment (1917–1991), involving both countries, provided a number of influential and revolutionary women writers on gender, such as Alexandra Kollontay, Nadezhda Krupskaya, Vera Zasulich, and Inessa Armand; what is more, Soviet socialism was often regarded in the West as a litmus test for revolutionary change in society and its effect on the emancipation of women.

HISTORY

Before 1917 married women in all social classes were essentially the property of their husbands. Czarist law proclaimed that the wife was obligated to obey and respect her husband as head of the family. The law explicitly permitted a man to beat his wife. Although competitive sport was a male preserve and no women's names are to be found in the lists of participants in pre-1917 championships, women in czarist Russia were allowed to take an active part in certain muscular, professional sports, such as wrestling and weightlifting. Since such events were largely confined to the circus, a certain voyeuristic, commercial motivation cannot be excluded. For example, Madame Atleta pressed 89.5 kilograms (197.3 pounds) and on one occasion raised 52 kilograms (114.6 pounds) with one hand.

In the political context of the Russian Revolution and Civil War (1917–1920), it is hardly surprising that solving the "woman question" was not high on the agenda. Yet, women's issues were not ignored. The Bolsheviks were committed to the liberation of women, and the principles of equality of the sexes and equal pay for equal work were enshrined in early legislation. Married women also gained a freedom previously denied them. Divorce was made simple, and marriage became a civil rather than a religious matter. Abortion was legalized on the grounds that it was a necessary evil. A Women's Department was set up in 1919 to disseminate the new policies among women, and under the leadership of Aleksandra Kollontay and Inessa Armand in the 1920s, it achieved a good deal.

In terms of sporting activities, the tone for the 1920s was set by the Bolshevik leader Vladimir Lenin, who derived from, and shared with, Karl Marx a belief in the potential of fully developed individuals. Lenin indicated the powerful force that sport might exert on women's emancipation: "If we can draw women into sport . . . we shall bring an entire revolution in the Russian way of life."

In the early years of the Revolution, therefore, one finds few inhibitions about women taking up any sports. In the 1920s and early 1930s, Soviet women took up a wide range of sports—including soccer (association football) and ice hockey.

From the 1930s onward, however, official Soviet policy began to discourage women from taking part in certain sports that male leaders believed to be contraindicated, harmful, or morally degrading. As a male writer was to put it years later, the prevailing view came to hold that, in choosing a sport, girls should be motivated by a beautiful figure, grace, and plasticity; boys by strength, stamina, skill, and speed. These changes occurred as the regime started to implement an industrialization program that was to hurl the whole of the country into a gigantic campaign to "build socialism" and transform the backward agricultural economy into an advanced industrial one.

It was at this time that women's issues were removed from the agenda, swallowed up in Stalin's five-year plans. The Women's Department was dissolved, and many of the earlier gains for women were weakened by a renewed stress on the nuclear family, by financial barriers to divorce, and by a ban on abortion that continued until 1955. The liberation of women in practical ideology now meant no more than participation in economic production and military effort. And so it remained until the mid-1980s.

THE COLD WAR ERA

Following the Allied victory in World War II and the Soviet Union's entry into the Olympic movement in 1951, communist leaders noted the world's regard for sports and decided that they were a suitable arena in which to demonstrate the superiority of their ideology. The major effort in sport competition became to win world, especially Olympic, victory over the leading capitalist nations, particularly the United States. One effect of this policy since the 1950s was to encourage the participation of Soviet women in every event in the Olympic Games.

Not only did Soviet women make up a large proportion of Soviet teams in multisport tournaments such as the Olympic Games, they also made an important, sometimes decisive, contribution to Soviet success overall. In the 1988 Summer Olympics in Seoul, Soviet women made up 35 percent of the Soviet team (overall, women constituted 20.5 percent of all competitors) and contributed 42 of the 131 Soviet medals (32%). In the seventeen track and field matches held between the United States and the Soviet Union between 1958 and 1981, the Soviets won thirteen times, compared to three American wins and one tie. Yet Soviet men won only five times, while the women won sixteen times, losing only once. In other words, if it had not been for the women, the Soviet Union would have lost most matches. This point was not missed by Soviet officials in striving for international success.

Sport, then, was the only area apart from space conquest—the first woman in space being the Russian Valentina Tereshkova—in which the Soviet Union had been able to demonstrate superiority over the United States. Such commitment to international success had far-reaching consequences for sport and gender: in the Soviet Union far fewer official prejudices were directed against high-level women's (Olympic) sport than was generally the case in the West. Indeed, Western women were able often to point to examples of Soviet women's success to gain more attention and acceptance for themselves. However, Western women returned the compliment in sports such as soccer, marathon running, and horse racing—all of which initially received social disapproval from male authorities in Russia and Belarus.

To sum up, attitudes regarding the participation of women in sporting activities have both reflected and reinforced beliefs about the social role and status of women in the Soviet Union. The reasons why there was official encouragement for women to engage in sport—and related physically exacting activities—must be sought in the state's economic, military, and social needs as well as its ideologies. The work of women was vital to economic progress, and sport was thought to help make workers physically fit, mentally alert, and disciplined. The important role of women in the Soviet economy was heightened by the dramatic reduction of males in the population as a result of World War II (about 20 million men died), and many women engaged in physically exhausting jobs (for example, 34 percent of road workers and 44 percent of heavy manual laborers were women in 1990). The physical and psychological characteristics required or developed by successful participation in sport were congruent with conditions that shaped Soviet notions about the "essential nature of femininity" and desirable feminine demeanor. In certain important ways, the qualities of physical vigor and competitiveness, which have traditionally been seen as masculine virtues in the West, were compatible with the ways in which women were expected to present themselves in everyday life in many parts of the Soviet Union. Both Olga Korbut (Belarussian) in gymnastics and Tamara Press (Russian) in the shot put, therefore, represented acceptable role models for young Soviet women.

WOMEN AND SPORTS IN POST-SOVIET RUSSIA

The political and economic instability that accompanied and followed the breakup of the Soviet Union in December 1991 disrupted women's sports as well as many other elements of life in Russia. At the international level, these effects were manifested in fewer women participating in

Russian figure skater Elena Sokolova performs her free program during the women's final of the ISU Figure Skating Grand Prix Cup of Russia in Moscow, in November 1998. She later won the competition. (AFP/Corbis)

events, as well as in the poorer quality of attending female athletes. For example, in 1988 the Soviet Union sent 162 women to the Olympics, but in 1992 the Commonwealth of Independent States team (comprised of Russia and other former Soviet republics) sent only 64 women. In 1996, the Russian Federation sent its own team, which had rebounded to include 157 women. However, they won fewer medals than in the past and were nearly invisible in the high-profile women's team sports of soccer (association football), basketball, softball, and volleyball. They also no longer dominated gymnastics. The most notable Russian woman athlete at the Olympics was Sveltlana Masterkova who took the gold in 800- and 1500 meter runs.

James Riordan

Bibliography

Riordan, James. (1978) *Sport in Soviet Society*. Cambridge, England: Cambridge University Press.

———. (1989) *Sport, Politics and Communism*. Manchester, England: Manchester University Press.